HITLER
AND
CHURCHILL

Also by Andrew Roberts

'The Holy Fox': A Life of Lord Halifax
Eminent Churchillians
The Aachen Memorandum
Salisbury: Victorian Titan
Napoleon and Wellington

HITLER AND CHURCHILL

Secrets of Leadership

Andrew Roberts

Weidenfeld & Nicolson
LONDON

First published in Great Britain in 2003
by Weidenfeld & Nicolson

A CIP catalogue record for this book
is available from the British Library.

ISBN 0 297 84330 3

Typeset by Selwood Systems, Midsomer Norton

Printed in Great Britain by
Butler & Tanner Ltd, Frome and London

Weidenfeld & Nicolson

The Orion Publishing Group Ltd
Orion House
5 Upper Saint Martin's Lane
London WC2H 9EA

To Peter Wyllie

Contents

Illustrations

Between pages 94 and 95:

Hitler with Blondi.[6]

Hitler with Eva.[1]

Hitler posing with children.[6]

A very rare shot of the short-sighted Hitler wearing glasses.[6]

Benito Mussolini in his bathing trunks.[1]

Churchill didn't much care what he looked like.[7]

Hitler deliberately dressed down to emphasise his simplicity *vis a vis* his generals.[8]

Goebbels sharing a joke with the Führer.[6]

You had to walk through nine hundred feet of increasingly splendid halls before you reached the Führer's study.[6]

The architect Albert Speer and Hitler admire their handiwork at the opening of the new Reich chancellery in 1938.[6]

Churchill walking the streets of london on 26th May 1940.[2]

Hitler's secretaries smoked when his back was turned.[6]

Hitler at a party in 1937 with two Father Christmases.[4]

Churchill with his daughter Mary.[2]

Finance minister Hjalmar Schacht salutes the Führer's bust in 1935.[4]

Kingsley Wood and Anthony Eden advise Churchill after a Cabinet meeting, only hours before he became prime minister on 10th May 1940.[2]

Chamberlain's wartime cabinet in October 1939.[8]

Between pages 126 and 127:

General Walther von Brauschitsch, Hitler and General Franz Halder operating Mission Command.[9]

Lieutenant-General Erich von Manstein.[8]

Air Chief Marshal Sir Hugh Dowding of Fighter Command.[2]

Bob Boothby, Churchill's close friend and confidant until he got involved in the sleaze story known as the Czech gold affair in 1941.[2]

Field Marshals Lord Alanbrooke and Bernard Montgomery with Churchill in France in 1944.[4]

Churchill, wearing military uniform, at the Teheran conference.[3]

Hitler inspects the damage after the Bomb Plot of 20th July 1944.[6]

Bruno Gesche, the commander of Hitler's SS Bodyguard.[10]

Some books have claimed that the Führer was gay.

A photo forged and then distributed as a postcard by the British Political Warfare Executive.[11]

Hitler wearing the Iron Cross 1st class; swastika armband and peaked hat.[2]

Churchill with a few favoured props: homburg hat, striped waistcoat, polka-dotted bow-tie and flamboyantly-arranged handkerchief.[2]

The author and the publishers offer their thanks to the following for their kind permission to reproduce images:

1 The Bildarchiv Preussischer Kulturbesitz
2 Hulton Getty
3 Popperfoto
4 Ullstein Bild
5 Voller Ernst
6 The Walter Frentz Archive
7 The Imperial War Museum
8 AKG London
9 Heidemarie Schall-Riacour
10 Bayerische Staatsbibliothek
11 Richard Garnett

Acknowledgements

Since this book has been written in large part to accompany a BBC2 television series, I should like to thank Laurence Rees, director of *Timewatch*, for conceiving the idea and the Controller, Jane Root, for commissioning the series. Laurence is living proof that eccentric individuality can survive even in the largest organisations. I have hugely enjoyed making *Secrets of Leadership*, and especially working with the programme's producers, Jonathan Hacker, Detlef Siebert, Dominic Sutherland and Andrew Williams. Dani Barry, Lucy Heathcoat-Amory, Suzanne Hughes, Helen Nixon, Kate Rea, Lorraine Selwyn, Nancy Strange and Mark Walden-Mills were also a delight to work with for their professionalism and charm. Detlef Siebert and Dominic Sutherland very kindly read the manuscript of this book for me; of course the responsibility for any errors that still infest it is entirely theirs.

I would also like to thank the following people for their help, either through conversations or correspondence I have had with them: Joan Bright Astlen, Paul Courtenay and Nigel Knocker of the International Churchill Society, Mr James Drummond, Professor Sir Michael Howard, Anthony Montague Browne, Philip Reed, Director of the Cabinet War Rooms, the Hon. Celia Sandys and Lady Soames. I would further like to thank Mr Richard Garnett for his hospitality at Hilton Hall and his permission to research in, and quote from, his father's papers relating to the Political Warfare Executive; M. Robert Varoqui who kindly showed me around the Maginot Line; Major Ian Park-Weir who explained Churchill's time at the Royal Military Academy, Sandhurst; Herr Hoffmann who was very generous with his time showing me the German High Command's wartime headquarters at Zossen; Oberregierungsrat Hans Meissner for making Göring's Air Ministry (today the German Finance Ministry) and Herr Dr Palt for making Goebbels's Propaganda and Public Enlightenment Ministry (today the Federal Ministry for Labour and Social Welfare) open to me;

Carole Kenwright and Judith Seaward were helpful during my visits to Chartwell.

I should also like to thank Chris Wren of the 11 Group Battle of Britain Operation Room at RAF Uxbridge; Wally Bennett, Andy Mahon and Stig Thornshon of the Warship Preservation Trust, Birkenhead, for allowing me the run of U-Boat 534; Fred and Harold Panton for allowing me on to their magnificent Lancaster Bomber 'Just Jane' stationed at East Kirkby, Lincolnshire; Harald Prokosch, head of the Siemens press department and Detlef Haumann, the maintenance manager of the Siemens Dynamo Works in Berlin; Squadron-Leader Ed Bulpett for a fascinating day at RAF Coltishall, Norfolk; Lieutenant Lucas Chevalier of L'École Militaire at Les Invalides, Paris; the FCO for allowing me access to Churchill's office in the Old Admiralty Building in Whitehall; the staff the Maison Blairon in Charleville-Mézières for permitting access to General Gerd von Rundstedt's Army Group A headquarters, Lieutenant-Commander Rupert Nichol for my visit to the minehunter HMS *Ledbury*, and Dr Wilhelm Lenz, Head of the Deutsches Reich department of the Bundesarchiv Lichterfelde. Allen Packwood of the Churchill Archive Centre at Churchill College, Cambridge, was also very helpful to Detlef and Dominic in their researches for this series, for which many thanks.

As always I am profoundly indebted to my publishing team: the extremely talented and professional editor Ion Trewin, agent Georgina Capel and indexer Douglas Matthews, all of whom I am proud to say are friends as much as colleagues. Many thanks also to Jane Birkett who did the copy-editing and to Joanne King for her excellent picture research. I should finally like to thank Leonie Frieda for typing the manuscript, and for everything good that is happening in my life.

This book is dedicated to Peter Wyllie, my friend of twenty years, for giving me the best piece of advice I've ever received. His career shows that he already understands the secrets of leadership.

Andrew Roberts
www.andrew-roberts.net
December 2002

Introduction

> 'I keep my eyes open and their evidence makes me thoughtful. The future is inscrutable but appalling; you must stand by me. When I can no longer restrain and control, I will no longer lead.'
>
> *Savrola* by Winston Churchill

'How can one hundred people be led by a single person?' That was one of the essay questions in my Cambridge University entrance exam and, although it has long fascinated me, it has taken me twenty years to get round to trying to answer it. Yet this question lies at the heart of history and civilisation. If one person could not command one hundred others there would be no wars, but neither could there have been any cathedrals, space exploration or philharmonic orchestras. The ability of one person to make a hundred others do his bidding is the basic building block upon which all collective human endeavour is based, for better and for worse. So how does it happen?

One might reasonably expect that because politics and society have changed so fundamentally over the centuries, so too would the nature of leadership. Since agrarian societies based on feudal obligation have been overtaken in the West by democracies based on representative institutions, we ought to be swayed by different imperatives and led by appeals to very different motives for action. Yet the astonishing thing is that even in an age that considers itself sophisticated and correspondingly cynical, in times of peril inspired leadership still relies to a large extent on the suspension of belief.

This unchanging vernacular is evident from the minimal alterations that have taken place in the language of leadership. To read

Pericles' Funeral Speech of 431 BC ('Athens crowns her sons'), or Cicero's 'Amongst us you can no longer dwell' speech against the usurper Catiline in 63 BC, or John Pym's 'The cry of all England' speech of 1642, is to appreciate that the stock of human emotions to which leaders appeal is limited and remarkably constant. Were we listening to those three orators today we would probably be equally as moved now as their audiences were then. This stock of emotions can be plundered, plagiarised, but above all learned. The purpose of this book is to examine how two absolutely opposite personalities both pillaged that short lexicon in their different ways in order to win the prize both knew only one of them could attain: victory in the Second World War.

When in 1941 the film director Sir Alexander Korda wanted to exemplify Britain's spirit of resistance to Nazism, he hired Laurence Olivier to play the eponymous role in Shakespeare's *Henry V*. The King's speech before the breach at Harfleur was directly analogous to the speeches that Churchill was making that year, even though more than three centuries separated them. True leadership stirs us in a way that is deeply embedded in our genes and psyche. If the underlying factors of leadership have remained the same for centuries, cannot these lessons be learned and applied in situations fortunately far removed from the life-and-death ones of 1939–45?

Leadership – like courage and even sincerity – can be completely divorced from the concepts of good and evil. Adolf Hitler was both brave and sincere in his promotion of his beliefs, despite the fact that they were loathsome. Only to study the leadership qualities of people of whose actions one approves would be to deny oneself the examples of some of the world's most influential leaders. Undoubtedly the greatest criminal of our own times, Osama bin Laden, is a leader none the less and deserving of our investigation into how he could persuade so many people to wreak so much destruction. Just as Field Marshal Montgomery kept a framed photograph of Erwin Rommel in his caravan throughout the Desert campaign, we should try to study our enemy's leadership techniques in order to be able ultimately to defeat him.

Our world is still recognisably that which the post-Hitler settlement of 1945 bequeathed us. The Great Powers, allowing for Russia's and Eastern Europe's shrugging off of Communism in 1989–91, are much the same as they were when the United Nations was set up in

San Francisco at the end of the war. Other than at the time of the implosion of Yugoslavia – which did not lead to any out-of-area conflicts – no European borders have altered. If one counts Korea as a United Nations police action, no wars have been fought directly between any Great Powers other than China's war with India in 1959. The past six decades have thus altered Europe less than in any similar period of time since the early Middle Ages. Decolonisation was already under way before Winston Churchill left office in 1955, and were he to return to earth today it would not take the Chiefs of Staff long to debrief him about the present state of the planet. Hitler – the Satan we cannot wholly put behind us – would need Hiroshima and Nagasaki to be explained to him, but the rest would be comprehensible enough. After all, he predicted in his bunker that the ultimate victors from his demise would be America and Russia, and although Germany's reunification might briefly excite him, the fact that it has turned out so peacefully and democratically would infuriate him satisfactorily. The events of 1939–45 still shape our world both with their lessons and their legacies. Hitler's and Churchill's continuing relevance to our lives is incontestable; Saddam apart, the West is presently enjoying those 'broad sunlit uplands' that Churchill promised us and Hitler tried so hard to raze.

That Churchill is still recognised as the personification of courageous leadership was indelibly underlined in the aftermath of the al-Qa'ida attacks on the United States of 11 September 2001. In their hour of pain and trial, Americans time and again turned to his example to express their deepest feelings about their sense of loss, their defiance and determination. Churchill once more emerged as a major figure in what can be called – after the title of one of his own books – 'the world crisis'. In his 2001 State of the Union address, President George W. Bush spoke of how, in their response to the attacks on America: 'We will not waver, we will not tire, we will not falter, and we will not fail.' It was a conscious echo of Churchill's broadcast to America of February 1941, in which he said: 'We shall not fail or falter; we shall not weaken or tire.' In his speech to the stricken survivors of the Pentagon on 12 September, the very morning after so many of their comrades had perished, US Defense Secretary Donald Rumsfeld said: 'At the height of peril to his own nation, Winston Churchill spoke of their finest hour. Yesterday, America and the cause of human freedom came under attack.'

Rumsfeld returned to the subject of Churchill several times afterwards and the following August he told three thousand members of the US Marine Corps in California that there were direct parallels between America's relative diplomatic isolation over the projected war against Iraq and Churchill's lonely stand against the appeasement of Germany in the 1930s. Everything that I have read about Churchill's 'wilderness years' leads me to conclude that there are indeed just such parallels.

When President Bush was shown around the Cabinet War Rooms during his visit to London in 2001 he described Churchill as 'one of the really fascinating leaders', and he asked the British Embassy in Washington to furnish the Oval Office with an Epstein bronze bust of him.[1] (Ronald Reagan had already hung a portrait of Churchill in the White House's Situation Room.) Today it is Churchill who, thirty-seven years after his death, is helping to provide the vocabulary and the vernacular for the spirit of defiant resistance that America wishes to project to the rest of the world. 'Winston Churchill and his words are endlessly quoted and approved,' reported the *Boston Daily Record*, and when the President visited the devastated area of Manhattan's Ground Zero, comparisons were drawn with the Prime Minister's morale-boosting tours of the East End during the Blitz. As he prepared for war against Iraq, the President let it be known that he was reading a book entitled *Supreme Command: Soldiers, Statesmen and Leadership in Wartime* by the American academic Eliot A. Cohen, one of whose chapters is devoted to Churchill's relationship with his Chiefs of Staff.[2] (On a more mundane level, the comedian Jim Carrey quoted Churchill when he presented his far-from-mundane one-million-dollar cheque to the charity fund set up for the families of the victims of 11 September.)

At the highly charged ceremony to promote scores of New York firemen to fill the ranks of their fallen colleagues, Mayor Rudolf Giuliani quoted Churchill and earned the *Washington Post*'s accolade of 'Churchill in a Yankee's cap'. (Not such an inconceivable image, in fact, since Churchill loved wearing eccentric and sometimes outlandish caps and hats.) When he visited Britain in February 2002, Mayor Giuliani told Alice Thomson of the *Daily Telegraph*: 'I used Churchill to teach me how to reinvigorate the spirit of a dying nation. After the attack I'd talk to him. During the worst days of the Battle of Britain, Churchill never stepped out of Downing Street and said, "I don't know what to do", or "I'm lost". He walked out with a direction and a purpose, even if he had to fake it.'[3]

'Even if he had to fake it.' One of the contentions of this book is that for much of the time between the completion of the evacuation from Dunkirk on 3 June 1940, and Hitler's invasion of Russia fifty-five weeks later on 22 June 1941, Churchill did indeed regularly have to fake it. For all his superb oratory during that period, Churchill did not really know how Germany was going to be defeated. Faking it is sometimes a crucial part of leadership, but as St Paul wrote in his first epistle to the Corinthians: 'If the trumpet shall give an uncertain sound, who shall prepare himself to the battle?' Churchill's certainty transmitted itself to the British people, even though in 1940 it was difficult to understand how on any possible rational analysis the war could be won.

Although both before and especially after the war, Churchill occasionally performed disappointingly in some of the high offices of state that he held, in those vital months of 1940–41 and for the rest of the conflict until 1945 he performed astonishing feats of leadership. At the heart of it all was a confidence trick of such staggering audacity that if he had not been proved right by events, he would probably have risked impeachment. (Of course if he had been proved wrong by events, and Britain had been successfully invaded, parliamentary retribution would have been the least of his worries.) This book will examine that benevolent confidence trick, as well as the malevolent ones employed by his antagonist.

The classical leadership paradigm

It has proved relatively easy throughout history for leaders to find people willing to kill for them; what has been far more difficult is to find people willing to die for them. People brought up in modern, rationalist-Christian Western countries have usually demanded at least the outside possibility of survival, but they have none the less volunteered in wartime for operations and units that have involved appallingly low survival-rates. The alternative that Shakespeare's Henry V offered to breaching the defences of Harfleur was, after all, to 'close the wall up with our English dead', and both twentieth-century world wars saw people willing to accept stupendously high attrition rates, especially in the infantry officer corps of the First World War and in Bomber Command in the Second. That was one kind of noble sacrifice; what the world saw on 11 September 2001 was its exact obverse image.

When Osama bin Laden was encouraging his followers to commit suicide, the methods he used seem to have been in essence indistinguishable from those employed by the Assassins in medieval times or the Mahdi and Khalifa in the Sudan in the 1880s and 1890s. They also seem to have borne a close resemblance to the Japanese *kamikaze* pilotry of 1944–5. Churchill, who fought against the Khalifa and was present at his army's final destruction at Omdurman in 1898, would immediately have recognised what he described (in a very different context) as 'a fakir of a type well known in the East'. The nature of this kind of charismatic pseudo-religious leadership – also exhibited by the cult leader Jim Jones when he persuaded over nine hundred of his followers to commit suicide in Guyana in 1978 – seems to be outside modern Western comprehension. Grigory Rasputin and some of the leaders of the earliest Crusades seem to have had something of the same appeal – Hitler certainly did – and it needs to be understood if the present threat to the West is to be overcome.

If bin Laden's leadership style is essentially Hitlerian in its vernacular and antecedents, and George W. Bush and his senior advisers look to Churchill for their inspiration, might not the War against Terror be legitimately seen as a re-fighting of the Second World War by proxy? I believe it can be, and the dichotomy between the charismatic Hitlerian versus the genuinely inspirational Churchillian techniques of leadership will be one of the central themes of this book. For the secrets of both types of leadership can be learned almost by rote, and harnessed to the benefit of anyone with an eye to history and the telling phrase.

Alan Bullock, in his joint biography of Adolf Hitler and Joseph Stalin subtitled *Parallel Lives*, demonstrated how many of the Nazis' totalitarian techniques were copied from the Bolsheviks. Of course the combined satanic but undeniable talents of Albert Speer, Joseph Goebbels and the film-maker Leni Riefenstahl made the Nazis' rallies far more visually impressive than the Red Square march-pasts so beloved of the Soviet Politburo, but the amplified showmanship of both regimes amounted to little more than a showbiz spectacle done by microphones, lighting effects, smoke and mirrors.

In that beautiful and subtle critique of the dictatorial technique, the 1939 Hollywood movie *The Wizard of Oz*, the hitherto-terrifying wizard turns out to be a dwarfish mountebank who is kept busy behind an imposing façade pulling levers that produce flames and furious noises. Hitler, Stalin, Mussolini and Franco, the film suggests, actually amounted to no more than this, if only the Western democracies had the courage, decency and intellect to stand up to them. Yet for all that we have discovered about these men's personal inadequacies, they were responsible for the massacre of so many innocents as to leave the twentieth century forever besmirched as, in one distinguished historian's phrase, 'The Age of Infamy'.[4] In real life, instead of flying off in his balloon back to Kansas, the wizard would have shot the Scarecrow, the Tin Man, Cowardly Lion and Dorothy (and doubtless Toto into the bargain).

'No sadder proof can be given by a man of his own littleness than disbelief in great men,' wrote Thomas Carlyle in *On Heroes, Hero-Worship and the Heroic in History*, yet is not the reverse more true? Is there not pathos in our constantly casting about for leaders, when we have not yet perfected the art of being mature followers, sceptical of attributing superhuman qualities to people who we know perfectly well are no more than flesh and blood like us? A mature democracy should cringe at these periodic bouts of hero-worship, like the embarrassment a mature woman feels about her early-teenage crush on the captain of the school lacrosse team. 'One of the most universal cravings of our time', wrote the American political thinker James MacGregor Burns, 'is a hunger for compelling and creative leadership.' It is a hunger that time and again has led to disaster, as when France cried out for leadership from Napoleon in 1799, Russia turned to Lenin in 1917 and compounded her error with Stalin less than a decade later, and no fewer than thirteen million Germans voted for Hitler in 1932. 'We won't get fooled again,' sang The Who in their eponymous political song. Yet we have been, time and again.

As Hitler's latest and finest biographer Sir Ian Kershaw pointed out in his 1987 book, *The 'Hitler Myth'*: 'The readiness to place all hope in "leadership", in the authority of a "strong man", has in itself of course not been peculiar to Germany. Promotion by threatened élites and acceptance by anxious masses of strong authoritarian leadership, often personified in one "charismatic" figure, has been (and still is) experienced by many societies in which a weak pluralist system is incapable of resolving deep political and ideological rifts and is perceived to be in terminal crisis.' Far from being, as Carlyle believed, a sign of bigness – or the absence of littleness – the glorification of leadership by 'great men' might merely be one sign of a country's Third World status.

Anarchist philosophers, and some modern libertarian thinkers, have argued with conviction that the underlying problem is the very existence of the concept of leadership itself, at least on a national scale. This also seems to be one of the complaints of the anti-globalisation protesters who descend on any town that is brave (or foolhardy) enough to host a summit of 'world leaders'. Were mankind to be able to organise itself in such a way that one man could not wield absolute power over a hundred, they argue, we would all be better off. Just as pure Marxists believe that the State would 'wither away' after the implosion of capitalism through self-contradiction, so anarchists such as Pierre Proudhon and Mikhail Bakunin contended that one day the very need for political leaders would eventually be dispensed with altogether. Yet although this argument has gained some ground since the war, especially in America during the 1960s and early 1970s, it is still as utopian as ever.

The briefest glance at the modern world shows how the ubiquity and visibility of 'world leaders' are, if anything, more in evidence today than at any time since 1945. Leaders have come to personify their countries in the public imagination and, even in an age of European integration, they have maintained a far higher public profile than might have been predicted even only thirty years ago. The influence that has led to this increase in the importance of world leaders – if not necessarily in their actual deployable power – does not look set to wane in the near future. This is largely due to the exponential increase in the speed and penetration of information technology, whereby more people in more places can be made aware far faster of more things that are happening. As the primary spokesmen for their countries, world leaders have taken full advantage of this development to raise their corporate profiles.

Far from meaning that we look more carefully at each issue the more conscientiously to be able to debate what is happening, the communications and information revolution has meant that we have bemusedly delegated more and more decision-making duties to our leaders. The 2002 Indo-Pakistan dispute over Kashmir was boiled down in the world's media to a stand-off between Prime Minister Vaypayee and President Musharref, and the issue of whether Osama bin Laden was dead or alive was considered more newsworthy than the liberation of Afghanistan itself from the Taliban. In 1780 the Whig MP John Dunning proposed the Commons motion that 'the influence of the Crown has increased, is increasing and ought to be diminished'. The same is today true of the influence of world leaders.

Leaders are likely to become more rather than less of a part of our daily lives because politics is being made ever simpler by the media, and nothing simplifies an issue better than to concentrate on the character of a single leader, or better still the personalities of two antagonistic ones. The need under universal suffrage to appeal to what is effectively the lowest intellectual common denominator in the electorate – at least among those likely to cast a vote – has inevitably led to the wholesale lowering of standards when it comes to persuasion, a process that politicians themselves nowadays wholeheartedly aid and abet.

Here is a single sentence from the peroration of William Gladstone's speech that destroyed Benjamin Disraeli's deficit-financing Budget of 1852 (and along with it the whole Tory ministry):

> I look back with regret upon the days when I sat nearer to many of my honourable friends opposite than I am now, and I feel it my duty to use that freedom of speech which I am sure, as Englishmen, you will tolerate, when I tell you that if you give your assent and your high authority to this most unsound and destructive principle on which the financial scheme of the Government is based – you may refuse my appeal now – you may accompany the right honourable gentleman the chancellor of the exchequer into the lobby; but my belief is that the day will come when you will look back upon this vote – as its consequences sooner or later unfold themselves – you will look back upon this vote with bitter, but with late and ineffectual regrets.[5]

It might have been one of the longer sentences of the Grand Old

Man's œuvre, but can you imagine anyone in modern politics uttering anything like it? Three-word verbless sentences, intellectually patronising sound-bites, references to footballing or soap opera catch-phrases – these are the stuff of modern political oratory.

The vocabulary of classical politics, involving speeches replete with literary and classical allusions, is simply not appropriate today because the decline in educational standards has made it impossible for much of the electorate to understand it, even if the politician himself has the intellectual wherewithal to deliver speeches of the necessary calibre. The great Whig lawyer and politician Lord Brougham said: 'Education makes a people easy to lead, but difficult to drive; easy to govern, but impossible to enslave.' It is a fearful thought that the opposite might also be true about the lack of education that is being imposed on the electorates of tomorrow.

This is not simply reactionary snobbishness – I have no desire to emulate the Princesse de Petitpoix in Disraeli's *Coningsby*, who felt it her duty in life 'to avenge the cause of fallen dynasties and a cashiered nobility' – but the fact remains that Gladstone, Disraeli, Rosebery, Balfour and Lord Salisbury believed in politics as an uplifting process, and they consciously sought in their speeches to educate almost as much as to persuade. Few political leaders today feel the same moral purpose in their speeches, and those who do seem to find it impossible not to sound like prigs.

With democracy has come demagoguery and, as Aristotle predicted, there is no more shameless type of government in the world than a perfect democracy, because it cannot admit of the possibility that its sovereign, the people, might ever be wrong. Social ills are blamed on political leaders today in a way that they rarely were under the old oligarchies. With blame comes the subconscious belief that leaders can change everything, even human nature. This absurd assumption is most evident at prime ministerial meet-the-people exercises, when Tony Blair is regularly asked to pass measures into law that would in earlier times rightfully be left to the bishops to implore through prayer, or in some cases the saints through divine intervention. Parliament could easily legislate that everyone should be kind and good, wrote Lord Salisbury in one of his *Saturday Review* essays in the 1860s, or that gravity should not cause window-cleaners occasionally to fall off window-sills, but there are limits to its true power.

The moment at which modern political leadership is most evident in peacetime comes during general election campaigns. These have always been toe-curling periods, hateful to anyone with even so much as a residual slither of human pride or dignity. The British election of 1992 saw a particularly low point in this regard, when the arguments were boiled down to accusations of 'double whammy' tax increases and the Government accused the Opposition of telling 'porkies' (which is cockney rhyming slang for lies).

What would Sir Max Beerbohm have made of it all? Consider his 1943 Rede Lecture on Lytton Strachey: 'This, they say, is to be the century of the common man. I like to think that on the morning of January 1st, in the year 2000, mankind will be free to unclasp its hands and rise from its knees and look about it for some other, and perhaps more rational, form of faith.' We have now passed that date, and there is no visible sign of anything but the same genuflection. If Francis Fukuyama's *The End of History and the Last Man* is correct in predicting the permanent global predominance of social democracy, there never will be.

'The wars of peoples will be more terrible than the wars of kings,' warned Churchill in his Commons speech on the Army Estimates in 1901. For, as he wrote in his novel *Savrola*, 'Chivalrous gallantry is not among the peculiar characteristics of excited democracy.'[6] Churchill, the paladin of democracy, underlined this problem when, one foggy afternoon in November 1947, he had a long day-dream about his father when painting in his studio at his country home, Chartwell. It was perhaps more of a vision, since according to his own handwritten account of the incident: 'I suddenly felt an odd sensation. I turned round with my palette in my hand, and there, sitting in a red leather upright armchair, was my father,' who had in reality died fifty-two years earlier. In the course of their 'conversation', the son told his father, who had been the founder of what was then called Tory Democracy: 'We have had nothing else but wars since democracy took charge.'[7]

Not only has democracy presided over the bloodiest wars in history, but some of them – such as Vietnam and the Gulf War – have been fought specifically in its name. When one fights for an idea rather than a particular geographical objective, such as Silesia or Alsace-Lorraine, it is almost impossible to compromise. Wars of democracy have tended to become wars to the knife; as a modern secular religion, democracy requires unconditional surrender. It despises compromise rather like the combatants of the eight wars of religion that France underwent between 1562 and 1595. The insistence on Germany's unconditional surrender in the world wars arguably elongated both, whereas earlier, eighteenth-century wars were limited dynastic affairs that generally ended when a province had been taken and a peace treaty could be signed. Churchill recognised this problem, and only managed to avert war against Franco's Spain in May 1944 by pointing out to the House of Commons: 'There is all the difference in the world between a man who knocks you down and a man who leaves you alone.' Had the Cold War of 1946–89 ever broken out into direct inter-superpower warfare it is likely that it would have ended only after massive destruction, because democracy, as Lord Salisbury said of militant Christianity, knows no middle way when faced with determined opposition.

The modern leadership paradigm

The thirteenth-century Sienese priest St Peregrino Laziosi is the patron saint of malignant growths, so it is presumably he who watches over the increase of the number of unelected public relations appointees who infest the British body politic to ensure that leaders are kept as far away as possible from the people they lead. Mr Wharton, in Trollope's *The Prime Minister*, 'was a Tory of the old school, who hated compromises, and abhorred in his heart the class of politician to whom politics were a profession rather than a creed'. Today's leaders in Britain and America – from all parties – are more and more drawn to politics as a profession, rather than out of a genuine sense of public duty, and have less and less 'hinterland', the current buzzword for non-political outside interests.

This process has been bad for the quality of leadership, since modern politicians find it almost impossible to resign on points of principle or for misdemeanours, having nowhere else to go in life. When in July 1954 Sir Thomas Dugdale, the Minister of Agriculture in Churchill's peacetime government, resigned over the compulsory purchase of land at Crichel Down before anyone had really suggested that he should, he returned to his traditional county pursuits with scarcely a backward glance at his severed career. Today ministers tend to hang on until they are threatened with dismissal. It is one of the least edifying spectacles in politics, and it further undermines the public's respect for their leaders.

This is not to argue that the leaders of the past were less ambitious than present-day ones, since they patently were not. As the British Prime Minister Lord Rosebery wrote in his biography of his friend and political opponent, Lord Randolph Churchill: 'The ambitious man who can watch without soreness the rise or success of a contemporary is much rarer than the black swan.'[8] It is merely to argue that the leaders of yesteryear tended to recognise when their time was clearly up, and go, in a way that is quite foreign to politicians such as David Mellor and Stephen Byers, whose grasps had to be slowly and painfully prised from the seals of office. In the fifth century BC Confucius said: 'There is no spectacle more enjoyable than to observe an old friend fall from a high roof', but the barely concealed *schadenfreude* which those two painfully prolonged resignations evinced in many other politicians – especially of their own parties – tended to disgust the public.

Politicians have long been drawn to the enjoyment of office for its own sake, regardless of where it might lead. When, in July 1834, Lord Melbourne was considering whether to accept King William IV's offer of the premiership, his notoriously outspoken private secretary Tom Young cried: 'Why, damn it all, such a position was never held by any Greek or Roman: and if it only last three months, it will be worth while to have been prime minister of England.' 'By God, that's true,' answered Melbourne. 'I'll go!' He did, and was prime minister for a total of six years and 255 days. Ambition *per se* is no bad thing in a leader, so long as it is allied to genuine talent, as it was in Melbourne's case. But as the former Tory Party Treasurer Alistair McAlpine found in John Major's Conservative Party: 'There is no room for either sentiment or principle in the lives of the overly ambitious.'

John Adair, the world's first professor of leadership studies, puts the importance of time and place in leadership succinctly when he says: 'It is difficult to be a great leader in Luxembourg in a time of peace.' Napoleon needed the Terror, Caesar needed the Gallic Wars and Churchill needed the Nazis to be raised to the pitch of greatness each achieved. (It must be said of Churchill, however, that had he died in April 1940 before becoming prime minister, he would none the less have already been a significant figure in twentieth-century politics.) One of the characters in A. N. Wilson's 'Lampitt Chronicles' emphasises the importance of historical opportunity succinctly when he observes of his own wasted life: 'I had never "done" anything: hard to see, after Suez, what one would "do", even if built with the same moral fibre of the old pioneers of Empire.'[9] Enoch Powell best enunciated this almost nihilistic feeling politically when he argued after Suez that the Empire no longer made sense and that the Commonwealth was no logical replacement.

In 1927 the American journalist Heywood Broun wrote of how, 'Just as every conviction begins as a whim so does every emancipator serve his apprenticeship as a crank. A fanatic is a great leader who is just entering a room.'[10] Leaders can appear before their time, and if it is not ready for them they can be forgotten, no matter how charismatic or inspirational they personally might be. Leaders need their John the Baptists more than they, their supporters, or history will readily admit. Oliver Cromwell required John Pym, General Franco needed General Mola, Gamal Abdel Nasser relied on General Neguib, and Ronald Reagan had to have his Barry Goldwater in order to pave their own ways to power. Tony Blair had the unaccustomed luxury of having two John the Baptists in Neil Kinnock and John Smith in order to make his ideas the more palatable and his path the smoother.

The process is often tough on the St John figure, as it was of course on the Baptist himself. They rarely get their rightful recognition and tend to be reminiscent of the Abbess del Pilar in Thornton Wilder's *The Bridge of San Luis Rey*, who 'was one of those persons who have allowed their lives to be gnawed away because they have fallen in love with an idea... before its appointed appearance in the history of civilisation'. Rather than being a fellow politician, 'the one who went before' is often an intellectual, someone whose thoughts make it possible for the leader to say and do things that would have been inconceivable even so much as half a generation earlier. Margaret Thatcher, for example, needed the economic views of Friedrich von Hayek, Milton Friedman, Sir Keith Joseph and Enoch Powell to be widely disseminated before she could undertake her wholesale free market reforms of the 1980s. She generously acknowledges these intellectual debts, but often leaders like to be seen as having constructed their ideology entirely on their own. Yet as Heine declared in *On the History of Religion and Philosophy in Germany*: 'Note this, you proud men of action. You are nothing more than the subconscious hodmen of the men of ideas ... Maximilian Robespierre was nothing but the hand of Jean-Jacques Rousseau, the bloody hand that drew from the womb of Time the body whose soul Rousseau had created.' Neither Hitler nor Churchill was preceded by a John the Baptist character; they were no one's subconscious hodmen.

Hitler and Churchill: their continuing relevance

In order to try to estimate the continuing power that the Second World War exerts over us, I collected a number of press cuttings over two weeks in March 2000, a fortnight chosen entirely at random, snipping out anything that related to the Second World War, a six-year period that had, after all, ended fifty-five years before. In those fourteen days Israel released Adolf Eichmann's diaries; the David Irving *v* Deborah Lipstadt and Penguin Books libel trial about the Holocaust began to hear the concluding evidence from each side; the Austrian would-be Führer Jörg Haider finally and with evident reluctance denounced Hitler as the most evil man of the century, a place he had hitherto reserved for Churchill and Stalin; it was proposed that the empty fourth plinth in Trafalgar Square be filled by a composite statue of 'Women at War'; claims for compensation or restitution for art looted by the Nazis were estimated at between £800 million and £2.5 billion; the 97-year-old Leni Riefenstahl was reported to have survived a helicopter crash in the Sudan, and was about to be played by Jodie Foster in a film about her life; handwritten notes of a speech made by Hitler to the Reichstag in 1939 fetched £11,800 at auction; Neville Lawrence, the father of the murdered black teenager Stephen Lawrence, likened the experiences of young black people in Britain to those of Anne Frank; a man dressed as Hitler was arrested attempting to gatecrash the Vienna Opera Ball; fine obituaries appeared of Harold Hobday who breached the Eder Dam with a bouncing bomb, and Dominic Bruce, the RAF officer who made no fewer than seventeen attempted breakouts from German POW camps, including Colditz; the Queen Mother's wartime correspondence about the Duke and Duchess of Windsor aroused much media interest; and SS General Walter Schellenberg's 1940 Nazi invasion plan of Britain was published, complete with the list of 2,820 people who were going to be arrested. The Second World War was thus continuing to make headlines, almost on a daily basis, even over half a century on. For us Tommies, the war is far from over.

This is partly because the story of the 1939–45 period, and especially the year between June 1940 and June 1941, goes to the very heart of Britain's self-perception as a nation. It has aspects that appeal to both the Right and the Left. For the Right, those 386 days when we 'stood alone', albeit with the invaluable support of the Empire and Commonwealth, and also the alliance of Greece, represents the ultimate expression of sovereignty, proving the inestimable benefits of national independence. For the Left, it was the time when Fascism as a concept, rather than merely the nations of Germany and Italy, was faced down by the forces of democracy as represented by what Churchill dubbed 'the Grand Coalition' which included Clement Attlee's Labour Party. Michael Foot once said that 1940 was too powerful a symbol to be confiscated by the Right, and it is partly because both sides of the political spectrum take ideological succour from the events of that year that our pre-eminent *annus mirabilis* has survived as such a potent totem. As *The Times* wrote in a leader on 5 June 1990: 'Many countries celebrate the day that their independence was won or their *ancien régime* overthrown. Neither is applicable to Britain, a country without a national day of its own ... Britain remembers a national year ... The iconography of 1940 cannot be very far from those with Britain on their mind.'

There is a tribe in East Africa in which the witch-doctor's primary duty is to predict what a former great chief would have done in any given set of circumstances, and both sides of the debate over the extent of British integration into the European Union draw great inspiration from Winston Churchill. Euro-federationists such as Michael Heseltine like to cite Churchill as supporting the concept of European unity, although he tends to fail to add that the war leader did not actually wish Britain to be a participant in it. Sir Edward Heath also enjoys reflecting that it is to prevent future wars of the sort in which he fought that the continent needs to federate. Similarly, those opposed to the Maastricht blueprint for Europe, such as Bill Cash MP and the historian Norman Stone – both of whose fathers died in the war – recall the disastrous results of trying to force Britain into a European superstate without her full-hearted consent.

It must always be back to 1940–41 that we return when we seek reasons for why Britons are proud to be so. There are plenty of things which Britain does very well indeed, but equally there always seem to be other countries that do exactly the same things better. It is hard to conceive of being proud of Britain simply because of pageantry, motor-racing, the pop music industry or the creation of the NHS, not least because Germany had its own national health insurance system far earlier. There has to be something more, and for many it is what Britain did over sixty years ago. Unlike any other Power, the British Empire stayed in the field from the start – except for the first two days from the German invasion of Poland – until VJ-Day signalled the end, and that is a cause for huge justifiable pride.

Such was the sense of catharsis generated by the war years that anything which took place afterwards was bound to be perceived as smaller, safer, more mundane, less magnificent. The post-war period in Britain has inevitably also been a post-heroic age. The Britain of Harold Wilson, Edward Heath and Jeremy Thorpe of the seventies simply could not hope to compare in terms of glamour and romance with that of Churchill, Eden and Montgomery of the early forties. Yet through all the various strains that were heaped on post-war Britain – the scuttle from Empire, periodic devaluations of sterling, mass New Commonwealth immigration, the Suez débâcle, appealing to the International Monetary Fund, British Leyland's industrial relations troubles, and the 1978–9 Winter of Discontent – the memory of 1940–41 was always a solace and a reminder that underneath all the humiliations there was a great nation.

Many another nation has had its golden age, its moment in history's limelight. The particular tragedy of my baby-boom generation is that ours should have been so recent. It is almost a recipe for nihilism, knowing that nothing can recapture that sublimely heroic period. Just as Greeks are still rightly proud of the achievement of fifth-century Athens, Frenchmen feel exalted when they contemplate the Arc de Triomphe (despite its presentation as victories of battles that France actually lost), Americans revere the Founding Fathers, and Mongolians still venerate (against strict government fiat) the memory of Genghis Khan, so we cannot wholly put behind ourselves the year in which, as T. S. Eliot wrote in his 1941 poem 'Little Gidding', 'History is now and England.'

There is little indication that interest in the war is lessening simply because its participants are leaving the stage, any more than interest in the Parthenon in Greece, Napoleon in France or the Constitution in America has waned with the death of their immediate protagonists and authors. The first quarter of the twenty-first century will see the Second World War veterans march off life's battlefield, but fascination with and admiration for their achievements will not die with them. Long after all the personal connections have been severed, the characters, events and lessons of what happened between 1939 and 1945 will be remembered by future generations. The re-introduction of the two minutes' silence on Armistice Day is an indication of the revived interest in, and veneration for, that time. Whenever I lecture on the war in schools I am repeatedly told by teachers that it is their pupils' favourite historical period by far.

Some people believe that Britain's obsession with the war is infantile, and even detrimental to the process of our maturing as a normal European state. They argue that the scars have largely healed, and are only picked open when hooligans sing xenophobic lyrics to the tune of 'The Dambusters' March' at international football matches. Yet the headlines of that fortnight in March 2000 ought to persuade them otherwise. As T. S. Eliot also put it in his poem: 'We are born with the dead: See, they return, and bring us with them.' Whether it is Swiss banks being sued by Jews demanding reparations, American schoolchildren venerating Hitler and then unleashing terror at Columbine High School, or audiences flocking to Spielberg movies such as *Schindler's List* or *Saving Private Ryan*, the echoes of Hitler's War will keep reverberating on and on, probably in ways that we cannot begin to guess at today.

Many factors would lead to final Allied victory and German defeat in World War II: not least the vast superiority in numbers and matériel. But Hitler's and Churchill's leadership also played a vital part in it. The lessons we can learn about how they behaved between 1939 and 1945 can help us in the way that we approach the far less momentous dilemmas of our own times. What were the leadership secrets that Hitler employed to mesmerise a nation? If we can see through him so easily today, why couldn't the German people then? Why were the warnings of his arch-opponent Winston Churchill not heeded when he was predicting precisely what Hitler was about to do next? He got it right in almost every respect, and such Themistoclean foresight is the essence of leadership. Unlike Hitler, Churchill had been educated and trained to exercise leadership since birth, yet he was not trusted with it until it was almost too late. Why not?

I believe that we need to understand how leadership works, how it is used and so often misused. We need to know what makes someone a good leader, but also how to spot all those tricks that would-be leaders use to try to gain our trust and support. We need to know how to identify the Führers of the future, because one thing can be taken for granted: next time they certainly won't be wearing the tell-tale jackboots and armbands.

Hitler and Churchill to 1939

'You know I may seem to be very fierce, but I am fierce with only one man – Hitler.'

Churchill to his new private secretary, John Martin

We are all familiar with the film footage of vast fawning crowds lining the streets to greet Hitler on his various journeys through the Third Reich in the 1930s. They were staged, of course, but the adoration on the faces of the ordinary Germans generally was not. How could such an unprepossessing specimen – with his absurd little moustache, rasping voice and staring eyes – have come to command such fanatical devotion?

To an extent rarely seen before outside a religious context, the phenomenon of Adolf Hitler allowed intelligent people to suspend the activity of that part of their brains which induces rationality. The German Minister of Defence, Field Marshal Werner von Blomberg, claimed that a cordial handshake from the Führer could cure him of the common cold. Field Marshal Hermann Göring said: 'If Hitler told you you were a woman, you would leave the building believing that you were.' There are endless further examples of intelligent people – men and women alike – who were spellbound by Hitler. One of his senior staff officers, General Walter Warlimont, recalled how: 'Hardly one of the great theatre commanders, when summoned to make a presentation or report at the headquarters, was proof against the overpowering presence of Hitler.'[1]

Churchill by contrast never seemed to exert this kind of personal, almost mystical power over others. While Hitler had charisma,

Churchill did not. How was it possible that Hitler instilled so much more awe and adulation than Churchill? And why, despite that, did Churchill ultimately prove the more successful leader? What made Hitler and Churchill leaders anyhow, and what special skills and techniques did they employ to induce millions to follow them?

Various attempts have been made to liken Hitler and Churchill to one another. As one historian of the Churchill family, John Pearson, has put it:

> In a number of respects Churchill and Adolf Hitler were uncomfortably alike. Both were ruthless men, obsessed with military power and a driving sense of private destiny. Both were self-educated, intensely nationalistic, and powerfully aggressive in the face of opposition. Both, too, were strongly egocentric characters, overwhelming orators, natural actors and mesmeric talkers, more than capable of dominating those who fell beneath their spell. Both ... [found] their relaxation in painting, speculative monologue and nocturnal screenings of their favourite films. There was even an uncanny similarity in the way both sketched out strongly autobiographical fantasies of their intended paths to power, Churchill in [his novel] *Savrola* and Hitler in *Mein Kampf*.[2]

Unfortunately, any useful insights this passage might contain were wrecked when the author went on to claim that Churchill 'might well' have acted in the same way that Hitler did in his rise to power, whereas in fact the idea of Churchill wading up to his spotted bow-tie in the blood of his political enemies is utterly ludicrous. Most powerful leaders – certainly not just Hitler and Churchill – are 'egocentric characters' who are 'powerfully aggressive in the face of opposition', but where Churchill argued down his opposition and defeated it by votes in Parliament, Hitler gunned down his opponents on the Night of the Long Knives and used Dachau and other concentration camps to dispose of the rest. Churchill would never have considered resorting to such tactics, even were Germany's internal stresses of the 1920s replicated in his own country. He did indeed intern Britons without trial under Regulation 18B in 1940, but he always considered it, in his own words, 'in the highest degree odious', and he released them as soon as he safely could. He reserved the use of gas for when – and if – the Germans invaded the British Isles, not as an instrument of genocide against civilians.

Churchill's nationalism was undeniably deeply felt and well-articulated, but it was never of the resentful, paranoiac and vicious kind that Hitler espoused. Rather than 'speculative monologue', Churchill actually excelled at dialogue and repartee; he would soon have tired of the unquestioning, mute, adoring audiences favoured by the Führer. Churchill was only 'obsessed with military power' in times of war; it just so happened that two of his periods of office coincided with the two most terrible wars of human history. In times of peace he concentrated on bringing in the legislation that forbade the employment of boys under fourteen in mines, introduced National Insurance, and gave one afternoon a week off for all workers. Furthermore Churchill's painting was done for relaxation and pleasure; Hitler painted houses for a living and ceased to do so when his need for cash eased.

The attempt to liken Hitler's *Mein Kampf* to Churchill's novel *Savrola* was perhaps the most absurd of Pearson's contrivances. Whereas the former book is a blueprint for Nazi Germany's quest for *Lebensraum* (living space) in the East and a treatise about the Aryan's racial superiority over the Slav, *Savrola* is a light romantic melodrama about the love affair between the wife of a president of a small European Latin republic and its leader of the opposition, the eponymous hero. Written in 1897 and published in 1900, *Savrola* does contain a few references to politics, including some neo-Darwinist references to the survival of the fittest among nations that reflected the standard eugenicist thinking of the day, to which Churchill subscribed, but that is where any similarity to *Mein Kampf* ends. It certainly did not sketch an autobiographical fantasy about Churchill's rise to power, not least because Savrola advocates the appeasement of the dictator Molara, leaves the country when the Revolution starts and does not attain power in Laurenia until the epilogue of the book in which everyone is living happily ever after.

Unlike *Mein Kampf*, *Savrola* was not a commercial success, and as Churchill admitted: 'I have consistently urged my friends to abstain from reading it.' It is easy to see why, with its absurd plot, one-dimensional characterisation and relentless clichés. Rats leave sinking ships, people stoop to conquer, petards are hoisted, the heroine loves the soil the hero walks upon, hours come, and 'All is fair in love and war'. It is also full of the politically incorrect remarks that one would expect from a work of its time: the King of Ethiopia has a 'black but vivacious' face, the lot of a woman is abdication and compliance, and of virtually the only working-class character in the book, we 'will read no more, for history does not concern itself with such'. The hero, Savrola, is a 32-year-old philosopher, amateur astrologist and statesman, who is drawn to politics more through ambition than his desire to contribute to the public good.

In almost every facet of their personalities, no two men could have been more different than Hitler and Churchill. The latter was a magnificent hedonist whose appetites were massive. On his way to the Quebec conference on the *Queen Mary* liner in 1943, for example, Churchill ate a meal comprising 'oysters, consommé, turbot, roast turkey, ice with canteloupe melon, Stilton cheese and a great variety of fruits, *petit fours* etc, the whole lot washed down by champagne (Mumm 1929) and a very remarkable Liebfraumilch, followed by some 1870 brandy'.

The question of Churchill's drinking is an important one. He used to say that he had taken more out of alcohol than it had taken out of him, but then all drinkers believe that. In his case, however, with an ox-like constitution that served him well until his ninth decade, it was no more than the truth. Although Hitler believed that Churchill was a hopeless alcoholic, the evidence suggests otherwise. Churchill was clearly joking when he refused a cup of tea on medical grounds, claiming that: 'My doctor has ordered me to take nothing non-alcoholic between breakfast and dinner.' In fact, as he wrote in his autobiography *My Early Life*, 'I have been brought up and trained to have the utmost contempt for people who get drunk.' His friend Professor Frederick Lindemann once calculated that Churchill had drunk enough champagne in his lifetime to fill half a railway carriage, but that he took over half a century to do so.[3] ('The Prof' was the master of what would today be termed political incorrectness, once asking a civil servant: 'What is this foolish proposal to abolish hunger?')

Accusations of alcoholism made by the former historian David Irving in his multi-volume biography of Churchill, which is the kind of hymn of hate that would have been written if the wrong side had won the Second World War, parrot the standard Nazi propaganda line. Fortunately, though, Mr Irving gives us enough evidence in his books to refute his own allegations. Thus, when he states that on one weekend at Chequers in August 1941 the (non-claret) alcohol consumption consisted of two bottles of champagne, one of port, a half-bottle of brandy, one of white wine, one of sherry and two of whisky, he also lets us know how many people were consuming them. Sunday lunch alone found Lady Horatia Seymour, Lord and Lady Cranborne, Lord and Lady Bessborough, 'a Rothschild and his wife', an RAF officer and the (admittedly teetotal) Canadian Prime Minister, William Lyon Mackenzie King, around the Churchills' table. Once one divides the amount of drink consumed by the number of meals served and then again by the number of family members and guests present (in this case at least nine) it no longer seems excessive, especially in view of the generous standards of entertainment in grand country houses of the day.[4] On Irving's own statistics, therefore, Churchill cannot be accused of alcoholism, unless it is argued that he drank the whole of Chequers' entertainment budget himself. As we know from the testimony of several of his private secretaries, who did the mixing, Churchill liked his brandies and whiskies heavily diluted with water and soda.

(The author Clive Ponting has also complained that Churchill and Eden drank expensive 1865 cognac together in November 1940, but one might legitimately ask: if they did not deserve the luxury of drinking vintage brandy as they fought to save civilisation, who did? Mr Ponting's biography of Churchill and his book *1940: Myth and Reality*, which consistently denies the heroism of Britain in her finest hour, makes him reminiscent of no one so much as the balding clerks in John Betjeman's poem 'Slough', who 'daren't look up to see the stars / But belch instead'.)

Hitler, meanwhile, can be accused – and indeed convicted – of being an anti-smoking teetotal vegetarian. He was not a complete teetotaller because he would, he said, occasionally 'swallow water or beer because of the dryness of my throat', as he testified in his 1924 trial after the so-called 'Beer-hall Putsch'. A special dark beer with an alcohol by volume content as hopelessly low as two per cent was later brewed for him by the Holzkirchen brewery of Bavaria. During the Second World War, Hitler once remarked that there was little that could be done to alter the eating and drinking habits of the people in the short term, but that after the war he would 'see to the problem'. The ghastly prospect of a low-alcohol cholesterol-free Reich beckoned the Aryan peoples after victory.

In private, Hitler was one of those holier-than-thou vegetarians who sometimes give that perversion a bad name. During the twenties, when a friend called Mimi Reiter ordered a Wiener Schnitzel, he pulled a face and said: 'No, go ahead and have it, but I don't understand why you want it. I didn't think you wanted to devour a corpse... the flesh of dead animals. Cadavers!' He called broth 'corpse tea', and would tell what he considered a humorous story about a deceased grandmother whose relatives threw her corpse into a brook in order to lure crayfish for their supper. To a guest who was eating smoked eel he once remarked that eels were best fattened with dead cats, and to ladies eating suckling pig he said: 'That looks exactly like a roast baby to me.' Quite apart from the rudeness to his guests and the sick imagery employed, the sheer irony of Adolf Hitler lecturing others on the immoral aesthetics of corpses and death is delectable.

Hitler was once presented with a lobster by Heligoland fishermen, but he wanted to ban the eating of such 'ugly and expensive' animals and did not like being seen eating luxury foods. During the first few months after coming to power he signed no fewer than three separate laws providing for the protection and proper treatment of animals, and in January 1936 his Government decreed that 'Crabs, lobsters and other crustaceans are to be killed by throwing them rapidly into boiling water. When feasible, this should be done individually,' since, after much debate at high government levels, officials decided that this was the most humane method of killing them.

Hitler also liked caviar, until he discovered how much was being spent on it and he then moved on to roe, since the idea of a caviar-eating leader was incompatible with his conception of himself. Churchill had a robust attitude to people of this sort, minuting to Lord Woolton at the Ministry of Food in July 1940: 'Almost all the food faddists I have ever known, nut-eaters and the like, have died young after a long period of senile decay... The way to lose the war is to try to force the British public into a diet of milk, oatmeal, potatoes etc, washed down on gala occasions with a little lime juice.'

Hitler was almost entirely devoid of any but the blackest humour, and until the last hours of his life was a bachelor unable to commit himself emotionally to another human being. Churchill, by contrast, was a family man, compassionate and rightly famed for his wit. Nor could their artistic tastes have been more different. Hitler knew much about classical music in general and was inspired by the works of Richard Wagner in particular. Churchill preferred military marches, Gilbert and Sullivan, the music-hall comedian Harry Lauder, and the school songs he had sung at Harrow and remembered with fondness for the rest of his life. As a child, Diana Mosley, a cousin via Churchill's wife Clementine, remembers him singing 'Soldiers of the Queen' 'and other ballads of his youth, beating time as he did so with his shapely white hand'.[5] When he was attending the Quebec conference Churchill 'made several of his entourage, including the fastidious [Permanent Under-Secretary at the Foreign Office Sir Alexander] Cadogan take part in the collective singing of old music-hall songs'.[6] Churchill was an exemplar of Noël Coward's quip in *Private Lives* about the potency of cheap music; he could not bear to hear the sentimental song 'Keep Right on to the End of the Road' because it made him cry.

Pretty much anything could induce tears in Churchill. Whereas many modern leaders struggle hard to manufacture genuine emotions, Churchill – who was essentially a Regency figure in the way that he openly exhibited his feelings – was regularly overwhelmed by them. If George W. Bush or Tony Blair were to cry in public it might well unnerve a large number of people during the War against Terror, but Churchill was so naturally lachrymose that he seems to have spent much of the Second World War in tears. 'I blub an awful lot, you know,' he once told his post-war private secretary, Anthony Montague Browne. 'You'll have to get used to it.' He soon did, not least when tears rolled down the Prime Minister's face as he contemplated the list of war dead at Boodle's Club in St James's. Churchill's earlier private secretary Sir John ('Jock') Colville explained how it was 'part of his character and quality, he wasn't scared to be emotional'.

Churchill wept at the news that Londoners were queuing for bird-seed to feed their canaries during the Blitz; after his 'Blood, toil, tears and sweat' speech; at the baptism of his grandson and namesake Winston; at the cheering of his announcement in the Commons of the attack on the French Navy at Oran; touring the East End during the Blitz in September 1940; at the end of the visit to Britain of the

American envoy Harry Hopkins; hearing of the sufferings of occupied France in June 1941;[7] watching Alexander Korda's movie *That Hamilton Woman* on the way to Placentia Bay; at the religious service on HMS *Prince of Wales* once there;[8] during the march-past after the Battle of El Alamein; on receiving the 1945 general election results;[9] at John Freeman's Address in Reply to the Gracious Speech in August 1945; at the first Alamein reunion at the Royal Albert Hall, meeting those blinded in the battle;[10] at Sir Stafford Cripps's funeral, and on many other occasions. The Duke of Windsor wrote to the Duchess at the time of King George VI's funeral in 1952: 'I hope to see Cry Baby again before I sail,' annotating: 'Nobody cried in my presence. Only Winston as usual.' It was rather un-English for a nineteenth-century aristocrat to wear his huge heart on his sleeve in this manner, but it was common in earlier times and entirely Churchillian.

(Anthony Montague Browne stayed on faithfully serving Churchill until the latter's death in January 1965, to the detriment of his Foreign Office career. It was he who had to register the death at Kensington Town Hall, choosing 'Statesman' over 'Retired' as the occupation of the deceased. Before the coffin was closed, Jock the marmalade cat, of whom Churchill was very fond, came into the bedroom, jumped into the coffin, peered into the still face, and went away, never to re-enter that room again. Montague Browne was the only non-family member to walk behind the catafalque at the State funeral. He recalled how, at the end of the long day of great national obsequies, he returned from Bladon churchyard in Oxfordshire 'submerged in a wave of aching grief for Britain's precipitous decline, against which [Churchill] had stood in vain'. When he got back to his flat in Eaton Place he discovered that it had been burgled. It is as good a metaphor for modern Britain as any.)

While it is impossible to imagine two men more different than Hitler and Churchill, as leaders they had much more in common than one might think. The key attribute shared by both men was an almost superhuman tenacity of purpose that they held on to throughout their long years of adversity and failure. Hitler's early career was anything but promising. Landsberg prison in Bavaria, where Hitler wound up in 1923, was a forbidding place, although he was treated very leniently there. He had just tried to seize power, but instead his 'Beer-hall Putsch' failed pathetically. Indeed, up to the age of forty, Adolf Hitler was a failure in almost every respect. For most of the 1920s his NSDAP (nicknamed Nazi) Party was headed nowhere. In the elections of 1928, for example, it polled a mere 2.6 per cent of the vote. Most people at the time regarded Hitler as the joke leader of a joke party, thankfully devoid of any political future.

Churchill fully appreciated what Hitler went through in these German wilderness years. In his 1937 book *Great Contemporaries*, he reprinted an article of 1935 in which he had said that the story of Hitler's 'struggle cannot be read without admiration for the courage, the perseverance, and the vital force which enabled him to challenge, defy, conciliate, or overcome all the authorities or resistances which barred his path' in what Churchill described as Hitler's 'long wearing battle for the German heart'. (With commendable éclat, Churchill even retained those – and other – generous words about Hitler in the 1941 reprint of that book.)

Unlike Hitler – who had every disadvantage necessary for success in life – Churchill had every privilege that so often presages mediocrity. He was born at Blenheim Palace straight into the apex of Britain's political establishment; his father, Lord Randolph Churchill, was Chancellor of the Exchequer when Winston was at prep school. He had been bequeathed a far easier start than Hitler, who was the son of a simple Austrian customs officer. The grandson of a duke, whose heir presumptive he was until the age of ten, Churchill had had a promising career as Home Secretary before disaster overtook him as First Lord of the Admiralty in the First World War. Through a combination of military misjudgement and appalling luck, his brainchild, the Gallipoli campaign, was a costly failure, and he was forced to resign from the Cabinet in ignominy. His wife Clementine always remembered it as the lowest point in her husband's life, when he reputedly even briefly considered committing suicide.

Yet he refused to be broken. Politics were so deeply in Churchill's blood that he discussed them with Lloyd George in the vestry when waiting to sign the register during his wedding, and he was not about to leave that world. By 1924 Churchill was himself Chancellor of the Exchequer and after serving for five years in that high post he once again chose the political wilderness when he resigned from the Shadow Cabinet to pursue a long, bitter and ultimately doomed campaign against Indian self-government. His calls for enthusiastic British prosecution of the Russian Civil War and his air of over-excitability during the General Strike did not add to his reputation; instead, along with his eccentric and seemingly self-interested support for King Edward VIII during the Abdication Crisis, these made him look like a hopelessly reactionary imperialist warmonger and maverick in the eyes of most Britons. It was only by a vote of three to two that he escaped being deselected by his own constituency. There was indeed a sense, after he had warned of disaster so many times over so many different issues over so long a period, that by the time he got round to warning about the size of the Luftwaffe, Churchill was no longer taken seriously. He had himself written of this phenomenon in *Savrola*, when he described Laurenia's anti-Molara press and the way that: 'The worst result of an habitual use of strong language is that when a special occasion really does arise, there is no way of marking it.... They had compared the Head of the State so often and so vividly to Nero and Iscariot, very much to the advantage of those worthies, that it was difficult to know how they could deal with him now.'[11]

For all but a few months in the 1930s, Churchill was yesterday's man. The writer Christopher Sykes called him 'a disastrous relic of the past' and even his friend the Canadian press baron Max Beaverbrook described him as 'a busted flush'. In 1931 there was a book published entitled *The Tragedy of Winston Churchill*. For a decade he was forced to spend much of his time at his home at Chartwell in Kent, painting, bricklaying and writing the biography of his great ancestor John Churchill, the 1st Duke of Marlborough. When the Tory MP Lady Astor visited Joseph Stalin in 1937, the Russian leader asked her about his old enemy's political prospects. 'Oh, he's finished,' she replied, a view of Churchill that would have been echoed by most other political commentators of the day.

Yet, like Hitler, Churchill clung unflinchingly to his beliefs, the principal one being that he was chosen by Providence to save his country. Despite widespread hostility and ridicule, he continued to warn against the threat of Nazi aggression. This started early; in March 1933 he pointed to 'the tumultuous insurgency of ferocity and war spirit' that was then raging in Nazi Germany. With Hitler only Chancellor for two months, Churchill drew attention to 'The pitiless treatment of the minorities' in Germany, and the way that she had 'abandoned her liberties to augment her might'. In particular he emphasised the rapid expansion of the Luftwaffe and the contrasting weakness of the Royal Air Force. Picturing the 'incalculable conflagration' which might be unleashed by an incendiary-bomb attack on London, Churchill was accused by the British Prime Minister Stanley Baldwin of being alarmist.

Part of the problem was that Churchill was not suited to subordinate posts. His restlessness and frustration, borne out by his unsuitability for other roles, misled nearly everyone about his leadership capabilities, but some of his colleagues recognised this early on. The Foreign Secretary at the time of the outbreak of the First World War, Sir Edward Grey, once remarked that: 'Winston, very soon, will become incapable from sheer activity of mind of being anything in a Cabinet but prime minister.' Churchill's decisiveness emerged as the vital quality required for national leadership, but he was not well suited for any position but chief executive. His energy, drive and encyclopaedic mind, when exercised in the subordinate positions he held throughout his career, simply alienated colleagues and superiors. Many of his peers viewed his move to Number Ten in 1940 with dread and alarm. The War Cabinet official Sir Ian Jacob wrote years later of how: 'They had not yet the experience or imagination to realize the difference of a human dynamo when humming on the periphery and when driving at the centre.'

Although Churchill longed for office in the thirties, afterwards he was hugely relieved that he had not been offered it, since it kept his hands entirely clean of any responsibility for the National Government's policy of appeasement. 'Over me beat invisible wings,' he later wrote. Throughout his life, Churchill believed he had been especially chosen by Fate for greater things and this was a key factor in his drive. Once, in the Great War, when his dugout was blown up by a high-explosive shell moments after he had left it, he said that he had 'a strong sensation that a hand had been stretched out to move me in the nick of time from a fatal spot'. Not by any means a conventional Christian, Churchill believed in a kind of providence that reserved him for a special destiny, although he had denounced such an idea in *Savrola*, when the hero tells the heroine: 'I have always admired the audacity of man in thinking that a Supreme Power should placard the skies with the details of his squalid future, and that his marriage, his misfortunes, and his crimes should be written in letters of suns on the background of limitless space. We are inconsequential atoms. ... I realise my own insignificance, but I am a philosophic microbe, and it rather adds to my amusement than otherwise.' As Churchill put it elsewhere, we are all worms, but he liked to think of himself as a glow-worm.

After he was run over by the Italian-American driver of a car crossing Fifth Avenue in 1931 he said: 'There was a moment ... of a world aglare, of a man aghast ... I do not understand why I was not broken like an eggshell or squashed like a gooseberry.' He might not have understood at the time, but he had his suspicions that Fate had especially marked him out to save his country. Therefore he continued to warn against the threat of Nazi aggression at every opportunity. (In a retort to Willie Gallagher, the only Communist MP in the Commons, Churchill said in 1944: 'I was for eleven years a fairly solitary figure in this House and pursued my way with patience; and so there must be hope for the honourable member.')

In one of the no fewer than seven hundred newspaper articles that he wrote – covering everything from iced water and corn on the cob to Mussolini and the rise of the Luftwaffe, for publications as diverse as *Cosmopolitan* and the *Pall Mall Gazette* – Churchill produced an essay on Moses that must have left readers in no doubt who Churchill believed would lead his people to the Promised Land. 'Every prophet has to come from civilisation, but every prophet has to go into the wilderness,' he wrote. 'He must have a strong impression of a complex society and all that it has to give, and then must serve periods of isolation and meditation. This is the process by which psychic dynamite is made.' All this self-referential philosophising must have been faintly irritating and ridiculous to many people in 1932, but it would have seemed very different eight years later, once the dynamite – psychic and physical alike – had exploded. If he had a political role model at this time, it was Clemenceau, of whom he wrote (surely semi-autobiographically) in *Great Contemporaries*: 'He was defeated in his constituency of the Var, and quitted its bounds under the taunts and insults of the mob. Rarely was a public man in times of peace more cruelly hounded and hunted. Dark days, indeed, and the leering triumphs of once-trampled foes!' But, years later in 1917, 'It was at that moment ... that the fierce old man was summoned to what was in fact the Dictatorship of France. He returned to power as Marius had returned to Rome; doubted by many, dreaded by all, but doomsent, inevitable.' Once in power, Churchill wrote of Clemenceau (while dreaming about himself): 'He looked like a wild animal pacing to and fro behind bars, growling and glaring; and all around him was an assembly which would have done anything to avoid having him there, but having put him there, felt they must obey.' A better description of the British Conservative Party in May 1940 could scarcely be imagined.

Although Churchill's daughter Mary Soames has correctly written that he 'had a strong underlying belief in a Providential God', she has also pointed out that he 'was not religious in a conventional sense – and certainly no regular church-goer'.[12] The primary duty of the Almighty Being in whom Churchill believed, but to whom he paid little overt obeisance, seems to have been to watch over the physical well-being of Winston Leonard Spencer-Churchill. On one occasion when a visiting cleric over-generously described him as 'a pillar of the Church', he answered: 'Well, I don't think that could be said of me. But I do like to think of myself as a flying buttress.' He enjoyed the hymns, conformed outwardly as an Anglican in the way that most Conservative politicians did at that time, approved of the Church's then role as a bulwark of social stability, and applauded the part it had played in the development of the nation state. Moreover, he used the Bolsheviks' atheism against them politically, and although, as his friend Sir Desmond Morton put it, he 'did not believe that Christ was God... he recognised him as the finest character who ever lived'. He particularly admired the courage that Jesus had shown in the manner of his death, an aspect in a man's character that always mattered greatly to Churchill.

He was not entirely joking when he wrote to his mother from India in 1897: 'I am so conceited, I do not believe the Gods would create so potent a being as myself for so prosaic an ending' as death in a skirmish on the North-West Frontier. When one considers how often and how closely Churchill brushed against the Grim Reaper's cloak in his long life it is hard to doubt that he might well have had an (admittedly somewhat blasphemous) point when he assumed that 'invisible wings' beat above him. For what was the actuarial probability of a man who lived his kind of life finally dying a nonagenarian? Consider the might-have-beens. He was born two months prematurely, after his mother took a fall out walking with the guns of a shooting party on the Blenheim estate, and had then taken 'a rough pony ride' back to the palace. Neither the London obstetrician nor his Oxford auxiliary could get there in time for the birth. Aged eleven, Churchill very nearly died of pneumonia at his Brighton prep school, a disease that was to recur during and after the Second World War. His son Randolph wrote that this attack in 1886 brought Churchill 'closer to death than at any time during his long and adventurous life'. His next brush was more self-inflicted, when aged eighteen he leapt off a bridge in a game of chase with his brother and cousin on the estate of his aunt Lady Wimborne near Bournemouth. He fell twenty-nine feet on to hard ground and knocked himself out for three days, rupturing a kidney. 'For a year I looked at life round a corner,' he recalled. He then nearly drowned in Lake Geneva.

The stories of his exploits in Cuba, where he witnessed action with Spanish forces, on the North-West Frontier of India with the Malakand Field Force, at the charge of the 21st Lancers in the Battle of Omdurman, and also in escaping from a Pretorian prisoner-of-war camp during the Boer War are well documented; indeed, the 21st Lancers' regimental motto of 'Death or Glory' seems neatly to encapsulate the options with which Churchill sought to present himself between 1895 and 1900. Yet this seeming daring of death did not end in his mid-twenties. He even survived a plane crash.

After his enforced resignation from the chancellorship of the Duchy of Lancaster as a result of the failure of the Gallipoli campaign in the Great War, Churchill took command of the 6th battalion of the Royal Scots Fusiliers in France. Not for him the château-generalship of so many senior Allied officers far behind the lines of that conflict. On occasion, when he was inspecting a trench or dugout, a German high-explosive shell would land on it just before he arrived or soon after he left.

Although Churchill was never subjected to an assassination attempt – a curious oversight in an otherwise eventful life – he did of course frequently court danger during the Blitz when he would climb up on to the roof of the Admiralty to watch the air battle, despite the ever-present danger of bullets, high explosives, shrapnel blasts and plane crashes. He was up there in September 1940, the same month that Buckingham Palace took a direct hit in the courtyard at only the other end of the Mall. Churchill, who hunted and took flying lessons, led a life that could have been cut off on more than a score of occasions before victory was won in the Second World War. Faith in his own star, in what he called his 'guardian' and 'guiding hand', was a necessary prerequisite for a leader who wanted to follow the kind of active existence that Churchill had chosen for himself.

The historian Paul Addison has characterised Churchill's spiritual beliefs as 'a concoction of ambition, historical myth, and a residue of religious conviction'. If they were what sustained his sense of self-belief during the months of doubt and despair after the Dardanelles catastrophe, who can hold them against him? There is anyhow a tremendous ambiguity to his true religious beliefs. When in a Shadow Cabinet meeting in June 1950 he referred to 'the Old Man' coming to his aid, he later had to explain that he had meant God, yet three years later, after his stroke, he told his doctors that he did not believe in the immortality of the soul and that death was 'black velvet – eternal sleep'. That is what he had called it in *Savrola*, half a century earlier, when the Laurenian president faced death 'and beyond he saw nothing – annihilation – black, black night'.[13]

Yet there is also an assumption that Heaven does exist in several of Churchill's letters, particularly the moving one that was to be delivered to Clementine were he to die in the trenches, in which he wrote: 'Do not grieve for me too much. I am a spirit confident of my rights. Death is only an incident, and not the most important that happens to us in this state of being. . . . If there is anywhere else, I shall be on the lookout for you.' In his book *Thoughts and Adventures* (1932) he also wrote: 'When I get to Heaven I mean to spend a considerable portion of my first million years in painting, and so get to the bottom of the subject.'

Because Churchill was, in his own words, 'lacking in the religious sense' – and lost any specifically Anglican faith he might have had by about the age of twenty-three – he developed an elemental, almost pagan belief in Fate and Destiny rather reminiscent of Napoleon's. But not Hitler's. For Hitler increasingly saw himself as the Supreme Being who could control Providence, something that was quite alien to Churchill's (admittedly also highly egotistical) belief system. If anything, Hitler had a yet more unshakeable faith in his own star, a certainty about his ability to guide Fate himself. He believed that it was down to Fate that he was born at Braunau am Inn, close to the German border, and that nothing less than 'Divine Providence' had sent him to Vienna to share the sufferings of the masses; and of course – just like Churchill – it had also been an unseen hand that had protected him in the trenches during the First World War when so many of his comrades had perished.

All of this, Hitler reasoned, must have been done for a purpose, which equally clearly must be a great one. By the summer of 1937 he believed himself to be utterly infallible, stating: 'When I look back upon the five years that lie behind, I can say, this was not the work of human hands alone.' Imagine the invincible self-regard it is necessary to have in order to tell the German people, as he did in one speech: 'That is the miracle of the age, that you have found me, that you have found me among so many millions. And I have found you, that is Germany's good fortune.' In this he was encouraged by the Nazi Party: comparisons of Adolf Hitler to Jesus were only disparaged by SS Gruppenführer Schulz from Pomerania, for example, because whereas Christ had had a mere twelve disciples, Hitler had seventy million.[14]

Hitler also called on his *Schiksal* (Destiny) and *Vorsehung* (Providence) when he simply wanted to avoid making a decision. He only really chose to make decisions when events or his opponents forced them upon him; otherwise, as the historian Karl Dietrich Bracher has said, his trust in Fate was part of the rationalisation of his instinctive dislike of having to take them. Hitler stated that he would not undertake an action, 'Not even if the whole party tries to drive me into action. I will not act; I will wait, no matter what happens. But if the voice speaks, then I will know that the time has come to act.' The belief that one is a recipient of voices in one's head is a well-known symptom of schizophrenia. If the sense of Hitler as a national Messiah became a new kind of faith for Nazi Germany, it was one in which he himself was an enthusiastic co-religionist.

The sense of all-or-nothing that Hitler and Churchill both espoused in their wilderness years was also a consequence of neither having independent means, at least until the success of their books – in Hitler's case *Mein Kampf* and in Churchill's *The Second World War* – made them financially secure. Although he was never as poor as Adolf Hitler was during his wilderness period, Churchill lived for many years teetering on the brink of bankruptcy. People tend to assume that because Churchill was the grandson of a duke and born in a palace, he was also rich, but the truth is very different. Almost throughout his life, and certainly before the publication of his wartime memoirs in 1948, Churchill's debts left him constantly bordering on negative net worth. The outgoings on his splendidly luxurious lifestyle nearly always amounted to as much as he earned from his journalism and ministerial salary. His financial situation was so precarious at the time of his wife Clementine's fourth pregnancy in the summer and autumn of 1918 that it is thought that she even offered to put up her baby for adoption by General Sir Ian Hamilton's wife after it was born.

In May 1915, when forced to resign over the Gallipoli débâcle, Churchill did not return to his ministerial salary of five thousand pounds per annum until Lloyd George appointed him Minister for Munitions in July 1917. In the meantime he had to survive on the pay of an army officer and a backbench MP, in the days when neither was large. Clementine was no heiress, and could contribute very little to the family's finances. So short of money were they in 1918 that when the lease ran out on their London home in Eccleston Square they had to move into Churchill's aunt Cornelia's house in Tenterden Street off Oxford Street. Worse was to come later that year when Churchill received a letter from the Ministry of Agriculture complaining that the land at his country home, Lullenden in Sussex, was not being fully cultivated, at a time when producing food was a duty incumbent on all British landowners. (The civil servant Sir Maurice Hankey recalled spending a tea-time with Churchill in 1917 'rambling around his wild and beautiful property'.) In his reply to the Ministry, Churchill had to admit that he simply had not got the capital to invest in the machinery necessary to cultivate his land.

Although his journalism was later to provide him with a large income, he wrote relatively little during the First World War, and it was to be several years before the income from his history of that war, *The World Crisis*, came on stream. With his reputation at its nadir after Gallipoli, he could also not call on the generous group of rich friends who were occasionally to bail him out during the wilderness years of 1931–9 and who at one point bought him a Daimler car for his birthday. For all his genius in other areas, Churchill was an inept financial speculator, who lost the 2002 equivalent of a quarter of a million pounds in a single day of the Wall Street Crash of 1929.

Both Hitler and Churchill, therefore, knew hard times, although they were hardly comparable since Hitler did not have the kind of friends who could bail him out to the extent of buying him a

Daimler. Yet both men shared a tenacity, an unshakeable belief in their mission no matter what others said of them, and it was largely this that gained them followers once the political circumstances had changed. Today we think of Hitler and Churchill as powerful leaders, but we tend to forget how unlikely their rise to power seemed to people at the time. Both had been failures, Hitler in the 1920s and Churchill in the 1930s. So how could they become leaders of their countries such a short time afterwards?

Creation of the national myth

Hitler used his time in Landsberg prison to write a book, or rather he dictated it to his acolytes Rudolf Hess and Emil Maurice, who were also serving prison sentences for their participation in the Beer-hall Putsch. It reads like a work that has been spoken by a man walking up and down a prison cell, letting out the frustrations of his captivity in his rambling fury. *Mein Kampf* is a dreadful work in every respect: a garbled, unfocused mixture of manic hyper-nationalism, twisted Darwinism and repulsive anti-Semitism. Rather like Karl Marx who reduced history to merely the story of class struggle, Hitler's history of mankind is no more than a racial struggle, and the ills of the world are put down to an international Jewish-Bolshevik conspiracy. The subjugation of allegedly inferior peoples such as the Slavs is offered as the recipe for Germany's salvation. Yet *Mein Kampf* also holds the secret of Hitler's startling rise to his position as the Führer of Germany.

The creation of an all-encompassing national legend is epicentral to the formation of a modern political movement. For Hitler, this was *Dolchstosslegende* (the stab-in-the-back myth). According to this explanation of Germany's defeat in the Great War, the surrender of November 1918 came not as a result of unsustainable losses on the battlefield, still less of bad generalship by men like Hindenburg or Ludendorff, or even the incompetence of the Kaiser, but because a sinister conspiracy of socialists and Jews had betrayed the honest brave German *Volk* (people) from within. This analysis, which historians agree has no evidential historical merit whatsoever, was drummed into Germans at every available opportunity by the Nazis.

On occasion, Hitler would retell German history from the time of

Arminius, the German who defied the Roman Empire, via the Emperor Barbarossa and Frederick the Great, creating a mythical heroic past for the whole of Germany which he could contrast powerfully with the humiliations of the 1919 Treaty of Versailles and which he put down to this alleged stab-in-the-back. In fact, of course, the defeat had been the result of German troops being stabbed in the front by the British, French, American and Canadian armies, rather than in the back by the Jews.

Even non-Nazis came to believe implicitly in the *Dolchstosslegende,* providing as it did the perfect psychological balm so desperately needed by a proud nation raw in defeat. In a biography published in 2002 it has emerged that in the 1920s the Prince of Pless, one of Germany's greatest aristocrats, was told by his father that he had dined the night before in the Pariser Platz in Berlin with the rich Jewish hostess Frau von Friedländer, who had allegedly told him:

> You don't perhaps realise that you nearly won the war because we were assisting you the world over and it was only because of us Jews that things went very badly for you afterwards. If you remember, in 1917 Balfour made his famous declaration in which he promised us a Jewish homeland in Palestine. Up to then we were on your side, because the Kaiser had promised us a homeland, but after the Balfour declaration it was decided that we should throw in our lot with the Allies. This we did and the whole power of our worldwide organisation worked in that direction. You don't realise, of course, the great mistake you made here in Germany and in Austria by allowing Jews to obtain commissions in your armies, because it gave us the possibility to collect information on every level, up to and including the General Staff and to get an insight into the workings of your military machinery, which we could never have achieved otherwise. This information we passed on to the Allies. So they always knew far in advance what your plans were and where and when the next military move was going to take place.

The Prince of Pless recalled that 'My father was quite upset. He could not get over the fact that his Jewish friends, whom he had known for years before the war and who had pretended to be loyal

German subjects and staunch friends and supporters of the Kaiser, in reality were all the time prepared to work against him if ordered to do so by their political leaders.'[15] If cultured aristocrats could have fallen for such ludicrous lies and conspiracy theories, how much easier would it have been for the less well-educated German masses?

However repugnant his core beliefs are to us today, in *Mein Kampf* Adolf Hitler offered a clear vision: that of a German *Reich* (Empire) that would one day dominate Europe. For a people who considered themselves downtrodden by sinister influences – however absurd the theories behind them – it proved irresistible. In his book Hitler wrote:

> If the German nation today, penned into an impossible area, faces a lamentable future, this is not a commandment of Fate. Neither is to revolt against this state of affairs an affront to Fate... Germany will either be a world power or there will be no Germany. And for world power she needs that magnitude which will give her the necessary position in today's world, and life to her citizens.[16]

Few people took this vision seriously at the time. Yet such was Hitler's invincible sense of self-belief that he let none of this deter him. He had a deep sense of mission. 'The Jews have not brought about the 9th November 1918 for nothing,' he told the Czech Foreign Minister, Franzisek Chvalkovsky, in January 1939. 'This day will be avenged.' This warped, paranoiac conspiracy theory displayed what most modern psychologists would diagnose as the primary symptoms of a psychopath. Yet he would have been a psychopath few people would have heard of had it not been for the crisis of capitalism known as the Wall Street Crash.

Everything changed dramatically for Hitler when the American stock market collapsed in New York in October 1929. Soon afterwards the Great Depression hit Europe, bringing unemployment to millions and widespread social unrest in its wake. In May 1928 the Nazis had won 2.6 per cent of the popular vote and only a dozen seats, but by September 1930 – when Germany had five million people unemployed – they won 18.3 per cent and more than a hundred seats in the Reichstag. The month after the Lausanne Conference of June 1932, which terminated Germany's reparations payments under the Versailles Treaty, the Nazis won 37.4 per cent. In that election, anti-democratic parties won a majority of the vote; for the first time in history a large modern state had deliberately voted against democracy. Now that Germany was riven by crises, Hitler suddenly gained what every successful leader needs: followers. Six months later he was Chancellor.

Churchill too had a strong, unshakeable vision: that of a powerful British empire based on civilised values. During the 1930s, in his study in his country house at Chartwell in Kent, he wrote many speeches warning of the dangers that Nazi Germany posed to Britain and the world. This is an excerpt from one he made to the City Carlton Club in September 1935, as Italian threats to Abyssinia (modern-day Ethiopia) became ever more menacing and Germany's Nuremberg Laws outlawed the Jews and made the swastika the official flag of Hitler's Reich:

> Germany is rearming on a gigantic scale and at an unexampled speed. The whole force and power of Nazidom are being concentrated on warlike preparations by land, sea and air. The German nation, under Herr Hitler's dictatorship, is spending this year at least six times as much as we are on the Army, the Navy, and the Air Force put together. German finance is a perpetuated war budget. I admire the great German people, but the rearmament of Germany, organized and led as she is now, must appear to anyone with any sense of proportion as the greatest and most grim fact in the world today.[17]

Recognising that Hitler's expansionist foreign policy must eventually mean war, Churchill time and again called for Britain to undergo a comprehensive programme of heavy rearmament. Few listened. He was variously denigrated as a 'fire-eater and militarist', a 'rogue elephant', or – by the *Daily Express* in October 1938 – as 'a man whose mind is soaked in the conquests of [the 1st Duke of] Marlborough'.[18] It was the same month that the Chamberlain Government had decided not to go to war with Germany over Hitler's plan to dismember Czechoslovakia, a stance that was greeted deliriously by the great majority of Britons. Clearly, Churchill's vision was completely out of tune with the times.

It was only on 15 March 1939, after the Nazis had marched in and occupied the rump of Czechoslovakia, that it dawned on the British people that Churchill might have been right all along about Hitler's true intentions. They understood how, in exploiting Britain's and France's lack of resolve, Germany was set to dominate Europe. Finally, after the warnings of half a decade, more and more people were willing to share Churchill's vision of a powerful alliance ready to defend freedom.

So both Hitler and Churchill gained followers through a vision which they clung to unflinchingly. Such a vision is the key to true leadership, and it is particularly powerful if the leaders have stuck to it through adversity, as both Hitler and Churchill did. Leaders give people a common goal with which they can wholeheartedly identify. Managers don't have that guiding vision. As Ronald Reagan put it: 'To grasp and hold a vision, that is the very essence of successful leadership – not only on the movie set where I learned it, but everywhere.'

Hitler's vision, of course, was a fantastically evil one, but this is not how the German people saw it at the time. While to us his ideas seem utterly foul, many Germans believed that he really did offer them a glittering vision for a better future. Of course, most of it was defined by what he was against, rather than what he stood for. He was opposed to socialism, Bolshevism, the Versailles Treaty, liberalism, the Jews, big business, democracy, and old-style Wilhelmine aristocratic conservatism. Saying what one is against is far easier (and often more effective) in politics than stating what one is for, and Hitler took this truth to new heights.

Oratory

'The power which has always started the greatest religious and political avalanches in history has been, from time immemorial, none but the magic power of the word,' wrote Hitler. For him, words were 'hammer blows' which had the power to 'open the gates to people's hearts'. He admired the impassioned oratory of the British Prime Minister David Lloyd George, saying: 'The speeches of this Englishman [*sic*] were the most wonderful performances, for they testified to a positively amazing knowledge of the soul of the broad masses of the people.' When it came to propaganda, the Nazis pioneered a vast range of innovative ideas. For example, they invented what are today called 'photo-opportunities', and Hitler's rallies were undeniably impressive spectacles involving tens of thousands of people marching in perfect step. Yet for all their visual extravagance, it was at the centrepiece of these rallies – his oratory – that Hitler knew he had to excel. To that end he trusted only himself to write his speeches, as did Churchill. Neither man resorted to the phalanxes of speech-writers so favoured by today's politicians.

In his public performances Hitler used the old show-business trick of making people wait for him in order to build up excitement and expectation, both prior to his appearance and even when he had already stepped up to the dais. He would survey his audience, grasping his military belt with its *Gott Mit Uns* (God With Us) motto on the buckle, for sometimes up to half a minute before starting to speak. Commencing relatively slowly and with a low, deep voice, it was not until the end that he ranted and screeched in the manner so often seen on newsreels. He would also speak through the applause just after it had begun to drop off, and would wind up with shorter and punchier sentences. Many of these techniques, very different from the ones in common use in the Western democracies of the thirties, have become standard practice in political speech-making today.

Tenacity and charisma alone would not have made Hitler Germany's Führer. He still needed to sell himself and his vision. In order to succeed, leaders have to be able to convey themselves and their message to the public, and the primary means has always been – and probably always will be – the set-piece political speech. For all the penetration of the written word, graphics, text messaging and video link-ups, nothing is so politically persuasive as the power of direct oratory. Even today, for all the modern public-relations gimmicks offered by television, radio, the Internet and multimedia, we still judge our leaders largely by their ability to move us through their oratory. Politicians who are poor public speakers rarely make great leaders.

Both Hitler and Churchill have rightly gone down in history as highly effective orators, but surprisingly enough public speaking did not come naturally to either of them. While both undoubtedly showed talent eventually, they had to work very hard to develop it. Hitler liked to have a warm-up act to heighten the audience's anticipation of his public appearances. In a speech to workers at the Siemens Dynamo Works in Berlin on 10 November 1933, it was performed by his Propaganda Minister Dr Joseph Goebbels. This speech, given only nine months after Hitler had become Chancellor, provides a perfect illustration of the sinister but masterful method by which the Führer managed to create a sense of community between himself and his audience. It is worth considering in some detail for the various methods he used to play upon the emotions of an audience who were not necessarily positively disposed towards him.

'German compatriots, my German workers,' Hitler began, 'if today I am speaking to you and to millions of other German workers, I have a greater right to be doing this than anybody else.' He was aware that many in that largely working-class audience were likely to have left-wing sympathies, yet within a minute he had won them over with a reference to his wartime service in the trenches, something that many of them had also undergone. 'Once I stood amongst you. For four and a half years of war, I was in your midst. And through diligence, learning – and, I have to say, hunger – I slowly worked my way up. Deep inside me, I always remained what I had been before.' His reference to the widespread food shortages undergone by Germany in 1918–19 was a master-stroke, one of several in that speech.

He continued: 'But I was not amongst those who worked against the interests of the nation. I was convinced that the destiny of the nation had to find representation if terrible damage to the whole people, sooner or later, was to be avoided. This separated me from the others.' Then came an attack on the Versailles Treaty. By restricting Germany to an army of one hundred thousand, without armour or aircraft and a navy with no larger vessels than ten thousand tons, the Allies had tried to protect themselves from a resurgent Germany after the Great War.[19] It was nothing like so harsh as the terms that Germany planned to impose on the rest of Europe if victorious, but it disbanded the German General Staff, provided for the occupation of the Rhineland until its terms were accepted, demanded financial reparations and contained a clause blaming Germany for deliberately starting the war. Though each was perfectly reasonable in itself, collectively the clauses of the Versailles Treaty amounted to Hitler's best (and indeed only) rational political argument. As he put it in his Siemens speech: 'The theory that victor and vanquished have to remain in their legal position for ever, this theory has led to a new hatred in the world, to perpetuate disorder, to uncertainty, to distrust on one side and fury on the other.' It was a hatred and fury that Hitler would spend the next decade doing everything in his power to stoke up and then unleash.

Hitler knew very little about economics, but he did know that his audiences probably knew even less. So it was to the financial aspects of Versailles that he turned next:

> The world was not pacified, as was explained at the time, but on the contrary, the world was plunged into ever-new haggling and ever-new discord. And the second thesis was equally mad: that you have to destroy the vanquished economically as well, so that the victor has a better economy. A mad theory, but one which runs like a red thread through the whole Versailles Treaty and which finally leads to the fact that for ten years they have tried, on the one hand, to burden the economy of a great people with an unbearable load, and on the other, to destroy it as much as possible, to cut off all its opportunities. We experienced the consequences of this. The way in which, in order to fulfil its economic obligations, Germany was increasingly forced to throw itself on to the export markets under any kind of conditions, the way in which the international competitive struggle began here and the way in which political debt was gradually changed into economic debts.

Economically this was drivel, not least because the Allies had early on begun to lessen Germany's debt burden, which was significantly reduced by the Great Depression too. Yet it worked rhetorically, which is all that mattered to Hitler as he got on to another favoured topic: the Jews. The chief aim of the speech was to promote rearmament without regard for international restrictions. It was obvious that this would damage Germany's international position, but Hitler made it clear whom he intended to take the blame:

> The struggle between the people and the hatred amongst them is being nurtured by very specific interested parties. It is a small, rootless, international clique that is turning the people against each other, that does not want them to have peace. It is the people

> who are at home both nowhere and everywhere, who do not have anywhere a soil on which they have grown up, but who live in Berlin today, in Brussels tomorrow, Paris the day after that, and then again in Prague or Vienna or London, and who feel at home everywhere.

At that point a man in the audience shouted out: 'The Jews!' Without pausing to consider him, or this, Hitler continued: 'They are the only ones who can be addressed as international, because they conduct their business everywhere, but the people cannot follow them.... I know one thing about those who today are agitating against Germany, about this international clique which libels the German people in such a way: not one of them has ever heard a bullet whistle past.' In fact, of course, the Jews had a distinguished record of fighting in the trenches during the Great War, as even the SS had to accept when, at the Wannsee Conference that planned the Final Solution in 1942, Reinhard Heydrich ordered that 'severely wounded veterans and Jews with war decorations (Iron Cross 1st class) will be accepted in the old-age ghettos' rather than being 'evacuated east'.[20]

Hitler never once actually mentioned the Jews by name in his Siemensstadt speech, but it was obvious to everyone to whom he was referring. It did not need the moron in the audience to shout it out. Hitler once remarked that if the Jews had not existed: 'We should have to invent them. It is essential to have a tangible enemy, not merely an abstract one.'[21] In the Nazi state, all social classes were supposed to be united in the so-called *Volksgemeinschaft* (people's community). Nothing creates more unity than a common enemy; hatred of the Jews thus constituted the backbone of Hitler's power. By overtly not mentioning the Jews by name in his speech, Hitler created another bond between himself and the audience, tacitly drawing them into his conspiracy.

The oration at the Dynamo Works continued, and by now he was indeed yelling:

> They should see that what I am saying is not the speech of a Chancellor, but that the whole people stands behind it as one man, man for man, woman for woman. What is bound together today is the German people itself. For centuries it has sought its destiny in

> discord, with terrible results. I think that it is time to seek our fate in unity, to attempt to realise our fate as an indivisible united community. And in Germany I am the guarantee that this community will not favour one side alone. You can see me as the man who does not belong to any class, to any caste, who is above all that. I have nothing but a connection to the German people.

This proclamation of the leader's classlessness and commitment to community was greeted with cheering and acclaim, along with the singing of the Nazi Party anthem, the Horst Wessel Song.

The German people, Hitler was emphasising, were completely separate from the Jews. Getting over this sense of the 'otherness' of non-Germans was just as important as emphasising the identity of the Aryan race itself.[22] The British philosopher Bertrand Russell believed that 'Few people can be happy unless they hate some other person, nation or creed', yet why did Hitler hate the Jews? It is a straightforward enough question, and central to the history of the twentieth century, but there is still no entirely satisfactory answer. Various different theories have been adduced, from his having caught syphilis from a Jewish prostitute, via his having been cheated by the Jewish Dr Eduard Bloch, who treated Hitler's mother for breast cancer, to the allegedly Jewish professors who turned him away from the Visual Arts Academy of Vienna. Yet could there be a far more sinister answer than these naïvely monocausal ones? Might it be that Hitler actually had nothing personally against the Jews, but just spotted that demonising them would be a rewarding political move?

In a recent ground-breaking book, entitled *Hitler's Vienna: A Dictator's Apprenticeship*, the historian Brigitte Hamann has gone so far as to argue that during his 1908–13 sojourn in Vienna, between the ages of nineteen and twenty-four, Hitler actually liked and got on well with several Jews. Her researches left no Viennese stones unturned, from Dr Bloch's account-books to the racial background of the Visual Arts Academy's examiners. As a result, she managed to delve deep into the psychopathology of the future Führer, with fascinating results.

Much of what Hitler wrote about his Viennese years in *Mein Kampf* turns out either to be exaggerated or untrue. What is incontrovertible, however, is that although Hitler knew and lived among Jews during his poverty-stricken period as a painter and opera fanatic, they treated him well and he displayed no overt signs of hostility towards them at the time. During all the tedious, endless later monologues about his dog days in Vienna, Hitler never mentioned having a bad experience with a Jew there. It is even possible to state that some of Hitler's best friends were Jews, such as Josef Neumann and Siegfried Läffner. Far from it being instilled in him by his brutal, drunkard father or his provincial Austrian background, Hitler only appears to have taken to anti-Semitism much later, probably an entirely cynical manoeuvre to enhance his political ambitions after the Great War. Poor, shy, untalented, utterly asexual, introverted, socially envious and monomaniacal, the young Hitler was, in Albert Speer's later words, 'an insecure stranger in a large metropolis' when he lived in Vienna. Instead of adapting his personality in order to fit in, as most normal people would have done, Hitler withdrew further into himself and blamed the Viennese for not appreciating him properly.

It was the petty resentments of this unhappy time in the Austrian capital that established many of the outlines of what turned into Nazism. All that was needed was a huge European war to create the necessary conditions in which the bacillus of his views could thrive. Right on cue, only a year after Hitler left Vienna, came the cataclysm of August 1914. The dictator had served out his apprenticeship, and once anti-Semitism was cynically slotted into his creed he was ready to wreak his havoc. Of course it makes little difference whether Hitler's anti-Semitism was born of personal distaste, perceived wrongs or political opportunism, but it seems that the last was the case.

The writer Frederic Raphael has an interesting new theory that is a psychological twist on the one about the Jewish doctor of Hitler's mother having cheated and/or misdiagnosed her. According to this thesis:

> If Dr Bloch failed to cure Frau Hitler's cancer, it is unlikely – not to say impossible – that in those days anyone could have. Nor does Hitler say so. That 'Adi' loved his mother is undoubted; so did Proust, who nevertheless, in a notorious *Figaro* article, defended matricide on the grounds that, after all, everyone sometimes longs

> to kill his mother. Is it too tricksy to suggest that Hitler, seeing his mother's sufferings, wished (humanely enough) that they would end but that, when they did, in her death, he felt so guilty that he transferred his shameful wish onto the Jewish doctor, who could then be the scapegoat for it?[23]

It probably is indeed far too 'tricksy', not least because Hitler might well have been among the millions of us who have never once wanted to harm our mothers, but it is certainly no wierder than many of the monocausal theories that have been produced to explain the Holocaust.

Some people consider that it is not just irrelevant where Hitler contracted his anti-Semitism but also morally wrong to investigate the issue too closely. They argue that it plays into the hands of people who, like David Irving, take the opposite view. As has been perceptively pointed out by the writer and critic Jonathan Meades, there is

> a school of charlatanism whose bickering adherents attempt to explain Hitler by inventing, or giving credence to, folkloric stories of psycho-sexual traumas: Hitler's mother was allegedly mistreated or misdiagnosed by a Jewish doctor and died; Hitler may have contracted syphilis from a Jewish prostitute – these speculations are hateful because they seek to make individual Jews culpable for the enormities their race was to suffer. There are, inevitably, one-ball theories and satanic abuse theories. There is the ludicrous tale of the infant Hitler having his penis bitten by a goat into whose mouth he was attempting to urinate.[24]

This last theory, if true, might explain much about Hitler, but presumably not his anti-Semitism. And even if Hitler was monorchid, that does not explain why thirteen million Germans voted for the NSDAP in 1932, since they were not told that he was short of a testicle (which, anyhow, he was not). What is interesting is not what drove him, so much as what drove the German people to abandon democracy and support a leader whose revanchism was so loudly proclaimed at every opportunity.

In his speech at the Siemens Dynamo Works it was only in carefully selected places that Hitler worked himself into a completely deliberate and well-rehearsed rage. For the most part, he did not rant and foam during his speeches, despite the fact that he is shown in that state in most of the footage one sees. Reinhard Spitzy, private secretary to the German Foreign Minister Joachim von Ribbentrop, recalled how once, after a good lunch with Hitler and his staff, a servant entered the room to announce that a British diplomat had arrived:

> Hitler started up in agitation. '*Gott im Himmel!* Don't let him in yet – I'm still in a good humour.' Before his staff's eyes, he then worked himself up, solo, into an artificial rage – his face darkened, he breathed heavily and his eyes glared. Then he went next door and acted out for the unfortunate Englishman a scene so loud that every word was audible from the lunch table. Ten minutes later he returned with sweat beading his brow. He carefully closed the door behind him and said with a chuckle, 'Gentlemen, I need tea. He thinks I'm furious!'[25]

Leaders have to be actors, and Adolf Hitler understood this very well, even if he was something of a ham one himself. In the early days of his career he studied the performances of a Bavarian comedian named Weiss-Ferdl in order to learn how to captivate an audience. Just like an actor, Hitler would endlessly practise his poses and gestures in front of the mirror in his shabby room in Munich's Thierschstrasse. Photographs exist of him also doing this much later in his career. It was in the streets and beer halls of Munich that Hitler plied his early trade as a political agitator, sometimes speaking to audiences as small as a dozen people. There he learned just how much his effect on the public owed to careful planning and preparation of material. Anyone who has tried to address an audience at Speakers' Corner in London's Hyde Park will know just how quickly the experience toughens one intellectually and emotionally, especially when it comes to dealing with chance hecklers and outright opponents.

Hitler would personally examine the acoustics of the beer halls so that he could change his tone and pitch accordingly. Once he made the mistake of delivering a speech on a Sunday morning. The audience was, as he later described, 'cold as ice'. From then on, he preferred to schedule his speeches for the evenings when his audiences were more receptive to his message. As he wrote in *Mein Kampf*: 'It seems that in the morning and during the day the human mind revolts against any attempt to have somebody else's will or opinion imposed upon it. In the evening, however, it easily succumbs to the domination of a stronger will.' (Professional actors bear out this contention; for some reason, audiences are far more receptive at evening performances than at matinées. It took a particular mind like Hitler's to put this phenomenon to a political use.)

Theatrical effects like martial music, seas of flags, massed ranks of storm troopers, and especially dramatic lighting – sometimes using military searchlights, sometimes hand-held flaming torches – were employed at meetings and rallies to increase the audience's receptiveness still further, and the Nazis pioneered means of propaganda that are now a commonplace in the modern political arena. The comparison to Churchill could not be more stark. He held few rallies and employed no spin-doctors or special effects. His preferred venue was the House of Commons or the wireless, where the audience physically present was relatively small. He relied on the power of the spoken word and the persuasiveness of the better argument. It wasn't demagogic tricks that made him the greatest orator of the twentieth century, but his exceptional command of the English tongue. As he wrote in *My Early Life*: 'I would make boys all learn English; and then I would make the clever ones learn Latin as an honour and Greek as a treat. But the only thing I would whip them for is not knowing English. I would whip them hard for that.'

Churchill was not a natural-born speaker; few people are. After a disastrous experience trying to address the Commons entirely from memory at the age of thirty, he abandoned the practice. Instead he would sometimes spend ten to fourteen hours preparing a single speech, occasionally to the accompaniment of gramophone records playing martial music, working and reworking it until he finally thought it perfect. As his friend Lord Birkenhead joked: 'Winston has spent the best years of his life writing impromptu speeches.' Churchill said that the best advice he ever got on parliamentary speaking came from the Tory politician and former Cabinet minister Henry Chaplin, who told him: 'Don't be hurried. Unfold your case. If you have anything to say, the House will listen.' It was advice Churchill put to good, and occasionally devastating, effect.

In *Savrola*, Churchill described the genesis of the hero's great speech in the Laurenian City Hall. It seems so plainly autobiographical an explanation of the process of creating a political oration that it bears repetition in full:

> His speech – he had made many and knew that nothing good can be obtained without effort. These impromptu feats of oratory existed only in the minds of the listeners; the flowers of rhetoric were hothouse plants. What was there to say? Successive cigarettes had been mechanically consumed. Amid the smoke he saw a peroration, which would cut deep into the hearts of a crowd; a high thought, a fine simile, expressed in that correct diction which is comprehensible even to the most illiterate, and appeals to the most simple; something to lift their minds from the material cares of life and to awake sentiment. His ideas began to take the form of words, to group themselves into sentences; he murmured to himself; instinctively he alliterated. Ideas succeeded one another, as a stream flows swiftly by and the light changes on its waters. He seized a piece of paper and began hurriedly to pencil notes. That was a point; could not tautology accentuate it? He scribbled down a rough sentence, scratched it out, polished it, and wrote it in again. The sound would please their ears, the sense improve and stimulate their minds. What a game it was! His brain contained the cards he had to play, the world the stakes he played for. As he worked, the hours passed away. The housekeeper entering with his luncheon found him silent and busy; she had seen him thus before and did not venture to interrupt him. The untasted food grew cold upon the table, as the hands of the clock moved slowly round marking the measured tread of time. Presently he rose, and, completely under the influence of his own thoughts and language, began to pace the room with short strides, speaking to himself in a low voice and with great emphasis. Suddenly he stopped, and with a strange violence his hand descended on the table. It was the end of the speech.[26]

'Rhetorical power', wrote Churchill, 'is neither wholly bestowed, nor wholly acquired, but cultivated.' He was a perfectionist, rather than a born orator, and in 1940–41 the result was indeed perfection. The cadences of Churchill's speeches of that year owed much to the hours when, as a young hussar subaltern stationed in India nearly half a century earlier, he had studied the historical works of Gibbon and Macaulay. Churchill created his own synthesis of the grandiloquent rolling sentences of the former and the biting wit of the latter. His oratory was also influenced by the late-Victorian rhetoric of William Gladstone, the Irish-American politician Bourke Cockran and his own father Lord Randolph Churchill, who was the most magnetic political orator of his day.

Churchill's grand, old-style idiom did not impress everybody; some found it insincere, others pompous, yet others derided him as a cross between a ham actor and a music-hall turn. There was even one point during the locust years of the 1930s when the House of Commons shouted him down when he tried to put the case for King Edward VIII during the Abdication Crisis. It was not really until 1940 that, in that supreme test of the British people, Churchill's rhetoric at last truly matched the perils of the hour to create the sublime beauty of the best of his wartime speeches. The defeat on the Western Front, the evacuation from Dunkirk, the Fall of France, the Battle of Britain, the Blitz, the threat of invasion – all produced speeches and phrases that will live for as long as does the English tongue.

In the summer of 1940, Churchill's speeches were just about all the British people had to sustain them. With Hitler in control of Continental Europe from Brest to Warsaw, even the Chiefs of Staff had no logical plan for victory. With neither Russia nor America in the conflict, all Britain could do was to hold on, grimly praying that something might turn up. Churchill could not really appeal to the head in his protestations of the certainty of ultimate victory, so he had to appeal to the heart.

Without having very much in the way of sustenance or good news for the British people, Churchill took a political risk in deliberately choosing to emphasise the dangers instead. Only three days after becoming prime minister he told the House of Commons: 'I have nothing to offer but blood, toil, tears and sweat.' He attempted no evasions about the nature of the task ahead, as his words swept away a decade of appeasement, doubt and defeatism, which he had once called 'the long, drawling tides of drift and surrender'. He unhesitatingly placed the conflict in the stark context of a Manichean struggle between good and evil, truth and falsehood, right and wrong. It was what Britons longed to hear. As he left the Commons he observed to his friend Desmond Morton: 'That got the sods, didn't it?'[27]

The effect was indeed extraordinary. As the writer Vita Sackville-West told her husband, the Information Minister Harold Nicolson: 'One of the reasons why one is stirred by his Elizabethan phrases is that one feels the whole massive backing of power and resolve behind them, like a great fortress: they are never words for words' sake.' The mention of Elizabethan England is instructive, for Churchill enlisted the services of the past to boost British morale, summoning up the ghosts of Drake and Nelson to emphasise to the people that Britain had faced such dangers and emerged victorious before. The subliminal message was that they would do so again. He was never above adapting successful lines for use in his speeches, both of his own and other people's; for example, his famous phrase about the RAF in the Battle of Britain might have owed something to Sir John Moore's declaration about the capture of Corsica in 1793: 'Never was so much done by so few men.'

Isaiah Berlin, in his essay-length book *Mr Churchill in 1940*, was at pains to point out how Churchill drew on 'an historical imagination so strong, so comprehensive as to encase the whole of the present and the whole of the future in a framework of a rich and multi-coloured past'. Churchill expected at least a working knowledge of British history from his listeners; he never talked down to them or patronised them by adapting his style to the perceived requirements of a modern mass audience. As Berlin put it: 'The archaisms of style to which Mr Churchill's wartime speeches accustomed us are indispensable ingredients of the heightened tone, the formal chronicler's attire, for which the solemnity of the occasion called.'

On 11 September 1940 Churchill broadcast to the nation on the likelihood of a German invasion, saying:

> We cannot tell when they will try to come; we cannot be sure that in fact they will at all; but no one should blind himself to the fact that a heavy, full-scale invasion of this island is being prepared with all the usual German thoroughness and method, and that it may be launched now – upon England, upon Scotland, or upon Ireland, or upon all three.

That speech was broadcast from deep within the Cabinet War Rooms, a bombproof underground complex of offices and private quarters in Whitehall. They had been constructed just before the war to house the central core of the government in the event of air raids. Churchill made this speech shortly after the first bombing raids on London, knowing that even if Hitler had decided not to invade, the Luftwaffe's bombers were likely to continue to terrorise British cities.

This was how he conveyed the conviction that Britain could take it, whatever might come:

> Therefore, we must regard the next week or so as a very important period in our history. It ranks with the days when the Spanish Armada was approaching the Channel, and Drake was finishing the game of bowls; or when Nelson stood between us and Napoleon's Grand Army at Boulogne. We have read all about this in the history books; but what is happening now is on a far greater scale and of far more consequence to the life and future of the world and its civilisation than these brave old days of the past.

Churchill made people feel that they were not alone in this struggle; they were walking with history. As an historian himself, he was in a perfect position to put Britain's plight in 1940 squarely in its historical context. To a people who were taught at school of the exploits of Drake and Nelson, this had an electrifying effect. Churchill had already demanded heroism from the British people when he appealed to the future millennium, with the words: 'Let us brace ourselves to our duties, and so bear ourselves that, if the British Empire and Commonwealth last for a thousand years, men will still say, "This was their finest hour."' Now he appealed to the past millennium, equating the situation with that of 1588 when the Spanish Armada bore down on Elizabeth I's England, and 1804 when Napoleon threatened to invade Britain. As prime minister, he once minuted to R. A. Butler at the Ministry of Education: 'Can you make children more patriotic? Let them know Wolfe won Quebec.' It not only worked with children; by mobilising British history in his support he encouraged people to think of themselves as being part of a long continuum, something which the huge success of books about the Napoleonic Wars during the Second World War implies was very successful.

In the context of today's politics and society, much of Churchill's argument and the vocabulary in which it was couched were of course deeply politically incorrect. Clive Ponting has complained of the way Churchill continually referred to 'our own British life, and the long continuity of our institutions and the Empire', instead of 'coming up with a view of the future designed to appeal to a modern democracy'. This was because Churchill realised that the British nation was primarily fighting for its very identity and continued existence, before any utopian ideas about decency and democracy, let alone equality and fraternity. He therefore appealed to the ancient, tribal belief that the British people then had in themselves, largely based on the deeds of their forefathers and pride in their imperial achievement. It is no longer really an idiom that politicians can turn to, but it helped save us then.

There are those, such as the late Lord Hailsham – he chose the singular forum of Radio 4's *Desert Island Discs* to adumbrate his theory – who consider the emergence of Winston Churchill as prime minister in May 1940, within hours of Hitler unleashing his Blitzkrieg upon the West, as a proof of the existence of God. No theologian, I prefer to subscribe to the opinion of the American broadcaster Ed Murrow on the phenomenon of Churchill in 1940: 'He mobilized the English language, and sent it into battle.' The printed page is not the correct medium for these speeches, of course. To feel the shiver down one's spine at Churchill's words only recordings will do. They alone can convey the growls, the sudden leonine roars, the lyrical sentences, the cigar-and-brandy-toned voice, the sheer defiance coming straight from the viscera insisting upon no surrender in a war to the death.

Churchill suffered from a slight stammer and a lisp, which affected his public speaking. Like his father, he had difficulty all his life pronouncing the letter 's'. As a young man he would try to remedy the problem by rehearsing such tricky phrases as: 'The Spanish ships I cannot see for they are not in sight.' Later, when he was on the American lecture circuit, he began to cure his lisp and the inhibitions that it had caused him. Although he worked hard at overcoming his speech impediment, he never mastered it entirely. 'Those who heard him talk in middle and old age may conclude that he mastered the inhibition better than he did the impediment,' his son Randolph later joked. Churchill's lisp is noticeable even in his most famous speeches that inspired the nation during the war, leading detractors to assume – wrongly – that he was slurring his lines due to drink.[28]

Hitler's Siemensstadt trick of not referring to his enemies directly was also occasionally used by Churchill, who made a radio broadcast in November 1934 on the probable causes of a future war, in which he warned of a 'nation of seventy millions a few air-hours away being taught that war is a glorious exercise', a clear, but indirect reference to Nazi Germany. Yet whenever he felt he was able to mention his enemies directly, he greatly relished it. His wartime estimations of Ribbentrop and Mussolini in particular were fine knockabout stuff, displaying part music-hall turn and part sincere disdain. Mussolini he variously described as 'this whipped jackal', 'a lackey and serf' and 'the merest utensil of his master's will'. His very pronunciation of the word 'Nazis', which he lengthened to sound like 'Narr-zies', illustrated his contempt for them. 'Everybody has the right to pronounce foreign names as he chooses,' was his robust maxim.[29]

Jokes, often with himself as the butt, were an essential part of Churchill's speeches. I have only come across one occasion when Churchill failed to get a joke: when Jock Colville, his private secretary, interjected (in a discussion on Montgomery's extravagant self-promotion) that the general had banned the Eighth Army bands from playing 'The British Grenadiers'. When Churchill asked why, Colville replied that it was because of the first line: 'Some talk of Alexander...' (General Harold Alexander was Monty's rival in the desert.) There was a gratifying laugh from the other guests around the dining-room table, but the next morning, to Colville's horror, he found that Churchill had taken the story seriously and had dictated a minute to the Chief of the Imperial General Staff that Montgomery's order be immediately rescinded. As Colville recalled: 'When I explained with embarrassment that I had only said it as a joke, he was far from amused.' That single rule-proving exception apart, Churchill was a man for whom humour was a vital part of life. He also had a tremendous propensity for the arresting, amusing simile such as: 'Punishing China is like flogging a jellyfish.' Witticisms tend to accrete to the genuinely witty – like Oscar Wilde, George Bernard Shaw and Noël Coward – even if they did not actually utter them, and Churchill has undoubtedly benefited from this phenomenon.

Hitler, while supposedly being a good mimic in private, almost never made jokes in public. Mimicry is anyhow something of a harlot's trick, and otherwise his humour was of the cruel kind; nothing amused him more than other people's discomfiture. After the war, Albert Speer recalled the cruel practical joke that Hitler and Goebbels had played on the Nazis' official foreign press spokesman, Ernst 'Putzi' Hanfstaengl, whose close personal ties to the Führer were a source of uneasiness to the rather splendidly titled Minister for Propaganda and Public Enlightenment. Hitler owed Hanfstaengl much; they had been friends since 1923 when he lent Hitler the $1,000 with which the Nazis began printing the *Völkischer Beobachter* as a daily newspaper. As a Harvard graduate, Hanfstaengl had given Hitler an air of respectability in polite social circles in the early days of the movement. None of this could protect him from the spite of Goebbels, however, who

> began casting aspersions on Hanfstaengl's character, representing him as miserly, money grubbing, and of dubious honesty. He once brought in a phonograph record of an English song and attempted to prove that Hanfstaengl had stolen its melody for a popular march he had composed. The foreign press chief was already under a cloud when Goebbels, at the time of the Spanish Civil War, told the table company that Hanfstaengl had made adverse remarks about the fighting spirit of the German soldiers in combat there. Hitler was furious. This cowardly fellow who had no right to judge the courage of others must be given a lesson, he declared. A few days later Hanfstaengl was informed that he must make a plane trip; he was given sealed orders from Hitler which were not to be opened until after the plane had taken off. Once in the air, Hanfstaengl read, horrified, that he was to be put down in Red Spanish territory where he was to work as an agent for Franco. At the table Goebbels told Hitler every detail: How Hanfstaengl pleaded with the pilot to turn back; it must all be a misunderstanding, he insisted. But the plane, Goebbels related, continued circling for hours over German territory. Finally the pilot announced that he had to make an emergency landing and set the plane down safely at Leipzig airport. Hanfstaengl... only then realized that he had been a victim of a bad joke... All the chapters of this story elicited great merriment at Hitler's table – all the more so since in this case Hitler had plotted the joke together with Goebbels.[30]

Hardly surprisingly, soon afterwards Hanfstaengl left Germany to live abroad in American exile, where he acted occasionally as an adviser to Roosevelt when the President wanted to delve into the mind of his chief antagonist.

Nor was that an isolated example: Goebbels understood how the Führer's sense of humour and fondness for these kinds of practical jokes could be used to promote himself and sideline potential opponents. True leadership involves noticing when one is being manipulated, but Hitler did not seem to do so with Goebbels, who was probably the most intelligent Nazi of the Third Reich. When a senior Party member Eugen Hadamowski set his sights upon promotion to control the Reichsrundfunk (the Reich broadcasting system), Goebbels decided to set up another elaborate joke. He had earmarked that job for one of his own cronies, but he suspected that Hitler might prefer Hadamowski, who before the Nazis came to power had won his gratitude for having organised very efficiently the public address systems for their election campaigns.

Albert Speer described Goebbels's cruelly brilliant campaign to undermine his *bête noire*:

> He had Hanke, state secretary in the Propaganda Ministry, send for the man and officially informed him that Hitler had just appointed him Reichsintendant (General Director) for radio. At the table Hitler was given an account of how Hadamowski had gone wild with joy at this news. The description was, no doubt, highly coloured and exaggerated, so that Hitler took the whole affair as a joke. Next day Goebbels had a few copies of a newspaper printed reporting on the sham appointment and praising the new appointee in excessive terms. He outlined the article for Hitler, with all its ridiculous phrases, and acted out Hadamowski's rapture upon reading these things about himself. Once more Hitler and the whole table with him was convulsed. That same day Hanke asked the newly appointed Reichsintendant to make a speech into a dead microphone and once again there was endless merriment at Hitler's table when the story was told.

With Hadamowski's credibility ruined behind his back (and probably with absolutely no justification) Goebbels was able to appoint his own man to the still vacant job. As Speer appreciated: 'From one point of view, Hitler was the real dupe of these intrigues. As far as I could observe, Hitler was in fact no match for Goebbels in such matters.... But it certainly should have given one pause for thought that Hitler allowed this nasty game to go on and even encouraged it. One word of displeasure would certainly have stopped this kind of thing for a long while to come.'[31]

Such practical jokes are hardly a high form of humour, and the knowledge that Hitler would be party to the humiliation of an efficient and hard-working official simply because he was alleged to be overambitious tells us much about the contempt he felt for the human race in general. Compare this to the superb sallies and brilliantly funny jokes of Winston Churchill and the dichotomy is obvious. (The genesis of perhaps Churchill's most famous joke, the punch-line of which is 'And you madam are ugly, but in the morning I shall be sober', can perhaps be found in *Savrola*, in which he wrote of President Molara's wife, Lucile: 'It is hard, if not impossible, to snub a beautiful woman; they remain beautiful and the rebuke recoils.'[32])

So many of Churchill's jokes are too well known to bear repetition here, but there is one that for some reason has not been included in the standard 'Wit and Wisdom' anthologies of his humour (perhaps because it might be apocryphal). After he had been lecturing in the United States in the thirties on the multifarious positive aspects and benefits of the British Empire, an aggressively anti-imperialist American woman asked a long question about British policy towards Mahatma Gandhi's independence movement, culminating in the words: 'So, Mr Churchill, what do you intend to do with your Indians?' 'Leastways, madam,' the great man is said to have replied, 'not what you did with yours.'

Hitler avoids Churchill

It had been Putzi Hanfstaengl who had nearly organised an encounter between Hitler and Churchill in August 1932, when Churchill was in Germany on a tour of Marlborough's battlefields as part of the research for his biography of his great ancestor. Churchill's son Randolph had covered Hitler's election campaign of the previous month for the *Sunday Graphic*, even flying in the putative Führer's plane from meeting to meeting, and he was keen for his father to meet the man who he was even then convinced 'will not hesitate' to plunge Europe into war as soon as he had built an army capable of so doing.[33] Hanfstaengl knew Randolph through his foreign press contacts, and so he and Churchill dined together at Churchill's hotel in Munich.

At the dinner Hanfstaengl spoke of Hitler 'as one under a spell' – his 'mission' over 'Red Spain' still being several years in the future – and told Churchill that since Hitler came to that same hotel at tea-time every afternoon it should be easy for him to engineer a meeting between them. According to Hanfstaengl's memoirs – which were written after he left Germany and so therefore might well have been heavily biased – Hitler was unhappy about meeting someone 'whom he knew to be his equal in political ability', adding: 'In any case, they say that your Mr Churchill is a rabid Francophile.' This showed that Hitler at least knew of Churchill by that stage of his career, and from later remarks of his it is clear that he had also read at least some of Churchill's autobiographical writings.

Hanfstaengl held out the hope that on one of the afternoons or evenings of Churchill's stay, Hitler – who had recently turned down the office of vice-chancellor in the declared expectation of soon being offered the chancellorship itself – might be curious enough about the British wartime First Lord of the Admiralty to come to the hotel to join Churchill, his daughter Sarah, Randolph, the *Daily Telegraph* owner Lord Camrose and Professor Lindemann for coffee. At the dinner that evening, Churchill had told Hanfstaengl, in a discussion about the 'extensive representation' of Jews in Germany's professions, to 'Tell your boss from me that anti-Semitism may be a good starter, but it is a bad sticker'.

Churchill never had the chance to tell Hitler anything directly because he did not appear, but the next day Hanfstaengl made a final attempt to talk the Nazi leader into meeting the man who was – unbeknownst to any of them – eventually to prove his nemesis. Hitler made precisely the same mistake that was being made by so many in British politics at the time; he had written Churchill off, telling Hanfstaengl: 'In any case, what part does Churchill play? He's in opposition and no one pays any attention to him.' Nor did Hanfstaengl's cheeky reply – 'People say the same thing about you' – serve to change his mind. Two days later Churchill and his party had left the city to return to England, with Hitler keeping away until they had gone.

One of the great interviews of history had thus been missed, possibly out of an inferiority complex on Hitler's part, but most likely owing to his acceptance of the received wisdom that Churchill was 'a busted flush' and not worth his time. If so, it should be added to the list of Hitler's fundamental miscalculations. Of course, it is impossible to surmise what might have taken place had the two men met, but if Churchill was tempted to relay his message about anti-Semitism it would hardly have lasted long or been much of a meeting of minds, particularly as neither spoke the other's language. More likely it would have resembled the weighing-in of two opponents before a boxing match. At its worst it could have been one of history's great disappointments, with a formal and mutually insincere exchange of pro-forma diplomatic *politesses* and some generalisations about their Great War experiences. Perhaps it is therefore better that it did not take place after all.

Charisma

Whereas Churchill never really projected charisma, Hitler radiated it. Churchill had a commanding personality that many people might mistake for charisma, but charisma is different. Charismatic leadership is based on the almost mystical qualities that followers attribute to their leaders. This form of power has no roots in tradition or basis in institutional authority; it acknowledges no constitution and is quite separate from the power of an elected statesman in a democracy. No one ever wanted to give Churchill dictatorial powers for life, as were accorded to Hitler. Churchill was the archetype of the inspirational leader but not regarded as superhuman, ethereal, or existing on a different plane from the rest of mankind. (Not everyone would agree with this estimation: the young scientist R. V. Jones, who was summoned to the Cabinet Room in June 1940 to explain the Luftwaffe's radio beam guidance system to Churchill, found that 'whenever we met in the war I had the feeling of being recharged by contact with a source of living power' which he naturally found exhilarating.[34])

There are endless examples of people who were spellbound by Hitler. How did he do it? Firstly, Hitler discovered early in his career that he could intimidate and dominate others simply by staring at them without blinking. It gave him an aura of determination and unshakeable conviction. As in the children's game of 'Who blinks first?' Hitler rarely blinked when he glanced at someone he wished to impress. It could be fantastically disconcerting to those who had no inkling of what he was up to. Albert Speer recalled that he once had a 'blinking duel' with Hitler over dinner. When Hitler stared at him, Speer decided to try to hold his gaze. Hitler kept staring at Speer, waiting for him to cave in. As Speer put it: 'Who knows what primitive instincts are involved in such staring duels ... this time I had to muster almost inhuman strength, seemingly for ever, not to yield to the ever-mounting urge to look away.'[35] Fortunately, at that moment Hitler had to attend to the request of the woman seated next to him, and so he had to break off the duel.

It helped that Hitler had his mother's eyes, which were an unusual shade of light blue with a strange admixture of greenish-grey. There are hordes of people who bear witness to the weirdly compelling effect that Hitler's eyes had upon people. The French Ambassador Robert Coulondre seemed transfixed by them, and the playwright Gerhart Hauptmann described seeing them as the greatest moment of his life. Martha Dodd, the American Ambassador's daughter, testified that they were 'startling and unforgettable'. Nietzsche's sister Elisabeth said of them: 'They ... searched me through and through.' Slightly protruding and almost lashless, the Führer's eyes had a curiously hypnotic effect, or at least they did once Nazi propaganda put it about that they did. A great deal in the creation of charisma is autosuggestion, for if Coulondre, Hauptmann and Dodd had not been told of the power of Hitler's eyes beforehand, they might well not have noticed them.

Of course there was more to Hitler's charisma than just his glance. Most people believe that charisma is a natural personal quality that one either has or does not have. It is in fact an acquired trait, and indeed something of a confidence trick. It is our perception that provides a leader with charisma; after all, no one is born charismatic. Nobody who knew Hitler as a corporal in the trenches of the Great War or as a failed artist in Vienna remembered him as being charismatic, or even much of a leader. He only acquired charisma through his political success and his own unceasing efforts to create a cult of his own personality. Hitler deliberately nurtured this status of infallible superman until millions proved willing to accept him at his own outrageously inflated estimation. His biographer Sir Ian Kershaw describes his state of mind by 1936 as one of 'narcissistic self-glorification'.[36]

Once we attribute an unchallengeable authority to a leader, he (or occasionally she) simply acquires charisma, which derives from the Greek word for spirit. Religious leaders sometimes have – at least in the eyes of their followers – charisma, because their authority is founded on faith. As a secular religion, Nazism was no different. The historian Michael Burleigh has shown how much Nazi ideology had in common with a religious cult, above all in its deification of the Messiah figure.[37] The authority of the Führer was beyond question, and Hitler deliberately emphasised the charisma that was attributed to him by nurturing this status of superman. He avoided being connected to anything likely to be unpopular or that could have made him look fallible. He rarely displayed emotion and deliberately kept himself detached from situations requiring the exhibition of ordinary human feelings.

Nearly everyone who knew Hitler personally confirms that it was hard to relax in his presence. Although cine film taken by his girlfriend Eva Braun shows that he was generally friendly and polite on social occasions, nevertheless genuine warmth or affection were entirely lacking. Instead Hitler chose to surround himself with an aura of unapproachability. He never developed a genuine personal relationship with other human beings; indeed his Alsatian, Blondi, was the closest he came to having a friend.

Until a few hours before his suicide, Hitler remained unmarried. Eva Braun was kept out of the public eye and was known only to his inner circle. All witnesses agree that Hitler never showed any real interest in her; she was attractive enough to look at and pleasant to have around, but that was about it, until her undeniably brave and devoted decision to stay with him to the very end. She wanted to die an honest woman, a legally wed German bunker-frau, and at least he accorded her that honour as the price of her willingness to join him in his suicide. Afterwards they probably parted company, since she had not done anything to justify her joining him on his journey over the Styx.

Public relations

Hitler liked to be photographed with children and animals, never quite kissing babies but undergoing all the rest of the debasing crudity of modern political photo-opportunities. His cultivation of an image of simplicity was perhaps one of his most effective public relations devices, maybe even more effective than the bombastic Nazi rallies. Joseph Goebbels was intent on presenting Hitler as 'the People's Chancellor', emphasising his simple tastes and closeness to the ordinary German. While many Germans perceived the Party officials as bigwigs – whom they nicknamed 'golden pheasants' – the Führer remained, in their eyes, 'one of us'. It is a populist propaganda trick used by many modern leaders. (Few are the American politicians who keep their jackets on in town-hall meet-the-people exercises nowadays.)

Despite being short-sighted, Hitler never wore glasses in public. His secretaries used an especially large font when typing his speeches because he felt that to be seen with glasses might impair his superman image.[38] He also avoided being photographed taking any sort of strenuous physical exercise. Nor would he let even his valet see him anything less than fully dressed. Once, when to Hitler's deep disapproval Mussolini was photographed in bathing shorts, the Führer said he would never allow that to happen to him; indeed, he expressed the fear that 'some skilled forger would set my head on a body in bathing trunks'![39] He was embarrassed to disrobe before a doctor and would never permit an X-ray of his sensitive stomach. He also refused to have a masseur, as suggested to him by Heinrich Himmler, the head of the SS. He liked to have his body covered at all times, and even in the hottest weather he wore long white underwear, as became apparent in the aftermath of the Bomb Plot when his trousers were blown off on the warm summer day of 20 July 1944.

By contrast, Churchill could not have cared less about his physical appearance. He almost never stood on his personal dignity, although he was always conscious of the respect that he felt ought to be accorded to what he occasionally called 'the King's first minister'. When Churchill was ill in Morocco in 1944 two retainers dragged him up a hill to a picnic in the Atlas Mountains using the tablecloth as an ungainly makeshift hammock. The complete absence of dignity involved in this mode of transportation could not have troubled him less. He could often be found at work in his dressing gown and slippers. He would sometimes unselfconsciously undress or take a bath in the presence of his staff and colleagues. On one occasion he even received a startled President Roosevelt as he got out of the bath, with the joke: 'The prime minister of Great Britain has nothing to hide from the president of the United States.' Churchill also had an inherently uncharismatic penchant for funny hats and fancy uniforms. He was the only prime minister, even including the Duke of Wellington himself, who ever wore military uniform while in office. In photographs taken with Roosevelt, one shows Churchill in the uniform of an honorary air commodore, another in the uniform of a colonel of the 4th Hussars, and yet another as an Elder Brother of Trinity House (the body that oversees the running of Britain's lighthouses). While most people will find such eccentric taste in clothes immensely attractive, it tends to make Roosevelt look Churchill's superior. In *Savrola*, Churchill had shown that he was aware of the advantages of dressing simply, even if he had not followed the advice himself. He described the eponymous hero entering the Laurenian State Ball: 'No decorations, no orders, no star relieved the plain evening dress he wore. Amid that blaze of colour, that multitude of gorgeous uniforms, he appeared a sombre figure; but, like the Iron Duke in Paris, he looked the leader of them all, calm, confident, and composed.'[40]

Certainly by the time Churchill became prime minister he seemed to care little about dress codes. In 1940 he invented what he called his 'siren-suit', a garment based on his bricklaying boiler suit only made in velvet, with a full-length zip up the front. While his office staff ridiculed it as his 'rompers', Churchill wore it even on some formal occasions, visiting troops or receiving foreign dignitaries. It was not appreciated at the Kremlin, where, he said: 'They thought I was pushing democracy too far.' It confirms what Hitler already knew: that by dressing down a leader can actually make himself more visible rather than less.

The Nazis, of course, loved dressing up. It is hard to imagine anything more grandiose than the full-dress uniform of Heinrich Himmler, until one comes to the uniform of Hermann Göring. He loved medals and even invented a few new ones, secure in the knowledge that he would be the prime candidate to receive them. Yet the uniform of Adolf Hitler himself had no gold braid, no epaulettes, no lapel badges, no sashes or orders, just the Iron Cross decoration of the simple but courageous soldier in the First World War, a Nazi Party badge and one other small badge. Hitler encouraged other Nazi leaders to dress flashily while he himself deliberately dressed down. This was part of his populist image as the 'People's Chancellor'. He was sending a message to the people that, unlike other leaders, he was so powerful that he didn't need special uniforms or insignia to emphasise it.

When in 1938 Hitler travelled to Rome for a meeting with Mussolini, he had special uniforms made for everybody accompanying him. The task fell to Benno von Arent, Reich Stage Designer and Reich Commissar for Fashion, whose talent for medal design earned him the nickname 'Tinsmith of the Reich' from Albert Speer. Arent was best known for his sets of operas and operettas, and the diplomats on the trip were dressed in frock coats heavily laden with gold braid. Only the Führer dressed, as usual, in a simple outfit. As he said: 'My surroundings must look magnificent. Then my simplicity makes a striking effect.'

A place of their own

Part of Hitler's entirely manufactured charisma was the result of the carefully co-ordinated photo-opportunities that portrayed him as a man in love with simplicity and Nature. To effect this, it was necessary to have both a good deal of privacy and a perfectly chosen base away from the city. Leaders need to be occasionally physically inaccessible in order to emphasise their power over events, and that was something Hitler well understood. The town of Berchtesgaden in the Bavarian Alps is inextricably linked with Adolf Hitler, whose country home, the Berghof, was built above the village of Obersalzberg, just up the mountain. Hitler was very proud of his long connection with the region that had begun when he went on an incognito visit to a fellow Fascist politician Dietrich Eckart before the Beer-hall Putsch. He stayed in several inns in the area over the years and later on bought a house that became the centre of a huge compound for the Nazi top brass. Martin Bormann, Hermann Göring and Albert Speer all had houses built on the hillside, largely in order to protect their all-important personal access to the Führer. Three thousand yards of concrete bunkers built for them underneath the hillside still exist, although much of the rest was blown up by the American Army in 1945 in order to prevent the site becoming a shrine to neo-Nazis. (It was a genuine concern; the hotel on top of the Gran Sasso mountain in the Abruzzi region of Italy from which Mussolini had been liberated in a daring paratroop coup incorporates a museum that nostalgically commemorates the SS commando unit's action.)

'Yes, there are many links between Obersalzberg and me,' Hitler reminisced to his cronies in January 1942. 'So many things were born there, and brought to fruition there. I've spent up there the finest hours of my life. It's there that all my great projects were conceived and ripened. I had hours of leisure, in those days, and how many charming friends!' If Hitler's ghost can be said to haunt anywhere, it is not in the anonymous, flattened area off the Wilhelmstrasse in Berlin where his bunker used to be, but up there on the Bavarian Alpine mountainside.

The Berghof itself was not the architectural masterpiece that Hitler believed it to be. For some reason the Führer loathed varnished furniture, preferring stripped pine. His biographer Norman Stone has described it as 'a building fit for an Ian Fleming villain. Huge slabs of red marble adorned it; looted pictures hung on the walls; there was a vast, thick carpet; a huge fire burning in the grate; oversized armchairs were placed an uncomfortable distance apart, in such a way that the guests would have to half shout their platitudes at each other as the sparks leapt from the fire in the gathering twilight.'[41] For his fiftieth birthday, the Nazi Party presented Hitler with the civil-engineering miracle of 'the Eagle's Nest', a stone building six thousand feet up, reached through the middle of the mountain, from which he could view the entire region, including his beloved Salzburg.

Yet the breathtaking panoramic scenery did not calm what passed for his soul. Paradoxically, those beautiful views seemed only to have helped Hitler to come to his most drastic decisions. It was while he was staying at Obersalzberg that he plotted to grab absolute power in Germany, that he hit upon the infamous Berchtesgaden plan to dismember Czechoslovakia, and where he planned the invasion of Russia. Joseph Goebbels, a regular visitor, regularly complained to his diary about the amount of time the Führer spent at Obersalzberg, but was gratified by the way that 'the solitude of the mountains' tended to spur his Führer on to ever more fanatical efforts. It was in late March 1933, while staying here, that Hitler decided upon a boycott of all Jewish businesses, services, lawyers and doctors across the whole Reich. Staggeringly beautiful scenery clearly had the opposite effect on Hitler that it tends to have on most other people; rather than softening and humanising him, it hardened his heart and filled him with dreams of racial domination. There was a legend that under one of the highest peaks of the Berchtesgadener mountain range, the Untersberg, the German Emperor Barbarossa lay sleeping, and it was thus no coincidence that the German invasion of Russia in June 1941 was codenamed 'Operation Barbarossa'.

In the summer of 1933 Obersalzberg became a place of pilgrimage for many Germans. As Sir Ian Kershaw has written: 'Such were the crowds of admirers trying to glimpse the Reich Chancellor that Himmler, as Commander of the Bavarian Political Police, had to lay down special traffic regulations for the Berchtesgaden area and to warn against the use of field-glasses by those trying to observe "every movement of the people's Chancellor".' In the end, such was the interest that the whole area had to be cordoned off during Hitler's afternoon walks in order to ward off the sightseers. So a tradition was begun of a daily march-past, when 'up to two thousand people of all ages and from all parts of Germany, whose devotion had persuaded them to follow the steep paths up to Obersalzberg and often wait hours, marched, at a signal from one of the adjutants, in a silent column past Hitler'. For one of his closest adjutants, Fritz Wiedemann, such unrestrained adulation had quasi-religious overtones, and it doubtless helped lead Hitler to believe himself to possess almost superhuman powers.

It was also in Bavaria that propaganda opportunities were given full rein. There are photographs of the Führer in traditional lederhosen leaning against a tree; the Führer with smiling, adoring, blond children; the Führer patting his Alsatian, Blondi; the Führer poring over architectural drawings of the cities he intended to build; a happy, relaxed Führer taking tea with Eva Braun; the Führer as Father of his Aryan people; a becloaked Führer welcoming distinguished guests such as David Lloyd George and the Duke of Windsor to the Berghof; the statesman at work, comforting the old, walking on a snowy hillside.

Having a place away from the city where he could think, write and entertain was important to Churchill too. Chartwell in Kent was bought in September 1922 for five thousand pounds, a knock-down price because it was dilapidated and had been put up at auction with a reserve of £6,500 but had received no bids. The only reason Churchill was able to afford it was because of a bequest from a first cousin once removed, Lord Herbert Vane-Tempest, who had been killed in a Welsh railway accident just at the time that Churchill had been appointed Colonial Secretary.

Churchill in addition had to spend almost twenty thousand pounds on renovating the house over the next eighteen months, and it was a constant drain on his resources for years afterwards, to the point when Clementine continually fretted that it would bankrupt them. It was nonetheless precisely the kind of retreat that a man who occasionally suffered from 'black dog' depression needed, commanding as it does superb views over the Kentish Weald that can only be uplifting to the spirits.

If Obersalzberg was the most Wagnerian and Teutonic place in Central Europe, there is no more quintessentially English county than Kent. Just as the Berghof's geographical situation and aspects encouraged Hitler in his dreams of conquest, so the Kentish Weald reinforced Churchill's determination to resist them.

Architecture

Hitler was obsessed with the power of architecture to emphasise his and Germany's new-found greatness. He would have wholeheartedly echoed Churchill's perceptive remark that: 'First we shape our buildings and then they shape us.' Hitler had megalomaniacal building plans for Berlin. While Goebbels staged huge rallies celebrating the quasi-religious Führer-cult, Speer was ordered by Hitler to build a new Reich Chancellery that would simultaneously impress and intimidate visitors, just a few hundred yards from Potsdamer Platz in Berlin. Nothing of it is left today; the site is now a block of flats and – rather imaginatively – a kindergarten. The blueprints show that Hitler's New Chancellery was some twenty times bigger than the old one that it augmented. The date of the New Chancellery's construction – 1938 – is highly significant since it was in that year that Hitler annexed Austria in March and the Sudetenland in October, thus winning two of his greatest foreign-policy objectives without recourse to war.

Setting out for huge territorial expansion in his quest for *Lebensraum* for the German people, Hitler was keen to make the greatest possible impression on foreign visitors. He explained to Speer, whom he had earmarked to be the architect of 'Germania', his new capital: 'I shall be holding extremely important conferences in the near future. For these, I need grand halls and salons that will make an impression on people, especially on the smaller dignitaries.' The New Reich Chancellery stretched a quarter of a mile. While its address was Voßstraße 2–6, this was not where the entrance was found. Speer purposely chose a seemingly illogical place for it on the side of the building, in the Wilhelmstrasse. This meant that an arriving dignitary had to walk along nine hundred feet of halls of ascending grandeur, with the imposing Marble Gallery at the centre, before reaching the Führer's study. Hitler was delighted with Speer's work, saying: 'On the long walk from the entrance to the reception hall they'll get a taste of the power and grandeur of the German Reich!'

Hitler's study was a vast room of twelve hundred square feet, adorned with ponderous chandeliers and an immense pastel-coloured carpet. The friezes of three great heads adorned the front panels of the Führer's huge desk: one of them was that of the Medusa with writhing snakes emerging from her head. In classical mythology, anyone who saw the Medusa fell instantly under her spell and was turned to stone. Hitler rarely did any work in this study; its sole purpose was to receive visitors and leave them in awe of his charisma and Germany's power.

Compare this to Number Ten Downing Street, a terraced house in Whitehall, which in size and style looks nothing special, at least from the outside. Roy Jenkins has described it as 'one of the most rickety large houses in London, built early in the eighteenth century, a well-known period for jerry-building'. Number Ten is a little like Dr Who's Tardis, with far more space than seems possible from the outside, since it sprawls into the area of neighbouring houses and connects with other parts of Whitehall through passageways that cannot be externally observed. It could therefore not be more different from the very showy but impractical Reich Chancellery. Even so, almost the entire working area of Number Ten would have fitted into Hitler's study alone.

Small wonder that it is nearly impossible for a British prime minister to develop the kind of charisma that Hitler projected. British political leaders before the war used to walk around the streets without the retinues of bodyguards, political advisers and aides that they have today, and this very approachability also made it hard for them to acquire charisma. Even during the war, Churchill would often walk from Downing Street to Parliament. Today, even in peacetime, prime ministers tend to be driven the three hundred or so yards, only wishing to walk the short distance when – as during the Queen Mother's funeral in 2002 – it is hoped that they might be able to make political capital out of it.

Props, logos and trademarks

Hitler and the Nazis mastered the use of props and trademarks through their uniforms, jackboots, swastika logo, armbands, flags, anthems, and the salute – which all bestowed a distinctive corporate identity on their party and followers. Even Hitler's most potent facial characteristic, his absurd little toothbrush moustache, went through various stages of development as he altered its width occasionally. Churchill also understood how politicians needed distinctive trademarks. In an essay on politicians' props – Gladstone's collars, Baldwin's pipe, and so on – he once wrote, disingenuously: 'I have never indulged in any of these.' Did he really think that normal people wore those homburgs, spotted bow-ties, high wing-collars, and smoked that size of Romeo y Julieta cigar? He adopted the V-for-victory sign in the summer of 1941, and he also owned literally dozens of hats: military and naval headgear, pith helmets, an Australian bush hat, Russian astrakhans, homburgs, panamas, top hats – one of which recently fetched £10,000 at auction – stetsons, even an American Indian chieftain's feathered war bonnet. He rarely inhaled cigars, but as he was about to walk into a public occasion he lit one up and advised the Tory MP beside him: 'Never forget your trademark!'[42]

Hitler, by contrast, was a fanatical non-smoker who considered tobacco to be 'the wrath of the Red man against the White man for having been given hard liquor'. It took the Führer to find a racial motive behind even smoking. The Nazis instituted the world's most powerful anti-smoking movement between 1933 and 1945, which instituted bans on smoking in public spaces, restrictions on tobacco rationing for women, and developed the world's most refined tobacco epidemiology, linking tobacco use to lung cancer for the first time. Fears that tobacco might prove hazardous to the physical well-being of the Aryran race meant that German doctors – half of whom were Nazi Party members by the outbreak of the war – led the campaign against smoking. Advertisements pointed out that while Hitler, Mussolini and Franco were all non-smokers, Stalin and Roosevelt puffed away on cigarettes and Churchill was rarely seen without his cigar.[43]

Yet for all these campaigns, German cigarette consumption actually increased during the early years of Nazi rule, from 570 cigarettes per capita per annum in 1932 to 900 in 1939. (In France during the same period it only rose from the same base figure to 630.) The German anti-tobacco activists complained to the Führer about the 'American-style' advertising with which they had to contend, but he was reluctant to act against the tobacco firms since they had declared themselves as early and enthusiastic supporters of his regime, to the point of bringing out a special brand of *Sturmzigaretten* (Brownshirts' cigarettes). They also provided an invaluable stream of revenue for Hitler's perennially hard-pressed Treasury, contributing no less than one billion Reichsmarks in the financial year 1937/38. By 1941 taxes on tobacco were providing around eight per cent of the Government's entire income and so were crucial for the war effort.

Despite the Luftwaffe and Post Office both banning smoking, as well as many factories, government and Nazi Party offices, rest homes and hospitals – and Himmler announcing a smoking ban on all uniformed SS officers on duty – consumption nonetheless continued to rise. Although some air-raid shelters provided special rooms, in general smoking was banned there, as it was on buses and trains in sixty of Germany's larger cities by 1941. The Nazis announced 'the beginning of the end' of smoking throughout the Reich when they increased tobacco taxes to their highest levels in November of that year. The result was that although more soldiers smoked than ever before (some 87.3 per cent), they were smoking

23.4 per cent fewer cigarettes. In 1940–41 Germans smoked an astonishing 75 billion cigarettes, enough to form a cylindrical block 436 feet high with a base of a thousand square feet.

People management

Who would you assume was better at people management – Hitler or Churchill? While Hitler kept himself detached and did not really care for anybody else but himself, he did look after his staff, who pretty uniformly adored him. When they fell ill, he visited them in hospital. He enjoyed giving presents on their birthdays and at Christmas, and even paid personal attention to selecting appropriate gifts. Some, like his valet, saw in him their second father.

Even up to her death in 2000 at the age of eighty-three, Hitler's favourite secretary, Gerda Christian, retained fond memories of the man she always – even after 1945 – called 'The Chief'. With him in the bunker until just before the end, she never afterwards had a bad word for her 'kind and fair' former boss. There is no leader so evil that he will not have his defenders. It was doubtless possible to find sixteenth-century Muscovites who would recall the reign of Ivan Vasilievich with nostalgia. He was a harsh Tsar, they would concede over their vodka, but he was fair and his torturing should be seen in its proper historical context. 'The Terrible' was really more a respectful term of endearment than any kind of criticism. Genghis Khan probably had supporters who would aver years later that he had had a bad press, probably didn't know what was being done in his name, was misunderstood, and anyhow at least he had made the yaks run on time. You always knew where you were, sentimental Transylvanians would recall, with Vlad the Impaler.

Eric Hobsbawm, who is regularly described as our greatest living historian – though heaven knows why while his near-contemporaries such as Robert Blake, Asa Briggs, Alan Bullock, Hugh Dacre, Antonia Fraser, Paul Johnson and Hugh Thomas are still breathing – has still not tired of pointing out how Joseph Stalin modernised the Soviet Union, and so could not have been all bad. Kim Il Sung, Fidel Castro, even Pol Pot have had their Western apologists. It is a well-known phenomenon that intellectuals and writers, who proclaim their objectivity and atheism at every opportunity, are often the first to worship naked power, and it seems that the more brutally that such power is exercised the more devout is the obeisance.

The remarkable hero-worship shown by intelligent and sensitive Englishmen to Napoleon, even while he had the Grande Armée stationed at Boulogne in 1804, is a fine example of this baleful phenomenon. In his book *Napoleon and English Romanticism*, the historian Simon Bainbridge chronicled what he calls the 'obsession' which Byron, Hazlitt, Wordsworth, Coleridge and Southey felt for the thrusting Corsican upstart. In politics, too, the Whigs sailed perilously close to treachery in their outspoken admiration for their country's enemy. While an undergraduate at Cambridge, William Lamb – later Lord Melbourne – wrote a Latin ode to Bonaparte, and his letters to his mother recorded joy at French victories and sorrow at Allied successes. He and Charles James Fox admired Napoleon's 'energy', in much the same way that British writers and aristocrats admired the 'energy' of Nazi Germany in the thirties. The historian Arthur Bryant went so far as to describe Hitler as 'the Unknown Soldier come to life' in June 1939, only three months before the outbreak of war, and he did not have Frau Gerda Christian's excuse of having known the Führer personally.

The way that intellectuals have been mesmerised by tyrants in the twentieth century, with genuinely brilliant men such as Jean-Paul Sartre and E. H. Carr falling in politically platonic love with Stalin, has had a terrible effect on the rest of their countrymen. Critical faculties were lulled, potential opposition stymied. What might perhaps be excusable in a young secretary who had seen little of life outside the Berlin bunker is entirely unforgivable in hardbitten hacks like Walter Duranty, the *New York Times* correspondent in Moscow in the thirties who actually witnessed Stalin's deliberate policy of famine-creation in the Ukraine and yet still wrote favourably about the Bolshevik regime. Another American journalist, Lincoln Steffens, famously went further and reported on his return from Russia: 'I have seen the future and it works.' Even now that Marxist-Leninism has been confined to the dustbin of history – except of course in China, Cuba, and the sociology departments of western campuses – and shown conclusively not to have worked despite seventy years of experimentation, the Hobsbawms remain unrepentant.

Just as apologists for the Kray twins are quick to argue that they kept the East End streets safe, and Irish republicans claim that the IRA are effective in combating small-time drug dealers, there seems to be no one too vicious to rate hagiography, however specious the grounds. There is also a certain perversity in human nature that makes us wish to say the opposite to everyone else, to be the child who points out the emperor's nudity. Of course, properly harnessed that impulse can sometimes even be good for democracy. Even when the American House of Representatives voted to declare war on Japan after the surprise attack on Pearl Harbor, one person – Mrs Jeanette Rankin of Montana – voted against it. She was one against 388, she was foolhardy and wrong but she was not browbeaten for her brave pacifist stand. Only dictatorships require absolute unanimity, and election results such as that in North Korea in 1985, where the Great Leader claimed to have won 100.0 per cent of the popular vote, often hint at weakness rather than strength.

For Frau Christian there was a final irony. 'I cannot complain about my time with the Führer,' she told friends. 'We were even allowed to smoke at a time in Germany when it was not the done thing for women to smoke.' As it was only after a long and painful battle against lung cancer that she died, so it might be argued that her boss even did for her in the end too.

Churchill, by contrast with Hitler, was a tough boss for whom to work. Very often he failed to display what he described in *Savrola* as 'That charm of manner of which few great men are destitute'. When it came to people management, he could on occasion be rude and sarcastic. His secretaries had difficulty in interpreting what they described as his 'inarticulate grunts or single words thrown out without explanation', and he could often be wounding to those who failed to grasp his intentions. 'Where on earth were you educated?' he would growl. 'Why don't you read some books?' Had Churchill exhibited the same kind of behaviour in today's working environment he could have wound up in front of an industrial tribunal. He had a terrible temper, although his great charm usually allowed him to unruffle feathers afterwards. To his credit, he was just as bad with colleagues and superiors as with underlings.

When, as Chancellor of the Exchequer in the 1920s, Churchill had a disagreement with the then Minister of Health, Neville Chamberlain, he was reported to have remonstrated with the Prime Minister, Stanley Baldwin, by marching 'about the room shouting and shaking his fist' and launching into 'a tremendous tirade'. Chamberlain thought Churchill's temper 'childish and contemptible' and wrote to Baldwin: 'Not for all the joys of Paradise would I be a member of his staff! Mercurial! A much abused word, but it is the literal description of his temperament!'

Under the terrible strain of leading the country in the summer of 1940, Churchill received a letter from his wife that read: 'There is a real danger of your being generally disliked by your colleagues and subordinates because of your rough, sarcastic and overbearing manner', and adding, 'I must confess that I have noticed a deterioration in your manner... and you are not so kind as you used to be.' Churchill took notice and tried to reform, but as the Australian Prime Minister Paul Keating used to say: 'Leadership is not about being nice. It's about being right and being strong.'[44]

Churchill even publicly acknowledged his rudeness in a speech in the House of Commons in June 1941, when he said:

> I do not think any expression of scorn or severity which I have heard used by our critics has come anywhere near the language I have been myself accustomed to use, not only orally, but in a stream of written minutes. In fact, I wonder that a great many of my colleagues are on speaking terms with me.

Taking advice

The very fact that Clementine Churchill was able to write to her husband so honest a letter was indicative of their strong, open, enduringly loving marriage. On 16 April 1908 Churchill wrote, in a courting letter to Clementine Hozier, 'What a comfort and pleasure it was to me to meet a girl with so much intellectual quality and such strong reserves of noble sentiment.' On 18 April 1964, fifty-six years, two world wars and two premierships later, and after the exchange of several hundred letters and telegrams, Clementine Churchill was writing to her husband to say that the three party leaders would like to call on him to mark the close of his parliamentary career. Their genuine love was apparent from the first; 'the empty bunny [bed] is melancholy,' he wrote when she was away. It is quite wrong to suggest, as did the Hollywood actor Kevin Costner in May 2001 – while producing no evidence whatever – that Churchill was ever unfaithful to Clementine. That Clementine might have had, in Mary Soames's phrase, 'a classic holiday romance' with the art dealer Terence Philip is a matter of historical contention. Under the sundial in the Golden Rose Walk at Chartwell was buried Clementine's souvenir of the brief fling, the corpse of a dove Philip gave her with the W. P. Kerr quotation:

> Here lies the Bali dove.
> It does not do to wander
> Too far from sober men,
> There lies an island yonder,
> I think of it again.[45]

(If Churchill was one of the 'sober men' to whom the rhyme was referring, it makes the verse yet more intriguing.)

This romantic streak notwithstanding, Clementine Churchill was something of a battleaxe. She did not have much time for many of her husband's most interesting friends, such as Lord Beaverbrook, Brendan Bracken and Lord Birkenhead, but she retained the valuable ability to silence men like Generals de Gaulle and Montgomery with her basilisk, Aunt Agatha-style glare. Anyone of lesser mettle would probably not have survived marriage to such a restless and demanding spirit as Winston Churchill. It was always in defence of him that her harshest words were said. At a lunch party given by the French Ambassador in 1953 she overheard the former Foreign Secretary Lord Halifax saying that her husband had become a handicap to the Tory Party, and viciously retorted: 'If the country had depended on you we might have lost the war.' By comparison with Clementine's open and equal relationship with Churchill, even several years into their relationship Eva Braun was still calling Hitler 'mein Führer' and it is inconceivable that she would have taken him aside to warn him of his effect on his subordinates, even if he had requested it.

It has been suggested that the reason why Hitler's relationship with Eva Braun did not result in marriage until he was fifty-six years old and hours away from death was because he was homosexual. According to a well-researched and well-argued, but ultimately unconvincing book entitled *The Hidden Hitler* by Dr Lothar Machtan of Bremen University, published in 2001, the Führer was about as gay as his depiction in Mel Brooks's *The Producers*. Machtan claimed that not only was Hitler a promiscuous homosexual before 1933 and a severely repressed one afterwards, but it is even argued that he instituted the Night of the Long Knives massacre of July 1934 to cover up this guilty secret.

Unfortunately, as is almost inevitable in theories of this kind, the evidence is at best doubtful and scrappy, and at worst mere insinuation. Although since the twenties there have been dozens of autobiographies published with titles such as *I Was Hitler's Pilot*, *I Was Hitler's Doctor* and *I Was Hitler's Valet*, no one has stepped forward with the sure-fire sensational bestseller *I Was Hitler's Lover*. Dr Machtan's explanation for this is that among the 150 people killed on the Night of the Long Knives were many Brownshirts and others who knew about Hitler's predilections and that this mass 'elimination of witnesses and evidences' was near total.

Dr Machtan's theory is open to any number of doubts, however. Joseph Goebbels is known to have loathed homosexuals: would he have been content to serve under and ultimately to kill himself, his wife and six children for a man he suspected of being one? Generals who were suspected of homosexuality found their careers ruined, and homosexuality was made a crime punishable by the concentration camp. Although Dr Machtan repeats much anti-Hitler propaganda from the twenties and early thirties in support of his case, this is inherently suspect by its very nature, coming as it did from Hitler's most committed political enemies.

After the posthumous 'outing' by historians and television documentary-makers of Lords Baden-Powell, Kitchener and Montgomery, it was perhaps inevitable that questions would be asked about a man who only enjoyed something in the nature of a shotgun wedding. Nor is it only the Führer's reputation that has been blackened. According to a former comrade of Hitler's from the trenches, his fellow soldiers used to put boot blacking on Hitler's penis when he was asleep in the trenches, an activity which Dr Machtan describes as 'evidently a common occurrence' in the German Army.

The person who made this and several other such claims about Hitler was a man called Hans Mend, nicknamed 'the Ghost Rider'. Although he did indeed serve in Hitler's unit during the war, Mend was a blackmailing paedophile who wound up in prison for sex offences and had a series of unrelated money grievances against

Hitler. His eventual death in Dachau is taken as evidence that Hitler had him silenced, but it might just as easily have been as a result of his other activities. Anyhow, Hitler allowed Mend to live for years after the Brownshirt leadership had met their death at his hands, which would have been a curious oversight if he had been primarily concerned with silencing those who knew about his secret past.

Far from being new, the accusation of homosexuality was regularly levelled at Hitler by German Social Democrat and Communist newspapers before 1933. It is hardly a taboo subject, as Dr Machtan claimed, since many of the tens of thousands of publications on Hitler have gone into this possible side to his personality, and into the nature of his relationships with Rudolf Hess and Albert Speer in particular. If we are to believe Dr Machtan, Hitler was an insatiably promiscuous and predatory homosexual who acted out his crushes on chauffeurs, fellow soldiers, Viennese rent-boys and casual street pick-ups, but for some reason, he says, 'we must limit ourselves to conjecturing how and to what extent the Hitler–Speer relationship bore a homoerotic imprint'. Dr Machtan would even have us believe that he only married the 'tomboy' Eva Braun – who chose to die with him, despite presumably knowing that she was merely his 'beard' – in order to put future historians off the scent of his homosexual past.

Professor Norman Stone looked deeply into the whole subject of the Führer's sexuality back in 1980 for his biography *Hitler*, and he came up with a far more credible theory than that of an active homosexual who suddenly changes on becoming Chancellor of Germany. Stone argued that Hitler was 'semi-sexless', and that he had only half the normal levels of testosterone in his blood: 'No one knew what was going on in Hitler's head, and he never revealed anything.' Furthermore he might still have been a virgin at thirty-five.

Stone believed that Hitler's one true love was architecture, which involves its own paradox, considering how many beautiful buildings he was instrumental in destroying. He had little or no use for either men or women as sexual beings, for the sex act would merely bring him down to their base level. He was close to Hess, who was not homosexual, and to Röhm, who was, and addressed them in the familiar as 'du', but that certainly does not constitute evidence that he ever sodomised either of them, or wished to.

Ernst 'Putzi' Hanfstaengl, who knew Hitler as well as anyone in the early days of the Nazi Party, thought him 'the repressed, masturbatory type', at least before it was in his interests to exaggerate about the sexuality of his former boss for the American secret services. Since Hitler probably did have an affair with his own niece Geli Raubal, which possibly led to her suicide in September 1931, at best he must have been bisexual anyhow. 'He was a very lonely man, but he was prepared to settle for a long romance with power,' was Professor Stone's verdict, and it is a vastly more convincing one than that presented by Dr Machtan.

Even if Hitler had been homosexual, it would be of absolutely no use in explaining what he did politically, or how he did it. His carefully created charisma aside, Hitler was a rather ordinary person. As the professor of modern history at Cambridge University, Richard Evans, has observantly pointed out: 'The only really extraordinary thing about Hitler was his talent as a rabble-rousing orator, a talent he discovered after the First World War almost by accident. For the rest, he seems to have been normal in his private life, unoriginal in his ideas, and fanatical but by no means exceptional among the ideologues on the far right in Weimar Germany in his visceral but ultimately politically motivated hatred of the Jews.'[46] Churchill, on the other hand, was an extraordinary individual according to virtually any criteria one cares to employ.

Delegation versus Meddling

Churchill was notorious for his tendency to micromanage and meddle in other people's business. On a professional level, he would today be termed a 'micromanager'. His private secretary during his time at the Treasury, Percy James Grigg, recalled: 'It might easily happen that the minutes of a single morning covered the whole region between the draft of an important state paper or ideas for the next Budget and some desired improvement in the make-up of files or the impropriety of the Office of Works supplying Czechoslovakian matches in a British Government establishment.'

Every morning, while still in bed, Churchill would churn out endless instructions and inquiries about anything that came to his most fertile and questing mind. Before lunch one day while Chancellor of the Exchequer in the 1920s, for example, he asked his financial secretary to look into the question of withholding any increase in teachers' salaries; he asked the Cabinet Secretary whether it was really necessary to increase the number of submarines based in Hong Kong; and inquired at the Foreign Office about the cost of their telegrams from Persia. This kind of micromanagement created tensions and made Churchill unpopular with some long-serving Treasury officials, who did not appreciate the Chancellor's attempts to interfere in matters that they thought could be perfectly adequately dealt with at the appropriate lower levels.

As Chancellor, Churchill also attempted to run the *British Gazette*, the Government's propaganda news-sheet during the General Strike of 1926, to the point that its editor tried desperately to have him kept out of the building where the newspapers were printed. During the first night's production he complained to the Prime Minister, Stanley Baldwin, that Churchill had tried 'to force a scratch staff beyond its capacity' and had 'rattled them badly'. Five days later he complained again: 'He butts in at the busiest hours and insists on changing commas and full stops until the staff is furious!' Even worse, Churchill seems to have insisted on showing the printing staff how to operate their own machines.

Hitler dealt with the business of government in a completely different way. He loathed holding meetings and reading reports and was very reluctant to put anything in writing. 'A single idea of genius', he said, 'is worth more than a whole lifetime of conscientious office work.' Churchill, by contrast, was a hard worker, who, in his own words, 'found I could add nearly two hours to my working day by going to bed for an hour after luncheon'. This regime, to whose efficacy the author can attest, did allow Churchill to be something of a pest to his staff during the war since it enabled him to stay up until around 2 a.m., which those who had not had the luxury of snoozing in the afternoon found exhausting.

Hitler was by contrast rather indolent. Whereas Churchill immersed himself in complex economic questions, although not always successfully, Hitler rarely bothered at all. 'I have the gift of reducing all problems to their simplest foundations,' he said in 1932. He knew what he wanted: no unemployment and massive rearmament. So he appointed Germany's leading economic expert, Hjalmar Schacht, as Minister of Economics and Plenipotentiary of Rearmament and then let him get on with the business of managing the economy. 'Inflation is lack of discipline,' Hitler told Schacht,

The eyes have it:
Hitler in 1930.

Churchill striding purposefully out of Downing Street on 4 July 1940, speech in hand, to tell the Commons of the sinking of the French fleet at Oran.

The League of Maidens (some more like matrons) worship their idol as Heinrich Himmler looks on.

The Reich Party Rally for Honour and Freedom at Nuremberg, 1936.

Churchill tiling a roof in his Wilderness Years, the seam of his overcoat ripped.

Churchill wearing his siren suit, or 'rompers', at Chartwell in 1939.

A laurel halo for the Führer in gaol at Landsberg.

General Werner von Blomberg believed that meeting Hitler could cure him of the common cold.

Hermann Göring thought that Hitler could make him believe he was a woman.

Chancellor of the Exchequer Winston Churchill, accompanied by his parliamentary private secretary Bob Boothby, his daughter Diana and his bodyguard Inspector W.H. Thompson, walks to the Commons to present his 1929 Budget.

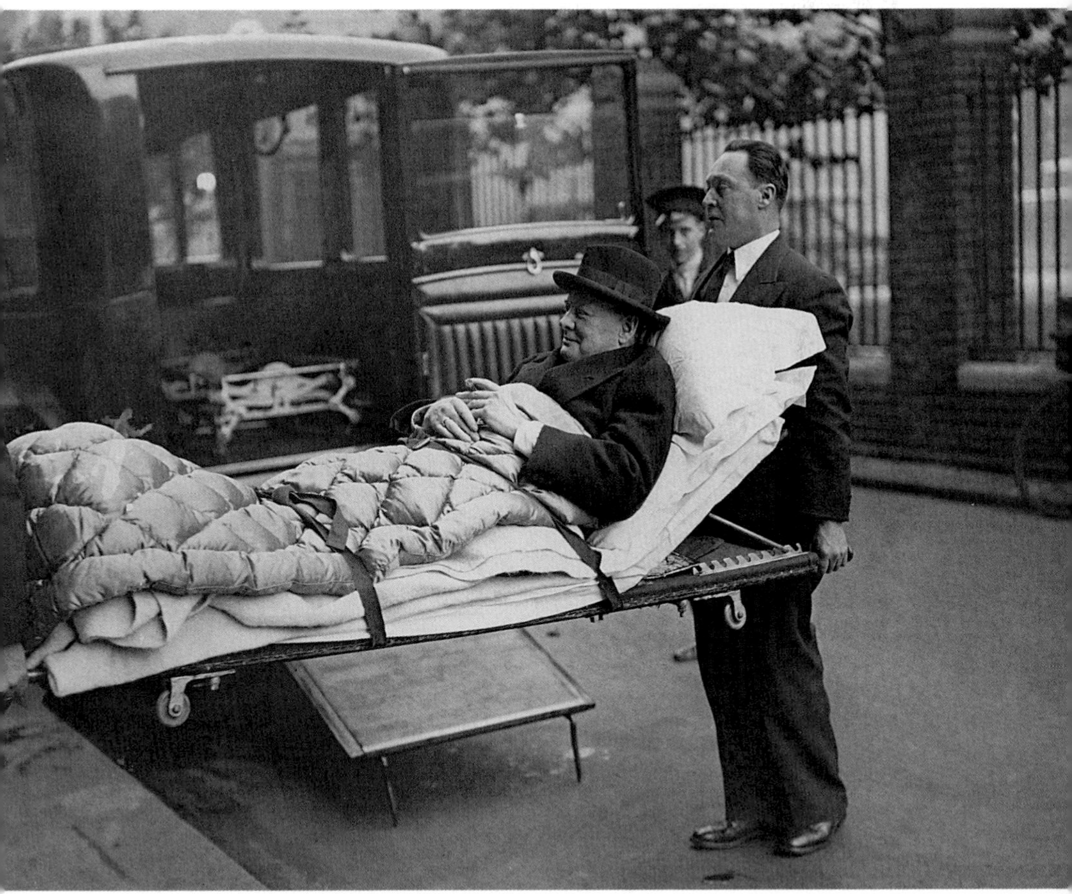

Churchill, still convalescing ten months after his accident on Fifth Avenue, is carried into his London home in October 1932.

The newly-elected Chancellor, in an uncharacteristically meek pose, meets his former commander-in-chief President Hindenburg at Potsdam on 21st March 1933.

The Führer inspects his troops outside the [Hradschin] Castle in Prague on the day of his unopposed invasion of the rump of Czechoslovakia, 15th March 1939.

The Munich comedian [Weiss-Ferdl] in his dressing room in 1930; Hitler studied his timing, delivery and techniques.

Hitler hamming it up for his favourite photographer Heinrich Hoffmann.

Churchill broadcasts from the White House in 1943.

'lack of discipline in the buyers and lack of discipline in the sellers. ... I will see to it that prices remain stable. That is what my Brownshirts are for.'[47] His economic views give the phrase 'command economy' an even more sinister meaning than the overtly statist one that it has already.

Schacht in fact generated a surprising economic upturn, but at a price. The deficit financing of Hitler's rearmament programme meant that after three years of a booming economy the food shops in Germany were running low of supplies by the mid-1930s. The Minister of Agriculture, Richard Darré, was worried about the situation. He bombarded Hitler's office with memoranda and tried for two whole years to gain an audience with the Führer, but in vain. Hitler wasn't interested in what he considered petty economic questions, which were better left to the experts.

Hitler only got personally involved when it became clear that his plans for military expansion were at risk. Schacht warned that Germany was heading for ruin unless the spending on rearmament was radically cut back but Göring understood better than Schacht what Hitler wanted to hear, he boasted: 'I know nothing about economics, but I have an unbridled will.' As Schacht was trying to restrict the rearmament programme, Göring sensed an opportunity both to please his boss and to extend his power base. He promised to provide a 'Four-Year Plan' that would supply both food and guns. So Hitler appointed him Reich Plenipotentiary of the Four-Year Plan and, within a few months, Göring had numerous experts for specific economic questions installed, who each competed with their counterparts in Schacht's Economics Ministry.

In May 1937 Schacht protested to Hitler about Göring's intrigues, but the Führer waved him away. He wanted nothing more to do with the matter and told Schacht to take it up with Göring directly himself. A few months later, Schacht saw no other course but to resign. This was a typical example of how Hitler ran the Nazi State. He wasn't interested in the details of policy or administration. Instead, he set the overall objectives and then let his subordinates fight it out among themselves.

The best way for a subordinate to deal with Hitler was to adopt the tactics of Colonel-General Walter Model, who used to avoid making requests of the Führer, always came up with forceful proposals that exuded energy, occasionally ignored orders that he judged impossible to execute, and very often simply presented Hitler with a fait accompli, reporting what he had already done. This very often worked, especially if Model managed to get him to believe that a particular strategy had been originally thought up by the Führer himself, in which case his support was assured. Model had a rough manner, but was absolutely loyal. Nicknamed 'the Lion of Defence' and 'the Führer's fireman', because Hitler switched him constantly from front to front attempting to hold up the Red Army's advance in 1944–5, Model finally shot himself on 20 April 1945.

Hitler even used to encourage competition between different areas of the state apparatus, promoting a kind of neo-Darwinist contest between ministries and acolytes. In the very opposite of the 'team-playing' management technique, Hitler never minded if some parts of his Government were at the throats of others. Thus the Foreign Minister Joachim von Ribbentrop was despised by the Propaganda Minister Joseph Goebbels, who was in turn loathed by the Party boss Martin Bormann, who was hated by the SS chief Heinrich Himmler, who was feared by the Armaments and Architecture Minister Albert Speer, who was disliked by the Luftwaffe commander Hermann Göring, who was in turn hated by Ribbentrop. Stirring this cauldron of seething animosities was the Führer, to whom they all ultimately and individually answered. This situation was patently absurd, but it suited Hitler well since it fitted in with his Darwinist views and secured his personal power, putting him in the position of ultimate arbiter between all the rival factions.

As an illustration of Hitler's technique, Albert Speer recalled how he

> took delight in having Ambassador [Walter] Hewel, Ribbentrop's liaison man, transmit the content of telephone conversations with the Foreign Minister. He would even coach Hewel in ways to disconcert or confuse his superior. Sometimes he stood right beside Hewel, who would hold his hand over the mouthpiece of the telephone and repeat what Ribbentrop was saying, while Hitler whispered what to answer. Usually these were sarcastic remarks intended to fan the Foreign Minister's suspicions that unauthorized persons might be influencing Hitler on questions of foreign policy, thus infringing his domain.

It was no way to run a government.

On the outbreak of war in 1939, Churchill was given the post of First Lord of the Admiralty, in charge of the whole naval theatre of operations. It immediately became evident that his exile in the political wilderness hadn't diminished Churchill's tendency to micromanage. From his office in the Old Admiralty Building – today called the Churchill Room – he bombarded both his subordinates and his Cabinet colleagues with memoranda that covered almost every aspect of the war. One naval officer confided to his diary: 'Winston Churchill is taking a great personal interest and tends to interfere with the sailors' business. He is an extraordinary man and has an astonishing grasp of the situation, but I wish he would keep to his own sphere.'[48] Churchill acknowledged this part of his nature, telling the House of Commons three years later: 'I am certainly not one of those who needs to be prodded. In fact, if anything, I am a prod.'

As he saw it, his 'sphere' as First Lord of the Admiralty extended far beyond responsibility for the Royal Navy. In a letter to the Foreign Secretary, Lord Halifax, on 10 September 1939, only a week after taking office, Churchill wrote to say that he thought that Halifax's friend, the British Ambassador to Italy Sir Percy Loraine, 'does not seem to understand our resolve', before going on to comment on telegrams from Egypt. He wound up with what read like a gentlemanly threat: 'I hope you will not mind my drawing your attention from time to time to points which strike me in the Foreign Office telegrams, as it is so much better than that I should raise them in Cabinet.' A few days later, Churchill sent Halifax a memorandum urging him to bring Bulgaria into the Balkan defence system. Meanwhile he was writing 'My dear Sam' letters to the Lord Privy Seal Sir Samuel Hoare, in which he questioned the need for petrol and meat rationing, entertainment restrictions, blackouts, and proposed the formation of 'a Home Guard of half a million men over forty'. This too had a final line that sounded dangerous: 'I hear continual complaints from every quarter of the lack of organisation on the Home Front. Can't we get at it?'

This propensity to interfere and micromanage is not unusual for energetic leaders, nor is it necessarily a bad thing. Hands-on management can be very effective, but it depends how it is done. The general problem with micromanagement is that the better people are at their jobs, the more they mind being told how to do them. Most of

Churchill's staff and colleagues were content to put up with his meddling only because he generated the vitality and fighting spirit that was so desperately needed. He was, in the words of one of his secretaries, not just 'a tremendous nuisance' but also 'a tremendous tonic'.[49] Thankfully it was the latter that prevailed. Churchill's energy and spirit more than compensated for all his faults and failures, and even for the Norway operation in the spring of 1940.

The idea for the operation had originally been Churchill's own. As early as September 1939 he had proposed cutting Germany off from some of its iron-ore supplies by mining the waters of Norway, which was neutral territory. Legal and diplomatic concerns delayed the operation for several months. When finally, in April 1940, the Royal Navy was sent towards Norway, the Germans struck first. Fully aware of Allied intentions, they occupied the major Norwegian ports before the British fleet arrived. After several weeks of fighting, the British did capture the key port of Narvik, only to have to evacuate it the following day. Soon Norway was in Hitler's hands and the world's greatest naval power had suffered a humiliating defeat. It is one of the many paradoxes of this period that it was the Norway débâcle that forced Chamberlain to resign and made Churchill prime minister, despite the fact that the First Lord bore far more direct responsibility for the unhappy Allied blunders during the operation than the Prime Minister. But leaders are often judged more by their spirit than by their actions, and usually rightly so. And Churchill possessed one key skill that great leaders need above all: the ability to inspire others.

Both Hitler and Churchill were able to draw on a powerful sense of nationalism during the war. Like Charles de Gaulle, who had 'a certain idea of France', Churchill had his own certain idea of what Britain was and could be, and it was an heroic one born of his (often over-romanticised) conception of British history. Hitler had no such instinctive understanding of the true nature of the German people and their innate national characteristics. He could play up to their anger and resentment, but it was the only tune in his repertoire, whereas Churchill could adjust his message to the changing times.

For all Churchill's talk of Trafalgar, Napoleon and Nelson, Hitler was still far from his Waterloo, as Churchill had to admit in July 1940 when he said that he hoped that by 1942 'the War will, I trust, take a different form from the defensive, in which it has hitherto been bound'. He was correct in his prediction, of course – late 1942 was to see the first great Allied victories of the war at El Alamein and Stalingrad – but he was still unable to provide any logical cause for optimism. He called for blind faith, and due to his leadership, oratorical skills and the lack of any honourable alternative, he got it.

Hitler too encouraged the belief that Germany's present struggle was an extension of its glorious struggles of the past. He presented himself as the spiritual descendant of the great German heroes in direct line of apostolic succession from giants such as the Emperor Barbarossa, Otto von Bismarck, after whom one of the greatest German warships was named, and Frederick the Great, whose exploits he had read to him by Goebbels as the Red Army marched on his Chancellery in April 1945.

Both Hitler and Churchill demanded great acts of sacrifice from their countries, a superbly counterintuitive form of leadership. The leadership manuals and books published by management gurus instruct us that: 'The fundamental task of leaders is to prime good feeling in those they lead. That occurs when a leader creates *resonance* – a reservoir of positivity that frees the best in people.'[50] For all the ghastly management-speak of that last sentence, the fact remains that people can feel good when making sacrifices, which can bring out the best in them – at least in wartime. Politicians do not always have to be resolutely upbeat in order to be popular. At dinner on 15 December 1940, during the Blitz, one of Churchill's junior ministers Richard Law put his finger on this truth when he told Churchill's private secretary that 'The secret of Hitler's power was his demand for sacrifice. The P.M. understood this and his own speeches were brilliant in that respect, but [the Minister for Labour Ernest] Bevin thought that he could buoy people up by promising them higher wages and better times. He was wrong.'[51]

The one thing that Churchill never asked the British people to sacrifice was hope. Before the entry of Russia and America into the Second World War in 1941, it was impossible to predict how Hitler was going to be defeated – even Churchill himself could not have known for certain – but his broadcasts none the less left no one in any doubt that it would eventually happen one day:

> It is a message of good cheer to our fighting Forces on the seas, in the air and in our waiting Armies in all their posts and stations,

> that we send them from this capital city. They know that they have behind them a people who will not flinch or weary of the struggle – hard and protracted though it will be; but that we shall rather draw from the heart of suffering itself the means of inspiration and survival, and of victory won not for ourselves but for all – a victory not only for our own time, but for the long and better days that are to come.

The driving force behind Hitler's charismatic leadership was the quest for power. Yet Churchill demonstrated that leaders don't need charisma or dictatorial powers to inspire others. After meeting Hitler people felt that he, the Führer, could achieve anything. But when people met Churchill they felt that they themselves could achieve anything. Genuine inspiration beats artificially-created charisma.

'Working towards the Führer'

One of Hitler's leadership techniques that proved very effective was the encouragement of the concept of what was called 'working towards the Führer', or carrying out tasks that it was felt would please him, even if he had not directly authorised them. Nowhere was this more in evidence in Nazi Germany than in the war against the Jews. Following Göring's take-over from Schacht, increasingly radical steps were taken to eliminate the Jews from the German economy. By April 1938 more than 60 per cent of Jewish firms had been liquidated or 'Aryanised'. In the course of 1938, following the Anschluss of Austria, anti-Jewish violence increased throughout the Reich. Hitler saw it as important for his international standing that he should not be personally associated with this anti-Jewish campaign as it gathered momentum. No discussion of the 'Jewish Question' was, for example, permitted by the press in connection with his visits to different parts of Germany in 1938.

The day after the assassination of Ernst vom Rath, the third secretary in the German Embassy in Paris, by the Polish Jew, Herschel Grynszpan, on 7 November 1938, local Party leaders instigated anti-Jewish demonstrations and pogroms all over Germany. On the evening of 9 November, Nazi leaders met in the Old Town Hall of

Munich to celebrate the fifteenth anniversary of the Beer-hall Putsch. By the time the reception began, vom Rath had died from his wounds. Goebbels wrote in his diary: 'I explain the matter to the Führer. He decides: let the demonstrations continue. Pull back the police. The Jews should for once get to feel the anger of the people.'

Goebbels seized upon the opportunity to improve his standing with the Führer, which had suffered greatly from the marital difficulties stemming from his relationship with the Czech film actress Lida Baarova. Here was his chance, by 'working towards the Führer' in such a key area, to win back favour. After Hitler had left the Old Town Hall, Goebbels gave an inflammatory speech suggesting that the Party should organise and carry out 'demonstrations' against the Jews throughout the country. The Party leaders relayed this immediately to their local offices, and Party and SA activists were turned loose on synagogues, lives and property.

Hitler was adamant that the SS itself was kept away from the Kristallnacht pogroms. The 'demonstrations' were meant to be seen as the 'spontaneous outburst of public rage', as Goebbels put it, and the involvement of the SS would have made the violence look far too much like an organised operation. In the event, few were fooled. Only six weeks after the Munich agreement had been signed, the true nature of the Nazi regime was once again highlighted for the world. Hitler hastened to dissociate himself from the events, but it is clear that Goebbels really had his full support, despite what his apologists have since tried to make out. In a secret speech to one hundred leading press men on the day after the pogroms, Hitler praised Goebbels's propaganda triumphs. A few days later, on 15 November, Goebbels's diary records that the Führer 'is in fine fettle. Sharply against the Jews. Thoroughly endorses my, and our, policies.' Indeed, Hitler now encouraged Göring to find a co-ordinated solution to the 'Jewish Question'.

Göring seized upon the opportunity to get a cash injection for his floundering Four-Year Plan. Insurance companies were told that they would have to cover losses, if their foreign business was not to suffer. As for the Jews, they were grotesquely enough held liable for the damage done to them. The insurance payments were made to the Reich, not to the Jews, and Göring imposed an 'atonement fine' of one billion marks on them. As from l January 1939 all Jews were to be completely excluded from the economy.

The overwhelming need on behalf of underlings to impress Hitler led to a radicalisation of Nazi policy. Kristallnacht taught the world, as if it had not had warnings enough – not least from Churchill – that Nazism was an evil creed that would most likely envelop the world in war. Economically, Göring's Four-Year Plan was simply not sustainable and the money spent on rearmament had somehow to be recuperated. War was the solution, and it was what Hitler had wanted all along. Churchill had been right. On the day war was declared, Neville Chamberlain appointed Churchill to his old post of First Lord of the Admiralty. Winston was back.

Hitler and Churchill from 1940

'War is a beastly thing now, all the glamour has gone out of it. Just a question of clerks pushing buttons.'

Churchill to Robert Bernays MP in the House of Commons tearoom in the 1930s

From the very first month of the war, during the period known as the 'Phoney War' or 'Sitzkrieg', while others were advocating caution, Churchill was agitating for action, not just at home, but abroad too. Yet his confidence in Britain's anti-submarine measures proved to be ill-founded. The carrier HMS *Courageous* was torpedoed in the Bristol Channel in September 1939. In the next month, a German submarine penetrated the defences of Scapa Flow and sank the battleship HMS *Royal Oak*. In the first nine months of the war, Britain lost 800,000 tons of shipping to a relatively small number of enemy submarines and magnetic mines. Yet in the late spring of 1940, Churchill publicly maintained that the Royal Navy had reduced the front line of the U-boat force to fewer than a dozen vessels. If this estimate had been accurate, the Navy would have nearly accounted for the better part of the whole front line of the German force. Unfortunately it was not, and Churchill had to arrange for the transferral to active duty of the Director of Anti-Submarine Warfare who kept telling him the truth.

On 20 January 1940 Churchill broadcast to the neutral nations, urging the Dutch, Belgians and Scandinavians to 'stand together with the British and French Empires against aggression and wrong'. This only encouraged Hitler to take a forestalling action. The captured records of Hitler's conferences reveal that in early 1940 he still considered 'the maintenance of Norway's neutrality to be the best course for Germany', but that in February he came to the conclusion that: 'The English intend to land there and I want to be there before them.' His definite decision to order an attack on Norway was taken a few days after Churchill had ordered the British destroyer HMS *Cossack* to sail into Norwegian waters and board the German ship *Altmark*, in order to liberate British prisoners. Churchill capitalised on this success and much was made of the event. The Norwegian Government protested against the violation of its territory, but their passive acceptance served to convince Hitler that Norway was actually Britain's accomplice, and it became the detonating spark of the pre-emptive action that he now ordered: the invasion of Norway.

On the evening of 9 April 1940, Churchill was enjoying a good dinner at the home of his Cabinet colleague, the Secretary of State for Air Sir Samuel Hoare. He was in a fine mood. A long-cherished project of his, the mining of Norwegian waters, was finally getting under way, and he hoped it would interrupt the vital German iron-ore imports from Scandinavia. Hoare recorded in his diary: 'Winston very optimistic, delighted with mine laying, and sure he had scored off the Germans. He went off completely confident and happy at 10.30.'[1] Yet when he returned to the Admiralty Churchill found that it was he and not the Germans who had been undermined. A large German naval force was reported to be steaming towards Norway. The next morning the Nazis captured the vital Norwegian port of Narvik and only a few weeks later all of Norway was in Hitler's hands.

Eduard Dietl, the German commander, had only two thousand mountain infantry and 2,600 sailors with whom to oppose 24,500 Allied troops, including the Norwegian 6th Division, so what had gone wrong?[2] The Germans had received excellent intelligence on British intentions; Churchill's designs had been let loose by none other than himself. He dropped a series of hints in a secret conference with neutral press attachés in London on 2 February that had soon become known to German Intelligence. By late March 1940 the world press had slowly filled with speculation about the Allied designs on Scandinavia and suspicions were raised further when it was discovered that Churchill's nephew, Giles Romilly, had been sent to Narvik.

By contrast, not a word of Hitler's own daring plan had leaked out.

A top-secret unit had been established within the German High Command, the Oberkommando der Wehrmacht (OKW), under Hitler's personal supervision. He appointed General von Falkenhorst in charge of the preparations for 'Weser Exercise'. To retain maximum secrecy, this soldier was at first given no maps to help him with this task. Instead he bought himself a Baedeker pocket-map of Norway and retired to a hotel room, returning in the afternoon with the plans to show Hitler, who instantly approved them. The Führer did not even mention a word of the scheme to Ribbentrop. It went off very successfully, the result of secrecy, daring and enterprise. Hitler himself called it one of the 'cheekiest operations' in recent military history, with good reason.

By contrast, Britain had a cumbersome governmental structure that tended to hold up operations of this sort. The Cabinet, the Foreign Office, the French, the Dominions and other important bodies had to be consulted – and world opinion had to be considered – before Churchill could violate Scandinavian neutrality by the mining of harbours. There was no single authority from which Churchill could swiftly obtain permission for such an operation. With so many parties involved in the decision-making, it was small wonder that the Germans were fully aware of British intentions.

Hitler's dictatorial powers made it much easier for him to keep his plans secret than for the British leadership. His Cabinet hadn't met since 1938 and it wouldn't do for the remainder of the war. And while the concerns of the British Foreign Secretary, Lord Halifax, did much to delay Allied action, his German counterpart Ribbentrop had been cut out of the decision-making process entirely. Such secrecy was in line with the Führer's Basic Order No. 1, which hung in every military office: 'Everybody must know only as much as is necessary to carry out his tasks, and then no earlier than need be.'

Yet during the Norwegian campaign, Hitler displayed a worrying loss of nerve. In a fit of funk over the situation at Narvik, the Führer had Field Marshal Wilhelm Keitel draft an order for the force there to withdraw to neutral Sweden and have itself interned. Only prompt action by a relatively junior officer, covering for his boss who was on sick leave, saved the situation. When Lieut.-Col. Bernhard von Lossberg received Hitler's message to the commander in Narvik at the OKW's Berlin office, he immediately sought out Keitel and Field Marshal Jodl and refused point-blank to send the Führer's order. It reflected, he said, the same loss of nerve that had lost Germany the Battle of the Marne in the First World War, which had led to four years of trench warfare and eventual defeat.

Jodl made it clear that he was in no position to countermand the order, but he found a way around the problem by sending another telegram to the commander in Narvik congratulating him on his recent promotion, while Hitler's orders were torn up. The following day Jodl explained to Hitler that the telegram had not been sent as it contradicted the congratulatory message that had just been telegraphed. Hitler's military staff were thus compensating for his own weaknesses. His second thoughts in the Norwegian campaign were no isolated incident either; the same thing was to happen in the French campaign during the summer of 1940. A close look at the famed Blitzkrieg success in the West reveals both the strengths and the weaknesses of Hitler's military leadership.

The Allied mentality before May 1940 can best be summed up in the two words: 'Maginot Line', the name given to the elaborate bulwark of French fortifications on the border with Germany. Constructed in the late 1920s and early 1930s, and named after the long-serving French Defence Minister André Maginot, it was considered the most advanced fortification system of its time and thought to be impenetrable to German attack. In reality, these fortifications contained the seeds of the most ignominious military defeat that France has ever suffered in her long history of subjugation and surrender. The French High Command expected a war with Germany to be a repeat of the trench warfare of the First World War. The Maginot Line was basically a Western Front in reinforced concrete. It was a model case of bad leadership; what the French High Command failed to appreciate was that history rarely repeats itself exactly and that leaders who cling to the recipes of the past are almost certain to fail. As Churchill joked in the House of Commons in 1944 on being warned to avoid the mistakes of 1914–18: 'I am sure that the mistakes of that time will not be repeated; we shall probably make another set of mistakes.'

When the Nazis prepared for their attack on France, they were clearly inferior in numbers and matériel. The Allies had more men, more guns, and more and better tanks. But the German Army had one inestimable advantage: it had better leaders. Their commanders recognised that the military circumstances had entirely changed since 1918. The Polish campaign had demonstrated the speed and destructiveness which a combined attack of panzers and Stuka dive-bombers could achieve. While the German High Command was preparing to unleash in the West this new form of warfare, dubbed 'Blitzkrieg' (lightning war), the British Parliament was engaged in a full-scale political crisis, as a significant proportion of the House of Commons revolted against the premiership of Neville Chamberlain.

Churchill takes charge

Between 7 and 10 May 1940 a sensational parliamentary coup replaced Neville Chamberlain, the incumbent wartime Prime Minister, with Winston Churchill, then First Lord of the Admiralty. Chamberlain, who had been one of the senior men responsible for the pre-war policy of appeasement, had presided over the mainly Tory National Government for three years and still enjoyed considerable support from the Conservative Party and in the country. A spontaneous outburst of anger at the British Expeditionary Force's poor performance in the recent Norwegian campaign, however, was about to be voiced in the House of Commons. With the Whitsun bank holiday approaching, it was agreed that the traditional debate on the adjournment of Parliament would be held on the issue of the military débâcle in Norway and the Government's general handling of the war so far. Unbeknownst to the Westminster MPs, Hitler was preparing to unleash his Blitzkrieg in the West, and as they met on the evening of Tuesday, 7 May 1940, an all-out German invasion of Holland, Belgium and France was only fifty-five hours away.

Few, if anyone, expected Neville Chamberlain's National Government to fall as a result of the debate, least of all the Prime Minister himself. Just before it began he told Lord Halifax that he doubted it would 'amount to much'. None the less, an extraordinary combination of factors – including inflammatory speeches from respected individuals, a lack of support from Tory backbenchers, a disastrous personal performance by the Prime Minister, incessant behind-the-scenes intrigues and deals, and an uncharacteristically lacklustre speech by Winston Churchill – meant that after two days of debate a new mood had settled on Westminster, one which forced Chamberlain from office.

One backbench Tory MP, John Moore-Brabazon, surreptitiously took some blurred photographs of what thereafter became known as the 'Norway Debate' with his tiny Minox camera from the Bar of the House, quite against Commons' rules. From these we can tell that when Chamberlain rose to defend the performance of his ministry the chamber and galleries were packed. The Prime Minister was at pains to explain away his complacent statement of 4 April that Hitler had 'missed the bus', which only four days later had been followed by Germany's attack on Norway, forcing British forces to evacuate the country from 2 May.

Facing regular interruptions from the Labour benches, Chamberlain soldiered through a long, self-exculpatory and uninspiring defence of his Government and himself. 'For my part I try to steer a middle course,' he said in a sentence typical of the whole speech, 'neither raising undue expectations which are unlikely to be fulfilled, nor making the people's flesh creep by painting pictures of unmitigated gloom.' It was hardly the leonine wartime leadership that Britain had enjoyed from the two Pitts, Lord Palmerston and David Lloyd George.

Answering him, Clement Attlee, the leader of the Opposition and of the Labour Party, struck some heavy blows against the planning, organisation and execution of the operations in Norway, arguing that the Government had entirely failed to learn from the lessons of Hitler's Blitzkrieg tactics as employed against Poland the previous autumn. 'The war is not being waged with sufficient energy, intensity, drive and resolution,' he said, quipping that Chamberlain had 'missed all the peace buses, but had caught the war bus'. In his peroration, Attlee proclaimed his confidence that Britain would win the war in the end, but in order to do so 'we want different people at the helm from those who had led us into it'.

Following him Sir Archibald Sinclair, the leader of the Liberal Party, drew attention to the way 'the complacent and, alas, ill-founded boastings of ministers contrast pitifully with the hard, swift blows of the German forces'. So far, so predictable. With a Tory majority from the 1935 general election of 249, the Government had little to fear if the debate went along strictly party lines. But after a pro-Chamberlain speech by the imperialist Tory backbencher Brigadier Sir Henry Page Croft and a crushing rejoinder from the Labour MP Colonel Josiah Wedgwood, who attacked Croft's 'facile optimism' and predicted a 'lightning strike' invasion of Britain, the fragile façade of party unity suffered its first crack.

Admiral of the Fleet Sir Roger Keyes, Conservative MP for Portsmouth, stood up in his full-dress naval uniform, complete with six rows of medal ribbons, and described the handling of the Norway campaign as 'a shocking story of ineptitude, which I assure the House should never have been allowed to happen'. Coming from the hero of the legendary Zeebrugge Raid of 1918, his views carried great weight. Of the many contemporaneous accounts of that day found in the diaries and correspondence of spectators, almost all refer to the power and authority of Keyes's speech. The admiral somehow managed to relieve his friend Churchill of any personal responsibility for the Norway débâcle, despite the fact that it had been almost entirely run from the Admiralty. 'The whole country is looking to him to help win the war,' he said of Churchill, before sitting down to much cheering.

Soon afterwards Leo Amery, a distinguished Conservative former Cabinet minister, rose to deliver another hammer blow against the Government front bench. Of diminutive height and not a naturally gifted speaker, Amery none the less carried extra weight because he sat for one of the seats in Chamberlain's home town of Birmingham and had himself been First Lord of the Admiralty. As his philippic progressed, Amery sensed that the mood of the House was with him, so he decided to take the risk of winding up his speech using the same words that Oliver Cromwell had employed in dismissing the Long Parliament in 1653: 'You have sat too long here for any good you have been doing. Depart, I say, and let us have done with you. In the name of God, go!' The effect was as dramatic as it was crushing for the Government, and is thought to have persuaded several MPs to vote against Chamberlain.

Oliver Stanley, the Secretary of State for War, tried his best to rescue the situation, and a couple of backbench National Government supporters also came to its defence, but by the end of the first day's debate it was clear, from one Labour MP's intervention, that it was not just the handling of the Norway campaign that was on trial, but the very existence of the Government itself.

By the time that Labour's Herbert Morrison opened the second day of the Norway Debate on Wednesday, 8 May 1940, the fate of Neville Chamberlain's National Government was indeed hanging in the balance. The first day had gone disastrously for ministers and it was obvious that a significant body of National Government supporters, mainly those who had opposed the appeasement policy in the thirties but also including the usual selection of disappointed office-seekers, sacked former ministers, rebels and 'awkward squad' types, were going to take this opportunity to try to oust Chamberlain by voting with Labour and the Liberals. The presence of several of the younger MPs in military uniform was felt to augur ill for the Government, considering the angry mood in the Armed Forces about what was seen as administrative incompetence. Even more worrying for the government whips was the number of usually loyal MPs who were considering either abstaining or absenting themselves altogether from the final division.

Morrison argued that 'the whole spirit, tempo and temperament of at least some ministers have been wrong, inadequate and unsuitable', citing by name Chamberlain himself, Sir John Simon the Chancellor of the Exchequer and Sir Samuel Hoare the Air Minister. He also announced that Labour had demanded a formal division at the end of the debate which would, he told MPs, 'broadly indicate whether they are content with the conduct of affairs or whether they are apprehensive about the conduct of affairs'.

At this point Chamberlain rose to accept the challenge, but in a very ill-advised manner. Mentioning 'my friends in the House', the Prime Minister said: 'I accept the challenge. I welcome it indeed. At least we shall see who is with us and who is against us, and I call on my friends to support us in the lobby tonight.' This was understandably characterised as a blatant appeal to narrow party loyalty at a time of great national peril, and as such it backfired disastrously.

Sir Samuel Hoare, the arch-appeaser of the thirties, spoke next and was badly mauled by a series of interventions from Admiral Keyes, the Labour front-bencher Hugh Dalton, and no fewer than seven other MPs. As Secretary of State for Air, Hoare was reduced to admitting that the RAF was 'not nearly big enough', a damaging remark from a government that had been in office for almost the whole of the previous decade.

Next to speak was David Lloyd George, who had waited eighteen years for his chance to revenge himself upon the men who had turned him out of the premiership in 1922. With his famed Welsh eloquence and reputation as 'the man who won the [Great] War', he contended that Britain was in a far worse position than in 1914, and blamed Chamberlain personally for his inability to 'rouse' and 'mobilise' the British Empire. It was a scornful, bitterly personal but highly effective attack. When heckled by a Tory backbencher, he sarcastically retorted: 'You will have to listen to it, either now or later on. Hitler does not answer the whips of the Patronage Secretary [Chief Whip].' Of Chamberlain's guarantee to Poland and the neutrals he said: 'Our promissory notes are now rubbish on the market.'

With Churchill ready to accept full responsibility for all that had taken place in Norway, Lloyd George made one of the most telling remarks of the whole debate and employed a powerful metaphor: 'The right honourable gentleman must not allow himself to be converted into an air-raid shelter to keep the splinters from hitting his colleagues.' His devastating peroration mentioned Chamberlain's appeal to the nation to make sacrifices for victory, concluding that: 'There is nothing which can contribute more to victory than that he should sacrifice the seals of office.'

Other major figures of the day such as Alfred Duff Cooper (who had resigned over the Munich agreement) and the former Labour minister Sir Stafford Cripps also spoke, and an intervention was also made by the young MP Quintin Hogg (later Lord Hailsham), but the House was waiting for Churchill to wind up the debate. It was not one of his vintage performances. He lost his temper, accusing the Labour MP Emanuel Shinwell of 'skulking in a corner' and angered the Labour Party with his jibes. His final plea to 'Let pre-war feuds die; let personal quarrels be forgotten, and let us keep our hatreds for the common enemy' went completely unheeded.

On the motion 'That this House do now adjourn', the Commons divided 281 in favour and 200 against, a government majority of eighty-one, far smaller than was normal in peacetime on a three-line whip. The rebels had included Lady Astor, Robert Boothby, Harold Macmillan, Quintin Hogg, John Profumo, General Spears, Lord Wolmer, Harold Nicolson, Leslie Hore-Belisha and of course Leo Amery and Admiral Keyes. Meanwhile there were rowdy scenes as two other rebels, Harold Macmillan and Earl Winterton, sang 'Rule Britannia!' until they were silenced by furious Tories. Labour MPs shouted 'You've missed the bus' at Chamberlain. In all, forty-one government supporters had voted against Chamberlain and around fifty had abstained. The Government was certainly very badly damaged, and as Chamberlain stalked out of the Commons chamber after the result was announced his survival as prime minister was clearly in grave jeopardy. Churchill had done his bit for the Prime Minister, but fortunately for him it was not enough. He had, however, shown the necessary loyalty not to be suspected of treachery by the Conservatives who were still overwhelmingly sympathetic to Chamberlain.

Although numerically Chamberlain's National Government had won the Norway Debate the previous evening by eighty-one votes, because the majority was normally well over two hundred it was considered a moral defeat. The Government's business managers tried to ascertain exactly how serious this was on the morning of Thursday 9 May, as they attempted to limit the damage in the time-honoured way, by doing deals. First the whips tried to find out from the rebels who had voted against the Government or abstained the previous night what price needed to be paid for the recovery of their support. Then Chamberlain's parliamentary private secretary, Lord Dunglass (later the Prime Minister Sir Alec Douglas-Home), brought some leading backbenchers into Number Ten to listen to their grievances and let it be known that Chamberlain was willing to sacrifice the Chancellor of the Exchequer, Sir John Simon, and the Air Minister, Sir Samuel Hoare, in order to stay in office.

That morning Chamberlain also personally saw Leo Amery to offer him either the chancellorship or the foreign secretaryship, which Amery steadfastly refused. By 10.15 a.m. Chamberlain seems to have realised that he might have to resign, so he sent for his friend, Foreign Secretary and ideological soul mate Lord Halifax. At their meeting the two men agreed that the Labour and Liberal parties had to be brought into the Government. Since it was very unlikely that Labour would come in under Chamberlain, the Prime Minister asked Halifax whether he would form a government instead, one in which Chamberlain pledged to serve under him. According to his diary, Halifax 'put all the arguments that I could think of against myself', primarily that of the 'difficult position of a PM unable to make contact with the centre of gravity in the House of Commons'.

Perhaps significantly, Chamberlain does not seem to have argued that the rules could be changed to allow a peer to sit in the Commons under emergency situations, although it is now known that he had taken secret soundings with the Government's law officers to establish how this might be achieved.[3] Instead he made the dubious prediction that little opposition could be expected in the Commons anyhow because it would be a coalition government.

The whole drift of the conversation gave Halifax a stomach-ache. He had neither expected nor planned for the actual premiership to devolve upon himself. When he returned to the Foreign Office after the 10.15 a.m. meeting, he told his under-secretary, Rab Butler, that although 'he felt he could do the job', Churchill would effectively be running the war so he 'would speedily turn into a sort of honorary P.M.', and therefore possibly be less influential in restraining Churchill than he would be if he remained Foreign Secretary, heir apparent and the most powerful Cabinet minister.

As for Labour, then meeting at their annual party conference in Bournemouth, Butler had had two conversations the previous evening with Hugh Dalton and Herbert Morrison, who both wanted Halifax to know that their party would enter a Halifax-led government; Dalton added that 'Churchill must stick to the war'. Attlee had also told Churchill's friend Brendan Bracken that Labour would be prepared to serve under Halifax.

With the support of the King, who believed that Halifax's peerage could be put 'into abeyance' in such an emergency, the outgoing Prime Minister Chamberlain, the Labour leadership and the vast bulk of the Conservative Party, the premiership was Halifax's for the taking, had he demanded it. However, he knew that his lack of interest and expertise in military matters was an inadmissible lacuna in a wartime premier. In January 1942 Churchill joked about the situation, telling the House of Commons: 'When I was called upon to be prime minister, now nearly two years ago, there were not many applicants for the job. Since then perhaps the market has improved.'

Before the crucial meeting at Number Ten, Churchill had lunch with Anthony Eden and Sir Kingsley Wood, at which Wood – a formerly loyal Chamberlainite – advised Churchill to hold out for the premiership itself. Churchill played the whole crisis superbly, making himself the primary candidate without in any way being seen to undermine the sitting premier. It was exactly the kind of deft political leadership that he had often not shown in a past full of boisterous romanticism, but in this moment he displayed his nerve to devastating effect.

When Chamberlain, Churchill, Halifax and David Margesson, the Chief Whip, met in the Cabinet Room at 4.30 p.m. on Friday 9 May, Halifax was in a sincere mood of self-abnegation. Churchill left a famous account of the meeting: 'I have had many important interviews in my public life, and this was certainly the most important. Usually I talk a great deal, but on this occasion I was silent.' Churchill claimed that only after a 'very long pause', which seemed longer than the two minutes' Armistice Day silence, did Halifax, almost out of embarrassment, blurt out that his peerage disqualified him from the premiership and Churchill realised that 'it was clear that the duty would fall on me – had in fact fallen on me'.

Written eight years after the event, Churchill's account is open to question. He got the time and date of the interview wrong and even omitted Margesson from it altogether. The anecdote had been told so often by Churchill in the meantime that it had acquired the barnacles of exaggeration that adhere to every well-sailed story. From the contemporaneous accounts that survive and from Margesson's own memory, as well as from other circumstantial evidence, it is thought that there was no 'very long pause' at all, but in fact Halifax 'almost immediately urged Churchill's greater fitness for leadership in war'.

One compelling new piece of evidence has recently emerged to suggest that there was indeed a silence, after which Churchill asserted his own fitness for the job, or at least Halifax's unfitness, which amounted to the same thing. Far from the mantle having fallen upon him, Churchill grasped it. In 2001 the letters and diaries of Joseph P. Kennedy, the United States Ambassador to London, were published, edited by his granddaughter. They record a visit that Kennedy made on 19 October 1940 to Neville Chamberlain, who was by then dying of cancer at his home in the country. After a wide-ranging discussion about the war and about his terrible state of health, Chamberlain spoke about the interview after the Norway vote. Kennedy noted:

> He then wanted to make Halifax PM and said he would serve under him. Edward as [is] his way, started saying 'Perhaps I can't handle it being in the H of Lords' and Finally Winston said, 'I don't think you could.' And he wouldn't come and that was settled.[4]

The capitalised word 'Finally' implies that a silence, or a long discussion, had in fact taken place, and then Churchill with brutal honesty agreed with Halifax 'and that was settled'.

Another interpretation is possible, which is worth mentioning only to dismiss. That is that the words 'he wouldn't come' refer to Churchill rather than Halifax, and meant that Churchill actually refused to serve in a Halifax government run from the House of Lords. Although this might fit the literary construction of Kennedy's sentence, such a construction would not fit the context of the political situation of the time, because Churchill would have been forced by patriotism to join a Halifax government in which the opposition parties were preparing to serve. There is no question of his holding out for the job through blackmail. Chamberlain clearly meant that Halifax 'wouldn't come' into the premiership. Equally, the historian David Carlton has put forward an ingenious theory that Chamberlain only saw Churchill as a stopgap prime minister to get Britain over the present crisis, after which he would replace him, and therefore secretly preferred Churchill to Halifax, whom it might prove impossible to dislodge later. This, too, is a theory too far, for all that it appeals to those who cannot overestimate the machiavellian nature of politicians.

Here was true leadership; Churchill believed he was the best man for the job and, by agreeing with Halifax, he made it clear that he wanted it. High posts like the British premiership rarely fall into people's laps unbidden; Churchill judged his moment and grasped it.

It still remained for Chamberlain to ask the Labour leaders whether they would join his Government or be willing to serve under someone else instead. When Attlee and his deputy leader Arthur Greenwood arrived at Number Ten they said that they would consult their colleagues in Bournemouth and telephone their decision the next day, but they also warned Chamberlain privately that Labour would be very unlikely to be willing to serve under him. After his speech at the Norway Debate, Attlee could hardly have said anything less. Within a matter of hours, at dawn on 10 May, Hitler unleashed his Blitzkrieg on the West. That Hitler attacked on the same day as Chamberlain resigned was one of the great coincidences of history, but that is all it was. There is no evidence that he chose the time because Britain was in the middle of a political crisis.

The first Cabinet meeting after Hitler's dawn attack in the West took place at 8 a.m. on Friday, 10 May 1940. The news was not wholly unexpected; indeed, less than a week earlier Halifax had warned all British embassies that it 'seems likely we are shortly to meet the full force of a German onslaught on ourselves'. The Cabinet heard how Belgium and Holland, both hitherto neutral, had been invaded in an attempt to outflank the Maginot Line, and thus deal a knockout blow to France. By the time of the next Cabinet meeting at 11.30 a.m. Chamberlain had concluded to his own satisfaction, but to few others', that the military situation was so serious that it justified postponing his resignation altogether. How could the Government change in the middle of such a crisis? he argued.

It was at this point that the Lord Privy Seal, Sir Kingsley Wood, hitherto a loyal Chamberlainite, bluntly informed the Prime Minister that, on the contrary, the new crisis meant that he had to step down immediately. The Air Minister, Sir Samuel Hoare, noted that 'No one said anything in the Cabinet except me. Edward [Halifax] quite heartless.' Many other ministers around the table, especially Winston Churchill but probably also including Halifax, felt that the dangerous new situation on the Continent actually made it more imperative rather than less that Chamberlain should go. What most did not know was that the day before, Wood had gone to Churchill to urge him to hold out for the premiership, or else he would soon be rewarded for this swift change of coat with the chancellorship of the exchequer.

When the Labour leadership telephoned from Bournemouth to say that the party would enter a coalition government, but not one formed by Chamberlain, it sealed the Prime Minister's fate. Crucially, however, they were in no position to decide who the new premier would be. It is quite wrong to think, as some politicians such as Roy Hattersley, Julian Critchley, Michael Foot and Barbara Castle persisted in doing for decades, that it was Labour that made Churchill prime minister. In fact, the party proclaimed itself just as willing to serve under Halifax at the time; the choice was therefore up to Chamberlain and the King. In such a small minority in the Commons, Labour was scarcely in a position to do anything else.

That afternoon, Chamberlain made one last effort to persuade Halifax to change his mind and take on the premiership, despite what seemed to have been agreed with Churchill the previous day. Lord Dunglass telephoned Henry 'Chips' Channon at the Foreign

Office to have him ask the under-secretary there, Rab Butler, to try to persuade Halifax to accept the job. When Butler went to the Foreign Secretary's room he was told that Halifax had gone off to the dentist and could not be contacted. So Chamberlain went to Buckingham Palace where King George VI accepted his resignation, and, as he told his diary, 'told him how grossly unfairly I thought he had been treated and that I was terribly sorry that all this controversy had happened'. When they got round to the subject of his successor, the King 'of course suggested Halifax' as 'the obvious man', but Chamberlain told him that Halifax 'was not enthusiastic'. The King did not exercise his right to ask Halifax directly, although he might have been able to change his mind with a personal appeal from the sovereign to a devoted public servant.

Instead it was Churchill who kissed hands, at 6 p.m. on 10 May. The King had not much wanted Churchill, possibly partly because of the irresponsible role he had played in support of his brother Edward VIII at the time of the Abdication Crisis. None the less, when it became clear that his constitutional duty was to appoint him, the King alleviated any awkwardness by making a joke. As Churchill recalled: 'His Majesty received me most graciously and bade me sit down. He looked at me searchingly and quizzically for some moments, and then said, "I suppose you don't know why I have sent for you?" Adopting his mood, I replied: "Sir, I simply couldn't imagine why." He laughed and said: "I want to ask you to form a Government." I said I would certainly do so.'

Churchill knew that his first action must be to invite Labour and the Liberals into what he later termed his 'Grand Coalition', so he asked Attlee and Arthur Greenwood to join a drastically slimmed War Cabinet of five, along with Chamberlain and Halifax. Churchill knew he had to treat the Conservatives well too, for, as he wrote to Chamberlain that evening: 'To a large extent I am in your hands.'

At 9 p.m. Chamberlain explained his resignation in a broadcast to the nation, urging it to support his successor. Our present Queen, then aged thirteen, told her mother that it moved her to tears. Meanwhile Churchill worked into the night, and as he went to bed at three o'clock next morning, he was 'conscious of a profound sense of relief. At last I had the authority to give directions over the whole scene. I felt as if I were walking with destiny, and that all my past life had been but a preparation for this hour and this trial.'

Hitler's route to Compiègne

On 21 June 1940 Hitler visited the French monument in Compiègne outside Paris that commemorated Germany's defeat in the Great War. An American newspaper correspondent, William Shirer, recorded the Führer's body language on that triumphant day:

> He steps off the monument and contrives to make even this gesture a masterpiece of contempt. ... He glances slowly round the clearing. ... Suddenly, as though his face were not giving complete expression to his feelings, he throws his whole body into harmony with his mood. He swiftly snaps his hands on his hips, arches his shoulders, plants his feet wide apart. It is a magnificent gesture of defiance, of burning contempt for the place and all that it has stood for in the twenty-two years since it witnessed the humbling of the German Empire.

A week later, on 28 June, Hitler did two things that were entirely out of character: he got up early and he went sightseeing. Like any dutiful German tourist, the Führer had prepared for the outing by reading up on the architectural highlights of Paris. As the convoy of black Mercedes-Benz limousines swept past La Madeleine towards the Arc de Triomphe, he delighted in showing off his detailed knowledge to his entourage.

At Les Invalides, Hitler gazed in silence at the tomb of Napoleon, that other European conqueror to whom the Führer frequently liked to compare himself. By now, Hitler believed that his leadership qualities made him, in the words of General Keitel, 'the greatest warlord of all times'. In just ten months the German Army had conquered half of Europe. Only the British and their imperial dominions and brave Greece remained defiant. Yet the method behind Hitler's initial successes as a war leader was, in time, to become his greatest weakness, and by capitalising on it Churchill was to set an example for anyone who aspires to leadership today.

When Hitler returned to Germany from his Blitzkrieg victory over France he was at the apex of his popularity. But Blitzkrieg, this new form of warfare, was not Hitler's invention. Nor was it Hitler who conceived the operational plan for the invasion of France. The credit for this must go to two generals, Erich von Manstein and Heinz

Guderian. As early as the early 1930s, Guderian had been advocating rapid panzer operations designed to take the enemy by surprise. Based on Guderian's ideas, Manstein developed the so-called 'sickle-cut' plan to outmanoeuvre French fortifications and render irrelevant their superior numbers in men and matériel.

Manstein wanted to mount an armoured assault through the forests of the Ardennes mountains, an area generally considered to be impassable to tanks. Conventional wisdom said it would be crazy to try to attack through there, but that is exactly why the German strategy was so successful. The panzer divisions were to attack where the enemy would least expect it. This would enable them to drive a wedge between the Allied forces by swiftly advancing to the Channel coast – just like the cut of a sickle. (The metaphor originated with Churchill.)

Most generals in the High Command favoured a much more conventional operation, and envisaged the main line of attack coming from the north, either side of Liège. They considered Manstein's panzer manoeuvre through the Ardennes mountains to be simply too risky. Manstein was hurriedly transferred to an insignificant post. But then the Führer intervened. To him, the unimaginative plans of the Army High Command (OKH) seemed to be no more than 'the ideas of a military cadet'.[5] Manstein's sickle-cut, on the other hand, signified a great risk but it had the crucial element of surprise to commend it. So Hitler ordered the OKH to adopt Manstein's plan.

This was a case of inspired leadership. Hitler realised that the operational plans of the High Command actually involved a greater risk than the seemingly reckless sickle-cut manoeuvre, because a conventional attack from the north was exactly what the Allies were expecting. Successful leaders don't gamble; they take calculated risks because they realise that sometimes the most dangerous thing you can do is not to take a risk at all.

Had it not been for Guderian's boldness and initiative, however, the German invasion may well have bogged down in World War I-style trench warfare. When on the third day of the invasion Guderian's panzers had reached the River Meuse, Hitler and the Army High Command ordered him to wait for the infantry divisions that were following as fast as they could. The result was the greatest traffic jam Europe has ever seen; columns of fifteen hundred tanks and one and a half million troops formed a tailback of 150 miles from the Meuse right back to the Rhine. Just as the blade of the sickle was beginning to cut deep, threatening to slice off the French and British forces in the north from their other armies in the south, the Führer was starting to have severe doubts. He was worried about the exposed flanks of the panzer spearheads under Guderian's command. Guderian knew that every day lost would give the Allies time to withdraw and regroup, so on 14 May he decided to ignore Hitler's orders and push forward, sweeping other divisions along with him.

The German Blitzkrieg of 1940 worked because the Allies feared a return to the costly stalemate of the First World War. But if one believes that the events of the past are going to replicate themselves precisely, one is almost guaranteed to fail. Hitler's entire career had been based on risk-taking, yet when it came to putting Manstein's daring plan into practice he showed a surprising lack of nerve, as he had in Norway.

On 17 May Franz Halder, the Chief of the Army General Staff, recorded in his diary: 'A really unpleasant day. The Führer is terribly nervous. He is frightened by his own success, does not want to risk anything, and therefore would rather stop us.'[6] Guderian was ordered to stop by the River Oise and wait for the infantry divisions to catch up. It was a major tactical mistake, showing that Hitler, although he was willing to take risks and employ Blitzkrieg tactics, astonishingly enough didn't really appreciate how they worked.

Guderian, on the other hand, fully appreciated that only speed and surprise protected him from a counter-attack. Vehemently protesting against the halt order, he relinquished his command. He only revoked his resignation after he had been given permission to undertake a so-called 'reconnaissance in force' – whatever that was thought to mean. Guderian decided to interpret it as a licence to act on his own initiative and to press on towards the Channel coast, which he hurriedly did.

Guderian's revolutionary form of mechanised warfare proved overwhelming and took the Allies completely by surprise. Ten days into the campaign, the first German units reached the mouth of the River Somme at the Channel coast. The sickle-cut was complete: the Allied armies in the north, including the British Expeditionary Force, were encircled. This was the worst day in British history for four hundred years. The British were about to lose their

Expeditionary Force of a quarter of a million men. There hadn't been a disaster like it since the English lost Calais in the sixteenth century. Yet the success of the sickle-cut operation cannot be credited to Hitler's leadership, but to Manstein's planning and the boldness and initiative of Guderian. Had Guderian stuck to Hitler's directives, it would have been all 'Krieg' and no 'Blitz' – a lightning war without the lightning and, quite possibly, a campaign with a very different outcome.

Would Guderian have got away with such initiative in the British Army? For his exploits in the French campaign, Hitler rewarded him with a promotion to lieutenant-general. There is a persistent belief in Britain that the Germans were like automatons, their soldiers blindly obeying orders, but it's a myth. Guderian was able to use his initiative because he was acting in accordance with the German principle of *Auftragstaktik* (Mission Command).

Mission Command

First developed by the Prussian Army in the nineteenth century and now official NATO doctrine, Mission Command means that headquarters confines itself to setting the objectives while leaving it up to the commanders on the spot to decide how best to achieve them. Success or failure – rather than obedience – is the ultimate criterion. Mission Command was the secret behind Hitler's startling victory over France. It is a crucial principle for effective leadership. The management gurus call it empowerment: leaders trust their subordinates and rely on their initiative and expertise. An important element was that everybody in the German Army was specifically trained to be able to take over the duties of the superiors in the event that they were called upon to take command.

Yet if the German Army's leadership was so efficient in 1939–41, how was it that these victories of the first years of the war were followed by ignominious defeats? The answer lies with the man who had appointed himself Supreme Commander of the Wehrmacht – Adolf Hitler. The fatal flaws of his leadership had already become evident in his Blitzkrieg against France. A key moment in the campaign took place in the Maison Blairon in the French town of Charleville-Mézières in the Ardennes close to the Luxembourg border, where Hitler came on the morning of 24 May 1940. This was the headquarters of General Gerd von Rundstedt, the Commander of Army Group A to the south-west of the encircled Allied forces. All German panzer divisions were under the command of Rundstedt, who was sixty-four years old and a general of the old school. He wanted his panzers to wait for the slower infantry.

The Commander-in-Chief of the Army, General Walther von Brauchitsch, and his Chief of Staff, General Franz Halder, strongly disagreed. They recognised that without continuing pressure the Allied forces would try to escape across the English Channel. On the night of 23 May, von Brauchitsch and Halder transferred command of the panzer divisions from Rundstedt to Army Group B in the north-east. Hitler learned of this change of command only on the following morning when he visited Rundstedt at his headquarters in Charleville-Mézières.

Von Brauchitsch and Halder had made the correct decision, but they had made it without their Führer. Hitler could not accept that the Army High Command had acted on their own initiative, as they were trained to do in accordance with the principles of Mission Command. Now, as victory was all but certain, the Führer was anxious to make clear that it was not his generals who were winning this campaign, but he himself. Since the Army were the only force in Germany powerful enough to depose him, all the kudos for the victory in the West had to be concentrated upon the Führer alone. He therefore immediately rescinded the transfer of command of the panzer divisions and authorised Rundstedt to issue a halt order to his Army Group.

It was this famous halt order that gave the Allies the necessary respite to evacuate 338,226 British, French and Belgian troops. No other decision of the Second World War caused such a storm of protest from German generals as the halt order at Dunkirk. Brauchitsch called several times on Hitler to have the order revoked – to no avail. The Führer gloated over the humiliation for the Army's Commander-in-Chief who, in his own words, felt 'forced to the wall'.

After it had become clear what a serious mistake he had made, Hitler claimed that he had intentionally spared the British to demonstrate that he wanted no war with them. Yet his true motives were very different. Hitler's decision to hold back the panzers had nothing to do with magnanimity towards Britain and indeed little to do with any strategic considerations at all. Its main purpose was to put the Army in its place, as modern historical scholarship has recently shown.[7]

Instead of the Army, Göring's Air Force was given the task of finishing off the encircled Allied troops. Hitler also wanted to give Himmler's SS enough time to move into position to join in the action at Dunkirk. By forcing the Army to share victory with Luftwaffe and SS, Hitler could be certain to receive the main credit for it.

The Luftwaffe failed ignominiously. When Dunkirk was finally captured, the vast proportion of Allied forces had been carried to safety across the English Channel to fight another day. Meanwhile the Führer had won a comparatively futile battle against the Army High Command. This was only the first of many grave errors Hitler made in the war. His striving to expand and protect his power base, even at the expense of military judgement, helped prepare the ground for his ultimate defeat. Hitler's army adjutant, Major Gerhard Engel, would later explain: 'Some of Hitler's decisions had nothing to do with military reasoning. They were only made to demonstrate to the head of the Army that Hitler was in command and nobody else.'[8]

Plain speaking from Churchill

It is hard to conceive how Hitler's new British adversary, Winston Churchill, could have refused to seek peace terms with the Nazis if the entire British Expeditionary Force had been captured at Dunkirk. As it was, Churchill turned the successful rescue of the Allied Army into a morale-boosting triumph in adversity. Being right about Hitler and the Nazis might have got Churchill to Downing Street in May 1940, but in order to stay there he needed to invent an entirely new kind of leadership – one that effectively abolished logic and appealed to the heart rather than to the mind. For the simple fact was that although Churchill had to tell the British people that the war was winnable, he himself did not have the first idea of how that could possibly be achieved. In a series of uplifting speeches he made a number of assertions about how the war might be won, each more improbable than the last.

He was imploring – as only remarkable leaders can, and only in extraordinary times – the public to feel rather than to calculate. If he had been proved wrong, he would have had to face the people's wrath for grievously misleading them. In the first speech he made as prime minister, in the House of Commons on 13 May 1940, Churchill was disarmingly honest when he admitted that he had 'nothing to offer but blood, toil, tears and sweat'. But he went on to offer much more than that when he said: 'You ask, what is our aim? I can answer in one word: Victory – victory at all costs, victory in spite of all terror, victory, however long and hard the road may be; for without victory there is no survival.'

By the time he spoke publicly again, six days later, the Germans had broken through the French defences to the north of the Maginot Line, and further suspension of belief was needed on behalf of the British people before they could imagine how they could possibly eventually prevail. Churchill did hold out hope for the French Army, saying: 'We may look with confidence to the stabilisation of the Front in France, and to the general engagement of the masses, which will enable the qualities of the French and British soldiers to be matched squarely against those of their adversaries. For myself, I have invincible confidence in the French Army and its leaders.'

It did not stay invincible, however, because only ten days later the British Expeditionary Force was being evacuated from the beaches of Dunkirk. But by showing indomitable courage himself, Churchill effectively shamed the British – who had for the past twenty years been zealous appeasers of Germany, and who had embraced the Munich agreement as enthusiastically as they had rejected him – into being heroic. His speeches assumed that they were actually looking forward to the coming attacks on the civilian population:

> There will be many men, and many women, in this island who when the ordeal comes upon them, will feel comfort, and even a pride – that they are sharing the perils of our lads at the front – soldiers, sailors and airmen, God bless them – and are drawing away from them at least a part of the onslaught they have to bear. Is this not the time for all to make the utmost exertions in their power?

By treating people in this way even before mainland Britain had fallen foul of attack, Churchill turned an understandably nervous and fearful people into heroes. Even if not everyone shared his confidence in ultimate victory, they were not about to spread defeatism by voicing their fears. This was a supreme act of leadership on Churchill's part. As he told the House of Commons on 4 June 1940:

> We are told that Herr Hitler has a plan for invading the British Isles. This has often been thought of before. When Napoleon lay at Boulogne for a year with his flat-bottomed boats and his Grand Army, he was told by someone 'There are bitter weeds in England.' There are certainly a great many more of them since the British Expeditionary Force returned... Even though large tracts of Europe and many old and famous States have fallen or may fall into the grip of the Gestapo and all the odious apparatus of Nazi rule, we shall not flag or fail. We shall go on to the end, we shall fight in France, we shall fight on the seas and oceans, we shall fight with growing confidence and growing strength in the air, we shall defend our Island, whatever the cost may be, we shall fight on the beaches, we shall fight on the landing grounds, we shall fight in the fields and in the streets, we shall fight in the hills; we shall never surrender.

'Long dark nights of trials and tribulations lie before us,' he warned in an especially bleak radio address. 'Not only great dangers, but many more misfortunes, many shortcomings, many mistakes, many disappointments will surely be our lot. Death and sorrow will be companions of our journey, constancy and valour our only shield. We must be united, we must be undaunted. We must be inflexible.' One man who immediately recognised the strategy behind Churchill's dismal honesty was Joseph Goebbels. 'His slogan of blood, sweat and tears has entrenched him in a position that makes him totally immune from attack,' wrote the Nazi propaganda chief in a magazine article entitled 'Churchill's Tricks'. 'He is like the doctor who prophesies that his patient will die and who, every time his patient's condition worsens, smugly explains that he prophesied it.' By preparing the public for bad news, Churchill denied the Nazis the full propaganda value of their victories. They could not wreck national morale if Britons had already heard the worst from the Prime Minister himself.

In his speech to the House of Commons explaining the evacuation from Dunkirk, Churchill knew that he had to hold out some hope – however slender – to encourage the British to fight on. The factor he chose to emphasise was the possibility, which he privately knew to be remote to the point of being negligible, that the United States might soon enter the struggle. In his peroration, he summoned up the prospect of carrying on the struggle 'until, in God's good time, the New World, with all its power and might, steps forth to the rescue and liberation of the old'. From his own conversations with President Roosevelt he knew that unprovoked direct American military intervention was still a very distant possibility, but to lead is to give hope, however false it might be.

The crucial point was that if the British people were being gulled, all but a tiny minority of them actually wanted to be. As professional confidence tricksters will affirm, in order for a 'sting' to be successful the 'mark' must at least subconsciously want to be taken for a ride. This is what happened to the collective subconscious of the British people in 1940–41; they believed Churchill because they willed themselves to, and because the only alternative – peace with Hitler – was simply too dreadful and dishonourable to contemplate. Yet if one had asked individual Britons rationally whether they truly believed it was possible to drag America into the war, or to blockade the whole European continent into surrender, or to defeat Germany by any of the other means that Churchill seemed to be holding out in that strange yet sublime thirteen-month period, they would have been hard put to explain the rationale behind his belief in ultimate victory.

Grasping plenary powers

Churchill had learned from the Dardanelles disaster of the Great War that it is a mistake, as he put it, 'to carry out a major and cardinal operation from a subordinate position'. He also wrote, 'My one fatal mistake was trying to achieve a great enterprise without having the plenary authority which could so easily have carried it to success.' With these memories, he decided to grasp exactly such authority when he came to power in 1940.

Wars are not won by evacuations, as Churchill said, and neither

Hitler with
Blondi.

Hitler with his other
blondie. Eva always called
him 'mein Führer', right up
to their shotgun marriage.

The Führer pioneered the politicians' photo-opportunity with children.

A very rare shot of the short-sighted Hitler wearing glasses; he feared such photos would damage his superhuman image.

When the Italian dictator Benito Mussolini was photographed in his bathing trunks Hitler exploded with derision.

Churchill didn't much care what he looked like.

Hitler deliberately dressed down to emphasise his simplicity *vis a vis* his generals.

Goebbels used humour to get round the Führer, and to undermine his rivals.

The architect Albert Speer and Hitler admire their handiwork at the opening of the new Reich chancellery in 1938.

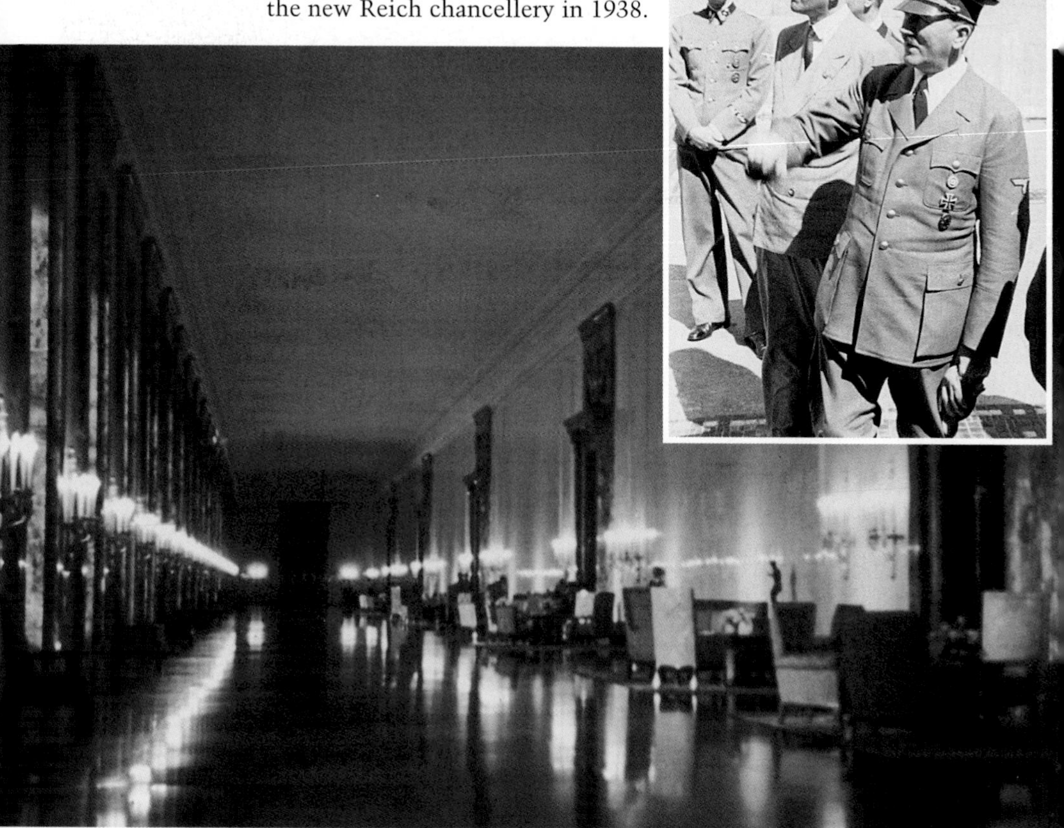

You had to walk through nine hundred feet of increasingly splendid halls before you reached the Führer's study.

Churchill would walk the streets of London even as wartime premier, as on 26th May 1940.

Hitler's secretaries smoked when his back was turned.

The Führer rated two Father Christmases at this party in 1937.

Hitler wanted to use the German diplomatic service to seduce Churchill's daughter Mary (left). It never happened.

Finance minister Hjalmar Schacht salutes the Führer's bust in 1935.

Kingsley Wood and Anthony Eden advise Churchill after a Cabinet meeting, only hours before he became prime minister on 10th May 1940.

Lord Salisbury looks down on Chamberlain's wartime cabinet in October 1939.

Back row, left to right: John Anderson, Maurice Hankey, Leslie Hore-Belisha, Winston Churchill, Kingsley Wood, Anthony Eden and Edward Bridges.
Front row: Lord Halifax, John Simon, Neville Chamberlain, Samuel Hoare and Lord Chatfield.

are they won by morale-boosting speeches alone. One of his first steps was to tackle the cumbersome and inflexible decision-making structure that he had inherited from Chamberlain. Churchill rightly complained that everything was 'settled for the greatest number by the common sense of most after the consultation of all'. Of the Committee of Imperial Defence, which was responsible for strategic plans but not for operations, he said that it represented the 'maximum of study and the minimum of action'.

Churchill's solution was to couple responsibility with the direct power of action. He didn't like purely advisory committees. War, he said, was 'more like one ruffian bashing the other on the snout with a club'.[9] He was equally straightforward when he complained to Harold Macmillan: 'Why, you may take the most gallant sailor, the most intrepid airman and the most audacious soldier, put them together – what do you get? The sum of their fears.' Macmillan recalled this being said 'with sibilant emphasis'.

Churchill had streamlined decision-making successfully as Minister of Munitions and at the Colonial Office during earlier periods in government. He recognised how it allowed the executives not to be smothered by detail and duplication. During the war his considerable organisational skills were brought into play as he sought to reduce overlaps in government and administration. He even had a gift for simplifying administrative language: the Local Defence Volunteers became the Home Guard, Communal Feeding Centres became British Restaurants, and so on.

At ten people, the War Cabinet was too large, just as it had been at the start of the Great War. One error was that it included the three service ministers, encouraged Cabinet discussions to become too broad, often extending to the making of operational plans. Chamberlain's attempt to solve this had been to form a Military Co-ordination Committee chaired by Lord Chatfield. It was charged with the mission of co-ordinating the efforts of the military services with the policy set out by the War Cabinet. It suffered from being advisory without control of any department, and without the power to give orders. In April 1940 the office was abolished under pressure from Churchill, who was none the less soon complaining that he had 'no power to take or enforce decisions'. When he became Prime Minister he halved the War Cabinet to only five members. 'The days of mere co-ordination were out for good,' one senior figure later wrote. 'We were now going to get direction, leadership, action – with a snap in it!'[10]

Churchill did not stop there. He immediately set about obtaining even greater powers, believing that, as he put it, strategic failure in war was due to 'the total absence of one directing mind and commanding will power'. Running a war by committee was bad enough, but on top of that there was no clear distinction between political and military decision-making. Creating the new office of Minister of Defence, taking the post himself and making the trusted General Ismay his personal liaison with the Chiefs of Staff was a political and administrative master-stroke. The new structure gave Churchill greater authority than any previous prime minister. He had placed himself in the direct line of responsibility for the creation of war plans and their execution, but he had not created an actual or new Ministry of Defence with all its costs and bureaucratic apparatus. As he warned Ismay, 'We must be very careful not to define our powers too precisely.' By keeping them flexible and nebulous, they were in effect far greater than if they had been circumscribed by Whitehall, Westminster or – more powerful than either – by precedent.

Churchill also immediately sought to reduce the number of committees. In particular he amalgamated many of the British military and civil missions to the United States which were burgeoning but whose responsibilities often overlapped. Two weeks after becoming prime minister he sent a memo to his Cabinet Secretary: 'I am sure there are far too many committees of one kind or another which ministers have to attend, and which do not yield a significant result. These should be reduced by suppression or amalgamation.' He despaired at collective decision-making through committees, on which the entire basis of British administration had for so long been centred.

Yet the new powers were not undemocratic; Churchill had not taken on autocratic powers but continued to work through the Cabinet because he knew that ultimately his power would always rest with the House of Commons, which in December 1916 had brought down the sitting wartime premier Herbert Asquith and in May 1940 had repeated the process with Neville Chamberlain. (The historian in Churchill would also have been reminded of Lord Aberdeen's fate during the Crimean War: British premiers who begin wars often do not get to finish them.) 'I am a child of the House of

Commons,' Churchill was to tell the United States Congress in December 1941. 'I was brought up in my father's house to believe in democracy. "Trust the people" was his message.... In my country, as in yours, public men are proud to be servants of the State and would be ashamed to be its masters.'

In practice, Churchill's streamlining of the system meant that he could push through controversial policies; one of these was the decision to use heavy bombers such as the Lancaster against German towns and cities. Under Chamberlain, bombing had been restricted to dropping leaflets and attacking naval targets. Air raids on land targets were off-limits, not only for fear of German retaliation but also for rather peculiar legal considerations. A Royal Air Force plan to attack military targets in the Black Forest had been rejected by the then Secretary of State for Air, Sir Kingsley Wood, with the words: 'Are you aware that it is private property? Why, you'll be asking me to bomb Essen next!'[11]

Churchill showed no such inhibitions and a few days after his assumption of the premiership he authorised attacks on military and industrial targets in Germany. When three months later, at the height of the Battle of Britain, the first German bombs fell on central London, Churchill bypassed both the Chiefs of Staff and the Secretary of State for Air and ordered Bomber Command directly to fly a reprisal raid on Berlin. Such swift decision-making would have been unthinkable under the structure of the previous government. And it was the right decision. For the next four years, strategic bombing would be the only means by which Britain could take the war to the German fatherland itself.

Other methods of taking control of the British war effort were Churchill's famous minutes, his 'prayers', and his 'Action This Day' tags. He had an astonishingly fertile mind: 'Winston had ten ideas every day,' his Chief of the Imperial General Staff Lord Alanbrooke used to say of him, 'only one of which was good, and he did not know which it was.' Roosevelt made a very similar remark, saying that the Prime Minister had a hundred ideas a day of which six were good (a much larger number if an even lower percentage).

Nothing was too minute a detail to escape Churchill's notice. He laid down the precise number of apes that should occupy the Rock of Gibraltar (twenty-four), tried to find out whether captured First World War trophy weapons could be reconditioned for use, worried about the animals in London Zoo during the bombing, and made sure that beer rations went to the fighting men at the front before those behind the lines. He even tried to discover whether wax might be used to protect the hearing of soldiers during bombardments.[12] Several of these requests, nicknamed 'prayers' because they often began 'Pray inquire…', were also tagged with a red marker demanding 'Action This Day'. On the very day that he became prime minister, 10 May 1940, for example, on top of all the other emergencies created by Hitler's assault in the West, Churchill came up with the idea that ex-Kaiser Wilhelm II be invited to defect to Britain from his exile in Holland. (It turned out to be one of Alanbrooke's nine or Roosevelt's ninety-four bad ideas and was not followed up.)

Sometimes Churchill's hands-on style simply went too far. His private secretary Jock Colville recalled how one night at Chequers:

> I was instructed, as usual, to ring up the duty captain at the Admiralty and find out if there was any news. There was none, and the duty captain promised to telephone immediately if anything of the slightest interest was reported. An hour later I was instructed to enquire again, and an injured duty captain reminded me of the promise he had given. When, at about 2am, I was bidden in spite of all remonstrations to try yet again, the angry officer, aroused from a few hours' sleep, let fly at me the full vocabulary of the quarter deck in times of crisis. Churchill, hearing a flow of speech, assumed that at least an enemy cruiser had been sunk. He seized the receiver from my hand and was subjected to a series of uncomplimentary expletives which clearly fascinated him. After listening for a minute or two he explained that he was only the prime minister and that he was wondering whether there was any naval news.[13]

Churchill wrote: 'Those who are charged with the direction of supreme affairs must sit on the mountain tops of control; they must never descend into the valleys of direct physical and personal action.' Yet, early in his premiership in 1940, he also admonished his staff that: 'An efficient and successful administration manifests itself equally in small as in great matters.' In his first few weeks as prime minister he even gave orders about the size of flag that flew outside the Admiralty. 'Churchill scrutinizes every document that has anything to do with the war and does not disdain to enquire into the most trivial point,' wrote one of his private secretaries. He gave orders about rabbits, how not to let the whisky industry suffer, and even altered the codenames of individual military operations.

Hitler also involved himself with the minutiae of fighting the war, at one stage personally banning horse-racing in Berlin, but there was one decisive difference between Hitler and Churchill: the Führer's orders were almost all issued by his private secretary, Martin Bormann, rather than being signed personally by him. Hitler himself put hardly anything in writing, which enabled him to deny his responsibility should things go wrong, or if they were too infamous to be directly connected with him. 'Never put an order in writing that can be given verbally' was his maxim. This enabled him (and his apologists, though with equal lack of credibility) to deny his responsibility for his crimes, up to and even including the Holocaust itself.

Churchill, on the other hand, had no difficulty about accepting responsibility. Indeed, on 21 April 1944 he told the House of Commons: 'I have no intention of passing my remaining years in explaining or withdrawing anything I have said in the past, still less apologising for it.' The following year he went further, saying: 'If I am accused of this mistake, I can only say with M. Clemenceau on a celebrated occasion: "Perhaps I have made a number of mistakes of which you have not heard."' Churchill had long been used to blame and indeed obloquy, and had developed a rhinocerine hide for criticism by the time the Second World War broke out. Anyone who had returned to active politics after the Gallipoli débâcle needed to be pachydermatous. As he wrote about something else in *My Early Life*, 'Everybody threw the blame on me. I have noticed that they nearly always do. I suppose it is because they think I shall be able to bear it best.'

Of course Churchill did not see why he should bear blame unnecessarily. In contrast to Hitler, he actually preferred things to be put in writing. As his wife Clementine advised General Sir Louis Spears: 'He often does not listen or does not hear if he is thinking of something else. But he will always consider a paper carefully in all its implications. He never forgets anything he sees in writing.' It had to be kept short, though, and entirely to the point. In July 1940 Churchill put out the following minute to the War Cabinet Secretariat and in large part he stuck to it throughout the war: 'Let it be very clearly understood that all directions emanating from me are made in writing, or should be immediately afterwards confirmed in writing, and that I do not accept responsibility for matters relating to the national defence on which I am called to have given decisions unless they are recorded in writing.'[14]

As the senior civil servant Lord Normanbrook recalled, this minute had a profound and immediate effect: 'Hitherto prime ministers wishing to seek information or to offer advice to a colleague had done so by letter – more often than not by correspondence conducted in their name by private secretaries. Now, ministers received direct and personal messages, usually compressed into a single quarto paper and phrased in language showing beyond doubt that they were the actual words of the prime minister himself.'[15] Minutes like this were usually written at the beginning and end of each day.

Churchill was one of the first modern political leaders to recognise the value of statistics and quantitative analysis. He appointed his friend Professor Lindemann to head his statistical office, which comprised about twenty people, including economists, at least one scientist, civil servants, and the usual retinue of clerk-typists to produce the reports. It soon proved invaluable to Churchill, who used data well. 'Do not think of making a case for a particular point of view,' he wrote. 'Let us just have the cold-blooded facts.'

Recognising himself to be an unusual creature, Churchill also wanted to ensure that abnormal people were allowed to thrive in the military and civil services. In a letter to Anthony Eden, the newly created Secretary of State for War, a few weeks after he became prime minister, Churchill wrote: 'We want live wires, and not conventional types.' Some six months later he wrote to Field Marshal Sir John Dill: 'We cannot afford to confine Army appointments to persons who have excited no hostile comment in their careers... This is a time to try men of force and vision and not be exclusively confined to those who are judged thoroughly safe by conventional standards.' As a result, thoroughly unconventional people like the half-mad Orde Wingate, the homosexual Alan Turing and the eccentric academics at Bletchley Park were permitted to make their significant contributions to the war effort. Churchill believed in using talent wherever he could find it, even if that meant looking beyond those who were conventionally qualified. In one letter to Field

Marshal Sir John Dill about the brilliant but unconventional tank general, Percy Hobart, Churchill wrote: 'It is not only the good boys who help to win wars. It is the sneaks and stinkers as well.'

The primary example of Churchill inserting the roundest possible peg in the squarest Whitehall hole was the promotion of his friend Lord Beaverbrook to Minister of Aircraft Production in May 1940, knowing that the threat of invasion could only be beaten off through air supremacy. 'The Beaver' was a Canadian press baron who was thought to have made his money by unscrupulous means and who thus had a controversial reputation, but who had been Minister of Information in the Great War and whose ownership of the *Express* newspaper group made him a power in the country.

Churchill was an exponent of what management gurus today call 'MBWA' – management by walking about. He constantly visited factories, gun emplacements, searchlight units, and so on. Soon after becoming prime minister he visited Fighter Command to see for himself what they required. Air Chief Marshal Sir Hugh Dowding told him he badly needed extra resources – pilots, night-defence capability, but most especially more planes. The major problem, Churchill quickly discovered, was the lack of available fighters. Churchill set about changing this by giving Beaverbrook his total support. He even overrode the objections of the King and others to appoint Beaverbrook a privy counsellor.

Fortunately, Beaverbrook soon proved highly effective. He used heavy-handed, often bullying techniques to get what he wanted and aircraft production soon significantly increased under his aggressive prodding. Resources were taken away from bombers, and he simplified the bureaucratic process to get at least a short-term boost in fighter production. His famous appeal for housewives' pots and pans for melting down did much to raise public awareness and morale, even if little of the metal produced found its way into actual aircraft.

At a meeting on 3 June, Sir Archibald Sinclair, the new Secretary of State for Air, reported that Britain was also dangerously short of pilots. During May fighter production had been critical, but now it was the number of pilots as well as of planes that had become the vital issue. Churchill told Sinclair that during a visit to Hendon he had noticed lots of pilots behind desks. 'Comb out the fluff and the flummery!' he ordered him in the authentic tones of a modern CEO. 'Keep me informed.'

By mid-August Sinclair had found more pilots to add to 'the Few'; he was helped by Churchill, overriding the complaints of the Royal Navy, to give Air Chief Marshal Dowding pilots borrowed from the Fleet Air Arm. The result of Churchill's leadership was that the overall number of fighter pilots rose despite the constant losses. The Germans, on the other hand, did not change a thing. They were very lethargic at the top level of the Luftwaffe; and in August Göring even went off hunting and playing with his train set.

On 15 September Churchill visited the headquarters of Fighter Command 11 Group on what turned out, coincidentally, to be the decisive day of the Battle of Britain. From there he watched the crucial air battle unfold and witnessed the glorious victory of the RAF. The success of that day meant that invasion was effectively no longer possible. On 17 September Hitler decided to postpone 'Operation Sealion' indefinitely, although it was not till 12 October that the invasion was formally called off, ostensibly until the following spring. In July 1941 it was postponed again by Hitler until the spring of 1942, 'by which time the Russian campaign will be completed'. Instead, on 13 February 1942 Admiral Raeder had his final interview on 'Sealion' and got Hitler to agree to a complete 'stand-down'. Yet Churchill recognised that the forging of a national commitment was stronger in the face of a perceived threat, so even after Ultra decrypts had informed him that the genuine danger had passed, he continued to warn of a possible invasion since he realised it was the perfect means to keep the nation focused and united.

If the Germans had invaded, and if the long history of British sovereign independence had come to an end in 1940, it would have happened in Neasden in north London. That was the location of the bunker to which Churchill and other senior government ministers were to move in the event of the Germans capturing central London, and where Churchill would have fought to the end. In his own words: 'If this long island story of ours is to end at last, let it end only when each one of us lies choking in his own blood upon the ground.' As he wrote of the death of the brave President Molara in *Savrola*: 'It often happens that, when men are convinced that they have to die, a desire to bear themselves well and to leave life's stage with dignity conquers all other sensations.'[16] So it might have been with Churchill. Although the Royal Family, Britain's gold reserves and the Royal Navy would have been evacuated to continue the struggle from Ottawa, Churchill was personally resolved to end it all in the nation's capital. (Of course, whether he would have been allowed to in the actual event is another matter, the exigencies of a real post-invasion scenario being impossible to predict, and a live prime minister in Canada being a lot more useful to the cause than a dead one in Neasden.) The Royal Family had a series of stately homes – including Madresfield Court in Worcestershire – to which they were going to be evacuated on their journey north towards embarkation from Scotland, and it is hard to believe that Churchill would not have also been prevailed upon to carry on the fight, especially if so ordered by the King. All such plans were of course kept strictly secret, because the primary purpose of the Government in the summer of 1940 was to counter any sense of defeatism, which had so sapped the will of the Continental Allies to continue the fight.

Defeating defeatism

In the midst of the Dunkirk evacuation in May 1940, Churchill circulated a memorandum to all Cabinet members and senior officials that read: 'In these dark days the prime minister would be grateful if all his colleagues in the Government, as well as high officials, would maintain a high morale in their circles; not minimizing the gravity of events, but showing confidence in our ability and inflexible resolve to continue the war until we have broken the will of the enemy to bring all of Europe under his domination.'

Stamping out defeatism, or worse still the supposed pro-Nazi Fifth Column that was thought to be operating inside Britain, was a central task for Churchill as he tried to lead the nation in 1940. In his post-Dunkirk speech he said that 'Parliament has given us the powers to put down Fifth Column activities with a strong hand, and we shall use these powers, subject to the supervision and the correction of the House, without the slightest hesitation until we are satisfied that this malignancy in our midst has been effectively stamped out.' One of the places this happened was at Ham Common in Richmond, where a secret MI5 base called Latchmere House was used to imprison the top forty suspected enemy spies in 1940–41, who were interrogated using methods expressly banned under the

Geneva Convention. Although little is known about this shadowy place – because the secret service files that cover it are even now still kept under lock and key – we do know that it was there that MI5 first broke and then 'turned' those who it believed were working for the Germans, with an almost complete success rate.

The process of countering defeatism elsewhere in the country was carried out with sometimes absurd over-efficiency, with ordinary people being arrested for doing no more than complaining about prices in bread queues. It was even made an offence to discourage people's belief in achieving victory.[17] In 1940 the literary critic Cyril Connolly was arrested in an Oxford hotel by military police because he 'seemed very interested' in the conversation of British officers near by. His Viennese-issued passport and editorship of a literary magazine led to an inquisition by no fewer than eight policemen, and he was only released once he proved that he had attended both Eton and Balliol College, Oxford.[18] One Leicestershire man got a two-year gaol sentence for saying in a pub that he 'couldn't see how we could win the war'. Yet neither really could the Prime Minister, who was even reduced to arguing in 1940 that Germany's subject peoples would rise against her if there was a bad winter.

During the Fall of France in mid-June 1940, Churchill broadcast to the people, saying that: 'We are sure that in the end all will come right.' With Hitler master of the European continent from Warsaw to Brest and from Narvik down to Naples, with Germany's non-aggression pact with Russia still holding, with Italy in the war against Britain, and with the Nazis having swallowed up eleven independent nations in two years, Churchill was rather reduced to the position of Mr Micawber in Charles Dickens's *David Copperfield*, who hoped against hope that 'something will turn up'. On 18 June 1940, in what has become known as the 'Finest Hour' speech, Churchill tried to set out the grounds upon which, as he put it, 'there are good and reasonable hopes of final victory'. But beyond saying that the Dominion prime ministers had endorsed the decision to fight on, and that the French might continue to resist – which they very largely did not – he still did not have any kind of rational recipe for eventual victory, for all the wonderful tone of his language. He argued that in one-to-one fighting in the air individual British pilots were superior to their German counterparts, and that the United States would shortly send immense supplies and munitions; but these were at best reasons why Britain might be able to survive, not explanations as to how an army could be landed on the continent of Europe that would capture Berlin, overthrow Hitler and win the war.

Churchill even held out the possibility that Germany might suddenly and inexplicably collapse simply out of superior British morale, citing what he claimed had happened in 1918: 'During that war we repeatedly asked ourselves the question: How are we going to win? and no one was able ever to answer it with much precision, until at the end, quite suddenly, quite unexpectedly, our terrible foe collapsed before us, and we were so glutted with victory that in our folly we threw it away.' A sudden and unexpected collapse in German morale was simply not a credible war plan. What Churchill knew was that the British Empire could not defeat Germany on its own; it desperately needed allies.

Finding allies

Even before he became prime minister, Churchill had hoped to draw a reluctant America into the war. After a lunch with Churchill on 5 October 1939, Ambassador Joseph Kennedy confided to his diary: 'I just don't trust him. He almost impressed me that he was willing to blow up the American embassy and say it was the Germans, if it would get the United States in.' Churchill understood earlier than anyone else in the wartime Government, especially after the Fall of France, that American help would be vital, and he embarked on a concerted effort of coalition-building even before he became prime minister, and despite the anglophobic American Ambassador. His offers to the United States culminated in a speech at the Mansion House on 20 November 1941, in which he promised that: 'Should the United States become involved in war with Japan, the British declaration will follow within the hour.'

Hitler, by contrast, completely underestimated the importance of alliances. There was a pragmatic side to him, as the Nazi–Soviet Non-Aggression Pact of August 1939 proved, but it was only ever intended as a short-term measure. As he put it in *Mein Kampf*: 'Tactical considerations matter.' When, a decade later, he discussed Germany's need for *Lebensraum* he said: 'That does not mean that I will refuse to walk part of the road together with the Russians, if that will help us... But it will only be in order to return the more swiftly to our true aims.'[19] The idea of staying faithful to the terms of a treaty the moment it was no longer advantageous to him was completely foreign to Hitler's way of thinking. His ideological aim of winning German living space in the East weighed far heavier than the moral or legal considerations of lesser beings.

Just as the Nazis underestimated the importance of alliances, so they had nothing but contempt for international agreements. Treaties were to them, in Göring's typically scatological expression, 'so much lavatory paper'. More often than not, Hitler failed to consult his allies about his next steps. Hitler not only broke his treaty with the Soviet Union, thus opening a war on two fronts; he also failed to inform his other allies, the Italians and the Japanese, of his plans for 'Operation Barbarossa'. He treated Italy with particular disdain, as the junior partner whose concerns and wishes could be readily ignored. As he said of that country: 'Mussolini might be a Roman, but his people are Italians.' Small wonder then that Mussolini decided, in his own words, to 'pay Hitler back in his own coin' when he attacked Greece only three weeks after being warned not to by Hitler at their meeting at the Brenner Pass on 4 October 1940. This possibly had a fateful effect on 'Operation Barbarossa'. As Mussolini's Greek offensive misfired badly, Hitler was forced to occupy Yugoslavia in April 1941 in order to come to Italy's aid. It was another lightning campaign, over in six weeks, but it probably helped to delay the invasion of the Soviet Union. Just how vital those six springtime weeks were became clear when the German Army only just failed to reach Moscow before the onset of the Russian winter.

Hitler also failed to inform his other ally, Japan, in the spring of 1941 about the impending invasion of Russia. Indeed he deliberately misinformed them, saying that 'Russia will not be attacked as long as she maintains a friendly attitude in accordance with the treaty'.[20] Had Hitler consulted with the Japanese before the German invasion, they might have been persuaded to invade Russia simultaneously. In the Russian Civil War, Japanese forces had fought in Siberia, and an attack from the East to coincide with Hitler's attack in the West could have been devastating to Russian morale. As it was, the Japanese High Command decided in September 1941 to postpone any military action against the Soviet Union and then three months later assaulted Pearl Harbor without warning the Germans, causing the United States to enter the war. Hitler's failure in coalition-building thus indirectly brought into being Churchill's strategic dream of a 'Grand Alliance' of the British Empire, the United States and the Soviet Union. Roosevelt's magnificent statesmanship ensured that a counterintuitive 'Germany First' policy was adopted, and Hitler's fate was thereby all but sealed.

Of course, for all of his public life since 1917 Churchill had shared Hitler's contempt for the Communist dictatorship in the Soviet Union. Indeed, even at the time of the publication of *Savrola* two decades before the Revolution, the chief villain was Karl Kreutze, a socialist revolutionary. Churchill had led the call for armed intervention against the Bolsheviks after 1918, and some of the greatest philippics of his career had been directed against the Soviets, in which he called them 'deadly snakes', 'cold, calculating, ruthless, patient', 'nothing lower', and even 'the nameless beast'. Yet none of these past views were allowed to bias Churchill against the opportunity of joining forces with the Soviet Union after Hitler's Blitzkrieg invasion of the USSR.

On 22 June 1941 Churchill broke the news of 'Operation Barbarossa' to the British people with the words: 'At four o'clock this morning Hitler attacked and invaded Russia. All his usual formalities of perfidy were observed with scrupulous technique.' He went on to pronounce the policy that: 'Any man or State who fights on against Nazism will have our aid. Any man or State who marches with Hitler is our foe.' He was thus prepared to subordinate his ideological prejudices to the greater cause. To his private secretary Jock Colville he had even remarked the night before the attack: 'If Hitler invaded Hell [I] would at least make a favourable reference to the Devil.'[21] Churchill was able to compromise: first by making concessions to the Americans, then by making an alliance with his old ideological enemy, Joseph Stalin. This willingness to compromise for the greater good is a characteristic of inspired leadership.

Speaking of his wooing of the Americans, Churchill once told Colville: 'No lover ever studied every whim of his mistress as I did those of President Roosevelt.' In 1941, when a new edition of his 1937 book *Great Contemporaries* was printed, Churchill included a laudatory article he had written about FDR in 1934, saying of his presidency: 'It is certain that Franklin Roosevelt will rank among the greatest of men who have occupied that proud position. His generous sympathy for the underdog, his intense desire for a nearer approach to social justice, place him high among the great philanthropists. His composure combined with activity in time of crisis class him with famous men of action.'[22] Later that year he described Roosevelt to the Canadian Parliament at Ottawa as: 'That great man whom destiny has marked for this climax of human fortune.'

This desperate desire to flatter and charm the Americans, and especially their leader, was noted by Roosevelt's minister Harold Ickes, who remarked that Churchill would have fêted the President's friend and personal representative Harry Hopkins even if he had been carrying the bubonic plague.[23] Yet Churchill could also make the subtlest of threats. Consider the wording of the message he sent to Roosevelt via the American Embassy in London on 15 June 1940, begging for American intervention before France capitulated:

> Although the present government and I personally would never fail to send the fleet across the Atlantic if resistance was beaten down here, a point may be reached in the struggle where the present ministers no longer have control of affairs and when very easy terms could be obtained for the British islands by becoming a vassal state of the Hitler empire. A pro-German government would certainly be called into being to make peace and might present to a shattered or a starving nation an almost irresistible case for an entire submission to the Nazi will. The fate of the British fleet ... would be decisive on the future of the United States because if it were joined to the fleets of Japan, France and Italy and the great resources of German industry, overwhelming sea power would be in Hitler's hands. He might, of course, use it with a merciful moderation. On the other hand he might not. This revolution in sea power might happen very quickly and certainly long before the United States would be able to prepare against it. If we go down you may have a United States of Europe under the Nazi command far more numerous, far stronger, far better armed than the new [world's].[24]

For all that politicians claim not to deal in hypothetical questions, in fact any conscientious ones must deal with alternative future possibilities all the time, and Roosevelt was no exception. 'After reading this,' his close adviser Henry Morgenthau minuted the President, 'unless we do something to give the English additional destroyers, it seems to me it is absolutely hopeless to expect them to keep going.' The result was the deal by which the United States gave Britain fifty destroyers in return for 99-year leases on various military bases in the western hemisphere. Churchill's methods were therefore not always as soft and soapy towards the Americans as his detractors tend to depict.

As the war progressed, Churchill had to accept that overall military strategy was increasingly dominated by his partners, the Americans and the Russians, who were contributing far more in terms of men, money and amounts of war matériel than Britain. For a long time in 1942 and 1943 Churchill nurtured the adventurous idea of 'rolling up Europe from the South-East' through the river valleys of the Balkans. While the Chief of the Imperial General Staff, Field Marshal Lord Alanbrooke, regarded such a venture as little more than what he called a 'pipe-dream', Churchill thought it was a realistic – and indeed preferable – alternative to 'Operation Overlord', the planned cross-Channel liberation of France. The Americans shared Alanbrooke's assessment, and Churchill finally conceded to this view and abandoned the idea. There was constant give and take between Churchill and the Chiefs of Staff, of whom he said in January 1944, 'They may say that I lead them up the garden path, but at every turn of the path they have found delectable fruit and wholesome vegetables.'

As the war progressed, Churchill found that his role was increasingly that of counselling rather than leading, let alone of controlling, Washington and Moscow. It is a position to which Hitler could never have adapted; whereas Churchill was an occasional tyro, Hitler could only ever be a full-time tyrant. 'What a small nation we are,' Churchill observed of the Teheran Conference with Roosevelt and Stalin in November–December 1943. 'There I sat with the great Russian bear on one side ... and on the other side the great American buffalo, and between the two sat the poor little English donkey.' None the less, the donkey developed an effective way to maintain its influence on the conduct of the war. It was the same method that Churchill's staff officers used against him when they wished to delay one of his favoured schemes or to dissuade him from a plan they judged impracticable – they agreed in principle at the outset and then tried to drown the idea in a sea of reasoned objection.

After the war Dwight Eisenhower, the former Supreme Allied Commander, said of Churchill:

> I had a very hard time withstanding his arguments. More than once he forced me to re-examine my own premises, to convince myself again that I was right – or accept his solution. Yet if the decision went against him, he accepted it with good grace, and did everything in his power to support it with proper action. Leadership by persuasion and the wholehearted acceptance of a contrary decision are both fundamentals of democracy.

Churchill would use every possible dialectical and emotional weapon to ensure that decisions did not go against him. According to the Director of Naval Intelligence Admiral Godfrey, these included 'persuasion, real or simulated anger, mockery, vituperation, tantrums, ridicule, derision, abuse and tears'. It took a tough man, such as Field Marshal Lord Alanbrooke undoubtedly was, to put up with these methods and often to overcome them.

Triumph of the will

Churchill recognised that many of Hitler's victories had come from the superior power of the dictator's will, and resolved to show that his own willpower was just as strong. In his broadcast of 14 July 1940, he said:

> I can easily understand how sympathetic onlookers across the Atlantic, or anxious friends in the yet unravished countries of Europe, who cannot measure our resources or our resolve, may have feared for our survival when they saw so many states and kingdoms torn to pieces in a few weeks or even days by the monstrous force of the Nazi war machine. But Hitler has not yet been withstood by a great nation with a will power the force of his own.

Churchill knew that part of the leader's task is to convince the people he leads that he has the necessary strength of will to fashion events, and not be merely swept along by them. His habit of sticking out his jutting jaw, almost in a caricature of a bulldog, emphasised this. He also somehow managed to turn his walking stick, which in any other pensioner might look like a sign of infirmity, into a potent symbol of defiance, as his statue by Ivor Roberts-Jones in London's Parliament Square eloquently demonstrates. He used his body language to convey the same message as his spoken language.

Although Churchill regularly and deliberately overestimated the chances of victory during 1940 and the first half of 1941, he never underestimated the dangers and difficulties. It made Churchill trusted as he took this stance to heights never seen before in politics. When the danger was real, as during the Battle of Britain in the late summer of 1940, the Prime Minister seemed almost to relish the long list of setbacks that had overcome Britain since he had taken office. It took an extraordinary leader in extraordinary circumstances to make an actual virtue out of such a series of catastrophes. In a speech he gave on 20 August 1940, he reported that:

> Rather more than a quarter of a year has passed since the new Government came into power in this country. What a cataract of disaster has poured out upon us since then! The trustful Dutch overwhelmed; their beloved and respected sovereign driven into exile; the peaceful city of Rotterdam the scene of a massacre as hideous and brutal as anything in the Thirty Years' War; Belgium invaded and beaten down; our own fine Expeditionary Force, which King Leopold called to his rescue, cut off and almost captured, escaping as it seemed almost by a miracle and with the loss of all its equipment; our ally, France, out; Italy in against us; all France in the power of the enemy, all its arsenals and vast masses of military material converted or convertible to the enemy's use; a puppet Government set up at Vichy which may at any moment be forced to become our foe; the Western seaboard of Europe from the North Cape to the Spanish frontier in German hands; all the ports, all the airfields on this immense front employed against us as springboards of invasion. Moreover, the German air power, numerically so far outstripping ours, has been brought so close to our islands that what we used to dread greatly has come to pass and the hostile bombers not only reach our shores in a few minutes and from several directions, but can be escorted by their fighting aircraft.

It was an appalling litany, but Churchill somehow managed to convert the very ghastliness of the situation into a strange kind of virtue. The allegation that Germany had won her victories by surprise, lies and trickery regularly resurfaced during his speeches, but now, he seemed to be arguing, the hitherto-trusting British were up to their own dastardly methods, and sheer moral superiority would see them through to victory. Again, this might seem utterly illogical in the context of modern warfare, but Churchill understood that it was moral courage that Britons needed in 1940 as much as sheer physical courage, arms and ammunition, and all his leadership skills were set to the task of providing it. He might not have been the right man to take Britain into the peace in 1945 or to lead her again in the fifties, but his leadership techniques were instrumental in persuading the British to persevere in the crucial thirteen months between the Fall of France and Hitler's invasion of Russia. Much of this was done by sheer willpower, and there is a certain irony in Leni Riefenstahl's choice of title for her film about Hitler, *Triumph of the Will*, since in the end it was Churchill's will that triumphed.

The use of creative tension: Churchill and Alanbrooke

'On no account must the contents of this book be published,' wrote Field Marshal Lord Alanbrooke on the opening page of his wartime diary, and it is easy to understand why.[25] As the 'master of strategy', the man Churchill had implored to become Britain's senior soldier, Alanbrooke was the repository of all the most important wartime secrets. Even when they were published in 1957 as part of a biography of Alanbrooke, the diary entries were heavily censored both on grounds of national security and for fear of antagonising powerful figures such as the then American President Dwight Eisenhower and the past and serving prime ministers Winston Churchill, Anthony Eden and Harold Macmillan.

In 2001 they were published unexpurgated for the first time, and although it had long been no secret that Alanbrooke did not always see eye-to-eye with Churchill on strategic matters, it was only then apparent that for much of the war he could hardly bear working with the Prime Minister. (Churchill, on the other hand, seems to have harboured no reciprocal ill-will towards Alanbrooke.)

Alanbrooke's influence on global strategy can hardly be

overestimated. It was he, more even than Churchill or the War Cabinet, who set out the stages by which Nazi Germany was going to be defeated. It was he who laid down the crucial sequence of North Africa, Italy and Normandy, as the prescribed path to Berlin. Once thought of as a typically strong, humourless, Ulster-born 'brass hat', it became clear that Alanbrooke was also a passionate man given to bouts of depression and elation, and also of fury against many of those with whom he had to work, especially Generals Marshall, Eisenhower and Patton, and much of the British political and military establishment.

Alanbrooke's painstaking approach often clashed with the more swashbuckling approach that came naturally to Churchill. It was the dichotomy between the chess player and the poker player. Yet Churchill never once overruled his Chiefs of Staff, however much he might have disagreed with them at times. The shadow of the Great War disaster at Gallipoli still hung over him, and he knew better than to trust his impulsive genius more than Alanbrooke's logical arguments. In his turn, Alanbrooke considered it his duty to prevent Churchill from getting Britain into another Gallipoli, a task in which he succeeded when quashing Churchill's plans for attacking in the Balkans in 1943 and Sumatra in 1944.

Although the minutes of the Chiefs of Staff Committee in the Public Records Office give the bare, factual outlines of what was discussed and agreed in the meetings, Alanbrooke's diaries flesh out the story and record the often volcanic rows that developed between the key players. Far from being the impassive, Olympian figures of wartime propaganda, Churchill and the British High Command were at times despairing of what to do next, and at bitter loggerheads over the way the war should be fought.

Where Churchill was romantic, boisterous and inspirational, the Chief of the Imperial General Staff was cautious, pessimistic, adamant and sober. Both men were combative, wilful, driven, and anxious to prevail. The personal tension between them eventually worked in Britain's favour, ensuring that grand strategy combined a mixture of Churchill's genius and Alanbrooke's professionalism. It was a pained, often exasperated working relationship that none the less helped to win the Second World War, even if it collapsed afterwards.

'Brookie wants to have it both ways,' commented Clementine

Churchill when his biography was published in 1957, after he had written a fulsome – if in the circumstances somewhat hypocritical – dedication in the copy that he sent Churchill. As Montgomery told the book's author, the historian Sir Arthur Bryant, Churchill was 'very angry indeed' at this, the first crack in the edifice of his wartime reputation. He would have been apoplectic if he had read what Alanbrooke and Bryant had already excised from the diaries.

Yet it must be recalled that Alanbrooke was often generous to Churchill in his journal and he regularly pointed out that it had been written at times of tremendous stress, often late at night, and as a way of letting off steam and thus preventing his irritation with his colleagues becoming apparent to their faces. The diaries therefore probably saved as many rows as they documented. In the major strategic arguments of the war, and especially in delaying the Second Front until June 1944 when the Allies were properly ready, Alanbrooke was proved right, and it was very fortunate that an admirable 'no man' was there instead of any weaker figure.

What saved Churchill from such potentially disastrous military blunders was that he respected people who stood up to him and did not mince their words. Indeed, it is to his great credit that he appointed Alanbrooke precisely because he knew he would stand up to him, something far removed from the standard practice in today's politics. As the American General George Patton once said: 'When everyone agrees, someone is not thinking.' Even the best leaders fail when they don't allow others to disagree with them; it was not a mistake that Churchill made.

Alanbrooke's diaries were a psychological safety-valve for a soldier who laboured under as great a weight of political and military pressure as any in history. As he snapped yet another pencil in half with the words 'Prime Minister, I flatly disagree', he was doing his duty better than any other Allied general on active service. Part of Churchill's greatness lay in the fact that he appointed Alanbrooke, and afterwards, however grudgingly, accepted his advice.

Part of his implicit self-belief stemmed from the fact that in one of his first major clashes with the Chiefs of Staff, Churchill's boldness had been proved correct. It was a very brave decision to reinforce the Middle East in July 1940, even while the Battle of Britain was being fought, involving sending nearly half of the available tanks around the Cape of Good Hope. Churchill's biographer Roy

Jenkins believes that without this signal victory over the Chiefs, 'Egypt might not have been held in 1941/early 1942, and the Western Desert could not have been the scene of Britain's first decisive land victory at the end of the latter year.'[26] This led Churchill, not unnaturally, to take a more belligerent stance towards the Chiefs of Staff than he might otherwise have done.

As a result, Churchill was occasionally allowed to prevail over the Chiefs' more cautious and wiser counsel. As the military historian John Keegan has written:

> Some of his initiatives resulted in actual disaster, such as his insistence, against American advice, in invading the Greek Dodecanese Islands in 1943. He also committed the cardinal military mistake of reinforcing failure, as by his decision to land the 18th Division in Singapore in 1942. It disembarked into Japanese captivity.[27]

Adopting his own staff's tactics of delay and veiled obstruction, Churchill succeeded in postponing 'Operation Overlord' until 1944, even though Stalin had been demanding a second front in the West ever since 1942, and Roosevelt aimed to launch the invasion in 1943. Fearing the disastrous consequences of a failed invasion, Churchill insisted that the Germans had to be weakened sufficiently before a cross-Channel operation should be attempted. He cunningly drew the Americans into diversionary campaigns in the Middle East and Italy, and thus prevented the premature launch of 'Overlord'. In retrospect, Churchill was absolutely right. It is more than doubtful that an invasion in 1943 could have succeeded, and the delay of 'Overlord' was arguably – after stiffening Britain's resolve in 1940–41 – Churchill's most important single contribution to the Allied victory.

Hitler on Churchill

'It's a queer business, how England slipped into this war,' Hitler told his guests at the Berghof on the evening of 18 October 1941. 'The man who managed it was Churchill, that puppet of the Jewry that pulls the strings.'[28] Not surprisingly, Churchill cropped up in Hitler's table talk almost as much as Hitler did in Churchill's speeches in the House of Commons, with quite as much bile but not a particle of the wit. 'I never met an Englishman who didn't speak of Churchill with disapproval,' Hitler told his henchmen on the evening of 7 January 1942. 'Never one who didn't say he was off his head.' He went on to claim that Churchill was in the pay of America, and that he 'is a bounder of a journalist'. As a result, the Führer believed, 'The opposition to Churchill is in the process of gaining strength in England. His long absence [in the United States] has brought it on him.' He then predicted that Britain might quit the war before the end. Five days later, on the evening of 12 January 1942, he returned to the subject, saying: 'Churchill is a man with an out-of-date political idea – that of the European balance of power. It no longer belongs to the sphere of realities. And yet it's because of this superstition that Churchill stirred England up to the war. When Singapore falls, Churchill will fall too; I'm convinced of it. The policy represented by Churchill is to nobody's interest, in short, but that of the Jews.'

Before the month was out, Hitler was considering how 'England can be viable only if she links herself to the Continent. She must be able to defend her imperial interests within the framework of a continental organisation.' The ideal time for that to happen would be once the Eighth Army had recaptured Benghazi, which they had done on Christmas Eve and which Hitler thought would re-establish British military prestige and was therefore the obvious 'psychological moment to put an end to the war'. The major problem was still Churchill, who 'had Russia at the back of his mind. Hitler didn't see that, if Russia were to triumph over Germany, Europe would at once come under the hegemony of a Great Power.'[29]

This concentration on his opponent was amounting to something of an obsession because, only two days later, at noon on 2 February, Hitler was back on the subject, opining that 'Churchill is like an animal at bay. He must be seeing snares everywhere. Even if Parliament gives him increased powers, his reasons for being mistrustful still exist. He's in the same situation as Robespierre on the eve of his fall. Nothing but praise was addressed to the virtuous citizen, when suddenly the situation was reversed. Churchill has no more supporters.' Four days later the Führer predicted that: 'A day will come, during a [Commons] secret session, when Churchill will be accused of betraying the interests of the Empire ... already several of his opponents are letting slip various disobliging remarks.' He then essayed a rather heavy gag: 'The English will have got nothing out of this affair but a bitter lesson and a black eye. If in future they make less whisky, that won't do any harm to anybody – beginning with themselves. Let's not forget, after all, that they owe all that's happening to them to one man, Churchill.'

Singapore fell on 15 February 1942, which brought Hitler to a new pitch of loathing, especially once it became clear that Churchill would not be ousted because of it. At dinner with Rommel three nights later, Hitler said that 'Churchill is the very type of corrupt journalist. There's not a worse prostitute in politics. He himself has written that it's unimaginable what can be done in war with the help of lies. He's an utterly amoral, repulsive creature. I'm convinced that he has a place of refuge ready beyond the Atlantic. He obviously won't seek sanctuary in Canada. In Canada he'd be beaten up. He'll go to his friends the Yankees.' The next evening, with Speer and Field Marshal Erhard Milch as his guests, Hitler discussed the terrible Russian winter that had descended on the German armies in the East: 'I've always detested snow; Bormann, you know, I've always hated it. Now I know why. It was a presentiment.'

Churchill felt that Hitler hardly needed a presentiment to know about the likelihood of it snowing heavily in Russia in winter. In a broadcast on 10 May 1942 he made the following sally:

> Then Hitler made his second great blunder. He forgot about the winter. There is a winter, you know, in Russia. For a good many months the temperature is apt to fall very low. There is snow, there is frost, and all that. Hitler forgot about the Russian winter. He must have been very loosely educated. We all heard about it at school; but he forgot it. I have never made such a bad mistake as that.

Four days after Hitler's attack on Russia, Churchill described him in a broadcast as 'A monster of wickedness, insatiable in his lust for blood and plunder'.

By the end of March 1942, with the British still not having overthrown Churchill, Hitler was starting to worry that Stafford Cripps might replace him. This led to an astonishing outburst from the Führer: 'I prefer the undisciplined swine who is drunk eight hours of every twenty-four, to the puritan. A man who spends extravagantly, an elderly man who drinks and smokes without moderation, is obviously less to be feared than the drawing-room Bolshevik who leads the life of an ascetic. From Churchill one may finally expect that in a moment of lucidity – it's not impossible – he'll realise that the Empire's going inescapably to its ruin, if the war lasts another two or three years.' What a tribute to Stafford Cripps that Adolf Hitler hated and feared him even more than Winston Churchill, and how self-deluding of Hitler to believe that Churchill would have ever been prepared to make peace with Germany after all that had taken place, even in order to save the Empire.

By 27 June 1942 Hitler had come up with a truly extraordinary plan to discover British intentions. In the course of a rant about the length of time Churchill and Roosevelt had been negotiating, from which he concluded that they had probably fallen out with one another, the Führer said: 'By far the most interesting problem of the moment is, what is Britain going to do now?' He believed that the job of finding the answer belonged to Germany's Foreign Office based on the Wilhelmstrasse, adding: 'The best way of accomplishing it would be by means of a little flirtation with Churchill's daughter. But our foreign office, and particularly its gentlemanly diplomats, consider such methods beneath their dignity, and they are not prepared to make this agreeable sacrifice, even though success might well save the lives of numberless German officers and men!'[30]

Quite how, in the middle of the Second World War, even the most 'gentlemanly' of German diplomats could have infiltrated the Auxiliary Territorial Service and achieved the seduction of the youngest of Churchill's three daughters – since Sarah and Diana were married, he presumably meant the nineteen-year-old Mary – was not explained. Hitler's propensity to micromanage campaigns clearly did not extend itself to those of the amorous type. The Führer was also exhibiting a bachelor's touching assumption that a father passes on the details of the higher conduct of the war to his daughter. (I am assured by Lady Soames that to her certain knowledge no such 'honey-trap' operation was mounted against her.)

By 1 July 1942 Hitler was still holding out hopes that Churchill would be overthrown in an internal coup, telling his guests that evening: 'For Churchill and his supporters the loss of Egypt must inevitably give rise to fears of a considerable strengthening of the popular opposition. One must not lose sight of the fact that there are already twenty-one members of parliament who openly oppose Churchill.' His accuracy was demonstrated when the very next day, in a motion of censure in the House of Commons, as Rommel pushed the Eighth Army back to El Alamein, Churchill's Government won by 475 votes to 25. 'I have never made any predictions,' the Prime Minister told the Commons, 'except things like saying Singapore would hold out. What a fool and knave I should have been to say it would fall!'

The next time that Hitler mentioned Churchill was a week later, on 9 July, when he made the fair point that the Prime Minister was wrong 'to portray his opponent in the manner in which Churchill has portrayed Rommel. The mere name suddenly begins to acquire a value equal to that of several divisions. Imagine what would happen if we went on lauding [the Red Army General] Timoshenko to the skies; in the end our soldiers would come to regard him as a superman.' In retrospect, it is hard to disagree with Hitler that the mythologising of Rommel as 'the Desert Fox' was a huge propaganda error by the Allies.

During Churchill's visit to Stalin in August 1942, Hitler again attempted to peer into the mind of his antagonist: 'I think Churchill was expecting some important development and went to Moscow hoping to return with the prestige of a great feat accomplished. They had had some great project in view, I am convinced: otherwise, why should they have sent the Mediterranean fleet to sea?' Of course it is part of the duty of a leader to try to understand what the opposition is thinking, but Hitler started out under such negative prejudices and absurd misapprehensions about Churchill – that he was drunken, near senile, and acting 'on the orders of his Jewish paymasters' – that he had no real chance of doing so. 'Churchill, the raddled old whore of journalism,' he ranted on 29 August 1942, 'is an unprincipled swine. A perusal of his memoirs proves it; in them he strips himself naked before the public. God help a nation that accepts the leadership of a Thing like that!'[31]

Churchill on Hitler

Churchill's strictures on Hitler were, as one might expect from such a master of parliamentary scorn, far less base, and they exhibited an understanding of Hitler's character that was entirely unreciprocated. He had made several positive references to Hitler in his journalism when the Nazis looked like a bulwark against German Communism, culminating in his remark in 1935 that: 'Those who have met Herr Hitler face to face in public business or on social terms have found a highly competent, cool, well-informed functionary with an agreeable manner, a disarming smile, and few have been unaffected by a subtle personal magnetism.' (Churchill had the moral courage to keep this sentence in the 1941 reprint of *Great Contemporaries*.) He also wrote of Hitler in that work: 'He it was who exorcised the spirit of despair from the German mind by substituting the not less baleful but far less morbid spirit of revenge.' Four decades earlier in *Savrola*, Churchill had written of the loathsome Iago-like private secretary Miguel who hailed from 'the infernal regions': 'He was small, dark, and very ugly, with a face wrinkled with age and an indoor life. Its pallor showed all the more by contrast with his hair and short moustache, both of which were of that purple blackness to which Nature is unable to attain.'[32]

It was in the early to mid-thirties that Churchill appreciated – long before anyone else of substance in British politics – that Hitler might develop into a greater threat even than the Communists. By June 1939 he was asking:

> Is he going to try to blow up the world or not? The world is a very heavy thing to blow up! An extraordinary man at the pinnacle of power may create a great explosion, and yet the civilised world may remain unshaken. The enormous fragments and splinters of the explosion may clatter down upon his own head and destroy him ... but the world will go on.

Just before the outbreak of war, on 20 August 1939, Churchill was painting with his teacher Paul Maze, and as he worked at his easel he now and again made statements about the relative sizes and strengths of the German and French Armies. 'They are strong, I tell you, they are strong,' he said, before his jaw clenched, showing Maze the iron determination of his will. 'Ah, with it all, we shall have him.'[33]

Churchill had much practice of trying to put himself in the position of his enemy in order to divine his intentions, not least in the war games played out at the Admiralty. He had even been present as a guest of Kaiser Wilhelm II at the German Army's manoeuvres before the Great War. So, at a meeting at Chequers with General Sir Andrew Thorne on 30 June 1940 to discuss a possible German invasion of Britain, Churchill tried to put himself in the Führer's place, saying that he was 'inclined to think that Hitler's plans have had to be changed: H. cannot have foreseen the collapse of France and must have planned his strategy of invasion on the assumption that the French armies would be holding out on the Somme, or at least on the Seine, and that the B.E.F. would either be assisting them or else would have been wiped out.' Churchill therefore did not subscribe to the theory that Hitler was a master strategist who had drawn up plans for the invasion of Britain after knocking out France in a six-week campaign.

He was right: Hitler had given no serious thought to an invasion of the British Isles, and only ordered the OKW planning staff to draw up detailed proposals for 'Sealion' in September, by which time it was too late to put into operation. General Thorne came away from the Chequers meeting with an interestingly counterintuitive view, telling Colville: 'Winston was more vital to this country than Hitler to Germany, because the former was unique and irreplaceable and the latter had established a school of leaders.' To which Colville made 'the obvious comment' that: 'Hitler may be a self-educated corporal and Winston may be an established student of tactics; but ultimately Germany is organised as a war machine and England has only just realised the meaning of modern warfare.'[34]

Churchill enjoyed personifying the struggle at every opportunity, calling Hitler 'That Man' and at one point saying of one of the Führer's peace offers: 'I do not propose to say anything in reply to Herr Hitler's speech, not being on speaking terms with him.' A key element in his tactics was the utter demonisation of Adolf Hitler, who – unlike Rommel – was permitted no redeeming features. 'By all kinds of sly and savage means he is plotting and working to quench for ever the fountain of characteristic French culture and of French inspiration to the world,' Churchill said of Hitler in a broadcast to the people of France on 21 October 1940. 'Never will I believe that the soul of France is dead.'

Churchill enjoyed using powerful imagery in depicting Hitler, as in his speech in the House of Commons on 9 April 1941, after a coup had taken place in Yugoslavia toppling the pro-Axis government: 'A boa constrictor, who had already covered his prey with his foul saliva and then had it suddenly wrested from his coils, would be in an amicable mood compared to Hitler.' Churchill concentrated on the person of Hitler when he sought to visualise the enemy for himself and others; it was an image that never failed to draw forth Churchill's eloquent and bottomless ire.

At Chequers on 2 May 1941, when the war news was terrible and Colville recorded the Prime Minister as being 'in worse gloom than I have ever seen him', Churchill sketched out for Averell Harriman, General Hastings 'Pug' Ismay and his private secretary Colville a world 'in which Hitler dominated all Europe, Asia and Africa'. In this *ad hominem* mood about his enemy he went on to envision a Middle East in which Suez was lost and 'Hitler's robot new order' ruled. 'With Hitler in control of Iraq oil and Ukrainian wheat, not all the staunchness of [the British population] will shorten the ordeal.' Each time when he might have justifiably used the words 'Nazis', 'Reich' or 'Germans' in this gloomy rodomontade, Churchill concentrated on the person of Adolf Hitler. (Of course he might well have been playing up this nightmarish future, in order to impress upon Roosevelt's envoy Harriman the need for immediate and generous aid.)

The next day, in a message he broadcast to the Polish people, Churchill again spoke of Hitler and the way that 'Every week his firing-parties are busy in a dozen lands. Monday he shoots Dutchmen; Tuesday, Norwegians; Wednesday, French or Belgians stand against the wall; Thursday it is the Czechs who must suffer; and now there are the Serbs and the Greeks to fill his repulsive bill of executions. But always, all the days, there are the Poles.'

The night before Hitler invaded Russia, Churchill – who knew it was going to happen from intelligence decrypts and had warned the Russians, but been ignored – was teased by Jock Colville as they walked on the lawn at Chequers after dinner. Colville jibed that his proposed support for the USSR was a complete *volte face* for such an arch anti-Communist. Churchill replied that 'he had only one single purpose – the destruction of Hitler – and his life was much simplified thereby'. It certainly was; whereas Hitler was fighting for a New Europe free of Jews, with *Lebensraum* in the East and German domination of the Slav peoples in perpetuity, Churchill could – at least until just before the end of the war – concentrate on the single task of extinguishing him.

Of course this did carry with it the dangers of occasional gross oversimplifications or worse, as when he told the House of Commons on 2 August 1944: 'The Russian armies now stand before the gates of Warsaw. They bring the liberation of Poland in their hands. They offer freedom, sovereignty, and independence to the Poles.' The Red Army was indeed standing outside the gates of Warsaw, but was cynically waiting for the uprising inside the city to be crushed by the Wehrmacht before moving in; once they did, they offered Poland neither freedom nor sovereignty, much less independence. Churchill's single-mindedness about the destruction of Hitler allowed him to make compromises even over the issue for which Britain ostensibly went to war in the first place.

Just because Churchill despised Hitler personally and rhetorically, it did not mean that he underestimated him politically. Staying in a villa at the Mamounia Hotel in Marrakech on 5 January 1944, he took a vote at dinner over whether Hitler would still be in power in Germany on 3 September that year, the fifth anniversary of the outbreak of the war. Seven people around the table, including Churchill's doctor Lord Moran, and the Czech leader Eduard Beneš – voted no. Four voted yes, including Lord Beaverbrook, Colville and the Prime Minister himself.

When the news came through of Hitler's death, Churchill made precisely the comment that one would expect from a man who admired personal courage above all the other virtues. In the middle of dinner on Tuesday, 1 May 1945, Colville brought in a copy of the announcement that was being broadcast by German radio, stating that 'Hitler had been killed today at his post at the Reich Chancellery at Berlin ... fighting with his last breath against Bolshevism'. Churchill's comment was: 'Well, I must say I think he was perfectly right to die like that,' to which Beaverbrook replied that it was just Nazi propaganda and he obviously had not.[35] Although Beaverbrook was correct, it showed Churchill's great generosity of spirit to accord his enemy the benefit of the doubt in such a way at such a time. (It turned out that the Nazis had withheld the announcement so that it might coincide with May Day, an important date in the German calendar.)

Seven years later in May 1952, and back at Chequers as prime minister, Churchill was quizzed by Montgomery as they walked along the monument hill above the house, making their way among the picnickers. How did the Prime Minister define a great man, asked the Field Marshal (who was probably fishing for a compliment): 'Was Hitler great?' 'No,' answered Churchill, 'he made too many mistakes.' They went on to discuss who could be classed as great, with Churchill fully accepting Jesus Christ's credentials because, among other reasons, 'the Sermon on the Mount was the last word in ethics'. In Churchill's view, therefore, it was Hitler's errors rather than his innate evil that disqualified him from the accolade of greatness. He had, after all, included Hitler among his *Great Contemporaries* in 1937, but that was before Hitler started making those mistakes for which Churchill came to despise him. Churchill too had made errors, but like a great leader – and unlike Hitler – he had learned from them.

Using secret intelligence

Churchill had certainly learned from the failure of the Norwegian campaign. One of the first things he did as prime minister was to ensure that he was kept personally informed of all the latest and most important intelligence. Not content with reading summaries and evaluations, he wished to examine personally the raw decrypts of the most important messages. Almost every day of the war, 'C', the head of the Secret Intelligence Service, sent over to Number Ten a buff-coloured box containing a selection of the most relevant items. This Ultra data derived from the success of the Poles in capturing an Enigma cipher machine and the staff of Bletchley Park in cracking the German military code.

A good illustration of Churchill's ability to keep his mind open and to try unconventional approaches can be found in his love of special operations. Nothing was too outlandish for the Prime Minister to consider in the war against Nazism. Churchill always had a special penchant for what he called 'funny' operations; he had a lifetime's fascination with spooks and codes, spying and secrecy. The appeal of unorthodox warfare chimed in well with his general wartime strategic concept for Britain: that a direct, full-scale, continental military engagement would cost more in terms of lives and resources than taking the more indirect route.

That had been the rationale behind the Gallipoli adventure in the First World War, and was to be the same behind the Italian and proposed Balkan campaigns in the so-called 'soft underbelly of Europe' in the Second. Between the wars, Churchill was a committed devotee to the theory that money spent on spying and collating information was rarely wasted. In 1909 he was instrumental in the creation of MI5 and on the eve of the Great War five years later he drew up the charter for the Admiralty's decrypting operation, codenamed Room 40.

From his time reporting to the Foreign Office when a subaltern in 1890s India, via his job of war correspondent in Cuba, to his active service behind the lines in the Boer War, Churchill nurtured his connections with British Intelligence. He made inspired use of the secret service in the Russian Civil War, in the U-boat war from 1914–15 and even during the General Strike. After the Second World War he continued to be an enthusiastic player of the great intelligence game, before going on to appreciate its use in the Cold War.

Churchill's close links with British Intelligence resulted in his being able to set up a private spy network which served him very well during his wilderness years.[36] During the war, using an operative called Alan Hillgarth, he also ensured that several of Franco's senior generals were successfully bribed to ensure Spanish neutrality. Lord Halifax tended to find it uncongenial to, as he put it, 'slip them envelopes on the golf links', but Churchill saw himself as merely acting in the great British bribing tradition of eighteenth-century diplomacy.

Churchill ensured that the fact that the Allies had cracked the Enigma code was known to only thirty-one people, codenaming it 'Boniface' to decoy the enemy into thinking that it all came from a single (necessarily very high-level) agent. Such was its sensitivity that one of those not informed about Ultra was Hugh Dalton – the director of the Special Operations Executive, whom Churchill had ordered to 'Set Europe ablaze!'.

'In wartime,' said Stalin first and Churchill soon afterwards, 'truth is so precious that she should always be attended by a bodyguard of lies.' The body set up to lie professionally for Britain was the Political Warfare Executive (PWE). In a house in Cambridgeshire the author has recently discovered an unpublished cache of PWE papers, documents and photographs that sheds fascinating new light on the way that the Allies planned to create chaos in Europe at the time of the D-Day landings in June 1944. This rich but hitherto untapped archive reveals the curious mixture of naïveté and ruthlessness that characterised PWE throughout its existence between 1938 and 1945.

The papers are those of David Garnett, which are held by his son Richard at Hilton Hall in Huntingdon.[37] In 1945 Garnett, the former Director of Training of PWE, was asked by the Foreign Secretary Ernest Bevin to write a secret history of the contribution the Executive had made to the war effort, for use in the Cold War in case of need. The result was so frank – indeed libellous – about so many prominent people in the Government and armed forces that it was distributed to only four people, at the War Office, Admiralty, Air Ministry and Foreign Office, and was then quickly buried in the archives of the Cabinet Office Historical Section. On its cover are the words: 'This Document is the Property of His Majesty's Government. SECRET. To be kept under lock and key. It is requested that special care may be taken to ensure the secrecy of this document.' It only finally saw publication in 2002, half a century after it was completed.[38]

Separate from Garnett's book are his private papers, which include his correspondence with scores of senior PWE officers. These cover a number of aspects of the work of the organisation that were not included in the secret history. Writing openly to their ex-colleague about their wartime experiences, many secrets were vouchsafed by these officers who otherwise would have gone to the grave with them. Just as with their secret sister-organisations MI5, MI6, Bletchley Park and SOE, such was the code of *omertá* surrounded PWE's wartime service that many of its officers felt that their duty to stay silent about its activities had not ended with the cessation of hostilities in 1945.

PWE was set up at the time of the Munich Crisis in 1938 to carry on the secret propaganda war against Germany along lines used in the First World War. Its purpose was to feed demoralising rumours to the Germans, by whatever means came to hand. In particular 'black' radio propaganda, which purported to come from within Germany but which was really being beamed from PWE's country headquarters at Woburn Abbey, was used to sow disinformation and misinformation in the homes of the Nazi enemy. Along with its American counterpart, the Office of War Information (OWI), PWE dropped no fewer than 265 million anti-Nazi leaflets on Germany,

Lieutenant-General Erich von Manstein, architect of the sickle-cut manoeuvre that led to the fall of France in 1940.

General Walther von Branschitsch, Hitler and General Franz Halder operating Mission Command fitfully in that campaign.

Air Chief Marshal Sir Hugh Dowding of Fighter Command – victor of the Battle of Britain.

Bob Boothby was Churchill's close friend and confidant until he got involved in the sleaze story known as the Czech gold affair in 1941.

Field Marshals Lord Alanbrooke and Bernard Montgomery with Churchill in France in 1944.

Churchill was the only British prime minister who wore military uniforms, at the Teheran conference he looked more like Stalin than Roosevelt.

Hitler was merely defenestrated in the Bomb Plot of 20th July 1944.

Bruno Gesche, the alcoholic commander of Hitler's SS Bodyguard, twice let off pistols when drunk, but kept his job.

Some books have claimed that the Führer was gay.

A photo forged and then distributed as a postcard by the British Political Warfare Executive. The caption quoted one of Hitler's speeches: 'What we have we hold.'

Hitler wearing the Iron Cross 1st class, swastika armband and peaked hat – his only insignia of rank.

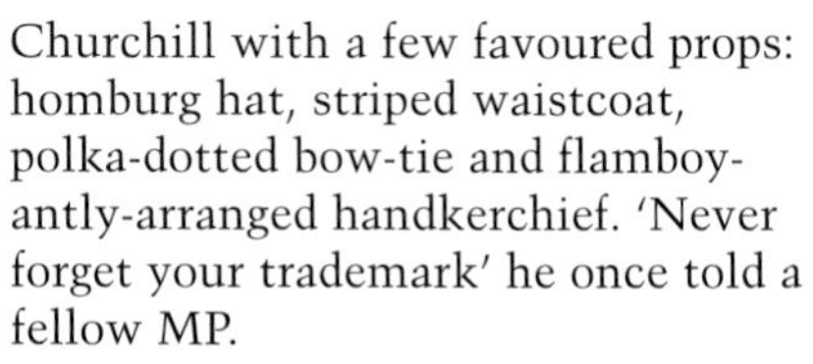

Churchill with a few favoured props: homburg hat, striped waistcoat, polka-dotted bow-tie and flamboyantly-arranged handkerchief. 'Never forget your trademark' he once told a fellow MP.

and broadcast hundreds of thousands of hours of propaganda of all kinds, including the frankly pornographic, which was designed to maximise listenership among ordinary German soldiers. It also spread bogus rumours such as the one that in 1940 the British had released in the English Channel two hundred man-eating sharks, imported from Australia, in order to eat Germans whose invasion boats had been sunk.

In a secret overview of the purpose of PWE, a senior officer, Lieut.-Col. R. L. Sedgwick, wrote: 'The fourth fighting arm, Political Warfare, attacks the mind. The chief forces which it employs are the dissatisfied elements in enemy countries or in enemy-occupied countries. Deceive your enemy, undermine his war effort, win the war of ideas.' This was to be done by 'bribery of newspapers, intrigue by women, personal flattery, sowing of internal dissensions, the setting of poor against rich and of rich against poor, young against old, soldier against general'. Rumours were to be sown in order 'to deceive and intimidate the enemy'.

Any organisation that called upon the diverse but undeniable talents of as varied a *galère* as Noël Coward, Raymond Mortimer, Freya Stark, Denis Sefton Delmer, John Wheeler-Bennett, Robert Byron, Sir Robert 'Jock' Bruce Lockhart, E. H. Carr and Richard Crossman could never have been a dull place to work, especially as some of the operations that they devised were often so bizarre. What is one to make, for example, of the dropping of large numbers of dead carrier pigeons into Germany with messages attached to their legs, in the hope of deceiving the Gestapo into thinking that a huge German resistance movement was in close touch with British Intelligence? Tens of thousands of counterfeit German ration books were also forged to create confusion, as well as stamps bearing Himmler's face, in the hope that people would rise in revolt against the idea of his becoming the next Führer.

We know from the autobiography of the head of PWE's 'black' propaganda unit, the ingenious ex-journalist Denis Sefton Delmer, that a large number of PWE's files were destroyed after the war. Garnett's newly declassified *Secret History*, along with the archive from Hilton Hall, allows us, more than half a century after the end of the war, to cast more light than ever before upon the workings of this fascinating, dedicated, but until now very shadowy organisation.

A 'Minor Sabotage Booklet' was proposed, which would advise

would-be resisters on the Continent how to help the Allies on D-Day (or 'Zero Hour' as it was rather transparently codenamed). Some of its suggestions were absurd and Heath Robinson-like, such as: 'Chemical devices. Strong laxatives, pernicious smells, harmless but bitter flavours for water, etc.' Other relatively harmless acts of resistance that were suggested were to call the fire brigade unnecessarily, 'to post all letters on one day and to post none at all on the next, to fill in all official forms wrongly, to queue up in railway stations asking how to get to some non-existent or hardly-known destination, to telephone the police station to complain that screams are coming from down the road'. It is hard to believe that these would have seriously inconvenienced the Wehrmacht on D-Day.

Other ideas would produce much more trouble for the Germans, such as the setting up of dummy roadblocks, the stencilling of false road signs, the mass puncturing of car and lorry tyres, and the cutting of field telephone wires. Finally there was advice on how to make incendiary bombs and tips on how to decapitate motorcyclists with wire strung between trees, which should always 'be placed at a slant so that when the rider is thrown off his machine it is into the ditch, where he will not be seen by the next motorcyclist'.

A postcard was mass-produced in December 1943 purporting to show Adolf Hitler masturbating, or at least holding his erect penis, with a broad grin on his face. Underneath the picture was a quotation from his Munich speech of November 1942, which translates as: 'What we have we hold.' A false news-sheet was also produced, allegedly by the OKW, denouncing this forgery, but reproducing it in full for the further delectation of anti-Nazi Germans.

A plan was made by the Director-General of PWE to flood Germany with 'ten times the amount of paper Reichsmark notes as there are in certain areas – particularly mining areas, the Sudetenland, Austria, etc, and starving Berlin. This will stop work in factories and mines, deplete stocks of goods in shops and produce chaos. Some parts of Germany will consume the goods of the rest.' It was feared, however, that the Germans might retaliate in kind, so the Director-General proposed as a pre-emptive measure to 'call in our own note circulation and replace it with a metallic currency'. The unimaginable costs and complications involved in putting such a plan into operation ensured that it never was.

Garnett's interview with the PWE operative M. Berman on 8

January 1945 finally clears up the mystery about the true extent of Noël Coward's contribution to the secret war effort. 'Mr Noël Coward was head of the French Department [of PWE] in Paris,' he stated. 'He was liaison officer for French propaganda. Lord Moore and Lord Strathallan assisted.' An undated, unsigned and uncopied 'Most Secret' document entitled 'Proposals for Joint P.W.E. and S.O.E. Action in Support of an Allied Invasion of Occupied Europe' provided for the selected assassination of quislings in the hours just prior to D-Day:

> In most countries there is likely to be a 'hard core' of traitors so compromised by their treachery that a fighting finish will be their only alternative to the lamp-post. This hard core is potentially dangerous at and about Zero Hour in relation to many of the activities being planned by or for patriots, and special measures against it are consequently worth contemplating. Planned liquidation in advance, even in a few cases, would obviously be of the highest importance.

Those quislings who could be 'kidnapped or taken into custody' and then 'blackmailed into turning King's evidence' would be expected to draw up 'lists of local traitors and their work; lists of prominent German (or other alien) civilians and their functions; names of persons or firms servicing the enemy; lists of stores and store-places; names of Gestapo agents and sub-agents; enemy plans in the event of retreat (i.e., scorched earth objectives); political movements secretly supported by the Germans', and so on. Among those who were deputed to undertake 'Operation King Rat' was the unlikely personage of the future royal dressmaker Hardy Amies.

In August 1941 Brigadier Ritchie Calder circulated a 'Most Secret' memorandum entitled 'Notes on Railway Sabotage', in which he went into loving detail about the best ways and places to destroy enemy trains: 'To secure maximum results a train should be derailed in a cutting (not on an embankment where the wreckage can be tumbled down the slope); in a tunnel (where there is no room for the breakdown cranes); on a bridge (so that the train falls over, damaging the parapet); or in a bottleneck of a marshalling yard (so that all operations are jammed).' Removing between five and ten sleepers on the bend of a track was his recommended method of achieving this.

There was further advice on how to damage points, signals, wagons, and axle boxes – 'remove the oil with a bicycle pump or pour in petrol, paraffin, water, sand, ashes or dirt'.

To celebrate the first anniversary of Battle of Britain Day, PWE considered calling a 'Tortoise Day' for 15 September 1941 during which Europeans would strike 'a blow for freedom by going slow'. 'Why sweat for the Germans?' they would be exhorted. 'Take your time. Where it normally takes one minute to walk from your cloakroom to your bench, make it take a minute and a half. If you go into a post office to buy a stamp, let it take longer. Engage the official in conversation. Let everything take longer than it usually does.' Again, it is doubtful that this would have made a significant contribution towards bringing the Third Reich to its knees.

The day before D-Day, the Oxford philosopher A. J. Ayer, then serving with the Inter-Services Research Bureau in Baker Street, approved a PWE leaflet entitled 'How to Live a Clandestine Life' that gave advice on how to survive on the run from the Gestapo. Among its tips were: 'Live in a friend's cellar, or out in the woods with a band of escapees. Assume a disguise, invent a story, choose a common – but not too common – name, remember a false date of birth and parents' names, leave before the curfews, never keep a scrap of paper, learn to use your memory, and avoid communicating with your family.'

Among the Hilton Hall papers is a copy of the 'Top Secret' letter that the Minister of Information, Brendan Bracken, wrote in January 1944 to General Brooks of PWE attacking the American Office of War Information, in which he described its directorate as 'incompetent, shifty and hare-brained'. In a coruscating paragraph that would undoubtedly have strained Anglo-American relations had it been made public, he went on:

> They have no consistent policy. The content of their hectic output depends upon American political considerations. The Polish vote, the Balt vote, the Jewish vote and above all the German vote will slant what politeness forces me to call their thinking. Their absurd actions followed by their gibbering explanations have earned them the contempt of most American newspapers. Why should we waste valuable time on this decaying and despised organisation? They will surely make you wallow with them in the squalid mess they created in America and wish to reproduce here.

Unsurprisingly, after this outburst, Brooks subsequently distanced PWE from OWI and cut it out of its next major operation, codenamed Operation Periwig. This was a PWE plan to get the Germans to waste time and energy by providing 'proof' of a vast number of Allied spies within Nazi Germany itself. Parachutes and other gear were dropped, bogus messages were broadcast in Morse code either side of the BBC news, and one message was sent in a simple code that it was intended that the Germans should crack, saying: 'Will meet you Monday 9.30 in the 4th row of the stalls in the Ufa cinema.' Since there was a Ufa cinema in almost every German town, it was hoped this would take up huge amounts of Gestapo manpower.

Of 330 live pigeons dropped over Germany, five flew home to Britain with messages written by their German finders. One that returned in April 1945 bore a message saying: 'There are no German military personnel in our village, Hellensen. As far as I know Lüdenscheid will not be defended because there are many hospitals in the town. The [Nazi] Party swine have all cleared out, leaving in civilian clothes. I am also a pigeon-fancier and send my greetings. Good fight.' Unsurprisingly, it wasn't signed.

No one enjoyed and supported these unorthodox ways of making war more than Churchill, who had an incredibly fertile mind for invention. One of his pet projects was for the creation of, 'for use in northern waters, a device for transforming icebergs, embellished with frozen wood pulp, into unsinkable air bases'.[39] Codenamed 'Habbakuk', from the biblical prophet who promised 'a work which you will not believe', Churchill tested the idea in his bathtub and a model of a Habbakuk was also built on Lake Patricia in Canada. This soon proved how impractical the idea actually was: it would have taken eight thousand men eight months working in arctic temperatures to build an iceberg carrier of the size required.

Another idea that Churchill championed was for floating harbours, codenamed 'Mulberry', to be used in Operation Overlord, the planned seaborne invasion of Normandy. Once again, the Prime Minister's bathtub was employed as the test site. General Ismay later recalled the scene as Churchill sat in 'a dressing gown of many colours' surrounded by his advisers, with an admiral moving his hand in the bath to simulate the effect of waves and a brigadier stretching an inflatable sleeve across the bath to show how it broke up the waves. It was, as Ismay reflected, 'hard to believe that this was the British High Command studying the most stupendous and spectacular amphibious operation of the war'. Amazingly, the Mulberry harbours did work and would turn out to be an important contribution to Operation Overlord, as they allowed the Allies to select landing zones away from the Germans' major gun emplacements and fortifications.

Sacking people

As well as not dismissing ideas out of hand, however impractical they might at first seem, another key rule to be found in management guides is that a good leader selects the right people for the right job. Yet that is only half the truth; what is just as important is that leaders sack the right people too. If they failed to live up to his expectations, Churchill could be ruthless even to his close friends. Bob Boothby, for instance, had been one of Churchill's most loyal allies in the Commons during the anti-appeasement struggle, for which Churchill, when prime minister, initially rewarded him with the post of under-secretary at the Ministry of Food. Yet when Boothby soon afterwards became entangled in a sleaze story known as the 'Czech gold affair', Churchill dumped his old friend ignominiously. Privately suggesting that Boothby should 'join a bomb-disposal squad', Churchill declared in Parliament: 'There are paths of service open in war time which are not open in peace; and some of these paths may be paths of honour.' Boothby duly joined a RAF bomber squadron, although he never forgave his friend for his lack of support.

Another close friend, Alfred Duff Cooper, the only minister to have resigned over the Munich agreement, was made Minister of Information. Once it became clear that he wasn't particularly well suited to the job, Cooper fell out with the press which soon ran ever more aggressive attacks against him. Their criticism focused on what they dubbed 'Cooper's Snoopers' – government informants who they claimed were ordered to evaluate the state of public morale and report back to the Ministry. The *Sunday Pictorial* held a 'Duff Cooper ballot' featuring an extremely unflattering picture of him and including a coupon saying: 'He gets £5,000 a year for being Minister of Information. Do you think he should hold office?'

Churchill didn't need any such ballot to show him that his friend had to be replaced and Cooper was sent away on a mission to the Far East. Although Churchill appointed him to important posts thereafter, he had in effect sacrificed a friend whom he had begun to see as a political liability. It was unfair on Duff Cooper, an extremely intelligent and talented man as well as a brave politician, but Churchill's primary concern had to be the interests of his Government and so Cooper had to go.

This kind of ruthlessness came even easier when administered against those who were not personal friends. The harsh treatment meted out to King Leopold III of the Belgians was such a case in point. Churchill needed a scapegoat for the 1940 defeat in the West, and the ideal person was the Belgian monarch who had capitulated to the Germans on 28 May, the day that the evacuations from Dunkirk began. Churchill blamed Leopold personally for the surrender, stating in the House of Commons on 4 June: 'Suddenly, without prior consultation, with the least possible notice, without the advice of his ministers and upon his own personal act, he sent a plenipotentiary to the German Command, surrendered his Army and exposed our flank and means of retreat.'

In fact, however, Churchill had been forewarned by his friend, Admiral Sir Roger Keyes, the liaison officer with the King of the Belgians, and according to Keyes he had not protested. As Keyes pointed out on several occasions:

> The Belgian Army at the time of its surrender was no longer efficient but on the verge of complete collapse. King Leopold had given repeated warnings that his troops were at the end of their tether, and of his fear of imminent catastrophe. It was beyond his power to ask the advice of his ministers, for his ministers had fled the country on the 25th, after vain efforts to persuade him to abandon his army and accompany them. The eastern flank of the B.E.F. was already widely exposed before the surrender; and the British commander-in-chief [Lord Gort], realising on the 25th that the Belgians were on the verge of collapse, and that the only way of saving the B.E.F. was to evacuate it, leaving the Belgian King to his fate, had from that moment initiated his own arrangements for guarding his route to the sea, though without acquainting King Leopold of his intentions.

When reasons of state dictated, however, the scapegoating of the King became an absolute political necessity and Leopold spent the rest of his life under the shadow of Churchill's inaccurate denunciation in the Commons. Almost alone of the non-German European royalties, Leopold was not invited to Princess Elizabeth's wedding in 1947.

Another example of Churchill's ruthlessness at the time was his order that the wounded should be the last people to be evacuated from the beaches of Dunkirk.[40] It made perfect military sense, of course, since the able-bodied were needed to defend Britain and it was initially thought that only 45,000 men could be brought home, but it was an extremely harsh order to give none the less. Or when he obtained the War Cabinet's permission in June 1940 to use mustard gas in Southern Ireland should the Germans land there, with the reasoning that although the storm troopers would have been issued with gas masks, the thousands of horses they would bring with them would probably not have been. Gas was also to have been used against the Germans on the beaches of southern England in the event of an invasion, with incalculable consequences for the civilian population of the south-coast towns, and for those who lived further inland were the wind to blow in that direction. To lead is to choose, and sometimes the decisions Churchill was forced to take were ghastly ones. Yet he never hesitated.

Hitler, of course, was ultimately far more ruthless than Churchill. A chilling example was the execution of those brave army officers who had plotted against him in 1944. They were hanged on hooks in Plötzensee prison in Berlin until they strangled to death. Hitler ordered: 'I want them to be hanged, strung up like meat-carcasses.' Some of them took as long as twenty minutes to asphyxiate.

Yet, while this shows Hitler at his most vindictive, documents in the Bundesarchiv in Berlin – which incidentally used to be the home of the SS Leibstandarte division that provided the SS Führer Escort, Hitler's bodyguard – reveal that he could be surprisingly forgiving to those who were loyal to him but guilty of misdemeanours. Hitler liked the company of those who had, in the words of Albert Speer, a 'flaw in the weave'. Gauleiter Karl Hanke said of him: 'It is all to the good if associates have faults and know that the superior is aware of them. That is why the Führer so seldom changes his assistants. For he finds them easier to work with. Almost every one of them has his defect; that helps keep them in line.' Immoral conduct, remote Jewish ancestry, or recent Party membership were all counted as flaws in the weave.

For the tasks that Hitler had in mind, particularly the undertaking of the Final Solution that was planned at the Wannsee Conference on 20 January 1942, it was important that his senior henchmen were absolutely not morally upright human beings. Albert Speer noted Hitler's genius at estimating the personality flaws in his lieutenants:

> He knew men's secret vices and desires, he knew what they thought to be their virtues, he knew the hidden ambitions and motives which lay behind their loves and their hates, he knew where they could be flattered, where they were gullible, where they were strong and where they were weak; he knew all this ... by instinct and feeling, an intuition which in such matters never led him astray.

The fact that he despised his fellow man thus helped a great deal. In the crimes he was going to commit, Hitler knew that he needed morally compromised, largely under-educated, utterly loyal accomplices and when he found one he knew he could trust – such as Bruno Gesche, the head of his bodyguard – he hung on to him far beyond the time when he should have been sacked.

The Nazi Party and SS files on Gesche reveal that he had a chronic drink problem. In 1938 he had to promise Himmler that he would abstain from alcohol for three years. Yet in 1942 Gesche once more got so drunk that he threatened a fellow SS officer with his drawn pistol. Himmler imposed another three-year prohibition on Gesche and sent him to the Eastern Front. The Bundesarchiv documents show how Hitler would not let down his former bodyguard. After Gesche was wounded, this man – who was an alcoholic and a security risk – was nevertheless called back to be by Hitler's side. It was not long before Gesche relapsed into old habits. On 20 December 1944, Himmler wrote to him:

> 1. You have again threatened a comrade with a pistol while intoxicated and fired shots senselessly.
>
> [...]
>
> 4. I shall give you the opportunity to serve in the Dirlewanger

Brigade and perhaps wipe out the shame you have brought on yourself and the entire SS, by proving yourself before the enemy.

5. I expect you to refrain from the consumption of alcohol for the rest of your life, without any exception. If your willpower has been so destroyed by alcohol that you are not capable of making such a decision, I expect you to submit your request to be released from the SS.

Gesche wasn't finally dismissed from the SS Führer Escort until just four months before the end of the war – this after many years of showing that he was a chronic drunkard. The indulgence shown him by Hitler was because he was what the Nazis called an 'old fighter from the years of struggle': he had joined the Nazi Party as early as 1922. Only one of Hitler's old comrades from that period could get away with so much.

The head of the Luftwaffe, Hermann Göring, was another, much more prominent example of Hitler's unwise loyalty to his cronies. A passionate hunter, Göring spent as much time at his country residence, Carinhall, as he did at the Air Ministry. As head of the German Air Force, Göring was all but a disaster. Time and again he promised more than he could deliver. At Dunkirk the vast majority of the encircled Allied troops were able to escape across the Channel, despite Göring having guaranteed that the Luftwaffe could finish them off by itself. He also promised that no single British bomber would ever reach Germany; if one did, Göring stated, his name would be Herr Meier (or Joe Bloggs, as we might say). As more and more German cities were turned into rubble, Germans would increasingly (albeit in private) refer to Göring as 'Herr Meier'.

At Stalingrad, Göring's assurance that he could supply the encircled Sixth Army by airlift encouraged Hitler to issue a halt order when a breakout would still have been possible. As it was, only a small percentage of the promised supplies ever arrived. Any responsible leader would have relieved a serial failure like Göring of his command, but not Hitler. Like Gesche, Göring had been with the Nazi Party since 1922; he had been badly wounded in the groin in the Beer-hall Putsch. This, and his personal loyalty to Hitler, were more significant in the Führer's mind than Göring's string of blunders as the Luftwaffe's Commander-in-Chief. It was not until the last days of the war that Hitler turned against Göring, and only then because he incorrectly believed that Göring was preparing to take over from him. Hitler had him arrested and ousted him from the Party and all his offices. To Hitler, personal and ideological loyalty was more important than professional aptitude and performance.

Hitler was loyal to his staff so long as he could rely on their loyalty to him. What he failed to recognise is that loyalty alone was not enough. A leader like Churchill could subordinate almost everything – be it his ideological or even his personal feelings – to the one goal he had set himself and his country: victory.

Hitler's appointment of Joachim von Ribbentrop to such a key post in the Reich as Foreign Minister was another example of his desire to have a henchman who had 'a flaw in the weave' rather than the most professional person available. Unlike Göring and Gesche, Ribbentrop came late into politics, only joining the Nazi Party in 1932 with the distinctly unprepossessing membership number of 1,119,927. He had acquired the prefix 'von' by paying a distant aunt to adopt him while his parents were still alive. (He later reneged on the payments.)

Despite the time he had spent in the United States before the Great War, Ribbentrop gravely underestimated the power of America at the time of Germany's declaration of war in December 1941. That miscalculation put the noose around his neck as surely as did the American GI who volunteered for the job at Nuremberg four years later. When the Allies questioned Ribbentrop's aunt-in-law about his whereabouts in May 1945, and asked which friends might be sheltering him, she truthfully told them that he didn't have any. His ignorance, incompetence and complete moral vacuity should have disqualified him for the post of foreign minister even in the Third Reich, but for Hitler they mattered less than his loyalty. Indeed, Ribbentrop's last words before the Nuremberg trapdoor opened were: 'Heil Hitler!'

As well as keeping the wrong people on because of their loyalty, one of the reasons for Hitler's failure as a leader was that he sacked some of his best commanders because of their perceived disloyalty. The Blitzkrieg pioneer Guderian was dismissed during the Russian campaign in 1941, only to be recalled in 1943. Erich von Manstein, the architect of the brilliant sickle-cut operation against France, was retired in 1944. One of Hitler's most senior commanders, Field

Marshal Gerd von Rundstedt, was dismissed and re-employed no fewer than four times. Sooner or later, almost every senior general was replaced by Hitler, no matter how able and experienced he was, because Hitler didn't trust the German military. In the course of the war no fewer than thirty-five field marshals and generals were dismissed by Hitler, more often for lack of loyalty than for perceived or actual military incompetence.

Churchill too enjoyed the company of those who had 'flaws in the weave'. His greatest friend before his tragic death in his late forties in 1930, F. E. Smith, Lord Birkenhead, was a heavy drinker. Max Beaverbrook was widely thought of as crooked. Brendan Bracken also had a shadowy background and was suspected of deliberately failing to quash the unfounded rumour that he was Churchill's illegitimate son. Averell Harriman had an affair with the wife of Churchill's son Randolph, but was not penalised socially for it by the Churchill family. Yet there is a world of difference between Hitler's case – where the flaws were held as a form of blackmail – and Churchill's, where they were indulged in the knowledge that those people who are closest to moral perfection are often crashing bores. One could be guilty of almost anything and remain in Churchill's entourage, but not of either cowardice or wilful dullness.

Hitler would indulge stupidity to a surprising degree, certainly far more than Churchill. Although neither man attended university, Churchill generally got on well with academics, whereas Hitler despised them. Of the fifty Reichleiters and Gauleiters who formed the élite of the Nazi leadership, only ten had completed a university education. While some had attended university classes for a time, the majority had never got beyond secondary school.

Although most of his generals fervently supported the Nazis' expansionist policy, Hitler had little confidence in their ideological and personal loyalty, so he resorted to naked bribery. Of course, it is not uncommon in military history for generals to be specially rewarded – after a war. Churchill's ancestor the Duke of Marlborough had received the Blenheim estate, and Wellington had been given Stratfield Saye by a similarly grateful nation. The government payments of £5,000 per annum (the same as a Cabinet minister received) made to Admiral Nelson's descendants only ceased under the premiership of Clement Attlee.

Yet Hitler was conspicuously generous towards his commanders while the war was still being fought. A large number of generals and field marshals received cheques for 250,000 Reichsmarks – about half a million pounds in today's money – that were signed by the Führer personally. Others were given huge tracts of land and grand homes. The estate of Glebokie in western Poland was a gift to General Heinz Guderian from his Führer. While such an act appears to demonstrate his generosity, in fact it illustrates Hitler's cunning in ensuring loyalty through unashamed bribery.

Glebokie belonged to a Polish aristocrat, who during the Great War had served in the German Army as an adjutant to General Hindenburg. Despite this, the Nazis put him in prison and his family was sent to a forced labour camp. General Guderian didn't seem to care about the rightful owner of the estate that Hitler had given him. After the war he never tired of pointing out his distaste for the Nazis, but he conveniently forgot that he had had no scruples in making himself an accomplice to Hitler's brutal occupation policy. When the officers who plotted against Hitler approached Guderian to join them, he declined.

Instead, when their plot had failed, Guderian chose to serve on the infamous 'Court of Honour' against them, which condemned them to death for violating their oath to the Führer. The estate in Poland must have had a bearing on his decision to remain loyal. For all the post-war protestations of the German officer corps about fighting for the honour of their fatherland, very often it actually came down to cash. Hitler's gifts to his generals would nowadays be called 'golden handcuffs'. These were payments designed to keep people loyal, even though genuine loyalty cannot be bought or sold.

In the British Army, things were taken to the other extreme. After the war, Lord Alanbrooke found himself so impoverished that he was forced to put his house on the market and move into the adjoining gardener's cottage. A keen ornithologist, Alanbrooke even had to sell his bird-watching books. Yet he wasn't devastated by his decline in material fortunes since he didn't expect the country to give him a grand estate. He lived his life according to a code of duty that was entirely unrelated to financial reward.

Churchill had no reason to distrust his generals' commitment to the cause they were fighting for, but that does not mean that he always believed in their professional competence. In the first three years of the war, Churchill frequently tried to interfere with his commanders in the field. In August 1940, for instance, he personally drafted a directive to the Commander-in-Chief for the Middle East that went into minute tactical matters and even contained instructions for the deployment of troops down to battalion level. On several occasions in the Desert War, Churchill harried commanders into rushed and poorly prepared offensives, often with disastrous results – at least until strong-willed generals like Harold Alexander and Bernard Montgomery taught him to trust them.

Alexander was given command of the Middle East in the summer of 1942, with Montgomery as commander of the Eighth Army, which opposed the Afrika Korps of Erwin Rommel. So far, the British had only experienced humiliating defeats at the hands of 'the Desert Fox' and Churchill was eager to see some successes. Just as with his previous generals in the Desert War, such as Auchinleck and Wavell, he attempted to meddle with Montgomery's and Alexander's commands and urged them to 'take or destroy' Rommel's Afrika Korps 'at the earliest possible moment'. Yet Alexander replied coolly, effectively telling the Prime Minister to back off. As El Alamein showed, Montgomery would not disappoint him either.

The Battle of El Alamein was not only a turning point of the war, it was also a turning point in Churchill's war leadership. He finally learned to trust his commanders in the field and let them do their jobs without his constant interference. It certainly wasn't easy for him to stop meddling. He had been a soldier himself, having attended the Royal Military Academy at Sandhurst, and had seen plenty of action, most recently in the First World War. He would have loved to exercise command himself, at all times and in all places. Before the age of twenty-five he had written two books, *The Malakand Field Force* and *The River War*, in which he had sought to give the British High Command the benefit of his advice in India and the Sudan.

Churchill was not the great military commander that his ancestor Marlborough had been. His outstanding leadership qualities were sometimes marred by a startling lack of judgement. Very often it was his romantic vision of war as an adventure that nurtured his military thinking, rather than a realistic appreciation of operational practicalities. One of his favourite schemes, for instance, was an invasion of Nazi-occupied Europe from Norway, an idea he repeatedly returned to throughout the war. Each time, the Chiefs of Staff were forced to prepare detailed operational plans for this scheme, if only to prove that such an enterprise was doomed to failure.

It is fascinating to see how Churchill's and Hitler's leadership styles developed during the course of the war: while Churchill involved himself less and less with the day-to-day military conduct of the war, Hitler became more and more the micromanager. This was largely because the victories of the German Army in the first two years of the war had led Hitler to believe himself to be an infallible military genius. Meanwhile the British defeats reminded Churchill that he himself was not one.

Ever since the time when the German Army had been checked at the gates of Moscow, Hitler became increasingly involved with operational details and even tactical matters that would have been much better decided by the commanders in the field. It was the very negation of the principle of Mission Command that had made the early Blitzkrieg campaigns so successful.

Such was Hitler's exaggerated self-belief that when, one day, he was whistling a classical tune and a secretary suggested that he had made a mistake in the melody, Hitler retorted: 'I don't have it wrong. It is the composer who made a mistake in this passage.'[41] Yet as the war progressed, Hitler forgot that it had often been the initiative of individual commanders that had won him his early victories.

As the war in the East dragged on, Hitler more and more played the part of a divisional commander rather than a commander-in-chief. It allowed him to forget for a while the grim realities of the overall situation as he concentrated on interfering with his battlefield commanders in individual operations thousands of miles away. 'The other day I called off an attack that was to procure us a territorial gain of four kilometres,' he boasted at one staff meeting, 'because the operation didn't seem to me to be worth the price it would have cost.' If Hitler had had a Cerberus like Lord Alanbrooke, he would never have been allowed to get involved in such detailed decision-making, but the very nature of the Nazi state made that impossible. The situation got so bad that by 1945 General Günther Blumentritt complained how one plan from Hitler

> came to us... in the most minute detail. It set out the specific divisions that were to be used... The sector in which the attack was to

> take place was specifically identified and the very roads and villages through which the forces were to advance were all included. All this planning had been done in Berlin from large-scale maps and the advice of generals ... was not asked for, nor was it encouraged.[42]

The contrast with the principles of Mission Command that had served Hitler so well in the West in 1940 could not have been more marked.

While Churchill had streamlined the decision-making process, Hitler operated a system of divide and rule that ensured that nobody but he could claim to have a comprehensive view of Germany's strategic situation. Yet the resulting fragmentation of command and blurring of responsibilities made effective military leadership all but impossible, as D-Day was to show. The 'Atlantic Wall', Hitler's fortification in Normandy, was designed to thwart an Allied attack across the Channel. It didn't succeed, of course, but the German failure was not primarily due to lack of armaments but rather to lack of leadership. Four years after the Blitzkrieg victory over France, the German command system was in a shambolic state.

The leadership technique that had helped Hitler to enhance his image of the charismatic, unchallengeable leader in times of peace proved to be his undoing in war, when he moved away from the rational – if albeit cynical and sinister – decision-making processes of his earlier years. This was particularly the case once the tide had turned in November 1942, the month both of Rommel's retreat after El Alamein and the encirclement of the German Army besieging Stalingrad. Hitler started to fit new information, especially discouraging news, into his already-formulated patterns of hopes and beliefs. Evidence that his strategy was failing was minimised, and he could not accept that the war was being lost even when he received a report from Albert Speer that actually contained the words: 'The war is lost.'[43] On 20 July 1944 the German opposition to Hitler finally got round to making a serious assault on his life.

Resistance to Hitler

A new Second World War myth is about to enter the liberal canon. For as well as being responsible for concentration camps (started in the Boer War), the oppression of Weimar Germany (as the economist John Maynard Keynes effectively argued in his book *The Economic Consequences of the Peace*), and of course the so-called 'genocidal' bombing of Dresden and Hamburg, a theory is now emerging that the British were also guilty of failing to give active support to the German resistance so that they found it impossible to overthrow Hitler.

The publication in 1996 of *Plotting Hitler's Death* by the distinguished German historian Joachim Fest took the argument a stage further even than earlier works by Patricia Meehan, *The Unnecessary War* (1992), and Klemens von Klemperer, *German Resistance against Hitler: The Search for Allies Abroad* (1993). Herr Fest unequivocally blamed the British Government for their 'lack of flexibility, their hostility, their blindness, and a political obtuseness that to all intents and purposes represented an alliance with Hitler'. He argued that 'Nazi propagandists and Allied spokesmen joined forces in a *de facto* coalition' in order to denigrate the German resistance. Several of the book's reviewers criticised Churchill and the British Foreign Secretary Anthony Eden for not doing more to support the plotters, and an editorial in *The Times* even argued that 'we too may wish to reconsider our wartime record' because of our 'misguided policy', which was only explicable because 'British leaders were fighting the wrong war'.

Yet far from being culpably blind or stupid, Churchill and Eden had sound, indeed politically unanswerable reasons for pursuing their 'perfect silence' policy towards the German resistance. As Fest, Meehan and Klemperer all acknowledge, there was no single resistance entity with which the British Government could reasonably deal to the exclusion of the others. There was little overlap between the Communist, Christian and military opponents of Hitler's regime. Even inside those circles that could genuinely pose a direct physical threat to Hitler's life there were wide differences over the intended outcome. Count Helmuth von Moltke's ideas for post-war democracy, for example, only involved elections for local councils and not for a national parliament. Claus von Stauffenberg and Karl Goerdeler wanted Germany to return to its 1939 borders, which of course included the re-militarised Rhineland as well as the Sudeten part of Czechoslovakia. Others, such as the politician Ulrich von Hassell, considered Germany's 1914 imperial frontiers desirable, yet they included parts of the very country, Poland, whose independence Britain and France had initially gone to war to defend in 1939. The possession of Alsace-Lorraine was another point of contention.

Furthermore, after June 1941, decisions over peace moves were no longer up to Britain alone. Once the war was being fought by the Soviet Union, and after December 1941 by the United States as well, it was unthinkable that Britain should enter into negotiations with any Germans behind the backs of her allies, especially after President Roosevelt's insistence in January 1943 on Germany's unconditional surrender as a precondition for peace. As one of the officials in the German Department of the Foreign Office, Sir Frank Roberts, put it in his autobiography, *Dealing with Dictators*: 'If Stalin got the impression we were in contact with the German generals, whose main aim was to protect Germany against Russia, he might well have been tempted to see whether he could not again come to terms with Hitler.'

The British Government's stance was succinctly summed up by Sir D'Arcy Osborne, the British envoy to the Vatican, who, when told by Pope Pius XII that the German resistance groups 'confirmed their intention, or their desire, to affect a change of government', answered: 'Why don't they get on with it?' It is also questionable what genuine support the Allies could actually deliver. Logistical support in terms of providing bombs or rifles was hardly needed by the German military, and moral support was of little practical help. Any promises about the Allies' attitude towards a post-Hitler Germany would necessarily have been contingent upon its political make-up, which might even have included senior Nazis. Anyhow, to be seen as being supported or influenced in any way by the Allies would have spelt disaster to any German opposition group attempting to form a post-Hitler government with the support of ordinary patriotic Germans.

British decision-makers had seen quite enough of the Prussian officer class between 1914 and 1918 to have much faith in its commitment to anything approaching democracy. For them, Prussian militarism was almost as unattractive as full-blown Nazism; national-conservative Germans were nearly indistinguishable from national-socialist ones. One can understand why Eden should have said that the July bomb plotters 'had their own reasons for acting as they did and were certainly not moved primarily by a desire to help our cause', however harsh that might sound in retrospect.

Insofar as the German generals were a homogeneous entity, rather than a group of competing and often mutually antagonistic individuals, their complicity in fighting one of history's most vicious campaigns was total. In Poland in 1939 the Wehrmacht were accessories to the crimes of the SS, but by 1941 they were full accomplices. The defeats in Russia and the July Bomb Plot were hardly coincidental. The British Government can be forgiven for suspecting that if Russia had been defeated, or if the Allies had been repulsed in Normandy the previous month, no bomb would have been placed under the man who had been followed unquestioningly by the German people during the first bloodless, and then highly sanguine, victories of 1938 to 1942.

Although the plotters were undoubtedly in Churchill's words, 'the bravest of the best', it remains unclear whether supporters of the Resistance spoke for very many other Germans beside themselves, even on 20 July 1944. Had Hitler died in the Bomb Plot he would not have been succeeded by some neo-Christian Democrat government, but probably by Heinrich Himmler, who controlled the SS. With Bormann merely a bureaucrat and Goebbels's influence largely dependent on the dead Hitler, Himmler would have exploited his formidable power base and most likely become the new Führer. Nor would much have been different had the vice-Führer, Hermann Göring, succeeded to the Nazi throne. The historian Peter Hoffmann has written that: 'Göring would have sought to rally all the state's forces by an appeal to *völkisch* and national-socialist ideals, by vowing to fulfil the Führer's legacy and to redouble the efforts to fight the enemy to a standstill.' If either Göring or Himmler had taken over and not made the many strategic blunders perpetrated by Hitler in the final months of the war, Nazi Germany might even have lasted longer. Furthermore, the average German soldier would doubtless have continued to fight on doggedly to protect his fatherland (and his mother's honour) from the rampaging Red Army.

An assassinated Hitler would also have provided the ideal new *Dolchstosslegende* once Germany was defeated. It would undoubtedly have been argued that just as Hitler was about to launch his war-winning secret weapons to destroy the Allied Armies, which he had spent a year purposely luring towards Germany, he was murdered by a clique of aristocrats, liberals, Christians and cosmopolitans whose treachery was evident since they were working in league with British Intelligence. It would have been a potent recipe for revanchism that would have resonated in Germany almost to this day.

In his 1947 book *The Last Days of Hitler*, the distinguished historian Hugh Trevor-Roper called the German Resistance 'a creature as fabulous as the centaur and the hippogriff'. But quite apart from the question of whether it was really quite as large and influential as its post-war advocates claim – it might well have swelled somewhat after the war, rather like the French maquis – the fact remains that the British had good reason for suspecting its contacts among the Resistance of being double agents. In November 1939 two MI6 officers were kidnapped at Venlo on the Dutch–German border by Gestapo agents posing as Resistance figures. Fest does not mention the incident, but Meehan acknowledges that it had 'serious and long-lasting consequences' in making the Foreign Office understandably suspicious of future advances.

Seen in this light, the offhand attitude of Sir Alec Cadogan, the Permanent Under-Secretary at the British Foreign Office – 'As usual, the German Army trust us to save them from the Nazi regime' – becomes easily explicable. After the resister Karl Goerdeler asked for Danzig to remain German, colonial concessions and a £500m interest-free loan before attempting to depose Hitler in December 1939, Cadogan was equally scathing. 'We are to deliver the goods,' he wrote, 'and Germany gives the IOUs.' The Foreign Secretary agreed. On the subject of what Neville Chamberlain termed 'Hitler's Jacobites', Lord Halifax complained: 'The Germans always want us to make their revolutions for them.' Judging by Herr Fest's book, little has changed.

'Assassination', said Benjamin Disraeli only a fortnight after Abraham Lincoln's death in 1865, 'has never changed the history of the world.' Was he right? Considering the baleful effect that Hitler's leadership had on the German people between 1933 and 1945, would it have been justifiable to have assassinated him? Papers released at the Public Records Office at Kew in 2000 showed that 'Operation Foxley', the various British Intelligence plans to kill Hitler, were quite well advanced but were prevented from being carried out by a policy decision taken from on high.

The question of whether the assassination of Hitler would have dramatically changed the course of the war goes to the heart of the ancient debate about whether history is primarily driven by what

T. S. Eliot called 'vast, impersonal forces' – so powerful that individuals, however seemingly influential, are in fact mere corks on history's waves – or whether great men, as Thomas Carlyle believed, determine by their own will what happens in human affairs. If Napoleon had been killed at the siege of Acre, or if Hitler had succumbed to 'Operation Foxley's' lethal cocktail of anthrax and bazookas, would the world be a different place?

Post-war American governments, or at least their Intelligence communities, seem to have cleaved to the 'great man' theory, authorising attempts on the life of Fidel Castro – once famously with exploding cigars – and bombing missions against Colonel Gaddafi in 1986 and Saddam Hussein in 1991. Although America has seen an inordinate amount of presidents (four) as well as other public figures such as Martin Luther King, Huey Long, Robert Kennedy and Malcolm X fall prey to assassins, it is still the most gung-ho of nations, willing to countenance an attack aimed specifically at an enemy leader, in a way that Wellington denounced as ungentlemanly when it was suggested that he fire a cannon directly at Napoleon during the opening stage of the Battle of Waterloo. By contrast with the Americans, Britain has been almost circumspect; indeed, it was said that the British politician Julian Amery's career never really prospered after he advocated that MI6 assassinate some of Britain's colonial troublemakers.[44]

Assassination as a policy tends to fare very differently when carried out in representative democracies with established power hierarchies than in feudal, tribal or dictatorial countries. Whereas the assassination of a president – McKinley or John Kennedy – or a prime minister – Spencer Perceval – merely results in the smooth substitution of a lieutenant, who is usually at pains defiantly to continue the same policies, it is different when the dead individual personifies the nation. If a war can be foreshortened, and a significant change of government effected by an *ad hominem* attack, such as on Saddam Hussein, it is hard to balk at such action.

The assassinations of Jean Paul Marat, Tsar Alexander II, Archduke Franz Ferdinand, Admiral Darlan, Reinhard Heydrich, Hendrik Verwoerd, Benigno Aquino, Father Jerzy Popieluszko and General Zia ul-Haq all had far-reaching political consequences – albeit often the opposite of what the assassins intended – because they took place in undemocratic countries. Those of Empress Elisabeth of Austria, King Humbert I of Italy, Jean Jaurès, Mahatma

Gandhi, President Diem of South Korea, Olof Palme, Indira Gandhi and Rajiv Gandhi, taking place in countries with representative institutions, did not, in Disraeli's typically flip generalisation, 'change the world'.

It is fairly safe to assume that Hitler's sudden death at the hands of the Special Operations Executive, by whichever of the splendidly James Bond operations was finally chosen for 'Operation Foxley', would have changed the course of the war, but for the better or worse? The war needed to be won by the Allies, but it also needed to be lost, comprehensively and personally, by Hitler himself. His suicide in the bunker after the total collapse of his dreams had to be the last chapter of the tale, the crucial prerequisite for the decent, democratic, peace-loving Germany we know today.

Before June 1944, Germany had wreaked far worse damage on the rest of the world than it had on her. To have concluded an armistice on the demonstrable fallacy that the war was begun and carried on by one man's will, rather than through the wholehearted support and enthusiasm of the German people, would not have produced the longest and most durable period of peace Europe has known for half a millennium.

A nation that had fought no fewer than five wars of invasion in the seventy-five years after 1864 needed to have the warlike instinct burned out of its soul. Only the horrors and humiliations of 1944 and 1945 could have achieved that. If they had been spared that ultimate calamity, somehow escaping Year Zero because of Operation Foxley, the Germans would not be the pacific democrats they undoubtedly are today. The ghastly, final scene of Götterdämmerung had to be played out, with Goebbels reading Thomas Carlyle's *Frederick the Great* in translation to Hitler in the Berlin bunker as the Red Army closed in. Ribbentrop, Kaltenbrunner, Streicher, Rosenberg and the rest could be hanged at Nuremberg, but Hitler himself needed to die by the one hand that would make his defeat truly complete – his own.

D-Day: Hitler's nemesis

Long before D-Day actually took place, Hitler was receiving contradictory reports on the time and location of the invasion from his three rival intelligence agencies. In line with Hitler's divide-and-rule principle, both the German Army and the Foreign Office had their own intelligence agencies, as well as Himmler's SS which ran the Sicherheitsdienst (SD). Each of these three agencies operated completely independently of each other, and often delivered contradictory analyses and reports. The British and Americans, by contrast, had a Joint Intelligence Committee that pooled and evaluated all incoming data, thereby rendering Churchill generally co-ordinated prognostications.

Even more serious for Germany was the fact that the commander responsible for the defence of France, Field Marshal von Rundstedt, had no direct control over many of the units operating in the area under his responsibility. Anti-aircraft units and parachute troops were under the control of Göring's Luftwaffe. The Waffen SS units reported only to Himmler. One Army Group was led by Rommel, but Rundstedt, although nominally his superior, was not permitted to give him direct orders. Two entire panzer divisions, held in reserve, were under the direct control of the High Command of the German Forces (the OKW), which in turn acted only on Hitler's orders. This greatly hampered Rundstedt's ability to manoeuvre fighting units effectively when the Allied landings began in the early hours of 6 June 1944.

Rundstedt immediately ordered the panzer reserves to speed towards the Channel coast to fling the Allies back into the sea before they managed to establish a firm toe-hold on the Continent, only to find himself reprimanded by the Army High Command (the OKH) for not having first obtained Hitler's authorisation. The panzer reserves were ordered to halt. But the Führer was not willing to give his authorisation and it was not until midday that Hitler finally reacted to the momentous news. It is not true that he was asleep, he was merely slow to make a decision. By the time he did so, the Allies had already seized the beachheads and Allied air superiority had made any large-scale movement of panzers during the day well-nigh impossible.

Churchill's promise to fight on the beaches had come true, but the fighting was not done at Brighton or Dover, but on the Normandy invasion beaches codenamed Juno, Omaha, Sword, Gold and Utah. Now it was only a matter of time before all of Europe would be liberated from the Nazi yoke. Yet the worse the military situation became for Germany, the more Hitler micromanaged, thereby making things even more dire than they were already. It was the very negation of the principle of Mission Command that had made Hitler's earlier Blitzkrieg successes possible.

After the Battle of the Odon had removed any chance that the Germans might have had to split Allied forces by striking at Bayeux, Rundstedt warned the OKW that the battle for Normandy was effectively lost. Field Marshal Keitel asked in despair: 'What shall we do?' Rundstedt's reply was harsh: 'Make peace, you fools.' He was relieved of his command and replaced by Field Marshal Günther von Kluge. A few days later, Rommel sent a letter to Hitler: 'Our troops are fighting heroically all along the line, but the unequal battle is nearing its end. In my view you should draw the necessary conclusions.' Kluge supported Rommel: 'Unfortunately, the field marshal is right.'

Yet Hitler would have none of this, especially when the failed assassination attempt of 20 July 1944 revealed a wide-ranging conspiracy against him within the High Command. His response was a ruthless purge of the military: 160 officers were executed, among them no fewer than two field marshals and seventeen generals. Rommel himself was offered no choice but to take poison.

The Bomb Plot weakened Hitler in other ways beyond the purely political. General Walter Warlimont of the OKH operation staff, who was injured in the blast, recorded how afterwards:

> Hitler himself was now quite obviously a sick man. His actual injuries on 20th July had been minor but it seemed as if the shock had brought into the open all the evil of his nature, both physical and psychological. He came into the map room bent and shuffling. His glassy eyes gave a sign of recognition only to those who stood closest to him. His chair would be pushed forward for him and he would slump down into it, bent almost double with his head sunk between his shoulders. As he pointed to something on the map his hand would tremble. On the slightest occasion he would demand that 'the guilty' be hunted down.

One original aspect of the Führer remained, however, and that was the well-advertised effect of his glance. A military adjutant who saw him only days before Hitler killed himself recalled how, although the rest of him looked like 'a sick and senile old man ... only in his eyes was there an indescribable flickering brightness ... and the glance he gave me was strangely penetrating'.

Warlimont noted how the attempt on his life led Hitler, not surprisingly, to mistrust his generals even more after July 1944, which made them correspondingly less likely ever to contradict him: 'His responsible advisers gave the immediate observer the disturbing impression that they were now guided, not by sober military considerations, but by a discipleship complex if possible more unquestioning than before.' As a result, Hitler proceeded entirely to scrap the doctrine of Mission Command that had served him so well in Poland, Norway, the Netherlands and France (at least before he intervened with the disastrous 'halt order' for the panzers before Dunkirk). In consequence, Warlimont further recalled of this post-July period:

> Hitler succeeded ... in setting the seal on his disastrous method of command by proclaiming as an order the principle that the sole responsibility of all commanders, even the most senior, was to carry out his orders unconditionally and to the letter. In face of the enemy a N.C.O. or private soldier had no right to question the soundness or likelihood of success of an attack ordered by his company commander; similarly the Supreme Commander of the Wehrmacht was not prepared to share responsibility for his decisions with commanders-in-chief of Army Groups or Armies. They were not allowed to ask to be relieved if they disagreed with his instructions.[45]

To make matters yet worse, Hitler's very survival of the Bomb Plot only served to reinforce his belief in his destiny. As Warlimont remembered:

> He was presumptuous enough to consider that it was 'Providence' which had preserved him on 20 July and now expected that other 'miracles' would give the war a new turn, although in earlier days he had heaped scorn upon the heads of any enemy leaders who had used this sort of language.

Churchill meanwhile used Hitler's survival as an opportunity for one of his most crushing broadsides. He had in the past referred to

Hitler as 'this bloodthirsty guttersnipe' and put Allied victories in Africa down in part to 'the military intuition of Corporal Hitler. We may notice the touch of the master hand. The same insensate obstinacy.' He had also refused to compare Hitler to Napoleon, since 'it seems an insult to the great emperor and warrior to compare him in any way with a squalid caucus boss and butcher'. Now, in September 1944, Churchill outdid even himself for scorn. Speaking in the House of Commons he said:

> When Herr Hitler survived the Bomb Plot ... he described his survival as providential. I think from a purely military point of view we can all agree with him. Certainly it would be most unfortunate if the Allies were to be deprived in the closing phases of the struggle of that form of warlike genius that Corporal Schicklgruber has so notably contributed to our victory.

As so often with Churchill's best jibes, it had the added but not wholly necessary advantage of being true. Three miracles had befallen Britain in the war, all of them the result of cardinal errors by Hitler: the 'halt order' of the panzers outside Dunkirk on 25 May 1940; the invasion of Russia on 22 June 1941; and the German declaration of war against the United States on 11 December 1941. None of these decisions had anything to do with Churchill, but they had collectively saved his cause. They had all come from one presiding mind. Leadership – in this case Hitler's catastrophically bad leadership – had been crucial. Truly great leaders understand how vital it is to listen to people who disagree with them. While Churchill engaged in debate, Hitler simply stifled it. In the end therefore, although totalitarian states are good at starting wars, democracies are better at winning them.

Conclusion

'History may regard Winston Churchill as the architect of the disastrous Gallipoli campaign or the maker of xenophobic speeches, but tonight we consider him, in philanthropic old age, as Churchill the European.'

Radio Times, November 2001

'Winston Churchill High School in Harare, Zimbabwe, will become Josiah Tongogara High, in memory of the commander of Mr Mugabe's 1970s guerrilla army.... Warren Park Primary School will become Chenjerai Hitler Hunzvi Primary School, immortalising the regime's chief rabble-rouser.'

Daily Telegraph, February 2002

'School Video On The War Gives Churchill Fourteen Seconds.'

Newspaper headline, 2001

What will they say of Adolf Hitler and Winston Churchill long after we are all dead? While there are still people alive who lost family members to Hitler's War, while we still live in a world the political contours of which are largely shaped by the post-Hitler settlement, it is impossible to be truly objective about them. What, though, will ordinary people make of Hitler and Churchill in 2145 or 2245, when they are as chronologically distant to our descendants as historical figures like Napoleon and Wellington are to us today?

Most of us fondly assume that Hitler will always be seen as another Vlad the Impaler, Attila the Hun or Ivan the Terrible – a hate-filled bloodthirsty tyrant and no more than that. As Sir John Keegan has put it: 'He belongs in the company of Genghis Khan, Tamerlane, Stalin and Mao Tse-tung, inhuman megalomaniacs all.

These men are, as the People of the Book have no difficulty in believing, in league with the Devil. May God rest their souls.'[1] Although in fifty years or so some revisionist biographies and television documentaries might occasionally attempt to rehabilitate the Führer, the judgement of posterity seems settled. But some distinguished thinkers, such as the American historian John Lukacs, are not so sure. Lukacs has identified a number of areas in which Hitler-revisionism has already made some (admittedly very limited) headway, and he fears that these will increase over time. Napoleon, after all, left over six million dead across Europe after two decades of wars of conquest, yet there is no shortage of intellectuals and writers who admire him today.

Lukacs believes that Hitler should be recognised as 'the greatest revolutionary of the twentieth century', superior even to Lenin in his ability to harness and then direct the politics of mass discontent, and that these ideas of nationalist triumphalism could still pose a threat in the future. His ultimate fear is that if Western civilisation melts away, and then threatens to disappear altogether, a danger lies before future generations. During a rising flood of barbarism, Hitler's reputation might rise in the eyes of ordinary people, who may come to regard him as a kind of Diocletian, a tough last architect of a desirable imperial order.[2] Fortunately, this outcome is hardly an immediate prospect, and if Western civilisation should ever dissolve to quite that extent, the state of Adolf Hitler's reputation will be among the last of our great-grandchildren's worries. Churchill himself said something to this effect in the House of Commons on 25 June 1941: 'If we win, nobody will care. If we lose, there will be nobody to care.'

In the Introduction to this book I tried to draw a distinction between the charismatic leader of Adolf Hitler's type and the inspirational one such as Winston Churchill. When we watch a magician performing his tricks at a children's party, half of us will stare at his hands trying to work out how he does them, while the other half of the audience will simply watch it for what it is, enjoying the sensation of being astounded. Natural sceptics will follow an inspirational leader, but be rightly suspicious of a charismatic one. In politics, therefore, scepticism is a healthy reaction that should be nurtured and encouraged.

The truth is that Hitler exerted far more power over people's imaginations and psyches than ever Churchill did. Hitler harnessed two of the most powerful, if vicious, of human emotions – envy and resentment – to his chariot wheels, and they took him an astoundingly long way. In the wake of the defeat of Germany and Austria in the Great War and their perceived ill-treatment in the subsequent Versailles peace treaty, it was pathetically easy to induce rampant self-pity in the German people. Indeed, Hitler was originally just one of a large number of competing far-right politicians trying to achieve this.

By contrast, neither envy nor resentment formed any part of Churchill's psychological make-up. The author John Julius Norwich recalls going to the cinema with his parents Alfred and Lady Diana Duff Cooper and with Winston Churchill: 'I remember a film about Irish peasants, during which he occasionally remarked: "Poor horse." And then at the end, he declared: "Envy – most barren of all vices."' The Germans' envy of the victorious powers of 1918, of their colonies and wealth certainly, but above all of their victory itself, made them easy victims for Adolf Hitler.

The Milgram and Asch experiments

'The art of leadership', wrote Tony Blair in 1994, 'is in saying no, not yes. It is very easy to say yes.'[3] Two famous experiments undertaken in America some years ago – the Milgram and the Asch projects – illustrate quite how easy it is for people to say yes, and they have very disturbing implications for the way we view the tractability of human nature. In the experiment conducted in 1963 by Dr Stanley Milgram, volunteers were required to test a man who was strapped on to a chair with an electrode attached to his wrists. The volunteer was told that the experiment was being undertaken in order to test human tolerance to pain. The man had been required to memorise a text, and if he repeated it correctly, the volunteer would simply do nothing. If he stumbled or erred, however, the volunteer was instructed to flick a switch on a rheostat that administered an electric shock to the man in the chair. These shocks got progressively more powerful as the errors increased.

In truth, of course, there was no electric charge at all, and the man was acting as he yelled out in pain. Yet the volunteers did not know that, and no fewer than 65 per cent of them blindly obeyed their instructions, going on to administer shocks of up to 450 volts, which would constitute a lethal dosage. The man's screams of pain did not prevent them continuing with the experiment. As Brian Masters has put it in his autobiography, *Getting Personal*, the Milgram experiment 'demonstrated beyond question that timid, kindly decent souls could become monsters if offered the chance'.[4]

Then there are the equally worrying implications of the Asch experiment, in which three people were shown three lines on a screen and asked which was the longest. Again, unknown to one of the volunteers, the other two were in fact experimenters. The longest of the lines was always perfectly obvious; the true answer was not in doubt, even to someone with the worst eyesight and meanest intelligence. After a couple of rounds in which they all chose the correct lines, the two experimenters began to choose the same wrong line, one that was identifiably and clearly shorter than the longest. At first the volunteer would protest and point out the truth, but astonishingly quickly he would go along with the opinion of the other two. The Milgram and Asch experiments show how easily people can be led, both into acting cruelly and – just as worrying – into disbelieving the evidence of their own eyes.[5]

Leading people to commit horrific crimes, as Hitler did in the Second World War, and then to deny the evidence of everything about them, was therefore not so hard a task as it might at first appear. Academic work done by the historian Christopher Browning of Princeton University on the notorious Reserve Police Battalion 101, which was responsible for thousands of deaths in the Final Solution in Poland, shows how respectable working- and middle-class citizens of Hamburg became genocidal killers. It seems that peer pressure and a natural propensity for obedience and comradeship – rather than anti-Semitism or Nazi fervour – turned entirely ordinary people into mass murderers.[6]

The lessons are as applicable to today as to 1941–5, as we are reminded by a glance at what happened in the 1990s in places like Rwanda and the former Yugoslavia. How could a people as civilised as the Germans have perpetrated the most ghastly crime of human history? Browning's central conclusion – that far more than just anti-Semitism drove Germany's infamous Reserve Police Battalion 101 to commit atrocities in wartime Poland – was attacked by the historian Daniel Goldhagen in his controversial book of 1996, *Hitler's Willing Executioners*.

Goldhagen argued that the recruits of Battalion 101, who were not selected in any sense for their Nazi ardour but who indeed joined up largely to avoid active service abroad, killed Jewish women, the elderly, and children 'for pleasure' because they had 'fun' on their 'Jew-hunts', where their 'demonological anti-Semitism' was translated into 'a widespread eagerness to kill Jews'. Anti-Semitism, the author maintained, was so ingrained into German culture, society and history that Hitler and the Holocaust were simply the inevitable results. All it took was for Hitler to provide the necessary leadership for genocide to take place.[7] The early 1940s provided the perfect – in the stock phrase of detective fiction – motive, opportunity and method. Yet German Jews were far better integrated in Germany than in most other parts of Europe in the twenties and thirties and, as Keegan has pointed out, 'in 1918 the Kaiser's Reich controlled all the *shtetls* in Europe, but harmed their inhabitants not at all'. Was it therefore much more a case of, as Milton Himmelfarb has memorably put it: 'No Hitler, no Holocaust'? So was Hitler's leadership the central feature of the tragedy?

Battalion 101 represented a cross-section of German society and no one was coerced into killing Jews or taking part in any atrocity. Browning believes that there was nothing peculiarly German about the Holocaust, except perhaps in the perpetrators' heightened respect for authority and readiness to obey orders, and that apart from a relatively small number of fanatical Nazis, few Germans generally approved of what was happening 'out east'. Yet neither did they actively disapprove; the vast majority of Germans were simply indifferent and did not want to be told about the details. Yet when called upon specifically to help in the genocide, between 80 and 90 per cent of the members of Battalion 101 acquiesced without undue complaint. After some initial squeamishness they 'became increasingly efficient and calloused executioners'. Only twelve of the battalion's five hundred members actually refused to shoot 1,800 Jews in the woods outside the Polish village of Jozefow on 13 July 1942. During the remainder of that seventeen-hour day of slaughter – interspersed with cigarette breaks and a midday meal – another forty-five members or so absented themselves for various reasons. The remaining 85 per cent simply got on with the job of shooting

Jewish women and children at point-blank range, even though they knew perfectly well that no retribution would have been exacted had they refused. 'At first we shot freehand,' one recalled. 'When one aimed too high the entire skull exploded. As a consequence, brains and bones flew everywhere. Thus, we were instructed to place the bayonet point on the neck.'

Using interrogation reports from the 1960s, it is possible to delve deep into the mindset of these killers. The reports make chilling but utterly compelling reading, as the authorities analyse the motives of men who for a large number of quite complex psychological reasons allowed themselves to become genocidal murderers. Most of these reasons – wartime brutalisation, 'segmentation', 'routinization', the desire for conformity and so on – do not end at the borders of Nazi Germany. We pride ourselves on the idea that the Holocaust could never have taken place in Britain, but in fact there were easily enough people in 1939–45 who would have staffed the gas chambers had they been erected in Argyll, Cardiff or the Home Counties.

Taking responsibility

Leaders take responsibility. When things went against Churchill he did not hesitate to take personal blame for them. In his speeches to secret sessions of Parliament he would readily admit to having made errors. Hitler, by contrast, constantly blamed others when the war began to go against him; first his generals and subsequently the whole German people, whom he wound up thinking unworthy of his genius. This dichotomy is well expressed by Churchill's willingness to visit bombed-out streets across Britain in order to raise morale, something Hitler flatly refused to do in Germany. Indeed, the Führer had curtains installed in his car. This distancing of himself from his people's suffering was undoubtedly an error for Hitler, who would probably have been received with adulation even up to 1944. His fear of being associated with images of failure and defeat meant that he passed up photo-opportunities that Churchill grasped enthusiastically. When, on 8 September 1940, Churchill started to cry at the sight of a flattened street in the East End of London, a local woman was heard to remark: 'Look, he really cares,' and the crowd cheered him spontaneously.[8] It helped, of course, that Churchill genuinely did care, and did not see people like Hitler did, merely as disposable units in his overall master-plan. Unfortunately for him, Hitler had no advisers who could change his mind. Successful leaders surround themselves with constructive dissenters; Churchill had Alanbrooke, Stalin had Marshal Antonov, Roosevelt had General George Marshall. Hitler, of course, received no such objective advice from 'no men'.

Hitler travelled very little during the war, just to his 'Wolf's Lair' headquarters in eastern Prussia, and four times to France – once to see Rundstedt, once to Paris to gloat at Compiègne, once to visit Marshal Pétain and Pierre Laval at Montoire and once to see General Franco at Hendaye. He was not much of a globe-trotter before the war either, having never visited Britain, America, Africa or the Far East. Some of his strategic blunders – especially his declaration of war against America in December 1941 – might have been avoided if he had been adventurous in early life and had an opportunity to discover for himself what the rest of the non-German world was really like. Churchill, by contrast, was by far the best-travelled Prime Minister in history: during the first four years of the war he covered no fewer than 110,000 miles, spending thirty-three days at sea and fourteen days in the air. It gave him a global strategic perspective entirely lacking in the mind of the Führer.

Knowing when to go

Part of the art of leadership is to know when to stop, but in common with all prime ministers of the twentieth century other than Lord Salisbury and Harold Wilson, Winston Churchill stayed on in office too long. As with so many of his predecessors, he was too easily convinced by arguments about his own indispensability, despite the fact that they were being made by progressively fewer and fewer people. When, in the summer of 1954, an old journalist friend told Churchill that 'quite a few of your Conservative friends are saying that it would be a good thing for the party if you were to resign some time fairly soon', the Prime Minister glanced at him and then around the Commons bar where they were sitting, before replying: 'You know, as I look at this room and think back over my long association with this House, I think this is a pretty good pub. And as I look at the faces in the House, I wonder why I should leave this pub until someone says "Time, please!" in somewhat stronger accents than those of my friends to whom you have been speaking.'[9]

Churchill ought to have emulated Cincinnatus and Garibaldi and left active politics at the time of his triumph in 1945. He could have retired to Chartwell to build walls, write books, paint pictures, and enjoy global secular canonisation. For, by 1945, the greatest adventure story of the century was very obviously over, and the 'Indian Summer' premiership of 1951–5, with its labour appeasement, political sclerosis, foreign-policy reverses and general air of nostalgia and complacency was not at all what an exhausted and poverty-stricken Britain needed. Like Ronald Reagan at Reykjavik at the end of his career, but with far less success, Churchill longed for a summit with the Russians that would earn him the unaccustomed soubriquet 'Peacemaker'. Unlike Reagan he did not speak for a superpower, and it was not to be.

When Churchill and his Conservative Central Office adviser Reginald Maudling sat down to write the leader's speech for the 1947 party conference, it slowly dawned on Maudling that Churchill had not actually read the Industrial Charter, the cornerstone declaration of party policy on all matters concerning the economy. So Maudling handed him a paragraph that summarised its provisions, concerning centralisation, high employment levels, strong trade unions, no denationalisation, equal pay for women, increased spending on training, joint production councils and partnership schemes between industry, government and unions. Churchill said there was a great deal in it with which he did not agree. 'Well, sir,' answered the hapless speech-writer, foreseeing difficulties and beginning to get flustered, 'this is what the party conference adopted.' 'Oh well,' replied Churchill, 'leave it in then.'

The 1951–5 ministry was not Churchill's finest hour. When he returned to Downing Street he brought with him piles of the red 'Action This Day' tags that he had attached to important papers during the war. They were put in a drawer and left there, never to be used. Inattention to detail, lack of interest in domestic and economic issues, and sheer laziness over policy were the besetting problems of the 'Indian Summer' premiership. It is a sign of the sclerotic nature of that ministry that even though the Prime Minister suffered a stroke in the summer of 1953, the Cabinet never noticed that anything untoward had happened. On the few occasions when the Prime

Minister intervened with his lieutenants' business it was to make matters worse.

Appeasement of growing trade union militancy only 'fed the crocodile' and introduced wage-induced inflation into the economy. The Chancellor of the Exchequer, R. A. Butler, was telephoned by Churchill just before Christmas 1954 to be told that he had solved the threatened rail strike. 'On whose terms?' inquired the worried Butler. 'Why, theirs of course, old cock!' replied a satisfied premier. If that was a leitmotif for a ministry which did not add to the lustre of Churchill's reputation. Its most enduring image must be the huge hearing aid that had to be placed in the centre of the Cabinet table so that the octogenarian Prime Minister and several of his more elderly wartime colleagues could hear what was being said. Churchill was, after all, already an old-age pensioner even when he came to the premiership in 1940.

When Churchill finally retired in April 1955 he failed to leave enough time for his successor, Anthony Eden, to settle in to the job before the Suez Crisis was upon him. 'Many people say that I ought to have retired after the war, and have become some sort of elder statesman,' he told the young scientist R. V. Jones in 1946, 'but how could I? I have fought all my life and I cannot give up fighting now!'[10] What had changed was the quality of his enemies; from the excitement of fighting Hitler in 1945 he had to make do with far less riveting foes such as an under-skilled workforce, an over-regulated economy and increasingly militant trade unions. His place in history secured by VE-Day, Churchill could have bucked the twentieth century's baleful trend of prime ministers holding on too long for their own or their party's good. But as Churchill had written in *Savrola*: '"Vehement, high, and daring" was his cast of mind. The life he lived was the only one he could ever live; he must go on to the end.'[11]

Churchill as an historian

The first thing Churchill did when he finally retired was to publish his great work of Anglo-American history, which he had been working on in fits and starts for decades. Leaders who wish to make a lasting mark on history need to be great writers as well as great orators, and Churchill's Nobel Prize for Literature was well deserved. 'In broad principle I shall be willing to undertake to write *A History of the English-Speaking Peoples*, their origins, their quarrels, their misfortunes and their reconciliation for the sum of £20,000,' wrote Winston Churchill to Newman Flower, the managing director of Cassell & Co. on 30 October 1932. The project would take four or five years, he expected. Yet because of the great events that overtook not only Churchill but also the English-speaking peoples themselves, this four-volume work was not published for another quarter of a century.

It was during the first few months of that period of internal Tory opposition dubbed his 'wilderness years' that Churchill came up with the idea of writing a work whose 'object was to lay stress upon the common heritage of the peoples of Great Britain and the United States of America as a means of enhancing their friendship'. It was an act of tremendous foresight, for a decade later those two countries, along with their dominions and dependencies, were to be in the forefront of the struggle to save civilisation.

Although there were sound political reasons for writing the book, the principal and immediate reason for its inception was financial. A prodigious spender with no inherited wealth, Churchill throughout his life relied on his pen and his parliamentary stipends to pay for his grand style of life, and having recently resigned from the Conservative Shadow Cabinet over the issue of Indian self-government he knew he could not expect any ministerial posts in the near future. In the event, it took a full-scale European war to get him back into His Majesty's Government.

So his *History* was from the outset intended to be a bestseller, as he wrote to one of his assistants, the Oxford historian Keith Feiling, 'a vivid narrative picking up the dramatic and dominant episodes and by no means undertaking a complete account'. This was not going to be yet another dry-as-dust semi-academic history of the British and their worldwide cousinhood, but a fast-flowing work of literature starting with Julius Caesar's invasion of England in 55 BC and ending in 1902 with Britain's victory in the Boer War.

Although Churchill engaged a number of leading historians to help him prepare drafts, to explain periods of history to him with which he was unfamiliar and generally to ease the process of research and writing, this was very much his own work – as the annotations on the various proofs make abundantly clear. In 1937, informing his wife Clementine of their precarious financial situation, he wrote about how the *History* was 'entailing an immense amount of reading and solitary reflection if justice is to be done to so tremendous a topic'. The final £15,000 of his advance was not payable until the delivery of the manuscript, which he hoped he could achieve in December 1939.

Of course the rise of Nazism was to interrupt his writing with increasing force over the following two years, but it is astonishing how Churchill was able to compartmentalise his life, snatching time from his campaign against the appeasement of Hitler to get on with his writing. As the war clouds seemed to be gathering over Czechoslovakia in August 1938, Churchill wrote to Lord Halifax about how he was 'horribly entangled with the Ancient Britons, the Romans, the Angles, Saxons and Jutes, all of whom I thought I had escaped from for ever when I left school'. Indeed, if anything, the work on his *History* might have been a useful distraction, for as he wrote to a friend during the Munich Crisis: 'It has been a comfort to me in these anxious days to put a thousand years between my thoughts and the twentieth century.'

The expectation that the publication would make up about one-third of his income for 1939 meant that it provided his principal daily occupation that year outside politics. A team of historians – some paid, others not – continued to help him in various capacities, from writing treatises, to giving private lectures at Chartwell, to checking proofs for factual accuracy. By the time of the *History*'s eventual publication these included some of the most distinguished men of their profession. F. W. (now Sir William) Deakin was Churchill's principal assistant; also lending their help at different times and in different capacities were Maurice Ashley, A. L. Rowse, Asa (now Lord) Briggs, J. H. (later Sir Jack) Plumb, G. M. Young, Alan (now Lord) Bullock and several other highly respected scholars. These historians, recalled Ashley, generally kept enough restraint on an 'exuberant' Churchill to ensure that his statements could be sustained by the historical facts.

'In the main,' Churchill wrote to Ashley in April 1939, 'the theme is emerging of the growth of freedom and law, of the rights of the individual, of the subordination of the State to the fundamental and moral conceptions of an ever-comprehending community. Of these ideas the English-speaking peoples were the authors, then the trustees, and must now become the armed champions. Thus I condemn tyranny in whatever guise and from whatever quarter it presents itself. All this of course has a current application.' Yet however many hours the 'current application' of his principles might have taken out of his day in the last months of peace, Churchill always somehow managed to find time to work on his *History*, to the point that he was busy revising the final chapter of the fourth volume on the very evening that Germany invaded Poland in September 1939.

The delivery date for his completed manuscript obviously had to be postponed, but even the outbreak of war did not entirely close down work on the *History*. The Phoney War found Churchill, who was by then First Lord of the Admiralty, trying to complete the series. F. W. Deakin had joined the 63rd Oxfordshire Yeomanry Anti-Tank Regiment, but was also correcting proofs in his (rapidly dwindling) spare time, while Alan Bullock prepared a ten-thousand-word section on Canada. 'I do hope you will be able to get on with this during the week as the matter is so important and the stress here is very great,' Churchill wrote to Deakin from the Admiralty on 6 October 1939. By 1940 Churchill's project was nearing completion, but so too was Hitler's, and after Churchill became prime minister in May the *History* had to be put on ice for the duration of the war, although the film rights were sold to the great Hungarian-American film producer Alexander Korda for £50,000.

It was not until the last week of 1945 – by which time Churchill had saved civilisation but lost the British general election – that he was able to continue work on his *History*. By then, of course, the English-speaking peoples had added the greatest chapters of their history to the tale, but it was decided not to extend the work to an extra volume to incorporate that. Churchill took his proofs of the book on board the *Queen Elizabeth* liner on his way to make his great 'Iron Curtain' speech in America, but no sooner did he return than another large-scale project was to intervene which would once again retard publication of his *History*.

Churchill considered it his duty to write six volumes of his war memoirs, and took advantage of his years in opposition to do this, helped by William Deakin. The work began in 1946 and the final volume, *Triumph and Tragedy*, also published by Cassell & Co., did not appear until 1954, by which time Churchill was once again prime minister, the Conservative Party having won the October 1951 general election. Yet again history had overtaken the *History*.

Ironically enough, it seems to have been Churchill's debilitating stroke in the summer of 1953 that led to the resuscitation of the project. His doctor Lord Moran had suggested that the Prime Minister should 'take up something that will calm your mind', at which Brendan Bracken, the former Conservative minister and Churchill's close friend, said: 'Well, why not finish *A History of the English-Speaking Peoples*?' As luck would have it, Bracken owned the journal *History Today*, which had been founded in 1951 and which was co-edited by his friend and former wartime assistant private secretary at the Ministry of Information, Alan Hodge. Hodge was something of a prodigy; he was only twenty-five when – after attending Liverpool Collegiate School and Oriel College, Oxford – he began writing avant-garde verse and collaborated with Robert Graves on *The Long Weekend* in 1940.

Co-editing the magazine with the author and poet Peter Quennell, in a highly productive partnership that lasted until Hodge's death in 1979, Hodge exercised, as *The Times* obituary of him states, 'a stewardship which was scholarly, imaginative and judicious'. He also published *The Past We Share* with Quennell in 1960, an illustrated history of Britain and America. Colleagues and friends of Hodge often lamented that his natural modesty contented itself with collaborative ventures rather than individual writings, through which he could have made a greater name for himself. A prime example of this was the way he headed the committee of historians who helped Churchill with the final research for *A History of the English-Speaking Peoples*.

A group of academics and historians was quickly brought together by Hodge to help Churchill, several of them the same men as had lent a hand before the war. 'I shall lay an egg a year,' Churchill announced to Moran, 'a volume every twelve months should not mean too much work.'

Aged seventy-nine, Churchill started to get the *History* ready for publication as he recuperated from his stroke. But on re-reading his early proofs he found that he wanted to recast the book substantially. The great events through which the world had passed in the intervening years since 1939 had put history into better perspective for him, and he wanted the work to reflect the wider lessons of history better than the first drafts had done. 'Hitherto after the opening chapters the story has been classified under titles of the reigns of kings,' Churchill wrote to Hodge. 'This was how we learned it at school. Of course it is not in accordance with the scale and temper of the work. We should consider only using monarchs for chapter heads when they represent some great phase or turning point in history.'

Magna Carta, the Hundred Years War, 'the Dawn of Parliament' and the Wars of the Roses were now to be given more emphasis than mere lists of monarchs, for, as Churchill put it: 'We are recording the march of events in what is meant to be a lively, continuous narrative. We are primarily concerned with the social and political changes as they occur, especially with those which have left their marks on today.' Churchill joked to his friend Lord Beaverbrook about this re-reading of his great work in the light of the Second World War: 'On the whole I think I would rather have lived through our lot of troubles than any of the others, though I must place on record my regret that the human race ever learned to fly.'

Just as Churchill had been working on the proofs the night that Hitler had invaded Poland in 1939, so he was revising them for the final time only two days after giving up his second premiership in 1955. This time no world event was going to be allowed to intervene. He had won the Nobel Prize for Literature in 1953 and had much to live up to, and, as he vouchsafed to friends, this was also to be his last literary endeavour. Talking to the historian A. L. Rowse from his bed at Chartwell in July 1955, Churchill admitted that he had been 're-reading the *History* he had written before the war, but he wasn't satisfied with it. However, there were people who would read it on account of his "notoriety".'

There were indeed; Cassell & Co.'s first print run of *A History of the English-Speaking Peoples* numbered no fewer than 130,000, with a further 30,000 being reprinted within a month. After that the reprints continued to come thick and fast, especially once the volumes – which were published between 1956 and 1958 – began to receive superlative reviews from historians such as C. V. Wedgwood, J. H. Plumb, Professor Michael Howard and Professor D. C. Somervell, scholars whose critical judgement was not blinded by Churchill's fame or grandeur. Even the notorious iconoclast A. J. P. Taylor wrote of the first volume, *The Birth of Britain*, that: 'It is one of the wisest, most exciting works of history ever written.'

Churchill fully deserved the massive critical acclaim that those volumes attracted when first published, and have continued to enjoy ever since. They should be read on their own terms, as a great work of literature, as much as – or perhaps even more than – a scrupulously accurate work of history. Pedants have been able to spot occasional sentences in which Churchill's natural exuberance and feel for the language or spirit of a story might have taken him over that thin dividing line between truth and myth – he cites (with caveats) Alfred the Great burning the cakes, for example – but the books are none the worse for that.

Churchill's place in history

'History,' declared Winston Churchill in his November 1940 panegyric to Neville Chamberlain, 'with its flickering lamp stumbles along the trails of the past, trying to reconstruct its themes, to revive its echoes, and kindle with pale gleams the passion of former days.' Churchill would probably have been very pleased by the historical cottage industry that has grown up around him and his reputation. Never far from controversy during his own lifetime, he would doubtless have taken enormous pleasure in defending himself from those who are today loosely called the 'revisionists'.

In one sense, of course, all history-writing is but a revision of the original version, and for some years after his death in 1965 writers about Churchill were merely seeking to restore the balance after the mass of hagiographies which had lauded him in the 1950s and early 1960s. Since then, however, and especially in the past decade, a new, highly critical tone has appeared. This is knocking, aggressively carping, and sometimes frankly contemptuous of Churchill and his achievements.

It has all had surprisingly little effect on the public perception of the wartime premier. The English-speaking peoples seem to have a settled view of Churchill's glory that no amount of historical debate will now alter. 'Churchill has a few detractors,' wrote the *Sunday Telegraph* on the fiftieth anniversary of VE-Day, 'but none has made much impression on the public view of him.' Today his popularity certainly shows no sign of abating. The numbers visiting his home, Chartwell, have been increasing steadily since it opened to the public in the year after his death; a United States warship was named after him in 2000, the first Englishman to be so honoured since the eighteenth century (although he was of course an honorary American citizen); more prosaically, a pair of his bedroom slippers recently fetched $10,000 at auction. He easily won the BBC's 'Great Britons' poll in November 2002, winning 447,423 votes, and was only just pipped at the post for Man of the Millennium by William Shakespeare in 1999, a defeat he would have taken much better than he did the result of the 1945 general election.

The virulence of the 1995 row over the purchase of Churchill's archives with money from the British National Lottery was a tribute to his continued pre-eminence in the national pantheon, as is the way in which both sides of the debate over the proper level of Britain's integration into the European Union attempt to appropriate his political legacy. When the would-be Führer of Austria, Herr Jörg Haider, criticised Churchill as a war criminal on a par with Hitler, it received far more attention than his other more immediate pronouncements about the widening of the European Union. When rioters daubed Communist and anarchist slogans on Churchill's Parliament Square statue on May Day 2000 there was a huge public outcry.

In the popular, non-academic sense at least, Churchill-revisionism is redundant. Like other national icons such as Lincoln, Washington and Napoleon – or his own antagonists Gandhi and de Gaulle – Churchill is so well-bunked that no amount of debunking books will have any appreciable effect on his standing. They continue to be written, of course, but they have the same impact on public perception as does a drawing pin stuck into the hide of a huge pachyderm. What in *Great Contemporaries* he called 'the grievous inquest of history' has sat in judgement on Churchill and has found that he has no case to answer. Only in certain historical and journalistic and outré academic circles is that verdict considered unsafe.

The first set of Churchill-knockers are the ideologists. From the author Clive Ponting on the Left across to David Irving on the far Right, these people have attempted to use various aspects of Churchill's career in order to make certain political points of their own. Depicting him as having a vicious or even evil personality, often by dragging quotations wildly out of context and ascribing motives so machiavellian that they might even have shocked Churchill himself, the ideologists rapidly lose the sympathy and patience of objective readers. If Churchill is so violently disliked by both extremes of the political spectrum, we rightly assume, he could not have been all that bad.

In 2001, admirers of Winston Churchill breathed a huge sigh of relief. For fourteen years, since the publication of David Irving's first volume on Churchill, they had been waiting to see what foul conspiracies the extreme right-wing historian might have managed to dig up in the hundreds of archives to which he had access yet in a 1063-page hymn of hate ironically entitled *Churchill's War: Triumph in Adversity* it was clear that he has not managed to land one single significant blow on the reputation of Britain's wartime leader.

All the old accusations were trotted out, of course: that Churchill was a rude, lying alcoholic who concealed Japan's intention to attack Pearl Harbor from the Americans, was behind the murder of Britain's ally the Polish leader General Sikorski, wanted to flatten Rome, and so on and so endlessly on. There were even a few new, equally groundless slurs; according to Irving's book, Churchill was also a flasher who enjoyed exposing himself to foreign statesmen, was responsible for tipping off the Nazis to the fact that Britain had broken their codes, and wanted MI6 to assassinate Britain's other ally, General de Gaulle.

There were a dozen such new accusations, most of which would be laughable if they were not so rabidly presented, complete with 160 pages of notes that were intended to look as if they backed them up. Yet when, for example, Irving claimed that the then Queen Elizabeth (the late Queen Mother) supported Hitler's peace offer in 1940, and that the proof was to be found in Box Number 23 of Lord Monckton's papers at the Bodleian Library in Oxford, I recalled from my own work on Monckton that that particular box had never been open to historians. Sure enough, the Bodleian Librarian officially confirmed to me that David Irving has not so much as seen the box, let alone opened it.

Many of Irving's assertions are completely contradictory. If Churchill 'invariably put the interests of the United States above those of his own country and its empire', why did he not warn the Americans about what was about to happen in Pearl Harbor? Or if

Mr Irving's notorious views on Auschwitz are correct – that Jews were not being systematically killed there – why should Churchill be held to account for not ordering the RAF to bomb the place? Mr Irving consistently wanted it both ways in his book, but equally consistently wound up getting neither.

Despite the book's subtitle, Irving sees no redeeming features in the man who had the temerity to defeat Adolf Hitler. Churchill's funniest jokes are dismissed as 'jibes'. The imperative need to meet President Roosevelt in early 1942 to co-ordinate a post-Pearl Harbor global military strategy against Germany and Japan is explained in terms of the Prime Minister's 'desire to hobnob at the highest levels'. He is accused of winning the war 'in spite of himself'. Yet whenever the evidence for Irving's claims is minutely examined by someone who has visited the same archives and handled the same original documents, it utterly fails to justify Irving's ludicrous allegations.

The selective quotation is legion. When Irving claimed that Churchill wished to 'eliminate' de Gaulle, what Churchill in fact recommended to his Cabinet colleagues was that they should consider whether they should 'eliminate de Gaulle as a political force and face Parliament and France upon the issue'. Irving's entire Pearl Harbor theory also rested upon an obvious misreading of the diary of Sir Alec Cadogan.

If Mr Irving really has, as his publisher's blurb suggested, spent twenty-seven years researching and writing *Churchill's War*, then he has wasted half a lifetime. 'For in its long series of silly, snide, unproven innuendoes he has ultimately achieved a rather pathetic piece of work. Instead of trying to rebuild his historical reputation, which was destroyed by his defeat in the Irving *v* Lipstadt and Penguin Books libel trial in 2000, he has produced a book that will only convince the most extreme right-wing conspiracy theorists.

When Irving writes that Churchill was of 'partly Jewish blood, although safely diluted', he is simply being offensive. When he claims that Churchill 'was ambivalent about why he was really fighting this ruinous war', he is ignoring the evidence of dozens of the finest speeches ever delivered in the English tongue, which explained to Britain and the world between 1939 and 1945, in utterly uncompromising language, precisely why Nazism had to be extirpated for human civilisation to survive and prosper.

When Irving alleged that the Duke of Windsor was forced to leave Portugal in August 1940 at British 'pistol point', he was merely writing rubbish. Irving's profession of 'shock' that Churchill turned a blind eye to the affairs of his daughter-in-law Pamela Harriman is based on a failure to appreciate the mores of Churchill's class and time. Churchill's supposed desire 'to see Rome in flames' is utterly disproved by his message to Roosevelt that: 'We ought to instruct our pilots to observe all possible care in order to avoid hitting any of the Pope's buildings in the city of Rome.'

A second strand of Churchill revisionism comprises a critique which seems to be growing in American libertarian and isolationist circles. In Patrick Buchanan's 1999 book, *A Republic, Not an Empire*, Churchill is denied a place on the side of the angels, and in a single half-hour speech at a recent history conference, the New York State University historian, Robert Raico, managed to level no fewer than thirty-two accusations against him. I have found that survivors of the London Blitz have their own comments to make on Mr Raico's statement that Hitler never had any intention of bombing their city and that Churchill was therefore wrong to advocate building a strong RAF in the thirties. According to Raico, Churchill was a crypto-socialist, an ethnic-cleanser, a war criminal and a 'stooge' of Stalin's. 'A man of blood and a politico without principle,' Raico described him in an article to support his thesis, 'whose apotheosis serves to corrupt every standard of honesty and morality in politics and history.' Rarely, I find, do the American libertarian revisionists take refuge in understatement.

Although he is British, the professional contrarian Christopher Hitchens was writing in an American publication, *Atlantic Monthly*, in April 2002 when he accused Churchill of being ruthless, boorish, manipulative, 'incapacitated by alcohol', myopic, and wrong about almost everything except the Nazis. He even accused Churchill of being 'vulgar and alarmist' for 'constantly drumming on the subject' of rearmament in the thirties, as though it was possible to be 'alarmist' about something like the rise of Adolf Hitler. In the course of his nineteen-page rant, entitled 'The Medals of his Defeats', Hitchens claimed that it was 'easy to imagine the R.A.F. helping the Wehrmacht in the Caucasus'. This is in fact an impossibility for anyone who is not an obsessive controversialist attempting simply to *épater les Churchillians*. Only a misunderstanding of the

War Cabinet minutes could have produced Hitchens's statement that in 1940 'Churchill more than once favoured limited negotiations with Hitler', when Churchill was actually putting the case to the War Cabinet *against* any such negotiations. Hitchens puts Churchill's opposition to German hegemony down to 'pure ambition', thereby ignoring the great mass of his writing and speeches and political actions over forty years in support of the concept of a European balance of power. Even Adolf Hitler himself recognised Churchill's commitment to that balance of power theory, which he considered outdated, but which he did not deny (see p.116).

In his attack on Churchill for ordering the shelling of the French Fleet at Oran, Hitchens ignores the fact that Britain could not have known that Vichy would not have handed their fleet over to Hitler – if that was indeed the case. We must be thankful that Churchill and not the uncharacteristically-gullible Hitchens was responsible for the security of Britain in 1940. When the writer then states of the Oran attack that Churchill's 'chroniclers prefer to skate over it or, where possible, elide it altogether', he is – unusually for so intelligent a polemicist – writing demonstrable rubbish. The episode has been discussed by Sir Martin Gilbert (in no fewer than twenty-seven pages), Roy Jenkins, John Keegan, John Lukacs, John Charmley, Joseph Lash, Philip Guedalla, Basil Liddell Hart, William Manchester, John Ramsden, Geoffrey Best, Norman Rose, A. L. Rowse, the present author, and, of course, by Churchill himself in the second volume of his memoirs.

Likewise, far from Churchill's retirement being 'a protracted, distended humiliation of celebrity-seeking and gross over-indulgence', in fact the four volumes of Churchill's *History of the English-Speaking Peoples* were acclaimed by academic historians and, as we have seen, are still in print over forty years later. After winning the Second World War, Winston Churchill had little reason or need to 'seek' celebrity. Yet it is only when Hitchens makes the claim that Churchill was responsible for deliberately putting the American liner *Lusitania* at risk in 1915 in order to bring the United States into the Great War that one starts to doubt whether Hitchens himself can really believe these ludicrous theses.

Churchill regularly used to joke that he knew that history would be kind to him because he himself would be writing it. Sadly, however, people who are uniquely disqualified by their lack of objectivity have been writing a great deal of history about him, and a good deal of cross-fertilisation goes on between them. Many of the quotations Mr Raico uses to illustrate his accusations are footnoted to have come from the work of Irving and Ponting; in turn Raico is quoted admiringly by Buchanan. Several of Hitchens's allegations seem to have originated from Irving. It is almost impossible to believe that these people have set out in genuine pursuit of historical truth, rather than to attack Churchill for the shock value (and sales) attendant on abusing such a totem figure of Anglo-American political culture.

Churchill is a powerful magnet for believers in conspiracy theories. The charge-sheet against him is as long as it is imaginative. Hardly a year goes by without a new book being published accusing him of luring Rudolf Hess to Scotland or having had prior knowledge of the bombing of Pearl Harbor or another such rank absurdity. He has been accused of engineering the Wall Street Crash of 1929 (in which he personally lost a fortune); a writer in the *Philadelphia Inquirer* has argued that if Churchill 'had been a little wiser in 1911, or 1919, neither World War II, nor the Korean, Vietnam nor Persian Gulf wars would have happened, nor the drug explosion, nor the vast [American] deficit'; some writers still maintain that he allowed the city of Coventry to be destroyed rather than risk revealing that Britain had cracked the Enigma code. The Internet has, needless to say, opened up an entirely new front on which Churchill revisionists can hallucinate, polluting cyberspace with ever more absurd fantasies. The excellent magazine *Finest Hour*, published by the International Churchill Society, has for years been collecting and systematically refuting these and dozens of other such allegations.[12]

A third and highly influential source of Churchill revisionism is provided by the press. Newspaper editors will readily affirm that Churchill stories make great copy, especially since the dead cannot sue for libel. We therefore see news stories in reputable newspapers which, had they been written in his lifetime, would have garnered Churchill hundreds of thousands of pounds in out-of-court settlements. According to some recent newspaper articles, Churchill was a drug addict who actively helped his daughter-in-law to cuckold his own son. He supposedly ordered Mussolini's assassination, and then tried to recover compromising documents relating to a secret Anglo-Italian peace deal he had allegedly tried to arrange. Churchill rarely smoked cigars, we have been told, but liked having lit ones around in order 'to accentuate his masculinity'.

According to various revisionists, he was also a plagiarist, an opportunist, a warmonger, a hypocrite, a fantasist, the true creator of Nazism – ingenious one, that – a terrible military strategist and a pathological liar. Someone has even written a book, which has inexplicably been catalogued according to its own estimation as non-fiction, stating categorically that Churchill helped Martin Bormann to escape from Berlin in 1945 and then found him a house near London in which to live out the rest of his days in comfort.[13] The advance offered to the author of this drivel was reputed to be in the region of a quarter of a million pounds, although it is said that it was not paid in full because the allegations did not stand up to scrutiny. As recently as September 2002 the Saudi Arabian Ambassador to London, Ghazi Algosaibi, wrote to *The Spectator* to claim that Churchill ordered troops to fire on suffragettes in 1917, an accusation that was comprehensively rebutted a fortnight later by the International Churchill Society.[14]

All that historians can do when faced with these patent absurdities is to stay calm, go back to the original documents and prime authorities – usually Sir Martin Gilbert's magisterial eight-volume biography with its fourteen companion volumes – examine the historical context and available evidence, and work out the truth as forensically as possible. Ninety-five times out of a hundred, Churchill comes off scot-free.

Of course Churchill is certainly not above all criticism. Quite obviously with a career so long and varied, involving twice crossing the floor of the House of Commons, and being called upon to make momentous decisions, his judgement on several issues can legitimately be questioned. Over issues such as the the Sidney Street siege of 1910, the Gallipoli débâcle, the partition of Ireland, rejoining the gold standard, the handling of the General Strike, Indian nationalism, the Abdication Crisis, Bomber Command's targeting policy, the 1943 'soft underbelly' strategy, the insistence on Germany's unconditional surrender, the refusal to help the July plotters, British official recognition of Soviet guilt over the massacre of Polish officers in the forest of Katyn, and the proposed bombing of Auschwitz, Churchill has been criticised by distinguished academics and responsible politicians and journalists, both during his lifetime and after it. Such criticism was and is fair enough, although this author personally believes that Churchill made the right choice in almost every single one of those cases, displaying a far better track record of good judgement than most of his contemporaries. What is now being seen, however, is not a reasonable and honest debate but a series of acerbic and hostile criticisms levelled at Churchill's very patriotism and honour.

By far the most cogent criticisms of Churchill's career, and the ones most capable of scratching the outer paintwork of the edifice of what is now an untarnishable reputation, are those that have been voiced by Dr John Charmley, Professor Maurice Cowling, and the late Alan Clark, who loosely make what might be called the British Tory nationalist critique. In January 1993, Dr Charmley published *Churchill: The End of Glory*, which he followed in 1995 with *Churchill's Grand Alliance: The Anglo-American Special Relationship 1940–1957*. Both were closely argued and well-written analyses of Churchill's personal responsibility for the collapse of British power in the twentieth century. Churchill is also blamed for preventing Charmley's hero, Neville Chamberlain, from successfully pursuing appeasement to its intended conclusion, namely a debilitating German–Soviet war in which both antagonists fought each other to a standstill and were left mutually weak and thus no threat to Britain or the West.

Churchill is further accused of effectively betraying the British Empire to the United States through naïvety and an over-exaggerated view of British post-war weakness, and also of letting socialism into Britain by the back door. This view is fundamentally flawed, in that it mixes up cause and effect and hardly allows for Churchill's limited alternatives by 1945. The Tory nationalist school none the less constitutes the most significant attempt to dislodge the great man from his Parliament Square pedestal.

It is worth while, therefore, to look closely at the contention that Britain ought to have made peace with Nazi Germany in 1940 or 1941. (Professor Cowling, by contrast, believes Britain should not have gone to war in the first place in 1939.) Far from saving the Empire, not fighting the war to the end would have been disastrous both for Britain and for the prospects of a civilised, peaceful, democratic Western Europe such as has existed since 1945. Any advantages that so craven a treaty might have produced would have been marginal, prohibitively expensive and probably also very short-lived.

Since before the time of the Spanish Armada of 1588 it has been British policy to oppose any hegemonistic Continental power which sought to control the Channel ports in Holland and Belgium from which an invasion of southern England might be launched. King Philip II of Spain, Louis XIV, Napoleon Bonaparte and Kaiser Wilhelm II all suffered significant reverses in successive wars over precisely this issue. To have left Hitler in undisputed control of these ports in 1940 would have entailed decades of danger, with astronomically high defence expenditure and the need for perpetual vigilance for the rest of the decade and probably beyond.

With Britain out of the war, Hitler would probably not have needed to swoop south into Yugoslavia and Greece in the spring of 1941. As was examined in the last section, he would thus have been able to launch his invasion of Russia six weeks earlier than he did, with divisions taken from France, the Low Countries and Africa as well as those he had originally earmarked in Germany and Poland. Even as it was, the Wehrmacht nearly reached Moscow's underground stations, captured Stalingrad and subjected Leningrad to a gruelling thousand-day siege. Had the Germans pushed the Soviets back beyond the Urals, Hitler would have been master of Europe from Brest to Sverdlovsk. Instead, Britain's alliance with Russia allowed the Allies – once Hitler's ill-advised declaration of war had brought the United States into the conflict against Germany – to supply the Red Army with five thousand tanks, seven thousand aircraft, fifty-one thousand jeeps and fifty-one million pairs of boots, assistance which contributed materially to its ultimate victory.

As the author Major-General John Strawson has asked of any peace negotiations that might have taken place in 1941:

> Would Great Britain have been left in possession of both her Royal Naval and merchant fleets, with absolute freedom of the seas for trading and other purposes? Would Italy have abandoned her African colonies? Would Greece and Albania have been free? Would Rommel and the Afrika Korps have quit Libya? Would Britain have been at liberty to maintain her armed forces at their – by 1941 – not contemptible level, and to deploy them where she wanted other than in Hitler's domains? What would Britain have said to France, the Low Countries, Denmark, Norway, and to Poland? Would Hitler have agreed – the agreement to have been

> subject to rigid verification measures – to cease research into and development of V-weapons, jet aircraft, new submarines – and nuclear weapons? Would he, after the subjection of all Eastern Europe including Russia, once more have declared that he had no further territorial claims? Would he have guaranteed the integrity of the British Empire? Or would the whole negotiated peace – on the bizarre assumption that it could ever have come off at all – simply have proved to be another Peace of Amiens, the truce between Great Britain and France of 1802–1803, during which Napoleon feverishly prepared for a resumption of hostilities?[15]

Merely posing this series of questions in itself highlights the improbabilities of a workable peace being successfully negotiated, let alone the dangers inherent in leaving Hitler as master of Europe.

Just as disastrous for Britain's hopes of long-term independence would be the scenario in which Stalin defeated Hitler, and the Red Army poured westward to Berlin and beyond, with no Anglo-American army in France and Germany to stop him pushing on further. Stalin's control of the Channel ports would have been no less dangerous to Britain's long-term independence in the late 1940s and 1950s than Hitler's.

Add to this the fact that Hitler was (albeit fitfully) undertaking his own nuclear research, while Stalin was learning about the Allied nuclear breakthroughs from his Western spies, and the necessity for full British participation in a drastically foreshortened war becomes obvious. For either dictator to have been left, perhaps for years, in control of Europe would have necessarily been disastrous for Britain's hopes of continued and genuine independence. Henry Kissinger once quipped of the decade-long Iran–Iraq War: 'A pity they both can't lose.' The risk of a Nazi–Soviet war resulting in something other than mutual defeat was too great a one for the British Government to take in 1940.

Furthermore, the great cause of trying to encourage the United States to adopt a 'Germany First' policy in the struggle to save civilisation would have been utterly wrecked if Britain had come to terms with Hitler after the British Expeditionary Force's evacuation from Dunkirk. It took the dogged resistance during the Blitz and the Battle of Britain to convince America of Britain's worthiness as an ally. Although Britain did indeed wind up in hock to America after the war, she would have been in no better financial state as a result of remaining in perhaps decades-long military readiness, waiting for the likely moment when Hitler suddenly revoked his peace treaty and attacked again. The Führer had, after all, reneged upon every other treaty he had ever signed.

Furthermore, the war had been going on at sea for nine months by the time of the Dunkirk evacuation; sailors had perished, ships carrying child evacuees to Canada had been torpedoed, and as a result British blood was up. To have made a palpably ignoble peace would have dealt a crushing blow to imperial pride and self-esteem, and would doubtless have caused severe internal ructions fatal to the sense of national unity fostered once the opposition parties entered Churchill's Government in May 1940. The demoralisation of the United Kingdom and her imperial allies was too high a price to pay to escape the perils of the Blitz; the only domestic political winners would have been the Communist Party and the British Union of Fascists.

As for the accusation that Churchill killed the thing he most loved: in fact, after the India Act of 1935 the British Empire was already well on the way towards self-governance. The Second World War accelerated that process, without doubt, but the great days of Empire were long over by the time that Churchill came to power in May 1940. On a more emotional level, what glory would there have been in the possession of an Empire mortgaged to Britain by the grace of Adolf Hitler?

To have made peace with Hitler in 1940 and thus to have forsworn the hope, however remote it might have seemed at the time, one day to liberate Europe from Nazism, would have been to condemn the continent to what Churchill that year famously termed 'a new Dark Age, made more sinister, and perhaps more protracted, by the lights of perverted science'. Hardly a European Jew could have survived the extermination process which had been begun on an *ad hoc* basis in Poland in September 1939, but became fully industrialised by 1942, if Hitler had been allowed undisputed possession of Europe and no Allied invasion had taken place in 1944, 1945, or any time thereafter. The Great Powers are presently enjoying their longest period of peace since the rise of the nation state in the sixteenth century; would that really have been possible if Hitler had been allowed to keep the spoils of his victory in 1940?

Churchill knew that to have made peace with Germany would be to have forfeited his own and his country's honour. In his panegyric to Chamberlain, after speaking of history's 'flickering lamp' trying 'to kindle with pale gleams the passion of former days', Churchill asked:

> What is the worth of all this? The only guide to a man is his conscience; the only shield to his memory is the rectitude and sincerity of his actions. It is very imprudent to walk through life without this shield, because we are so often mocked by the failure of our hopes and the upsetting of our calculations; but with this shield, however the fates may play, we always march in the ranks of honour.

Despite the unrelenting efforts of his revisionist detractors, Winston Churchill marches there still.

Notes

Introduction

1 Christopher Hitchens, *Atlantic Monthly*, April 2002, p. 121
2 *Daily Telegraph*, 29 August 2002
3 *Daily Telegraph*, 12 February 2002
4 Johnson, *Napoleon*, p. 193
5 Brian MacArthur (ed.), *The Penguin Book of Historic Speeches*, 1995, pp. 300–1
6 Churchill, *Savrola*, p. 156
7 Gilbert, *Winston S. Churchill*, vol. 8, p. 369
8 Rosebery, *Lord Randolph Churchill*, p. 81
9 A. N. Wilson, *Watch in the Night*, p. 32
10 *New York World*, 6 February 1928

Hitler and Churchill to 1939

1 Warlimont, *Inside Hitler's Headquarters*, p. x
2 Pearson, *Citadel of the Heart*, p. 243
3 Brendon, *Churchill*, p. 126
4 Irving, *Churchill: Triumph*, p. 62
5 Mosley, *Life of Contrasts*, p. 47
6 Brendon, op. cit., p. 110
7 *BBC History Magazine*, May 2001, p. 7
8 Patrick Kinna in Sir Martin Gilbert's 1992 TV biography of Churchill
9 Ibid.
10 Letter from Ian Weston-Smith, 1 May 2001
11 Churchill, *Savrola*, p. 50
12 Mary Soames, 'Winston Churchill: the Great Human Being', 9th Annual Crosby Kemper Lecture, 21 April 1991, p. 7
13 Churchill, *Savrola*, p. 226
14 Jablonsky, *Churchill and Hitler*, p. 260
15 Luke, *Hansel Pless*, p. 73
16 Hitler, *Mein Kampf*, pp. 740–2
17 Rhodes James (ed.), *Churchill Speaks*, p. 603
18 *Daily Express*, 5 October 1938
19 Grint, *Art of Leadership*, p. 267
20 Roseman, *Wannsee*, p. 113
21 Rauschning, *Gespräche mit Hitler*, p. 223
22 Grint, op. cit., p. 297
23 *Spectator*, 26 January 2002

24 *The Times*, 16 July 1998
25 Irving, *Churchill: War Path*, p. 20
26 Churchill, *Savrola*, p. 88
27 Brendon, op. cit., p. 143
28 Jablonsky, op. cit., p. 209
29 *The Observer*, 5 August 1951
30 Speer, *Inside the Third Reich*, p. 151
31 Ibid, pp. 187–8
32 Churchill, *Savrola*, p. 79
33 Gilbert, *Winston S. Churchill*, vol. 4, pp. 446–7
34 Prof. R. V. Jones, 'Churchill as I Knew Him', 10th Annual Crosby Kemper Lecture, 29 March 1992, p. 10
35 Speer, op. cit., pp. 155–6
36 Kershaw, *Nemesis*, p. xvi
37 Burleigh, *Third Reich*, pp. 253–5
38 Overy, *Interrogations*, p. 38
39 Waite, *Psychopathic God*, p. 42
40 Churchill, *Savrola*, p. 99
41 Stone, *Hitler*, p. 86
42 Irving, *Winston S. Churchill: Triumph*, p. xviii
43 Proctor, Robert N., 'The Anti-Tobacco Campaign of the Nazis', www.freerepublic.com
44 *Time* magazine, 9 January 1995
45 Soames (ed.), *Speaking for Themselves*, p. 390
46 *Sunday Telegraph*, 12 July 1998
47 Jablonsky, op. cit., p. 270
48 Gilbert, *Winston S. Churchill*, vol. 6, p. 166
49 Ibid., pp. 59–60
50 Goleman, Boyatzis and McKee, *New Leaders*, p. ix
51 Colville, *Fringes of Power*, p. 319

Hitler and Churchill from 1940

1 Gilbert, *Winston S. Churchill*, vol. 6, p. 216
2 Keegan, *Second World War*, p. 38
3 Roberts, *Holy Fox*, p. 201
4 Smith (ed.), *Hostage to Fortune*, p. 476
5 Engel, *Heeresadjutant bei Hitler*, p. 75
6 Burdick and Jacobsen, *Halder War Diary*, p. 85
7 Frieser, *Blitzkrieg-Legende*, p. 392
8 Engel, op. cit.
9 Brendon, *Churchill*, op. cit., p. 140
10 Hayward, *Churchill on Leadership*, p. 73
11 Spears, *Assignment to Catastrophe*, p. 216
12 Wheeler-Bennett (ed.), *Action This Day*, p. 50
13 Ibid., pp. 52–3
14 Ibid., p. 20
15 Ibid., pp. 19–20
16 Churchill, *Savrola*, p. 307

17 Hinsley and Simkins, *British Intelligence*, vol. 4, p. 47
18 Thompson, *1940*, pp. 134–8
19 Kershaw, *Hitler Myth*, pp. 13–14
20 Jablonsky, op. cit., p. 159
21 Colville, *Fringes of Power*, p. 382
22 Churchill, *Contemporaries*, p. 343
23 Brendon, *Churchill*, p. 156
24 Kimball (ed.), *Churchill and Roosevelt*, pp. 49–50
25 Danchev and Todman (eds), *Alanbrooke War Diaries*, p. xi
26 Jenkins, *Churchill*, p. 629
27 *Daily Telegraph*, 29 August 2002
28 Trevor-Roper (ed.), *Last Days of Hitler*, p. 95
29 Ibid., p. 264
30 Ibid., p. 505
31 Ibid., p. 630
32 Churchill, *Savrola*, p. 22
33 Gilbert, *Winston S. Churchill*, vol. 4, p. 1103
34 Colville, op. cit., p. 180
35 Ibid., p. 404
36 Stafford, *Churchill and the Secret Service*
37 Richard Garnett's papers at Hilton Hall, Huntingdon
38 Garnett, *Secret History of PWE*
39 Gilbert, *Winston S. Churchill*, vol. 7, p. 455
40 Brendon, *Churchill*, p. 147
41 Jablonsky, op. cit., p. 22
42 Ibid., p. 256
43 Ibid., pp. 241–2
44 Author's 1993 conversation with the late Lord Hume, p. 184
45 Warlimont, op. cit., p. 463

Conclusion

1 John Keegan, *Daily Telegraph*, 18 July 1998
2 John Lukacs, *Hitler of History*
3 *Mail on Sunday*, 2 October 1994
4 Masters, *Getting Personal*, pp. 57–8
5 Bryan Appleyard, 'Leaders of the Pack', *Sunday Times* magazine, 20 January 2002
6 Browning, *Ordinary Men*
7 Goldhagen, *Hitler's Willing Executioners*
8 Jenkins, op. cit., p. 635
9 Willans and Roetter, *Wit of Winston Churchill*, p. 106
10 Jones, op. cit., p. 11
11 Churchill, *Savrola*, p. 43
12 In order to subscribe to *Finest Hour*, contact *www.winstonchurchill.org* or write to PO Box 1257, Melshaven, SN12 6QQ
13 Creighton, *Op. JB*
14 *Spectator*, 7 and 21 September 2002
15 Strawson, *Hitler and Churchill*, pp. 502–3

Bibliography

All books were published in London unless otherwise stated. The dates given are not for publication, but only for the edition used.

Adair, John, *The Effective Leadership Masterclass*, 1977
Addison, Paul, *Churchill on the Home Front*, 1992
Alldritt, Keith, *Churchill the Writer: His Life as a Man of Letters*, 1992
Ashley, Maurice, *Churchill as Historian*, 1968
Beevor, Antony, *Stalingrad*, 1998
Berlin: The Downfall 1945, 2002
Below, Nicholas von, *At Hiler's Side: The Memoirs of Hitler's Luftwaffe Adjutant 1937–1945*, 2001
Berlin, Isaiah, *Mr Churchill in 1940*, 1949
Best, Geoffrey, *Churchill: A Study in Greatness*, 2001
Bethell, Nicholas, *The War Hitler Won*, 1972
Birkenhead, Earl of, *Churchill 1874–1922*, 1989
Blake, Robert, and Louis, William Roger, *Churchill*, 1993
Brendon, Piers, *The Dark Valley: A Panorama of the 1930s*, 2000
Winston Churchill: A Brief Life, 2001
Browning, Christopher R., *Ordinary Men: Reserve Police Battalion 101 and the Final Solution in Poland*, 1992
Buchanan, Patrick J., *A Republic, Not an Empire: Reclaiming America's Destiny* (Washington DC), 1999
Bullock, Alan, *Hitler: A Study in Tyranny*, 1952
Hitler and Stalin: Parallel Lives, 1991
Burdick, Charles, and Jacobsen, Hans-Adolf, *The Halder War Diary 1939–42*, 1988
Burleigh, Michael, *The Third Reich: A New History*, 2000
Callaghan, Raymond A., *Churchill: Retreat from Empire*, 1984
Carlton, David, *Churchill and the Soviet Union*, 2000
Carter, Violet Bonham, *Winston Churchill as I Knew Him*, 1965
Charmley, John, *Churchill: The End of Glory*, 1993
Churchill's Grand Alliance: The Anglo-American Special Relationship 1940–57, 1995
Churchill, Winston S., *Savrola*, 1900
Secret Session Speeches, 1946
Great Contemporaries, 1962
Thoughts and Adventures, 1990

Clark, Alan, *Barbarossa: The Russian-German Conflict 1941–1945*, 1965
Cohen, Eliot A., *Supreme Command: Soldiers, Statesmen and Leadership in Wartime* (New York), 2002
Colville, John, *Fringes of Power*, 1985
Coote, Colin (ed.), *Maxims and Reflections of Winston Churchill*, 1947
The Other Club, 1971
Cosgrave, Patrick, *Churchill at War: Alone 1939–40*, 1974
Cowles, Winston, *Churchill: The Era and the Man*, 1953
Cowling, Maurice, *The Impact of Hitler: British Politics and British Policy 1933–1940*, 1977
Creighton, Christopher, *Op. JB*, 1996
Danchev, Alex, and Todman, Daniel (eds), *War Diaries 1939–1945: Field Marshal Lord Alanbrooke*, 2001
Day, David, *Menzies and Churchill at War*, 1986
Eade, Charles (ed.), *Churchill by his Contemporaries*, 1955
Ehlers, Dieter, *Technik und Moral einer Verschwörung. Der Aufstand am 20. Juli 1944* (Bonn), 1964
Engel, Gerhard, *Heeresadjutant bei Hitler 1938–1943* (Stuttgart), 1974
Evans, David, *Telling Lies about Hitler*, 2002
Fest, Joachim, *Plotting Hitler's Death: The German Resistance to Hitler 1933–1945*, 1966
Fraser, David, *Alanbrooke*, 1997
Frieser, Karl-Heinz, *Blitzkrieg-Legende der Westfeldzug 1940* (Munich), 1996
Garnett, David, *The Secret History of P.W.E.*, 2002
Gilbert, Martin, *Winston S. Churchill*, 8 vols, 1966–1988
Churchill's Political Philosophy, 1981
Churchill: The Wilderness Years, 1981
The Second World War, 1989
Churchill: A Life, 1991
In Search of Churchill, 1994
Giuliani, Rudolf, *Leadership*, 2002
Goldhagen, Daniel, *Hitler's Willing Executioners: Ordinary Germans and the Holocaust*, 1996
Goleman, Daniel, Boyatzis, Richard, and McKee, Annie, *The New Leaders: Transforming the Art of Leadership into the Science of Results*, 2002
Grint, Keith, *The Arts of Leadership*, 2001
Grunberger, Richard, *A Social History of the Third Reich*, 1971
Guedella, Philip, *Mr Churchill: A Portrait*, 1941
Hamann, Brigitte, *Hitler's Vienna: A Dictator's Apprenticeship*, 1999
Hardwick, Joan, *Clementine Churchill: The Private Life of a Public Figure*, 1997
Hart, B. H. Liddell, *History of the Second World War*, 1970
Hayward, Steven, *Churchill on Leadership*, 1997
Hinsley, F. H., and Simkins, C. A. G., *British Intelligence in the Second World War*, vol. 4, 1990
Hitler, Adolf, *Mein Kampf*, (Berlin: 162nd–163rd reprint, Eher Verlag), 1935

Hough, Richard, *Winston and Clementine: The Triumph of the Churchills*, 1988
Irving, David, *Hitler's War 1942–1945*, 1977
The War Path: Hitler's Germany 1933–1939, 1978
Churchill's War: The Struggle for Power, 1987
Churchill's War: Triumph in Adversity, 2001
Jablonsky, David, *Churchill and Hitler: Essays on the Political-Military Direction of Total War*, 1994
Jenkins, Roy, *Churchill*, 2002
Johnson, Paul, *Napoleon*, 2002
Keegan, John, *The Second World War*, 1989
Churchill's Generals, 1992
Kemper III, R. Crosby (ed.), *Winston Churchill: Resolution, Defiance, Magnanimity, Good Will*, 1996
Kershaw, Ian, *The 'Hitler Myth': Image and Reality in the Third Reich*, 1989
Hitler 1889–1936: Hubris, 1998
Hitler 1936–1945: Nemesis, 2000
Keynes, John Maynard, *The Economic Consequences of the Peace* (New York), 1971
Kimball, Warren F. (ed.), *Churchill & Roosevelt: The Complete Correspondence*, 3 vols, 1984
Kraus, René, *The Men Around Churchill*, 1971
Lamb, Richard, *The Ghosts of Peace 1935–1945*, 1987
Lash, Joseph P., *Roosevelt and Churchill 1939–1941*, 1977
Lawlor, Sheila, *Churchill and the Politics of War 1940–1941*, 1994
Lee, J. M., *The Churchill Coalition 1940–1945*, 1980
Lipstadt, Deborah, *Denying the Holocaust: The Growing Assault on Truth and Memory*, 1993
Lord, Walter, *The Miracle of Dunkirk*, 1982
Lowenheim, Francis L., Langley, Harold D., and Jonas, Manfred (eds), *Roosevelt and Churchill: Their Secret Wartime Correspondence*, 1975
Lukacs, John, *The Hitler of History*, 1997
The Duel: Hitler vs Churchill 10 May–31 July 1940, 1990
Churchill: Visionary, Statesman, Historian, 2002
Luke, Michael, *Hansel Pless: Prisoner of History*, 2002
Machtan, Lothar, *The Hidden Hitler*, 2001
MacArthur, Brian (ed.), *The Penguin Book of Historic Speeches*, 1995
Manchester, William, *The Caged Lion: Winston Spencer Churchill 1932–1940*, 1988
Martin, Sir John, *Downing Street: The War Years*, 1991
Masters, Brian, *Getting Personal*, 2002
Meehan, Patricia, *The Unnecessary War: Whitehall and the German Resistance to Hitler*, 1992
Megargee, Geoffrey P., *Inside Hitler's Command* (Kansas), 2000
Middlebrook, Martin, *The Battle for Hamburg*, 2000
Montague Browne, Anthony, *Long Sunset: Memoirs of Winston Churchill's Last Private Secretary*, 1995

Moran, Lord, *Winston Churchill: The Struggle for Survival 1940–1965*, 1966
Moriarty, David, *A Psychological Study of Adolf Hitler*, 1991
Mosley, Diana, *A Life of Contrasts*, 2002
Overy, Richard, *Interrogations: The Nazi Elite in Allied Hands 1945*, 2001
Parker, R. A. C., *Churchil and Appeasement: Could Churchill Have Prevented the Second World War?*, 2000
Parker, R. A. C. (ed.), *Winston Churchill: Studies in Statesmanship*, 1995
Pearson, John, *Citadel of the Heart: Winston and the Churchill Dynasty*, 1991
Pelling, Henry, *Winston Churchill*, 1974
Ponting, Clive, *Churchill*, 1994
Ramsden, John, *The Age of Churchill and Eden*, 1995
Man of the Century: Winston Churchill and his Legend since 1945, 2002
Rauschning, Hermann, *Gespräche mit Hitler* (New York), 1940
Redlich, Fritz, *Hitler: Diagnosis of a Destructive Prophet*, 2000
Rees, Laurence, *The Nazis: A Warning from History*, 1997
War of the Century: When Hitler Fought Stalin, 1999
Horror in the East, 2001
Rhodes James, Robert, *Churchill: A Study in Failure 1900–1939*, 1990
Rhodes James, Robert (ed.), *Churchill Speaks 1897–1963: Collected Speeches in Peace and War*, 1981
Roberts, Andrew, *'The Holy Fox': A Biography of Lord Halifax*, 1991
Eminent Churchillians, 1991
Roberts, Frank, *Dealing with Dictators: The Destruction and Revival of Europe 1930–70*, 1991
Rose, Norman, *Churchill: An Unruly Life*, 1994
Rosebery, Lord, *Lord Randolph Churchill*, 1906
Roseman, Mark, *The Villa, The Lake, The Meeting: Wannsee and the Final Solution*, 2002
Sandys, Celia, *Churchill Wanted Dead or Alive*, 1999
Smith, Amanda (ed.), *Hostage to Fortune: The Letters of Joseph P. Kennedy*, 2001
Soames, Mary (ed.), *Speaking for Themselves: The Personal Letters of Winston and Clementine Churchill*, 1998
Spears, E. L., *Assignment to Catastrophe, vol. I: July 1939–May 1940*, 1954
Speer, Albert, *Inside the Third Reich*, 1995
Spotts, Roderic, *Hitler and the Power of Aesthetics*, 2002
Stafford, David, *Churchill and the Secret Service*, 1997
Stewart, Graham, *Burying Caesar: Churchill, Chamberlain and the Battle for the Tory Party*, 1999
Stone, Norman, *Hitler*, 1980
Strawson, John, *Hitler and Churchill in Victory and Defeat*, 1997
Thompson, Laurence, *1940*, 1966
Thorne, Christopher, *Allies of a Kind: The United States, Britain, and the War Against Japan 1941–1945*, 1978
Trevor-Roper, Hugh, *The Last Days of Hitler*, 1947
Trevor-Roper, Hugh (ed.), *Hitler's Secret Conversations 1941–1944*, 1961

Waite, Robert, *The Psychopathic God: Adolf Hitler*, 1993
Warlimont, General Walter, *Inside Hitler's Headquarters 1939–1945*, 1964
Watt, Donald Cameron, *How War Came: The Immediate Origins of the Second World War 1938–1939*, 1989
Wheeler-Bennett, John (ed.), *Action This Day*, 1968
Willans, Geoffrey, and Roetter, Charles, *The Wit of Winston Churchill*, 1954
Willmott, H. P., *The Great Crusade: A New Complete History of the Second World War*, 1989
Wilson, A. N., *A Watch in the Night*, 1996
Wilson, Thomas, *Churchill and the Prof*, 1995
Woods, Frederick, *Artillery of Words: The Writings of Sir Winston Churchill*, 1992
Young, Kenneth, *Churchill and Beaverbrook*, 1966

Index

In this index WSC stands for Churchill; AH for Hitler

KT-419-988

the Write Stuff

the Write Stuff

Evaluations of Graphology—
The Study of Handwriting Analysis

OOO

Edited by

Barry L. Beyerstein & Dale F. Beyerstein

Prometheus Books • Buffalo, New York

Published 1992 by Prometheus Books

96 95 94 93 92 5 4 3 2 1

Library of Congress Cataloging-in-Publication Data

The Write Stuff: evaluations of graphology, the study of handwriting analysis / edited by Barry L.Beyerstein and Dale F. Beyerstein.

p. cm.

Includes bibliographical references.

ISBN 0-87975-612-8—ISBN 0-87975-613-6 (pbk.)

1. Graphology. I. Beyerstein, Barry L., 1949- II. Beyerstein, Dale F., 1952-

BF891.W75 19991

155.2'82—dc20

91-21698

CIP

Printed in the United States of America on acid-free paper.

This volume is lovingly dedicated to the memory of
Hilliard Harris William Beyerstein(1907–1990)
who taught us it is most important to think for ourselves
when the majority perceives something as obvious.

Contents

Acknowledgments

The editors of this volume would like to express their appreciation to their fellow contributors for the cooperation, good humor, careful thought, and hard work they have so generously lent to this project. The friendly help of Doris Doyle and Mark Hall at Prometheus Books has been instrumental at every stage, both in completing the volume and improving it. The excellent editorial and substantive suggestions of Dr. Lillian Leiber have added significantly to the quality of the chapters with which she assisted. Our profound thanks to them all. The assistance of Elliott Marchant and Deborah Nijdam is also gratefully acknowledged. Finally, we would like to express our love and thanks to Susie, Elsie, Lindsay, and Loren for their support and encouragement and for the many weekend and evening activities with BLB and DFB that they gave up so this book could be produced.

Section One

Introduction and History

1

General Introduction

Dale F. Beyerstein and Barry L. Beyerstein

The editors' interest in graphology (handwriting analysis) was piqued a couple of years ago when one of us (BLB) was phoned by the *Vancouver* (Canada) *Sun* to comment on the results of a piece of investigative journalism that would prove to be very embarrassing to local politicians. Apparently a local graphologist had approached employees of the Vancouver School Board with a solution to a serious problem. In the past few years, in schools across North America, there have been several cases of teachers who have been charged with sexual offenses against their students. School administrators are concerned with the welfare of their students, and rightly wish to prevent teachers from harming innocent children. One feels powerless to think that the many tests, evaluations, and checks that are given to applicants for teaching positions, and those already employed in the system, do not detect those people with sexual tendencies that could do so much damage to innocent lives. So, if one is offered a foolproof method that will detect these malefactors prior to their causing this harm, it would be a dereliction of duty to turn it down, would it not?

That was the gist of the offer made by a local graphologist to a harried and scientifically ill-informed school board official: the graphologist claimed to be able to detect pedophiles with unfailing accuracy, and offered a "scientific test" to prove it! Give him (without the writers' knowledge) some samples of handwriting, and he would find the pedophile! The story gets a bit murky at this point, since the Vancouver School Board, and the bureaucrat responsible, understandably do not like to talk about it. The graphologist, on the other hand, does, and tells several *conflicting* stories about it. But the kernel of the story appears to be this: the graphologist was presented with ten (or, on other accounts, nine) handwriting samples —the school board doesn't, for obvious reasons, like to say *whose*, or how they got them—and he did his analyses. Much to his surprise, he found that nine (or was it eight?) of the samples were written by pedophiles *or potential pedophiles!* The graphologist was very proud of himself, having seen through the little twist in the experiment that might have caught him off his guard! He thought that he would be given one pedophile in the sample; but by his reckoning, there were more, and he caught them all! It was at this point that the local media thought this little backroom experiment was worthy of the public's attention.

Fortunately, BLB was not totally unprepared to comment when the reporter called. As a twelve-year-old, he was introduced to graphology in the way a great number of "professional" graphologists were: by buying a book from the occult section (now it would be the New Age section) of the local bookshop, and immediately began analyzing his friends.

The editors of this volume found that most of the graphologists they have debated over the years were introduced to the subject through short, non-credit night school courses offered by a local school board, community college, or university continuing education division. Some had taken a home study course through the International Graphoanalysis Society of Chicago, while many, including the graphologist who approached the Vancouver School Board, had made up their own system which they declined to divulge to anyone (and which, of course, had never undergone scientific evaluations). Several who were charging corporations for their services admitted having read only one popular book on the subject before "going into business."[1] In addition to the graphologists' lack of professional accreditation and scanty background in relevant academic specialties, the authors also typically found them eager to join the skeptics in condemning competing analysts' brands of graphology as "unscientific." Nonetheless, they remained steadfast in asserting their own scientific legitimacy. We have always asked in such encounters for published evidence that we might have overlooked that would substantiate their claims. Most promised but sent nothing, a few sent us self-published tracts, one sent us an uncritical article from *Playboy*; the few items received from practicing graphologists that were more substantial, we have reviewed in our contributions to other sections of this book. The obvious isolation of these graphologists from relevant fields of research and their lack of agreement on key issues within the discipline were disconcerting, to say the least.

In response to media queries about the school board case, BLB, having grown up and become a psychophysiologist instead of a graphologist, first searched for his boyhood text on graphology. It was hard to locate, but one does not part readily with something that cost that many weeks' allowance. Rereading it after all those years, he was astonished to find there was virtually no difference between its claims and procedures and those touted by the very latest graphology books. BLB next decided to run a computer database search to see if there was any independent support for graphological claims in the scientific literature. The results of the survey showed the scientific case for graphology to be exceedingly weak. Furthermore, polling university colleagues who specialize in psychological measurement and the psychology of individual differences produced a mere handful of reputable psychology texts in English that even mentioned graphology, and they did so only to dismiss it as a pseudoscience. Believers in graphology are virtually non-existent in North American psychology departments but some can be found in Europe and Israel. In preparing his chapters for this volume, BLB was forced to rely on garage sales, New Age booksellers, self-published tracts by graphologists themselves, and the occult sections of the local libraries to find the majority of the pro-graphology works he reviewed.

Returning to the saga that drew the editors into the graphology debate—the chairman of the Vancouver School Board was a thoughtful man as well as an astute politician. He was well aware of the damage that can be done to an individual's reputation by calling him a potential pedophile, and of the damage that can be done to the school board's budget if such a charge could not be substantiated. As soon as the story broke on the local Canadian Broadcasting Corporation (CBC) TV station, he immediately put a stop to use of graphology in the Vancouver school system, blaming their flirtation with it as the work of an overzealous underling. The media were understandably very sensitive to the issue of fairness in hiring and promotion in the workplace, and editorialized sternly about use of graphology in personnel matters. The *Vancouver Sun* even published its first ever handwritten editorial (see Fig. 1)! Not only that, reporters began to dig around, and discovered that seven municipalities surrounding Vancouver were using graphology, or, as some of their mayors would have it when cornered, "experimenting with" or "considering" it. As well, several private companies, including banks, credit unions, and construction companies, were discovered to be using it.

At this point, the junior editor of this volume (DFB) got involved. The British Columbia Civil Liberties Association (BCCLA), of which he is a director, has had a long history of dealing with questions of fairness in employee relations, including privacy considerations. They immediately jumped into the conflict, in cooperation with the Society of British Columbia Skeptics, an organization that supports the goals of the Committee for

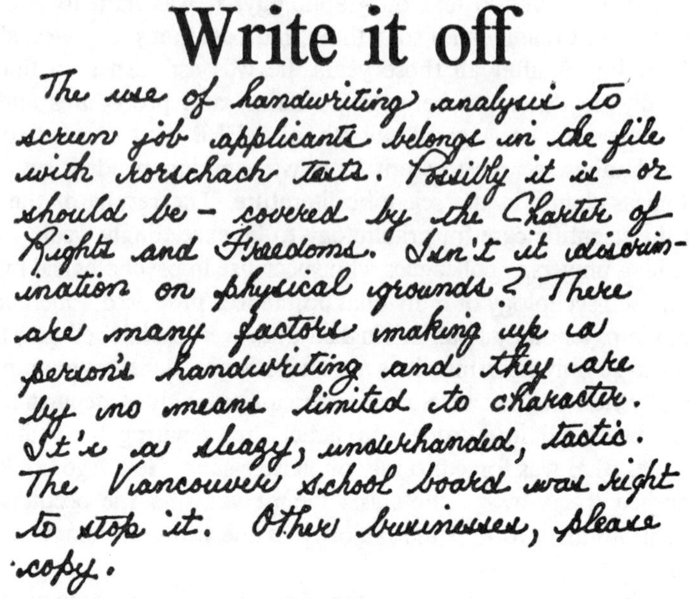

Write it off

The use of handwriting analysis to screen job applicants belongs in the file with Rorschach tests. Possibly it is—or should be—covered by the Charter of Rights and Freedoms. Isn't it discrimination on physical grounds? There are many factors making up a person's handwriting and they are by no means limited to character. It's a sleazy, underhanded, tactic. The Vancouver school board was right to stop it. Other businesses, please copy.

Figure 1.

the Scientific Investigation of Claims of the Paranormal (CSICOP): education in scientific and critical thinking, and investigation of occult paranormal or pseudoscientific claims. The BCCLA's position on testing of employees in the workplace, whether for drugs, dishonesty, or general competence, is that testing must, first of all, be for attributes that are relevant to the job, and second, be the least onerous method of getting this required information—for example, the testing must not be unduly invasive of privacy. Third, the results of these tests must be kept confidential. But fourth, and most important for our present purposes, the test must be able to accurately detect the traits it promises to detect, and not lead to serious accusations—such as pederasty, dishonesty, or incompetence—that could ruin a person's career despite being unfounded.

The two editors of this volume provided the BCCLA with a brief on graphology, which provided our answer to the fourth question posed above: whether graphology's claims to accuracy in determining these traits could be justified. The BCCLA and the Skeptics provided arguments to the local municipalities and businesses using graphology, based on the available scientific information, which showed conclusively that the use of graphology as a personnel selection tool was unfair, given its demonstrated poor accuracy in scientific tests. The upshot of this campaign was that six of the seven municipalities, and most of the private companies, gave up on graphology. But the most interesting finding from this process was not about graphologists, but personnel managers. It became clear to us very quickly that they had chosen graphology on the basis of testimonials of fellow personnel managers and from the sales pitches of the graphologists. None of them had checked out the scientific literature on graphology until we presented it to them; and very few of them were conversant with the scientific literature on personnel selection and testing presented in chapter 11. Thus we saw the need for a collection such as this that would provide the necessary readings on the subject in one book. This also leaves us with the question of why graphology *seems* to work when it cannot pass careful scientific tests. This issue is dealt with in several places in this volume, notably chapters 13 and 16.

The B.C. Skeptics wanted to do more than refer to already published studies of graphology. They wanted to do replications of these studies, as well as new research. They offered to do studies of local graphologists, and contacted the professional associations of graphologists to engage their cooperation in these tests. But to no avail—most graphologists just are not very interested in scientific tests of their claims, it would seem. The closest the Skeptics got to a test was when a Toronto graphologist agreed to be tested, and after getting quite a bit of media attention, stopped off in Vancouver on a cross-country media and speaking tour to meet with them. Following the advice of James Randi, the Skeptics produced a written protocol for the test. The graphologist, confident that she would pass the test with flying colors, initialed the protocol and returned to Toronto. All that was necessary for the signature on the final protocol was for her to name an agent to oversee BCS operations in Vancouver (choosing subjects, observing to ensure that the protocols in Vancouver were followed properly, etc.), and for the graphologist to choose the passage from a book that the subjects who were to be tested would copy out. But, after having got all the media attention, she then backed out! After several attempts at telephone conversations to determine why she was stalling at her end, which were terminated by the graphologist hanging up, it became clear to us that this graphologist was far more interested in the publicity she derived from promising to do the test than in actually doing the test. The working graphologists that we have interviewed and/or debated on TV and radio have turned out to be an unimpressive lot. Most were sincere, but ill informed, even about their own field, let alone the scientific method and scientific principles of personnel selection. We began to wonder whether we were for some reason getting a biased sample, or whether Canadian graphologists and those from the northwest corner of the United States really were representative of graphologists in general.

We had an opportunity to answer this question in November of 1988.

This collection of papers grew out of a session on graphology at the 1988 CSICOP meeting in Chicago. BLB planned and chaired that session, and Edward Karnes and Richard Klimoski presented papers there. Their contributions in this volume are revised and expanded versions of their papers in that session. As is the case with many of the sessions at CSICOP conferences, the aim was to invite the leading practitioners and defenders of the field undergoing scrutiny to present the best evidence they have for their discipline—i.e., whatever they think should convince open-minded skeptics. Skeptics (in this case, Klimoski, Karnes, and B. Beyerstein) then offered their reasons for thinking that the evidence for the claims made by defenders is deficient. Rose Matousek, president of the American Association of Handwriting Analysts, and Felix Klein, vice-president of the Council of Graphological Societies, presented papers at this session, but they did not accept an offer to write up their talks for this volume. In any case, we do not feel the loss, since they chose not to present the material we requested when we invited them to participate in the Chicago panel, viz., scientifically acceptable data from research, by themselves or anyone else, attesting to the accuracy of graphology as a personality test or personnel selection device. The talks by these official representatives of two of the largest graphological associations in the U.S. concentrated instead on descriptions of their methods and numerous testimonials from satisfied customers. We had specifically recommended that they do not include the latter, because they cannot count as scientific evidence. Every astrologer, palm reader, tea leaf reader, and medium we have ever met has had his or her legion of clients who attest to the seeming accuracy of the reader's wares—why this is so, despite lack of scientific credibility of these character reading techniques, is explained by several authors in this book, e.g., Dean et al. (chapter 13). Matousek also chose to spend much of her time in the session attacking (on irrelevant grounds) fellow panelist Richard Klimoski for publishing the results of a carefully controlled study of graphologists he had conducted. Matousek's organization had originally approved the methodology, in addition to funding and participating in the study, but had tried, unsuccessfully, to suppress its publication when the results failed to substantiate the graphologists' claims.

The two graphologists on the CSICOP panel also unwittingly provided a demonstration of their penchant for post hoc reasoning when they showed slides of sample analyses they had done. They pointed out "obvious" signs of writers' characteristics exemplifed in the writing samples. The problem was that they admitted knowing in advance of doing the analyses what the writers were like!

The aim of this collection is the same as the CSICOP session: to present to the open-minded reader an overview of the best evidence available on both sides of the dispute about graphology. With this in mind, we invited papers from the leading critics of graphology, and specialists in personality, cognitive psychology, and psychological testing who were willing to assess graphologists' claims against the standards that are used in their fields. The response from this group was most encouraging. All the people we asked graciously agreed to write original essays for this volume. On the other hand, the response from the graphological community was less heartening. Perhaps because we are not graphologists ourselves, or known supporters of it, most graphologists did not think that our project deserved their support. Whatever the reason, we could not get from graphologists original essays defending graphology. So, we did the next best thing: we went to the published literature.

Our criteria for selection of pro-graphology chapters were the following: first, we wanted papers from practicing graphologists who were respected by their peers—those who, despite the wide disagreement to be found in the graphological community, would be recognized by graphologists as competent spokespersons for graphology. Second, we wanted representatives of a cross-section of the various schools of graphology. Third, we wanted those who had done original research themselves, and who were familiar with the best research of others in the field; i.e., we asked for papers that referred to what the proponents considered to be the best empirical research, so the open-minded reader would have a good bibliography to follow up. And fourth, we wanted papers that were originally published in respectable places. Most of the works on graphology are popular books, where references to empirical studies are not given (despite the fact that many graphologists who charge fees receive much of their training from such books), or self-published pamphlets or monographs. Interested readers can examine these popular books in the New Age section of their nearest bookshop, so there is no point in including excerpts from that material here. The self-published items from individual graphologists or societies are more difficult to obtain, but we decided against including any of the manuscripts we have in our possession on grounds of fairness. It would be too easy to make graphology look simply foolish by including a representative sample of this "pop-psychology" material. So we have included instead material that was addressed to a scientific or scholarly audience. Fifth, a point related to the fourth: we wanted graphologists who were respected by the scientific community; who would know the language of the sciences and be able to speak to those people who were interested in the evidence that graphologists had to offer. And last, we thought it was important to include material from foreign graphologists. North American graphologists often defend themselves against the charge that very little serious scholarly work is available to defend graphology by saying that all the good work is done in Europe.

We are pleased that one of Europe's most prominent graphologists, Oskar Lockowandt, responded to our request to summarize the scientific support for graphology as he sees it. We are also pleased that James Crumbaugh, the graphologist whom fellow handwriting analysts cited to us most frequently as their preferred spokesperson, agreed to contribute his statement in favor of the Graphoanalytic approach.[2] (Dr. Crumbaugh was invited to participate in the 1988 CSICOP panel on graphology, but other commitments prevented him from appearing. Unfortunately, the International Graphoanalysis Society declined repeated requests to send a representative in his stead.) We also thank Patricia Wellingham-Jones for permission to reprint one of her recently published graphological studies which we include as a representative example of current research being done by graphologists.

This book is divided into six sections. The first, which includes the present introduction, deals primarily with historical, cross-cultural, and definitional issues. It also includes a chapter by Joe Nickell that distinguishes his profession—that of a questioned document examiner—from the practice of graphology. The two are quite distinct in aims, philosophy, and practice, but are often confused in the public mind.

The second section presents the case for graphology as stated by two of the world's most respected and widely published graphologists, James Crumbaugh and Oskar Lockowandt.

Section Three weighs the scientific status of graphology according to the criteria of the philosophy of science (D. Beyerstein) and examines the underlying rationale for believing that particular characteristics of people are related to the configuration of their script (B. Beyerstein).

In Section Four, critics of graphology present their objections from the standpoints of personality assessment (Bowman), organizational psychology and personnel selection (Klimoski), psychological measurement theory (Dean), cognitive psychology (Dean et al.), and neurophysiology (B. Beyerstein).

Section Five presents representative empirical studies by a graphologist (Wellingham-Jones) and by psychologists skeptical of its utility (Karnes and Leonard). The results of these studies are interesting in their own right but are also included in order that the reader might compare the methodologies, experimental controls, statistical procedures, etc., used in studies that do and do not find support for graphology.

Given the possible consequences for one's professional advancement and reputation raised by use of a debatable assessment tool such as graphology, it is only a matter of time until parties who feel aggrieved by its use will seek redress in the courts, as they rightly did with regard to polygraph testing in the workplace. Thus in the final section of this book, we have asked two lawyers to address the practice of graphology in light of relevant statutes and precedents in the U.S. (Reagh) and Canada (Carswell). Recent legal restrictions on use of polygraphs have created a vacuum that graphologists have been eager to fill. Employers' desperate desire for a quick fix for problems of employee honesty and productivity has made them vulnerable to certain graphologists' hard-sell tactics and inflated, unsubstantiated claims. One particularly disturbing aspect of some of the advertising we have been seeing recently is that it informs prospective clients that one of graphology's great advantages is that it can be used without applicants or employees even being aware they are being evaluated! This was one of the selling points allegedly made by the graphologist who approached the Vancouver School Board, offering to identify sexual deviants in the teaching ranks.

The editors of this book would be remiss if they did not admit at the outset their strong skepticism about the value of graphology. Their dubiousness is based, however, on graphology's violation of well supported principles within areas of the editors' own professional expertise and a careful reading of both the pro- and anti-graphology literature. The editors have attempted to give the proponents of graphology in this volume ample opportunity to include any scientific evidence for its utility they wish, and to refute the skeptics as they see fit. The proponents were chosen for their prominence in the published literature and on the strong recommendation of numerous practicing graphologists.

Herbert Spencer (1829–1903) wisely wrote:

> There is a principle which is a bar against all information, which is proof against all argument and which cannot fail to keep a man in everlasting ignorance. That principle is, "Condemnation before investigation."

We invite the reader to enter into an open-minded investigation of the evidence for and against the practice of graphology.

NOTES

1. It is an especially worrying sign when the majority of popular books on a subject and the instructional "texts" most "professionals" in a supposedly technical field learn from and consult regularly are one and the same. This we have found to be the case repeatedly in our interactions with practicing graphologists.

2. In this volume, "graphology" and "handwriting analysis" will be used interchangeably to refer to any system that claims to discern personality, aptitudes, attitudes, proclivities, or medical data from the configuration of written letters, words, or sentences, or their distribution on the page. "Graphoanalysis" is a regis-

tered trademark that refers exclusively to the copyrighted system of handwriting analysis taught by the International Graphoanalysis Society (see chapters 2, 7, and 9, this volume).

2

A Brief History of Graphology

Joe Nickell

This historical overview should provide the reader with some background to the graphology debate. Dr. Nickell emphasizes the historic and present connection of graphology with mystical and occult doctrines, a point taken up again in chapters 3 and 9. This does not, by itself, refute graphology. After all, medicine and astronomy had some of their origins in doctrines that we know today—or even were known at the time—to be pseudoscientific, as graphologists like to point out. So the reader should look at Dr. Nickell's other contribution in chapter 4, as well as Oskar Lockowandt's review of the modern literature in chapter 5, and Barry Beyerstein's chapter 9, as well as both chapters in Section Five, before deciding what to conclude from this.

Graphology—the alleged science of divining personality from handwriting—is a branch of that large, amorphous field known as "character reading," and its roots are ancient.[1]

One of graphology's antecedents is physiognomy. In Old Testament times, when few could write, character was thought to be revealed in the face. And so it was said that "the shew of their countenance doth witness against them" (Isaiah 3.9).[2] A treatise attributed (falsely) to Aristotle compared man's features to those of animals as a means of indicating character traits. Thus, sharp-tipped (doglike) noses belonged to those who were irascible; large, round noses (like those of lions) were found on the faces of magnanimous persons; thin, hooked noses (comparable to eagles' beaks) were common to people who were noble but grasping; and so on.[3]

The first step toward the ultimate development of graphology was the recognition of individuality in handwriting, and this was accomplished by the time Jewish laws were collected and written down in the Mishnah (ca. A.D. 70–200):

> These when they come of age may be believed when they testify of what they saw while they were yet minors: A man may be believed when he says, "This is my father's handwriting," or "This is my teacher's handwriting," or "This is my brother's handwriting." . . .[4]

It appears that the rudiments of graphology were also familiar to the Romans. The second-century historian Suetonius drew inferences about the character of Augustus from his examination of Augustus's handwriting.[5] As well, the Emperor Nero is said to have remarked that he was distrustful of a particular man in court because "his handwriting showed him treacherous."[6] A more emphatic endorsement of the validity of graphology came from the eleventh-century Chinese artist and philosopher Kuo Jo Hsu, who said: "Handwriting can infallibly show whether it comes from a person who is noble-minded, or from one who is vulgar."[7]

Apparently the first attempt to explicate the perceived relationship between handwriting and personality was made by a seventeenth-century Italian physician named Camillo Baldi (or Baldo, 1547–1634). In 1622, Baldi published in Capri his *Trattado come da una lettera missiva si conoscano la natura e qualita dello scriviente* (*Treatise on a Method to Recognize the Nature and Quality of a Writer from His Letters*). Baldi wrote:

> It is obvious that all persons write in their own way. . . . These . . . traits of character can be recognized in any handwriting. . . . Yet it is necessary to observe carefully whether the characteristics of handwriting recur, moreover whether they are in any way artificial. . . .[8]

Baldi initiated the analysis of handwriting by dividing it into its various elements. However, his treatise generated relatively little interest,[9] although some itinerant magicians were said to have gone "from castle to castle practicing the new art."[10]

A similar treatise was written by Marco Aurelio Severo (1580–1656), and more than a century later, J.K. Lavater (1741–1801) included a chapter on the subject in his *Physiognomische Fragmente* (*Physiognomic Fragments,* 1774–78). Still another work was produced by Johann Christian August Grohmann (1769–1847).[11]

Modern interest in graphology is attributed to a circle of the French Catholic clergy in the nineteenth century. About 1830, this group of churchmen—including the Archbishop of Cambria, the Bishop of Amiens, and Abbé Louis J.H. Flandrin—began to involve themselves in the study and interpretation of handwriting.[12] This ecclesiastical impetus, according to one commentator, "may account for the severity of judgment still to be found in some French graphology."[13]

It was a disciple of this group, Abbé Jean-Hippolyte Michon (1806–1881), who established the term *graphology,* founded the Society of Graphology in Paris (1871), and set forth the results of his studies in several treatises, including *Les Mystères de l'écriture* (*The Mysteries of Handwriting,* 1872); *System de graphologie* (*System of Graphology,* 1875); and *La Méthode pratique de graphologie* (*Practical Method of Graphology,* 1878).[14] Michon attempted to give graphology a systematic basis and to associate isolated "signs" or elements (*i*-dots, *t*-bars, flourishes, etc.) with particular character traits.[15]

Michon's *analytical* approach contrasted with the *intuitive* approach of medieval Chinese philosophers like Kuo Jo Hsu and of certain eighteenth- and nineteenth-century intellectuals and amateur graphologists like Johann von Goethe, Thomas Gainsborough, Edgar Allan Poe, and Robert Browning. In an attempt to better understand a writer's personality, these intuitive practitioners would often trace over the script, thus supposedly getting a "feel" for the person's character.[16]

Although Michon had addressed the need for systemization (a requisite for graphology to lay claim to being a science), his "fixed signs," according to one critic, "were so numerous and arbitrary that they invariably contradicted one another unless some coordinating factor was introduced, and he made no effort to resolve the contradiction by a more general theory of personality. . . ."[17]

That task fell to Michon's pupil, Crepieux-Jamin (d. 1840), who eventually broke away from his teacher's system. He took instead a more *holistic* approach, stressing that a specimen of writing must be comprehended as a whole, to which the various signs and features contributed in different degrees. As he asserted, "The study of elements is to graphology as a study of the alphabet is to the reading of prose."[18]

French researchers continued to dominate the field of graphology until near the end of the nineteenth century, when the focus shifted to Germany. Wilhelm Preyer related the physical movements of writing to mental processes and, in 1895, advanced the notion that handwriting is essentially "brain writing."[19] (This concept is discussed in chapter 14.) Georg Meyer, a German psychiatrist, argued that emotion was expressed through all psychomotor functions, not just handwriting, and he suggested the need for a new science, *characterology,* in addition to graphology. Meyer also advocated a common vocabulary for the two "sciences."[20] His suggestions were taken up by Ludwig Klages. According to Klara G. Roman, in her *Encyclopedia of the Written Word:*

> In establishing laws and principles of graphology and characterology, Klages assumed a "science of expression" that postulates two forces within man: "mind," which binds and inhibits him, and "soul," which frees and develops him creatively. According to Klages these two forces, always dynamically at variance, influence all of man's behavior and are most crystallized in his *expressive movements*—a term coined by Klages—that is to say, walk, gesture, gait, speech, mimicry, writing, and so on. All such bodily movements, actualizing the tensions and drives of the personality, have a common form *level or style that is consistent with the individual's general motor* behavior and *rhythm* of movement. It is particularly in handwriting, where the movements between the two forces are caught, that they are most accessible for study and interpretation.[21]

Klages set forth his theories in five books and was mentor to an entire generation of German graphology enthusiasts.[22]

Subsequently, Professor Max Pulver of the University of Zurich extended Klages's theories into the field of psychoanalysis. To the usual measurements of letter height and width, Pulver added depth (i.e., pen pressure), which he linked to the individual's libido. He also sought to evaluate the "symbolic" aspects of handwriting and to interpret them much as one would interpret symbols in dreams.[23] His *Symboliker der Handschrift* (*Symbolism of Handwriting*) was published in 1930. According to one author:

> Interested in the psychology of the unconscious, he saw the clean white page as world space, to be filled by entering it according to one's nature, be it quickly but hesitantly, slowly and with eyes constantly turning backward to the past, or in an eager, all-embracing rush. He noted the upward reaching of the spiritually inclined, and the downward plunging strokes made by earthy natures. But he was also aware that many of these impulses are unconscious, that we are governed as much—or more—by those thoughts and feelings which never surface, as by our conscious attitudes and decisions.[24]

Further developments took place elsewhere—including Belgium, Hungary, and the Netherlands. And in England, Robert Saudek, a Czech, sought to modify the European speculative approach by using more quantitative methods. In his experiments in the 1930s, he employed devices to measure pressure and even used slow-motion photography to study writing movements.[25]

In the United States, June Downey was one of the earliest experimenters in the field, following the lead of French and German researchers. Her book, *Graphology and the Psychology of Handwriting,* which appeared in 1919, was based on earlier German and French notions of writing as expressive movement. In 1933, Harvard's Gordon Allport and Phillip E. Vernon published their *Studies in Expressive Movement,* which presented their view that handwriting was part of a person's total expressive nature (a view stemming from the theories of Meyer and Klages).[26] (See also chapter 14, this volume.)

Today, the status of graphology reflects its somewhat checkered past, and it often seems not far removed from the time when wandering conjurers disseminated the "art." Competing theories vie for favor, nowhere more than in America where some thirty-two different graphological societies—some "using methods which are not easily combined with other systems"[27]—attempt to advance the ancient belief. Lacking significant scientific or scholarly endorsement, but attracting criticism from many quarters,[28] the various practitioners often advertise their services in tabloids and occultish publications like *Fate* magazine. Their ads in *Fate* share pages with those hawking other forms of character reading, divination, crystal power, and the like. Similarly, book catalogs often reflect graphology's kinship with the mystical. For example, a Barnes & Noble catalog advertises a graphology text under the heading "The Occult," along with such books as *The Ghost Hunter's Guide, How to Read Hands,* and *The Evidence for Visions of the Virgin Mary.*[29]

In Europe, where various French, German, Swiss, and other theories represent a patchwork system, belief in the validity of graphology is apparently much stronger among university psychology professors than it is among their North American counterparts. However, the situation there is not always as favorable to graphology as is sometimes claimed.[30] In any event, acceptance is no substitute for proof. As Martin Gardner observes in his classic work, *Fads & Fallacies in the Name of Science:*

> One of the major difficulties in all forms of character reading research is that no really precise methods have yet been devised for determining whether an analysis fits the person or not. Wide margins on a written letter, for example, are supposed to indicate "generosity." Is there anyone who would not feel that such a trait applied to himself? People are generous in some ways and not in others. It is too vague a trait to be tested by empirical method, and even good friends may disagree widely on whether it applies to a given individual. The same is true of most of the graphological traits. If you are told you have them, you can always look deep enough and find them—especially if you are convinced that the graphologist who made the analysis is an expert who is seldom wrong.

After describing the need for appropriate tests of the claims made by graphologists, Gardner concludes:

> Until a character analyst can consistently score high on [such] tests . . . his work will remain on the fringes of orthodox psychology. The fact that millions of people were profoundly impressed by the accuracy of phrenological readings suggests how easy it is to imagine that a character analysis fits the person analyzed—provided you know exactly who the person is![31]

Gardner's statement—made in 1957—continues to be valid today. It is time to realize that the Emperor of Graphology has no clothes.

NOTES

1. Etymologically, graphology (from Greek words for *writing* and *doctrine*) means the study of handwriting.
2. See also Ecclesiastes 8.1.
3. "Physiognomy," *Encyclopaedia Britannica,* 1960, 17: p. 886.
4. Ketuboth, 2.10. (See Herbert Danby, *The Mishnah: Translated from the Hebrew* [Oxford: Oxford UP, 1933], p. 247).
5. Suetonius, *History* 2.87 (cited in "Graphology," *New Catholic Encyclopedia,* 1967, 6: p. 704).
6. Quoted in Huntington Hartford, *You are What You Write* (New York: Macmillan, 1973), p. 43.
7. Ibid.
8. Quoted in "Handwriting," *Encyclopedia Britannica,* 1960, 11: p. 149.
9. Werner Wolff, *Diagrams of the Unconscious* (New York: Grune & Stratton, 1948), pp. 5, 357; "Handwriting," p. 149.
10. Hartford, p. 49.
11. "Graphology," p. 704; Wolff, pp. 5, 364.
12. "History of Graphology," in Klara G. Roman, *Encyclopedia of the Written Word: A Lexicon for Graphology and Other Aspects of Writing* (New York: Frederick Ungar, 1968), p. 174; Margaret Gullan-Whur, *The Graphology Workbook: A Complete Guide to Interpreting Handwriting* (Wellingborough, England: Aquarian, 1986), p. 11.
13. Gullan-Whur, p. 11.
14. Ibid.; Wolff, pp. 5, 366; Roman, p. 174; Hartford, p. 50.
15. Roman, p. 175.
16. "Handwriting," p. 149.
17. Hartford, p. 50.
18. Roman, p. 175.
19. Ibid.
20. Ibid., pp. 175–176.

21. Ibid., 176.
22. Ibid.; Hartford, p. 52.
23. "Handwriting," p. 150; Hartford, p. 56.
24. Gullan-Whur, p. 12.
25. Roman, p. 178.
26. Ibid.
27. Gullan-Whur, p. 13.
28. Particularly vocal against the claims of graphologists has been the distinguished Committee for the Scientific Investigation of Claims of the Paranormal—a scientific watchdog group including Carl Sagan, Isaac Asimov, and others.
29. Barnes & Noble's "Winter Reading" catalog, February-March 1987, p. 49. (Other headings on the same page are "Fortune Telling" and "Astrology & Magic.")
30. See also Oskar Lockowandt, "On the Development of Academic Graphology in the Federal Republic of Germany After 1945," *The Graphologist* 4(1): pp. 2-8 (Spring 1986).
31. Martin Gardner, *Fads & Fallacies in the Name of Science* (New York: Dover, 1957), pp. 296-297.

3

By a Man's Calligraphy Ye Shall Know Him: Handwriting Analysis in China

Barry L. Beyerstein and Zhang Jing Ping

Graphologists often point to the age and ubiquity of their art as though this implies validity. They argue, for instance, that because it was widely accepted in ancient China that a writer's character could be discerned from his or her calligraphy, this counts as evidence in favor of modern graphology. Similarly, western graphologists often claim that handwriting analysis enjoys greater official acceptance in modern China than in the West, but they present little evidence that this is so or that this alleged endorsement is based on scientifically acceptable data. What proponents neglect to state is that Chinese graphology arose from the same sorts of augury and divining practices as western graphology and is thus open to the same criticisms (see chapter 9, this volume).

In fact, raising the Chinese connection actually arouses further doubts about graphology. As Barry Beyerstein points out in Chapter 14, it reduces the already low *a priori* credibility of graphology to demand that the physical substrate of each personality trait must unerringly connect with the same set of writing features in every writer of the Roman alphabet and a quite different set in every writer of an idiographic script such as Chinese. It strains credulity even further to think that not only would personality mechanisms have to modify hundreds of features of copybook letters in exactly the right pattern to reflect the individuality of every person who learns one system of written symbols, but must also be able to automatically lock their influences onto a totally different set if he or she should learn another arbitrary system for encoding language. It would be an interesting test to see if a Chinese graphologist analyzing the Chinese script of a group of bilingual writers would make the same attributions as a western graphologist analyzing the same writers' Roman script. Given the frequent lack of agreement among different schools of western graphology, the editors would not expect high concurrence cross-culturally.

In addition to its long and varied history of magical divination practices, China can also take credit for the world's oldest system of objective selection tests. The ancient Chinese civil service examinations represent the first attempt to select public administrators on the basis of merit rather than social standing. Graphologists have sometimes taken the fact that penmanship counted in these written exams to mean that the detection of moral stature and character from script had, at this early date, already made the transition from occultism to the realm of objective testing. Though historical accounts by westerners dispute this, the senior author of this chapter was delighted to have an opportunity to examine claims about Chinese graphology first hand when he was invited to spend part of a sabbatical year at Jilin University in the People's Republic of China. There he met a very capable collaborator, Zhang Jing Ping, who examined Chinese historical materials and surveyed modern popular sources, looking for references to handwriting analysis and any objective tests that might have escaped western critics. His search confirmed that, in accord with the western sources cited in this chapter, and contrary to some graphologists' claims, reading personality from calligraphy did not enter into the ancient Chinese civil service examinations. Divination from calligraphy does, however, form an interesting thread in the Chinese folk tradition, one that survives, as in the West, despite scientific doubts about its accuracy.

During his stay in China, Barry Beyerstein also had the opportunity to speak with various officials and academics interested in personnel selection. He found that these officials were eager to catch up on developments in western psychological testing that had previously been unavailable for political reasons and that they were quite happy to leave graphology where they feel it belongs—in the realm of folk superstition.

INTRODUCTION: PROPHECY IN ANCIENT CHINA

Although graphology as practiced in the West has not emerged as a separate profession in China, the notion that an individual's personality and future prospects are encoded in his or her handwriting has long enjoyed a place among Chinese divination practices.[1] It is part of a tradition, rooted in ancient Taoist mysticism, that assumes the magical power of written symbols to access the spiritual world and thereby to inform, to protect, or to cure (Legeza 1975).

China's ancient civilization has produced an amazing variety of occult methods for reading personality and foretelling the future (Bloomfield 1983; Loewe 1981; Needham 1956, ch. 14; Ronan 1978, ch. 10). Ronan (1978: 202) lists "glyphomancy" (augury by scrutiny of writing) as a common divination practice in ancient China. It coexisted with other methods that interpreted facial features, palms, dream imagery, geologic formations (geomancy), patterns of strewn milfoil sticks (which evolved into the hexagrams for the divinatory book, *The I Ching)*, and, of course, the alignments of heavenly bodies (astrology). Some of the very earliest examples of Chinese writing are archeological relics (c. 1400 B.C.E.) that record oracles' interpretations of the surface cracks produced by roasting tortoise shells or the shoulder bones of certain large mammals (Loewe 1981; Ronan 1978: 192). Obviously, it is but a small step to interpreting the lines in writing itself.

Given this climate of belief and the visual and symbolic richness of Chinese written characters,[2] it is not surprising that interpretation of pictographs (or "ideographs" as they are also known) would emerge as a mantic practice. The rarity and power of literacy itself was so great in earlier times that it often acquired a magical aura (Zusne and Jones 1989: 196–198; 248–250). According to Legeza (1975: 9),

> a profound belief in spiritual powers of calligraphy was very probably already present even in the formative period of Chinese civilization (i.e. during the first millennium B.C.), and was largely responsible for the survival of the Chinese idiographic script. For it is significant that, despite several attempts at reform, the Chinese civilization has always shown reluctance to adopt an alphabetic script.

Like the western divining methods discussed in chapter 9, Chinese augury is based on the assumption that supernatural powers will guide intuition and free association toward the "correct" meanings of arbitrary signs or omens. The rationale for extending the mental associates of these ambiguous stimuli to people or events is the magical "law of similarity" (Ronan 1978: ch. 10; B. Beyerstein, ch. 9, this volume). Western graphology is based upon the same trust that symbolism suggested by the shapes and positions of letters will be magically reenacted in the writer's life. But while the supernatural connection was taken for granted by Chinese glyphomancers, it is strenuously denied by most European and North American graphologists. Nonetheless, as chapter 9 of this book demonstrates, claims by the latter to have abandoned their magical roots are less than convincing.

According to Loewe (1981: 40), the history of Chinese divination has followed a course familiar to observers of western graphology—the initial meanings of signs were arrived at by intuition and free association, supposedly with the aid of supernatural inspiration. But once these revelations were recorded, readings tended, thenceforth, to be a fairly mechanical process of matching an individual's signs with codified interpretations found in the sacred texts. Like the rules of modern graphology, these were passed down reverently and seldom, if ever, tested or revised.

Chinese calligraphy, like all other forms of writing, originated as pictorial representations, but the pictographs have come to represent sounds rather than objects (DeFrancis 1984: 137). DeFrancis (1984: 133) puts to rest the prevalent western misconception that modern Chinese characters remain mere facsimiles, i.e., that they portray objects and actions visually, without the restrictive intermediary of phonetics. On the contrary, modern Chinese characters represent sounds by symbolizing objects whose names sound like the phonemes (the smallest sound units of a language) they are to convey. But, although they have become highly stylized and simplified, Chinese characters are still more obviously related, visually, to their pictographic origins than are the many alphabetic systems for representing phonemes. Thus they present an even richer substrate than western alphabets for eliciting free associations and pareidolia (see ch. 9) for oracular purposes.

Bloomfield (1983, ch. 8) describes a number of descendants of ancient Chinese augury that persist in Chinese communities around the world. Among them is a procedure that can be traced back at least to 722 B.C.E. and employs methods not unlike those of western graphologists. A Taoist priest of the Tang Dynasty (618–907 C.E.), Tsui Wu Yih, is revered as a master of this technique.

> The questioner first writes down a Chinese character—anything that comes into his head. Then the fortune-teller goes on to dissect the character and tell him what it all means. This can give rise to a considerable meaning because all Chinese characters, unlike the Roman alphabet, have many elements of other words in them. It is this multiplicity of concepts in each character that makes Chinese poetry so difficult to translate. . . . Obviously a written language so rich in elements is ready made for the fortune-teller's rhetoric. (Bloomfield 1983: 143)

Paralleling the Chinese prophetic tradition is another longstanding heritage of skeptical thought (Needham 1956: 365–395). Chinese skeptics have raised doubts about glyphomancy that sound rather like western criticisms of graphology (Bloomfield 1983). The Chinese critics were chagrined, first of all, by glyphomancers' unbridled freedom to pick and choose parts of characters, realign, and reassemble them. They were further upset by the augurers' use of analogical and associative thinking to play upon the multiplicity of homophones, puns, visual resemblances, etc., in Chinese writing. Doubters charged that this meant readings were bound to be an arbitrary outpouring of the reader's (perhaps unconscious) prejudices, intuitions, and flights of fantasy.

In addition to glyphomancy and use of written incantations in hopes of securing a desirable future, China has also had a tradition of personality reading by impressionistic appraisal of calligraphy. It is to this analogue of western graphology that we now turn.

CALLIGRAPHY AND PERSONALITY

Since the writing tools of the ancient Chinese, waterbrush and prepared ink, are different from those in common use today, there are distinct differences in the calligraphy produced by traditional and modern implements. The nuances of brush technique allow more scope for personalization of characters. This, plus the effects of officially-mandated simplifications of the script in recent years, means that ancient and modern calligraphy should be considered separately. The six basic strokes used in traditional Chinese characters are the following:

一 丨 丶 丿 乙 亅

The modern, simplified characters taught today have been reduced to combinations of five basic strokes:

丶 一 丨 丿 乙

In ancient China, nearly all calligraphers assumed that their calligraphy was a precise expression of their inner nature. Calligraphy itself was regarded as much more than just a means of conveying facts. It was an important aspect of Chinese culture, essentially an art form. As with poetry, painting, music, or dance, it was taught that through subtle embellishments of brush strokes, calligraphers could express thoughts, feelings, ideals, and ambitions, independently of the semantic content of their script. It was taken for granted among the literate elite that one's temperament, sentiments, and innermost soul were revealed for all to see when one put brush to paper. As the tenth century Chinese artist and critic Liu Xi Zai remarked in his famous work *The Generalizations of Chinese Art*:

> Calligraphy is the thing that manifests man's knowledge and learning, ability and talent, ideals and aspirations; in short, just man himself in nature.

This view is neatly encapsulated in an old aphorism, well known throughout China: "By a man's calligraphy ye shall know him." In part, this simply recognizes that calligraphers may intentionally embellish their work as an artistic statement, but it also incorporates an idea more akin to western graphology, namely, that unintentional adornments of written characters reveal precise aspects of personality. As claimed by some "holistic" schools of western graphology, these qualities are supposedly conveyed to others impressionistically, by a sort of intuitive "resonance" rather than by any intellectual or analytical process.

At the very least, it is universally accepted that writers of Chinese characters impart individually recognizable qualities to their script, just as writers of the Roman alphabet do. It is this personal imprint, which emerges despite standardized instruction, that gives handwriting analysis its appeal in both the East and West. It feels as though it ought to work. But despite this surface plausibility, the assumption that writing encodes specific personality traits remains to be proved. It is not a given to be accepted merely because it seems to make sense intuitively. As B. Beyerstein points out in chapter 14, individuality in script is more likely to be due to variations in bio-mechanical factors and bio-cybernetic programs controlling writing movements than to the graphologists' assumption that precise personality traits commandeer unique writing movements.

OBJECTIVE VS. SUBJECTIVE TESTING IN ANCIENT CHINA

Regardless of how it might arise, the distinctiveness of an individual's calligraphy was of concern to the officials who set the stringent civil service exams that became formalized in China around 200–100 B.C.E. (DuBois 1965; Bowman 1989). By 622 C.E., open, competitive examinations were taking place at regular intervals. Candidates who had been previously screened for their moral stature and basic literacy were allowed to sit formal written examinations in this, the world's first attempt to select public administrators objectively on the basis of merit. In the Chinese civil service examinations we see the earliest example of a split that was to occur much later in the West, between those attempting to develop objective measures of individual differences (see chs. 10 and 11) and those who rely on subjective, intuitive, and magical means of evaluation (cf. ch. 9).

By the time of the Ming Dynasty (1368–1644 C.E.) the civil service exams had become quite standardized, with successful candidates funneling through district and provincial screenings to the national selections in Beijing.

At the district level, required compositions were evaluated on several criteria including their "beauty of penmanship and grace of diction" (Martin 1870, quoted in DuBois 1965: 31). The best and the brightest were eligible to proceed to the provincial capital where they vied for the coveted title of "Promoted Scholar."

At this level, according to Martin, each examination was marked with a cipher and re-copied by an official scribe so "that the examiners may have no clew to its author and no temptation to render a biased judgement." Interestingly, Martin's observations show that the Chinese were already aware at this early date of two prime requirements of modern psychological measurement: "blind" rating of test materials and the need to secure independent agreement among more than one rater. These are precautions western graphologists still routinely violate more than six centuries later.

The "Promoted Scholars" advanced to the pinnacle of the selection system in Beijing where the emperor himself set the themes upon which candidates were required to write. Hanging in the balance was a place in the Imperial Academy. At this stage, interpretation of the Confucian classics dominated the content of the examinations and preference was given to those exhibiting outstanding verbal cleverness and the ability to construct elegant arguments almost like those of modern word games (Bowman 1989).

Also at this rarefied level,

> [p]enmanship reappears as an element in determining the result, and a score or more of those whose style is the most finished, whose scholarship the ripest, and whose handwriting the most elegant, are drafted into the college of Hanlin, the "forest of pencils" [and] recognized as standing at the head of the literary profession. (Martin 1870, quoted in DuBois 1965)

The Chinese selection system, being open to men (and at certain times also to women) from any background and based strictly on ability, was an influential model when competitive civil service examinations were finally adopted by France, the United Kingdom, the U.S.A., Canada, and other nations. The Chinese examiners recognized that a relatively small sample of relevant behavior, obtained under controlled conditions, could yield an estimate of performance in a wider range of situations. The key word here is "relevant," for the intention was to sample behaviors that had a reasonable chance of predicting performance on the job (for a modern perspective, see Klimoski, ch. 11). Where handwriting counted in assessing candidates for the Chinese civil service, it was considered a measure of esthetic, manual, or spatial abilities, not a magical index of personality.

Though the content of the Chinese examinations was criticized at the time as being too esoteric, Huang Chi, an official of the examining board, defended the selection system in 1655. In effect, he argued that it measured certain general mental abilities of the sort that are recognizable to modern psychologists (Jang 1990). Penmanship played a part to be sure, but it was only evaluated, quite reasonably, for its own sake or as a gauge of artistic flair or proficiency on spatial or mental imagery tasks. In the days before mechanical printing (also a Chinese invention), and especially in a style-conscious court, pleasing, legible script was a reasonable part of a public official's job description.

At a more abstract level, calligraphy was also deemed useful in assessing other pertinent abilities. For instance, in addition to including the appropriate content in his or her answer, the candidate was required to make it fit a specified page format on the first and only attempt. Thus the examinations, in addition to sampling memory, verbal agility, and educational attainments, tested the candidates's spatial skills and ability to reconcile the conflicting demands of accommodating to traditional constraints while still exhibiting creativity. Though an individual's moral status was important in selection for the ancient Chinese civil service, there is no evidence that the examiners thought they could discern such attributes from the candidate's calligraphy. The admirable restraint of the examiners in this regard did not, however, deter prevalent folk beliefs in the occult powers of calligraphy. It continued to be widely supposed that personal qualities were encoded in writers' script.

It is interesting, given the differences in their idiographic and alphabetic writing systems and so many other aspects of Chinese and European culture, that many of the same folk beliefs about writing emerged, apparently independently, in both populations. As Warner and Sugarman (1986) point out, ordinary westerners who have no training in graphology exhibit some agreement in the free associations they make to certain features of handwriting. These tend to be commonsense connections such as associating a large signature with self-importance, for example. Though the validity of such attributions is questionable, there seems to be a natural tendency to extend the traits a script reminds one of to the person who wrote it. Humans everywhere seem to have a strong bent for this sort of magical attribution, as seen by the widespread appeal of the "law of similarity" (see ch. 9).

Parallels in popular beliefs about writing in China and the West suggest interesting universalities in how intuition and free-associative processes work. For instance, in both cultures it is widely felt that hard-to-read handwriting betrays the writer's antisocial tendencies and intention to stifle communication. Also in both cultures, folk diagnoses of this sort typically have built-in loopholes to save the system when its ascriptions don't fit or might prove embarrassing, i.e., verbal sleight-of-hand that renders the procedure effectively unfalsifiable. For example, the junior author of this chapter found that, despite the predominantly negative connotations ascribed to illegible writing in China, it was also believed that some indecipherable handwriting is merely the result of a hasty or energetic nature that cannot be bothered to make neat, conventional characters.[3] He also found that it is conventional wisdom in China, as in the West, that happy people will tend to accentuate their uphill strokes and that their dot-like strokes will thicken at the end.

Chinese handwriting interpreters apparently share other beliefs with western graphologists, such as the following. If bar-like strokes are wavy or dots appear more like curves, or the endings of words show an upswing, this supposedly indicates a sense of humor. Similarly, handwriting interpreters in both cultures assume that people who like to do things in a big way, to "make a splash," as it were, will write with a large hand. Small writing in both societies suggests the writer has a penchant for concentrating on details.

In China, as in the West (cf. chapter 9), it is popularly held that perusal of the calligraphy of historical figures will confirm one's casual impression that there are written correlates of personality and occupation. The calligraphy of intellectuals is believed to have a tender, delicate nature; military heroes are reputed to have bold, unconstrained calligraphy. Upright, resolute people are expected to write with a firm, vigorous hand and artists' calligraphy is said to have a picturesque, poetic quality. Scholars and professional caligraphers are thought to impart a certain profundity and academic quality to their writing.

When asked what support there is for these popular beliefs, Chinese adherents, like their western counterparts, fall back on anecdotal evidence. Best known in this regard are historical figures who are also honored as calligraphy masters and whose distinctive styles are reputed to mirror their personalities. Among those often cited are the eminent Tang Dynasty writer Han Yu (768–824 C.E.), the Song Dynasty poet Su Shi (1036–1101 C.E.), and his contemporary, the statesman and writer Ou Yang Xiu (1007–1072 C.E.).

Because of such examplars, and especially the eleventh-century artist and philosopher Kuo Jo Hsu (see ch. 2), it has long been believed in China that expert calligraphers themselves may be particularly adept at judging personality from the calligraphy of others. This is alleged to include the ability to discern noble-mindedness from vulgarity, caution from recklessness, and maturity from naivety. Supposedly, one can also divide the observant from the dull-witted, the easy-going from the irascible, and the trustworthy from the treacherous. Also revealed are liberalism versus conservatism, realism versus idealism, kindheartedness as opposed to callousness, etc. As with western graphology, some of the foregoing may seem slightly more plausible than others, but a search of Chinese sources by the junior author of this chapter revealed no empirical studies to back up any of these assertions.

Like their western counterparts, Chinese supporters of handwriting analysis make the mistake of concentrating exclusively on anecdotal evidence that is consistent with their position; i.e., they regard the fact that some people exhibit both the written sign and the putatively related behavior as "proof" the technique is valid. As Dean (ch. 12) and B. Beyerstein (ch. 9) show, a proper test must compare the incidence of these supportive cases with that of people who have the writing feature but lack the personality trait and those who have the personality trait but not the allegedly correlated written sign. The critics in this volume show that when these rules have been scrupulously followed, the result has not been flattering to handwriting analysis.

READING PERSONALITY FROM WRITING IN MODERN CHINA

Just as there is debate among western graphologists over the relative merits of "molecular" versus "holistic" ways to discern personality from writing, there have been similar disagreements in China. In the West, the trend in graphology seems to be away from interpreting small portions of letters in favor of reliance on more "holistic" impressions (see Crumbaugh, ch. 7 and Nickell, ch. 2). But in China developments seem to have followed the reverse path. While the attributions discussed in the foregoing sections could be considered "global" impressions of the overall impact of writing, more recent opinions in China regarding interpretation of calligraphy focus on individual differences in formation of the five basic strokes that comprise modern Chinese characters (see above). To some extent, this has coincided with adoption of western writing implements, replacing the more variable brush and ink, and with official attempts to simplify and standardize the characters themselves.

We have looked in vain for scientific evidence regarding handwriting analysis in China. It seems that the Chinese scientific establishment considers it a holdover from old folk superstitions, not worthy of empirical study.[4] This is significant because other traditional practices with a mystical past, such as acupuncture and herbal medicine, are being scrutinized by reputable Chinese researchers because they can demonstrate some efficacy. Occultists practicing handwriting analysis, for their part, appear to be content to remain in the mystical camp. There is no indication they are trying to acquire a gloss of authority for their divining practices by pretending to be scientific disciplines.[5]

When the senior author of this chapter was a visiting professor in China, he was unable to find any credible experts in relevant fields who believed that precise personality traits were encoded in writing. This does not preclude the possibility that some ostentatious people might choose to express their flamboyance in certain features of their writing or that artistic or meticulous people might do likewise. But evidence to support the contention that there are unique written signs of, say, sincerity, benevolence, hostility, or promiscuousness is no better in the Chinese than the western literature.

NOTES

The authors would like to acknowledge the assistance of Elsie Zhang and Elliott Marchant in the preparation of this chapter.

1. Divination is also known as augury. Diviners assume supernatural forces will guide them in interpreting signs or omens to foretell the future or discern information about individuals. Almost any random, complicated stimulus can be the starting point for the process of free association that leads to the interpretation. For a more detailed discussion of the related concept of "pareidolia," and divination in general, see chapter 9 of this volume. A good history of Chinese divinatory practices can be found in Loewe (1981).

2. To avoid confusion, we shall use the term "character" in this chapter to refer to a single Chinese ideograph, and not in its other common usage as a synonym for personality makeup.

3. Whether the more or less charitable interpretation will be deemed appropriate is usually decided by the well-known "halo effect." This is the tendency to rate someone's unknown attributes more or less favorably, depending upon how one feels about aspects of him or her that are already known. Examples of this in western graphologists' judgments can be seen in chapter 9.

4. In the recent drive to modernize the Chinese economy, identification of talent has become a priority and interest in scientifically based selection procedures has burgeoned. Contact with worldwide developments in the psychology of individual differences had previously been discouraged for political reasons. Handwriting analysis does not seem to be finding a place in this resurgent interest in testing.

5. This is quite unlike the case of other Chinese occult practices such as Qi Gong, which are actively seeking unearned respectability by developing into full-blown pseudosciences (Kurtz 1988).

REFERENCES

Bloomfield, F. 1983. *The Book of Chinese Beliefs*. New York: Ballantine Books.

Bowman, M. L. 1989. "Testing Individual Differences in Ancient China." *American Psychologist* (March): pp. 576–578.

DeFrancis, J. 1984. *The Chinese Language: Fact and Fantasy*. Honolulu: University of Hawaii Press.

DuBois, P. H. 1966. "A Test-Dominant Society: China, 1115 B.C.–1905 A.D." In *Testing Problems in Perspective,* edited by A. Anastasi. Washington, D.C.: American Council on Education, pp. 29–36.

Jang, K. 1990. "The Imperial Chinese Civil Service Examinations: Observations from a Modern Measurement Perspective." Unpublished manuscript. Dept. of Psychology, University of Western Ontario, London, Ontario, Canada.

Kurtz P. 1988. "Testing Psi Claims in China: Visit by a CSICOP Delegation." *The Skeptical Inquirer* 12(4): pp. 364–375.

Legeza, L. 1975. *Tao Magic: The Secret Language of Diagrams and Calligraphy*. London: Thames and Hudson.

Loewe, M. 1981. "China." In *Oracles and Divination,* edited by M. Loewe and C. Blacker. Boulder, Colo.: Shambhala, pp. 38–62.

Needham, J. 1956. *Science and Civilization in China.* Vol. 2: *History of Scientific Thought.* Cambridge: Cambridge University Press.

Ronan, C. A. 1978. *The Shorter Science and Civilization in China: An Abridgement of Joseph Needham's Original Text.* Vol. 1. Cambridge: Cambridge University Press.

Warner, R., and D. Sugarman, 1986. "Attributions of Personality Based on Physical Appearance, Speech, and Handwriting." *J. of Personality and Social Psychology* 50(4): pp. 792–799.

Zusne, L., and W. Jones. 1989. *Anomalistic Psychology: A Study of Magical Thinking.* Hillsdale, N.J.: Lawrence Erlbaum.

4

Handwriting: Identification Science and Graphological Analysis Contrasted

Joe Nickell

As a practicing Questioned Document Examiner, Joe Nickell shares with others in his profession the annoyance of being confused with graphologists. The concern with this widespread misapprehension goes deeper than the annoyance all professionals feel when their profession is confused with another by the public (e.g., the podiatrist who must continually tell laypeople that he or she specializes in feet, not babies).

Drawing the distinction, as Nickell does here, between questioned document examination and graphology helps to deal with one of the major reasons pseudosciences survive. People do not believe questionable or patently false notions merely out of stupidity; they believe them because they first of all accept sensible notions, and then are lulled into suspending their critical faculties; thus allowing in the nonsense which follows. We might refer to this as the principle that *"Nonsense rides piggyback on sensible things."* Most defenders of questionable practices begin their discussions by referring to truisms that everyone accepts, or facts that were discovered by legitimate sciences. It is even more difficult to separate sense from nonsense when one is confused about which professions defend which, or worse, the same professional defends both. In some jurisdictions, graphologists are recognized as Questioned Document Examiners. And graphologists do share some beliefs with the latter, as Nickell points out. But the *differences* he notes between determining common authorship and personality traits are, he argues, more important.

Following a lecture I had given on "historical investigation"—which included a segment on certain documents I had authenticated as well as several I had exposed as forgeries—an elderly woman raised her hand. What did I think of graphology, she asked. I replied, all too briefly, that I had no doubt that personality affected one's handwriting, but that I questioned whether one's personality could be gleaned from one's handwriting alone. The woman persisted, but with some confusion. Perhaps it was Graphoanalysis she was referring to. I replied that while Graphoanalysis is alleged to have a scientific basis, I was skeptical of it as well. Still she insisted—as if to prove its validity—that it is used as "evidence in court."

It was only later, as I was driving home, that I finally realized what the woman had probably intended: She was inquiring about handwriting *comparison,* the work of respected forensic experts like those she had no doubt seen on TV detective shows.

As this incident demonstrates, the lay person may not always understand the differences between the examinations conducted by the document examiner and those performed by the graphologist—instead lumping both under the imprecise heading of "handwriting analysis." Actually, the graphologist attempts to divine from handwriting the largely subjective and elusive quality of a writer's personality, whereas the questioned document examiner is concerned with a panoply of more or less objective problems, including detecting forged handwritings, uncovering alterations in documents, identifying authorship of anonymous writings, and the like. For example, I recently exposed as forgeries some notes, ostensibly by Charles Dickens for his novel *Great Expectations,* and I demonstrated that some letters received by a newspaper from supposedly different persons were authored by a single individual who had altered her handwriting to hide the fact.

Nevertheless, there *are* superficial similarities between the two approaches. The graphologist, like the scientific document examiner, studies such individual features as pen pressure, the slant and speed of writing, the form of connecting strokes, and similar characteristics.[1] Both consider the implications inherent in forged and disguised writings, such as might be found, for instance, in a "poison pen" letter.[2] States one graphological text, "It is practically impossible either to disguise one's own handwriting completely or to copy the handwriting of another person beyond the range of detection."[3] A standard text on document examination agrees with the former premise but notes that "imitation of the handwriting of another is one of the most effective disguises of one's own handwriting."[4]

In fact, both graphology and questioned-document examination share a basic concept: the individuality of handwriting. As it is expressed by a prominent graphologist, Werner Wolff, in his 1948 *Diagrams of the Unconscious:*

> Both conscious and preconscious movements are learned. Even if many children have the same teacher and learn to make letters in the same way, each child's writing will nevertheless show an individual pattern. This variation cannot be explained by the immediate conditions of writing such as paper, pen, or position of the body, because the variation remains stable, allowing us to identify each child's writing in many repetitions even if we alter the conditions intentionally, as by giving different kinds of paper and pens, and changing the positions of the body.[5]

Similarly, a noted document expert, Ordway Hilton, states in his *Scientific Examination of Questioned Documents:*

> Writing is a conscious act. Still, through repeated use, the actual formation of each letter and word becomes almost automatic so that the experienced writer concentrates most of his conscious thought on the subject matter rather than the writing process itself. Thus, writing comes to be made up of innumerable subconscious, habitual patterns, which are as much a part of the individual as any of his personal habits or mannerisms. Writing is more, however, than a set of subconscious habits. It is a living, gradually changing part of the writer, and is far from a mechanical reproduction prepared by the complex human mechanism of muscles and nerves which are called into play to produce it. It is influenced by a mental picture of copybook form, modified by individual taste and the writer's ability to imitate that which is in his mind. Physical and mental conditions at the time of writing may affect it. Whether it is a criterion of personality is debatable, but that it is individual to each and every person is an established fact. Therefore, it can be identified, and the identification is based upon all of the elements which combine to create its individuality.[6]

(See Figure 1.)

The fact that handwriting exhibits traits which can identify an individual has been recognized since ancient times. Indeed, as early as the third century, Roman jurists established guidelines for making legal comparisons of handwriting based on "resemblance or similitude of hands."[7] But there are other factors that reflect a person's individuality—fingerprints, for instance, and facial features—yet few graphologists would urge us to believe in physiognomy (the attempt to read character from facial features). And few would suggest that fingerprints offer any more credible basis for divining character than do the lines studied by palm readers.

Nevertheless, by analogy if not by science, handwriting has long been held to mirror personality. (See chapter 2: "A Brief History of Graphology.") What was lacking, however, according to Adrian Furnham, lecturer in psychology at London University, was "not a method of analysis so much

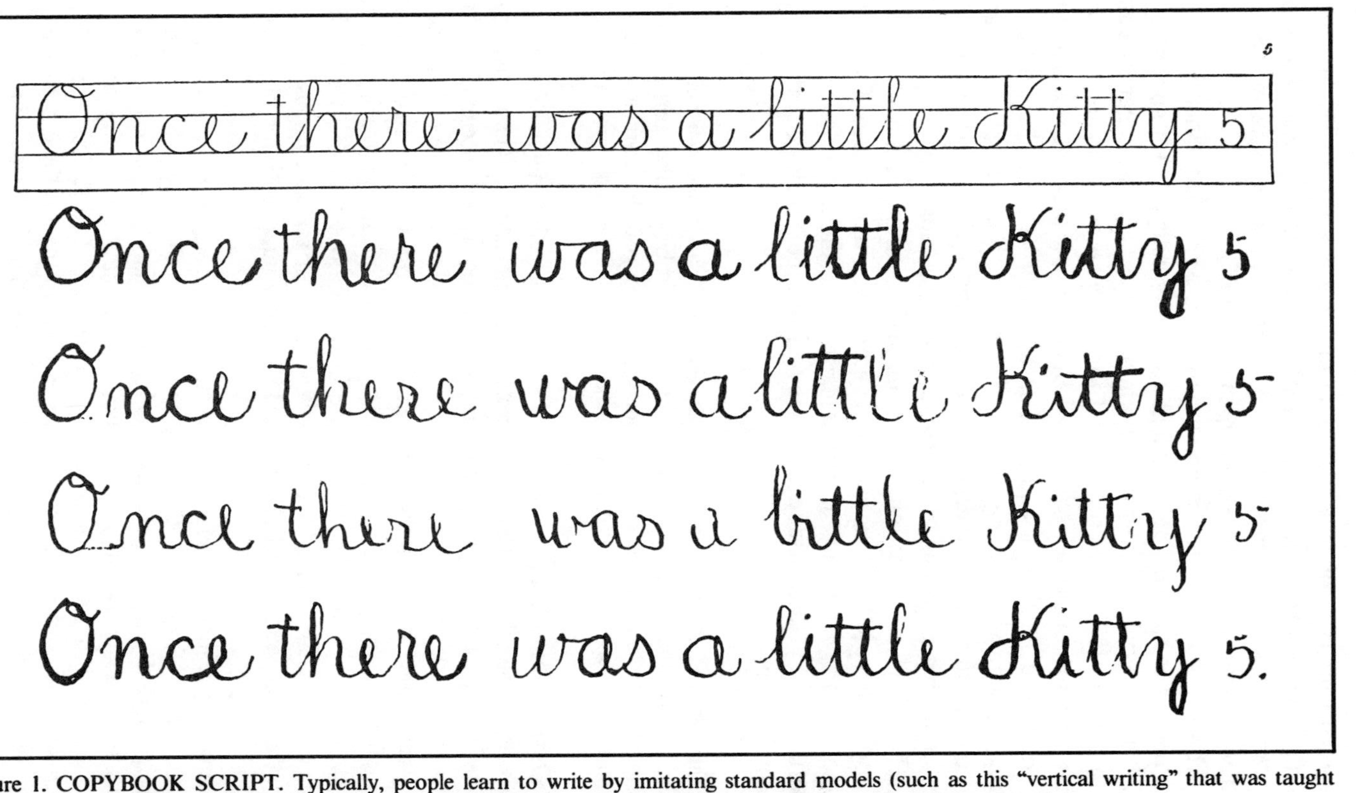

Figure 1. COPYBOOK SCRIPT. Typically, people learn to write by imitating standard models (such as this "vertical writing" that was taught in American schools from about 1890–1900). Over time, individuality increasingly develops. (Collection of Joe Nickell)

as a theory of how or why individual differences are manifest in handwriting."[8] In any case, evidence that handwriting accurately reflects personality variables is at best equivocal and, in most cases, is negative.[9] (Such evidence is treated at length elsewhere in this book.)

This is not to say there is nothing that can be gleaned about a person from his or her handwriting. Although most graphologists will not attempt to do so, lay people can correctly determine a writer's sex from handwriting approximately 70% of the time.[10] And forensic texts such as Albert S. Osborn's monumental classic, *Questioned Documents,* generally agree that not only sex but a number of additional factors may be gleaned from handwriting, though with varying degrees of certainty. For example, there are particular features that may indicate nationality, such as certain capital-letter forms that are common to German writing systems.

Then there are clues, not only from spelling and punctuation errors but also from the letter forms and certain other traits, that point to illiteracy.[11] Indeed, the alleged ability of graphologists to distinguish criminals from noncriminals by their handwriting may merely be predicated on socio-economic status.

> Criminals tend to come from lower socioeconomic classes than noncriminals, and socioeconomic class does seem to be reflected in handwriting, perhaps as a function of better education and more emphasis on good handwriting in the upper as opposed to the lower ranges of the socio-economic class structure.[12]

Other features that a scientific document detective might observe in handwriting include the tremor attributable to old age or illness (see Fig. 2),[13] as well as certain features that may suggest the writer's occupation. An obvious example is the "court hand" of old English documents—an elaborate script used by members of the legal profession who reportedly "made something of a racket of it" because it was so difficult for the lay public to read.[14] Or a telegrapher might have inadvertently revealed his trade by a characteristic five-words-to-a-line writing, even in an anonymous letter.[15] Still other occupations might be reflected in handwriting, as Hilton observes:

> Elementary school teachers have for the most part a neat, legible hand closely imitating copybook style. Draftsmen may reveal their occupation through their numeral styles or particular letter forms. Many accountants have a small precise handwriting, while other occupational groups have writing peculiar to their profession or trade. Interpretation of these signs must of course be done with caution as within each group there is the exceptional person who fails to conform, and there are many groups which have no occupational habits.[16]

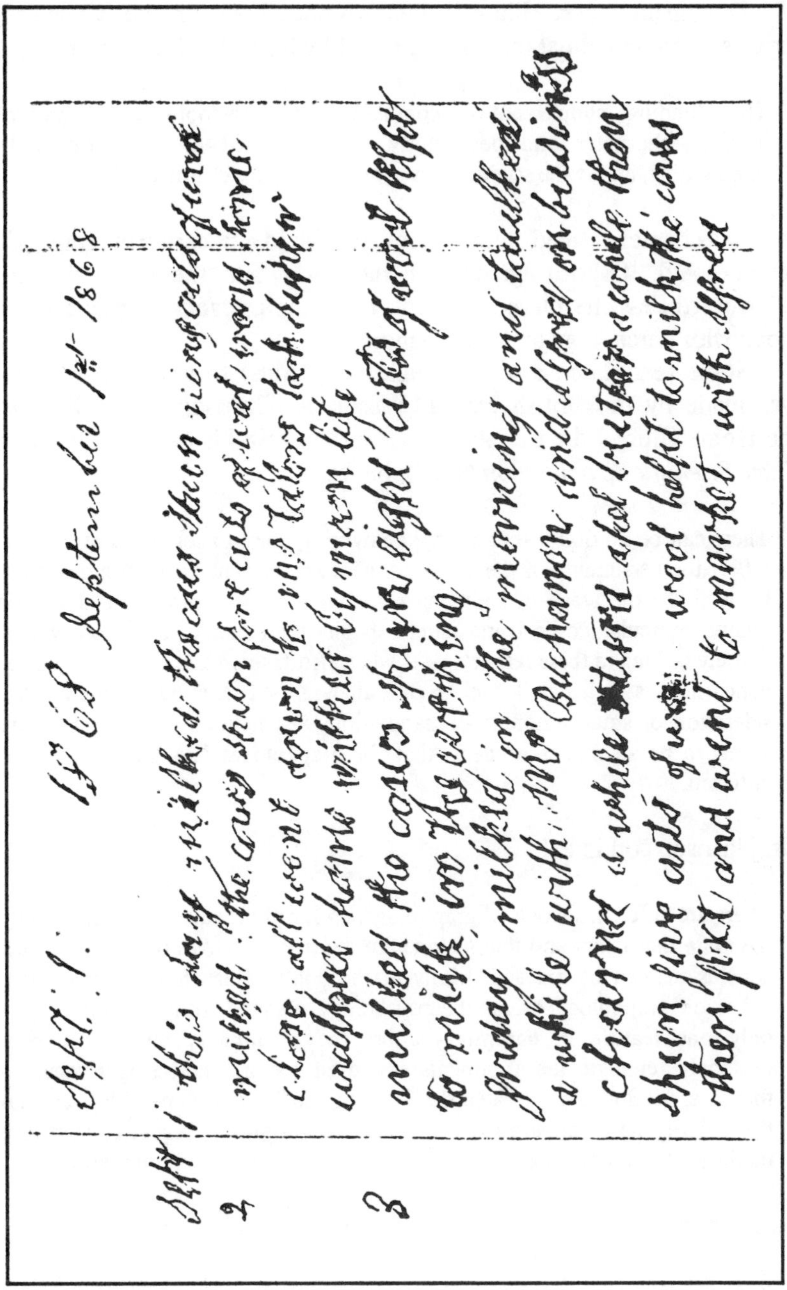

Figure 2. TREMULOUS WRITING—like this extreme example from a woman's diary of 1868—can result from a variety of causes, including illness and old age. (Collection of Joe Nickell)

Document expert Hilton is quick to note, however, that while certain aspects of an individual may be suggested by his or her handwriting,

> These findings should not be confused with a graphological analysis of writing—character and personality reading based on the individual's handwriting, an art the scientific basis of which is not clearly established.[17]

In a chapter entitled "Graphology and the Identification of Handwriting [graphology]," Osborn agreed with those who felt "there is something in it." Nevertheless, he placed graphology in the category of pseudoscience, along with phrenology and physiognomy.[18]

Some years later, a very thoughtful response to graphological claims was made by the British expert, Wilson R. Harrison, then Director of the Home Office Forensic Science Laboratory. In his *Suspect Documents: Their Scientific Examination* (1958), he stated:

> There can be no doubt that every handwriting does, to some extent at least, reflect the personality of the writer. A neat and elegant handwriting is more likely to be the work of someone who has at least a modicum of artistic ability, muscular control and careful habits than that of a person who is entirely lacking in these respects. It is when efforts are made to extend general conclusions and a detailed character analysis is attempted from the consideration of small amounts of handwriting—sometimes a single signature seems to be all that is needed—that the graphologist lays himself open to criticism.

Dr. Harrison continued:

> There are different schools of graphology, each with its adherents, who stoutly maintain that theirs and theirs alone are the true principles on which correct conclusions can be reached. Many of the books which have been written, either on graphology or on the psychology of handwriting, seem to have only one feature in common—whilst the preliminary chapters appear reasonable enough, the arguments employed become increasingly vague as they are developed in greater detail, until finally it becomes obvious that the majority of the conclusions of any graphologist must be reached by intuitive methods, since they appear to have little or no experimental foundation.

Harrison was pessimistic about the future of graphology:

> It is unlikely that graphology will ever be raised to the status of an experimental science because of the formidable difficulties certain to be encountered in assembling and analysing numerous specimens of the handwriting of a

great many people whose character and capabilities, both realised and latent, are known. This would be an essential preliminary if the principles on which character assessment is to be accomplished are to be sufficiently reliable to allow the conclusions of graphologists to be seriously considered in the courts.[19]

An interesting exchange between an advocate of graphology and a noted document expert, Ordway Hilton, took place in 1985 in the pages of the prestigious *Journal of Forensic Sciences.* Not only had Hilton spoken somewhat disparagingly of graphology in his 1956 book on questioned documents (as quoted earlier), but in 1980, he had branded it a "rather dubious art" that "has nothing to do with scientific questioned document examination as practiced in this country."[20] (The distinction is not always clear outside the U.S. and England.)[21]

The 1985 exchange began with the criticism by Dr. Niyogi, a toxicologist, of a 1983 article by Hilton.[22] Dr. Niyogi asserted:

Document examiners [have] ignored the aspect of determining personality from handwriting. Above all, the decision to write comes from brain [sic]. The hand obeys the command of brain, so we see writing on the paper. In other words, it is not only handwriting but brainwriting.[23]

In his article, Hilton had pointed out that "Any two writings by different individuals usually contain some similarities, sometimes a great number, but the differences should distinguish between the writers." Dr. Niyogi offered a suggestion. Perhaps, he thought, "personality traits in handwriting analysis" could assist the document examiner in distinguishing between the writers.[24]

Hilton responded:

Dr. Niyogi's letter shows a lack of understanding of the work of a questioned document examiner and how the identification of handwriting differs from graphological analysis. The identification of handwriting and graphological determinations of character traits are two very different disciplines that he chooses to treat as one.

The production of handwriting involves a complex physical act. Between the brain and the moving hand and fingers is an extensive muscle and nerve system that must be trained to react in a coordinated way to produce the finished writing. Thus writing is more than simply "brainwriting" as Niyogi and some graphological writers term it. Writing can be changed by intensive practice, and it can deteriorate over a period of time by lack of proper attention to its production. Physical factors such as injury to the arm or hand can change a person's handwriting.

Hilton added (in part):

> Niyogi's references to personality traits and his suggestion that document examiners should apply these to handwriting identification is an easy route to error in identification problems. Graphologists find similar personality traits in very different handwritings, that is those that can easily be distinguished by the identification processes. If one is inexperienced in identification of handwriting, overdependence on these traits in an identification problem can lead to serious error.[25]

Notwithstanding such statements, there are qualified document examiners who are also practitioners of the "emerging science"[26] of graphology. In a study of data published in 1976, I found that slightly more than half of semi-professional and professional graphologists offered themselves as consultants in questioned-document identification. Only about one in four, however, were members of peer-review organizations such as the International Association of Questioned Document Examiners.[27]

Figures were not available for the number of questioned-document examiners who profess a belief in graphology, but as Osborn said, if an English or American expert who testifies in court "believes in the subject he usually conceals the fact."[28] Osborn also concluded:

> As practiced at least, this alleged science has no value in identifying the author of a writing, and its exaggerations and unjustified inferences are likely to lead to loose thinking and weakening credulity. When the reports of practicing graphologists are more than mere generalities of wide application—which they usually are—they consist as a rule of positive inferences from ridiculously frail or misinterpreted data. This tendency toward exaggeration no doubt partly arises from the common tendency of devotees of various half-sciences and occult subjects to become partly self-hypnotized and self-deluded. . . .[29]

Osborne's thoughts—if not his "brainwriting"—exhibit the praiseworthy traits of critical thinking, honesty, and wisdom. If he, and his colleagues, seem harsh in judging graphology, it is not because of an unwillingness to consider the claims made in its behalf; rather, it is because those claims have not been substantiated by scientific investigation.

NOTES

1. Compare, for example, Barbara Hill's *Graphology* (New York: St. Martin's Press, 1981), pp. 5–6, with Charles E. O'Hara's *Fundamentals of Criminal Investigation* (Springfield, Ill.: Charles C. Thomas, 1973), p. 786. Of course, the *manner* in which these features are studied can be markedly different.

2. See Hill, pp. 121–27, and Werner Wolff, *Diagrams of the Unconscious* (New York: Grune & Stratton, 1948), pp. 144ff. and 178; cf. Albert S. Osborn, *Questioned Documents,* 2nd ed. (1929; reprinted, New Jersey: Patterson Smith, 1978), *passim* (see especially pp. 147 and 270ff.).

3. Huntington Hartford, *You Are What You Write* (New York: Macmillan, 1973), p. 245; Hartford is citing earlier texts.

4. Osborn, pp. 18, 212.

5. Wolff, p. 3.

6. Ordway Hilton, *Scientific Examination of Questioned Documents* (Chicago: Callaghan & Co., 1956), p. 136.

7. John I. Thornton and Edward F. Rhodes, "Brief History of Questioned Document Examination," *Identification News* (January 1986): p. 7.

8. Adrian Furnham, "Write and Wrong, the Validity of Graphological Analysis," *The Skeptical Inquirer* 13 (Fall 1988): p. 64.

9. Ibid., pp. 64–69. For a book-length study, see Abraham Jansen, *Validation of Graphological Judgments* (The Hague, Netherlands: Mouton, 1973).

10. Furnham, p. 68.

11. Osborn, pp. 410–11.

12. Terrence Hines, *Pseudoscience and the Paranormal* (Buffalo, N.Y.: Prometheus Books, 1988), p. 296.

13. Osborn, pp. 112–13; Hilton, p. 128.

14. Mary A. Benjamin, *Autographs: A Key to Collecting* (New York: Dover, 1986), p. 155.

15. Illustrated in Osborn, p. 139.

16. Hilton, pp. 129–30.

17. Ibid., p. 127.

18. Osborn, pp. 435–48.

19. Wilson R. Harrison, *Suspect Documents: Their Scientific Examination* (New York: Frederick A. Praeger, 1958), pp. 518–19.

20. Ordway Hilton, letter to editor, *Journal of Forensic Sciences* 25 (1980): p. 469.

21. Osborn, pp. 441–42.

22. Ordway Hilton, "How Individual Are Personal Writing Habits?" *Journal of Forensic Sciences* 28 (1983): pp. 683–85.

23. S. K. Niyogi, letter to editor, *Journal of Forensic Sciences* 30 (1985): pp. 6–7.

24. Ibid.

25. Ordway Hilton, letter to editor, *Journal of Forensic Sciences* 30: p. 8.

26. Hartford, p. 232.

27. I selected the 91 "professional" and "semi-professional" graphologists listed in Paul W. Landrum and Betty Tucker, *Who's Who in Graphology and Questioned Documents World-Wide* (Hixson, Tenn.: Unique Books, 1976), including an "update section." There were 52 (or 56.5%) who offered their services as questioned-document examiners, and 24 (or 26%) who were members of the International Association

of Questioned Document Examiners and World Association of Document Examiners.

28. Osborn, p. 442.

29. Ibid., pp. 442–44.

REFERENCES

Blotnick, Srully. 1985. *Otherwise Engaged: The Private Lives of Successful Career Women.* New York: Facts on File.

Chassler, Sey. 1986. "The Women Who Succeed." *Working Woman* 86–87 (January): pp. 102–103.

Gaeddert, William P. 1987. "The Relationship of Gender, Gender-related Traits, and Achievement Orientation to Achievement Attributions: A Study of Subject-Selected Accomplishments." *Journal of Personality* 55 (4): pp. 687–710.

Gallup, George, Jr., and Alec M. Gallup, with William Proctor. 1987. "What Successful People Have in Common." *Reader's Digest.*

Halcomb, Ruth. 1979. *Women Making It: Patterns and Profiles of Success.* New York: Ballantyne Books.

Harrison, A. A., M. Moore, and M. H. Rucker, 1985. "Further Evidence on Career and Family Compatibility Among Eminent Women and Men." *Archivo de Psicologia, Neurologia e Psichiatria* 46 (1): pp. 140–155.

Jacoby, Susan. 1988. "Roots of Success." *Family Circle Survey* (April 5): pp. 1–8.

Lawrence, Timothy L., and Brian H. Kleiner. 1985. "The Keys to Successful Goal Achievement." *Journal of Management Development* 6 (5): pp. 39–48.

Moch, Adrienne. 1983. "Psychologist Explores Keys to Success in Love, Money." *Profitline* 3 (9).

Roman, K. G. 1968. "The Psychogram, Its Background and Uses." In *Handwriting Analysis Workshop Unlimited,* ed. C. Cole. Campbell, Calif.: E.C.F. Cole.

Roman, K. G., with G. Staempfli. 1956. *Das Roman-Staempfli graphologische Psychogramm [The Roman-Staempfli Graphological Psychogram].* Berne: Ausdruckstunde.

———. 1968. "The Profile-in-the-Circle: A Graphological Psychogram." In *Encyclopedia of the Written Word: A Lexicon for Graphology and Other Aspects of Writing,* ed. K. G. Roman. New York: Frederick Unger. [Reprint of 1956 article.]

Sheehy, Gail. 1981. *Pathfinders.* New York: Bantam.

Wellingham-Jones, P. 1989. *Successful Women: Their Health and Handwriting.* Tehama, Calif.: PWJ Publ.

Section Two

Graphologists Present Their Case

5

The Present Status of Research on Handwriting Psychology as a Diagnostic Method

Oskar Lockowandt

The present selection appeared first as a chapter in Muller and Enskat (1961) and was updated in 1976, translated into English, and made available in North America in the Journal Supplement Abstract Service of the American Psychological Association, volume 6 (1), 4, ms # 1172. Slight grammatical alterations have been made by the editors to the version which appears here. Since it was meant to be an overview of the literature, none of the experiments cited here are described in sufficient detail for the reader to evaluate them. However, it is interesting to compare Lockowandt's opinion of the value of certain studies which the reader knows firsthand; or to compare Lockowandt's opinion with somene else who discusses the same experiment; e.g., the reader may wish to compare what Lockowandt has to say about the study by Frederick (1968) with Dale Beyerstein's discussion of the same experiment in chapter 8.

Unfortunately, many of the papers cited here are not available in English. However, Lockowandt's discussion gives the reader an idea of the breadth of studies done by European graphologists. The reader may also wish to consult Geoffrey Dean's chapter 12, which reviews some of the same studies cited by Lockowandt. Dean's advice in that chapter is to ask how big the *effect size* is in the studies reported. Lockowandt gives us this information about some of the experiments he discusses. Where Lockowandt reports this, the reader may wish to look at what Dean has to say about how useful graphology has been shown to be. Also, the reader may wish to read Lockowandt's own assessment, given twelve years after this review was first published in English, of what has been demonstrated about the validity of graphology. That assessment appears in Lockowandt's chapter 6.

Since the first appearance of this review in 1961, the principles of handwriting psychology have been explored more intensively than ever before. This research activity has concentrated on verifying the assertions of handwriting psychology. Muller and Enskat (1965) and Muller and Mattes (1966) have addressed the issues in handwriting research in their studies and have included it in their theoretical framework. The most recent critical analyses of experimental verification studies are those of Prystav (1969, 1971a, 1971b). From these and other studies, we will present an overview of the methods and results of controlled studies of handwriting psychology.

HANDWRITING PSYCHOLOGY AS A PSYCHODIAGNOSTIC DISCIPLINE

Handwriting psychology owes the progress reflected in modern validation research to psychological diagnostics. The application of today's psychometric methods to handwriting, especially as advocated by graphometrists, rests on the same assumptions regarding the scientific and theoretical position of handwriting psychology as do other branches of psychology. In light of current developments, one can no longer safely consign graphology to the realm of expressive psychology. Many critics (such as Kirchhoff 1926, 1962, 1965, 1968) exclude graphology completely from the science of expression, on the grounds that handwriting is detached from the person and from bodily awareness of its working materials and, instead, include it in the methodological repertoire of psychological diagnostics. This viewpoint may be too extreme. Writing and the written product are similar to the self-recorded responses made to the stimulus conditions of a test; in both cases a person's attributes, psychic structure, personality development, etc., are assessed by self-recorded behavioral characteristics. The present author adopts a position midway between expressionistic and test psychology. Handwriting psychology occupies a special position within test psychology, because, unlike the testing situation, no new behavior is required, only the activation of long-practiced skills.

How the debate on the scientific and theoretical position of handwriting psychology will be resolved remains to be seen; the ultimate conclusion will depend upon the results of further research. In the overwhelming majority of controlled studies currently available, however, handwriting psychology is considered a psychodiagnostic discipline. Three principles, which hold for the entire field of psychology, characterize both the progress and direction of research: the objective reality of human behavior and experience, the ability to control research conditions, and the reduction of speculative ideas to empirically verifiable questions. The preferred methods for testing handwriting psychological statements have been defined by these principles.

PREREQUISITES FOR VALIDATING THE PRINCIPLES OF HANDWRITING PSYCHOLOGY

The most important prerequisite for validation research is the quantifiability of handwriting characteristics. Quantifiability means more than measurement in the physical sense, because only a few handwriting characteristics can be handled in this way. In psychometry, quantification has a broader meaning; it requires that each handwriting trait be assigned a definite place on a scale. The type of scale (nominal, ordinal, interval) dictates which type of statistics is used to analyze the data.

Many basic handwriting factors are easily scaled, because they appear to be unidimensional (that is, they vary along a single dimension). Other, more complex factors such as movement flow, regularity, and distribution are multidimensional (that is, they vary along several dimensions simultaneously). The number of dimensions of highly complex factors such as the expressive quality of rhythm is unknown but is probably very large. Until now, the experimental treatment of these highly complex factors, which are vitally necessary for handwriting interpretation, has been greatly oversimplified, and they have usually been scaled as if they were unidimensional, if they are scaled at all. This practice has been aptly criticized, for research methods must be suitable to the material being studied. Thus, multidimensional scales, such as those developed by Torgerson (1958), should be used for these complex factors. A simple writing factor is assigned a single point (or value) on a single unidimensional scale, whereas a complex writing factor will be assigned a single point on each of a number of dimensions and, therefore, needs to be represented as a spatial configuration.

Two further assumptions can only be touched on here: the unequivocal definition of the writing factors and their range of variability or fluctuation. Except for impression characters, it has not been difficult to define writing factors, but the scaling of very changeable handwriting samples is still problematical. Proposals for the psychometric solution of these problems have been put forward by Stein Lewinson (1956, 1964) and Lockowandt (1968). In addition, research in handwriting psychology must meet standard experimental conditions with regard to the selection of research subjects, statistical methods, and writing materials. These issues have been discussed by Wallner (1961a).

METHODS OF VALIDATING HANDWRITING PSYCHOLOGY

The following questions are commonly asked in handwriting validation research, and they must be answered scientifically if handwriting is to be recognized as a useful diagnostic instrument: Can handwriting factors be measured or evaluated accurately? To what extent do handwriting psychologists agree on the measurement or evaluation of graphic factors? Can production variables such as writing pressure and writing speed, which are recordable only in the act of writing, be reliably ascertained from an evaluation of the fixed writing picture? How confidently can factors measured from the writing picture be evaluated? Does handwriting vary with changing time and circumstances?

These questions are answered in the following review of studies of handwriting reliability. Reliability refers to the degree to which the behavior under study—in this case, handwriting—is reproducible and to the degree to which measurement or evaluation of that behavior is reproducible. It is prerequisite for validity. It can be investigated with respect to both the writing features themselves and to the meanings derived from them. As the questions posed above suggested, various aspects of reliability remain to be explored. On the graphic characteristics level, objectivity, stability, and consistency of the trait have attained particular importance in the studies done so far. On the interpretation level, it is necessary to determine the degree of agreement among several judges (interjudge reliability) and the consistency in the interpretations made by a single judge.

If the reliability of handwriting and handwriting analysis can be established, we will need to answer the following questions: Are the interpretations derived from the handwriting features valid? Have they a diagnostic use? Which areas of personality do they illuminate? Can intelligence, emotionality, and other traits be inferred from the handwriting? How confidently can these areas of personality be identified?

Validity is the degree to which a psychological diagnostic procedure, including handwriting analysis, actually measures the personality trait it purports to measure. It is the goal for which all other researches are only necessary preliminaries. Like reliability, it can be investigated either in terms of the writing characteristics themselves or in terms of the interpretations of handwriting characteristics. The validity of writing characteristics has been examined by a variety of methods, including correlation of single features with criteria, multiple correlation, factor analysis, and contrast group comparisons. Contrast group methods and fractionated and construct validation have been used to study the validity of interpretations. The statistical bases of these methods can be found in Lienert (1969), and an overview of quantitative testing methods in handwriting psychology can be found in Lockowandt (1968).

THE RELIABILITY OF HANDWRITING CHARACTERISTICS

OBJECTIVITY

If statements about the attributes of the writer are to be derived from his or her writing characteristics, then it must be possible to identify these characteristics objectively. That is, the identification of these characteristics must not be a product of wishful thinking on the part of those describing them. For a long time, the objectivity of handwriting characteristics had always been assumed, but more recent studies in handwriting psychology have addressed themselves to the problem of objective identification for both measured and evaluated characteristics. Objectivity is here operationally defined as the degree to which the measurements and/or the ratings made by several handwriting psychologists of the same graphic characteristic correlate with each other.

Birge (1954) and Wallner (1961b) investigated the metric objectivity of measurable variables. Birge had two graphologists independently measure five metric writing variables from fifty writing specimens. The correlations between the measurements made by the two graphologists were extremely high (average $r = .97$). Wallner had one graphologist rate and measure eleven metrically measurable writing characteristics in 107 handwriting specimens. His results were also highly favorable (average $r = .90$). This research shows that measurable characteristics are reliable.

Groffmann and Fahrenberg (1960) analyzed the writing speed complex and isolated three types of speed: pen speed, performance or output speed, and subjective haste. The objectivity of the ratings made of these factors by handwriting psychologists and by laymen was tested by Lockowandt (1961) and by Wollenweber (1961). Pen or speed could be objectively rated, but performance speed could not because of experimental error. Also, the handwriting psychologists reached a high level of agreement on their rankings of subjective haste.

Characteristics which are rated are less reliable (or objective) than those which are measured. Studies by Wallner (1961c, 1962) showed that the objectivity of rated or ranked characteristics is largely dependent upon their complexity; very complex characteristics can be judged objectively only with great difficulty. Nevertheless, his studies yielded unexpectedly favorable results. His five judges used a seven-point rating scale to rate flow of rhythm, an unquestionably complex characteristic, in 100 unsorted writing samples. The overall agreement among judges was high (average r = .59). Other rated characteristics, especially impression qualities, have shown a satisfactory degree of objective judgment. Nevertheless, the reliability coefficients so far reported for complex writing characteristics are too low to be used in validation studies.

Wallner's (1962) study provides further information with regard to the differences in objectivity between rated and measured characteristics. The objectivity of impression qualities was approximately .17 correlation points below that of corresponding measurable characteristics, even when the latter were judged rather than measured. A study by Hofsommer, Holdsworth, and Seifert (1965) corroborates these results. They found a substantial difference between the objectivity of measured and rated characteristics (treatment of margins: r = .98; and stiffness of pen grip: r = .41). These results provide a realistic estimate of the true differences in objectivity.

The experiments discussed so far do not, however, represent the practical work of the handwriting psychologist, who does not classify impressionistic qualities that have been chosen by others, but who makes his or her own selection from an array of impressionistic characteristics that are presented in the form of adjectives. Muller (1957) has examined this selection process in an experiment in which ten handwriting psychologists were asked to assign to twelve handwriting samples the twenty most suitable adjectives from a list of 150 impressionistic characteristics. These impressionistic qualities were divided into twenty-four groups of adjectives that were related in meaning. The inter-rater agreement of the handwriting psychologists was 42.5%; that is, on average, they agree on eight of the twenty selected qualities. It is interesting that consensual agreement—that is, agreement based on the significance of the adjective in the context of the entire handwriting sample—is higher than agreement based on the meaning of the adjective in isolation (68.5% vs. 42.5%). Searching for consensual agreement closely parallels the practice of handwriting psychologists in their everyday work. The difficulty of judging highly complex impression qualities is illustrated by a marginal finding; as a rule, male handwriting psychologists prefer different impressionistic qualities from those selected by female handwriting psychologists.

STABILITY

Handwriting psychology seeks to discern psychic attributes through handwriting as collective signs and draws conclusions from observed and recorded writing behavior about the dispositions and attributes that determine these behaviors. In accordance with basic hypotheses of personality theory (Graumann 1960), handwriting psychology assumes that these attributes are not subject to continual, substantial alteration but are relatively, though not rigidly, constant.

It is further assumed that the relative constancy of these personality attributes corresponds to the relative intra-individual constancy of writing movements and writing characteristics. Therefore, a person's typical system of handwriting must not vary substantially if one is to draw conclusions from it about the permanent attributes of the writer. This constancy is called stability or repeated measurement (test-retest) reliability. Handwriting stability is defined as the relative constancy of handwriting characteristics over time and under different circumstances. It is, of course, a prerequisite for validity, but it can be studied independently of it.

An accurate assessment of stability can be achieved only by systematic variation of writing conditions and of time intervals. The few studies on stability which have been done to date have concerned themselves with the effects of different instructions on the constancy of handwriting characteristics (e.g., normal pace compared with increasing speed to maximum tempo) and with time intervals of ninety minutes to two months.

Harvey (1934) found, with an interval of two months between first and second writings, an average stability coefficient of $r = .77$, with values ranging from $r = .48$ for the size of capitals, to $r = .85$ for the size of middle zones. Bearing in mind that the second writing was produced under rapid dictation, these results can be considered highly favorable. Fischer (1962, 1964) reported even greater stability in handwriting samples produced a week apart ($r = .80$–$r = .93$). Fahrenberg and Conrad (1964) confirmed these results using an interval of ten days.

More recent research from the Psychological Institute of the University of Freiburg in Breisgen (Beiersdorf, Derleth, and Kupper, all cited in Prystav 1971a) has yielded remarkably high stability coefficients under varying experimental conditions. Most values were beyond $r = .80$, many were beyond $r = .90$. These studies used time intervals ranging from ninety minutes (Beiersdorf) to three weeks (Derleth and Kupper).

All of these studies dealt with the stability of measurable characteristics. Prystav (1969) is the only investigator to study the stability of a characteristic —writing pressure—which cannot be measured, but must be evaluated. Using an interval of six weeks and a four-point scale, he obtained an average agreement of r = .90 in the rating of this characteristic.

Lockowandt and Keller (1975) examined the stability of children's handwriting. Two handwriting specimens were collected from each of 120 male and female pupils, ranging in age from ten years to twelve years, eleven months. The interval between the first and second specimens was two years. Six handwriting psychologists and ten laymen had the task of determining which handwriting samples were written by the same child. These judges showed a significant level of agreement in matching pairs of samples, thereby demonstrating that the handwriting of children represents a stable graphometric product.

Since the birth of handwriting psychology, the individuality of handwriting has been one of the basic axioms of the discipline; and this axiom has never been seriously questioned with regard to the handwriting characteristics of the graphically mature and graphically practiced person. There was much doubt, however, that the handwriting of those who are graphically immature and unpracticed showed similar individuality. It was believed that the handwriting of children was so likely to change during their developmental stages as to render valid interpretation impossible.

The results of the Lockowandt and Keller (1975) experiment, as well as those from the first genetic stability research performed by von Bracken (1934), have shown clearly that handwriting becomes individualistic at an early stage, as early as the first year of school. This individuality can be observed during the entire period of schooling. It is more pronounced in the handwriting of boys than of girls, and it increases with age. It is particularly significant that individually shaped graphic movements are manifested during the first years of school, because they are complex characteristics of a coordinated total movement, even though this coordination is not yet fully developed. The distortion of the microdynamics of writing during puberty is not so drastic that the basic personality of the adolescent cannot be reflected in handwriting. With certain reservations, therefore, the interpretation of children's handwriting is justified (see also Ajuriaguerra and Denner 1964).

CONSISTENCY

Consistency studies address the question as to whether and to what extent the individual measurements in a *single* writing specimen are in accord with each other. Consistency is also known as split-half reliability, because the measurements or ratings from one-half of the specimen (e.g., the even-numbered) are correlated with those from the other half (e.g., the odd-numbered). Consistency determinations are particularly important for evaluating how representative of the specimen the measurements are. The more variations there are in an intra-individual characteristic, the greater the number of individual measurements required for accurate evaluation.

Studies by Timm (1965, 1967), Fischer (1962), and Prystav (1969) and those by Derleth, Kupper, and Beiersdorf (see Prystav 1971a) have yielded high consistency coefficients for metric handwriting characteristics. Almost all the coefficients reported are greater than r = .85, most are beyond r = .90. A comparison of Fischer's consistency values, based on twenty individual measurements per characteristic, and Prystav's, values based on ten measurements, clearly supports Wallner's hypothesis that ten individual measurements are sufficient to establish the consistency of metric writing characteristics. The consistency coefficients from the two studies scarcely varied from each other.

In general, lower consistency coefficients are obtained for rated or evaluated characteristics than for metric characteristics. Timm found r = .94 for measured characteristics, r = .89 for simple ratings, r = .82 for complex ratings, and r = .73 for impressionistic characteristics. Prystav's (1969) values for rated characteristics are even lower; they vary from r = .15 to r = .47 for impressionistic characteristics (lively – rigid), from r = .12 to r = .47 for complex characteristics (right-tending–left-tending), and from r = .29 to r = .86 for simple ranked characteristics (curving – straight).

Much more favorable results were obtained by Hofsommer, Holdsworth, and Seifert (1965) and by Wallner (1968), apparently because of the optimal conditions under which the research was carried out. Markedly different writing samples were selected, the samples were presented simultaneously, and forced classifications were made. Prystav reached the same conclusion: "The astonishingly high reliabilities of these writers have now mainly theoretical importance as indicating values of graphological evaluated characteristics obtainable under the best possible conditions" (1969, 127).

When measurable characteristics are compared with evaluated characteristics under research conditions similar to those of actual practice, evaluated characteristics have shown relatively little consistency. Because of their complexity and their unknown dimensional structure, the definition of these characteristics is still imprecise. Only more uniform definition of evaluated characteristics, combined with the use of comparison and model writing samples, as Muller and Mattes (1966a, 1966b) have shown, can lead to better results. Further research on the consistency of evaluated characteristics is warranted, because they appear to be very useful diagnostically (Babst 1971).

THE RELIABILITY OF HANDWRITING INTERPRETATIONS

Of all the cognitive processes used in handwriting psychology, interpretation—the assignment and judgment of meaning—is the least well understood. It involves cognitive operations by which a multiplicity of combinations and chains of reasoning are integrated in ways that are difficult to explicate and describe, so there is ample opportunity for the use of subjective judgment.

Handwriting interpretation is dependent on a multiplicity of factors. It is influenced by the size and quality of the writing specimen, by the spontaneity and evocativeness of its formation, by information concerning its origins, by the information content and semantic richness of the writing, and by conditions specific to the writer. The methods of evaluation used also affect the interpretation process, that is, by the precision with which the writing characteristics are defined, the ways in which graphic factors are combined and modified, the specificity and generality of the essential rules of interpretation, and the recognition of measurement errors such as central tendency and halo effect.

The personality of the judge has a major influence on the kind of interpretation that is made. His qualifications, his personal and practical experience, the nature of his training (e.g., pluralistic or dogmatic), and his ability to make specific judgments will all play a part in his interpretation. And finally, the purpose for which the judgment is to be used will determine how detailed and extensive the interpretation will be. The nature of the interpretation will vary depending on whether, for example, the writing psychologist is asked to evaluate specific qualifications such as leadership ability for a particular occupation or to evaluate general characteristics such as sociability or vitality.

In terms of the psychology of thought, the interpretation process itself can be regarded as a process of gathering and assimilating information, from which a global picture of the psychological attributes of the personality emerges. This global picture is then steadily differentiated and, if need be, restructured on the basis of the information gleaned from the written material (Daul 1966; see also the description of the interpretation process by Lockowandt 1973 and chapter 8 of this volume).

OBJECTIVITY: INTER-INDIVIDUAL AGREEMENT

Reliability studies of graphological interpretations are concerned with the extent to which several judges agree in their interpretation of the same handwriting sample, regardless of whether their diagnostic judgments are correct. The earliest and frequently cited work on this topic was done by Crider (1941). Two handwriting psychologists ranked eighteen handwriting samples on nine personality characteristics. Overall agreement between the judges was low (average rho = .18). Crider's study was, however, methodologically flawed; his judges were very different in their qualifications, and the written material was scanty. Although Crider's findings cannot be taken as an accurate estimate of inter-judge reliability, his study pointed up the need for better research design.

Among the small number of studies on reliability of interpretation, the works of Hofsommer, Holdsworth, and Seifert (1965), Wallner (1965, 1969), Schneevoigt (1968), Cohen (1969), Reichold (1969), and Volz (1969) are of particular importance because of their wide scope and more exacting methodology. Hofsommer and colleagues had three handwriting psychologists rate leadership ability among foremen (n = 322) on a seven-point scale. They found a high and statistically significant level of agreement among all judges (average rho = .74). This result, unusually favorable for handwriting psychology, is all the more unusual because the attribute to be judged was quite broad and the handwriting samples had not been written under standardized conditions (the candidates had written to apply for jobs using their own writing implements).

A much lower level of agreement among their three handwriting psychologists was found in their judgments of the success of technical school students (n = 57) (average rho = .39), but overall, at least four of five coefficients were significant. Their three handwriting psychologists were able to reach a highly significant level of agreement (average rho = .62) in their evaluations of the abilities of office workers.

It is usually assumed that the reliability of graphological judgments is influenced by the nature of the writing (e.g., spontaneous writings vs. those designed to be pleasing to the reader) and by the writing instrument (pen vs. pencil). However, Hofsommer, Holdsworth, and Seifert (1965) demonstrated that such influences are only slight. Handwriting psychologists generally assume that the personality of the writer is relatively constant across situations, so the special circumstances of the writing has little influence on their evaluations. The value of this expanded research for handwriting psychology cannot be overstated. It provided, for the first time, a methodologically faultless demonstration that handwriting psychologists use binding yardsticks of judgment and agreed-upon cognitive schemata in the complex process of interpretation.

The fundamental finding that handwriting interpretations are produced by something other than chance has been successfully replicated with other populations and other research techniques. Wallner (1965) had eighty-nine writing samples rated by six handwriting psychologists on 12 dimensions such as movement tempo, mood swings, perceptual faculty, temperament, and contact ability. Of the 180 rater intercorrelations, 93% were significant at or beyond the .05 level. This high reliability value, which the author achieved in later study (Wallner 1969), leaves little doubt about the stability of the judgment processes used by handwriting psychologists.

Wallner (1965) was also able to show that the effect on their interpretations of the judges' qualifications was substantial. The judge who had no university training in psychology and scarcely any practical experience deviated considerably from the combined ratings of his colleagues. Furthermore, the content of the writing specimens did not explain the high-level agreement among the judges; the one judge who did not understand the language of the writing specimens (Swedish) did not differ in his judgments from the other judges.

That handwriting psychologists can make reliable judgments of such specific attributes as intelligence has been demonstrated by Schneevoigt (1968) in a painstaking experiment. The results of two intelligence tests served as the intelligence criteria, and five out of six concordance coefficients were statistically significant. Schneevoigt also found that the more varied the expression of the intelligence in the writings of the subjects, the greater the degree of agreement among the raters—a finding of particular relevance to handwriting psychologists, many of whom prefer a broad concept of intelligence (see Lockowandt, chapter 8).

In spite of the favorable evidence currently being amassed on the objectivity of interpretation, it must be remembered that interpretative judgments are, in general, less reliable than judgments of graphic characteristics. Better results must await more analysis of the interpretation processes themselves.

STABILITY: INTRA-INDIVIDUAL CONSTANCY

How stable are the judgment processes of handwriting psychologists? If the same psychologist evaluates the same handwriting specimen at two different times, how similar are his two evaluations? Although we do not yet know how long the time interval between repeated interpretations should be in order to rule out memory effects, the results to date suggest that handwriting psychologists are constant in their judgments.

Crider (1941) presented a handwriting psychologist with the same writing sample he had rated on twelve personality traits one month earlier. Agreement between the two ratings was significant on all twelve traits (average rho = .82), including the writer's intelligence, emotional stability, and self-confidence.

Reichold (1969) has confirmed that handwriting psychologists derive their interpretations from a clear cognitive frame of reference. After an interval of three months, a handwriting psychologist evaluated ninety handwriting specimens on adjustment to the environment, self-confidence, perseverance, foresight, and maturity. Stability coefficients for the five dimensions ranged from r = .78 to r = .88. Both studies used only one judge, so more extensive studies are needed to establish the generalizability of these early results.

The interpretation of a writing sample is the product of complicated processes of selection, ordering, and combination. The studies by Crider and by Reichold indicate that the judgments of handwriting psychologists were not accidental but were based on firm methodological rules.

THE VALIDITY OF HANDWRITING ANALYSIS: GRAPHIC CHARACTERISTICS

Validity is the accuracy with which a diagnostic or assessment procedure measures what it is supposed to measure. It is usually assumed—incorrectly—that the same general concept of validity is equally applicable to every diagnostic method, including handwriting psychology. A diagnostic method is not, however, valid or not valid. On the contrary, each test of validity must be considered in terms of the research sample and the criteria used in that particular study. Accordingly, there is only a "differentiated validity" (Michel and Iseler 1968); that is, a test of handwriting is able to make valid assertions about some criteria, but not about others. Validity research, then, can be compared to exploring new territory; every study—insofar as it is methodologically sound—expands the informational and practical possibilities of a diagnostic method.

The validity of handwriting analysis is operationally defined as the degree to which the handwriting characteristics of a sample of individuals correlates with specific, precise criteria such as scores on tests, responses to questionnaires, or ratings by supervisors. It must be emphasized that negative results from such studies do not necessarily speak against the validity of handwriting psychology. A low correlation, by itself, may reflect either the low validity of the criterion employed in the study or the low validity of the handwriting analysis. A validity study can only be considered satisfactory when the reliability and validity of the criterion have been established. In the meantime, studies in which handwriting characteristics were correlated with test results must be critically evaluated (see Muller and Mattes 1966a and Prystav 1969 for critical historical reviews of validity research). Furthermore, the choice of appropriate criteria is critical. We believe that internal criteria such as test scores must be replaced by external criteria such as professional and academic success or occupational achievement.

CORRELATION OF INDIVIDUAL GRAPHIC CHARACTERISTICS WITH CRITERIA

Secord (1948) and Wallner (1966) investigated the validity of individual handwriting characteristics by correlating them with specific criteria. Secord tried to validate the Stein Lewinson (1942) scale by using such personality characteristics as mood state and affective ability, but without success. Wallner's results were equally disappointing. These validation techniques have been dismissed by graphologists, because they do not take into account the holistic nature of handwriting, and instead cultivate an atomistic view of graphic characteristics (see Angermann 1970). In view of the results to date, it is unlikely that simple graphic variables will correlate significantly with the criteria used. Such relationships are possible, however, in the case of complex characteristics such as those used by Wallner (e.g., regularity, maturity of the writing) in his, so study of these validation procedures cannot be entirely rejected.

To date, none of the factor analytic studies (discussed in detail below) which have generated large correlation matrices (as many as 29,000 coefficients per test) has led to satisfactory results, when only the correlations between single graphic characteristics and criteria are taken into account. To be sure, many significant relationships between writing characteristics and criteria are found, but the correlations are too low (usually on the order of $r = .15$) to permit accurate prediction of criteria. There is no point, therefore, in citing the individual relationships that have been found.

There are a number of factors that may serve to reduce the correlation between handwriting characteristics and criteria. The computation of the product-moment correlation is based on statistical assumptions that are not always fulfilled. The most important of these assumptions is that the two things being correlated are related to each other in a linear fashion. When this is not true, the degree of actual relationship will be systematically underestimated. See Timm (1965) and Prystav (1969). It is not yet known whether curvilinear relationships are more frequent than linear relationships in handwriting psychology as Wallner (1970) has assumed.

It is also possible that the relationship between graphic characteristics is affected: there may be a three-sided distribution in an uncontrolled way by other (moderator) variables. The theory of "moderated regression," proposed by Saunders (1956), was used for the first time by Konttinen (1968) in the psychology of children's handwriting. In addition, the correlation can be reduced if the criterion is unreliable or if the writing characteristics are unreliable, as might be the case with a subjectively evaluated trait that is assessed by a single rater.

MULTIPLE CORRELATION

Handwriting psychology has always objected to simple correlation studies on the grounds that it is impossible to predict any criterion from a single graphic characteristic. This objection is remedied by multiple correlation techniques (also called multiple regression analysis), in which several graphic characteristics are combined in the prediction of criteria. Multiple correlation was introduced into handwriting psychology by Timm (1965, 1967) and pursued by Linster (1969), Prystav (1969), and Wallner (1970).

Linster (1969) has presented the most promising results thus far. He was able to predict an extensive spectrum of ability and personality characteristics from graphometric variables. Regression coefficients of .65–.85 were found between writing variables and specific aspects of intelligence, achievement, interpersonal behavior, relationship to environment, emotionality, and personal maturity. Intelligence was manifested as intellectual agility, theoretical ability, logical thinking, and imaginativeness. The graphometrically definable traits included both quantitative and qualitative performance. Tolerance (r = .85), good fellowship, restraint, and discretion were the forms of contact behavior most precisely defined. Environmental adjustment could be differentiated by handwriting psychology as open-mindedness, activity, drive for dominance, passivity and adaptability, overall behavior, openness, and self-criticism. Affectivity included the distinction between robust and sensitive emotionality.

These findings show the wide range of behavior and dispositions that can be identified with confidence from handwriting, even on the level of graphic characteristics. Although the research results are still clear enough for practical application, they are plausible in terms of handwriting psychology. The use of multiple regression techniques has shown that graphological characteristics are endowed with psychological meaning.

FACTOR ANALYSIS

Factor analysis starts with the intercorrelation of a large number of characteristics and then determines which characteristics cluster together to form a smaller number of basic components or factors that are responsible for the handwriting, ability, or personality under investigation. Factor analytic studies aimed at revealing the basic dimensions or factors of handwriting have been carried out by Lorr, Lepine, and Golder (1954), Droesler (cited in Unkel 1964), Fischer (1964), Adolfs (1964), Seifert (1965), and Stein Lewinson (1968).

Attempts to use factor analytic methods to validate handwriting psychology have been made by Fahrenberg (1961), Conrad (1964), Unkel (1964), Fahrenberg and Conrad (1965), Timm (1965, 1967), Lockowandt (1966, 1968), Wallner (1971), Linster (1969), Prystav (1969), and Paul-Mengelberg (1971). This branch of research is still in flux, but several general statements can be made.

Factor analytic studies of graphometric variables have yielded many different factors that help reveal those aspects of handwriting that may be important for assessing ability and personality. Unfortunately, the task is not complete. Most writing variables occur in several factors, thereby obscuring the clear identification of independent factors. Furthermore, there is no unanimity as to the number of factors required for a complete description of handwriting. Prystav (1969, 282) concluded from his review that there are "about 10 principal factors which share importantly in coining the 'basic framework' of writing and above all in regard to movement; and around 15 specific factors, which contribute predominantly to the individual shaping of the writing picture." Although there are theories of handwriting psychology that postulate a small number of basic dimensions—or even a single basic dimension—they undoubtedly oversimplify what is actually a complex situation.

To date, factor analytic studies of handwriting have been successful in predicting the following criteria: (1) intelligence as measured by the Raven test, by the Intelligence-Structure Test of Amthauer, and by Wechsler's Full Scale Intelligence Quotient and Deterioration Index; (2) several kinds of psychomotor performance such as finger coordination, finger-hand speed, and arm movement; and (3) the psychic regulation mechanism derived from the Color Pyramid Test (Schaie and Heiss 1964), acheivement motivation, vital energy, and psychic balance. However, the vast amount of work done so far on factorial validation of handwriting is not in proportion to the still scanty results. An economical construction of future research is urgently needed.

CONTRAST GROUP PROCEDURES

The contrast group method of validation involves the selection of two groups that differ markedly from each other with respect to a particular characteristic. These groups are then tested to determine whether they can also be differentiated on the basis of the criterion variable. In handwriting psychology, these groups can be formed either on the basis of marked differences in handwriting characteristics or in personality characteristics. Both methods have been employed with varying degrees of success. The use of extremely different groups increases the likelihood that they will also differ on the criterion, but this approach has little practical application, because the extreme characteristics required for this method are not usually found in the situations in which handwriting psychology is customarily used.

Only Land (cited in Adolfs 1964) and Birge (1954) have used the contrast groups method to validate individual handwriting characteristics. Land constituted his groups on the basis of two handwriting characteristics, slant and alignment. From two hundred handwriting samples, he selected four groups of ten samples each, one with normal slant, one with extreme left slant, one with normal alignment, and one with extremely sloping alignment. The Pressey-X-O test, which identifies group differences in emotionality, served as the criterion. Land found that writers with extreme handwriting characteristics—i.e., left slant and down-sloping alignment— were more emotional than those with normal characteristics—a result in full accord with the interpretive hypotheses of handwriting psychology.

It is not clear, however, whether each of the two graphic signs chosen by Land, slant and alignment, is independently related to emotionality, or if they are the only or the most critical graphic signs associated with emotionality. Lockowandt (1966) has shown, for example, that slant is significantly correlated with the following writing characteristics: extent of upper loops ($r = -.41$), size of upper length ($r = -.38$), and distance of upper signs from the word body ($r = -.35$). Thus, the stronger emotionality reported by Land could also be attributed to the characteristics that are highly correlated with slant. It is better, therefore, to proceed not from individual graphic characteristics, but from writing factors which represent clusters of related graphic characteristics.

Birge (1954) chose the opposite route from Land and divided his research sample on the basis of personality characteristics. A total of 685 students ranked each other on five dimensions: intelligence, emotional stability, dominance, culture, and sensibility or high-strung temperament. From this sample of students, groups of twenty-four subjects were selected so that two subjects with the most extreme ratings for each dimension were to be found in each group. Thus in each group two were highly intelligent, two unintelligent, etc. Correlations of the differences among twenty-two handwriting variables for the groups judged most extreme yielded no significant relationships with the five ability and personality characteristics. It is likely, however, that this study was flawed by the use of personal judgments made by naive observers, which are known to be affected by such tendencies as the halo effect and the projection of the rater's own unconscious problems onto the person being rated.

The use of the contrast group method for validating specific handwriting characteristics has been neglected in handwriting psychology even though positive results can be obtained, as Land's experiment has demonstrated. The method would probably be more fruitful if groups were formed not on the basis of specific graphic signs, but on the basis of graphic dimensions of a higher degree of abstraction (factors). Thus, for example, contrasting groups might be formed on the basis of their Writing Expansion, a general factor which has been identified in several factor analyses and which has a generally agreed upon definition.

THE VALIDITY OF HANDWRITING INTERPRETATIONS

Contrast Group Methods. The contrast group method can also be used to study the validity of interpretations made from handwriting analyses. Much of this research had dealt with the writing of children.

The distinguished developmental theorist Gesell (1906) was the first to study the relationship between quality of handwriting and gender, school achievement, general intelligence, motor skills, and experimentally determined writing dexterity (n = 4361 schoolchildren). His results are noteworthy: (1) From the first grade on, boys showed a greater tendency than girls to uncoordinated writing. (2) From the fifth grade on, girls were more accurate than boys. (3) Sex differences manifested themselves clearly by the age of about ten and a half years. (4) The accuracy of handwriting in primary school children varied directly with school achievement. Among these primary schoolchildren, it was found that the inaccurate writer was also less accurate and less conscientious in the rest of his or her school performance. This author has used the Chi-square test to analyze Gesell's data and has found all the differences he reported to be statistically significant (Lockowandt 1970a, 310).

Oinonen (1961) divided 122 first and second graders into those with good and those with poor handwritings and found significant correlations between handwriting quality and intelligence (r = .38) and between handwriting quality and school performance (r = .60). The combined correlation of handwriting and intelligence with school performance was, predictably, even higher (r = .74 in the first grade and r = .70 in the second grade), indicating that school performance can be predicted with a high degree of accuracy by a combination of intelligence and handwriting assessment. Thus, both Gesell and Oinonen were able to demonstrate the partial validity of children's handwriting and to show that Klages's judgment regarding the "inferior handwriting form" (1927, 233) and the poverty of expression in children's handwriting was not justified.

Hueskins and Schuler (quoted in Lockowandt 1972) also tested the validity of children's handwriting using the contrast group method. Performance on the Pauli-Test served as the criterion for 295 children, age 10–12, and 299 children, age 13–16 years. The performance structure of the Pauli-Tests could be predicted with a high level of statistical significance for the younger group but not for the older group of children. The average biserial correlation coefficient for the younger group was r = .27 for boys (ranging from r = .13 to .48) and r = .44 for girls (ranging from r = .45 to .53). It is especially noteworthy that positive results could be obtained using a very specific criterion and unpracticed judges.

In contrast to these characteristic-centered studies were the group studies based on contrasting personality characteristics. Grunewald-Zuberbier (1966) used the type of contrast group procedure used by Birge (1954), in that she looked at differences in handwriting among three groups of children: children in institutions, children in correctional facilities, and normal children. She assumed that there would be substantial differences in personality among the three groups of children. One of her most important findings was a difference in the variability of writing characteristics (size, width, regularity, interval between words, and space between lines) between children in institutions and normal children. Institutionalized children who were behavior problems because of excessive impulsivity (Aggressions) showed greatly increased variability. Grunewald-Zuberbier interpreted the differences she found for the constructive writing components, Activity and Control, to mean that the children from institutions, unlike normal children, were characterized by increased Activity drive and decreased Control. She also found evidence against the dogmatic assertion of Klages (1927) that children's writings show poverty of expression.

It is difficult to find groups of adults who, because of highly unusual life histories, show clearly distinguishable personality structures. A very interesting research program involving extreme groups of people was conducted by Paul-Mengelberg (1965). She compared the qualitative and quantitative handwriting characteristics of two groups of disturbed adults with those of a normal control group. Group A consisted of persons who had returned home after long periods in Russian prisoner-of-war or labor camps; Group B consisted of politically oriented persons who had spent long periods underground or in concentration camps. Group A and B showed prominent symptoms of premature aging, which were manifested by a much higher biological age as compared to chronological age.

Paul-Mengelberg was able to differentiate the three groups on the basis of their handwriting characteristics. Groups A and B both showed a syndrome of strikingly disturbed handwriting characteristics, but Group A showed a more uniform graphic symptomatology than Group B. The author attributed the uniform symptomatology of Group A to the frequent occurrence of such disorders as organic brain damage from head injury or deterioration from the aftereffects of systemic disease like typhus. Group B was characterized by severely neurotic symptomatology, including anxiety and restlessness, fears of death, and irritability. In subsequent studies (1971a, 1972), Paul-Mengelberg added a group of compulsive personality types to her original research sample. Further analysis of the expanded sample confirmed the limited graphic performance possibilities of the brain-injured by contrast with the varied writing performance of the neurotic subjects, whose conflict structures were as varied as the circumstances underlying their neuroses.

Lockowandt (unpublished) used a contrast group procedure to compare the writing actions of children who were dyslexic with those of children who were not dyslexic. The children were asked to copy a text from the blackboard, while their writing movements and the movements of their heads were filmed. The first ninety seconds of the films were evaluated graphometrically, and significant differences were found between the two groups.

The value of handwriting psychology for the assessment of ability and personality gains further support from a very original study by Frederick (1968), carried out in collaboration with the Institute of Applied Psychology in Saltsjobaden, Sweden. Its goal was the identification of fifty-five male and female suicides from their handwriting. From the typed text of each suicide's writing specimen, three handwritten copies were prepared by control subjects. Five handwriting psychologists, five detectives, and five secretaries served as judges. Their task was to select from the four specimens presented the one that was in the suicide's own writing. All five handwriting psychologists showed highly significant percentages of successful choices, and the accuracy of their choices was clearly superior to that of the detectives and the secretaries.

The handwriting validity values obtained from comparison group studies are generally very high. Nevertheless, it must be acknowledged that the differentiation of comparison groups on the basis of handwriting interpretation is not always successful. For example, it has not been possible to discriminate psychotics from normals using handwriting psychology (Pascal and Suttell 1947, Frederick 1965). The reasons for this failure are not known, but the clinically variable ways in which psychosis is manifested makes it unsuitable as a validity criterion.

Content Validity. Early evidence for the validity of handwriting interpretation came predominantly from studies using matching procedures. In this case, handwriting psychologists would either judge the writing of persons unknown to the researchers (a procedure used by Binet 1906 and Bobertag 1929), or they would match their judgments against judgments based on clinical evaluations or the results of tests. In all these studies, global comparisons were made in accordance with the precepts of Allport and Vernon (1933): "If we are to attain the most adequate validation, the script as a whole and the personality as a whole must somehow be compared."

Eysenck reported (1961) that the interpretations of a handwriting psychologist were greater than chance performance matched with brief psychiatric descriptions. There are also well-known matching experiments of

Powers, a collaborator of Allport and Vernon, who obtained greater than chance agreement between personality judgments and handwriting interpretations. These studies were particularly welcome to traditional graphology because they supported the holistic character of graphological assessment. They have, however, been criticized by psychometrically oriented handwriting psychologists such as Fahrenberg (1961) and Prystav, because the nature of the matching process remains unclear.

Recognition of the weaknesses of holistic matching methods soon led to attempts to validate individual interpretive statements. We will pass over the early and well-known studies by Marum (1945), Eysenck (1948), and Castelnuovo-Tedesco (1948)—all of which yielded positive results, despite methodological flaws—and report some of the more recent work on the validity of handwriting psychology.

Hofsommer, Holdsworth, and Seifert (1962) investigated the accuracy with which two handwriting psychologists could predict success at a Swedish school of forestry. Fifty-four students were rated by two handwriting psychologists on a set of attributes that the authors assumed would determine success in this institution: emotional stability, vital energy, strong will power, and intellecutal versatility. The critical validation criterion was the average school report record for twenty-three subjects after one and a half years of training. The results are surprising and demonstrate that prognosis by handwriting can be very accurate. Validity coefficients for the two judges combined ranged from rho = .17 to rho = .78 (average rho = .55), and almost all of them were statistically significant. These results are particularly important because they successfully replicate the most positive early validation study by Castelnuovo-Tedesco (1948).

Hofsommer and Holdsworth (1963) reported equally favorable results from a study in which a handwriting psychologist attempted to predict from the handwritten autobiographies of 141 candidates their degree of pilot aptitude after a year and a half of basic training. The authors hypothesized that the following personality characteristics were important: ability of tolerate psychic stress, method of working, and social adaptability. At the end of the training period, the judgments of the handwriting psychologists were correlated with the dichotomous criteria "suitable for further training" or "not suitable for further training." As demonstrated by the significant biserial correlation coefficient (r = .36), the handwriting psychologists could predict the general vocational suitability of pilots with a considerable degree of confidence. They could also predict achievement in advanced training for the sixty-one candidates who had been selected for the basic course (rhotau = .41). They could not predict the training results for the twenty-four aspirants in the final stage of training, but this result is not surprising in view of the homogeneity of the group. It is astonishing that so specific a characteristic as qualification for fighter pilot could be predicted by handwriting, especially because it had not previously been known that it was determined by psychological motivation.

Relationships between single personality factors and handwriting variables have been confirmed and expanded in a series of studies reported by Wallner (1963a, 1963b, 1965). He was able to show that many psychic attributes such as temperament, distractibility, need for recognition, verbal ability, logical reasoning, ability to achieve, motivation to achieve, and intelligence could be evaluated reliably by handwriting psychology. In his studies of intelligence, Wallner achieved a triple replication of the same results with different research samples, thus demonstrating that intelligence can be reliably assessed by handwriting analysis.

It should be noted that Wallner applied rigorous standards of test construction in his experiments. He devised and standardized scales for such attributes as speed of movement, contactability, and need for recognition. He also repeated some of his experiments with different samples of subjects, following the warning by Mosier et al (1951) that validity coefficients decrease when the same tests are applied to different groups of individuals.

On the whole, the rigorous tests of content validity have demonstrated the validity of handwriting analysis. Unfortunately, however, the validity coefficients from all the studies reviewed are relatively low. The reason does not lie in the low validity of handwriting psychology but in the lack of semantic congruence between the evaluations of writing and psychological criteria.

Construct Validity. The concept of construct validity, which seems to hold out great promise for handwriting psychology, derives from Cronbach and Meehl (1955). It is not a fundamentally new method of validation but a structured combination of a number of validation methods that have in common one theoretical assumption: one proceeds not from a specific test or writing behavior to a behavior criterion, but from behaviors to attributes, psychic structures, dispositions, dimensions—from the observable to the non-observable. In other words, given an observable behavior, what are the attributes or internal psychological structures of the individual that are likely to mediate or produce that behavior?

These attributes and structures have been called constructs. No assumptions are made as to the nature of constructs except that they are not open to direct observation. They are, however, necessary for explaining the uniformity of a person's behavior.

The theoretical development of a construct requires a well-grounded theory from which several hypotheses are derived. Different behavioral characteristics are then interpreted on the basis of these hypotheses. The process of construct validity is thus a continual process of modification of the underlying theoretical system and reinterpretation of empirical findings in the light of modified constructs.

Traditional graphology, the oldest graphological diagnostic method, offers an abundance of interpretative propositions, which are derived from specific theories and which can be considered as empirically testable hypotheses. They are, however, not easily understood. For research purposes, it is important that these hypotheses be formulated as narrowly, clearly, and unequivocally as possible.

Fervers's (1948) noteworthy study of construct validity is illustrative. Twenty research subjects were injected intravenously with Eunarcon to produce sleep. Afterward, they were required to empathize in their handwriting with different groups of people—laborers, maidservants, monks, nuns, kings, and queens. The handwritings produced from the "inner person" in this way showed the typical forms and characteristics of the person with whom the writer empathized. The basic structure of the writer's script was preserved, but with an overlay of the collective features of the imagined group. The writing samples produced as if the writer were farmer were full of energy, powerful but clumsy and unrefined; the writing produced as if the writer were the monk was weak, delicate, intellectual, precise, and refined.

Fervers's study stimulated further investigation of pharmacologic effects on the motor aspect of writing. These later experiments made precise and specific predictions about the alterations in handwriting to be expected after induction of a drug with known psychological effects. They also used better quantitative methods. Grunewald (1967) carried out an exacting study of the effects of the central nervous system stimulant Peripherin and the depressant Evipann, and he described the resulting disturbances of coordinated movement. His descriptions of the changes that occur in writing after electric shock (for example, the loss of writing coordination) are especially impressive. There have also been informative studies of the effects of alcohol, such as those by Rabin and Blair (1953), Detrey (1954), Tripp, Fluckiger, and Weinberg (1959), and Gerchow and Wittlich (1960). All of these studies document the progressive deterioration of graphomotor performance with alcohol, the expansion of the writing motoric, and the decreasing precision of form.

There have been numerous handwriting studies of monozygotic and dizygotic twins. The results of work by von Bracken (1939a, 1939b), Wanscher (1943), Goldzieher-Roman (1945), Norinder (1946), and Ostlyngen (n.d.), to name only the most important thematic studies, have been contradictory. Collectively, they come to the paradoxical and surprising conclusion that monozygotic twins differ more in their handwriting behavior than do dizygotic twins. Several explanations of this phenomenon have been offered. Von Bracken proposed a sociopsychological explanation, that is, that monozygotic twins tend to cultivate asymmetrical social behavior; whereas Goldzieher-Roman proposed a genetic explanation, that is, that monozygotic twins are opposite in handedness.

There have also been several studies aimed at delineating developmental changes in handwriting. Longitudinal studies by Kircher (1926), Goldzieher-Roman (1936), Legrun (1929), and Ajuriaguerra (1964) have described evolution of the functional structure of the writing of hyperkenetics from insufficient movement control to sureness and restraint. A complete genetic validation of handwriting is, however, yet to be done (see Lockowandt 1970a for a critical overview of genetic studies).

Construct validation of handwriting has also been attempted using the theories of constitutional psychology, which posits that different personality types or attributes are associated with different body types. Steinwachs (1952) used the triadic schema of Kretschmer (1943), and Pascal (1943) used the somatotype system of Sheldon. They found not only quantitative but also structural typological differences in handwriting as a function of body type, but most of the differences were confined to measures of speed and pressure.

A number of criticisms can be leveled at much of the research on the construct validity of handwriting: that only elementary graphometric variables were used; that an oversimplified functional model of the brain physiology of writing was used as the basis for the mechanisms of activation and control; and that the writing was produced under exceptional conditions. On the other hand, the experimental precision with which these studies were conducted is impressive.

SUMMARY

The reliability of handwriting is well established for simple measured and ranked characteristics. The results of most studies have yielded values that are typical for psychological test procedures. The results are more variable for complex writing characteristics; some are adequate, some inadequate. With more rigorous attempts to specify the multidimensionality of these characteristics, higher reliability coefficients are to be expected.

The reliability of graphological interpretations is surprisingly high (Prystav 1969, 1971a, 1971b), indicating that handwriting psychologists have gone beyond a restricted evaluation yardstick to a unified cognitive schema of interpretation. Thematic studies have shown that an extensive analysis of the interpretation process is indispensable.

The results of validity studies correlating individual characteristics with criteria are predominantly negative, but validation studies using multiple correlation have yielded more positive results. Factor analytic research has been productive, but not uniformly so.

Contrast group studies of specific writing characteristics have led to inconclusive or conflicting results. They have been more successful at validating interpretations of handwriting. Especially noteworthy are the studies on children's handwriting (Lockowandt 1970a), on groups who had experienced extreme conditions (Paul-Mengelberg 1965), and on suicides (Frederick 1968). Accordingly, handwriting must be regarded as an efficient diagnostic instrument.

Most content validity studies have yielded positive correlations with criteria (see particularly the work of Wallner 1961–1971 and of Hofsommer, Holdsworth, and Seifert 1962, 1965). Many psychic dimensions can be diagnosed with confidence using prevailing research techniques and conditions. The unimpressive size of the coefficients can be attributed to the lack of semantic congruence between graphological and psychological judgments. Lockowandt's (1969c) critical overview of construct validity research shows that handwriting has proved itself valid in many respects and that the shortcomings found can probably be remedied.

This review indicates that the results of reliability and validity studies in handwriting psychology are not uniformly positive. There are two possible explanations for the negative findings reported. First, some authors lack sufficient knowledge of the relationships and conditions of handwriting psychology and, therefore, are misled by inadequate and unsuitable experimental procedures. They ignore the recent scientific reorganization of handwriting psychology, and they continue to attack the discipline as it existed in the early stages of its development. They continue to engage in "validation research" such as the handwriting games of Hull and Montgomery (1919), which can assume unfair importance in places such as America where the climate is already hostile toward handwriting psychology. Future researchers will avoid these fallacies if they acquire a thorough grounding in the history, methods, and practical efficiency of handwriting psychology before launching their investigations—a prerequisite for validation studies in any area of psychology.

Second, many validity studies have failed to separate the effects of the handwriting system used from the personality of the handwriting psychologist using the system. Until this is done, one cannot determine whether negative results reflect the failure of the graphological instrument or of the handwriting psychologist. It is necessary, therefore, to understand the psychologist's methods of working, the source of impression qualities, and the complicated process of interpretation. We still do not know the role played by his kinesthetic experience, his adherence to specific forms of impression, his practical experience, and his constant errors of judgment.

Despite the problems that remain to be solved, it is clear that there is no justification for the view that the findings of handwriting psychology are the result of chance or mere accident. The research reviewed demonstrates that there are orderly, lawful relationships between handwriting and personality, aptitudes, and behavior. There is no doubt that the methodology of handwriting psychology can be expanded and refined, and it is hoped that this review will help stimulate such efforts.

REFERENCES

Adolfs, K. 1964. "Faktorenanalytische Untersuchung der gebrauchlichsten Handschriftvariablen." Dissertation, University of Freiburg.

Ajuriaguerra, J. de, und A. Denner. 1964. *L'ecriture de l'enfant.* Neuchatel.

Allport, G., and P. Vernon. 1933. *Studies in Expressive Movement.* New York, Macmillan.

Angermann, Ch. 1970. "Messen und Deuten." *Zeitschr. f. Menschenkunde* 34: pp. 262–279.

Babst, E. 1971. "Zur Objektivität und Reliabilität der Handschrift-Beschreibung mittels Eindruckscharakteristiken." Thesis, University of Berlin.

Binet, A. 1906. *Les revelations d'ecritures d'apres un controle scientifique.* Paris.

Birge, W. R. 1954. "An Experimental Inquiry into the Measurable Handwriting Correlates of Five Personality Traits." *J. of Personality* 23: pp. 215–223.

Bobertag, O. 1929. *Ist die Graphologie Zuverlässig?* Heidelberg.

Bracken, H. v. 1934. "Die Konstanz der Handschriftenart bei Kindern der ersten Schuljahre." *Nederlandsch Tijdschrift voor Psychologie* 1: pp. 541–554.

———. 1939a. "Untersuchungen an Zwillingen über die quantitativen und qualitativen Merkmale des Schreibdrucks." *Zeitschr. angew. Psychol.* 58: pp. 367–384.

———. 1939b. "Das Schreibtempo von Zwillingen und die sozialpsychologischen Fehlerquellen der Zwillingsforschung." *Z. f. menschl. Vererbungs- u. Konstitutionslehre*: p. 58.

Broeren, W. 1964. "Über die Zuverlässigkeit der Beschreibung von Sprechstimme und Handschrift." Thesis, University of Heidelberg.

Castelnuovo-Tedesco, P. 1948. "A Study of the Relationship between Handwriting and Personality Variables." *Genetic Psychol. Monographs* 37: 167–220.

Cohen, R. 1969. *Systematische Tendenzen bei Persönlichkeitsbeurteilungen.* Bern und Stuttgart.

Conrad, W. 1964. "Untersuchung über die Faktorenstruktur der Handschrift." Thesis, University of Freiburg.

Crider, B. 1941. "The Reliability and Validity of Two Graphologists." *J. Appl. Psych.* 25: pp. 323–325.

Cronbach, L. J., and P. E. Meehl. 1955. "Construct Validity in Psychological Tests." *Psychol. Bull.* 52: pp. 281–302.

Daul, H. 1966. "Das Deuten in der Graphologie. Eine methodologische Untersuchung der Struktur und Prinzipien graphologisch-diagnostischer Interpretation." PhD Dissertation, University of Heidelberg.

Detrey, M. 1954. "Handschriftveränderungen unter Alkoholeinfluss." *Ausdruckskunde* 1: pp. 9–12.

Eysenck, H. J. 1948. "Neuroticism and handwriting." *J. of Abnormal and Social Psychology* 43.

———. 1961. *Dimensions of Personality*. London, pp. 5ff.

Fahrenberg, J. 1961. "Graphometrie." PhD Dissertation, University of Freiburg.

Fahrenberg, J., und W. Conrad. 1964. "Eine explorative Faktorenanalyse graphometrischer und psychometrischer Daten." *Zeitschr. exp. angew. Psychol.* 12: pp. 223–238.

Fervers, C. 1948. "Experimentelle Untersuchungen der Schrift nach Einführung mit Eunarcon intravenos." *Grenzgeb. der Medizin* 1: pp. 89–93.

Fischer, G. 1962. "Die faktorielle Struktur der Handschrift." PhD Dissertation, University of Vienna.

———. 1964. "Zur faktoriellen Struktur der Handschrift." *Zeitschr. exp. angew. Psychol.* 11: pp. 254–280.

Frederick, C. J. 1965. "Some phenomena affecting handwriting analysis." *Percept. and Motor Skills* 20: pp. 211–218.

———. 1968. "An Investigation of Handwriting of Suicide Patients through Suicide Notes." *Journal of Abnormal Psychology* 73: pp. 263–267.

Gerchow, J., und B. Wittlich. 1960. "Experimentelle und statistische Untersuchungen über alkoholbedingte Persönlichkeitsveränderungen in der postresorptiven Phase." *Bund für alkoholfreien Verkehr e. V.*

Gesell, A. L. 1906. "Accuracy in Handwriting as Related to School Intelligence and Sex." *Am J. Psychol.* 17: pp. 394–405.

Goldzieher-Roman, K. 1936. "Studies on the Variability of Handwriting: The Development of Writing Speed and Point Pressure in School Children." *J. of Genetic Psychol.* 49.

———. 1945. "Untersuchungen der Schrift und des Schreibens von 283 Zwillingspaaren." *Schweiz. Z. f. Psychol. und ihre Anwendung* 6.

Graumann, C.-F. 1960. "Eigenschaften als Problem der Persönlichkeitsforschung." In *Persönlichkeitsforschung und Persönlichkeitstheorie,* Lersch, Ph., und H. Thomae. Göttingen.

Groffman, K. J., and J. Fahrenberg. 1960. "Experimentelle Untersuchungen zum Problem der Schreibgeschwindigkeit." *Psychol. Forschg.* 26: pp. 114–156.

Grünewald-Zuberbier, E. 1967. "Aktivierung und Kontrolle bei verhaltensschwierigen Kindern im Bereich der Graphomotorikm." *Psychol. Beitrage* 9: pp. 503–524.

Grünewald, G. 1966. *Dynamik und Steuerung der Schreibmotorik.* Köln and Opladen.

Gubser, F. 1972. "Inwieweit sind 'Führungseigenschaften' graphologisch fassbar?" *Industrielle Organisation* 4: pp. 147–154.

Harvey, O. L. 1934. "The Measurement of Handwriting Considered As a Form of Expressive Movement." *Char. and Pers.* 2.

Heer, G. M. 1970. "Schulerfolg im Spiegel der Handscrift." Thesis, University of Zurich.

Hofsommer, W., and R. Holdsworth. 1963. "Die Validität der Handschriftenanalyse bei der Auswahl von Piloten." *Psychol. u. Praxis* 7: pp. 175–178.

Hofsommer, W., R. Holdsworth, and T. Siebert. 1962. "Zur Bewahrungskontrolle graphologischer Diagnosen." *Psychol. Beitrage* 7: pp. 397–401.

———. 1965. "Reliabilitätsfragen in der Graphologie." *Psychol. u. Praxis* 9: pp. 14–24.

Hull, C. L., and R. P. Montgomery. 1919. "Experimental Investigation of Certain Alleged Relations between Character and Handwriting." *Psychol. Rev.* 26.

Kircher, R. 1926. "Experimentelle Untersuchung der Entwicklung des Schreibens während der Volksschulzeit, besonders im ersten Schuljahr." *Arch. f. d. gesamte Psychol.* 54: pp. 313–354.

Kirchhoff, R. 1962. "Das Verhältnis von Graphologie und Ausdruckskunde." *Zeitschr. f. Menschenkunde* 26: pp. 320–337.

———. 1962. "Methodologische und theoretische Grundprobleme der Ausdruckskunde." *Stud. Gen.*

———., ed. 1965. *Ausdruckspsychologie.* Band 5 des *Handbuchs der Psychologie.* Göttingen.

———. 1968. Ausdruck: "Begriff, Regionen und Binnenstruktur." *Jahrbuch für Psychologie und Psychotherapie.*

Klages, L. 1927. *Zur Ausdruckslehre und Charakterkunde.* Heidelberg.

Konttinen, R. 1968. *Relationships Between Graphic Expansivity and Extraversion as a Function of Anxiety and Defensiveness.* Helsinki.

Legrun, A. 1929. *Die Schreibgelaüfigkeit der Schulkinder.* Wien-Leipzig.

Lienert, G. A. 1969. *Testaufbau und Testanalyse.* Weinheim, privately circulated.

Linster, H. W. 1969. *Eine Validitätsuntersuchung graphometrischer Variablen.* Zul.-Arbeit: Freiburg i. Brg.

Lockowandt, O. 1961. *Reliabilitätskontrolle und Validitätsuntersuchung zum Problem der Schreibgeschwindigkeit.* Freiburg i. Brg., unveröffentl.

———. 1966. "Faktorenanalytische Validierung der Handschrift mit besonderer Berücksichtigung projektiver Methoden." PhD Dissertation, University of Freiburg.

———. 1968. "Faktorenanalytische Validierung der Handschrift mit besonderer Berücksichtigung projektiver Method." *Zeitschr. exp. angew. Ps.* 15: pp. 487–530.

———. 1968. "Quantitative Uberprüfungsmethoden in der Graphologie." *Zeitschr. f. Menschenkunde* 32: pp. 232–253.

———. 1969. "Über das Konzept einer konstruktiven Validierung der Handschrift." Part I. *Zeitschr. f. Menschenkunde* 32 (1968): pp. 426–437; Part II. *Ebendort* 33 (1969): pp. 57–83.

———. 1970a. "Die Kinderhandschrift—ihre diagnostischen Möglichkeiten und Grenzen." *Zeitschr. f. Menschenkunde* 34: pp. 301–326.

———. 1970b. "Le probleme de la garantie dans la psychologie de l'ecriture." *La Graphologie* 119: pp. 21–41.

———. 1972. "Empirische Untersuchungen zur Validität der Kinderhandschrift."

Zeitschr. f. Menschenkunde 36: pp. 293–311.
———. 1973. "Der Prozess der Urteilsbildung in der Schrift-psychologie." *Zeitschr. f. Menschenkunde* 37 (1973): pp. 135–154.
Lockowandt, O., and C.-H. Keller. 1975. "Beitrag zur Stabilität der Kinderhandschrift." *Psychol. Beitrage* 17: pp. 273–282.
Lorr, M., L. T Lepine, and J. V. Golder. 1954. "A Factor Analysis of Some Handwriting Characteristics." *J. Pers.* 22: pp. 348–353.
Marum, O. 1945. "Character Assessments from Handwriting." *J. Ment. Sci.* 91: pp. 22–42.
Michel, L., and A. Iseler. 1968. "Beziehungen zwischen klinischen und psychometrischen Methoden der diagnostischen Urteilsbildung." In *Person als Prozess.* Festschrift zum 65. Geburtstag von Prof. Dr. Phil. Robert Heiss, herausgegeben von K. J. Groffmann und K. H. Wewetzer. Bern und Stuttgart.
Mosier, Ch. I., E. E. Cureton, R. A. Katzel, and R. J. Wherry. 1951. Symposium: "The Need and the Means of Cross-Validation." *Educ. Psychol. Measmt.* 11 (5).
Muller, W. H. 1957. "Über die Objektivität von Anmutungsqualitäten in der Handschrift." *Psychol. Beitrage* 3: pp. 364–389.
Muller, W. H., and A. Enskat. 1961. *Graphologischen Diagnostik.* Bern und Stuttgart.
———. 1965. *Grundzüge der Graphologie.* In *Ausdruckspsychologie,* edited by R. Kirchoff, Göttingen.
Muller, W. H., and H. P. Mattes. 1966a. "Die Grundhypothesen graphologischer Diagnostik und der gegenwärtige Stand ihrer empirischen Überprufung." *Acta Graphologica* 17.
———. 1966b. "Zur Objektivierung der Schriftbeschreibung." *Zeitschr. f. Menschenkunde* 4: pp. 361–379.
Norinder, Y. 1946. "Twin Differences in Writing Performance: A Study of Heredity and School Training." Lund.
Oinonen, P. 1961. "Poor Handwriting as a Psychological Problem." *Acta academiae paedagogicae Jyvaskylamisis.* Jyvaskyla, 21.
Ostlyngen, E. n.d.. *Über erbliche und umweltliche Bedingungen.*
Pascal, G. R. 1943. "Handwriting Pressure: Its Measurement and Significance." *Character and Personality* 11: pp. 235–254.
Pascal, G. R. and B. Suttell. 1947. "Testing the Claims of a Graphologist." *J. Personality* 16: pp. 192–197.
Paul-Mengelberg, M. 1965. "Die Symptome der Veralterung in der Handschrift." *Zeitschr. f. Menschenkunde* 29: pp. 3–27.
———. 1971a. "Beziehungen zwischen dem Abbau-Quotieten im Hawie und der Intelligenz-Baurteilung auf Grund der Handschrift." *Zeitschr. f. Gerontologie* 4: pp. 208–216.
———. 1971b. "Schreibmotorische Störungen bei ehemaligen Kriegsgefangenen und Verfolgten." In *Spätschaden nach Gefangenschaft und Verfolgung,* edited by H. J. Herberg. Herford.
———. 1972. *Die Handschrift von ehemaligen Kriegsgefangenen und politische Verfolgten.* Bonn.

Prystav, G. 1969. "Beitrag zur faktorenanalytischen Validierung der Handschrift." Dissertation, University of Freiburg.

———. 1971a. "Reliabilität graphometrischer Schriftebeschreibung (Part I: Merkmalsebene)." *Zeitschr. f. Menschenkunde* 35: pp. 70–94.

———. 1971b. "Reliabilität graphologischer Beurteilungen. (Part II: Interpretationsebene)". *Zeitschr. f. Menschenkunde* 35: pp. 95–110.

Rabin, A., and H. Blair. 1953. "The Effects of Alcohol on Handwriting." *J. Clin. Psychol.* 9: pp. 284–287.

Reichold, L. 1969. "Die Reliabilität und Validität graphologischer Aussagen. *Zeitschr. f. Menschenkunde* 33: pp. 198–210.

Saunders, D. R. 1956. "Moderator Variables in Prediction." *Educ. Psychol. Measmt.* 16: pp. 209–222.

Schaie, K. W., and R. Heiss. 1964. *Color and Personality.* Bern and Stuttgart.

Schneevoigt, I. 1968. *Graphologische Intelligenzdiagnose.* Bonn.

Secord, P. F. 1948. "Studies of the Relationships of Handwriting to Personality." *J. Pers.* 17: pp. 430–448.

Seifert, T. 1965. "Faktorenanalyse einiger Schriftmerkmale." *Z. exp. angew. Psychol.* 11: pp. 645–666.

Stein Lewinson, Th. 1956. "Graphische Darstellung der Handschriftlichen Dynamik." *Ausdruckskunde* 3: pp. 145–180.

———. 1964. "Die dynamische Kurve und der Leistungsquotient." *Graphol. Schriftenreihe* 6.

———. 1967. "Klages in Zeitalter der Psychometrie." *Zeitschr. F. Menschenkunde* 31: pp. 1–33.

———. 1968. "Entwicklung mit Hilfe des Elektronenrechners." *Zeitschr. f. Menschenkunde* 32: pp. 393–413.

Stein Lewinson, Th., and J. Zubin. 1942. *Handwriting Analysis.* New York.

Steinwachs, F. 1952. "Konstitutionstypische Grundkurven der Handschrift und ihre pathologischen Veränderungen." *Z. Psychoth.* 2.

Sulzer, F. 1949. *Angst, Verdrängung, Hemmung und Unlust im Schriftausdruck.* Leiden.

Timm, U. 1965. "Graphometrie als psychologischer Test?" Dissertation, University of Freiburg.

Timm, U. 1967. "Graphometrie als psychologischer Test?" *Psychol. Forschg.* 30: pp. 307–356.

Torgerson, W. S. 1958. Theory and Methods of Scaling. New York.

Tripp, C. A., F. A. Fluckiger, and G. H. Weinberg. 1959. "Effects of Alcohol on the Graphomotor Performances of Normals and Chronic Alcoholics." *Percept. Mot. Skills* 9: pp. 227–236.

Unkel, H. 1964. "Eine Faktorenanalysis graphometrischer und psychometrischer Daten." Working paper, University of Freiburg.

Volz, D. 1969. "Zur Objektivität und Reliabilität graphologischer Beurteilungen." Working paper, University of Freiburg.

Wallner, T. 1961a. "Bemerkungen zu W. H. Muller's 'Untersuchungen über die Objektivität von Anmutungsqualitäten in der Handschrift.' " *Psychol. Beiträge*

5: pp. 585–596.

———. 1961b. "Experimentelle Untersuchungen über die Reliabilität direkt metrische messbarer Handschriftvariablen." *Zeitschr. f. Menschenkunde* 25: pp. 49–78.

———. 1961c. "Reliabilitätsuntersuchungen an metrisch nicht messbaren Handschrifvariablen." *Zeitschr. f. Menschenkunde* 25: pp. 1–14.

———. 1961d. "Undersokningar av tillfortitligheten i bedomningar baserade pa grafologiska metoder." Thesis, University of Stockholm.

———. 1961e. "Über Zusammenhänge zwischen Merkmalen der Handschrift." *Zeitschr. f. Menschenkunde* 25: pp. 113–121.

———. 1962. "Neue Ergebnisse experimenteller Untersuchungen über die Reliabilität von Handschriftvariablen." *Zeitschr. f. Menschenkunde* 26: pp. 257–269.

———. 1963. "Konstruktion und Reliabilität von geeichten numerisch-beschreibenden Skalen." *Diagnostica* 9: pp. 139–155.

———. 1963. "Über die Validität graphologischer Aussagen." *Diagnostica* 9: pp. 26–35.

———. 1965. "Graphologie als Objekt statistischer Untersuchungen." *Psychol. Rdsch.* 16: pp. 282–298.

———. 1966. "Zusammenhänge zwischen Prognosedaten, Handschriftenvariablen und Ausbildungsergebnissen." *Zeitschr. f. Menschenkunde* 30: pp. 380–387.

———. 1967. "Orientering i skriftpsykologins teori och forskningsresultat." *Nordisk psykologi* 19: pp. 162–173.

———. 1968. "Zusammenhänge zwischen graphischen Variablen und Persönlichkeitsbeurteilungen." *Zeitschr. f. Menschenkunde* 32: pp. 438–445.

———. 1969. "Die Reliabilität schriftpsychologischer Begutachtungen." *Zeitschr. f. Menschenkunde* 33: pp. 191–197.

———. 1970. "Der prognostische Wert von Tests und Handschriftenvariablen bei Eignungsuntersuchungen." *Zeitschr. exp. ang. Psychol.* 17: pp. 316–356.

———. 1970. "Planung und Durchführung von schriftpsychologischen Untersuchungen." *Zeitschr. f. Menschenkunde* 34: pp. 280–300.

———. 1971. "Der Unterschied zwischen Schriftpsychologie und Graphologie." *Psychol. u. Praxis* 15: pp. 1–8.

Wanscher, J. H. 1943. "The Hereditary Background of Handwriting: An Investigation of Mono- and Dizygotic Twins." *Acta Psychiat. Kbh.* 18: pp. 349–375.

Wolfson, R. 1949. "A Study in Handwriting Analysis." Ph.D. thesis, Columbia University.

Wollenweber, H. 1961. "Experimentelle Untersuchungen zur Frage der Abhängigkeit der Feder- und Leistungsgeschwindigkeit von der Schriftgrosse." Working paper, University of Freiburg.

6

The Problem of the Validation of Graphological Judgments

Oscar Lockowandt

The following chapter was originally presented at the First British Symposium on Graphological Research, held in Oxford, UK, in August, 1987. An abridgment was published in *The Graphologist,* the journal of the British Institute of Graphologists in the Summer 1988 issue (Lockowandt 1988). It was originally written by Dr. Lockowandt in German, then translated into English by Brenda James and Natalie Marby. This version relies on both the original translation of the talk and the published paper, and the editors have made some slight changes to the translation.

Lockowandt candidly admits to graphologists that in the studies he and his colleagues have conducted the validity coefficients are too low to demonstrate graphologists' abilities to predict intelligence quotients: "Here we see that graphologists, using handwriting as a basis, are clearly not capable of diagnosing the intelligence quotients (or standard values) which result from the various kinds of intelligence tests in use" (p. 92). Thus, on this point Lockowandt finds himself in agreement with the skeptics in this volume, as well as being somewhat less optimistic than he was in 1976 when he published the original version of chapter 5. However, he parts company with skeptics over what conclusions should be drawn from this.

Lockowandt offers three reasons for graphologists' failure: First of all, he maintains that graphologists mean something different by "intelligence" than what has been traditionally meant by psychologists who devised the intelligence tests that were used as the criterion in his and his colleagues' experiments. On this matter he will find a fair bit of support from psychologists, who will readily agree that ordinary language notions of intelligence are not the same as those presupposed by standard intelligence tests. To deal with this problem, Lockowandt introduces the notion of the "graphological concept of intelligence," which he equates with the German word *Bildung*. However, note that he offers no evidence in this paper that graphologists can reliably or validly measure this attribute either.

Second, he wonders whether the differentiations in intelligence measured on standard IQ tests really are measuring anything significant in the sense of our determinations of intelligence in real life. While this is an issue about which all competent psychologists are acutely aware, we shouldn't allow this *tu quoque* response to obscure the point that graphology does not allow us to make the fine discriminations about intelligence that cannot be made by standard IQ tests. If Lockowandt is right in maintaining that these differences are not worth making, the question then arises why we need to pay anyone to discern what common sense tells us about for free—and this point would apply to graphology no less than to other tests.

Third, on page 96 he suggests that graphologists may be measuring something that is independent of that which is measured by standard personality tests. Hence it would be no surprise that the validity of graphological judgments appears quite low. This is possible, but Lockowandt fails to mention a consequence of his speculation that could be tested: If these traits really were being accurately measured by graphologists, we would expect to find a fair degree of inter-rater *reliability* amongst graphologists, even though we do not find a high *validity*. (See Bowman, chapter 10 for the distinction between these.) But we do not find this.

Lockowandt distinguishes between three models of testing for validity of graphological assessments. Model 1a compares *graphological characteristics* of the writing sample being analyzed (e.g., the relative heights of capital and lower case letters) with the *criterion* (e.g., the results of a standard IQ test). It thus serves to answer the question whether there is a correlation, say, between making large capital letters and intelligence. Model 1b attempts to compare *graphological judgments* (i.e., the *judgment of the graphologist* that the *subject who produced the handwriting* is intelligent), which will (in some way, depending on the particular theory held by the graphologist) be determined by the graphologist's assessments of the graphological characteristics and the criterion. Lockowandt admits that the studies he cites in the following paper, whether following model 1a or 1b, simply demonstrate low-validity coefficients.

Lockowandt proposes a third sort of testing, which he calls *processual validation*. The basic idea is one with which Bowman (chapter 10) agrees: most ordinary language personality terms are vague, ambiguous, or otherwise unclear. So, when the graphologist produces his *judgment*, Lockowandt maintains that the reason it is not accepted may be because of this indeterminacy in meaning, and not the graphologist's inability to discern personality traits. So, the point of processual validation is essentially to clear up this indeterminacy by having the person who disagrees discuss the matter with the graphologist, until they can agree upon common meanings. Lockowandt suggests that it will often be discovered that the two parties do not disagree after all; they had just been involved in a terminological misunderstanding; and once this is resolved, they will all agree that the graphological judgment really did fit the client all along. The obvious rejoinder to this proposal is that it calls into question the standard scientific method for determining validity of tests, as outlined in chapter 8 and by Klimoski in chapter 11. Those who are familiar with the debate about psychic mediums or channelers will see a parallel: the alternate explanation for their seeming accuracy is the subjective validation effect (see chapter 13). Unless this hypothesis can be ruled out, we do not have good evidence for the validity of the technique.

Second, it appears Lockowandt has simply conflated a scientific test of graphology with the usual operation of graphologists in personnel situations: note the example that Lockowandt uses, p. 100, which is not of an experimental situation testing graphology, but an *application* of graphology. Evidence that graphology "works" that is derived from this type of "case study" approach might be valuable if graphology had already been validated in a proper scientific test; but it cannot serve as a *replacement* for such a test. See Dean et al. in chapter 13 for a discussion of the worth of anecdotal evidence.

Lockowandt's processual validation also creates problems with practical applications of graphology in personnel selection. Compare Klimoski's requirement, described in chapter 11, that a personnel psychologist must compile a job description and worker requirements *before* beginning to assess candidates for a job. The personnel psychologist should try to eliminate, from the very beginning, the sorts of ambiguity and vagueness Lockowandt discusses, and not to try to resolve them *after* the candidates are recommended for the job.

Also worthy of note is Lockowandt's discussion of the experiment he carried out, reported on pp. 90–91. He reports that he examined 690 possible correlations out of over 7,000, and found 46 of these variables to be correlated with IQ scores. Instead of beginning with a prediction, as described in chapter 8, Lockowandt was just looking for correlations in a large volume of data. If one goes on "fishing expeditions" when analyzing data, it will be no surprise that one will find positive correlations aplenty if one keeps searching long enough. In this case, Lockowandt found positive correlations between his graphological measurements and intelligence test scores 8 percent of the time.

Lockowandt realizes what the problem is here: ". . . so that even if some of the correlations should be purely by chance, the obvious correlations—about 8 percent of the total—remain significant" (p. 91). The reader should draw his or her own conclusions about whether the fact that there are some significant positive correlations out of this large sample really matters. *Some* correlations are bound to be positive by chance alone: perhaps *these* are the ones. What is required is an independent replication of this study; but Lockowandt reports no such studies that find these correlations repeated.

Last, on p. 89, Lockowandt points out that there has been no "clear, comprehensible and irrefutable" refutation of graphology. Some readers may quibble at this, depending on their definition of "clear, comprehensible and irrefutable." For example, it is arguable that the study by Karnes and Leonard in chapter 16 meets this standard, as does Klimoski's two studies done with Rafaeli, reported in chapter 11, and Dean (chapter 12) cites a number of studies that are possible candidates. However, the main point is that it is not up to the critics to offer studies refuting graphology; the onus of proof rests on the defenders of it. And Lockowandt is not prepared to state of any experiment that he discusses in this chapter or his chapter 5 that it offers "clear, comprehensive and irrefutable" evidence in favor of graphology either.

STANDARD MODELS OF VALIDATION

THE NEED FOR VALIDATION

Academic recognition of handwriting analysis has once again become problematical. Some believe that the validity of graphology must first be proved before it can gain access to the hallowed halls of the university. This view, which is shared by many of my colleagues, is not only wrong, but also short-sighted. Up to now there has never been a clear, comprehensible, and unimpeachable refutation of the claims of handwriting analysis. Daring assumptions of the past are being revived in order to discredit graphology for good. One of them is Guilford's (1964, 271ff) absurd explanation that differences in handwriting are due to the anatomy of the hand. This view was offered earlier by Carus (1938, 325–326) and later by Pawlik et al. (1973). But these criticisms are wide of the mark, and they obscure the most important reason for including graphology in the university.

If graphology is to be studied scientifically, it must be studied in the university. This point becomes especially important when we realize that, outside the university, graphology has been called upon to judge the abilities of individuals, and these graphological judgments have been used to determine status of individuals in many important ways. The social acceptance and, widespread use of graphology in nonacademic spheres make it necessary to raise it to a scientific subject. Both unquestioning acceptance of graphology's powers and outright rejection of graphology on the basis of untenable arguments are founded on irrational attitudes. What is needed is a *critical attitude of mind,* which we have taken as the basis of our work.

I shall present in this chapter some thoughts on the validity of graphological judgments. For the sake of easier comprehension, I shall mention only a few studies; but you may be sure that every one of my statements can be confirmed empirically. You will find the necessary data in chapter 5.

One theoretical approach to graphology maintains that it is unnecessary to prove the validity of graphological statements because handwriting is a form of human expression and can, therefore, be just as revealing as facial expression. It asserts that in the same way that we immediately understand laughter and a person's feelings by looking into his face, we can instantaneously determine a person's character by looking at his handwriting. This almost parapsychic ability is given the name "intuitive knowledge" (*Kennerschaft*) as if, thereby, all problems have been solved. I consider this theory to be incorrect for two reasons. First, contrary to the elaborate argumentation of Ludwig Klages, handwriting is *not* an expression, but rather an act, a work, a thing (an *ergon*) that is separated from the person (Kirchhoff 1962). Second, it is unfortunately the case that many graphological judgments of individuals are inaccurate. In going through cases in our research seminar, we have come across judgments made by fully trained graphologists which prove to be completely incorrect. Evidence of recurring misinterpretations of handwriting and the ethical issues that are raised by those mininterpretations make it absolutely necessary to carry out validity tests.

CRITERION-RELATED VALIDATION

If we acknowledge that validity tests are necessary, then we are faced with the problem of selecting or devising the most appropriate tests. The most important and most frequently used method is *criterion-related validation.* A criterion-related validation study of handwriting analysis could start, for example, with the individual characteristics (such as slant or expansion of height) of one person's handwriting, and then determine whether any of these graphic characteristics are correlated with that person's scores on various tests, such as objective tests of intelligence or projective tests of personality. We carried out such a test with 100 subjects (Lockowandt 1966). In order to determine each of 69 different graphic characteristics, we carried out a total of 28 measurements randomly throughout each handwriting sample.[1] Approximately 800 to 1,000 measurements were carried out on each handwriting sample.

Each subject took a variety of tests, including an intelligence test (Amthauer's Intelligenz-Struktur-Test) and the Holtzman Inkblot Technique, a variation of the Rorschach Test. The correlation coefficients between our 69 handwriting characteristics and the total standard score on the intelligence test ranged from 0.20 to 0.40. Of the 690 possible coefficients,[2] 46 were significant.

What conclusion can be drawn from these results? First, it is clear that there are relationships between the handwriting characteristics we measured and the intelligence test results. In the total experiment we looked at 102 criterion variables, which, when correlated with each of the 69 handwriting variables, yield a total of 7,038 correlations. Thus, even if some of the correlations occurred purely by chance, the obvious correlations—about 8 percent of the total—remain significant. It must be noted, however, that all the correlation coefficients are much too low. The largest coefficient ($r = 0.35$) suggests that there is a connection between the width and increasing size of the left margin and certain aspects of the intelligence test. We graphologists have always taken such a correlation for granted. The significance of the left margin is different from that of the right margin in that the left margin is indicative of reflection and conscious detachment, which are qualities relating, in a broad sense, to a person's intelligence.

I have presented this selection of results from our experiments because they are typical. Using the same number of handwriting characteristics, two of my colleagues, Timm (1965) and Prystav (1971), have correlated these handwriting characteristics with the findings from other diagnostic methods such as questionnaires. The same results were obtained repeatedly: correlations of the most varied kind were evident, the coefficients were statistically significant, but in general they proved to be far too low. It was irrelevant which criterion was chosen.

VALIDATION ON THE INTERPRETATION LEVEL

I am well aware that graphologists will be dissatisfied with the experimental studies I have described. I am a graphologist myself, and I too am dissatisfied. The graphologist is justified in criticizing them, because they do not examine the *judgment itself*, nor do they take into account the ways in in which the *overall impression* can alter the significance of individual handwriting characteristics. This shortcoming we call the *interpretation limitation.*

To remedy this shortcoming, my colleague, Michel, devised another method of validation (Michel 1969). Let us refer to the traditional criterion-related validation of graphology as *Model 1a: Validation at the graphological characteristics level.* Model 1a attempts to find correlations between selected handwriting characteristics and criteria such as test scores. The graphologist, his intuitions, his conclusions, and his thought processes are not taken into consideration. The aim of Michel's alternative, however—call it *Model 1b: Validation on the interpretation level*—is to draw special attention to these inner processes, but only in the sense that it demands from the graphologist the solution of the assessment task, without requiring that his or her processes become explicit. These two models are illustrated in Figure 1.

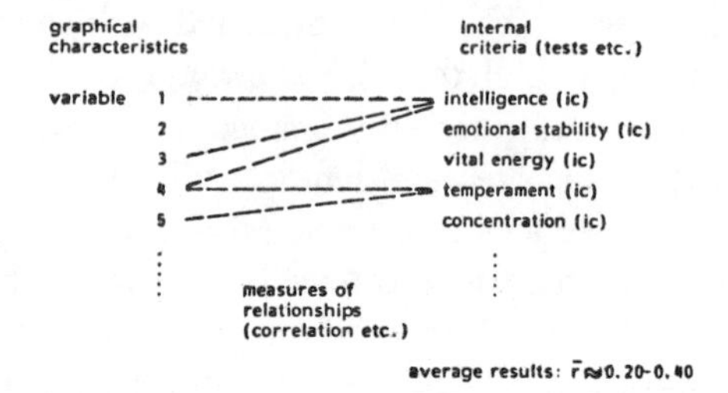

Model 1a. Validation on the graphical characteristic level

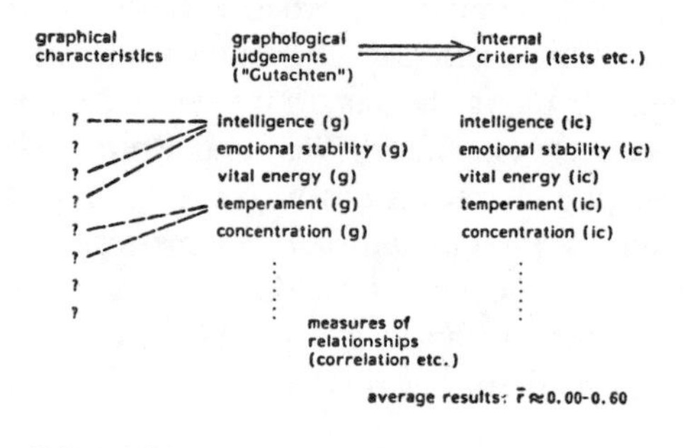

Model 1b. Validation on the interpretation level

Figure 1.

Model 1a can also be criticized because it limits the array of graphic characteristics that can be studied. It is possible that we select those handwriting characteristics which are easy to work with, but which are of little diagnostic significance. This criticism does not apply to Model 1b, because here it is up to the individual graphologist to decide which characteristics will be used as the basis of his or her graphological judgment. The disadvantage of this approach is that, when negative results are obtained, it is not clear whether they are due to the handwriting (that is, the assessment instrument) or to those interpreting it.

Michel (1968) used the Model 1b approach in a series of careful studies in which he correlated graphological judgments of intelligence with data from intelligence tests, teachers' judgments, and semester reports. The handwriting samples of seven students whose intelligence quotients covered a wide range (see Table 1) were given to several graphologists to rank according to judged intelligence quotients.

TABLE 1

IQ SCORES OF SUBJECTS IN MICHEL (1968)

Subject	IQ Score
1	88
2	116
3	98
4	110
5	133
6	127
7	122

Table 2 shows the correlations (Spearman rho) between the ranking of graphological judgments of intelligence and the rankings based on intelligence tests and other sources. With the exception of the results with the Raven's test, however, the results are generally disappointing.

We can see that the results obtained with Models 1a and 1b are discouraging for the validity of graphology. There is only a single experiment —that combines both Models 1a and 1b—which has yielded more promising results (Castelnuovo-Tedesco 1948). We have tried for several years to reproduce these experiments (Lockowandt 1979). Unfortunately, we did not succeed, so we could conclude only that unknown factors, which cannot be found in the description of the experiments, must have been at work. A personal consultation with the author also failed to shed light on the subject.

But is the situation really so bleak? Let us look critically at these experiments and see what conclusions we can draw from them.

TABLE 2

	Concord-ance (rho)	IST	WAIS	Raven	Teacher's judgment	Term report
Experiment I	.25	.16	.27	-*	.27	.27
Experiment II	.59	.37	.16	.66	.46	.40
Experiment III	.64	-.36	-.09	-.18	-.08	-.19
Mean	.47	.06	.11	(.24)	.22	.16

*Raven-test not used.

Table 2. Mean concordance and validity coefficients of the graphological diagnosis of intelligence in three studies by Michel (1968).

PROBLEMS WITH CRITERIA AND PROBLEMS WITH VALIDATION

My major objection to such experiments is that they *oversimplify* the nature of the graphologists's diagnostic work. Let us take a closer look at the most widely used criteria, intelligence tests. Here we see that, using handwriting analysis, graphologists are unable to determine the intelligence quotients which result from the intelligence tests now in use. It does not necessarily follow, however, that graphologists are incapable of assessing a person's intelligence from his handwriting.

The use of intelligence test scores as criteria in studies of the validity of handwriting analysis is based on a premise which has by no means been proved—namely, that intelligence quotients are a valid measure of a person's intelligence. After many decades of research into intelligence, it has become clear that intelligence tests provide only a one-sided, limited assessment of intelligence. Therefore, it can be argued that graphologists can, indeed, determine a person's actual intelligence from his handwriting, but not the artificial intelligence scored in standard tests. In our practical and controlled examination of individual cases, we have become convinced that graphological analysis can accurately assess true intelligence.

By a detailed analysis of the diagnostic process, we increased our understanding of the *graphological* concept of intelligence. This concept can be best described with the German word *Bildung*—the sum of a person's cultural development—for which there is no English equivalent. Graphologists know from experience that it is not possible to determine very special talents and abilities from a person's handwriting; even the special talents of a genius cannot be recognized, as the handwriting of Einstein and of the artist Kathe Kollwitz have clearly demonstrated. On the other hand, it is not difficult to differentiate between an "educated" and an "uneducated" person by looking at their handwriting. As used here, the term "education" (*Bildung*) can perhaps be equated with "knowledge of life" or a "discriminating attitude to culture." What is *not* meant is the ability to complete a sequence of numbers or to create an analogous word pattern or other simple cognitive tasks. What *is* meant is a person's "general state of culture" or what Lewin called a person's "degree of differentation." Or, it may also be similar to the difference between "crystallized" and "fluid" intelligence as proposed by Cattell.

In his excellent phenomenological work on intelligence, the Swiss graphologist Pulver (1949) also presented an extended concept of intelligence, composed of five types of intellectual behavior: ordering and arranging, intentional application, abstraction and ideation, intensity and concentration (an auxiliary function), and sheer comprehension. Without going into the details of his analysis, I should like to state only that our daily systematic work has shown that graphological diagnosis can indeed be accurate and valid, if one uses this broad concept of intelligence. Although it is very difficult to find adequate measures for these components of intelligence, graphologists have been right not to shrink from or ignore such difficulties and to avoid basing validity tests, for purely methodological reasons, on limited and inadequate understanding of intelligence. When experimenters fall prey to this temptation, one can observe what Maslow (1970) called "overstress on technique": the view that a research finding has value only when it has been done "cleanly," that is, in a methodologically correct way.

The studies described above contain clear indications that the extended concept of intelligence (*Bildung*) is the one that is most suitable for graphological diagnosis. My colleague Timm (1965), for example, has found a sizeable correlation between school education (as determined by levels of school qualifications) and several arrangement characteristics of writing such as the distance between words and between lines (multiple R = .59).

In the experiment cited earlier, Michel (1964) tested only concurrent validity, that is, the extent to which the graphologists' assessment of intelligence agreed with the results of an intelligence test. In this regard, Michel has noted that:

> The concurrent validity of new tests is sometimes determined by correlation with tests with a high validity result. Here, of course, we are only checking

> whether the old test can be substituted by the new. *Therefore, negative results do not necessarily go against the new test.* (Michel 1964, 53; emphasis added)

His assertion is indeed correct, and it is unfortunate that he did not apply it to his own experiment.

Formal tests cannot, of course, embrace all of reality. Each test can gain access to only a limited number of the many characteristics that constitute the whole person. Furthermore, test results are *internal* criteria for testing graphological validity, in that they are produced by the same source as the handwriting that the graphologist analyzes. But experiments conducted to date indicate that the validity of graphological analysis is best tested by using *external* criteria, such as the judgments of teachers and supervisors.

It is strange that the validity of handwriting analysis has so often been tested on the basis of characteristics which it neither wanted to assess nor pretended to be able to assess. The fact that its results so seldom agree with those of other evaluation techniques may well be an indication of its *independence* and its unique access to an individual's personality—an access which is impossible with any other method.

FAILURE TO CONSIDER THE INTERPRETATION PROCESS

Another important criticism of the usual methods of validating graphology is that research carried out to date has examined only *universal graphic characteristics* and has ignored the interpretation process of the handwriting analyst. Even if research had established the psychological significance of each graphic characteristic, it would still be necessary to understand the individualistic interpretation processes of the graphologist.

Let us assume, for example, that we wish to validate handwriting analysis by means of the Rorschach Test. Take the relationship between form and color in the Rorschach Test, which is said to reflect emotional impulse and emotional regulation. These emotional tendencies can also be determined from handwriting by analyzing the relationship between motion and form. Assume, further, that we found for a number of individuals that there was a high correlation between the overall motion-to-form characteristic of handwriting and the form-color sequence of the Rorschach. Although this result would be a valuable demonstration of the connection between handwriting and character, it would have limited practical value for the handwriting analyst, who can make use of it only to the extent that it fits into his or her individualized process of interpretation. Even in those studies, like Michel's (1964), in which the handwriting analyst has been free to use his own methods of interpretation, the results have been disencouraging, because the very process of interpretation has been ignored.

A NEW MODEL OF GRAPHOLOGICAL VALIDATION: PROCESSUAL ASSIMILATION

In order to understand and conceptualize the interpretive processes on which the processual assimilation model is based, we drew on three sources of information: (1) our observations of our own interpretive processes; (2) our observations of other qualified handwriting analysts whom we asked to "think out loud"; and (3) our process analyses of the cognitive operations used to generate model reports.

The processual assimilation model can perhaps best be introduced by an experience common in our practice. A graphologist receives instructions to analyze a person's handwriting and prepares his report, which he hands over to the head of a personnel department. To his great disappointment, he is told that his report is unfounded and incorrect. The story could end here, as would be expected by opponents of handwriting analysis. But it is possible that the graphologist or the personnel manager or both of them feel that the work had been too superficial; so they decide to discuss the entire text again, in detail. Perhaps they divide it into individual statements—a technique known as *fractional validation.* At the end of this concerted effort at mutual understanding, the graphologist and the personnel manager discover, to their surprise, that they agree to a great extent, without one having forced his ideas on the other. The conclusions they have reached constitute *objective evidence.* How is this possible?

This process—which we call *procedural agreement*—is of central significance for the validation procedure. Unfortunately, handwriting analysis is expected to reach a level of achievement which is not expected, for example, of medicine. It is expected to be speedily produced and unwavering in accuracy, like William Tell's aim at the apple. What is not appreciated is the fact that handwriting analysis requires a kind of dialectic operation to work out the actual circumstances. Every well-meaning and critical researcher realizes that the validity of statements is not of a dichotomous nature; it is not all or none, but in certain stages of the validation process —a process which can last for several years in difficult cases—it may vary considerably. Validity may be very low or even zero at the beginning of the process, but after long and deep discussion it may reach a high level. I should like to stress that these changes may arise without forced group agreement, but simply from feelings of objective inadequacy.

What has actually happened in the course of this processual change in validity and of what importance is this observation for our problem?

Both experts speak a *different language;* each codes his or her communications in a language that is very different from that of the other. It is important to emphasize that we are not dealing with a linguistic-semantic problem. These language differences are only a symptom of something different; they merely characterize the superficial aspect of the situation. In general, little would be achieved if one expert should try to explain his vocabulary to the other, but it can be used as a starting point, in order to rid language of misunderstandings and errors. Here is an example from my colleague, Mr. H. Hartmann.[3] In a graphological reference submitted by an applicant, special emphasis was placed on his vitality, which was considered to be a positive attribute. He was not given the job, however, because it was feared that this vitality would have an adverse effect on the female members of the staff. "The potential employer had thus interpreted the very general term 'vitality' in a selective manner (that is, in the sense of sexual activity) and thus completely reversed its positive connotation" (Hartmann, 1970, 78).

Let me emphasize again that it is not the differing language codes which are decisive. Rather, it is *what* is coded. The two language codes are founded on different conceptual frames of reference or different theories of personality or motivation, which have different origins. The frame of reference of the handwriting analyst has developed from his daily involvement with "curdled" or fixed individual movements that record themselves and that are *oriented from standard handwriting.* The genesis of his frame of reference is thus graphogenotic. On the other hand, the frame of reference of the personnel manager, who generates the external criterion, has evolved from his long involvement with his subordinates, his knowledge of average work rates, and his experience with the attributes that promote work effectiveness and social compatibility.

These differences among experienced experts can lead to large discrepancies in the interpretation of the same observations. Fiedler (1984) has pointed out that experts cannot always digest important observations dispassionately. Judgment may be distorted by one's conceptual schema, by selective perception, by the self-fulfilling prophecy—seeing what one expects to see—and by the dominance of the hypothesis. Thus, a hypothesis is not always abandoned, even when facts clearly discomfirm it. It is essential, therefore, that the handwriting expert be constantly aware of his or her conceptual framework and, as recommended by Dettweiler (1980, 1984), acquire psychologically believable self-experience in the diagnostic of handwriting psychology.

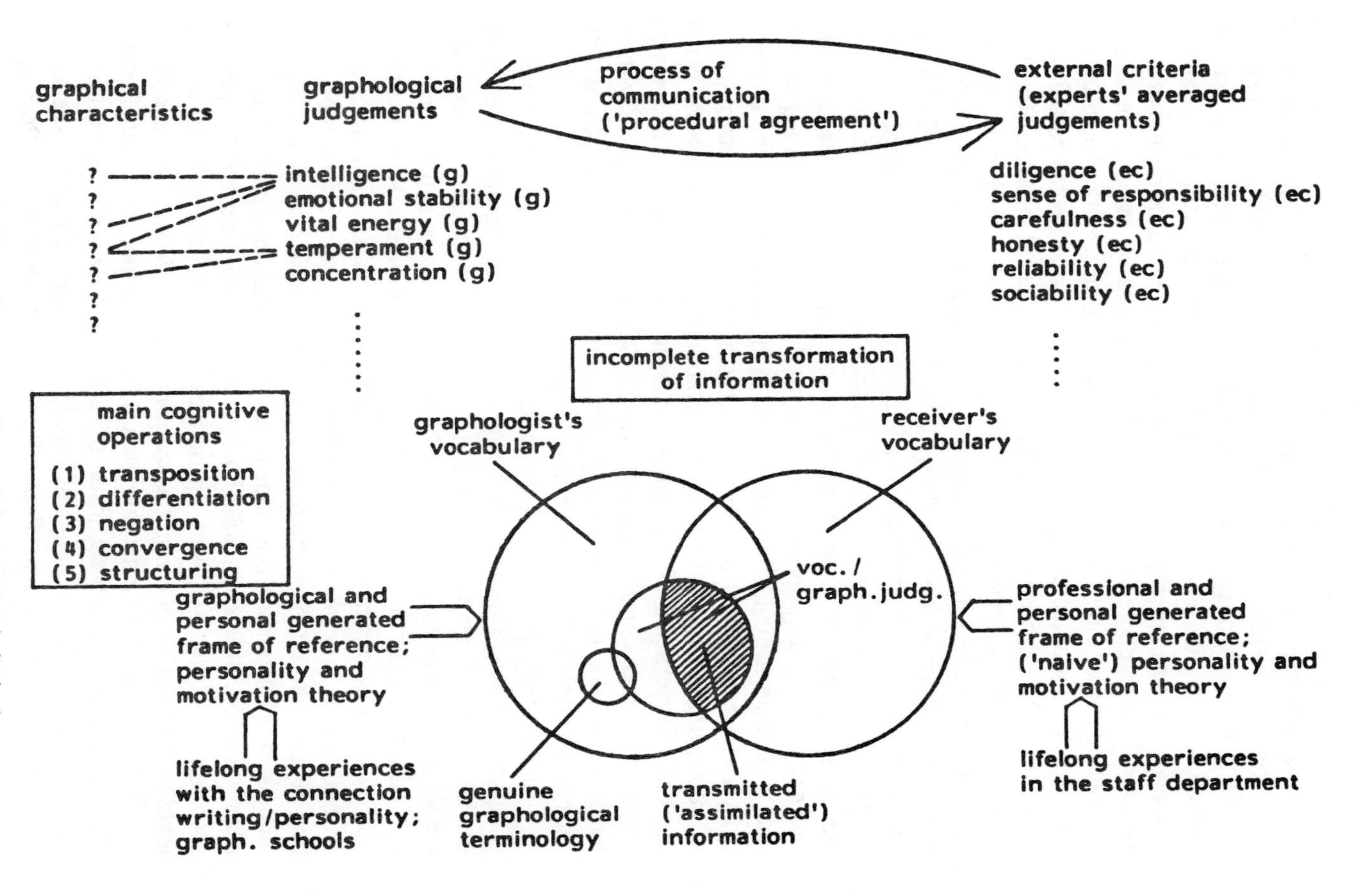

Figure 2. Validation in the form of 'processual assimilation'

Model 2 represents our current view of the process of validation. Figure 2 shows how the model works, using our example of the graphologist presenting the results of his analysis of employees' handwriting samples to the personnel manager. Once internal criteria are replaced by external criteria, such as the expert assessments and judgments of the personnel manager, the validation process involves a very complex *communication process.* The graphologist generates his judgments by means of a variety of cognitive operations, including transposition, differentiation, negation, convergence, and structuring. These are, in turn, embedded as partial operations in a broader meaning-centered and recentered process. Relations that tend to be homogeneous and configurations that tend to be syndromatic are combined in this process (Lockowandt 1973, Jager 1984). We mark the judgments that are derived by this method with the index (g), in order to separate them from those judgments based on external criteria.

Expert judgments which are diagnostically founded in different theories of personality or conceptual frames of reference are marked by the index (ec). Now, the process of gradual mediation, procedural agreement, and processual assimilation begins. Communication between the graphologist and the personnel manager produces an incomplete transformation of information—in part, because the vocabulary of the two experts is not identical. Some items of information can be exchanged and assimilated because of shared comprehension horizons. Others cannot, especially those which are unique to handwriting-psychological terminology, such as Pulver's (1949) concept of "depth-tension."

Although the transfer and assimilation of information may never be complete, we are convinced that two very different frames of reference can be connected by means of language. Thus, it is naive to assume that the validation process consists of nothing more than one expert's declaring the individual assertions of the other correct or incorrect. What is needed instead is an *intermediary process* in which a transformation takes place on both sides. In terms of radio technology: to convey information, it is first necessary to establish the same wavelength. In the case of handwriting analysis, it is necessary that individual statements be rephrased in such a way as to establish comparability between the two systems. This process should not be confused with operationalizing; *the process at issue here involves the creation of conditions that make correct judgments possible.*

These processes of externalization, transformation, and objectification that make possible the comparison of different frames of reference are idiosyncratic and, therefore, must be brought forth anew for each expert.

Consider, for example, Pophal's concept of "degree of stiffening," a handwriting characteristic that is intended to encompass the behavioral characteristics of both inhibition and disinhibition. The word "inhibition" may be part of a sales manager's vocabulary, but it does not mean the same as "degree of stiffening"; and if it is used in the lay-psychological sense, it may well obscure rather than elucidate the intended sense. In our own research we have found that the most commonly used metaphor for inhibition, the brake, fails to capture what the author actually meant. The term "inhibition" is commonly mistaken for the neurotic state of inhibition. For Pophal, however, inhibition is a normal psychological and physiological constituent of the movement of writing, without which it would not even exist. The possible psychopathological manifestations of stiffening are of only secondary interest.

In view of these conceptual differences, it may be difficult or even impossible for a sales manager to understand that a salesman's writing should show degree of stiffening III, perhaps with a tendency toward II if more indulgence is demanded, or toward IV if more power of resistance and a higher tolerance of frustration are considered necessary. If, however, the sales manager's life experiences prevent him from appreciating these distinctions, he will consider the handwriting-based psychological assessment entirely false. The discernment of the respective connection of explanation and the transformation of judgments into statements are necessary in this case in order to make a comparison at all possible.

The process of arriving at such judgments has seldom been given such extensive consideration and treatment. Only a single work with this declared aim has come to our attention, that based on Max Hall's (1928) psychotechnique, which has since fallen into oblivion. Hall's work dealt with the value of handwriting analysis as a method for selecting mercantile apprentices. He found a high level of agreement between the psychological judgments of a single handwriting psychologist and information obtained from six mercantile experts (total rho = .86; the values for the six experts ranged from .68 to .86). Hall explained the high correlations as follows: "The amount of correlation is only then clear when the mistakes, which are made by competent judges in the quantification of both items of information, are very little" (Hall 1928). These findings are particularly striking, because the judgments of the experts were completely independent of each other. It is possible that this experiment was conducted under unusually favorable conditions and that the use of a single handwriting psychologist may limit the generalizability of Hall's result. Nevertheless a close analysis and replication of this experiment would be worthwhile, especially because it is so carefully described.

CONCLUSIONS

1. Internal criteria such as the results of tests or questionnaires should not be used in attempts to validate handwriting analysis. Internal criteria fall short of the demands of handwriting analysis, either because it is not known precisely what they assess, or because it is known that they assess only limited aspects of the information provided by handwriting analysis.

2. Attempts to validate should use external criteria, which in most circumstances would be the judgments of experts in the field of practice (e.g., staff managers). The experts should function as independently of each other as possible, so that, for example, each would assess the employee's personal references independently of the others and then generate an average assessment through group discussion. The experts should go through a similar process to create an average judgment of the graphological assessments. The correlation between these two average assessments constitutes the measure of validity. It is important that the experts should not work with global reports, but with individual statements.

3. It is essential that the communication process between the experts in the field of practice and the handwriting analysts be kept free of disturbing influences. In pilot studies, we have found that failure to control such influences impedes the clear communication of judgments, not the ability to make judgments. In these situations, special attention must be paid to the way in which information is transmitted.

4. Should the judgments diverge, that is, in the absence of validity, one should first look for possible errors in the transmission of information and then recheck the experiment. As we know from initial experiments, such errors can be avoided by giving the professional expert and the handwriting analyst the opportunity to gain deeper insight into each other's perspective, so as to clarify differences in conceptual framework, views of being evaluated, and the requirements of the position to be filled.

5. Finally, we believe that such validation experiments demand a radical change of view, a shift in focus. We must direct our scientific skill toward working out an appropriate criterion for handwriting analysis. Above all, we must try to bring clarity into the communication process with all its possible obstacles. Hall's (1928) study demonstrates that such experiments are much more complicated than those that have been conducted to date on the validity of handwriting analysis. We firmly believe that, "If we are faced with the choice of dealing with either (1)

experimentally simple problems that are however trivial or invalid, or (2) experimental problems that are fearfully difficult but important, we should certainly not hesitate to choose the latter." (Maslow 1970, 21)

SUMMARY

This chapter discusses the problem of establishing the validity of psychological judgments based on handwriting analysis. After preliminary remarks concerning the need for a scientific approach to the problem, the two most commonly used models for criterion-based validation are described and criticized in detail. Their two most important defects are their lack of fit with the subject and their total dependence on internal criteria. We then suggest a recentering of the whole perspective in order to solve the validity problem. The process of passing a judgment should be cleared up in a body, and above all, external criteria should replace internal criteria, and judgments by professional experts should be made via discussion among all the experts involved. Until the new model is fully elaborated, the process of validation should be viewed as a complicated process of communication, which is susceptible to disturbance and in which clarification and transformation of information is necessary. These ideas reflect our efforts to drive back quantitative methods of examination in psychological assessment and to find the way back to qualitative methods of research.

NOTES

1. The randomizing process was as follows. In order to ensure that the measurements were random throughout the sample, we divided the sample into four quadrants, and took three measurements on the edges, the first possible measurement from the border of the page, and so on. In addition, we took four measurements from the center of the sample, for a total of 28 measurements. In order to ensure the accuracy of each measurement we used a magnifier with a scale.

2. We used Subtests 70–79 of the Intelligenz-Struktur-Test, making a total of 10 x 69 = 690 possible correlations.

3. I would like to express my thanks to Mr. Hartmann for the many important insights and items of scientific information he has provided over the years.

REFERENCES

Carus, C. G. 1938. *Symbolik der Menschlichen Gestalt.* 4th ed. Dresden.

Castelnuovo-Tedesco, P. 1948. "A Study of the Relationship Between Handwriting and Personality Variables." *Genetic Psychological Monographs* 37: pp. 167–220.

Dettweiler, Ch. 1980. "Die Tiefenpsychologische Dimension der Schriftpsychologie." *Angewandte Graphologie und Charakterkunde* 28(2): pp. 5–21.

———. 1984. "Zum Selbstverständnis des Schriftanalytikers (Schriftpsychologen)." *Angewandte Graphologie und Charakterkunde* 32(2): pp. 46–50.

Fiedler, K. 1984. "Diagnostische Fähigkeiten und Diagnostische Erfahrung." In *Diagnostische Urteilsbildung in der Psychologie,* edited by R. S. Jager et al., pp. 303–327.

Guilford, J. P. 1964. *Persönlichkeit.* Weinheim, 1964.

Hall, M. 1928. "Die Schriftbeurteilung als Methode der Berufsauslese." *Psychotechnische Zeitschrift* 3(1): pp. 65–81.

Hartmann, H. 1970. *Psychologische Diagnostik.* Stuttgart.

Jager, R. S. et al., eds. 1984. *Diagnostische Urteilsbildung in der Psychologie: Grundlagen und Anwendungen.* Göttingen.

Kirchhoff, R. 1962. "Das Verhältnis von Graphologie und Ausdruckskunde." *Zeitschrift für Menschenkunde* 26(3): pp. 320–337.

Lockowandt, O. 1966. "Faktorenanalytische Validierung der Handschrift mit Besonderer Berücksichtigung projektiver Methoden." Ph.D. Dissertation, University of Freiburg.

———. 1973. "Der Prozess der Urteilsbildung in der Schriftpsychologie." *Zeitschrift für Menschenkunde* 37(3): pp. 135–154.

———. 1979. "Bericht über das Symposion Schriftpsychologie in Mannheim." In *Bericht über den 31. Kongress der Deutschen Gesellschaft für Psychologie in Mannheim 1978.* Vol. 2, edited by L. Eckensberger, pp. 331–350. Göttingen.

Maslow, A. H. 1970. *Motivation and Personality.* New York, p. 21.

Michel, L. 1964. "Allgemeine Grundlagen Psychologischer Tests." In *Psychologische Diagnostik,* edited by R. Heib, p. 53. Göttingen.

———. 1969. "Empirische Untersuchungen zur Frage der Übereinstimmung und Gültigkeit von Beurteilungen des Intellektuellen Niveaus aus der Handschrift." *Archiv für die gesamte Psychologie* 121: pp. 31–54.

Pawlik, K., M. Amelang, B. Heinze, and W. Beyer. 1973. "Zur Abhängigkeit graphometrischer Variablen von Merkmalen der Anatomie und Psychomotorik." *Zeitschrift für Experimentelle und Angewandte Psychologie* 20(4): pp. 630–652.

Prystav, G. 1971. "Reliabilität graphometrischer Schriftbeschreibung (Part I.)" *Zeitschrift für Menschenkunde* 35: pp. 70–94.

Pulver, M. 1949. *Intelligenz in Schriftausdruck: Eine Studie.* Zürich.

Timm, U. 1965. "Graphometrie als psychologischer Test? Eine Untersuchung der Reliabilität, Faktorenstruktur und Validitat von 84 Schriftmerkmalen." Ph.D. Dissertation, University of Freiburg.

7

Graphoanalytic Cues

James C. Crumbaugh

This chapter is a slightly revised version of Dr. Crumbaugh's contribution to the *Encyclopedia of Clinical Assessment,* volume 2 (San Francisco: Jossey-Bass Inc., 1980).

After his introduction, Dr. Crumbaugh provides a brief history of graphology up to Bunker's founding of the Graphoanalysis movement in 1929. The reader may wish to compare this section with Nickell (chapter 2). Section II outlines Graphoanalytic procedures. Dr. Crumbaugh distinguishes between two sorts of handwriting traits: *primary,* which can be determined from a single feature of handwriting, such as the position of the stroke on the *t,* and *evaluated,* which are inferred from two or more primary traits. Dr. Crumbaugh maintains that Graphoanalysis can discern emotions, optimism, loyalty, logical thinking, impulsiveness, prejudice, diplomacy, selfishness, and fears, as well as many other traits. However, he specifically asserts that Graphoanalysis cannot diagnose mental or physical disease. He also expresses doubts about graphotherapy, a movement which asserts that changing one's handwriting changes the associated personality traits.

Dr. Crumbaugh endorses the notion of holism criticized by Dale Beyerstein in chapter 8 and Dean et al. in chapter 13, as well as the idea that clinical judgment on the part of the Graphoanalyst is required to produce valid predictions of a handwriting subject's character.

Graphoanalytic cues are based on a particular system of graphology or handwriting analysis, which in turn is one form of graphokinesics or expressive movements made graphically. Interpretation of all forms of graphokinesics for the purpose of assessing the personality and character of an individual is based on the fundamental assumption in clinical psychiatry and psychology that personality is expressed by or projected into all of the individual's responses to the environment. The person may respond in either of two ways: (1) verbally, by describing a perception or interpretation of an ambiguous stimulus such as a Rorschach inkblot; or (2) manually, via such expressive movements as projective drawing or handwriting.

Projective techniques of the verbal type include: (1) the Rorschach, Holtzman, and other inkblot tests; (2) the Murray Thematic Apperception Test (TAT), which requires the person to interpret ambiguous pictures of persons and objects, and which contains more structure than inkblots but is still open to broad interpretation; (3) the Shneidman Make a Picture and Story Test (a variant of the TAT); (4) the Twitchell-Allen Three Dimensional Apperception Test, which offers small objects for both visual and kinesthetic perception; and (5) the tautophone test, which uses ambiguous recorded sounds that can be free-form like inkblots or more structured like the apperception tests—to name but a few. Most projective methods have been of the verbal type, and most of these have involved visual perception.

The chief projective techniques of the expressive movement type are the various forms of projective drawing or writing tests: (1) the Goodenough (1926) Draw-a-Person Test and the Buck (1948) House-Tree-Person Test, which require the person to draw his or her own version of persons or objects; (2) the Mira (1940) Myokinetic Test, which requires a blindfolded subject to draw free-hand different types of lines in various planes with each hand alternately; and (3) handwriting analysis. Of these, the Goodenough and the Buck tests are the most widely used, although most clinicians "crystal ball" the drawings and do little in the way of objective scoring. Nevertheless, many practitioners believe that they are among the most revealing of all projective methods, even though studies have failed to demonstrate their validity. Although responses to the Mira Myokinetic Test are scored more objectively, the test is complicated to administer and has never been widely employed. Handwriting analysis offers the advantage of being more amenable to precise measurement, while at the same time allowing the seasoned analyst to bypass detailed measurement and to make global interpretations based on a subjective fusing of the relationships among the data.

Sign interpretation, the attempt to tie specific personality traits to specific signs or features found in inkblots, drawings, or handwriting, has never been well validated for any projective technique, and it is often said that the validity is in the clinician and not in his tools. Global interpretation has consistently been superior to sign interpretation, which means that what is actually valid is the experience of the clinician in putting together in a totally unanalyzable way the overall picture of personality yielded by the complex interaction of all the signs. Since the meaning of a sign changes depending on the other signs with which it occurs, a sign cannot be interpreted in a constant manner from one person to another. (Allergists experience the same problem: a patient may not be allergic to an apple as such but may respond severely to the combination of an apple and an orange.)

Handwriting analysis not only permits the experienced clinician to make global interpretations, but it also offers the novice or the less expert practitioner adequate quantification to depend on until holistic expertise is developed. The same can be said for the Rorschach, but not for most projective methods. Handwriting analysis has other advantages: (1) The sample of writing can be taken by a clerk without expenditure of professional time. (2) It can be obtained without the person knowing what it is to be used for. (3) Samples can be obtained from most people over a span of many years, since most people have kept something they have written by hand at most key periods of their lives. Thus, longitudinal studies of personality can be carried out more easily than with other techniques of evaluation, because test data are usually not available from earlier stages of life.

Background and Current Status

Probably the first organized attempt to analyze handwriting was that of Camillo Baldi, an Italian scholar and physician.[1] While a professor at the University of Bologna in 1622, he published his *Treatise on a Method to Recognize the Nature and Quality of a Writer from His Letters.* The next published work was by Johann Kasper Lavater (1741–1801), a Swiss scholar of personality at the University of Zurich. These early publications interested many intellectuals but had little following as a possible method of personality analysis, for the simple reason that very few people could read and write.

As education became more widespread in the nineteenth century, handwriting analysis rapidly gathered interest. It was practiced far more as an art than a science, but often with amazing intuitive skill, by such figures of the period as Goethe, Poe, the Brownings, Leibniz, Balzac, Dickens, and many others. It is said that Gainsborough achieved the lifelike quality of his portraits by having before him, while painting, a handwriting specimen of his subject. He felt that the handwriting enabled him to capture the essence of the subject's personality.

In France serious study of handwriting was undertaken by Abbé Louis J. H. Flandrin and the Archbishop of Cambrai. Their real contribution, however, was the training of their assistant, Abbé Jean Hippolyte Michon, who published in Paris in 1875 the most scholarly work on handwriting up to that time. Entitled *The Practical System of Graphology,* Michon's work coined the generic term for handwriting analysis. He tirelessly studied hundreds of graphic signs which were presumed to indicate specific personality traits, and his system because known as "the school of fixed signs."

In the late nineteenth century, a discipline of Michon, Crépieux-Jamin, expanded his master's studies and modified to some degree the rigid one-to-one relationship that Michon assumed to exist between handwriting strokes and personality traits. But the basic theory of isolated signs remained dominant in French schools of handwriting analysis.

Near the turn of the century, Crépieux-Jamin interested the great French psychologist Alfred Binet (who devised the first intelligence tests) in handwriting analysis as a technique for testing personality. Binet's experiments indicated that handwriting experts could distinguish successful from unsuccessful persons by their writing with an accuracy of 61 to 92 percent, a remarkable accomplishment in view of the crude methods of the day. Binet was also able to determine, to a considerable degree, the intelligence and honesty of writers, but not their age or sex. These findings have been verified in the graphoanalytic system of handwriting analysis.

In Germany also there were serious students of handwriting during the last half of the nineteenth century. William Preyer at the University of Berlin demonstrated an essential similarity between handwriting, foot writing, teeth writing, opposite-hand writing, and even crook-of-the-elbow writing; and he noted that "all writing is brain writing." Later, psychiatrist Georg Meyer showed important differences between spontaneous writing and written material that had been copied.

The most prominent name in German handwriting analysis became —and remained for some years—that of Ludwig Klages. He coined the term *expressive movement* to refer to all motor activities performed habitually, automatically, and without conscious thought: walking, talking, gesturing, facial responding, and especially handwriting. But while Klages' influence was strong in Germany for a time it did not spread, because his system was esoteric and subjective, intuitive in the extreme, complex, and mixed with an intricate personal philosophy that made it incomprehensible and of dubious authenticity to serious scholars.

Although Klages' work was not widely followed by handwriting experts elsewhere, his name had gathered enough momentum in German circles (which were the most respected in science of the time) to cause many scholars to evaluate the validity of handwriting analysis by appraising the validity of his system. When American psychology developed from the historical foundations of German psychology, which was the cornerstone of the scientific study of the mind, many early American psychologists did the same.

Graphoanalysis, founded by M. N. Bunker in 1929, has been called a protest against both the atomistic, one-to-one sign graphology that typified the French school and the broad, sweeping, intuitive graphology of the German school. This middle-of-the-road compromise position drew heavily from the then new Gestalt school of psychology, which insisted that people must be studied as dynamic wholes and that these wholes are more than the sum of their individual parts. Bunker based this method of personality evaluation through handwriting on this fundamental Gestalt concept. Thus, he emphasized that the interplay of related traits produces an overall effect that is different from that of any single trait, and that the holistic or global personality pattern can be produced by a variety of single-trait combinations, all of which must be learned by experience.

Until his death in 1961, Bunker developed his school and continued to augment its teachings by empirical studies of the handwriting specimens of various personality types. Following Bunker's death, V. Peter Ferrara of Chicago assumed the leadership. Holding a master's degree in psychology, Ferrara emphasized sound validation research to support the concepts of Graphoanalysis and to modify those that did not prove valid.

Graphoanalysis now has certified practitioners in all states of the union and in most countries of the world. It has a wide variety of practical applications. The chief areas of use are: (1) in business and industry (Fullmer, 1971; Rast, 1966), where Graphoanalysts assist personnel specialists in selecting job applicants with specific aptitudes, in job placement and promotion, and in the determination of character in credit risks; (2) in schools (International Graphoanalysis Society, 1975), where Graphoanalysts help vocational counselors determine areas of aptitude and help teachers determine the patterns of personality that cause the student to have trouble in school or the school to have trouble with student; (3) in mental health clinics and hospitals (Root, 1966; Watanuki, 1963), where Graphoanalysts help psychiatrists and psychologists understand the personality structure, traits, and psychodynamics of patients (it should be noted that Graphoanalysts do *not* offer diagnoses of either mental or physical illnesses, and they do not do therapy); and (4) in forensic or questioned-document work, where Graphoanalysts serve as expert witnesses in authenticating legal instruments (International Graphoanalysis Society, 1975).

Graphotherapy, training the person to use in his or her writing those strokes that usually represent desirable traits and to eliminate those strokes that usually imply undesirable traits, has been explored, but it is in a strictly experimental stage at present. It is not taught in Graphoanalysis or permitted by the code of Graphoanalytic ethics except in collaboration with mental health specialists in a clinical setting. The validity of this type of therapy is questionable. Although favorable results have occurred with graphotherapy, they can also be explained as placebo effects. Further, the face validity of such therapy is poor; there is no apparent reason why traits *reflected in* handwriting but *not caused by* handwriting should yield to a manipulation that is unrelated to their cause.

CRITICAL DISCUSSION

DESCRIPTION OF GRAPHONALYTIC PROCEDURES

Graphoanalysis consists of the following steps: First, a *perspectograph*—an analysis of the first hundred upstrokes that appear in the sample of writing—is constructed. This sample is preferably a full page or more of spontaneous writing made with a pencil or ballpoint pen on unruled paper, without the individual's knowing that it is for analysis. The rules for determining and measuring these upstrokes are rather complex. The final measure is the percentage of each of seven degrees of slant found in the writing, from far forward to far backward. Each upstroke is marked and measured by a specially constructed gauge, and each of the seven degree spans of the gauge indicates a degree of emotional responsiveness of the writer. In general, far-forward writing is found in extremely emotional persons, while backward writing indicates emotional constraint and blockage (see Fig. 1). This characteristic becomes important in determining the way in which many traits found in one's writing will affect one's behavior. The percentage of each slant span is plotted on a bar graph for reference as other traits are revealed. The interpretation of slant is demonstrated in Figure 1.

Figure 1. Levels of Emotional Responsiveness

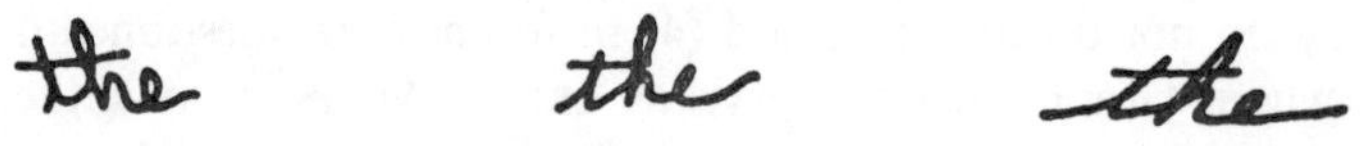

(a) Withdrawal

(b) Objectiveness

(c) Intense responsiveness

The second step in constructing a Graphoanalysis is completion of a special worksheet that lists some one hundred "primary" personality traits and some fifty "evaluated" traits. A primary trait is one that can be determined from a single-stroke formation. For example, temper is indicated by t-bars made to the right of the t-stem. An evaluated trait is one that must be inferred from two or more other traits. For example, timidity is a product of low self-confidence, shyness, self-consciousness, and clannishness. It should be noted that graphoanalytic definitions of traits are often different from those most commonly employed among mental health disciplines, but personality theorists differ so much among themselves that few uniform definitions are possible. Both primary and evaluated traits are rated as to intensity in the handwriting sample on a three-point scale in which "X" is slight, "XX" is moderate, and "XXX" is strong.

The worksheet is divided into trait groups, which serve to delineate the personality. Among these groupings are:

1. Emotions, revealed by slant and depth of writing, as shown in Figure 1.

Figure 2. Mental Processes

(a) Comprehensive thinking

(b) Cumulative logical thinking

(c) Exploratory or investigative thinking

2. Mental processes, revealed by such traits as comprehensive, cumulative, and exploratory thinking, as demonstrated in Figure 2. The sharp points of the *m* and *n* in 2a show comprehension: the rounded tops of the loops of the same letters in 2b show logical thinking; the wedges of the *m* and *n* in 2c show investigative thinking. Mental processes are intensified by traits like conservatism, generosity, optimism, loyalty, positiveness, broad-mindedness, and tenacity; they are reduced by such traits as impulsiveness, pessimism, prejudice, and narrow-mindedness.
3. Social behavior, supported by such specific traits as diplomacy, frankness, humor, optimism, poise, and self-reliance; negated by such traits as clannishness, selectivity, selfishness, and impatience, as illustrated in

Figure 3. Note the tight loops of the *m* and *n* in 3a, which indicate repression, and the spread loops in 3b, which indicate the opposite.

Figure 3. Social Responsiveness

many many

(a)
Repression

(b)
Uninhibition

Fears and defenses, and the degree and type of adjustment, are indicated by such traits as caution, bluff, dignity, decisiveness, pride, tenacity, and persistence. Special aptitudes are evaluated for the fields of business (diplomacy, decisiveness, determination, and initiative), science (creativity, imagination, and analytical thinking), mechanics (manual dexterity, precision, rhythm, and the like), and other areas. Further illustrations of stroke interpretations in the determination of personality traits are shown in Figures 4 through 10.[2]

The low t-bar in Figure 4a reveals a lack of self-confidence, while the high t-bar of 4b indicates strong will power. Figure 5a shows simplicity or modesty in the small *a* of *Ann,* while 5b reveals ostentation in the large *a.* Figure 6a shows frankness in the closed *a* of *and;* 6b shows self-deception in the initial loop of *a;* and 6c shows purposive or intentional deceit in the double loop of *a.* Figure 7a demonstrates abstract imagination in the large upper loop of the letter *l,* while 7b reveals materialistic imagination in the large lower loop of the letter *g.* Figure 8a portrays depression or pessimism in the downward slope of the word *many,* while 8b indicates optimism in the upward trend of the word. Figure 9a shows strong determination in the bold downstroke of *y,* while 9b shows weak determination in the short, light downstroke of this letter. Figure 10a reveals close attention to details in the closely dotted *i,* while 10b portrays inattention in the high, removed dot of the *i.*

These cues will not be "sure fire" for any individual, but if the reader will check a given cue against the personalities of a dozen or so people whom he knows well and who show it in their writing, he will find that most of these people show the trait represented by the cue. Of course, in a given case the cue meaning may be modified by overriding counter-

Figure 4. Approach to Achievement

the the

(a)
Lack of
self-confidence

(b)
Strong
will power

Figure 5. Levels of Social Appeal

ann ann

(a)
Simplicity,
modesty

(b)
Ostentation

Figure 6. Levels of Honesty

and and and

(a)
Frankness

(b)
Self-deception or
rationalization

(c)
Intentional
deception

Figure 7. Levels of Imagination

(a)
Abstract
imagination

(b)
Materialistic
imagination

Figure 8. Attitude toward Life

(a)
Depression
Pessimism

(b)
Optimism

Figure 9. Levels of Determination

(a)
Strong
determination

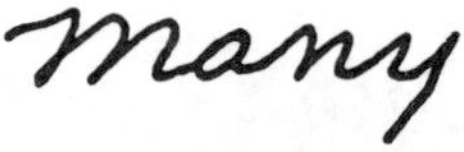

(b)
Weak
determination

Figure 10. Levels of Attention

(a)
Close attention
to details

(b)
Inattention

cues, and the true interpretation is based on the relationship among cues and, therefore, requires broad clinical experience. Before this experience can be acquired, the many variations of each handwriting stroke and the probable meaning of each variation are studied. After mastering these elements, the student is coached and given practice in creating from the mass of data collected a personality picture that shows the trait interactions and the effect of these interactions in producing the individual's unique personal Gestalt.

When the worksheet has been completed, the true skill of the Graphoanalyst is tested by his ability to put all the data together into a unified, meaningful Gestalt or pattern, which yields a valid picture of the personality of the writer. Graphoanalysis, like the Rorschach or any other good projective technique, is thus not a cut-and-dried mechanical process but a dynamic means of assessment that can be learned only through broadly based experience. The fundamentals and the basic procedures can be taught in school, and the neophyte must depend on them while he or she gradually accumulates the experience that is necessary for accurate clinical judgments based on intuitions about the meaning of the various patterns of traits. Here again is a demonstration of the adage that the validity of a projective technique is in the clinician and not in the instruments. The beginner can, with mastery of the instrument of Graphoanalysis, offer much helpful information about the writer's personality and style of dealing with life situations, but only years of practice will make him a master of the art.

THE QUESTION OF VALIDITY

The theory of handwriting analysis rests on solid ground as a projective technique of the expressive movement type, but historically it has been dismissed as pseudoscience, because early psychologists reacted negatively to the intuitive and imprecise systems of early graphology. Psychologists have often acknowledged in elementary textbooks that handwriting *should* reveal personality and graphology that has good face validity—it looks as if it should work. But they maintain that because empirical studies have failed to establish the validity of graphological systems, they must be classed with astrology, phrenology, and the like. Thus, the majority of psychologists turned to other projective techniques of expressive movement such as projective drawing. Projective drawings have long been a part of the armamentarium of many clinical psychologists, even though there is little evidence for their validity (Murstein, 1965). In more recent years, many authors have reexamined the evidence, particularly that for Graphoanalysis, and have concluded that graphology is not a pseudoscience. Ruch (1967, p. 117), for example, states: "Although many psychologists feel [graphology] has no more value than palmistry or reading tea leaves, it has been studied scientifically in recent years by rigorously controlled methods. The general conclusion is that graphology may eventually prove to have value in predicting personality traits." Within the last ten years, more and better validity research has appeared, and a number of psychologists, psychiatrists, and other physicians have begun to take training in Graphoanalysis.

The question of validation continues to be raised by critics, most of whom are psychologists. While some have seen the advantage of graphology and have taken the training, the majority apparently feel that the methods in which they already have been schooled are the only assessment burdens they wish to assume. Perhaps this is understandable in view of the fact that the training required to become expert in handwriting analysis is at least as demanding as that required to master the Rorschach. (It should be noted that this is the situation in America; in Germany many universities have required training in graphology as part of the work for a Ph.D. in psychology.)

The chief validation studies are cited and abstracted in a brochure published by and available from the International Graphoanalysis Society (1970). These and later studies have demonstrated a scientific basis for the assumption that handwriting can be as valid in personality assessment as other major projective techniques. The work of Eysenck (1945), Wolfson (1949), Weinberg, Fluckiger, and Tripp (1962), and Crumbaugh and Stockholm (1977) has shown that it is easier to establish the validity of global or holistic interpretations of handwriting samples than of the atomistic, molecular, or isolated sign approach to interpretation. The same is true of other projective techniques, demonstrating once again that validity is primarily in the clinician rather than in the technique. Only experience blended with good intuitive judgment makes for valid assessment, whatever instrument is used. Further validation evidence has been offered by Fluckiger, Tripp, and Weinberg (1961), Mann (1961), Naegler (1958), and Thomas (1964).

Even the infant shows personality tendencies in graphic movements, and these tendencies do not disappear in old age. While handwriting reflects the motor decline of advanced age, neither age nor sex can be assessed by handwriting. Education (beyond basic literacy), socioeconomic status, race, ethnicity, and vocation have no bearing on the ability of Graphoanalysis to determine character and personality, although vocational aptitudes and interests are reflected in handwriting.

As has been noted, neither mental nor physical disease can be diagnosed by Graphoanalysis, but handwriting often provides information that helps the physician make a better estimate of the cause of symptoms. IQ is never determined by the Graphoanalyst, but the level of intellectual efficiency can be estimated. Graphoanalysts can help those professionals who are charged with responsibility for almost all types of disorders—though they do not assume this professional responsibility themselves—by offering a picture of personality patterns that often yields helpful clues to the presence of underlying organic factors in the etiology of psychiatric disorders.

PERSONAL VIEWS AND RECOMMENDATIONS

The present state of Graphoanalytic art and science warrants its practical use by well-trained Graphoanalysts in a variety of working situations, although neither Graphoanalysis nor any other single assessment technique should ever be used alone in making important life decisions. Neither handwriting analysis nor any other psychological test of personality should determine whether one enters a certain occupation, gets credit, and so forth. Test results must be combined with clinical, educational, demographic, and all other relevant data. The validation of Graphoanalysis is neither better nor worse than that of most other projective techniques. While all of them leave something to be desired in "hard-core" validation, no experienced clinician doubts that any one of them may constitute a useful tool in the hands of a practitioner who believes in it, studies it deeply, and gains broad experience in the relationships between the responses it elicits and the patterns of behavior and personality traits it reveals.

NOTES

1. The historical material in this section is taken primarily from Lecture No. 3 of the general course of the International Graphoanalysis Society.
2. Constructed by Teresa Croteau-Crumbaugh, MGA, Master Graphoanalyst.

REFERENCES

Buck, J. N. 1948. "The House-Tree-Person Test." *Journal of Clinical Psychology* 4: pp. 151–158.

Crumbaugh, J. C., and E. Stockholm. 1977. "Validation of Graphoanalysis by 'Global' or 'Holistic' Method." *Perceptual and Motor Skills* 44: pp. 403–410.

Eysenck, H. J. 1945. "Graphological Analysis and Psychiatry: An Experimental Study." *British Journal of Psychology* 35: pp. 70–81.

Fluckiger, F. A., C. A. Tripp, and G. H. Weinberg. 1961. "A Review of Experimental Research in Graphology, 1933–1960." *Perceptual and Motor Skills* 12: pp. 67–90 (Monograph Supplement 1–V12).

Fullmer, T. P. 1971. "The Use of Graphoanalysis in Personnel Selection." *Best's Review* 72(2).

Goodenough, F. L. 1926. *Measurement of Intelligence by Drawings.* Yonkers, N.Y.: World Book.

International Graphoanalysis Society. 1970. *An Annotated Bibliography of Studies in Handwriting Analysis Research.* Catalogue No. G1059. Chicago: International Graphoanalysis Society.

———. 1975. *Field Reports from IGAS Students and Graduates: The Many Varied and Successful Uses of Graphoanalysis.* Catalogue No. G623 0475. Chicago: International Graphoanalysis Society.

Mann, W. R. 1961. "A Continuation of the Search for Objective Graphological Hypotheses." Ph.D. dissertation, University of Ottawa.

Mira, E. 1940. "Myokinetic Psychodiagnosis: A New Technique for Exploring the Cognitive Trends of Personality." *Proceedings of the Royal Society of Medicine* 33: pp. 173–194.

Murstein, B. I. 1965. *Handbook of Projective Techniques.* New York: Basic Books.

Naegler, R. C. 1958. *A Validation Study of Personality Assessment Through Graphoanalysis.* Catalogue No. 309. Chicago: International Graphoanalysis Society.

Rast, G. H. 1966. "The Value of Handwriting Analysis in Bank Work." *Burroughs Clearing House* 50: pp. 40–41ff.

Root, V. T. 1966. "Graphoanalysis—An Aid in Solving Human Relations Problems." *Hospital Topics Magazine* (July).

Ruch, F. L. 1967. *Psychology and Life.* 7th ed. Glenview, Ill.: Scott, Foresman.

Thomas, D. L. 1964. "Validity of Graphoanalysis in the Assessment of Personality Characteristics." Master's thesis, Colorado State University.

Watanuki, H. H. 1963. "Graphoanalysis: A Tested Tool in Clinical Counseling." *Journal of Graphoanalysis* 3(12): pp. 11, 13 (July).

Weinberg, G. H., F. A. Fluckiger, and C. A. Tripp. 1962. "The Application of a New Matching Technique." *Journal of Projective Techniques* 26: pp. 221–224.

Wolfson, R. A. 1949. *Study in Handwriting Analysis.* Ann Arbor, Mich.: Edwards Brothers.

Section Three

Philosophical Underpinnings of Graphology

8

Graphology and the Philosophy of Science

Dale F. Beyerstein

In this chapter, Dale Beyerstein examines the rationale behind a scientific experiment: What *should* it be attempting to prove? This chapter complements the discussion of Dean, Kelly, Saklofske, and Furnham in chapter 13 of the biases which corrupt our common sense when we attempt to assess the efficacy of a method of personality assessment such as graphology. Dean et al. show why it is necessary to be able to minimize the chances of these biases leading our judgment astray. Beyerstein maintains that the scientific method is the best we have to acheive this end. Dean in chapter 12 provides a discussion of the concept of *effect size,* which is what we attempt to measure by a scientific experiment. Bowman in chapter 10 discusses the special pitfalls of experiments to determine personality traits. Section IV of this chapter provides the reader with a guide showing where to find the information contained in the typical scientific paper. A well-written scientific paper ought to provide the reader who is not used to reading scientific literature the information necessary to assess the argument. In Section V this guide is applied to an analysis of one of the most often cited papers providing evidence for graphology. The reader is also encouraged to apply the tools discussed here to the three original experiments discussed in this volume, Wellingham-Jones in chapter 15, and Karnes and Leonard in chapter 16.

INTRODUCTION

"Is graphology scientific?" This question surfaces almost every time graphology is discussed, but it cannot be answered until we decide what we mean by "scientific" in this context. That is the main purpose of this chapter. But before tackling this question, we should look at why people think that it is an important one to ask. Graphologists claim to discern personality traits with some degree of accuracy. Most people think that a scientific technique for determining personality traits will be more accurate than an unscientific one. So, the question whether graphology is scientific is often asked in order to throw light on the question whether graphology *works.*

If our real interest is in the latter question, we do not need to worry *directly* about whether graphologists themselves follow the scientific method, even if we do believe that a scientific assessment is generally more reliable than one which is not scientific. To say that one technique is more reliable than another does not commit us to holding either that the first is perfect, or that the second is utterly worthless. Therefore it is *possible* that graphologists may have stumbled upon an assessment technique which works, at least tolerably well, quite by accident. That is, they might not be able to *describe* what they do in terms familiar to scientists, and they might not be *aware* that their techniques are functionally equivalent to those used by a scientist. Nevertheless, at least some of the graphologists' techniques might be in accordance with the scientific method. Of course, even on this assumption, most of us would maintain that graphology would work even better if the hit-and-miss techniques used by unscientific graphologists were to be replaced with ones that are more scientific. This is the view of many people who defend graphology at the same time as they extol the virtues of the scientific method. No doubt they are embarrassed by some of the people practicing graphology, who are also practitioners of astrology or their pseudosciences, and who make pronouncements and use methods that cause scientists to cringe. But, after all, most sciences that are respectable today had their origins in pseudo- and proto-scientific practices.[1] So, the hope of many who defend graphology is that it can be put into a scientific framework; and in the meantime, we can gain from the valuable insights into personality that graphology has to offer. Note that this position is compatible with the one taken by the graphologists contributing to this volume, Crumbaugh, Wellingham-Jones, and Lockowandt.

Nevertheless, we should not allow defenders of this position to beg the question whether graphlogy does work. We must *independently verify* the judgments of graphologists. We need a "yardstick," or in technical talk, a *criterion*, by which we can measure personality traits of subjects, and with which we can compare the judgments of personality traits independently arrived at by the graphologists. Such a criterion must come from a method of personality assessment that is arrived at by the scientific method. So, we must at this stage concern ourselves with the question about what constitutes a scientific method of personality assessment, in order to determine what will serve as an adequate criterion. Again, the graphologists contributing to this volume endorse this requirement. Once we have decided on the necessary conditions for what makes the criterion a scientific measure, we can compare the criterion with the graphologists' ways of doing things, as Richard Klimoski does in chapter 11. Thus, if it does turn out that the graphologists' personality assessments measure up fairly well against the criterion, the hope is that graphologists can borrow whatever it is that makes the criterion scientific, and thereby improve their accuracy.

So much for one reason for discussing the scientific method in this chapter. A second, and more important reason is that the authors in this volume all refer to studies, done either by themselves or by others, purporting to demonstrate the validity, or lack of validity, of various types of graphology. But there is disagreement, not only amongst these experts, but also amongst most others, over which studies are properly done and which really represent any *important* evidence in favor of graphology. Many executives of companies that are considering graphology as a hiring tool, and many people who simply want to find out about graphology out of curiosity, find this disagreement amongst so-called experts bewildering. A question I have often heard from laypeople is, "If the experts cannot agree, how can the layperson hope to come to an informed opinion by reading these studies?" And the answer to this rhetorical question then serves as their justification for doing their own type of test. This usually consists of hiring the graphologist and seeing what he or she can do. But such a test is just not very reliable, for reasons outlined by Dean et al. in chapter 13 of this volume. Human reason and observation unaided by the scientific method are impotent to deal with a complex question such as the validity of graphology. Fortunately, it is not as difficult as many people suppose to read a scientific paper critically and make up one's own mind about the evidence presented. After I present the analysis of what makes a good scientific test, and an argument for why such tests are necessary, I offer a short guide to the standard format of papers in most scientific disciplines. I shall show there that, in a good scientific paper, what may appear at first to be very intimidating is really a straightforward way of presenting the information necessary for the reader to decide whether the experiment under discussion was a good test of a theory. Of course, not all scientific papers are well written; but at least my discussion should give the reader criteria which will allow the reader to discover this quickly and put the paper aside in favor of another worth his or her time. As a practical illustration of how to read a scientific paper I offer a critique of what is most often cited as one of the very best papers presenting scientific results in favor of graphology (Frederick 1968).

GOOD SCIENTIFIC TESTS

THE SCIENTIFIC, THE NONSCIENTIFIC, AND THE UNSCIENTIFIC

T. H. Huxley described science as "organized common sense." Its major virtue is to provide a method for *testing* claims about how the world works, or proposed *explanations* of these workings. For present purposes, we will call these claims or explanations *theories.* A scientific theory deals with the empirical world. This is the world that we perceive through our senses, or which *cause* things to happen that we can perceive through our senses, as in the case when a proton passes through a cloud chamber and (via a complicated causal chain) produces a blip on a monitor which can be perceived by the naked eye. However, common sense theories also attempt to describe the empirical world. Anyone can come up with claims about the empirical world, and some of these are bound to be correct. The difference between a scientific and a common-sense theory is this. When we describe a theory as scientific, we are not so much interested in the *content* of the theory—what it actually *states*—as we are in whether it is of the sort that can be tested by the scientific method. This requires qualification: of course it is thanks to what the theory states that we are able to find ways of testing it. For example, a theory about God's intentions cannot be tested by the means available to science; therefore the *content* of such a theory will not be scientific, but rather theological. But the point remains that, so long as the theory is testable by the scientific method, a theory will count as scientific, even if it contradicts previously accepted scientific theories, or seems on the face of it absurd.[2] Also, we must remember that to say that a theory is scientific is not to endorse it as *true*, since there have been, and will continue to be, many false scientific theories. And, conversely, to say that a theory is *not* scientific is not to say that it is *false.* Science is *one* method of getting at the truth, but there are disciplines other than science that state true propositions. Take logic, for example: despite some differences of opinion amongst philosophers of logic about the correct *analysis* of logical truth, they will all agree that there *are* logical truths, and furthermore, that they can be discovered independently of the methods used in the sciences.[3] So, not all truths are discoverable by science.

Note that I was careful to use the description "*not* scientific" above, rather than "*un*scientific." There is a distinction. The latter carries with it the idea of being *contrary to* science. Logic, as I just implied above, is not contrary to science; it is simply another discipline with a different methodology. Logic, the formal study of patterns of reasoning that are valid or invalid, does not use the scientific method described below to arrive at its results. Nevertheless, scientists *use* logic in their reasonings—when they reason correctly, at any rate; thus logic is *consistent with* science. On the other hand, to be *un*scientific is to be contrary to science in (at least) one of three ways.

The first way of being unscientific is to think that claims require no justification, no evidence to back them up, when obviously they do. Of course, to think this is not just to be unscientific, it is to be irrational. This mistake can be referred to as an *absence of skepticism.*

The second way is to use a method of testing a claim which is incompatible with the scientific method, *where the scientific method is appropriate.* Let us refer to this as the *alternative paradigm* approach.

The third way of being unscientific is to *abuse* the methodology of science by attempting to do science properly but failing at it. Let us refer to this as *mistaken methodology.*

Absence of Skepticism. Often skeptics will compare graphology to what most graphologists will agree are pseudosciences: phrenology, astrology, or the like. For example, see Barry Beyerstein's parallels between graphology and sympathetic magic in chapter 9. Graphologists will often take umbrage at this. They will point out that the *content* of the theory of graphology is nothing like that of, say, astrology. They will point out that astrologers assert the existence of causal relationships between the positions of planets or stars at the time of one's birth and human personality traits without having the faintest idea of what *mechanisms* might be responsible for these relationships. Or astrologers will be more precise in asserting what mechanisms are responsible, but these mechanisms are ones that are totally at variance with what modern science tells us. On the other hand, graphologists maintain that the theory behind graphology is, on the face of it, plausible and consistent with what we—and more importantly, scientifically trained psychologists—know about human personality. Handwriting, they say,[4] is a bit of behavior, which expresses personality traits, just as style of dress or characteristic facial expressions. In other words, this claim has *face validity* (see Bowman, chapter 10, and Klimoski, chapter 11). This response is problematic for two reasons. First, what seems plausible on the face of it just may not be plausible once we examine the assumptions in more detail. On this point see Barry Beyerstein's discussion in chapter 14.

Second, this response by the graphologist misses the point of the comparison the skeptic is making. The skeptic usually has in mind not the content of the theory, but the attitude toward *justification* of theories that graphologists sometimes take. The skeptic's point is that graphologists, like practitioners of pseudosciences such as astrology or biorhythms, sometimes do not see the need to look for evidence for their claims, and when they do, they are willing to settle for evidence that is not very good.

The big difference between someone with a skeptical, scientific cast of mind and someone who lacks it is in the way these two types of people deal with something that "seems obvious on the face of it." The former type will notice something that seems obvious and then ask how one might go about *testing* whether it is really so. The latter will simply assume that no further testing is required, *since* it is so obvious that it is so. The former, of course, will often discover that which appears obvious *is* in fact the case, after some further investigation. If so, she will not think that she wasted her time doing this further investigation; she will have enjoyed the testing procedure itself as a satisfaction of her curiosity, and will have gained a deeper insight into the phenomenon in question for her trouble. The latter, on the other hand, simply views further examination of "the obvious" as a waste of his time—he is too anxious to *apply* this insight to confirm it first. Furthermore, this sort of person views anyone who asks for further evidence as questioning his integrity, as obstructive, or—worst of all, in this person's view—as *negative!*

Both skeptics and believers realize *in principle* that not every immediate insight that tells us something "obvious" about the world really will pan out in the end; but it is only the person with the scientific temperament that has a chance of discovering that things really aren't this way after all. On occasion, this sort of person will be thankful to discover that she has made a mistake before wasting a lot of time. And she will certainly be thankful to someone else who takes the trouble to present her with evidence that things are not as she originally thought. The person who lacks a scientific temperament, on the other hand, has often committed himself—and his *ego*—so deeply into this insight that he will be very unhappy to find out that things are not really as he thought, and it is for this reason that he sees the skeptic as being "negative."

But it is acknowledged by almost everyone, except those in the heat of debate with a skeptic, that the best defense against the frailties of our intuition is the scientific method and the skepticism which is its underpinning. The problem is, however, that there are many defenders of the *principle* of open-minded skepticism who fail to put it into *practice* when their cherished beliefs are at stake.[5] Dealing with this sort of defender of graphology consists mainly in asking them to live up to the standards of evidence that they profess.

Alternative Paradigms. Not all graphologists share this commitment to the scientific method, however. My colleagues and I have proposed scientific tests to graphologists who have refused, offering the reason that graphology is an art, not a science. By this remark we take them to mean that their judgments are based on some kind of intuition, which is not reducible to, or duplicated by, the methods of the sciences. We have countered with the argument that using the scientific method is the best way of determining whether graphology works or not, quite apart from the question how the graphologist views the status of his or her profession. That is, the graphologists we have encountered have not yet demonstrated that they can use graphology to discern personality traits that are opaque to non-graphologists. Until they demonstrate this there is nothing that requires explanation by intuition, or non-Newtonian, non-linear, non-Western, or non-*anything* paradigms. However, some graphologists have argued that the scientific method gives us no knowledge of any value about human personality. This extreme view is, as I have just emphasized, not taken by the graphologists contributing to this volume, and it is not shared by any of the personnel managers using graphologists with whom I have had discussions. The latter have been quite insistent that they would not be using it if they did not think that it had the status of a science. So, I shall not take the time to refute this position here, because the people who are interested in this book do not really believe it. The point of this volume is to debate the scientific status of graphology. There are, I admit, people who reject the scientific method as a means of arriving at truth —or at least *probable* truth—about the empirical world. But the onus of proof is on them to describe their favored alternative to the scientific method clearly enough for me to assess it. I have no idea how to assess their usual handwaving about "intuition," "alternative paradigms," or mystical sources of enlightenment.

There are some defenders of graphology who try to hold *whichever* of the above positions that will work best. They will begin by holding that the scientific method demonstrates the validity of graphology, and thus are in a position to cash in on the rewards that can be had in this society by anyone offering a service that has been "scientifically proven," until they are confronted with the data, which they have not previously bothered to consult. Instead of examining those data, and either rebutting them or revising their views, they simply switch to the "alternative paradigm" position and maintain that scientists don't really know anything anyway. This is an obvious rhetorical trick, and I emphasize that it is not used by the defenders of graphology in this book. Nevertheless, it is common enough amongst defenders of graphology that I should mention it in passing. The response to it is obvious: simply keep asking for the evidence.

Mistaken Methodology. This is the kind of problem encountered in orthodox science all the time. Science has evolved by refining methods to deal with this problem: the peer review process, publication of the methods used in experiments in order to get criticism from colleagues that will correct methodological flaws, replication of experiments in order to uncover these flaws, and so on. Since these problems are commonly found in orthodox science, it is not surprising that we find them in graphology as well. But insofar as graphology really is scientific, methodological problems should be no more problematic for graphology than any other science. Scientists who criticize graphological experiments on methodological grounds are paying graphologists the respect of treating graphologists in the same way that they treat their colleagues. In the next two sections I describe the rationale behind the methodology accepted by other sciences, and argue that there is no reason why graphological claims, if they are true, cannot be shown to be true by the methods consistently practiced in orthodox psychology.

THEORIES, HYPOTHESES, PREDICTIONS, AND TESTS

Let us return to Huxley's point about science being organized common sense. A good experiment is just one that organizes our search for evidence for or against the theories. To criticize an experimental design is just to say that it is badly organized for that purpose. Now we shall look at what constitutes a good experimental test of a theory, and what fails to meet these standards.

A good scientific test is one that will provide evidence for or against a theory. By "good test" I do not mean one that *verifies* the theory being tested; I mean one that provides unambiguous evidence *either* in favor of the theory *or* against it. How does a test do this? I shall take up this question in the "Scientific Experiments" section, but first we should look at the elements involved in a scientific test.

Theories. Since theories are complex—consider quantum mechanics, or a theory about the mechanisms of evolution—they will consist of many individual statements which should be true or false independently of each other. To be more precise, the statements of a theory fit together into subsets of statements, with entailment relations between members of the set, but typically not between them and statements that form part of another subset.[6] It is for this reason that it is possible to *modify* a theory by changing one part of it, while leaving other parts relatively intact. However, some statements of a theory are more central to it than others; and a rough idea of how central a given statement is in a theory is captured by seeing how many statements it entails. Roughly speaking, the more central a statement is in a theory, the more statements it[7] entails.

So whole theories cannot be tested all at once if they have any complexity; an experiment will test a *part* of a theory. If the part survives the test, this will add support to the theory as a whole, if the part fails the test, then the theory will require modification. Perhaps just that part that failed will require modification, but in some cases the entire theory will have to be revised in order to leave a consistent package. When we are devising a test of a theory, one thing that matters is what we already think of that theory. If we think that the theory is basically sound, then we usually perform tests of minor parts of a theory. We are looking to extend the theory and apply it to a new range of cases, or to "fine tune" it: to modify small details. On the other hand, if we think that the theory is mistaken, we try to test a central tenet of the theory, to get to the heart of the matter and show what is fundamentally wrong with it.

Hypotheses. In either case, the part of the theory that will be tested will be that which entails a *hypothesis*: a statement that something or other will be the case under certain conditions. For example, "Pure water freezes at 0° Celsius at air pressures normally encountered at sea level" is an hypothesis in our sense.[8] It is a common-sense assertion, but also one that follows from certain statements in the theory of thermodynamics. The verification of the hypothesis is what provides evidence—though not *conclusive* evidence, as we shall see in a moment—that the theory is true. The refutation of the hypothesis provides evidence—though, again, not *conclusive* evidence—that the theory is false. We shall come in a moment to the explanation of how this works. But the most important point for the moment is that, if the testing of the hypothesis is to play this evidential role for the theory, then the hypothesis must be one that is entailed by the theory we are ultimately trying to get evidence for. We do not want to be in the position, after the test has been conducted, of not knowing whether the experiment has provided worthwhile evidence for or against the theory. So, it is essential that we be clear before we examine the results of the experiment whether the theory really does entail the hypothesis. And in order to determine this, both have to be clearly and unambiguously stated.

Predictions. If the above hypothesis is true, then it, along with other statements will entail another statement, such as "the thermometer will read

0° at the moment this water turns to ice." Call this latter statement a *prediction*.[9]

Initial Conditions. Obviously the mere fact that water freezes at 0° C does not *by itself* entail that a given thermometer will read 0°. The thermometer must be accurate, working properly, immersed in the water in a certain way, and a whole host of other conditions must be met. Call all these conditions *initial conditions.* For our simplified present purposes, we can think of the description of the initial condition as the description of how an experiment was set up and conducted, and how the measurements are made—anything, in short, which might affect whether or not the prediction comes true in the experiment.

SCIENTIFIC EXPERIMENTS

In a scientific experiment we begin with a hypothetical statement of the form "*If* water freezes at 0° C, *and* <DESCRIPTION OF INITIAL CONDITIONS>, *then* the thermometer will read 0° C at the conclusion of the experiment."[10] Schematically, this statement looks like this:

FIGURE 1

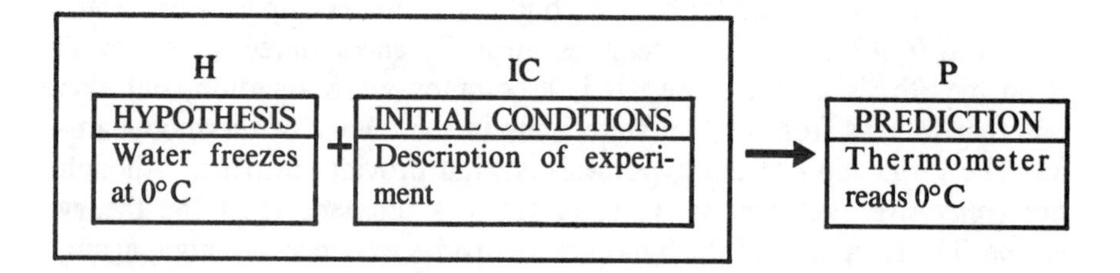

So, we assume that the hypothesis is true, and we do our best to see that the initial conditions are the way we described them, and then check to see whether the prediction turns out to be true.

Confirmation of Theories. When we get the prediction we were expecting, we take the hypothesis to be confirmed. What we have done here is to make use of an argument with the following form:

If **H** *and* **IC** *then* **P** (1)

P

H

But now we see the reason why scientists insist that the confirmation of a hypothesis in an experiment does not establish that hypothesis with certainty: an argument of this form is invalid. A valid argument is one that satisfies the following property: *It is impossible for the premises of the argument to be all true while the conclusion is false.* If an argument is not valid, then it is invalid. The sense of *impossibility* we have in mind is that it is not just *accidental* that we happen to have true premises and a true conclusion of a given argument; this must be guaranteed by the form of the argument. However, consider another instance of an argument with the same form:

If Harry visits us *and* Isabella Calls us, then the telePhone rings. (2)

The telePhone rings.

Harry visits us.

Here we do have the possibility of true premises and a false conclusion: the telephone rings on occasions when Harry is not visiting us. Therefore, it is possible to have true premises and a false conclusion with this form of argument, and it is invalid. Since the scientific argument is of this form, it is invalid. That is why the truth of its premises is no guarantee that the conclusion is true also., So, using this argument, we have not established *with certainty* that the hypothesis being tested in an experiment is true just because we get the expected prediction (Giere 1984 and Hempel 1979). However, all is not lost. What this argument does for us is to *increase the probability* that the hypothesis is true; and with each succeeding replication of the experiment, the probability of the hypothesis gets successively closer to 1 (certainty), without ever reaching it. Philosophers use the admittedly horrid term "*probabilification*" to refer to the kind of support that premises offer for their conclusions in these types of arguments. The type of argument that *probabilifies* (as opposed to *entails*) a conclusion is *inductive* (as opposed to *deductive*).

Thus we can see one of the reasons why replication is important in science. Even though an experiment yields the expected prediction, and we are reasonably confident that the initial conditions were as described, we cannot be sure that the prediction came true *because* the hypothesis is true. It is always possible to construct an *alternate* hypothesis, such that it, along with these same initial conditions, will *also* entail that prediction. Fortunately, we often have reasons other than those derived from an experiment for preferring one hypothesis to a rival one. Such considerations turn on how well each hypothesis serves to explain this experimental result *as well as* other similar results and observations. For more on this, see Quine and Ullian (1978).

Disconfirmation of Theories. How do experimental results count as evidence against a theory? They do so by disconfirming a hypothesis which is entailed by the theory. In the example we used before, the hypothesis that water freezes at 0° C will be severely weakened by the experiment if we carry it out under the same initial conditions as I described previously, and find that the thermometer reads something other than 0° C. The argument for the falsity of the hypothesis makes use of the same first premise in the argument for the truth of the hypothesis. The difference in the two arguments is that in this case, the prediction is false:

$$
\begin{array}{l}
(H \,\&\, IC) \rightarrow P \\
\text{Not } P \\
\hline
\therefore \text{Not } (H \,\&\, IC)
\end{array}
\qquad (3)
$$

This argument is valid, as the reader can see for herself by substituting another argument for the same form. However, it does not establish the conclusion we were looking for, namely the falsity of the hypothesis *simpliciter*. Our conclusion is equivalent to denying *either* the hypothesis *or* that the initial conditions in fact held (perhaps the thermometer isn't reading accurately anymore?—maybe we aren't really at sea level?). Nevertheless, if we accept the claim that the initial conditions really were as described, we do have conclusive proof that the hypothesis is false. We construct the following argument, making use of the conclusion of the previous one, and pay attention to what we are saying when we have a statement of the form "Not (H & IC)":[11]

$$
\begin{array}{ll}
\therefore & 1.\ \text{Not } (H \,\&\, IC) \\
 & 2.\ \text{Not } H \textit{ or } \text{Not } IC \\
\therefore & 3.\ IC \\
\hline
 & 4.\ \text{Not } H
\end{array}
\qquad (4)
$$

This conclusion follows with the certainty of a deductive argument. Hence the oft-repeated claim that a scientific hypothesis can be refuted, but not verified. What we have seen from this discussion is that it can be verified, as long as we do not take verification to involve 100 percent certainty but rather *probabilification*; and it can be refuted as long as we are able to settle legitimate disputes about whether the initial conditions in the experiment are really satisfied.

Verification of Theories. What does the verification of a hypothesis tell us about the theory which entails it? As I said in a previous section, the degree of support that the theory receives from a verified hypothesis will depend upon how central the hypothesis is in the theory. For example, the Big Bang theory entails the claims that some photons which were released a few hundred thousand years after the Big Bang are still travelling around in the universe. Along with certain theoretical statements that the wavelength of a photon expands as the universe expands, this will yield the hypothesis that some of these presently existing photons are now of a certain wavelength. This hypothesis, along with suitable initial conditions describing the way the aerial on your TV set picks up photons, yields the prediction that you will see evidence of the Big Bang amongst the "snow" on your TV screen (Ingram 1989).

If that prediction is verified, this will lend support to the Big Bang theory. But the hypothesis that the photons will have just the wavelength that allows them to be picked up by a TV is not as central to the theory as many other parts. It is arrived at by calculations based on the age of the universe and its expansion rate. These calculations in turn could be revised if new data were to come to light; and these revisions would not significantly affect what is central to the Big Bang theory, viz., that the present universe grew out of a single, much denser collection of matter which is now expanding outwards *at some rate or other.* Therefore, the fate of this prediction about what you will see on your TV set will not determine the entire fate of the Big Bang theory though its failure might cause some revisions to it.

A second, related point that determines the degree to which a successful prediction supports a theory has to do with whether rival theories also make this prediction. For example, in the previous example, the Big Bang theory holds that only about 4 percent of the snow on your TV screen is from these photons left over from the Big Bang. Hence the vague prediction that you will see snow on your screen does little to support the theory, since other theories (accounting for the other 96 percent) also predict this snow. The success of this prediction also confirms these other theories. As I pointed out before, it is always possible to construct *inconsistent rival* theories to your favorite theory. What gives your theory the leg up against these competitors is its ability to predict something that none of the rival theories does; or, failing that, at least to make a much more *accurate* prediction than those of the rivals. This is often referred to as a *risky* prediction. The success of a risky prediction does much more to probabilify a theory than the success of a prediction which is also entailed by the rival theories. So, the kind of experiment that provides the best test for any theory will be one that determines whether a risky prediction is verified under conditions where we can be assured that the initial conditions are present.

TESTING GRAPHOLOGICAL HYPOTHESES

We are now in a position to examine what would constitute a good test of a graphological hypothesis that will in turn provide evidence for or against a theory of graphology. Our first problem is that there are many different schools of graphology, each consisting of rival theories. See Nickell (chapter 2) for an account of the three broad schools of graphology. However, our task is made easier by the fact that anything properly called a theory of graphology will consist of the claim that certain personality traits are correlated with certain features of handwriting. We need not concern ourselves with the differences of opinion amongst graphologists about *why* these traits are correlated in the way that they are, or which traits are correlated with which personality traits. All we need is a statement of a correlation entailed by that theory. That will serve nicely as a hypothesis to test. In order to tell whether the hypothesis has been demonstrated or refuted it must be stated clearly and unambiguously. For example, the hypothesis might be, "Handwriting which slants to the right at least *X*° is correlated with *Personality Trait T* (e.g., gregariousness) in the general population at a level which is statistically significant"; where *X* is a precise number, so we can be clear whether this condition is satisfied or not, and *T* specifies some trait which we can readily measure and agree whether the trait is displayed or not.[12] If this hypothesis is true, then it, along with suitable initial conditions, will entail a prediction which we can test. In fact, there are two types of validation studies, based on different hypotheses and different predictions, commonly used in testing graphology.

Lockowandt in chapter 6 identifies three types of validation, which he calls *validation at the graphological characteristics level* (Model 1a), and *validation on the interpretation level* (Model 1b). Jensen (1973:2) draws a similar distinction. His third type, *processual validation*, does not fit the scientific methodology under discussion, so I shall defer discussion of it to my section "A Diversion." In Model 1a, what are tested are the putative correlations between handwriting traits and personality traits. Note that the claim that there are such correlations is central to graphological theory. Once it is agreed how to measure the handwriting traits, *non*graphologists could measure them just as well as graphologists. For example, it would not take a graphological theoretician to discern that the width of the margin at a certain point on the page was 1.66 centimeters. Thus an experiment of this sort provides the strongest evidence for graphology, since there will be no question whether the prediction is true or not.

In Model 1b, on the other hand, what is being tested is the hypothesis that graphologists have the ability to make reliable or valid judgments of personality traits. Note that this hypothesis *presupposes* the hypothesis involved in Model 1a: that is, we must presuppose that there really are correlations between the handwriting and personality traits, and it is *this* correlation the graphologist is noticing in order to make his or her reading of the subject. As we shall see, it is just this presupposition that is called into question in debates between graphologists and skeptics. Let us now turn to Model 1a.

VALIDATION OF GRAPHOLOGICAL TRAITS

The hypothesis being tested in Model 1a is that there are correlations between a graphological trait *G* (e.g., handwriting slanting upwards on the page) and a personality trait *T* (e.g., gregariousness). In a good scientific test, the *strength* of this correlation would be given, but we must at least be told that the correlation is *statistically significant* (which means that it is unlikely that this difference is the result of chance) if we are to have anything to test. The best test of this hypothesis would be to gather a randomly selected subset of the population at large, further divide this group into those that clearly satisfied condition of having the graphological trait of slanting handwriting (call these people "Group 1") and those who do not (call these "Group 2," or the *control* group). Then, our prediction would be that the number of people in Group 1 who were gregarious exceeded those in the control group by an amount that was statistically significant. The reason that we require merely that there be *more* gregarious people in Group 1 than in the Group 2, rather than that *everyone* in Group 1 display *T*, while *no one* in the control group display it, is twofold. First, the correlation between the handwriting trait and the personality trait may be less than 1—that is, less than perfect; so we would not expect everyone in Group 1 to have *T*. Second, *T* may be correlated with other graphological traits as well (perhaps fat loops on their *l*s), and thus if some people in the control group make fat *l*s, they may be gregarious as well. Here is the prediction in this sort of experiment in the form of a histogram:

FIGURE 2

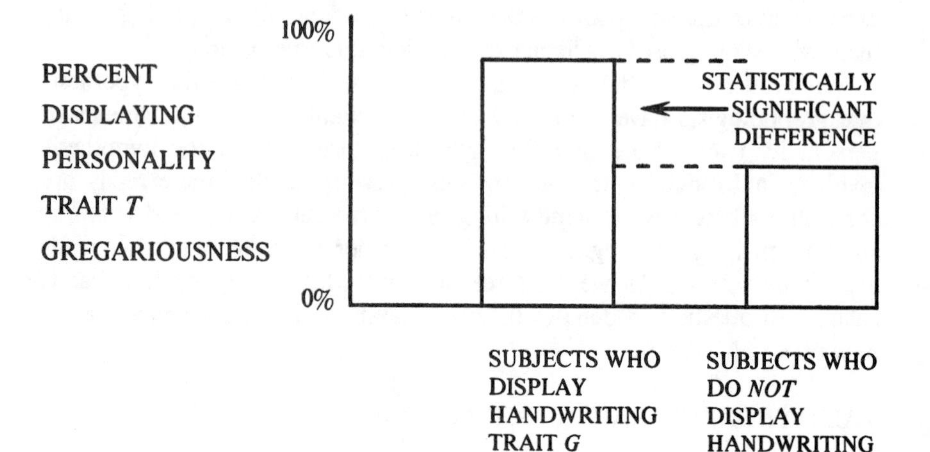

A more immediate problem is that most ordinary-language personality terms are vague and open-ended. You, dear reader, are gregarious some of the time, and your Presbyterian friends think that you are too much so sometimes, despite the fact that your friend Aloysius who is the profit margin at Clancy's Bar is continually telling you to loosen up and socialize more. For more on this, see Marilyn Bowman in chapter 10. In order to know whether the prediction can be verified or not, we must have a *criterion* of *T*: some independent measure of gregariousness—perhaps a psychological test which everyone agrees is unambiguous, precise, valid, and reliable enough as a measure of *T* to make a good test. If we are testing some controversial matter such as graphology, we must be especially careful to choose a criterion which is agreed upon by all parties to the dispute to be a good measure of the trait in question. Marilyn Bowman and Richard Klimoski discuss this point further in chapters 10 and 11, respectively. Once we have solved the problem of agreeing on the criterion, we would be in a position to know whether there are more gregarious people identified as belonging to Group 1 than in the control group, which would be the *prediction* of such an experiment.

The *hypothesis (H)* is that graphological trait *G* is correlated with personality trait *T*, but this by itself does not entail the *prediction (P)* that *G* will be found more frequently amongst members of Group 1 than the control group *in this test*. Whether this is so will depend upon *how G and T are measured*, and by whom (by someone competent?). Furthermore, description of how the test was done has to be added to *H* in order to entail *P*. The statement of these initial conditions has to make it clear that it is on the basis of measuring *G* that subjects were assigned to Group 1, and on the basis of measuring the *absence* of *G* that people were assigned to the control group. But often the trouble with graphological traits is that their measurement is a very subjective affair, and the only way we can ensure that the measurement is not corrupted by the person "knowing" that *G* "must" be present *because H is true*, and the writer of the specimen possesses *T*. After all, what is being tested is *H*, and this will not be tested if subjects could have been assigned to their groups on the basis of the graphologist *already knowing* whether the subjects possess *T*. Under these conditions, *whether or not H is true, P* will come true. Thus, the most important initial condition in such an experiment is that the graphologist be unaware of any test subject's score on the criterion: that is, he must be *blind*. And, in order to *ensure* this, the experimenter who determined *T* must not be in a position to pass this information on to the graphologist accidentally or unknowingly by transmitting unintentional cues.[13] The experimenters who deal with the graphologist must be blind to these results as well. We call an experiment *double blind* if both these groups lack knowledge in advance of the criterion.

The second crucial initial condition arises from the fact that the hypothesis under consideration is that it is the handwriting characteristics themselves that are correlated with the personality trait, and not other traits of the subject that happen to be revealed to the graphologist in the *content* of the handwriting. So, when we are testing *H*, we do not want to confuse the issue by allowing the graphologist to come to know of these personality traits from the meanings of the phrases in the handwriting sample itself. In our example, where gregariousness is the trait being tested for, we would not want the handwriting sample to be a personal letter, in which the subject recounts all the parties he has been to in the past few weeks. The content of the handwriting sample must be *controlled* to ensure that none of the information would allow the graphologist to determine the personality traits of the subject by good old common sense. Otherwise, the common-sense hypothesis will explain the success of the prediction as well as the graphologists' hypotheses, and we therefore derive no evidence for graphology from the test. As obvious as this requirement is, it is flouted by most of the studies cited by graphologists in support of their theory.

There are other important initial conditions, specifying how the measurements are to be made, how the criterion was selected, and so on. The following table summarizes where we are at the moment:

FIGURE 3

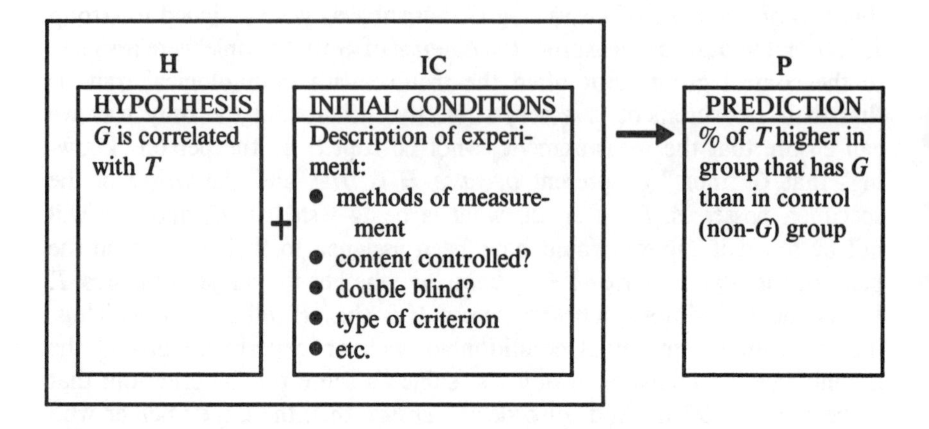

VALIDATION OF GRAPHOLOGISTS' JUDGMENTS

The second type of test, which Lockowandt calls *validation on the interpretation level* (Model 1b), involves testing the graphologist, rather than *directly* testing the claim that there is a correlation between graphological and personality traits. Of course, the assumption behind Model 1b is that the graphologist discerns personality on the basis of examining graphological traits; otherwise this kind of test would not support or provide evidence against graphology. So this type of test provides *indirect* evidence for or against the hypothesis that there are correlations between graphological and personality traits. The advantage, if it can be called that, of a 1b type test is that the particular correlation need not be specified. The focus of the experiment turns on the question whether the graphologists tested can discern any personality traits in the samples they analyze. If they cannot, then the question *what* they are analyzing is moot. But the disadvantage of this type of experiment is that if it provides evidence that the graphologists are discerning *something*, it gives us no indication of what that something might be. A further hypothesis would have to be formed about what the correlation might be, and then a model 1a-type experiment would have to be done.

The *hypothesis* being tested in a 1b-type experiment is a double-barrelled one: (1) there are certain (perhaps unspecified) correlations between graphological and personality traits; and (2) the graphologists being tested can discern these traits.

The *initial conditions* involved in the 1b test will be identical to those of 1a: in a well-designed test, they will ensure that the graphologists being tested are making their assessments of personality *only* on the basis of information contained in the handwriting samples they are working with, and not from any other source.

Given this complex hypothesis and these initial conditions, the *prediction* will be about graphologists' success at determining personality traits. But it cannot simply be that they will determine these traits: it has to be that they will do so *at a greater rate* than they would do if they did not have the graphological traits to work with. How much greater? Given the initial conditions, we are assuming that the only information available to the graphologists is the graphological traits in the sample. So, if the graphologist does *not* use these, he or she would be reduced to guessing, and in a properly run experiment we would be able to determine the rate of successful guesses we could expect by chance. For example, perhaps there are five possible traits to be guessed at, so we would expect by chance a subject would get 20% right, plus or minus the margin of error for a sample of that size. Therefore, the prediction we make in an experiment of this sort is that the graphologist will make *more correct guesses than expected by chance*, and, of course, the difference must be statistically significant.

FIGURE 4

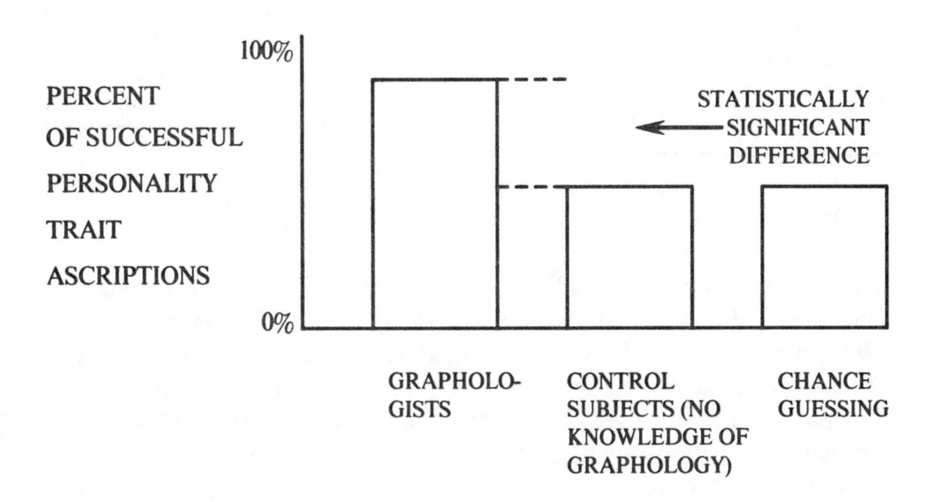

A variant of this experiment is based on the notion that, under the initial conditions assumed, a *control group* of non-graphologists would also lack any information they could use to determine personality traits. There would be no clues provided them, such as knowing that the subject who wrote the handwriting sample they are analyzing spent 25 years as a successful copy editor, which would lead to the likely guess that the subject was good at paying attention to subtle details. Also, since the control is assumed to be naive with respect to graphology, she would be unable to determine personality traits from the graphoanalytical traits in the sample. So, the control group should do no better than chance at guessing subjects' personality traits. On the other hand, as in the previous experiment, the graphologists should be able to exceed chance.[14] Therefore, the prediction in this experiment is that the graphologist should be able to do significantly better than the non-graphologist. Figure 5 shows the schema of this experiment:

FIGURE 5

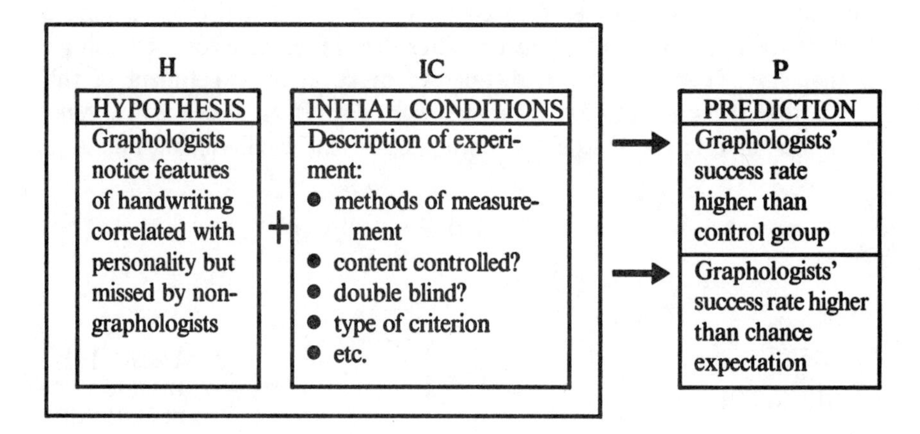

A DIVERSION: GRAPHOLOGY'S SPECIAL PLEADING

Graphologists historically did not arrive at their claims about correlations on the basis of validation studies of the Model 1a sort described in the preceding "Validation of Graphological Traits" section. Instead, as Nickell points out in chapter 2, the correlations they claim are ones that have been posited by a particular graphologist after a certain length of time observing handwriting, or that have passed down for generations by those who are members of a particular school. Given the levels of statistical sophistication in the past, this comes as no surprise. What is surprising is the paucity of these types of studies in modern times. Lockowandt (1966) is a welcome exception to this rule. This study is referred to by Lockowandt in chapter 6. There are comparatively more studies of the Model 1b sort: for example, Klimoski and Rafaeli (1983) and Rafaeli and Klimoski (1983), discussed by Klimoski in chapter 11; Karnes and Leonard in chapter 16; Wellingham-Jones in chapter 15; and Frederick discussed below. But, as Dean demonstrates in chapter 12 and Lockowandt admits in chapter 6, these studies do not offer a convincing case for graphology. Why aren't more and better studies done to settle the issue? Graphologists have two excuses for not doing either kind of study, to which we now turn.

Holism. When graphologists are criticized for not doing a model 1a-type of validation experiment, their standard defense is to argue for holism. Holism is the view that "the whole is more than the sum of its parts."[15] In graphology, this cashes out as the view that a single handwriting trait, such as the slope of the crossbar of the *t*, is not simply correlated with a personality trait such as enthusiasm or pushiness. Rather, a handwriting trait will mean one thing when associated with some other handwriting trait such as long descenders on letters such as *p* or *q* but quite another when associated with another handwriting trait such as thin loops on letters such as *l*. Therefore, some graphologists maintain that model 1a-type studies simply will not work: we cannot measure the influence of one handwriting trait in isolation; the only way of evaluating the influence of these traits is by examining the handwriting sample as a whole.[16]

But there are two problems with this line of defense. The first, explicated by Dean, Kelly, Saklofske and Furnham in chapter 13, is that if graphologists were right about this, they never would have discovered it using the methods they profess to use.

The second problem is that it is not clear what graphologists' claims to evaluate personality from handwriting samples could *mean*, unless they hold that, *everything else being equal*, a particular handwriting trait *G* will be found together with a particular personality trait *T*. That is what is meant by saying that there is a *positive correlation*, though less than 1, between *G* and *T*. And graphologists do make assertions of such correlations all the time. For example, consider Mahoney (1985:251) on the *t* crossbar: "An ascending slant connotes enthusiasm and an uplifted spirit. Those who allow their enthusiasm free reign in the world of dreams and hopes for the future exhibit this characteristic *t*." Now this certainly sounds like an unqualified assertion of a correlation, even if it isn't so clear how strong the correlation is in her view (no correlation coefficient is given), or what "enthusiasm" really amounts to and so we would be hard pressed to suggest a criterion for it.

But never mind. If we cannot get the graphologist to solve these problems for us, the problem is not holism, but simple vagueness. We will not know what hypothesis is to be tested, and we will not know whether the prediction is fulfilled or not. However, if we could get these problems solved, and if such a correlation exists, it will be possible to discover it by simply choosing a large enough group who make slanting *t* crosses, and a large enough control group who do not exhibit that handwriting trait, and measuring both groups against a criterion that operationally defines "enthusiasm" or an "uplifted spirit."[17] What constitutes "large enough" groups in this case will depend upon a number of things. First of all, the strength of the correlation: the weaker the correlation, the larger the groups will have to be for the correlation to show itself. Second, we will have to decide between two strategies about how to deal with all the other handwriting variables which might be connected with the personality trait, and which confound our problem. One strategy is to start with large enough samples of randomly chosen subjects, so that we have good reason to believe that all these other traits will be found in equal numbers in the experimental and control groups. Then it will not matter if some of these variables do mask the correlation. Remember that the claim being tested is that, *everything else being equal*, uplifting *t*s are correlated with an enthusiastic personality. The second strategy is to *ensure* that there are the same amounts of the other handwriting traits present in the control and experimental groups. Then they should cancel each other out, and a difference in frequency of enthusiasm between the two groups should be thanks to uplifting *t*s.

This is just the method called *control by random variation*, and it is successfully used for testing the efficacy or side effects of new drugs. If it works in pharmacology, despite the fact that the human body is an interrelated system with hundreds of variables compounding the picture, there is no reason that it should not work in graphology despite large numbers of interrelated variables. And this method works in orthodox psychology, despite the fact that even lower animals such as rats are integrated systems with hundreds of variables to deal with; not to mention the fact that with humans, psychologists regularly abstract from thousands of variables to find correlations between just two. Graphology simply cannot engage in special pleading—there is nothing special about handwriting variables that is not the case with the traits psychologists routinely handle. The main point here is that if holism in handwriting is true, it would not prevent us from discovering correlations between handwriting and personality traits by doing proper large-scale validity studies. In fact, if the problems were as thorny as the graphologists maintain, this would be the *only* way we could discover such correlations; they would never have come to the attention of graphologists, given the hit-and-miss methods they traditionally employ, as is pointed out by Dean et al. in this volume.

Processual Validation. Lockowandt describes a method in chapter 6 which is a rival to the two standard types of validity study discussed earlier. Its main advantage, he claims, is that it deals with the perennial disagreements over interpretation of personality characteristics that occur between graphologists and lay people such as personnel managers or supervisors. It is because of these disagreements, Lockowandt argues, that many people mistakenly come to the conclusion that graphologists fail to determine people's personalities accurately. As I described in the "Graphological Traits" section above and Klimoski describes in chapter 11, the normal way of handling this type of problem in science is to reach agreement *in advance* about what the prediction is really stating. This involves eliminating the vaguenesses in the personality judgment made by the graphologist, and in the criterion that is used to determine whether or not the prediction counts as accurate. As Klimoski shows, it is seldom a problem in industrial psychology to reach such an agreement prior to doing the study. But Lockowandt's method has the advantage for the graphologist of making it impossible for the graphologist ever to fail a validation study. Where there is disagreement between a lay person and a graphologist about a given subject's personality, what is required is:

> . . . a kind of dialectic operation in the original sense. Every well-meaning, but at the same time critical, researcher will come to the conclusion that the validity of statements is not of dichotomic nature, it is not either true or false, but in certain stages of this process—a process which can last for several years in difficult cases—it may vary considerably. At the beginning it may be very low or even zero; however, after long and deep discussion it may be high.

In other words, if the lay person accepts the graphologist's analysis, it is validated; if he does not, the process simply carries on until the lay person accepts it! As Randi says of the strategy of the psychic, "When you win, you win, and when you lose, you win." Not bad for the graphologist—but it's not science either. It is impossible to test a hypothesis without already agreeing in advance what hypothesis is to be tested and what will count as success or failure of the prediction.

WHAT A SCIENTIFIC EXPERIMENT PROVES

It might be thought that, because skeptics are "out to disprove graphology" whereas believers are "out to prove it," skeptics and believers in graphology will run entirely different experiments. In fact, the experiments themselves and the logic behind them should not differ no matter who is running them. Even if the *expectations* about the outcome of the prediction differ in the two groups, both will test *the same* hypothesis, and also the same prediction. For example, in a Model 1b-type experiment, the prediction will be that the graphologists being tested *can* discern personality traits by discerning the handwriting traits correlated with them. If the prediction turns out to be true, then skeptics and believers must both use the argument form (1) given above, along with the assertion that no other rival hypothesis would make the same prediction, to argue that the hypothesis is probabilified. If it is false, then skeptics and believers must both use argument forms 3 and 4 to argue that the test shows that the hypothesis has been disconfirmed. Of course, believers *expect* to use the argument for probabilification, while skeptics *expect* to use the argument for disconfirmation, while a person with a completely open mind would not have any idea until the data is in which arguments she will be using. However, it is highly unlikely that a person who has invested enough time to be in a position to conduct this type of experiment competently would be so unfamiliar with the issues to have an open mind *in this sense.* But this really does not matter. Unless skeptics or believers have some supernatural ability to *make* their expectations come true, any difference in the truth or falsity of the prediction of the experiment will be because of a difference in the initial conditions. Believers who are already convinced of the truth of graphology may be less willing than skeptics to entertain alternate hypotheses, and therefore may be less likely to design controls in the experiment that will rule them out. They may also be convinced by the prowess of the particular graphologists they are studying, to the degree that they do not bother to use all the care necessary to prevent the graphologists from picking up information from non-graphological sources.

Defenders of graphology often are quick to point out that "all" the skeptics have shown by showing the prediction to be false in an experiment is that *this particular* hypothesis has been disconfirmed—that *this particular (group of) graphologist(s)* could not demonstrate their abilities in *this particular experiment.* From this evidence alone, we cannot generalize to the conclusion that graphology is worthless. Of course this is true, for the reasons outlined above ("Scientific Expeirments"). But to say that "all" the skeptics have managed to prove is the above is like my admission that "all" I have been able to prove about the existence of Santa Claus is that he has never come down *my* chimney. But, given that none of my friends have reported a visit, and that I have reasons to suspect reports that he has visited other people, and that there are theoretical reasons for finding this existence claim implausible, I think that my skepticism about Santa Claus is more than just a peculiar prejudice. The main reason for this is that, properly, the onus of proof is on the believer in Santa Claus, not on me, the skeptic. And so is the onus on the defenders of graphology. Thus, the skeptic who presents negative results is presenting a very strong case, given the lack of positive results from controlled experiments from believers.

Testing an alternate hypothesis. Skeptics who are convinced by the rationale which parallels the Santa Claus reasoning just given must still confront the most ubiquitous—and, unfortunately, the *best*—argument in favor of graphology: Why do so many people, who are not fools, believe it works, *unless it does*? Dean et al. (chapter 13) discuss 23 biases that influence us toward thinking that a system of discerning personality traits, such as graphology, astrology, or phrenology, works even when it does not work. The most commonly discussed bias is the *Barnum Effect*, discussed in chapter 13, Bowman (chapter 10), and Klimoski (chapter 11). It is incumbent upon skeptics to offer experimental evidence to show that the Barnum Effect can explain people's tendency to believe that graphology works even if it doesn't. Karnes and Karnes (chapter 16) describe an experiment probabilifying the Barnum Hypothesis. In a crucial experiment, we test *the same prediction under the same initial conditions*. If the prediction comes out *true*, then this will support the graphological hypothesis; if it comes out *false*, it will support the Barnum Effect hypothesis.

So, in this type of experiment, an outcome which supports graphology cuts against the Barnum Effect, and vice versa. At least it does so on the presupposition that is defended by most graphologists, that their clients' claims to be able to match the personality profile with their own personality is evidence that graphology works. Most graphologists are not in a position to deny this, since it is the strongest argument they know of in favor of their discipline.

To sum up this section, then, there are two types of experiments that you will encounter. The first will test a hypothesis entailed by graphology. If the prediction entailed by this hypothesis is verified by the experiment, then this supports graphology; if it is falsified then this puts the ball in the believers' court: it is up to them to show other evidence that supports their belief. The second will test a hypothesis maintained by skeptics who attempt to explain why people believe in graphology despite the paucity of experiments of the first sort which support graphology.

HOW TO READ THE SCIENTIFIC LITERATURE

We turn now to the scientific literature reporting on the experiments that are offered in support of, or as evidence against, graphology. The first problem that might trouble the reader is that he or she was not there when the experiment was done, and hence must rely upon the honesty and integrity of the researchers. However, skepticism has its natural limits, and those limits are reached when further doubt is very unlikely to save one from error, and is likely to prevent one from accepting the truth. Given that authors are exposing themselves in public and placing their reputations on the line, we have some reason to have confidence in what they publish. Academics do suffer from being exposed as frauds or incompetents. Journals suffer as well, as do the reputations of their editors. So, despite the worries raised recently about fraud in science by authors such as Kohn (1988), Savan (1988), and others, we should remember that these authors were in a position to gather their data precisely because the fraud-detecting mechanisms did work, albeit more slowly than would be ideal. Thus, unless we have reasons to the contrary, we are not very likely to go far wrong by accepting the data presented in a journal that has a solid reputation.[18]

As it turns out, the usual way readers are led astray—intentionally or otherwise—is not by what *is* said that is false, but by what is *not* said about the initial conditions. The most common example of this is the lack of a clear statement about whether the test was double blind: whether the experimenter who was in contact with the graphologist being tested knew the information (e.g., the results of the criterion) the graphologist was trying to discern. Sometimes we are not given precise information about how well the graphologist knew the authors of the handwriting samples, and thus was influenced by something other than the handwriting. Usually we are told whether the handwriting samples were copied from the same source (e.g., a book or a magazine), in which case we do not have to worry about the graphologist getting information from the *content* of the handwriting (except for unintentional spelling mistakes, which can be revealing). However, many graphologists refuse to work from such samples, claiming that they are not "spontaneous," and for some reason never clearly specified, this prevents them from giving an accurate analysis. So, in many cases, graphologists work from personal letters, or, since the major interest in graphology is in personnel selection, many experiments are conducted using job application letters. This material is rich in personal information: obviously, someone applying for a job requiring an engineering degree is almost sure to have one, even if the letter doesn't say so; and age, place of birth, previous job history, and other relevant information gives the graphologist who can put two and two together, even subconsciously, an enormous edge. There is a reason why people so often resort to stereotypes about other people: they often *work*. Despite the fact that there are so many exceptions, if we follow them, we can often discern enough about a person to appear to be psychic (Hyman 1981), or to have knowledge about a person from a testing method such as phrenology or palmistry. But in journal reports, space is at a premium; and so we do not see the contents of the handwriting, and thus can only guess about how much the content influenced the graphologist's assessment.

Fortunately, the scientific journals have over the years established a standard format for papers, so it is easy to find the information that is available to evalute the experiment being reported. Psychology journals, where one is most likely to find a properly controlled study on graphology, almost universally follow this format. There are generally four sections to a scientific paper, each of which contains the elements I have discussed above.

The Introduction. The typical paper begins with an introduction, whether it is so labeled or not, which outlines the derivation and the importance of the problem being investigated, the results of other relevant research, etc. It is from this discussion that we get an idea of the theory that the authors are defending or attacking. Sometimes we have to piece together the theory from several places in the introduction and in the "Discussion" section (which I mention below), rather than finding it clearly stated in one place. We will also find here the statement of the *hypothesis* being tested, and the *prediction* that is expected, given that the hypothesis is true. This is the most important thing to look for in this section, but it is also important to ask the question raised above, whether the hypothesis being tested is really entailed by the theory being discussed. Some very good experimentalists are not as good theoreticians, and despite the fact that they go on to describe a very elegant experiment which provides very good evidence for the hypothesis, all this is for naught if the hypothesis isn't after all entailed by the theory. If this is so, then providing strong evidence for the hypothesis doesn't provide evidence for the theory being discussed.

Method Section. The introduction is usually followed by a section entitled "Method," wherein the procedures of the experiment—what I referred to above as the *initial conditions*—are described. It is here that the reader will look for conditions that would permit the prediction to come true even if the hypothesis were false—that is, if *some other* rival hypothesis were true instead. This problem is usually referred to as *confounding of variables.* As I said above, it isn't worth one's while at this stage to *simply* doubt that the initial conditions really were as described. The reader wasn't there, so he or she cannot determine this any better than the experimenters could. And, if a clever fraud took place, the experimenter can be expected to have covered his or her tracks sufficiently well that it cannot be discerned from an armchair several miles away, and several months or years later. However, what the reader can do is to ask herself whether the experimental design is inappropriate to determine whether these initial conditions are present. The "Method" section should describe the way measurements were taken, what instruments were used, and what precautions were taken to prevent the graphologist from gaining information through channels other than the handwriting. Central among these safeguards is the "double blind" condition. Questions about these procedures are relevant, and not just idle skepticism. And the most fruitful questions will be ones that will suggest modifications to the experimental design for a replication of the experiment. If there are legitimate doubts as to whether the initial conditions were as described, the modifications needed are ones that will more clearly determine this in a replication. Suggesting these modifications is therefore the positive contribution the skeptic can make, as opposed to simply doubting.

Results. In the third part, usually headed "Results," the author(s) state whether the prediction entailed by the hypothesis was verified or not. Again, as with doubts about initial conditions, doubts about whether the prediction came true are best settled by paying attention to the statements in the "Methods" section about how the effects were measured.[19]

Discussion. In the last section, the authors generally go on to discuss what they think they have proved, and careful authors point out what they have *not* proved. Also, we want to know whether what the graphologists managed to discern in the experiment was very imoprtant in two senses. First, we are interested whether the probabilification of the hypothesis being tested provides such support for graphology. Second, if it does provide theoretical support, most of us are interested in whether graphology has any *application* as a diagnostic tool—for example, in personnel selection. Careful readers will pay close attention at this point to Geoffrey Dean's advice in chapter 12: ask *how big* the effect size is. Perhaps the effect size is so small—even if it is highly statistically significant—that graphology would be useless as a selection tool. Or, perhaps the effect size is respecable, but there are a number of other methods of discerning the trait in question that are much better.

But paying attention to this question is pointless until we examine the first question about importance raised above. Even if the hypothesis is probabilified by the experimental result, the question about the centrality of the hypothesis still remains, and it is very easy for authors to overestimate this.

My examination of the literature convinces me that reports which satisfy *all* the criteria mentioned above provide negative results for the central claims of graphology. I know of no study published in English that unequivocally satisfies all the criteria, including the double-blind condition, *and* supports graphology. Lockowandt cites in chapter 5 a number of studies published in German which he advocates as examples of good tests; but he does not provide the details necessary for us to examine them here.

Since they are not available in English, the skeptical defender of graphology who reads no German, and who knows my professed position on graphology, may not want to trust my summary. So I shall present in the next section a test to which the reader may defer.

A SAMPLE SCIENTIFIC PAPER

The study which is most often cited by graphologists who pay attention to the scientific literature as one that provides strong evidence for graphology is Frederick (1968).[20] This study appeared in the *Journal of Abnormal Psychology*, a respected, peer-reviewed scientific journal. We have no difficulty in identifying the hypothesis being tested and the prediction which would probabilify it. The initial conditions are described carefully enough for us to see in general how the experiment was conducted, even if there are crucial details which I wonder about below. If all the experiments on graphology displayed *at least* this degree of rigor in their design, I would have no hesitation in describing graphology as a discipline backed up by careful scientific method. As for the degree of support this experiment provides for graphology, I have reservations which I shall outline in a moment; but I must emphasize that the criticism to follow is not directed at the author, since in his discussion section he never claims to have established a central tenet of graphology.

The hypothesis which was tested is neatly laid out in the "Discussion" section (p. 266):

> A priori, it seems reasonable to believe that there might be something operating within an individual at the time he is preparing to commit suicide which would reveal itself in a motor-expressive act such as handwriting.

In other words, if the various theories of graphology are true, Frederick maintains that the above hypothesis should be verified. Now for the *caveat* that I mentioned above: As Nickell mentions in chapter 2, the one tenet which is central to all schools of graphology is that handwriting traits are enduring qualities which correspond to long-term personality characteristics, such as nervousness or honesty. Notice that the probabilification of Frederick's hypothesis in this study does nothing to bolster this tenet of graphology. As I just said, this is not a criticism of Frederick; for he nowhere claims that it does. However, many supporters of graphology who cited Frederick to me implied that it did. What it does support is a claim only tangentially related: viz., that graphologists can detect very transitory features found in people's handwriting under extreme circumstances. Second, we should be clear about how little consolation the probabilification of this hypothesis provides for graphology as a practical diagnostic tool: as a help in preventing suicides, it is of no use to be able to detect agitation or nervousness in the suicide note. If the person contemplating suicide is available for study, the agitation or nervousness will be observable in many other ways; and if the note is all we have left to study it is too late. Frederick candidly admits (p. 266) that in an earlier study (1965) a trained graphologist could not distinguish between the handwritings of hospitalized psychotic patients and those from a control group of non-hospitalized people matched for age and sex. As Frederick puts it, "[a]pparently the writing of non-hospitalized psychotics as a group is devoid of clear-cut expressive signs such as anxiety, depression, aggressiveness, etc., which permit it to be distinguished from that of non-hospitalized persons" (ibid). Thus, a potential suicide has to be very close to the actual event before the agitation or depression will be manifested in the handwriting; thus my claim to its very limited efficacy.

Thus, Frederick's two studies taken together provide evidence going against the claims usually held by graphologists, that they can discern long-term personality traits. It is at most the transitory ones that graphologists can discern. And this is bad news for those who argue for graphology's efficacy as a personnel selection tool; for it is precisely the former that they offer to tell prospective employers about, and graphologists claim that one of the virtues of their system is that it doesn't confuse the discerning personnel manager with transitory features of the person that show up in a handwriting sample because of nervousness about the job application itself, or a fight with a spouse the morning that the handwriting sample is done. So, beware of a graphologist who tries to sell you a deal on personnel selection by citing Frederick. This graphologist either hasn't read it or understood it, or hopes that you won't.

Still, the above criticism says nothing about the quality of the experiment. So, I now turn to the question whether this hypothesis, along with the initial conditions, entails the prediction. First, the initial conditions: Frederick took 45[21] actual suicide notes, and had three independent persons, matched for age and sex with the suicide, copy them onto paper matched to the original suicide note, thus providing three control notes for each genuine note. The 45 sets of four notes were presented to three groups of subjects—one experimental group and two control groups. Group 1 consisted of five graphologists, and two control groups were comprised of subjects ignorant of graphology: one was comprised of five detectives, and the other of five secretaries. All subjects were to choose the genuine note from the four notes in the set, for each of the 45 sets presented. The object of these conditions was to ensure that whatever motivated the choice, it would not be the content of the note, since this was the same for all the notes of the set, nor the telltale signs that were independent of graphological characteristics. Thus the assumption was that the *only* marks that would distinguish the genuine suicide notes from the controls were graphological cues available to the graphologists but opaque to the non-graphologist control subjects. The expected frequency of hits for each subject would be between 11 and 12, if that subject were reduced to random guessing. Seventeen guesses would be statistically significant—17 or greater would occur only about twice in 100 such experiments if nothing but random variation were present.

Given these initial conditions, the prediction expected was essentially a two-part one: (1) that the graphologists' success rate would be statistically significant (i.e., 17 or better), while the non-graphologists would be in the range expected by chance 95 times in 100 (between 6 and 16 correct guesses); and (2) that the differences between the experimental and control groups would be statistically significant.

The results appear to be a very strong vindication of the hypothesis—see Table 1.[22] Both of these predictions were confirmed by the actual results. In a preceding section I said that the verification of a risky prediction—that is, one not made by the other rival theories—counts much more in favor of the theory than one which is made by all the rival theories as well. So, what we should now ask is whether some *alternate* hypothesis explains these results as well or better. That is to say, could some other hypothesis, along with these initial conditions, *also* explain these experimental results? To answer this question, we need to examine the initial conditions of the experiment a bit more closely.

As I already mentioned, the first thing to check for in the "methods" section is a statement about whether the test was conducted "double-blind." Here is what Frederick tells us (p. 264):

> In most instances, the experimenter himself was not fully aware of which note constituted the original since they were arranged by the research assistants and co-workers.

This leaves open the possibility that in *some* instances the experimenter *was* fully aware of which of the four choices was the original note—and the *really* skeptical amongst us may wonder whether in the remainder of the cases, he was *partially* aware. In any event, the possibility of the experimenter *unwittingly* cuing the graphologists toward the correct choice is there in this protocol, by Frederick's own guarded admission. Note my emphasis on "unwittingly": I am *not* suggesting anything like fraud. As some parapsychologists have finally discovered, after skeptics spent years

TABLE 1

JUDGE	NUMBER CORRECT	LEVEL OF SIGNIFICANCE
Graphologists		
1	30	10^{-8}
2	25	0000119
3	30	10^{-8}
4	28	.00000001
5	27	.00000007
Detectives		
1	16	.0753
2	14	.2159
3	15	.1327
4	11	.5911
5	15	.1327
Secretaries		
1	16	.0753
2	15	.1327
3	12	.4543
4	16	.0753
5	13	.3252

trying to convince them, many cases of supposed telepathy are more readily explained as instances of transmission of information by subtle, though wholly prosaic means that were opaque to both sender and receiver. For just one of the many discussions of this problem, see Hines (1988:82–84). A quick glance at Table 1 will reveal that these sensory cues would have to be effective in only a third of the graphologists' guesses in order to provide the difference between their success rates and those of the controls. Of course I have no idea what role subtle sensory cues played in obtaining these results. My point is that this is an alternate hypothesis not ruled out by the experimental design; and therefore Frederick's hypothesis is not shown to be superior to it by this experiment. Obviously we need a replication of this experiment, with this alternative ruled out by ensuring that it is double blind.

A second problem does not reveal itself in Frederick's discussion, although he did say something that made me want to do some more investigation. Describing the subjects, he states (p. 264):

> The graphology judges were all fully qualified professional European psychologists trained at the universities of Berlin, Freiberg, Stockholm, Basel, and Munich. One was a former university professor. American detectives and secretaries served as control judges.

So the graphologists had a further advantage over the control judges: an academic training in psychology. Does the training in psychology explain (part of) their higher success rate? We do not know, and therefore need a further study to test this alternate hypothesis. But that is not my main worry. The graphologists were European, and the controls were American.[23] So, it would appear that either the experimental or the control group was at a disadvantage because of a language barrier. Which group was it? To answer this question, we need to know the language in which the original suicide notes were written. Frederick doesn't say. Also, I *presume* that the control notes were written by people fluent in that language as well, though again Frederick does not say. So I speculate. For these speculations, it would be helpful to know where the experiment was conducted. Again, Frederick doesn't say, but Lockowandt (chapter 6) provides us with a clue. He reports that the experiment was carried out in collaboration with the Institut fur Tillampad Psykologi (Institute of Applied Psychology) in Saltsjobaden, near Stockholm, Sweden. Presumably that is where the suicide notes came from. But where did the Americans in the control groups come from? At the time Frederick worked at Patton State Hospital in Patton, California. Did he test control groups in the United States? If so, it would be no surprise that Americans, unfamiliar with Europeans' handwriting, may have missed subtle cues available to the European graphologists. Of course, these cues would be useful if the graphologists had access to other information about the subject which could be correlated with the actual person who committed suicide. And, indeed, this information was in some cases made available to the judges (p. 264):

> Each note was given an identifying number with the date on each [writer of the original suicide note] such as age, sex, and method of suicide recorded on a separate sheet of paper. This was available to judges who cared to use it. In some instances, religion and place of birth were also noted; in others, they were not.

So, if the information provided to the judges suggested the nationality of the writer of the suicide note, and the control notes were written by people from a different country or region from the suicide note writer, the graphologists may have done better than the control judges by using information other than graphology. That is, the graphologists and the control judges may have both known from the information provided that the actual suicide was in her 50s, born in Stuttgart, and had access to drugs readily available to a veterinarian, since ingesting drugs prescribed only for dogs was the method of suicide. But the European graphologists, and not the Americans, might have seen a lot of samples of middle-aged European veterinarians' handwritings, and further, be aware of the writing styles taught in Stuttgart schools just after World War I. We do not have to postulate that the European graphologists were able to identify all three controls on this basis. Being able to eliminate even one control by these means increases the judge's chances of a hit on a particular trial from .25 (4 choices) to .33 (3 possible choices).

We do not even have to speculate that the graphologists were *consciously* using this information in this way. But some graphologists do pride themselves on being able to identify handwriting from the region or country where particular handwriting features are taught. Goldberg (1986) reports that he lost a case of scotch in a bet with a graphologist who claimed to be able to do just this. So, even though it is impossible to tell how much of an advantage this added information in fact was to the graphologists, the fact that it was available is enough to ask that the experiment be replicated with this source of information eliminated.

Given the above, we are not in a position to say that Frederick's hypothesis is supported in this experiment. We have equal grounds for the hypothesis that the graphologists were able to outperform the control group simply in virtue of being more familiar with the characteristic handwritings of the authors of the notes, or that they were on some trials accidentally cued toward the correct answer by an experimenter who knew the correct target. And third, I suggested (note 21) a problem with the execution of the experiment that may have magnified the differences between the graphologists and the control judges. I do not maintain that I have *proved* that any one, or any combination, of these problems suggests an alternative hypothesis that accounts for these data better than Frederick's hypothesis. But my last point about the evidence we get from scientific experiments is that I do not have to. The burden of proof is on the defender of graphology to show that Frederick's hypothesis is more probable than an alternative hypothesis suggested by my criticisms. The standard way of doing this is to replicate this experiment, changing the initial conditions to rule out these problems that I have noted, and then to see whether a similar prediction gets verified. In the 22 years since this experiment was done, no such replication has been reported.

CONCLUSION

Even non-scientists should have little difficulty in analyzing the evidence presented in a paper published in a scientific journal. The reader can test this claim by trying her hand at analyzing the two papers presented in Part Five of this volume, by Wellingham-Jones and Karnes and Leonard. The reader who lacks independent verification of the facts or results presented in the paper, or the statistical tools to calculate the results for herself, is not at the disadvantage she might feel at first blush. She can rely upon the integrity of the authors, and the perspicacity of the journal editors to catch some mistakes in the data or statistics. Anyway, the real problems in scientific papers are to be found in the *arguments from* these data.

The reader is not so fortunate, however, in dealing with most of the publications from graphological organizations or popular books touting graphology. Most of the evidence presented for graphology in these publications consists of anecdotal evidence and testimonials from satisfied customers. Or worse, many books in this *genre* offer signatures or short handwriting samples of famous people from which we are asked to "infer" their personalities. For example, Paterson (1980:21–26) shows us that we can see "reaching for the stars" in Neil Armstrong's signature, "concentration" and "efficiency" in Bertrand Russell's, and that the murderer Crippen was "headstrong, aggressive, and hard." Where data are presented, often a little digging is required to extract it. In most cases, however, no useful data at all are presented. In this case one might adopt the strategy that works very well at the used car lot: If the salesman doesn't know the answers to your questions, or seems unwilling to provide the answers, wise consumers remember that there are other cars available, even if the sales pitches do not make them sound so attractive.

NOTES

1. A reflection for a moment on this point will show us what is wrong with the graphologists' explanation for why so many psychologists, at least in North America, reject graphology. Defenders of graphology maintain that this is because psychologists are in competition with graphologists, and therefore the former have financial reasons to denigate the latter. However, psychologists also have financial reasons to borrow anything which works. Therefore, we have reason to suspect that if graphology proves to have anything going for it, psychologists will take over graphology. The acceptance of hypnotism by some psychologists is an example of this phenomenon. Note I am not maintaining that hypnotism has much therapeutic value (see Baker (1982), Hilgard (1979), and Zusne and Jones (1982) for reasons to doubt this. My point is rather that, *despite* the suspiciousness of hypnotism, so many psychologists have demonstrated their open-mindedness (perhaps to the degree of *credulity*) on the matter, precisely because they *think* that it works. Defenders of graphology may retort that all I have shown is that the attitude toward graphology is like the attitude of many psychologists toward hypnotism before it became more widely accepted. But this response simply takes us back to the place in the argument from where this red herring sidetracked us: *how reliable is the evidence that graphology works?*

2. Of course, it is not a simple matter to state what is required to make a theory testable. Fortunately, we do not need to provide a full account of this for our purposes. Readers wishing to pursue the vast literature that has accumulated around Karl Popper's (1968) first attempt at stating the requisite conditions might wish to begin with the papers collected in Section II of Grim (1982). This section also includes the gist of Popper's orignal article.

3. The reason that there are different methodologies for different disciplines is that there are truths about different kinds of things. The majority of philosophers (though not all—for a dissenting viewpoint, the best place to start is with Mill 1970 and Quine 1960 and 1961) hold that the objects of mathematics and logic are different *kinds* of things from the objects of science. That is why different methodologies are appropriate to study them. We need not concern ourselves with the disputes in philosophy of mathematics or philosophy of logic over how similar the methods of logic are to the methods of science. Furthermore, I take it that I need not bother to justify the claim that graphology makes straightforward empirical claims: e.g., that there is a correlation between this feature of handwriting and that personality trait is about as good an example of an empirical claim as I can think of.

4. But not all of them—see the qualifications in Lockowandt.

5. As evidence of how widespread the respect for the *principle* of open-minded skepticism is, note the numbers of defenders of graphology who begin their defense with "I used to be skeptical, but . . . ," and then carry on with their evidence. But this evidence is almost always anecdotal, not the sort that would convince someone who was genuinely skeptical.

6. Another term for "theory" is "model." As an orrery or planetarium pro-

vides a *visual* representation of the solar system which demonstrates the relationships between planets, moons, etc., so an astronomical model provides a representation *in words* of these sorts of things, and also of more abstract notions such as causal or correlational relationships. See Giere (1982) chapters 5 and 6 for a more comprehensive discussion of this.

7. In conjunction with other statements—very few statements entail much by themselves.

8. Some may object to calling this statement a hypothesis, on the grounds that it is so firmly established. Indeed it is; and this points out an ambiguity with this term. (In fact, it is the ambiguity used by "Creation Scientists" in order to state that the theory of evolution is "just a hypothesis.") "Hypothesis," as defined in the *Oxford English Dictionary,* is "A supposition or conjecture put forth to account for known facts; *esp.* in the sciences, a provisional supposition from which to draw conclusions that shall be in accordance with known facts, and which serves as a starting point for further investigation by which it may be proved or disproved and the true theory arrived at." Thus, a hypothesis is *provisional,* and if it is confirmed by the facts, we should call it something else. Since the statement about water freezing (and also the theory of evolution) is so well confirmed by experimental evidence, we should call it something else. Perhaps we should; since there is a second sense of "hypothesis" which definitely does not fit: "A groundless or insufficiently grounded supposition; a mere assumption or guess." But, as I shall point out below, an experiment *never* confirms a hypothesis with certainty; so there is a sense in which all scientific claims are taken to be provisional: they are all subject to *possible* revision by further data, even if the probability of having to revise them is extremely low. (The theory of evolution fits into this category.) And there is a third sense of the term that fits the sense that it is used in the discussion below: "In *logic,* the supposition or condition forming the antecedent . . . of a conditional [If . . . then . . .] proposition." It is in order to capture this third sense that we call a statement, even when rendered highly probable, a hypothesis.

A second reason for objecting to calling the statement about the freezing point of water a hypothesis is that it is *now* counted as *true by definition*: We simply would not count a substance as water unless it froze at 0° C. This is true, but first, it was an empirical discovery (which has since been amply confirmed) that led to this definition; and second, if *per impossible,* water suddenly ceased to freeze at 0°, scientists would abandon this definition.

9. Ideally, such a prediction will be in the form of an *observation statement* (see Quine [1960:42–45]) and Quine and Ullian [1978] for a definition). Roughly, an observation statement is one that is true or false, and can be *determined to be* true or false independently of the theory that entails it. The reason why "the thermometer reads 0° " serves as an example of an observation sentence is that it can be determined to be true or false independently of the theories of thermodynamics which entail it on a particular occasion. Although there is a great deal of controversy over whether there really are any pure observational sentences, and this leads some philosophers to question whether we really can test theories by

the method described here (the problem of *incommensurability of theories*), I sidestep this question here and refer the reader to Newton-Smith (1981), especially chapter 2.

10. Often this hypothetical statement is referred to as the prediction. This is a perfectly sensible use of the term, but the way we are using the term "prediction," it refers only to the *consequent* of this hypothetical statement.

11. The move from (2) to (3) in the argument below is justified by a Rule of Inference often called *Disjunctive Syllogism.* It tells us that to deny a conjunction—to say "not (H & IC)"—it is sufficient to deny *either one* of the conjuncts ("not H *or* not IC"). (This is the reason that the sign on your local transit system reads [with the logician's brackets added for clarity] "No Smoking *or* Drinking," not "No Smoking *and* Drinking." If it read the latter, you could satisfy the ordinance by smoking, as long as you refrained from drinking at the same time.)

12. Experimental psychologists call this attempt to make the personality trait measurable *operationalizing.*

13. Readers who are familiar with the skeptical literature on parapsychology are already aware of the necessity of double-blind conditions in paranormal research. Psychologists are well aware of these problems in their experiments that need to be handled by double-blind conditions, especially since the publication of Rosenthal (1966). And it is no answer to this requirement to design an experiment so that measurements are made with protractors or even more sophisticated instruments; so that despite the fact that the graphologist knows what results are expected, the measurements are "objective" and can be read only one way. Rosenthal (1966) provides numerous examples that belie this assumption. A further recent example is given in Maddox et al. (1988) of evidence for homeopathy, published in *Nature,* gathered by a simple procedure of counting tiny spots on a microscope slide that turned blue. Maddox et al. present convincing evidence that more blue spots were counted on the slide than were actually there, precisely because the experimenter *expected* there to be more.

14. Is there any necessity to design the experiment so that the control group performs at chance expectations? Could we design the experiment so that the graphologists and the controls both have access to non-graphological information about the subjects? The Frederick experiment described below does this, and we see from it why this strategy is a bad one. First, it enormously complicates the question of what the expected rate of success without using graphology should be: we must not only determine how an *ideal* subject would use this information to improve her score over chance expectation, but we must predict how successfully subjects will *actually* use it in this experiment. Secondly, if the graphologist does better than the non-graphologist, this *could* be because the graphologist is using the non-graphological informmation better than the non-graphologist; and therefore a further experiment would be required to rule out this hypothesis.

15. For an excellent discussion of the original roots of holism in philosophy of biology, see Brandon (1985). His careful distinction between reductionism and mechanism in philosophy of science takes the wind out of arguments for holism in contemporary science; and his account of the original holism propounded by

Jan Smuts and J. S. Haldane as a *non*-vitalistic theory demonstrates how little succor New Agers can take from the position they have corrupted.

16. This line of argument is maintained not only by the gestalt school, which maintains explicitly this holistic assumption that it is not single traits that are correlated with personality, but rather global features of handwriting such as width of margins (see Nickell in chapter 1); it is also maintained by the trait school which does profess to deal with individual features of handwriting such as thinness or thickness of loops on *l*s. The latter school does hold that it is individual traits that matter, but they also fall back on holistic assumptions when asked for validation studies that demonstrate this.

17. This may not be so easy, since we would first have to get handwriting analysts to tell us what these terms *mean*. If they cannot agree, then the problem has nothing to do with the assumption of holism; it would simply be the case that they are not measuring anything at all.

18. Now, it might be held that the strictures that work to keep scientists honest when they are publishing in peer-reviewed scientific journals are not to be found, or are to be found to a lesser extent, in graphology journals. Even when they are peer-reviewed, the peers are those that are already inclined to accept the claims in question; and, in the climate of disbelief of graphology's claims found among North American psychologists and other scientists, the editors of and reviewers for graphology journals might be expected to be less critical of data which serve as good ammunition against the critics. As well, most North American graphologists are not very well educated. However, first of all, these comments apply to a *much* lesser degree to European graphology journals. Secondly, a much more important point: the skeptic who has to resort to accusations of fraud simply does not know his business. Methodological problems of the sort outlined in this chapter are sufficient to dismiss graphology's claims until better studies are done; and much of what appears in graphology journals simply isn't scientific evidence from a study. Much of what appears there consists of testimonials, anecdotal evidence, and the like.

19. One might worry about what has come to be known as the "Bottom Drawer Effect": if an experiment does not get significant results, obviously it is not going to get submitted for publication. Graphology experiments will almost always involve a prediction that a (the) subject(s) will do significantly better than expected by chance. The minimum level of above chance significance is "significance at the .05 level," meaning that if we repeated this experiment 100 times, we would expect only 5 results to be as high—*or low*—as this (we are talking about the end points on the classic "bell curve"). So, one might worry that the study you are reading is just one of the five, and the other 95 never saw the light of day. This is one reason why extraordinary claims usually have much higher levels of significance than the .05 standard. But, of course, an examination of the study itself will never settle this question for you. All you can do is to seek out further literature to determine whether this study has been replicated.

20. All page references in this section are to this article.

21. Originally 55, but 10 were discarded for what appear to be plausible reasons. One thing to be careful about, however, in evaluating a written report of an

experimental protocol, is to see whether the author clearly reveals *when* the protocol was changed to handle some sort of unforeseen problem. If one is suspicious, one might suspect unconscious selection of data in order to magnify an observed effect. For example, note Frederick's description of how these sets were determined to be unsuitable, and thus discarded:

> The control judges [i.e., the non-graphologist judges—*DFB*] were also used to assist in picking out any potential biases among the notes. For example, if the paper or blood smear on a note was thought not to be genuine, if the writing appeared on the back where it did not belong and could be noticed, etc., these could constitute a bias. Although such phenomena were not unequivocal in influencing the choices by the judges in any of the notes, to be certain that no biases were present 40 of the original 220 notes [i.e., 10 actual suicide notes and the three controls associated with each of them—*DFB*] were discarded from the final computation. (p. 264)

First of all, Frederick is to be commended for informing us of this change. For, what it suggests is that these 10 notes are ones that *were* identified correctly by (a significant number of) the control judges, and would have been identified correctly by the experimental group (graphologists) as well. Assuming that on average only 5 of the 10 notes could be identified by all subjects (graphologists *and* controls), then, from the results indicated in Table 1 (p. 265), at least 6 of the 10 control subjects would have achieved success rates significant at the .05 level, whereas without counting these notes, *none* of the control subjects did. Of course, this would not explain the highly statistically significant difference in success rates of the experimental (graphologist) group and the control group; nor would it explain the fact that the graphologists' success rate is highly statistically significant with these notes excluded. However, it raises the possibility that the graphologists noticed and made use of biases that they kept to themselves. *Of course* I do not know that this was the case; I merely raise the possibility as a reason for wanting this study replicated.

22. Those readers familiar with statistics may wish to consult Tables 1, 2, and 3 of Frederick (1968) for other statistical analyses which suggest a fair degree of inter-rater reliability amongst the graphologists, but none amongst the controls. On the other hand, those readers who are familiar with experimental design may want to examine the full description of the experimental protocols before bothering with this. The reader who agrees with my conclusion that the protocols are fundamentally flawed will agree that it wasn't chance that explains these results, but that the study doesn't demonstrate that it was noticing graphological cues either. Coming up with alternate explanations will not be aided by examining the statistics.

23. An explanation for Frederick having to go to Europe to find graphologists with a significant background in psychology is ready to hand: People with such dual training are much more common in Europe. Oskar Lockowandt, the author of chapters 5 and 6, is a psychologist trained in graphology, and is not that unusual. But, although there are notable exceptions—J. C. Crumbaugh, the author of chapter 7 is one—people trained in both disciplines in North America are pretty thin on the ground.

REFERENCES

Baker, Robert A., B. Haynes, and B. Patrick. 1982. "Hypnosis, Memory and Incidental Memory." *American Journal of Clinical Hypnosis* 25(4): pp. 253–262.

Brandon, Robert. 1985. "Holism in Philosophy of Biology." In Stalker and Glymour 1985, pp. 127–135.

Forer, B. R. 1949. "The Fallacy of Personal Validation: A Classroom Demonstration of Gullibility." *Journal of Abnormal and Social Psychology* 44: pp. 552–564.

Frederick, Calvin. 1965. "Some Phenomena Affecting Handwriting Analysis." *Perceptual and Motor Skills* 20: pp. 211–218.

Frederic, Calvin. 1968. "An Investigation of Handwriting of Suicide Persons Through Suicide Notes." *Journal of Abnormal Psychology* 73 (3): pp. 263–267.

Giere, Ronald. 1984. *Understanding Scientific Reasoning,* 2nd ed. New York: Holt Rinehart and Winston.

Goldberg, L. 1986. "Some Informal Explorations and Ruminations About Graphology." In *Scientific Aspects of Graphology,* edited by B. Nero. Springfield, Ill.: Charles Thomas, pp. 281–293.

Grim, Patrick, ed. 1982. *Philosophy of Science and the Occult.* Albany, N.Y.: State University of New York Press.

Hempel, Carl. 1979. *Philosophy of Natural Science.* Englewood Cliffs, N.J.: Prentice-Hall Inc.

Hilgard, Ernest R. 1977. *Divided Consciousness: Multiple Controls in Human Thought and Action.* New York: Wiley.

Hines, Terence. 1988. *Pseudoscience and the Paranormal.* Buffalo, N.Y.: Prometheus Books.

Hyman, Ray. 1981. "Cold Reading: How To Convince Strangers that You Know All About Them." In *Paranormal Borderlands of Science,* edited by Kendrick Frazier. Buffalo, N.Y.: Prometheus Books, pp. 79–96.

Ingram, Jay. 1989. "The Big Bang on Cable." In *The Science of Everyday Life.* Markham, Ontario, Canada: Viking.

Jensen, Abraham. 1973. *Validation of Graphological Judgments: An Experimental Study.* The Hague, Netherlands: Mouton.

Klimoski, R. J., and A. Rafaeli. 1983. "Inferring Personal Qualities Through Handwriting Analysis." *Journal of Occupational Psychology* 56: pp. 191–202.

Kohn, Alexander. 1988. *False Prophets: Fraud and Error in Science and Medicine.* Oxford: Basil Blackwell.

Lockowandt, O. 1966. "Faktorenanalytische Validierung der Handschrift mit Besonderer Berücksichtigung projektiver Methoden." Ph.D. dissertation, University of Freiburg.

Maddox, J., J. Randi, and W. Stewart. 1988. "'High Dilution' Experiments a Delusion." *Nature* 334 (28 July).

Mahoney, Ann. 1989. *Handwriting and Personality: How Graphology Reveals What Makes People Tick.* New York: Ballantine Books.

Mill, John Stuart. 1970. *A System of Logic.* London: Longman Group Limited. (Originally published 1843)

Newton-Smith, W. H. 1981. *The Rationality of Science.* London: Routledge and Kegan Paul.

Paterson, Jane. 1980. *Know Yourself Through Your Handwriting.* Montreal: The Reader's Digest Association (Canada), Ltd.

Popper, Karl R. 1968. "Science: Conjectures and Refutations." In *Conjectures and Refutations.* New York: Harper & Row.

Quine, Willard Van Orman. 1960. *Word and Object.* Cambridge, Mass: The MIT Press.

———. 1961. *From a Logical Point of View.* New York: Harper & Row. Especially "On What There Is," and "Two Dogmas of Empiricism."

Quine, Willard Van Orman, and J. S. Ullian. 1978. *The Web of Belief.* New York: Random House.

Rafaeli, A., and R. J. Klimoski. 1983. "Predicting Sales Through Handwriting Analysis." *Journal of Applied Psychology* 68: pp. 212–17.

Rosenthal, R. 1966. *Experimenter Effects in Behavioral Research.* New York: Appleton Century Crofts.

Savan, Beth. 1988. *Science Under Siege: The Myth of Objectivity in Scientific Research.* Toronto: CBC Enterprises.

Stalker, Douglas, and Clark Glymour, eds. 1985. *Examining Holistic Medicine.* Buffalo, N.Y.: Prometheus Books.

Zusne, Leonard, and Warren H. Jones. 1989. *Anomalistic Psychology: A Study of Magical Thinking.* Hillsdale, N.Y.: Erlbaum.

9

The Origins of Graphology in Sympathetic Magic

Barry L. Beyerstein

In her book, *Crime and Sex in Handwriting* (London: Constable and Co., 1981, p. 11), Patricia Marne writes:

> Although the Ancient Chinese and Romans accepted that there was a relationship between handwriting and personality, it was not until comparatively recently that graphology could lay claim to being a science, following clearly defined rules, and producing findings accurate enough to be used in personnel work in the professions, and in commerce and industry, to assess character and suitability. Furthermore, serious practitioners have had to fight against popular misconceptions that associate graphology with fortune telling and forecasting the future.

In chapter 9, Barry Beyerstein suggests the misconception lies with Marne and her colleagues, not the skeptics. Beyerstein reminds us that there is much more to being a science than "following clearly defined rules." Tarot reading, for instance, has clearly defined rules—the crucial distinction between science and pseudoscience is the way in which their rules are derived and validated. Another fundamental difference is that a putative science must produce a plausible theory to explain *why* its objects of study are linked in lawful and predictable ways. In chapter 14 of this volume, Barry Beyerstein shows why the graphologists' preferred causal explanation (viz., the "brainwriting" rationale) is untenable on scientific grounds. What, then, *is* the underlying rationale for graphology? In the present chapter, Beyerstein shows, by examining a broad range of graphological publications, that the causal force is still—although rarely acknowledged—the ancient principle of magical corrrespondence.

* * *

> Where any conviction remains in the existence of a supernatural order, . . . mantic practices are likely to persist. They are likely to flourish in proportion to men's recognition of their own weakness, and consequent need for help in solving problems beyond the scope of human competence.
>
> M. Loewe and C. Blacker, *Divination and Oracles*

In chapter 14 of this volume I question the scientific status of graphology, criticizing the hypothetical mechanisms modern practitioners invoke to explain relationships that were postulated long ago between writing and personality. It is my task in this chapter to show that, scientific pretensions notwithstanding, handwriting analysis has not really abandoned its origins in ancient principles of magical correspondence.

MAGIC VERSUS SCIENCE

At the dawn of the scientific era, Francis Bacon (1561–1626) wrote that "knowledge is power." The methods he, Galileo, and others developed for realizing that power emerged from incomparably older, but similarly motivated, attempts to understand, predict, and control an often threatening world. The details of how the scientific attitude gradually distanced itself from its roots in tribal magic are lost in antiquity but the conjectures of many anthropologists, psychologists, and philosophers of science converge upon a few major themes. Though differences of opinion remain, there is little doubt that both magical and scientific thinking stems from the desire for a hedge against uncertainty by harnessing unseen but lawful forces assumed to govern worldly events.

Lacking an understanding of the true causes of weather and natural disasters, or of crop and hunting failures, accidents, illness, and death, our early ancestors were understandably desirous of ways to circumvent their apparent arbitrariness. In his classic work, *The Golden Bough* (abridged and updated by Gaster 1959), the Scottish anthropologist Sir James Frazer (1854–1941) suggested how the primitive search for such magical protections probably evolved into scientific notions of cause and effect (for good discussions, see Monte 1975, ch. 1; Alcock 1980, ch. 2; Zusne and Jones 1989, ch. 2). The scientific and magical worldviews share the belief that it is humanly possible to uncover and exploit the immutable, impersonal, and non-obvious rules that determine natural phenomena.

Based on his observations of extant non-technological societies, Frazer argued that the search for magical powers began with attempts to recognize regularities in the chaotic stream of experience. Primordial science diverged from magical thinking when it began to insist that these regularities, once intuitively grasped, must be submitted to the acid test of empirical validation. Frazer suggested that the seeds of the scientific attitude were sown when a few "shrewder minds" started to suspect the inherent unreliability of magic. Others who noticed this elasticity between rituals and their intended effects took the alternate route of inserting wilful, vain, or whimsical deities into the causal chain. They envisioned an animistic world governed by capricious spirits who must be flattered, cajoled or bribed to permit desired events. By contrast, both magical and rudimentary scientific thinkers viewed the cosmos as an orderly and non-capricious system, though their relative success in bending it to their liking it came to differ sharply.

Despite centuries of evidence attesting to the superiority of the scientific approach, the sorts of magical thinking described by Frazer are far from extinct in modern industrial societies. This has been strikingly documented by observers of popular culture (e.g., Basil 1989; Schultz 1989) and by empirical research (e.g., Shweder 1977; Marks and Kammann 1980; Rozin et al. 1986; Zusne and Jones 1989).[1]

Shweder (1977) sees this persistence of magical thinking as a result of the general disinclination of normal adults to distinguish the truly causal from the merely coexistent in their everyday experience, coupled with an equally strong bent for seeing symbolic, personally meaningful relationships between unrelated objects or events. As Dean et al. discuss in chapter 13, we are all prone to make predictable blunders of this sort when we rely on informal reasoning to infer causality in complex situations. Driving these errors are numerous mental short-cuts called "cognitive heuristics" (Tversky and Kahneman 1974; Nisbett and Ross 1980). Among other things, they contribute to the illusory validity of various pseudoscientific practices when we evaluate them subjectively rather than by formal logic and statistical tests.[2]

The penchant for seeing intentionality and meaning in random coincidence, the basis of most superstitious beliefs, is so pervasive that it is even demonstrable in laboratory pigeons (Skinner 1948), not to mention any gaming table in Las Vegas. It underlies all divination procedures[3] and attempts to sway events by magical means. At its core is the assumption that perceived similarity, in and of itself, permits physical interaction between the phenomena that are felt to be alike.[4] The fallacy here is what Zusne and Jones (1989) call "reification of the subjective," the tendency to accord causal power in the external world to symbolic or metaphorical relationships conceived wholly in one's mind.

Believers in magic are not wrong in assuming that events are subject to lawful, hidden influences, but in their conceptualization of the nature of these influences. It is these ancient but erroneous views of influence that science has discarded, but which live on in the rationales for various occult and pseudoscientific practices. These range from telepathy, water dowsing, homeopathic medicine, faith healing, and astrology to divination practices such as the I-Ching, Tarot, numerology, and palm reading—and, as I intend to show, to graphology.

MAGICAL CORRESPONDENCES

The bedrock of all magical thinking is the notion of "sympathy," the idea that "like-begets-like." This vague notion of "likeness" permeates the occult and pseudoscientific realm. Sympathy can arise from spatio-temporal contiguity (contact magic) or symbolic association in the mind of an observer (homeopathic magic).

According to the *Law of Contagion*, a mystical "essence" passes between animate or inanimate objects that come into contact. The transfer of this ill-defined influence ensures that these objects retain an affinity for one another after they are physically separated. Because of their magical "sympathy," and in defiance of all criteria listed in note 4 at the conclusion of this chapter, an action directed toward one member of the pair supposedly engenders similar effects in its now distant partner. Practices such as voodoo, for example, maintain that mutilating hair or nail clippings or an item of clothing discarded by the intended victim will similarly devastate their former owner.

Lest we think only untutored rustics are susceptible to such delusions, consider the following examples. One, beloved by the vast readership of supermarket tabloids, is the "psychic archaeologist" who claims to describe the long-dead owner of an artifact simply by holding the object and "absorbing its vibrations." Another remnant of magical beliefs (though rarely recognized as such) can be seen at "celebrity auctions" where admirers will pay a princely sum for a pair of socks once worn by Robert Redford. Even in research settings with avowedly non-superstitious people, a surprisingly large percentage say they would feel uncomfortable if asked to don Adolph Hitler's shirt (Rozin et al. 1986).

More central to the present discussion is a related staple of magical thinking, the *Law of Similarity*. Here, it is similarity in the mind of the observer that mystically connects unrelated objects, people, or events. Things that superficially resemble one another are deemed to share fundamental properties so that the image becomes interchangeable with the object. As with contagion, the image retains a magical affinity with its referent so that the vicissitudes of the image are reenacted in affiliated objects.

A classic instance is that of astrology, which began when some ancient observer of the night sky mentally connected dots of starlight to create images of bulls, rams, crabs, fish, warriors, etc. These free associations were, of course, quite arbitrary—different cultures were reminded of quite different entities by the same random patterns, just as assorted patients see diverse things in the diagnostician's inkblots.[5] In the case of astrology, these products of human imagination allegedly take on a life of their own, imprinting the attributes of each image upon people they "contact," i.e., those born when that pattern occupies the appropriate sector of the sky. "As above, so below," the old adage goes.

Operation of the law of similarity, or magical correspondence, is apparent in the traits astrologers claim these constellations impart to people. Those born under the sign of Aries (the ram) absorb ramlike impulsivity and wilfulness; Geminis (affected by the image of the twins) are infused with a vacillating, self-divided nature; and (alas!) poor Tauruses like myself are condemned to bullish lives of plodding obduracy.

It is my contention that graphology, like astrology, sprang from the same widespread tendency to assume that similarities perceived in the mind have causal force beyond one's private feelings and imagination. Psychologists have found that ordinary people with no knowledge of graphology tend to extend their impressions of total strangers' writing styles to the writers themselves (Warner & Sugarman 1986). The traits they impute are derived in the same intuitive, common-sense way that spawned graphologists' beliefs—e.g., people with big signatures are deemed to be dominant and powerful. There is, however, no reason to believe that these naive attributions, based as they are on questionable cultural stereotypes, are necessarily accurate.

These days, graphology enjoys a surface plausibility that astrology lacks because graphologists invoke, however inappropriately, mediating mechanisms that sound, at first blush, scientifically respectable. That advantage would evaporate, however, if it could be shown that the purported links between signs and personality are metaphorical rather than physiological as graphologists claim. In chapter 14, I show why we should reject the claims for a neurophysiological basis of graphology. It is time now to support my counterargument that the rationale for graphology remains today, as it was at its inception, belief in the magical potency of symbolism and allegory.

THE ORIGINS OF GRAPHOLOGY

Graphologists whom I have debated have been proud of the antiquity of their craft. They imply that its longevity attests to its validity but, of course, the durability of racism and sexism exposes the weakness of this argument. Graphologists implicitly concede this point when they reject (as they usually try to these days) any affiliation with astrology, a much older scheme for character reading than their own.[6] Nevertheless, I maintain that the underlying rationales for graphology and astrology are identical. I assert this on the following grounds. First, both systems ascribe characteristics to people by extending to them symbolic and metaphorical attributes of arbitrary signs or images. Second, those signs, their meanings, and their supposed powers of coercion, are wholly mental constructs produced by the free associative capacity of the human imagination, as shown below. In short, for both astrology and graphology, the image governs the object—the quintessence of magical thinking.

SYMBOLISM IN WRITING

Their magical lineage would count little against modern astrologers or graphologists if they had repudiated ancestral misconceptions in favor of empirically verified mechanisms—as astronomy did with astrology and chemistry did with alchemy. Many graphologists claim they have done this but, on the contrary, my survey of their books and articles reveals veneration rather than renunciation of ancestral follies. Take for instance the esteem still accorded Ludwig Klages (1872–1956), the "founder of modern handwriting psychology" (Lewinson 1986). The father of the "expressive movement" rationale I criticize in chapter 14, Klages based his "Science of Expression" on a string of dubious, unsupported assumptions about writing movements. In order to link writing movements to character, he appeals constantly to magical forces masquerading as scientific mechanisms. In the end, they boil down to the same old metaphorical correspondences. At the conclusion of the longest series of nonsequiturs in recent memory, Lewinson (1986: 7) sums up why Klages's "intuitive philosophy" for interpreting mystical symbolism in writing should be taken seriously: "The mind would not appear in action at all, if it were not coupled with the vitality of the person." Whatever this and her other equally obtuse generalities might mean, Lewinson (1986: 8) somehow thinks it supports Klages's postulate that

> [t]here is unity of character in all the volitional movements of any individual. Every personal movement will assume that manner of movement which is

> characteristic of the individual. . . . Consequently, the handwriting is a volitional movement and must necessarily carry the individual stamp of any personality.

As usual, Klages asserts that which is to be proved. No definitions are given for any of the key terms and no reason to concede their existence except belief in his equally nebulous cosmic forces. One of these is "rhythm," a basic attribute of the soul, according to Klages. Lewinson explains that "Klages used rhythm as a psychic yardstick anchored in the Cosmos." On this unpromising foundation Lewinson bases her exegesis of Klages's allegorical system, starting with his idea that writing is

> formed by the personal "guiding image" and is markedly influenced by the individual's sense of space. It is a rhythmic movement condition, in which each single movement reflects the entire personality, the sum total of the writer's intellectual, emotional and physical tendencies. (p. 9)

Hard as I tried, I was unable to find any suggestion of a mechanism that could connect rhythm of writing movements to these attributes, other than a mysterious "will and feeling" of the soul that crops up regularly in Lewinson's impenetrable presentation of Klages's muddled dogma. His magical leap from written symbols to human conduct and the sweeping overgeneralizations typical of graphology are apparent in the following rendition of Klages's thought.

> Writing is systematized conduct . . . demonstrated in the regular stopping and starting of the pen. Connected writing can be considered an unnatural connection of natural life-factors, while disconnected writing can be considered unnatural disconnection of natural life-factors. The activity of logical connecting is extreme in cases of non-observance of the natural pauses in movement. The positive interpretation of connectedness is logical activity and a gift for synthesis and dialectic, deliberation, calculation, etc. (Lewinson 1986:11)

Of course, not a shred of evidence is offered to back up any of the tortured logic in this chapter in a self-proclaimed "scientific handbook" of graphology (edited by Nevo 1986).

Magical thinking is equally prevalent in the musings of the influential Swiss graphologist, Max Pulver (1889–1952). Pulver (1931) pronounced, by fiat as usual, that the mind approaches a blank page as a metaphor for the world—a testable hypothesis perhaps, but hardly something to be accepted on faith. For Pulver, ascending extensions of letters symbolized an uplifting, spiritual nature while descending ones indicated preoccupation with base motives such as material goods and sexual pleasure. Here we see a touching holdover from simpler times when pristine spirits dwelled in the heavens, far above the grubby world below.

A more recent disciple is Rose Matousek (1987) who adopts a view of the symbolic interconnectedness of the world that would have been quite acceptable to the Oracle of Delphi.[7] E.g., Matousek (1987: 10) asserts, "The performance of writing coincides with universal symbolism of moving forward and backward, into and out of, and challenging or withdrawing, just as with body gestures." As an article of faith, she accepts the graphological dogma that people whose script relates symbolically to certain maneuvers will behave in a like fashion—another clear example of assuming that which is to be proved. Matousek feels no need for proof because it is self-evident to magical thinkers that symbols command their referents in the real world (e.g., writers of open letters are open people).

Rand (1961: 44), to his credit, shows at least some minor discomfort with the looseness of this attribution process but he quickly gets over it. He agrees that graphologists' ascriptions seem like "superficial analogies" but he circumvents this to his satisfaction, though not to mine, by saying graphologists learn "to cultivate the technique [sic] known as 'empathy,' the ability to imitate various gestures, to feel the same impulses as the scriptor [i.e., writer]." Thus, he cascades one variant of sympathetic magic upon another.

Rand (1961: 45) asserts that his graphological "theory of motor tendencies" has a "sound theoretical justification." By this he means that written signs are "best understood by their general character—whether they are efficient or inefficient, progressive or retrogressive, etc." What in people's writing actually corresponds to these concepts is hopelessly vague as usual, but this does not hinder the usual leap of faith that the writer will have comparable tendencies. Rand's justification for why people's character would conform to their handwriting is that it is "palpably obvious" (i.e., he blithely trusts in face validity instead of seeking empirical evidence—see Bowman, ch. 10, and Klimoski, ch. 11, for the dangers of this approach).

Matousek (1987) realizes the need for some rationale beyond face validity, however. Oblivious to the fact that she is trying to justify magical relationships with her misconstruals of scientific data, she engages in the kind of naive neurological argument for graphology I criticize in chapter 14. She never considers what a tall order it would be to evolve a brain mechanism that could ensure someone's behavior conforms to interpretation of a symbol in his or her script which, in turn, just happened to remind someone of those behaviors (and often reminded other interpreters of something else).[8]

REVERSE CAUSALITY AND GRAPHOLOGY

A sure sign of magical thinking is that it permits the interchange of cause and effect and thus, reverse causality (i.e., effects can precede their cause). A prime example is the branch of graphology known as "graphotherapeutics" (de Sainte Colombe 1972). Not content merely to assert that character is revealed by symbolism in handwriting, this bizarre offshoot claims that altering a feature of a client's writing will eliminate the undesirable trait it represents. Once again, the author tries to justify this with an amusingly simplistic theory of brain function. As he says on p. 15:

> Character sets the individual pattern of each handwriting and is inseparable from it; consequently, a voluntary handwriting change, once achieved, produces a corresponding change of character. How is this possible? The circuit established between brain and graphic gesture by the nervous system is two-way. Thus, the ability of the brain to influence the writing hand is reversible.

De Sainte Colombe's book bristles with the pseudoscientist's love of neologisms, nonsequiturs, name dropping, reference to unpublished research, unreasonably high cure rates unsubstantiated by data, and misappropriation of scientific sounding but vacuously applied terms. The traits he attributes to writers are the usual metaphorical ones (e.g., light pressure means timidity, "no fighting spirit," or "possibly low blood pressure") (p. 117). Baselines that rise, then fall

> signif[y] a lack of perseverance. These people make a fine start . . . but their energy soon melts, and they give up easily. (p. 92)

But take heart, the remedy for this personal shortcoming is simple: straighten out the baseline and you straighten out the client.

To his credit, Crumbaugh (ch. 7) expresses doubts about the efficacy of graphotherapeutics, though he seems less concerned about graphology's metaphorical basis in general. I invite the reader to compare Crumbaugh's metaphorical interpretation of the slant of letters to that derived from de Sainte Colombe's (1972: 84) "graphometer." Whether the connection between symbol and behavior is conceived of as one-way or two-way, it is still magical if it is based on allegory and has no plausible mediating mechanisms other than scientifically discredited brain connections and the Law of Similarity.

Bunge (1984) reminds us that a reliable sign of a pseudoscience is lack of progress in a field; i.e., reverence for the founders' revelations rather than constant revising of theories in light of improved methods and new empirical data. The examples in this chapter show that, despite claims to the contrary, graphologists today are still wedded to the same metaphorical underpinnings the field has always espoused, ones modern psychology has repeatedly shown to be unreliable.

HOW NOT TO DEVELOP A PSYCHOLOGICAL TEST

As Bowman (ch. 10) and Klimoski (ch. 11) describe, psychology has learned from frustrating experience that development of valid personality and ability measures requires procedures quite the reverse of those followed by the founders of astrology and graphology. The scientific psychologist's search for a valid trait indicator starts by identifying a generally accepted criterion for the quality the test will ultimately identify. I.e., a set of attributes widely agreed to exemplify a trait such as introversion, gregariousness, leadership, or whatever. A large group of people acknowledged to possess the criterion attributes is then assembled and closely scrutinized to see what other characteristics invariably accompany the trait of interest. The hope is that some of these correlates could be used as simpler, cheaper, more convenient indicators of the desired trait.

Mathematical correlations are calculated between the criterion measure and each of these potential test items and those most strongly related to the criterion are retained for the next round. This set of provisional test items is then given to a new, randomly selected sample of people to see if those who score highly on them are in fact strong exemplars of the criterion behavior—and, of course, low scorers must lack the trait. On the basis of this information, the test battery is further refined and tried again on yet another sample of people (for details see Schmitt, Neal, and Klimoski 1991). Only after several iterations of this procedure would an ethical psychologist release the test for use in situations where it could significantly affect people's life prospects.

Contrast the foregoing with the origins of astrology and graphology where the signs came first and the empirical validation stage was skipped altogether. The originators of these character-divining schemes first noticed some symbols—in the heavens and on a page, respectively. We might ask what determined which of many possible patterns qualified as one of these signs? The answer is the subjective impression of the observer (see the section on pareidolia below). Those configurations that reminded the selector of certain actions, players, or events were assumed, by the principles of magical similarity, to have some sympathy, affinity, or predictive value with respect to their referents in the world.[9]

In later examples, culled from the graphological literature, note the nature of the disputes when graphologists disagree about what attribute a given sign indicates. The conflict never involves conflicting empirical data, but invariably stems from differing subjective preferences for one versus another of the many equally possible mental associations the sign might trigger (and hence what trait to attribute to the writer). But first, let us look at how such associations come to be formed initially.

PAREIDOLIA—THE BASIS OF GRAPHOLOGY

The kindling of imagery by random patterns is familiar to every schoolchild who gazes at billowing cloud formations in the sky and sees majestic beasts, clashing legions, or gallant ships of the line. Psychologists refer to the products of this imagination process as "pareidolia" (Zusne and Jones 1989: 77–79). They are the basis of all divining schemes. Divination involves intuiting scenarios or personal descriptors from the free associations triggered by random patterns such as lines on the palm, smoke in the air, entrails of oxen, tea leaves in a cup, or scribbles on a page.

A rejoinder I frequently encounter from believers who concede the magical origins of graphological signs is to deny that modern practitioners rely on these sorts of cues any more. Crumbaugh and other supporters of Graphoanalysis,[10] e.g., downplay the significance of single letter shapes that would suggest pareidolia directly. They prefer to derive "holistic" impressions by noting similar "strokes" that a writer employs as parts of many letters. Nonetheless, the examples of sign-trait correspondences Crumbaugh cites (ch. 7) still analogize these strokes to behaviors in ways reminiscent of the symbolic systems of Klages, Pulver, Matousek, and de Sainte Colombe, described earlier. E.g., backslanting strokes, for Crumbaugh, as for every other graphologist I've encountered, allegedly indicate people who "draw back" from social interaction.

ON WHAT DO GRAPHOLOGISTS BASE THEIR ASSERTIONS?

The many graphological publications I reviewed before beginning this chapter were depressingly similar to other areas of "pop-psychology" I have criticized elsewhere (e.g., Beyerstein 1990). I sampled, I think fairly, from a broad spectrum of graphological works, ranging across different schools and historical periods and from academic treatises to the worst of the dime-store "know thyself" paperbacks. As noted earlier, a striking feature of graphology, like other areas of "pop psychology," is the vague usage of scientific-sounding concepts such as "rhythm," "tension," "dynamics," "sensitivity," "forcefulness," and "energy." In keeping with the folk psychology out of which graphology emerged, no operational definitions of such terms are given and insufficient evidence is supplied to back up the bald assertions that they are represented in people's script.

Rand (1961: 46), in a model of pseudoscientific discourse, constantly borrows terminology from the legitimate scientific literature but uses it in idiosyncratic and inapproprite ways. Examine, if you will, his use of terms such as "pure psychomotor impulse," "kinaesthetic impressions," "psycho-physical significance." See also Matousek's use of "energy discharge," below, and Rand's (1961: 44) mutilation of the concept of "empathy," mentioned earlier.

The graphological systems I encountered were also essentially unfalsifiable.[11] They are replete with ad hoc arguments for explaining away inconsistencies and thus clearly unscientific. I leave it to the reader to decide if Lockowandt's "processual validation" procedure (see ch. 6) would pass any fair adjudication of its falsifiability as defined by Dale Beyerstein in chapter 8. Likewise, Lewinson's (1986: 9) espousal of "the criterion of double meaning (plus and minus) of every graphological sign" allows each indicator to mean one thing or its virtual opposite! Hardly a testable theory.

Several other manifestations of pseudoscience (cf. Bunge 1984) were common in the works I reviewed. These include: (1) reliance on unvalidated, "common sense" notions of traits and motives derived from everyday language and folk psychology; (2) unfamiliarity with relevant scientific research and methodologically weak[12] or non-existent empirical support for their own views; (3) lack of standardization and practitioner accreditation in the field as a whole and constant bickering over key concepts by contending factions; (4) reliance on subjective estimation in place of rigorous mathematical operations; (5) a consistent tendency to assume that which is to be proved; (6) failure to derive acceptable theoretical explanations and mechanisms; (7) highly selective use of confirming examples and ignoring of contrary evidence; and above all, (8) magical thinking and its underlying conceptual error, "reification of the subjective."

Let us now examine some representative examples of the magical underpinnings of graphology. To highlight graphologists' reifications of metaphorical correspondences, I have preserved their exact wording in quotation marks or drop quotes, where appropriate.

GRAPHOLOGICAL SIGNS OF GENERAL INTERACTONAL STYLE

Matousek (1987: 7) interprets people's scribbles as an index of how they "discharge energy," her term for irascibility. Zigzag doodlings, with their preponderance of straight lines, remind her of lightning bolts in a stormy sky. Therefore, she says, these individuals are prone to aggressive, explosive discharges of energy. This sort of doodler is supposed to be brusque, argumentative, and, like a bolt from the blue, "goes to get what he wants." For Matousek, angularity signifies tenseness, so if scribbles change direction abruptly, it means the writer is subject to similar springlike snaps of mood. Paterson (1978: 17) embellishes this theme, branding writers of "sharp" letters as lacking sensuality and possessing a "Puritan streak." In short, jerky writers are just plain jerks.

On the other hand (no pun intended), billowy, curvy scribbles remind Matousek (1987: 7) of clouds blown by soft breezes. So this doodler must release energy in "free and sweeping impulses." In place of the uptightness of the angular scribbler, this halcyon soul has a "malleable and sensitive temperament which 'rolls' with the punch." Similarly, Teltscher (1971: 22) agrees with virtually every other graphologist that writers of smooth, rounded script are amiable, kind, gentle, and yielding—obviously people with no rough edges who go with the flow.

Despite the lack of credible evidence, a few of the foregoing ascriptions might seem at least intuitively plausible (if one accepts the dubious "expressive movement" argument I have criticized in chapter 14), but it is hard to find any rationale for the following claims of script-personality correlations other than sympathetic magic.

SIGN YOUR LIFE AWAY—ONE PICTURE IS WORTH A THOUSAND WORDS

Graphologists also like to extrapolate to people the characteristics of objects found in their doodlings. Roman (1952: 36), e.g., reads into a woman's sketch of a top-heavy pile of books evidence that "plainly reveals [her] instability." Is your employer or fiance combing your wastebasket?

In the same pictographic vein, Teltscher (1971, ch 11) provides a chapter full of delightful examples of how signatures of famous people reflect their callings. He finds resemblance to musical notation in the signatures of Mozart and Lehar and "swordlike strokes" in those of Field Marshalls von Bismarck and von Blucher. Count Ferdinand von Zeppelin's autograph has a blimp-like quality and a local bishop's has a "large upper loop [that is] formed like a mitre, and the downward stroke resembles a pastoral staff." If Teltscher's carefully selected examples represent anything more than pareidolia, he fails to convince us by showing that these people included these flourishes in their signatures *before* embarking on their careers—and that inappropprite occupational symbols could not be just as easily read into the signatures of the professionals he chose. Also, he fails to note how many high achievers' signatures bear no resemblance whatever to their occupations.

Sara (1956), Smith (1970), Paterson (1980), and Surovell (1987) join Teltscher (1971) among the worst offenders as purveyors of this sort of highly selective, after-the-fact "proof" for their craft. They present samples of handwriting of famous individuals and then proceed to pick and choose those symbols in their writing that happen to be remind them of their well-known biographies. If graphologists could identify these sorts of signs *in advance* of knowing whose writing it was (admittedly difficult if the signee is a celebrity, but lots of very high achievers are not well known outside their professions), they might gain some credibility with this sort of theatrics. What the critics of graphology in this volume amply demonstrate is that handwriting analysts cannot pass this kind of "*blind*" test, their protestations notwithstanding.

Graphologists consider the signature especially important because it is supposed to be a "perfect pen print in miniature of what a more complete sample of your handwriting would indicate" (Holder 1958: 71). But again, there's the usual bit of waffling: there may be slight inaccuracy because people sign as they would like to have others view them. They may not have quite reached their ideal state yet. But signatures can be amazingly revealing, according to Matousek (1987: 16): a married woman who signs her given name bigger than her married surname betrays an unhappy marriage.

I-WITNESS TESTIMONY

Next to the signature, the personal pronoun "I" is the graphological "ego symbol." Matousek (p. 15) calls it the "private self estimate." Just like magic, Smith (1970: 37) says, "An inflated ego is shown by the inflated upper loop which makes the *I* tower above the others." Matousek (pp. 15–16) claims that the person who makes the *I* taller than other capitals shows that his or her "ego is trying to reach commanding heights." But if we minimize our *I*s, we "don't elevate ourselves substantially. . . . self importance has a diminished value."

Ornateness is also a useful clue to self-regard. "Beware of the man or woman who makes capital letters which are very ornate. These people are vain to the point of vulgarity . . . [and] will do anything to get attention," says Smith (1970: 30). Kurdsen (1971: 89) particularly dislikes coarse, ungraceful capital *M*s, equating them with coarse, vulgar people.

GENERAL ORIENTATION AND INTERESTS—THE TWILIGHT ZONE

Given the nature of handwriting, it is not surprising that spatial metaphors abound in graphology. A recurrent theme is the assumption that a writer's primary devotions are reflected in the proportionality of the upper, middle, and lower segments of his or her letters, the so-called "zones." The upper zone contains the stems of letters such as *d*, the lower zone the stems of letters such as *g* or *y*, and the mid zone accommodates the body of the letter. In the best traditions of sympathetic magic, clients are saddled with folk psychology labels that have no theoretical basis other than their symbolic association with the concepts of "upper" and "lower."

Roman (1952: 140) sees nothing wrong with a supposedly scientific enterprise being founded on such shaky assumptions. She justifies the three zone concept, for instance, by reference to the mystical numerological significance of the number three—after all, there is heaven, earth, and hell, the Christian Trinity, and the anatomical divisions of head, thorax and abdomen. Roman's system is the basis of the one still used by Wellingham-Jones whose work appears as a sample of modern graphologists' research in chapter 15.

Never bashful about reifying metaphysical symbolism, Rand (1961: 45) claims that prominent upper extensions reveal up-beat concerns such as intellectual pursuits, imagination, spirituality, and idealism—the "higher" aspirations, as we say. Conspicuous middle zones mean a practical, "down to earth" person, and those who exaggerate the lower zones of their letters are supposedly "low life" types who probably also try to submerge these predilections from general view. Elaborate lower extensions expose a preoccupation with material interests, physicality, sexual conduct, and social ambition—the "baser" pursuits.

In this way, graphologists type writers as imaginative vs. reality oriented or animated by idealism and spirituality as opposed to instinctual desires, physical needs, and mundane concerns. Why so? because thoughts are experienced up in the head and are supposed to be inspired by "lofty" concerns whereas folk wisdom places avarice, instincts, gut level feelings, and the gonads, conceptually as well as anatomically, in the nether regions. Imagination and intellect are up; elimination, regurgitation, and procreation are down, so look to the homologous portion of the writer's script for their manifestations.

Paterson (1978: 11) agrees that those whose swollen loops dangle too far below the line may be a bit too "sensual" for polite company but shows how to spot the solid citizenry. They are the ones whose letters exhibit copybook equality of their upper, middle, and lower zones, showing that they, like their script, are blessed with "a good sense of proportion," whatever that might mean.

Exegesis of the spatial metaphor can get quite detailed. For instance, Martin (1969: 78) asserts that long, stiletto-like lower loops indicate love of money—obviously "sharp" operators. Long, bulbous (dare I say well hung?) lower loops signify strong sexual urges. Short, pudgy lower loops, reminiscent of little paunches and lunchbags, betoken preoccupation with food. But on p. 27, Martin (1969) says these urges could be subconscious, so we needn't worry if the writer doesn't overtly conform to his or her analysis, or even disavows the reading. The system is beautifully unfalsifiable, and on that ground alone, unscientific.

Since individual letters have upper, middle, and lower zones, they too are ripe for symbolic interpretation. Crosses on *t*s can go up or down like mercury in a thermometer and are used analogously by graphologists. Smith (1970: 20) says a high *t* cross is a sure sign of an "idealist," but be careful because a weak high cross reveals a "day dreamer." Unfortunately, Crumbaugh (ch. 7) won't attend this *t*-party—he thinks high *t*-bars indicate a high degree of will power.

Whether or not this fine level of analysis is valid is one of the sources of dispute among the different schools of graphology. Though Crumbaugh's Graphoanalyst colleagues demur (see ch. 7), the vast majority of handwriting analysts say very precise attributes can be gleaned from such minute features of single letters. Despite the Graphoanalysts' deprecating attitude toward the other, "occult" schools of graphology (their president's term for the competition), my survey finds them following the same beaten paths. E.g., Stockholm (1988), publishing in *The Journal of Graphoanalysis* (the self-proclaimed "World voice of scientific handwriting analysis"), says of a young client:

> This boy has a mental quality which is usually ascribed to adults—abstract understanding. It is most clear in the tall upstrokes of the *h*s. It denotes an ability to grasp or understand abstract concepts. This gift is invaluable in working with abstract subjects. . . .[13]

At least since Heraclitus in the first century B.C., the unconscious has always been portrayed metaphorically as beneath the conscious so, naturally, one looks below the line for evidence of seething instinctual urges. Matousek (1987: 10) reiterates the justification for this assumption she shares with Pulver, Roman, Rand, and others:

> We write on a real or imaginary line, or base line, which divides conscious activities that are above from subconscious activities below. In graphology

the baseline is also considered the line of reality because all letters should "touch base" or make contact with it.

And why can we be so confident of these attributions that we might decline to hire or marry a denizen of the wrong zone, or worse yet, suspect him of pilfering from the stock room? According to Rand (1961: 45), the proof is self-evident.

> It is unnecessary to cite any rhetorical expressions associating aspirations with ascent, directing thought up and away, to the firmament, or those identifying corporeality with the earth, focusing attention downward. It would not be denied that they are well-differentiated symbolical expressions everyone knows.

In poetry or figurative language the connotations of words add variety and convey subtleties of meaning. As figures of speech, metaphors and the images they invoke can be engaging and informative. But as the power by which signs or omens supposedly command their referents, they are magic, not science. Having come to the bottom of this section on the symbolism of elevation, I must share one of my favorite up-down metaphors, one Oscar Wilde with his fine ear for nonsense never intended to reify: "We are all lying in the gutter, but some of us are looking at the stars."

SIZING YOU UP—YOUR PERSONAL PERSPECTIVE

Another favorite spatial metaphor in graphology is size. According to Teltscher (1971: 29), large writing means that one's outlook on life is broad. This person thinks big, possibly to the point of pomposity. Saudek (1924: 272) warns us, "If absolutely commonplace formations are found in a conspicuously large handwriting, they express the self-important arrogance of a blockhead."

As one might expect, diminutive writing purportedly reflects modesty:

> The modest person who conducts himself unostentatiously to avoid attracting attention does not need so much space, either in life or in his writing. (Teltscher 1971: 29)

But this too can have its down side. Small writing, says Teltscher, may be a sign of "a narrow outlook and lack of confidence." Paterson (1980: 9) agrees that petite letters indicate a modest person who shuns publicity, but they may also reveal feelings of inferiority. Martin (1969: 23) nicely sums up the orthodox interpretation of size: large script means the writer is interested in generalities (the broad picture); small writing reveals a person who is detail minded, i.e., one who dotes on trees rather than forests.

Smith (1970: 30) claims that wide-based, upper-case letters indicate a gullible person. Kurdsen (1971: 55) says that narrow base capitals are a sign of skepticism. Though my letters lack this feature, I certainly have the trait.

UPS AND DOWNS AND THE BOTTOM LINE

Lots of things go up and down, literally and figuratively. This provides graphologists with another of their favorite metaphors because baselines can ascend or descend. When they go downhill, so, apparently, does everything else. But when they are on the upswing, the sky's the limit (see, e.g., Crumbaugh, ch. 7, or Smith 1970: 9). For Holder (1958: 70) descending baselines mean a fretful, easily discouraged person who lacks ambition. In the extreme, lack of mental alertness and ill health are indicated. The person whose baselines are on the skids is usually subject to depression, pessimism, and despondency, but some caution is necessary before you refuse to hire or marry this alleged sad sack. That is because, as Smith (1970: 9) warns us, descending baselines could also mean nothing more than the fact that the writer penned the sample on her lap or simply needed glasses!

Sara (1956: 48) introduces another weasel factor—downsloping lines mean pessimism, as claimed, but it could just be temporary. It's noteworthy that graphologists claim that writing is so permanently fixed by personality that it cannot be disguised while they are also eager to explain away mistaken attributions by saying the trait really was there when the sign was written but it was only temporary.

The Law of Sympathy is hard at work in Paterson's (1980: 18) explication of the descending baseline: The "writer who always lets his lines slip away is possibly a pessimist, always feeling he is being dragged down." Teltscher (1971: 135) temporarily eschews magical connotations, attempting instead a bit of folksy physiologizing to account for why those in the doldrums take their baselines down with them. Pessimism, sorrow, disappointment, and resignation are accompanied by drooping of our bodies, he says—"We always think of the word 'droop' when we're depressed." This causes the arm to fall "back against the body because of its drooping posture, and the writing will . . . droop and sag."

Then there are the fortunate ones for whom it's "ever onward and ever upward." Sara (1956: 48) sees in their rising baselines evidence of a hopeful attitude. These people are ambitious, upwardly mobile, and not easily discouraged. Teltscher (1971: 135) finds exhilaration in this uphill struggle for the summit. Like a jet poised to take off, their "whole lines tend to rise," signifying their soaring moods and aspirations. But how deep are those feelings? Read on.

EMOTIONAL INTENSITY: THE PRESSURE IS ON

Matousek (1987: 12) analogizes intensity of pressure to intensity of feelings. Roman (1952: 263), in keeping with her Freudian bent, expresses this in terms of libidinal energy.[14] In general, heavy pressure means intense feelings, indelibly driven into the page, as it were. It follows (if we don't stop to ask why), that such a writer is as stubborn and difficult to change as his etched-in script. Martin (1969: 31) depicts the heavy-handed writer as the proverbial bull in the china shop, i.e., insensitive to others' reactions. Sara (1956: 69) also sees heavy pressure as a sign of forcefulness, an extrovert. For Rand (1961: 88, 90) it is proof of pugnacity, vulgarity, and willpower.

Conversely, light pressure means a flighty, changeable personality. This writer

> skims across the surface . . . of the paper, emotional impacts are relatively slight so that long term prejudice doesn't set in. (Matousek 1987: 12)

For Martin (1969: 30), light pressure means a sensitive person—a lightweight who frets over every nuance and is easily swayed by others.

Exemplifying the unfalsifiability of graphology, Sara (1956: 68) makes a strong assertion and then provides herself an escape hatch. She accepts the conventional wisdom that light, threadlike writing means the writer is sensitive, easily influenced, and introverted. But her next line provides the excuse when these predictions fail to materialize. She admits one can find light writing in hard-driving, outgoing people who seek responsibility and positions of leadership. She resolves the apparent contradiction by asserting that their writing (which, by definition, cannot lie) reveals that they're really shy and retiring underneath but trying doubly hard to compensate outwardly.

THE WIDE OPEN SPACES

In one of the few graphological ascriptions that makes any non-magical sense, Teltscher (1971: 34) asserts that stingy people cramp letters, words, and lines together to save valuable paper.[15] Generous people, he says, are "prodigal of space and paper." Their letters are wide, words widely spaced, and margins generous. But the magical metaphors are not far behind.

Paterson (1980: 11) agrees narrow writers can be "economical to the point of meanness" but adds that this narrowness also reflects a tendency to "hold restricted views." She says the writer of broad letters spreads himself around. He "likes elbow room to think and move freely, and prefers to travel." If the lines run together, Sara (1956: 54) says it's thrift, but many other graphologists think it's proof of a muddled thinker whose thoughts rub together.

Rand (1961: 115) can't decide for sure whether crowding of words signifies parsimony or confusion of ideas, but Holder (1958) would opt for stinginess if there were additional negative signs such as the angularity discussed above. Absence of terminal strokes would clinch the case, for the miserly would surely be too close-fisted to finish their words properly.

Paterson (1980: 18) finds people who leave large gaps between words are "clear minded" but they can be lonely because "they don't mix easily." One wonders why such a writer wouldn't just be "spaced out" or simply an "air head." According to Paterson, small spaces between words "mean that the writer likes people around him most of the time. He can be indiscriminate about his choice of friends."

LEFT, RIGHT, AND YOUR SLANT ON LIFE

In discussing Crumbaugh's differences with de Sainte Colombe over "Graphotherapeutics" above, we encountered another favorite graphological symbol, backward and forward slant. Paterson (1980: 9) speaks for the profession in regarding left-leaning writers as passive—"unwilling to go out and fight the world." She says they stand back, hold back their emotions, and are typically found in jobs such as back-room research and work dealing with history and the past.

Right slanters, for Paterson (1980: 9), are active; they rush "forward to meet other people." They show their feelings and their "heart almost always rules the head." Stockholm (1988: 8), of the more-scientific-than-thou Graphoanalytic School, adopts her inferiors' interpretation of slant, finding evidence of "emotional withdrawal" in a client's backhand script. Roman (1952: 184) ascribes the same general significance to slant, but prefers to equate left slant with defiance, upright writing with self-reliance, and rightward slant with a compliant nature.

ISN'T IT TIME YOU WROTE?

Rand (1961: 48) maintains the canonical view of slant but adds a time dimension (time, for some reason, always progresses from left to right). Rand analogizes right-leaning writing to progressiveness: "freedom from restrictive ties with past experience." As we saw above, Paterson thinks historians' interest in the past is coded in their back-slanting letters. For Matousek (1987: 11), any suggestion of horizontal movement also symbolizes a time line:

> where we are, where we're heading and where we've been. Going back [leftward] symbolically represents a return to the past, to ourselves, and to the comfort of home.

Longstanding cultural superstitions and biases against leftness are common in graphology (see Roman 1952: 145). They are particularly prominent in Rand's (1961: 48) treatise. He finds leftward motions retrogressive, "unnatural, time-consuming, inefficient." Quite the opposite are right-slanting, right-thinking writers.

VARIABILITY—NOT THE SPICE OF LIFE

For most graphologists, irregularity in writing is bad because variable writers are variable people. Such a writer is "disorderly, lacks discipline," and is unsure of what he wants to do (Paterson 1980: 13). But again the hedge: these may be highly original thinkers. Regularity in writing indicates a steady, disciplined, orderly individual—it is typically found among members of the armed forces and civil servants, says Paterson. Paterson's magical underwear shows when she tells us (1980: 10) that varying slant means "an unpredictable person with *changing inclinations*" [emphasis added].

FOLK PSYCHOLOGY AND GRAPHOLOGY

Modern psychology only began to achieve real explanatory and predictive success when it replaced vague everyday language and folk explanations with operationally defined, empirically validated constructs. Old folk nostrums are able to explain little, in part because of their excessively symbolic nature but mainly because they offered little beyond old adages and aphorisms as after-the-fact rationalizations. The fact that mutually contradictory aphorisms are available to cover any and all situations seriously limits their explanatory utility: e.g., "Look before you leap" vs. "He who hesitates is lost"; or, "Absence makes the heart grow fond" vs. "Out of sight, out of mind"; or, "Birds of a feather flock together" vs. "Opposites attract." Reading the graphology texts I did, I was constantly reminded of this kind of "wise old uncle" advice, which, as Krebs and Blackman (1988) demonstrate, is satisfying but notoriously unreliable.

Some areas of psychology, notably Freudian psychoanalysis, have not gone as far in purging this sort of post hoc reasoning as more scientifically minded practitioners would like. However, authors following Ellis (1956) are aware of this shortcoming and are making strong efforts to operationalize key psychoanalytic concepts and tie them to empirical observations.

The constant use of folk psychology terms and concepts in the graphological literature, and especially the way they are allegorically linked to written signs, allows graphologists to fudge the value to be placed on any given interpretation. Everyday language can be a delightfully slippery thing. After all, as Bertrand Russell reminded us, "I am firm; you are obstinate; he is pig-headed."

Not only are graphologists' trait descriptors ambiguously defined, but the signs that supposedly indicate them are open to the same freedom of interpretation. Oddly, Rand sees this as a virtue rather than a weakness.

> The fact that several meanings are given one sign does not indicate vagueness and uncertainty, but rather discriminating distinction. (1961: 40)

For instance, in some of the many sample analyses I read, vertical writing was considered evidence of an upright, upstanding, self-controlled citizen. In others, it signified a repressed, uptight martinet. On de Sainte Colombe's (1972: 84) graphometer, when the needle, like the letter slant, is vertical, the writer is poised, calm, and self-reliant, and has "a neutral attitude toward most things." Disinterest or rigidity? Admirable self-control or stifling repression? Take your pick.

Kurdsen (1971: 53) provides another example of the nonfalsifiability of graphological judgments. He toes the party line at first—backhand means aloof, reserved, self-contained, and undemonstrative, BUT slanting too far left means the writer is really highly emotional but has suppressed it. What counts as "too far" is left to the subjective opinion of the graphologist. Martin (1969: 20) also admits she encounters left-slanting writers who are unexpectedly dynamic, friendly, and outgoing. But she can see that it's obviously a facade designed to keep people from really getting close to the repressed recluse within.

MIXED MESSAGES: SIGNS IN COMBINATION

The ability to modify interpretations when combining signs is another source of graphology's unfalsifiability, especially because the combinatorial rules are so loose. E.g., Rand (1961: 91) concedes that there's more art than science in determining the meanings of signs taken together. According to Rand (1961: 40):

> It will be realized when interrelationships are studied that a group, or cluster, of related signs is a more specific indicator of behavior than any single sign. In the process of analysis the graphologist does not evaluate one sign without searching for another corroborating sign or opposing ones. It is nevertheless true that many single graphic signs manifest quite definite, if not absolutely specific, traits.

Crumbaugh (ch. 7) also advocates forming a "holistic" impression of the client by merging several indicators from a sample of writing because, in combination, a sign might suggest something different from what it would by itself. However, a recent publication of the Graphoanalytic school he represents asserts, "The dot above the letter *i*, if firm and round, tends to indicate loyalty; if circled, it's a sign of independence."[16] Despite their "holistic" rhetoric, the "strokes" Graphoanalysts interpret seem to me just as molecular as other analysis schemes I reviewed. Stockholm (1988: 9), for instance, can apparently detect "fear of ridicule" in the fact that a client's "second *l* [in the word *still*] extends up a little higher than the first *l*." Ultimately, though, the "molecular versus global" debate is a red herring because, as Dean et al. (ch. 13) point out, a holistic impression, if it is to have any reliability at all, must be a lawful synthesis of influences contributed by individual signs. The possibility that, in combination, signs might indicate something different than they do individually is not at issue. Such interactions are often found in orthodox psychology. But if the global impression of the Graphoanalyst is not based on a repeatable recognition and integration of the components that contribute to the overall impression, then the holistic technique is even more open to the criticism that its pronouncements are merely pareidolia foisted upon the client. This leaves us with the question of where the presumed meanings of Graphoanalysts' "strokes" came from originally, for even if the same combination of signs repeatably elicits the same character sketch, it could still be invalid because the signs themselves were based on magical correspondences to begin with.

As we have seen, graphologists typically say single signs are only suggestive but then go on to discuss single signs they obviously consider conclusive—until someone points out counterexamples. Then the post hoc excuse making begins. As with astrology, there's a built-in fudge factor—if the applicable descriptor doesn't fit, it's because there's another interacting sign that modifies the first. Rand admits many people's writing contains contradictory signs that must be individually weighted (to his credit, he admits this is a source of bias). Advocates of "holistic" approaches rely on the graphologist's intuition to form the necessary synthesis. But even if the individual sign meanings were valid, Dean (ch. 12) presents evidence that the human cognitive apparatus cannot accurately track the effects of that many interacting variables simultaneously. Computers might help here, but only if the initial assumptions are valid. Otherwise, no amount of correct data processing will save faulty input—it's G.I.G.O. ("Garbage In, Garbage Out"), the computer scientist's nightmare.

Let us now turn to some examples of how the magical attributions of graphology can most easily damage innocent reputations, namely, imputations of sexual and criminal misconduct.

SEXUALITY AND SEXUAL ORIENTATION—THROWN FOR A LOOP

There being specialists within every calling these days, it's not surprising that some graphologists concentrate on matters carnal. In her graphological guide to the amorous, called *Lovestrokes*, Harriette Surovell (1987: 57) endorses the widespread conviction that hanky-panky is revealed by what goes on below the line (e.g., "peculiar loops" mean sexual "kinkiness"). Hannah Smith (1970: 30) concurs that "a great variety of, and irregularities in, lower loops indicte sex [sic] deviation." Smith also informs us that if one of the lower strokes of a *y* or *f* is stronger than the other, this shows a temporary lack of interest in or ability to enjoy sex—something common in the writing of those contemplating divorce, she says. But Surovell notes that the gender of the writer must also be taken into consideration. Unclosed lower loops in a woman's script indicate orgasmic dysfunction but in males they mean unfulfilled sexual fantasies. If lower loops descend into the upper zone of the next line, this suggests inability to control sexual impulses (Surovell 1987: 58). Before you chuckle, remember these people offer advice to the police!

It's always seemed odd to me that graphologists presume to pass on total strangers' sexual orientation and practices when they decline to guess their gender—something ordinary citizens can guess from writing at a greater-than-chance level. Could this have something to do with the fact it's hard to prove or disprove allegations about highly personal sexual tastes, but a graphologist's ascription of gender is patently easy to check?

Surovell (1987: 120), in typical good taste, shows that a savvy graphologist would not have been deceived by the late Rock Hudson's facade of heterosexual panache. The clear indications of homosexuality she finds in Hudson's signature would have been more impressive if they had been noticed *before* the details of his tragic life and death became common knowledge. A similarly after-the-fact approach to classification is seen in Smith (1970: 34). The court's wisdom in incarcerating a "criminal homosexual" was confirmed by Smith who found obvious evidence of his "perverted excitement" in the "tangled loops" in his writing. Again, with 20:20 hindsight, Smith (p. 152) finds "crooked shapes below the baseline show the emergence of perversion."

All of this would be but a humorous example of human gullibility if there were not such dire consequences that could befall those labeled in such a cavalier fashion. A Vancouver graphologist recently offered to help weed out—surreptitiously, of course—the practicing (and potential!) pederasts in the local teaching ranks. He claimed 100 percent accuracy for a method that he would not even disclose to me. More shocking yet, he actually received a favorable hearing from several school district bureaucrats (for details, see ch. 1)! Increasingly, we also find graphologists making irresponsible attributions of dishonesty and violent tendencies based on nothing more than the magical correspondences discussed above.

DISHONESTY, CRIMINALITY, AND VIOLENCE—THE PEN MIGHT REVEAL THE SWORD

Graphologists' attributions of these disreputable tendencies are as ill-founded as their sexual lore, but there is much more disagreement among individual analysts as to what to look for when blackening someone's reputation in this area. Let us hope that if your employer hires a graphologist, you benefit from the luck of the draw. Rand (1961: 115), for instance, says an undulating (i.e., serpentine) baseline reveals a snake-in-the-grass. But for Martin (1969: 18), a wavy baseline means only a moody person who has his ups and downs. Similarly, for Smith (1970: 24) lack of dots on *i*s denotes nothing more sinister than absentmindedness, but Rand (1961: 116) regards undotted *i*s as among the "chief signs" of a "treacherous thief."

In presenting this argument, Rand demonstrates the preferred way of dealing with disconfirming facts in a pseudoscience. Along the way, he has to account for why the sample he reproduces has incriminating *i*s but also contains open-topped *o*s. He and others regard the latter as a sign of trustworthy openness (like "Little open mouths," says Sara [1956: 111]). Kurdsen (1971: 96) agrees; open-top *a*'s and *o*'s mean both a talkative and a generous person (the letters remind him of open purses). Because Rand's sample criminal had been demonstrably secretive, devious, and avaricious, he decided that, in this case, the inconveniently open *o*s must mean "he would, under conditions safe to himself, be frank, but at other times mislead by pretending to be candid." Postdiction is a wonderful thing.

Similarly, Rand (1961: 116) has to explain away the long terminal endings on words in a sample of "criminal handwriting." That is because he had previously dubbed such extensions a sign of generosity. He waffles by saying that this miscreant "would be generous for the end-purpose of getting more than he gave."

For Saudek (1924: 244), ovals closed at the top but open at the bottom are a mark of dishonest, insincere persons—something is definitely rotten beneath the surface. To be fair, Saudek, of all the authors I reviewed, relied least on blatant pareidolia and metaphor in his scheme. He also tried to introduce some degree of quantification of actual writing behavior by measuring muscle movements. However, he devised a cumbersome, convoluted system for translating strokes into speed values that he then proceeded to interpret in highly questionable ways. For all his commendable attempts at experimental rigor, I found no evidence that Saudek's work has influenced modern experts on the psychomotor control of handwriting (see ch. 14). Even graphologists today seem only to pay homage to his memory while they continue to apply their much more simple-minded metaphorical interpretations.

Saudek listed ten general indicators of dishonesty in writing, any four of which he though were sufficient to impugn the writer's trustworthiness. In addition to the aforementioned ovals, they included such sins as (1) evidence of "a slow act of writing," (2) writing that conveys "a very unnatural impression," (3) "decomposing, spineless structure," (4) "touching up the letter formations," (5) pen frequently lifted from paper, (6) important parts of letters omitted, and so on. The evidence he presented in favor of his scheme looks impressive at first glance, but would never pass by today's methodological standards. Nonetheless, Saudek is to be commended for at least attempting to validate his techniques empirically, something all too rare in a field founded on subjectivism and free association.

Knowing in advance the details of someone's felonious background is a great advantage in ferreting out "obvious" signs of their criminality. Many of the books I reviewed presented samples of convicts' scripts with analyses that showed that the signs were so clear that we should have locked them up before they committed their crimes—or at least denied them jobs in our organizations. Teltscher (1971: 231) found indisputable signals in a proven malefactor's wavy baseline, backhand slope ("standoffishness"), cramped style ("pettiness, narrow mindedness"), long lower loops ("extreme materialism"), and weak *t*-bars ("opportunistic, given to following the path of least resistance"). Smith (1970: 19) also thinks weak *t*-bars mean weak wills—and thus susceptibility to temptation.

None of these authors thought it necessary to present anything but supportive examples. The need to determine the percentage of non-criminals who have "criminal" signs and criminals who lack the definitive signs seems to have escaped them. Such evidence probably wouldn't faze graphologists anyway, for if the signs were found in a non-criminal's writing, they would claim he had larceny in his heart that just hadn't manifested itself yet.

Such is the quality of thought that could cost you your job and your reputation. Every graphologist I've debated, and most of the ones I've read, has had his or her anecdotes about detecting employees with their hands in the till. None had demonstrated this under the kind of controlled conditions one would think the gravity of the charge would demand.

When the *Vancouver Province* (January 26, 1988) alleged that Hannah Smith had been offering graphological advice to the Canadian National Parole Board, she strenuously denied it. But her 1970 book reveals a keen interest in alleged signs of criminality in handwriting. She proudly reprints (1970: 7) acknowledgments of her help from high officials in the Canadian penal system (who presumably do influence parole decisions) and her own admission, on page 35, that she had supplied "complete analyses" of the writing of an accused bank robber and murderer for her sister, Simma Holt. Holt was then a reporter for the *Vancouver Sun,* doing a story on the accused, and wanted to know his "real character" before championing his cause in western Canada's largest newspaper. Holt was subsequently appointed to the National Parole Board where she claims to have stopped relying on her sister's insights into the criminal mind when deciding which convicts were worthy of release. Let us examine the quality of these insights.

We can rest easy knowing that those rehabilitating the rapists and murderers in our penal institutions are getting the finest psychological advice available when they consult someone who believes, as Smith (1970: 22) apparently does, that double crosses on *t*'s are diagnostic of "a schizophrenic or split personality." Though readers of the popular press might confuse schizophrenia with a split personality, those who scrape through my introductory psychology course never do. Why a split personality would double its (their?) *t*-bars remains a mystery to all but the magically inclined. The real mystery to me is why a double crosser wouldn't be a con artist instead.

In a book marketed by Canada's most prestigious publishing house, and containing little else but symbolic interpretations, Smith (1970: 28) displays her forensic acumen:

> Although I do not care for symbolic interpretations in graphology, there is an *f* that resembles a gun and which was found extensively in the writings of Jesse James. It can mean a killer, if the accompanying writing is illiterate, brutal, immature, or angry. The self-same *f* can also be found in the writing of a very depressed intellectual who is becoming suicidal.

Smith (1970: 49) also says having *t*-bars shaped like clubs "shows an ability to be brutal" and "whiplash" *t*-bars mean viciousness and sadism (p. 146). But there's still hope; Kurdsen (1971: 106) says writers of whip-shaped *t*-bars are just practical jokers. Rand (1961: 154) takes Kurdsen's side on this one: wavy *t*-bars just mean humor. Elsewhere, though, Kurdsen does find sadistic signs in the written arsenal. On p. 127, he suggests that arrows in doodlings indicate a calculating, cruel temperament.

Toting up the sinister manifestations, Surovell (1987, p. 105) informs us that

> [t]he graphological indicators for violent tendencies are: lots of angles, excessive pressure, sudden stoppages, changes in direction, increased pressure at the end of a stroke. . . .

LEGIBILITY

Of course, anyone so cruel would not wish it to be widely known, so suspicion is immediately cast upon those whose writing is illegible, especially if his or her signature is a scrawl. That is because legibility supposedly indicates a desire to be clear and a lack of concealed or ulterior motives. But, for graphologists, illegible writers are dead as the employment office doornail: ". . . *illegible formations not attributable wholly to haste or carelessness or physiological defects, are attributable to deception, concealment, dissimulation*" (Rand 1961: 49, emphasis in original). But before we pass sentence in absentia, Holder (1958: 54) charitably interjects that illegibility might merely indicate a "less accurate thinker."

Nonetheless, an illegible signature would be the proof we await. The writer is thereby hiding his or her true self—engaging in a "cover-up" or laying a "graphic smokescreen." This according to Matousek (1987: 16) who seconds Teltscher (1971: 231) on this vital matter.

GRAPHOLOGICAL SIGNS OF HEALTH AND AGE

It is obvious that any disease that affects sensory-motor coordination, produces fatigue or tremor, or lowers attentiveness can lead to deterioration in handwriting. However, the evidence that specific syndromes or symptoms are symbolically represented in script is about as good as that for sign-personality correspondences.

Though all graphologists seem to think they can spot mental illness, criminality, philandering, pederasty, closet alcoholism, and real or potential drug abuse, fewer of those I encountered claimed to diagnose physical illnesses. Those who did were far from timid, however. E.g., Kurdsen (1971: 93) and Holder (1958: 147) assert that ragged or broken upper loops are a symptom of heart trouble. Kurdsen (p. 94) also says broken lower loops indicate infirmity of the legs or feet. Smith (1970: 31) regards a complete break between upper part of the letter and its lower loop as a sign of weakness in the lower back or legs. De Sainte Colombe (1972: 117) asserts that low writing pressure is diagnostic of low blood pressure. The magical connection is too obvious to require comment.

Another basic disagreement among graphologists concerns signs of aging. Hanna Smith (1970: 13) says age isn't evident in writing but Graphoanalyst Emilie Stockholm (1988) claims it is. Rose Matousek (1987: 17), in siding with the nays, exemplifies the verbal sleight of hand so typical of graphology: ". . . it is not possible to determine age from writing because there are mature young people and immature older people." As with graphologists' refusal to guess gender, it's too easy to check an age estimate and very easy to weasel with an amorphous concept like maturity.

DO CHARACTER READINGS BASED ON MAGICAL CORRESPONDENCES REALLY WORK?

It is incumbent upon purveyors of services, before money changes hands, to document their efficacy. Consumers demand truth in advertising from toaster manufacturers, why not from those who offer to reveal their aptitudes, personalities, or state of health? This is especially true when people's reputations, personal relationships, and livelihoods are at stake and they may not even know they are being assessed.

In this chapter, I have cast doubt on graphology because, like astrology, it is essentially a divination process where metaphorical interpretations are attributed to people by magical means. Nonetheless, if graphology could substantiate its claims of efficacy, its supernatural origins would be irrelevant. If it cannot pass fair scientific tests of validity, we must also ask why so many people believe it can?

As the critics in this volume show, in properly controlled studies where clients are asked to find the reading done specifically for them in a stack of anonymous astrological or graphological sketches, they are no more likely to select their own than anyone else's. Moreover, giving an identical, randomly chosen, astrological or graphological description to a large number of people who assume it was done specially for them elicits a remarkably high estimate of its apparent specificity and accuracy from everyone. This has been shown repeatedly in well-controlled experiments such as that by Karnes and Leonard (ch. 16). When the opportunity for capitalizing on this so-called "Barnum effect" is eliminated, it becomes clear that the illusion of accuracy in non-scientific character readings stems from subtle embellishments the client unintentionally reads into the actual text (see Dean et al., ch. 13).

The mental operations that contribute to the "Barnum effect" are a by-product of the habitual modes of thought we use in making sense of the ambiguities of everyday experience; i.e., they are similar to the cognitive biases that spawned astrology and graphology in the first place. It is a fundamental drive of human cognition to "make sense" out of whatever we encounter —so strong is this urge that we often perceive relevance and meaning where none exists. This tendency to produce a plausible interpretation of the facts at hand is so ingrained that when we encounter a character reader's description we are unaware that we are unconsciously infusing the meaning and significance into the bare bones of the reading (see Hyman 1977, Dickson and Kelly 1985, and Dean et al., ch. 13). I invite you to see for yourself whether the relatively few publications in respectable, refereed scientific journals that support graphology[17] incorporate the stringent controls described in the foregoing references. That is, do they have the necessary controls to prevent these subtle cognitive biases, in graphologist as well as client, from spuriously making the reading seem accurate and revealing?

P. T. Barnum attributed his success to the fact that he "had something for everyone." Likewise, as we've seen, graphologists' readings tend to be sufficiently vague, broad, and inconsistent to encompass anyone. Take for instance the double-speak in a pre-employment assessment I recently received, done by the Handwriting Resource Corporation of Phoenix, Arizona. On page 3 of HRS's slick, no doubt computerized, "Comprehensive Profile" one finds client 264-84-1259 described as possessing the following strengths "to a very high degree (Intensity 90–100)": "task-oriented, motivated by projects and work assignments." Only to a slightly lesser degree is he/she "persistent and steadfast." But on the next page, under "weaknesses," we see the same person also rated in the highest possible category for "unstable and unpredictable emotions" and undisciplined, uncontrolled behavior." Also among #1259's purported strengths are that he/she is "direct and outspoken" and "truthful, honest and sincere [and] will not mislead others." But under "weaknesses" HRC finds that #1259 "exaggerates and distorts the truth" and engages in "unkind and inconsiderate treatment of others" . . . "to a high degree (Intensity 80–90)." For some reason, the "very high degree" of "advanced conceptual skills" and "clever problem solving capabilities" revealed in his/her script apparently doesn't prevent him/her from having "poor concentration skills" and "unsystematic disorganized thinking" and paying "little attention to details" . . . "to an above average degree." On one page it's "flexible thinking" (good), on the next it's "disorganized thinking" (bad). Under strengths, he/she is listed as highly "logical and reasonable." Under weaknesses, his/her "judgment is subjective, based on emotional reactions." HRC finds #1259 "adventurous," "challenge oriented" and eager to "consider risky opportunities" but simultaneously racked by "feelings of uncertainty" and anxiety and "too concerned with self protection." He/she is also "outgoing and friendly" on page 3, but becomes "unkind and inconsiderate of others," and "lack[ing] in tact and diplomacy" by page 4. I'm sure all of these contradictions could be explained away given enough pop-psychology bafflegab, but that would be small comfort to the job candidate or the prospective employer who paid good money for this mass of contradictions.

Astrologers, Tarot readers, palmists, phrenologists, mediums, and graphologists counter scientific demonstrations of their inadequacies by parading legions of satisfied customers. Such reliance on personal testimonials and the subjective impressions of practitioners has been shown repeatedly to be a weak currency, as research on the "Barnum effect" clearly demonstrates. Unless there is valid research to support the sign-behavior attributions and the Barnum-type sources of illusory validity have been scrupulously eliminted with approppriate "blind" controls, testimonials count for nought.

COULD PROPERLY DONE STUDIES OF HANDWRITING REVEAL VALID CORRELATES OF PERSONALITY?

I have never maintained that it is impossible, in principle, that some aspects of writing could correlate with certain personality traits, just that this has not been satisfactorily demonstrated—for the various reasons cited by the critics in this volume. Nevertheless, I do have strong a priori doubts that any existing school of handwriting interpretation could ever withstand proper scientific scrutiny. That is because the putative sign-trait correlations of all extant schools were and remain rooted in magical thinking. The meanings they ascribe to signs were derived from unvalidated free associations—pareidolia triggered by crude resemblances between script configurations and the various human attributes they supposedly indicate. Extension of these attributes from sign to writer in the absence of empirical evidence and a believable causal mechanism is pure sympathetic magic.

As I have shown, the arbitrariness and subjectivity of the pareidolia process accounts for the disagreements among warring schools of graphology. All disputants leap to the conclusion, however, that their particular interpretation is the true predictor of how the writer will behave. They can't all be right, but they can all be wrong.

As long as subjective interpretation of symbols remains the basis of graphology, it cannot claim scientific status. Furthermore, until graphologists produce a plausible, scientifically testable physical mechanism that could mediate the connection between symbol and behavior (along the lines I describe in chapter 14) they will remain open to charges of occultism or pseudoscience. And finally, until graphologists eschew folk psychology and become cognizant of the methods and data of modern scientific personality research they will continue to be relegated to the fringes.

To the extent that the graphologists included in this volume have tried to demonstrate empirical relationships between writing and personality, their attempts to improve upon "pop-psychology" handwriting analysis are commendable. While I still see major methodological problems in the graphologists' best research to date, their attempts to abide by the rules of scientific personality research are to be encouraged. It remains my prediction, however, that valid correlations, if any, that might eventually emerge from improved research methods will not be strong enough or specific enough to justify the use of graphology in job selection, criminal detection, marriage counselling, and the like (cf. Dean, ch. 12). The relationships, if any, will be modest, common-sense ones, apparent to anyone, and will hardly require graphological training to notice them. E.g., careful, neat writers might, as a group, tend to be more fastidious than messy writers. Even so, I doubt that such a restricted sample of behavior would be a reliable indicator of a global personality type, and the weakness of the correlation would make it doubtful as a predictor for any particular individual. I certainly know many neat people with atrocious handwriting and neat writers whose homes and offices look like disaster areas. Obviously, it is bad enough when one tries to extrapolate from a little sample of behavior to something straightforward like neatness but, as I show in chapter 14, traits such as kindness, promiscuity, and suspiciousness that have no obvious correlate in script or unique control center in the brain could hardly be represented in writing unless one engages in the magical fallacy of reifying the subjective. I will accept graphologists' data to the contrary if it meets the methodological criteria set by the best experts in psychological measurement. To date, this has not been the case.

SUMMARY AND CONCLUSION

To reiterate, in constructing a valid psychological test, researchers start with a pool of potential test items and no preconceptions about what the eventual battery will look like. They choose, by rigorous empirical methods, those items from a large pool that happen, for whatever reason, to correlate reliably with carefully measured criterion behavior—no matter how irrelevant or counterintuitive the items finally selected may seem. Graphologists' reliance on intuitively satisfying pareidolia to diagnose traits immediately brands them as holdovers from the pre-scientific era of sympathetic magic. Far from enhancing their believability, the fact that graphologists' and astrologers' signs bear an explicit symbolic resemblance to the traits they purportedly indicate actually detracts from their credibility. Modern psychology and physiology provide no reason to think valid correlates of complex traits should be so transparently obvious.

A field that exhibits so many of the attributes of pseudoscience listed by Bunge (1984) and lacks credible mediating mechanisms as outlined in note 4 of this chapter cannot claim scientific status. If it is founded on allegorical interpretation of signs, it is all the more suspect. Above all, such divination is unscientific because it is uncheckable—there is no objective way of resolving interpretational disputes. The Danish physicist and poet Peit Hein had this fatal flaw in mind in his *Ode to Freud:* "Everything is concave or convex; so everything has something to do with sex."

NOTES

1. It is ironic that the success of the scientific method has been so great that even the most blatantly antiscientific practices today feel they must claim scientific status (see, e.g., Seckel 1988).

2. See also the discussion of the "subjective validation" effect by Marks and Kammann (1980). A demonstration of its ability to create a false sense of accuracy in graphologists' assessments is provided in the experiment by Karnes and Leonard in chapter 16. A good discussion of how widespread deficiencies in quantitative reasoning skills lead to popular acceptance of unsupportable claims is contained in Paulos (1988).

3. "Divination" refers to any practice of augury, the attempt to foretell events, select persons for particular tasks, etc., by subjectively interpreting symbols, signs, or omens ordained by a "higher power" (Loewe and Blacker 1981). Graphologists

claim they do not foretell the future; however they ascribe traits to people that would be of no interest or use whatsoever if having them did not predict how their possessor would act in a job, marriage, ethical dilemma, etc. They also say what they do is not supernatural, but in this chapter I document the magical basis of graphologists' extrapolation of signs to people. Whether practitioners realize it or not, the interpretations of signs in handwriting were not arrived at in a scientifically acceptable manner, but by processes of augury.

4. According to scientific canons, an event occuring at one time and place cannot produce an effect, locally or elsewhere, unless a finite period elapses between the two events and unless that interval is occupied by a causal chain of physical mechanisms operating successively and continuously between the two times and two places (Broad 1949). Pseudosciences and magical thinking are almost defined by their misappropriation of scientific terms such as "ether," "resonances," "vibrations," "energies," "balances," "planes," and "dimensions" in order to make it sound as if their mysterious influences meet these scientific criteria. At present, the only scientifically accepted forces that can cause interactions among physical entities are the strong and weak nuclear forces, gravity, and electromagnetism. For a good discussion of these limitations on magical interactions, see Rothman (1988). It is axiomatic among occultists, nevertheless, that mental power can affect things in the world without any mediation by these physical forces (B. Beyerstein 1988). A characteristic feature of magic is that there is no conceivable physical mechanism to mediate physical effects—they "just happen" by wishing and expressing the right incantations.

5. Unreliable as the Rorschach ("inkblot") test is as a diagnostic tool, at least all its users claim is that, because there is no inherent meaning in the pattern, the patient's free associations might reveal preoccupations, turmoils, fears, etc., that could be worth exploring. No claim is made that there is only one "right" association to the pattern or that answers reveal anything beyond that patient's state of mind *at the time.*

The serious objections to the Rorschach test arise when diagnosticians insist on reading unprovable symbolic interpretations into patients' overt utterances—much as graphologists routinely do with writers' scripts. Graphologists often compare what they do to Rorschach testing. Seeking support from such a questionable technique hardly seems prudent, but even the alleged parallels are doubtful. That is because, while it is conceivable (though not well documented) that triggering free associations with random stimuli might cause *ideas* of special concern to the patient to "pop up," there is no reason to believe learned patterns of muscle activity in the hand and arm would go to the trouble of acting out subtle, symbolic representations of the writer's character, any more than hair growth would. This would be doubly so if the "true meaning" could only be revealed by a highly trained graphologist. Why did the human species supposedly go to the trouble of encoding all this hidden material in script if there was no one to recognize it between the time writing emerged and the first graphologists came upon the scene?

6. Though most graphologists today wish to be seen as scientific practitioners, and thus downplay any affiliation with astrology, the two professions have long been closely intertwined in Europe, particularly in Germany (Howe 1984; Sklar 1977). Perusal of the classified ads in "New Age" tabloids or a visit to any "Psychic Fair" reveals continuing alliances between these two disciplines on this side of the Atlantic. Prominent graphologists such as Stephen Kurdsen (1971) who invite mediums like Jeane Dixon to write the foreword to their books or Dorothy Sara (1956) (former president of the American Graphological Society) who write books touting both graphology and occult phenomena show that magical interests remain close to the surface in the profession.

Until graphologists do more than simply deny this occult connection and replace the magical allegories that still underlie their craft with plausible mechanisms that meet the criteria I outline in chapter 14 and in note 4 above, they have only themselves to blame if they are held in low esteem by the scientific community. The graphologists invited to appear in this volume were selected because they have adopted the scientific approach by attempting to validate their methods empirically.

7. Lest I be accused of picking unrepresentative exemplars to criticize, I should note that at the time we debated in a public forum in Chicago in 1988, Rose Matousek was president of the American Association of Handwriting Analysis. Likewise, Dorothy Sara, Emilie Stockholm, and Klara Roman, whom I cite frequently, are establishment figures in their field. Sara served as president of the American Graphological Society, Stockholm is Dean of Instruction of the International Graphoanalysis Society, and Roman is highly touted by most graphologists because she is one of the few in a field generally taught in brief mail-order and night school courses who ever lectured at a large American university. In the examples cited throughout this chapter, the reader will see that they and the others mentioned indeed represent the mainstream of graphological thought.

8. Of course, graphologists could maintain that the causal arrow points in the opposite direction (e.g., open people are compelled to make open letters), but a mechanism that could assure that is equally improbable on neurological gounds, as I discuss in ch. 14.

9. Some of the early drafters of the rules for handwriting analysis probably reversed the process, starting with a subjective sense of the person and then looked for symbolic correspondences in his or her writing; e.g., "He seems to be a forward person, so what features in his script remind me of forwardness?" The metaphorical nature of the search is the same whether it was the script or the person that was examined first. It is the lack of empirical validation of the perceived likenesses and the slavish adherence to "the tried and true ways of the old masters" that disqualifies graphology as a scientific pursuit.

10. Graphoanalysis is a registered trademark that refers exclusively to the proprietary method of handwriting analysis taught by the "Chicago School" founded by M. N. Bunker. For further information on this school and its scathing denunciations of the other "unscientific" schools of handwriting analysis, see note 16.

11. For a definition of falsifiability and an explanation of why it is a crucial

requirement for a scientific theory, see Dale Beyerstein's discussion of graphology and the philosophy of science in chapter 8.

12. The most glaring and widespread shortcoming is the lack of proper "blind" control conditions. These include shielding the graphologist from knowledge of who the writer is and from other sources of information about the writer, including the often-revealing content that might be in a sample to be analyzed if it is part of a job application, for instance.

13. This passage also reveals the graphoanalyst's unfamiliarity with a vast body of research on cognitive development stemming from the work of Jean Piaget. It indicates that adolescents of this boy's age *are* usually capable of comprehending abstract concepts. One has to question the advisability of taking psychological advice from someone unaware of the work of the most cited developmental psychologist of the century.

14. Most of the criticisms directed at graphology for "reifying the subjective," i.e., assuming that symbolic relationships explain or determine psychological mechanisms, apply with equal force to the systems of Freud and his disciples. Freudian psychoanalysis has frequently been attacked for similar pseudoscientific attributes, including unfalsifiability. See Ellis (1956) regarding attempts to salvage useful insights in Freud's work while eliminating these shortcomings.

15. Even if utilizing every corner of a sheet might suggest economical use of paper, it would still be a huge leap of faith to assume that someone who is parsimonious in this situation would necessarily be equally tight-fisted in any or all other settings. See Bowman (ch. 10) regarding the problem of generalizing from small samples of behavior to broad behavioral dispositions. It is such generalizations that most need the kind of empirical validation that graphologists rarely provide.

16. From the 1982 promotional pamphlet by the International Graphonanlysis Society, Inc., *Enjoy the Rich Rewards of Graphoanalysis*. In an accompanying letter, the society's president, V. Peter Ferrara, dismisses all other schools of graphology as "non-scientific," "hit-or-miss" systems that disagree among themselves. He dubs the competition "guesswork" and "a kind of parlor game." Ferrara goes on to say that the founder of Graphoanalysis, M. N. Bunker, "one of the authentic geniuses of our age, . . . recognized that handwriting is a basic symbolism which reflects the writer's individual rhythm." Here we see the same old assumption that symbolic relationships determine real events. What a "writer's individual rhythm" might mean is anybody's guess, but it sounds rather like a bit of borrowing from the "unscientific" system of Klages discussed earlier.

In a 1988 symposium I was asked to organize, we tried to include a representative sample of prominent critics and proponents of graphology. The Graphoanalysts (who, as we've seen, pride themselves on their scientific status) were the only major school to refuse our repeated requests to send a spokesperson to this scientific forum. This despite the fact that the session was held in their hometown of Chicago.

17. Even fewer of the published studies favoring graphology are found in the highest quality journals with the most stringent peer-review standards and which do not charge authors for publication.

REFERENCES

Alcock, J. 1980. *Parapsychology: Science or Magic?* Oxford: Pergamon Press.

Basil, R., ed. 1988. *Not Necessarily the New Age: Critical Essays.* Buffalo, N.Y.: Prometheus Books.

Beyerstein, B. L. 1988. "The Brain and Consciousness: Implications for Psi Phenomena." *The Skeptical Inquirer* 12(2): pp. 163–173.

———. 1990. "Brainscams: Neuromythologies of the New Age." *Intl. J. of Mental Health* 19: pp. 27–36.

Broad, C. D. 1949. "The Relevance of Psychical Research to Philosophy." *Philosophy* 24: pp. 291–309.

Bunge, M. 1984. "What Is Pseudoscience?" *The Skeptical Inquirer* 9(1): pp. 36–46.

de Sainte Colombe, P. 1972. *Graphotherapeutics: The Pen and Pencil Therapy.* New York: Popular Library.

Dickson, D. H., and I. W. Kelly. 1985. "The 'Barnum Effect' in Personality Assessment: A Review of the Literature," *Psychological Reports* 57: pp. 367–382.

Ellis, A. 1956. "An Operational Reformulation of Some of the Basic Principles of Psychoanalysis." In *Minnesota Studies in the Philosophy of Science,* edited by H. Feingel and M. Scriven. Vol. 1, pp. 131–154,

Gaster, T. H. 1959. *The New Golden Bough: A New Abridgement of the Classic Work by Sir James George Frazer.* New York: New American Library.

Holder, R. 1958. *You Can Analyze Handwriting.* Englewood Cliffs, N.J.: Prentice-Hall.

Howe, E. 1984. *Astrology and the Third Reich.* Wellingborough, U.K.: Aquarian Press.

Hyman, R. 1977. " 'Cold Reading': How to Convince Strangers That You Know All About Them." *The Zetetic* 1(2): pp. 18–37.

Krebs, D., and R. Blackman. 1988. "The Science of Psychology and the Psychology of Common Sense." In *Psychology: A First Encounter,* pp. 27–31. San Diego, Calif.: Harcourt Brace Jovanovich.

Kurdsen, S. 1971. *Graphology: The New Science.* New York: Galahad Books.

Lewinson, T. S. 1986. "The Classic Schools of Graphology." In *Scientific Aspects of Graphology,* edited by B. Nevo, pp. 5–46. Springfield, Ill.: Charles Thomas.

Loewe, M. and C. Blacker, eds. 1981. *Oracles and Divination.* Boulder, Colo.: Shambhala Publications.

Marks, D., and D. Kammann. 1980. *The Psychology of the Psychic.* Buffalo, N.Y.: Prometheus Books.

Martin, R. C. 1969. *Your Script is Showing.* New York: Golden Press.

Matousek, R. 1987. *Graphology and the Phenomenon of Writing.* Self-published, 820 West Maple Street, Hinsdale, Ill. 60521.

Monte, C. F. 1975. *Psychology's Scientific Endeavor.* New York: Praeger.

Nevo, B., ed. 1986. *Scientific Aspects of Graphology: A Handbook.* Springfield, Ill.: Charles Thomas.

Nisbett, R., and L. Ross. 1980. *Human Inference: Strategies and Shortcomings of Social Judgement.* Englewood Cliffs, N.J.: Prentice-Hall.

Paterson, J. 1980. *Know Yourself Through Your Handwriting.* Montreal, Quebec: Reader's Digest Assn.

Paulos, J. A. 1988. *Innumeracy: Mathematical Illiteracy and its Consequences.* New York: Hill and Wang.

Pulver, M. 1931. *Symbolik der Handschrift.* Zurich: Orell Füssli.

Rand, H. A. 1961. *Graphology: A Handbook.* Cambridge, Mass.: Sci-Art Publishers.

Roman, K. G. 1952. *Handwriting—A Key to Personality.* New York: Pantheon Books.

Rothman, M. A. 1988. *A Physicist's Guide to Skepticism.* Buffalo, N.Y.: Prometheus Books.

Rozin, P., L. Millman, and C. Nemeroff, 1986. "Operation of the Laws of Sympathetic Magic in Disgust and Other Domains." *J. Personality and Social Psychology* 50(4): pp. 703–712.

Sara, D. 1956. *Handwriting Analysis.* New York: Pyramid Books.

Saudek, R. 1929. *Experiments with Handwriting.* New York: William Morrow.

Schmitt, J., J. Neal, and R. Klimoski. 1991. *Research Methods in Human Resources Management.* Cincinnati: South-Western Publ.

Schultz, T. 1989. *The Fringes of Reason.* New York: Harmony Books.

Seckel, A. 1988. "A New Age of Obfuscation and Manipulation." In *Not Necessarily the New Age,* edited by R. Basil. Buffalo, N.Y.: Prometheus Books, pp. 386–395.

Shweder, R. A. 1977. "Likeness and Likelihood in Everyday Thought: Magical Thinking in Judgments About Personality." *Current Anthropology* 18(4): pp. 637–658.

Skinner, B. F. 1948. "Superstition in the Pigeon." *J. Experimental Psychology* 38: pp. 168–172.

Sklar, D. 1977. *The Nazis and the Occult.* New York: Dorset Press.

Smith, H. M. 1970. *Between the Lines: The Casebook of a Graphologist.* Toronto: McClelland and Stewart.

Stockholm, E. 1988 (January). "Comparison of Traits Typical of 'Juniors' and 'Seniors.' " *Journal of Graphoanalysis*: pp. 3–10.

Surovell, H. 1987. *Lovestrokes: Handwriting Analysis for Love, Sex and Compatibility.* New York: Harper and Row.

Teltscher, H. O. 1971. *Handwriting—Revelation of Self.* New York: Hawthorne Books.

Tversky, A., and D. Kahneman. 1974. "Judgment Under Uncertainty: Heuristics and Biases." *Science* 185: pp. 1124–1131.

Warner, R., and D. Sugarman. 1986. "Attributions of Personality Based on Physical Appearance, Speech, and Handwriting." *J. Personality and Social Psychology* 50 (4): pp. 792–799.

Zusne, L., and W. Jones. 1989. *Anomalistic Psychology: A Study of Magical Thinking.* 2nd ed. Hillsdale, N.J.: L. Erlbaum Assoc.

Section Four

Critiques of Graphology

10

Difficulties in Assessing Personality and Predicting Behavior: Psychological Tests and Handwriting Analyses Contrasted

Marilyn L. Bowman

In chapter 10, Marilyn Bowman tackles one of the most controversial issues in psychology: the nature of personality. Although the scientific literature in this field has been plagued by misconceptions and false starts, Bowman shows that there are increasing areas of consensus. As these well-established data have emerged, they have cast increasing doubt upon various character-reading schemes that originated in the pre-scientific era of folk psychology. Modern research has revealed subtleties and complexities in the seemingly straightforward concept of a personality trait that "pop-psychologists," relying on overly simplistic, intuitive views of personality, have failed to address. This isolation, plus their failure to provide supporting research of their own, has seriously damaged their credibility in the scientific community. The pop-psychologists' lack of motivation to familiarize themselves with the latest personality research is partly due to its highly technical, mathematical nature and partly to the fact that the old folk-psychology notions of personality seem so plausible despite their inability to withstand empirical scrutiny. Heavy reliance by popular character readers, including most graphologists, on these dubious conceptual holdovers challenges their claim to describe people and predict their behavior accurately. A prime shortcoming, discussed by Bowman, is their failure to note the degree to which situational factors can modify the effects of internal dispositions.

Bowman also shows that pre-scientific character-reading schemes have paid insufficient heed to the conceptual pitfalls and measurement problems inherent in deriving accurate personality scales. She raises these methodological issues in her discussion of the two most fundamental requirements of a scientifically acceptable psychological test: reliability and validity. She then assesses the published research on graphology in light of these standards and deals with the question of why personality readings that fall far short of those standards can still seem remarkably accurate (the "Barnum Effect," examined in greater detail in chapter 13 by Dean et al. and chapter 16 by Karnes and Leonard). In the present chapter, Bowman also emphasizes the dangers of relying solely on the face validity of personality measures, the strongest selling point of most non-scientific assessment techniques.

In arriving at his or her own conclusion about the scientific credibility of graphology, the reader should compare the critiques in Bowman's chapter and Klimoski's (chapter 11) with the defenses offered by Lockowandt in chapter 6 and Crumbaugh in chapter 7, as all of these chapters revolve around the key issues of reliability and validity of psychological measurements.

* * *

Personality, the pattern of a person's stable and enduring psychological traits, is a common-sense idea. Most of us believe that we can describe the personalities of ourselves, our friends, and our family with some degree of accuracy. We ascribe to the people we know such traits as honesty, friendliness, sociability, or anxiety. We form our impressions from everyday behavior that we have seen or heard about; from the ideas, plans, hopes, and fears that we have heard expressed; from our observation of the impressions made on others; and from our knowledge of personal histories. Most of us believe that we can describe some of our friends more accurately than we can others and that, of the qualities we discern in a particular person, some are more central than others to the personality of that person. Furthermore, we often try to predict the behavior of people we know from what we have discerned about their personality traits.

The qualities that we use to describe ourselves and others are similar to the qualities used both by graphologists and psychologists in their formal assessments of personality. Hundreds of such personality attributes have been formally studied by personality psychologists in the twentieth century, and from these studies we have learned that descriptions of personality that seem intuitively simple and obvious are, in fact, complicated and readily influenced by many subtle factors.

The Stability of Personality

Despite the conviction most people hold that they *know* what kind of person they are and that they *know* that one friend is stubborn and another is generous, it turns out that some attributes are less enduring than they appear, and that they appear to be stable mainly because we usually interact with people only in a narrow range of specific situations. Behaviorist psychologist Walter Mischel, in his famous book *Personality and Assessment* (1968), showed that behavior can be significantly changed by situational conditions. At its most extreme, this position suggests that there may be no stable personality traits of any significance. This challenge to the conventional idea of personality as a conglomerate of relatively enduring traits stimulated two decades of active investigation into the stability of personality and the predictability of behavior.

Mischel's analysis raised the possibility that some of the qualities we observe and assume are stable might be illusions of our own need for cognitive consistency and predictability in our interpersonal relations. It suggested that we may conveniently ignore certain behaviors in our friends if we think they are not typical of them. If Mischel's ideas are correct, they also mean that if we use our current ideas about a person to predict his or her behavior, we would often be wrong, because that person's behavior would be more strongly influenced by situational forces than by his or her personality traits. For example, a person might be scrupulously honest in all matters dealing with personal income tax, and yet engage in petty pilfering in a particular job setting. If Mischel were asked the question: "How honest is this person?" he might reply, "It depends upon the circumstances," and he might decline the invitation to draw any conclusions about that person's *trait* of honesty.

Mischel was able to demonstrate that for many of the personality attributes traditionally studied by psychologists, the observed behavior was readily altered by situational influences. Thus, he forced researchers to look more closely at the stability of behavior across time and the consistency of behavior across situations. Two decades of complex research have taught us that there are individual differences in behavioral stability, that some behaviors are more responsive to situational influences than others, and that some situational forces have a greater influence upon behavior than do others. We have learned that there is no simple one-to-one relationship between a personality trait and behavior. John Doe may be generally an extroverted person, but how extroverted he will be will depend on whether he is at a party with close friends or at a formal dinner with his boss.

Nevertheless, our intuitive notions about our ability to identify the personality traits of our friends and family have not been invalidated. Kenrick and Funder (1988) concluded from their review of two decades of research that many personality traits are indeed powerfully related to behavior and that many criticisms of personality stability have been tested and been found wanting or limited in effect. Mischel's own attempts to understand these complexities have contributed important evidence that key or prototypic aspects of behavior appear to be consistent across both situations and time (1976). The cumulative effect of this vigorous research activity has been to identify more clearly several of the factors affecting behavior: most importantly, personality, abilities, and situational features. Predictions about behavior that are based solely on personality descriptions will be less accurate than those based on all three elements, and this will be equally true for psychologists and graphologists.

We have learned that certain attributes of the environment interact with personality to influence the actual behaviors that occur in specific situations. If environmental features are powerful (i.e., visible and well-defined), then individual differences in behavior are generally reduced. For example, in a place of worship during a formal service, behavior is largely constrained by the demands of the situation, and the behavior of most individuals will be predicted more accurately by knowing the nature of the situation than by knowing the personality attributes or mental abilities of the people there (Mischel 1976). If, in contrast, situational forces are weak (i.e., ambiguous as to the participants and the events unfolding), then it is more likely that individuals will call upon their own memories, and thoughts, and propensities to create their own interpretations of the event and that they will react in line with their individual interpretations. Under these circumstances, there will be much greater variation in behavior among individuals, and the behavior will depend more on internal, enduring personality and mental ability attributes than on situational influences.

We have also learned that certain psychological attributes are more enduring and stable than others. Decades of research indicate that general *mental ability* is a stable and consistent human trait. Kangas and Bradway (1971) showed, for example, that IQ scores obtained at age fourteen correlated .85 with scores obtained at age thirty and .68 with scores obtained at age forty-two.

Individual *interests* represent another family of psychological attributes that has shown significant long-term stability. Correlations in the .80s have been reported for scores obtained at three-year intervals on tests of vocational interests (Campbell 1977), and correlations as high as .40 have been reported between scores obtained as long as thirty-six years apart (Campbell 1971). Similarly, satisfaction with life at age thirty is strongly predictive of occupational and life satisfaction as much as thirty years later (Sears 1977).

Stability has also been established for a number of personality traits. Paul Costa and Robert McCrae (1985), researchers with the National Institute of Aging, concluded from their extensive longitudinal studies that there are five broad and basic dimensions of personality that are stable across time and consistent across situations: Neuroticism, Extroversion, Openness, Agreeableness, and Conscientiousness. Scores measuring these qualities may be obtained from a wide range of psychological tests, such as the Minnesota Multiphasic Personality Inventory (MMPI), the State-Trait Personality Inventory, and the Myers-Briggs Type Indicator. Other personality traits, such as impulsivity, shyness, social anxiety, and attitudes to authority, turn out to be less stable or consistent.

In describing personality, it is necessary to distinguish between a person's current, transient, psychological state and a deeper, more enduring trait. By knowing a person's state (e.g., depressed), we can often make accurate short-term predictions about the behavior that will ensue, but prediction over the long term will be poor. In contrast, by identifying an enduring personality trait, we can make (on average) accurate predictions over long time spans, but we would be less accurate in predicting behavior in single, specific situations. For example, a person might customarily be extroverted, but on a particular day might feel worried about an upcoming examination. If we assessed his or her personality on that day, it would be important to identify both the state of anxiety and the more enduring trait of extroversion, even though extroversion might not be prominent in that person's behavior or attitudes that day.

The importance of differentiating between transient and enduring aspects of behavior applies equally to conventional personality assessment and to graphology, although graphology has focused on enduring personality traits as the basis for predicting behavior. Thus, studies of the long-term consistency or reliability of personality traits are particularly important in evaluating the analyses and predictions made by graphologists. At the time Mischel first raised these issues, it was not clear if all traits were equally susceptible to environmental influences. We now know that some personality traits are, indeed, more stable than others.

We also know that the behavior of some individuals is more stable than is the behavior of others. This means that scores on a reliable and valid personality test will generate relatively accurate predictions about behavior for those individuals whose behavior is stable, but relatively inaccurate predictions for those whose behavior is changeable (Bem and Allen 1974). For example, a major longitudinal study that followed young people from adolescence to adulthood showed that the more stable individuals were those who had been particularly well-adjusted from the start. In contrast, those whose behavior was changeable had shown high tension and disequilibrium from the earliest time onward, and the nature of the changes they went through was unpredictable (Block 1971).

For truly adaptive functioning, individuals should be flexible enough to choose from their repertoires of personality and ability characteristics those behavioral responses that best match the needs of the situation. They should not be entirely driven either by situational or personality factors. Difficulties in matching behavior to environmental constraints are found, for example, in people with schizophrenia. Their behavior is described as overdetermined in that their internal preoccupations and their behavioral predispositions are so powerful that they determine behavior without reference to important environmental cues, with the result that their behavior is sometimes inappropriate. Any personality assessment procedure, including graphology, that focuses primarily on static personality attributes and ignores the complicated ways in which environmental influences interact with personality to produce behavior will be relatively inaccurate in predicting behavior.

To summarize: We know that behavior is largely the outcome of a person's mental abilities, personality traits, and the situations the person is in at the moment; that some situations have a stronger effect on behavior than do others; that some personality traits are more stable than others; and that the behavior of some persons is more stable than is the behavior of others.

Difficulties in Predicting Behavior

Personality descriptions form part of the more challenging task of predicting behavior, and predicting complex human behavior is a notoriously difficult task. How accurate are we likely to be if we want to predict the behavior of a specific person, whom we will call Jane Doe?

If the behavior is one that occurs frequently among people like Jane Doe (e.g., premarital celibacy in some religious sects, anorexia nervosa in ballet dancers), we could accurately predict Jane Doe's sexual or eating habits if she came from either of these groups, simply because those habits have high *base rates* in those groups. Furthermore, we would not even have to see Jane Doe or know anything about her (except her group membership) in order to make accurate predictions about these kinds of behavior. The same principle applies if we are trying to predict for an individual group member a kind of behavior which occurs rarely in that group (e.g., fraud among nuns). In other words, for behaviors that occur either with high or low base rates in identifiable groups, we can, on average, predict with good accuracy whether a member of the specified group is likely to engage in that behavior.

Prediction of individual behavior from group or population base rates becomes much more difficult when the behavior we are interested in occurs with a moderate rate of frequency (e.g., divorce) or when the behavior is one that is considered undesirable by society (e.g., drug abuse, violent behavior). Predicting on the basis of population frequency alone that a specific married couple will divorce will be accurate only 30–40% of the time. Predicting that a specific person will engage in undesirable behavior, even when that behavior has a high base rate in the group from which the individual comes (e.g., drug abuse in certain inner-city groups) has such potentially damaging consequences for the individual that, fortunately, psychologists are reluctant to predict from group base rates alone.

We can improve the accuracy of our predictions if we know something about the individual's own base rates for the behavior we are interested in. It is here that personality assessment techniques can play an important role. If we know, for example, that Jane Doe is a chronically anxious person, we can predict with reasonable confidence that she will be anxious in a job interview or a courtroom appearance. Conversely, if we know that Jane Doe is not depressed, has never entertained thoughts of suicide, and, indeed, considers suicide immoral, we can predict with reasonable confidence that she is not at significant risk for suicide.

This is not to say that knowledge of the personality of the person whose behavior we are trying to predict will insure that our predictions will be accurate. As we have seen, personality is not the sole determinant of behavior. It has been shown that, even when we know something about the personalities of the people whose behavior we want to predict, we are often inaccurate in predicting such behaviors as suicide among institutionalized mentally disturbed patients, violent behavior among incarcerated criminals, or theft among employees (see Farberow 1981; Mulvey and Lidz 1985; Saal and Knight 1988). Nevertheless, the use of reliable and valid techniques for assessing personality can lead to more accurate predictions of individual behavior than those based on group base rates alone.

Graphology: Stability of Behavior and Reliability of Assessment

Graphology uses a specific type of expressive behavior, handwriting, as the source of inferences about current personality traits and as the basis for predictions about behavior. In a sense, handwriting samples are analogous to the response individuals make on standardized personality tests. And, just as with personality test responses, we need to know how reliable over time and how consistent over situations an individual's handwriting is.

Documenting the stability of a person's responses is a standard procedure in the development of personality tests. A common method for determining the stability or reliability of responses to personality tests is to administer the same test to a number of people at different times and then examine the correlations for each person among his or her responses to the same test at different times (test-retest reliability). For example, the California Psychological Inventory (Gough 1957) has eighteen scales with test-retest reliabilities ranging from .57 to .77.

To determine the test-retest reliability of the graphic features of handwriting, multiple handwriting samples should be obtained from the same individuals at a number of different times. Each sample should be blind-scored (i.e., without knowledge of the author of each sample) according to formal script criteria; and, finally, correlations should be calculated between the scores for the different samples from each individual. Because handwriting analysis involves detailed judgments about script features, individual differences in judgment contribute error which usually results in lower test-retest reliabilities than are obtained for objectively scored tests, a common finding in all assessment situations where scores are based on human judgments.

The reliability of the graphic features of scripts can also be assessed by obtaining multiple script samples from each person on a single occasion, scoring these samples blind, and then correlating the scores from the different samples produced by each person. This method would give us an index of the *internal consistency* of the individual's writing, another type of reliability that is routinely determined for personality and mental ability tests. The 1955 Wechsler Adult Intelligence Scale, for example, has internal consistency (reliability) values ranging from .93 to .97. Saudek (1929), one of the classic writers on handwriting analysis, insisted that the analyst must examine many samples of an individual's writing, thus implicitly recognizing the need for internal consistency and test-retest reliability long before there was a scientific literature on these psychometric issues. In his own work on forgery detection, he used numerous samples before making his judgments.

What is the evidence that a given individual writes in an identifiably similar manner under different circumstances and at different times? Fluckiger, Tripp, and Weinberg (1961) reviewed almost three decades of research on the use of such physical measures as pressure of pen on the paper, grip pressure, and speed of writing for identifying individual handwriting characteristics. They noted that many devices had been invented to measure these physical aspects of writing but that, in fact, few studies had ever been done to determine if they were reliable in the writing of any given individual. They were able to locate several early studies that showed that handwriting can vary if the subject's central nervous system was strongly influenced (e.g., by alcohol or drugs, or after electroshock or hypnosis), but these extreme conditions do not speak directly to handwriting consistency under normal conditions. More recent studies of handwriting (e.g., Sovik, Arntzen, and Thygesen 1986) have shown that handwriting can change significantly with training. In addition, Rafaeli and Drory (1988) suggest that both individual and group or demographic characteristics may affect the consistency of an individual's handwriting.

Despite this modest evidence that the characteristics of an individual's handwriting can be altered, Klimoski and Rafaeli (1983) concluded from their review of many studies that, overall, a person's handwriting is reasonably stable across time. Reliability values have ranged from .77 to beyond .90, indicating that a person's handwriting can be reliably identified from the graphic features of his or her script. This graphic stability makes possible the forensic analysis of scripts for investigations of forgeries (see chapter 4).

Typical graphological analyses are not based solely on objective scores, but also on subjective judgments of specific script characteristics. These judgments may be of the yes/no variety; that is, a particular script feature is either present or absent; or they may be quantitative ratings of the size, intensity, etc., of specific features. Error will be introduced into the scoring of script characteristics if the person making the judgments is inconsistent in assigning scores or if different judges assign different scores to the same characteristic. These problems of intra- and interjudge reliability occur not only in handwriting analysis, but in all assessment procedures which cannot be scored objectively.

Such procedures, known in psychological assessment as projective techniques, customarily allow the person being evaluated much latitude in responding. For example, a person might be asked to describe "What might this be?" when shown a series of inkblots (Rorschach Inkblot Test, Rorschach 1942); or a person might be asked to create a dramatic story for each of a series of pictorial scenes (Thematic Apperception Test, Murray 1943). The relatively unstructured responses people make are then examined in order to identify and score features that are believed to be psychologically meaningful. In contrast, objective psychological tests markedly limit the range of responses allowed, and many well-established personality tests allow only Yes/No or True/False responses or numerical ratings of specific traits and behaviors.

In the case of handwriting analysis, the reliability of scoring judgments can be improved if the graphologist uses formal measurement devices to score features: rulers can measure letter size, protractors can measure slant, charts can provide prototype examples. Although some systems of graphological analysis accept the use of objective scoring aids, others reject them on the grounds that the best analysis is based on a holistic interpretation of many factors, including subtle qualities that do not lend themselves easily to objective measurement. To the extent that a graphology system does not assess specific features, scoring reliability cannot be determined, although the reliability of interpretations can be tested.

Intrajudge reliability in handwriting analysis can be assessed by determining the consistency with which a judge makes the same judgments of the same handwriting samples at different points in time. Most studies of the reliability of individual judges have examined the consistency of the inferences about personality made from the scripts, rather than the consistency in judging specific graphic features such as pressure or speed, or specific script features such as long loops or circles for dots. For example, Sonneman and Kernan (1962) reported highly consistent intrajudge reliability (correlations of .64–.85) for five ratings of psychological attributes inferred from two handwriting samples collected at two different times. In general, however, intrajudge reliability of handwriting analyses is rarely assessed or reported either for script features or for inferences about the personality traits of the writers. It is of interest that several of the early studies reviewed by Fluckiger, Tripp, and Weinberg (1961) were able to identify several personal characteristics of graphologists (e.g., experience in the visual arts, gender) that were associated with intrajudge consistency.

Interjudge reliability is the degree to which different judges make the same judgments of the same scripts. It has been studied more extensively than has intrajudge reliability. The results of early studies suggest that the greatest agreement among judges occurs when judgments are based on a small number of broad categories or on well-defined script features (Fluckiger, Tripp, and Weinberg 1961).

Furnham and Gunter (1987) found correlations as high as .89 between two raters of three highly specific script features. Galbraith and Wilson (1964) reported an interrater reliability of .78 between the ratings made by three handwriting judges of five personality traits, but Rafaeli and Klimoski (1983) found a median interjudge correlation of only .45, when inferred personality traits were rated. Jansen (1973) found interjudge reliability of trait inferences equally low both within and among several groups of handwriting analysts, including a group of trained graphologists. Similarly, Vestewig, Santee, and Moss (1976) reported significant differences among six experienced Graphoanalysts in their judgments of ten of the fifteen traits assessed, indicating low interjudge reliability. Keinan, Barak, and Ramati (1984) also reported low interjudge reliabilities, .20–.37 for six graphologists' ratings on thirteen scales. Overall, the range of interjudge agreement found in these studies indicates that graphologists often differ substantially in their ratings and interpretations of the same handwriting samples.

If judges, even those trained to a level of proficiency in a standardized training program such as Graphoanalysis (a registered trademark name), fail to agree with each other on the important psychological inferences to be made from script samples, what is to be done? Rafaeli and Drory (1988) point out that it is possible to reduce the statistical error that is associated with differences in ratings among judges, simply by using a single judge in each study. They do not recommend this practice, however, because if such a study generated significant results, we would never know if they were the result of the graphology method or of that graphologist's particular talents. If the graphology method is the source of the promising findings, then the results of the study could be generalized to others trained in that method. In contrast, if the results were an artifact of one graphologist's special talents, then they cannot be generalized.

Improvement in interjudge agreement on psychological rating scales can be achieved if specific names and descriptions are provided for the features important for each judgment to be made. For example, if anxiety is being rated on a 5-point scale, high interjudge agreement can be attained if the relevant behaviors for each of the five points on the scale are clearly described, and if judges are trained to reach high levels of agreement using these criteria. These techniques have been used in the development of many assessment procedures (including psychiatric diagnostic evaluation) with considerable success and with high levels of interjudge agreement. Standardized scoring criteria for handwriting analysis have not been developed to the same degree, although some commercial graphological services now use privately developed templates to classify some script features for later computerized summing. The use of computers to sum scored features does not, of course, improve the reliability of the total scores, since scores for individual features are still based on human judgments. The use of script templates should, however, improve the reliability of those judgments.

In summary: The graphic features of handwriting are stable enough that a given person's handwriting can be identified with good reliability by a well-trained judge. Psychological inferences derived from handwriting are less reliable because of error introduced by both intra- and interrater variation.

Validity of Assessment Procedures

All methods of assessing personality, abilities, interests, or temperament must be reliable, but reliability alone is not sufficient to make an assessment procedure an effective one. It is also necessary to demonstrate that the technique is valid; that is, that it measures what it purports to measure, whether it be extroversion, intelligence, anxiety, or an interest in music. Validity is usually established by demonstrating that there is an orderly relationship between the results of the assessment (e.g., test scores) and an independent index of the personal quality in question. A ruler, for example, is a reliable instrument for measuring the length of an earlobe, but we could not claim that it is a valid instrument for measuring creativity, unless we could show that there is an orderly relationship between earlobe length and creativity. In 1891, the Italian criminologist Lombroso claimed that geniuses and madmen were both characterized by short height, crooked bones, and pallor. All these qualities can be reliably measured, but none has ever been shown to be related either to genius or to mental disorder.

If we take an arithmetic test, score high, and are then told that we have a high level of arithmetic skill, what we are told makes good common sense. In more formal terms, the arithmetic test has high *face validity,* because it measured what it appeared to be measuring. But suppose we take the same arithmetic test, score low, and then are told that we have a high level of anxiety. The arithmetic test would have low face validity, because it appears to be measuring arithmetic skill, not anxiety. In fact, performance on tests of mental arithmetic does tend to decline as anxiety increases (Knox and Grippaldi 1970), so arithmetic tests may be more valid as tests of anxiety than their low face validity would suggest.

The degree to which a test does or does not measure what it appears to measure can only be determined empirically. This is especially true in personality assessment where it is known that scores may be distorted by many factors such as unconscious habits or deliberate bias. It is also known that personality test items sometimes measure the opposite of what they appear to be measuring. On the MMPI, for example, certain items with a paranoid quality contribute to the paranoia score if they are *denied,* while others contribute to that score if they are *endorsed* (Dahlstrom, Welsh, and Dahlstrom 1972). Some personality tests include items that are designed to detect deliberate bias on the part of subjects; these items look as if they are measuring one attribute when they are in fact validly measuring something quite different. Thus, it is important to distinguish between the face validity of an assessment technique and its real validity.

Handwriting analysis has a high claim to face validity. It is intuitively appealing to think that the expressive behavior of writing bears a meaningful relationship to our psychological attributes. I have noted earlier that a person's handwriting is reliable across time and consistent across situations. Also, writing is closely linked with our use of language, an important behavior for revealing many dimensions of our inner life. At first glance then, psychological descriptions based on handwriting analysis have a reasonable kind of appeal, and it is easy to believe that important personal qualities are revealed in our writing. The face validity of handwriting analysis is one of the reasons why graphology continues to be of interest in the general population, why personality reports based on handwriting analysis are often enthusiastically received by the script writers, and why it has been repeatedly studied by personality psychologists in the hope of using it in research and clinical assessment.

Gordon Allport and Philip Vernon, leading twentieth-century researchers and theorists in personality, published their investigations of handwriting analysis in their classic book *Studies in Expressive Movement* in 1933. In it, they expressed their disappointment with the lack of validity in handwriting analysis. Guilford, another major personality researcher, came to a similar conclusion more than twenty years later (Guilford 1959), and a more recent review of the literature (Klimoski and Rafaeli 1983) yielded no evidence for the validity of graphological analysis. Nevertheless, the technique has such a strong appeal to face validity that interest in it continues. Face validity often plays such a troublesome role in personality assessment research, by distracting us from the necessary empirical evidence, that one personality researcher has even suggested that "It may . . . be beneficial for any test *not* to have high face validity" [my emphasis] (Furnham 1986: 392).

The face validity of graphological analysis is also enhanced by the "Barnum effect," so named because of the readiness with which people suspend disbelief and accept the exaggerated claims of circus hawkers. In personality research it refers to the willingness with which people accept descriptions of their personalities when they believe the descriptions were made especially for them. The effect is robust if the accounts include mildly negative comments, followed by flattering comments. Paterson, who was the first to report the Barnum effect (see Blum and Balinky 1951), gave the same standard personality report to a group of businessmen, on the pretense that each report was based on observations and findings specific to each man. The men almost invariably accepted the reports as valuable, accurate, and specific descriptions of their own individual personalities.

The Barnum effect has been extensively studied ever since and is a well-established phenomenon. Snyder (1974), for example, confirmed the Barnum effect in experimental studies in which descriptions that were random and independent of the participants were presented to them in the form of horoscopes. Similarly, Karnes and Leonard (chap. 16, this volume) have shown that both authentic graphologists' reports and invented Barnum reports are accepted by subjects with equally high levels of credulity and that both are preferred to reports based on data from reliable and valid personality tests. Karnes and Leonard attribute this finding to the ambiguity and the generality of both the fictitious and the genuine graphology reports. Vestewig, Santee, and Moss (1976) also found that subjects were unable to differentiate bogus reports from Graphoanalysts' reports. A review of similar findings appears in chapter 13 of the present volume

Cognitive dissonance is another phenomenon that may contribute to the readiness with which people ascribe truth and accuracy to graphological reports. Cognitive dissonance (Festinger 1957) refers to the tendency people have to experience psychological discomfort if there is a discrepancy, or dissonance, between two attitudes a person holds or between an attitude and that person's behavior. The inclination, then, is to reduce the dissonance and the accompanying discomfort by changing one of the attitudes or by changing the discrepant behavior.

Take the case, for example, of a couple who marry despite great family opposition and then gradually realize they are badly suited to one another. Cognitive dissonance theory predicts that they will tend to distort or deny their true negative feelings in order to reduce the dissonance between their behavior (marrying in defiance of opposition) and their true feelings (unhappiness).

Cognitive dissonance has been widely studied in experimental and real-life situations, and it is a robust phenomenon. Because handwriting analysis is looked upon with some skepticism in North American culture, a person who goes against negative public opinion and submits to an analysis has in effect set the stage for possible cognitive dissonance. Thus, even if some parts of the report seemed to be incorrect, the person would be inclined to accept the analysis as a whole, because he would need to reduce the discrepancy between his initial decision and the actual, partly unsatisfactory outcome.

Personality research has demonstrated that certain personality qualities are regarded more favorably than others. For example, extroversion is viewed more positively than introversion, and high emotionality is considered an undesirable quality (Furnham 1986). To the extent, therefore, that personality analysis ascribes well-regarded personality attributes, it is likely to be well received.

We also know that a report that identifies psychological attributes that occur with a high frequency in the population will be (accurately) perceived as accurate, even though the attributes identified may be trivial. This phenomenon has been labeled the "Aunt Fanny effect" (Tallent 1958), because a skeptic reading such a report would be justified in saying, "Yes, and so's my Aunt Fanny, and so what?" The naive reader sees correct information but does not stop to think how general it is.

As we noted earlier, once it has been shown that an assessment technique (whether it be handwriting analysis or a personality test) generates reliable responses, it is necessary to demonstrate that the responses or the scores assigned to those responses are related to actual behavior in a regular and and meaningful way. It is the actual behavior, either current or future, that is the criterion against which the validity of the test procedure is measured. Thus, before we can use any assessment technique with confidence, we have to determine its *criterion-related validity.*

The personality tests that are commonly used have been developed to meet specific standards of test construction. The validity of a new personality test can be established by examining the relationships between responses from the new test and the responses obtained from other tests whose reliability and validity have already been established. Ideally, the responses from the new test should be highly correlated with the responses from other tests that measure the same traits or behaviors and poorly correlated with those from tests that measure different traits and behaviors. Furthermore, these relationships should hold whether or not the new and old tests are similar in format.

This system of test validation (the multi-trait–multi-method matrix) was devised by Campbell and Fiske in 1959, and it represents an ideal for psychological test construction. An assessment procedure that meets these criteria is said to show both convergent and discriminant validity, because it yields scores that converge with measures with which they should agree and that differ from measures with which they should disagree.

Further validation procedures include studies designed to determine whether demographic variables such as age, gender, or ethnicity significantly affect test scores, and studies designed to relate scores on the new test to past life experiences, real world behaviors, or self-reports of feelings, attitudes, and ideas. The results of these validation studies are then used to construct tables of normative scores from which one can determine, for example, whether the score of a particular person indicates a level of anxiety that is within the normal or the pathological range for a person of that age, gender, etc.

In concurrent validity procedures, the scores of individuals on the new personality assessment procedure can be correlated with their scores on a theoretically relevant psychological test, with ratings made by people who know the individuals well, or with behavior observed in a standard setting. Predictive validity procedures use such criteria as subsequent performance in a training program, sales productivity in a company, or response to drug treatment.

In general, objective psychological tests yield higher correlations with behavioral criteria than do projective assessment techniques. Because handwriting analysis shares many features with projective personality tests, it is not surprising that similar problems in establishing validity are found with both techniques.

Projective tests can be scored using well-defined scoring systems such as those devised for the Rorschach by Klopfer et al. (1954) or by Exner (1974), or they can be interpreted in an impressionistic, holistic way by a person experienced with the technique. If holistic methods of interpretation are used, the intra- and interjudge reliability of the interpretations can be evaluated, but the validity of the assessment technique is difficult to determine. To the extent, however, that formal scores are generated, these scores can be studied for both reliability and validity. Furthermore, if formal scoring methods have been developed, judges can be trained to a standard of reliability in scoring. A similar process could easily be applied to training judges to make reliable handwriting judgments so that they identify script features with a high level of agreement.

It is at the stage of relating test scores to psychological criteria (i.e., establishing criterion validity) that projective techniques often meet with difficulty. From 1930 to 1960, projective techniques were widely used to generate hypotheses about personality features, usually conceptualized in terms of Freudian or other instinct-oriented theories. Decades of studies, however, encountered major difficulties in validating these interpretations; as a result, many psychoanalytic hypotheses were abandoned. More recent work has attempted to use the Rorschach and other projective techniques to identify different perceptual styles in information processing, and there is evidence to suggest they may be useful for identifying perceptual problems associated with brain damage (e.g., Lezak 1983).

Because handwriting analysis is essentially a projective technique, validation studies are equally necessary to test its claim to validity. First, however, we have to consider the characteristics of the writing sample from which inferences about the personality or behavior of the writer will be drawn.

There are several kinds of handwriting samples, each with its advantages and disadvantages. If the sample is obtained from spontaneous writing, it may be written quickly and carelessly, whereas if it is copied or dictated text, it is usually produced more slowly and carefully (Saudek 1929). Also, spontaneous script contains idiosyncratic rather than standardized material, and it often includes autobiographical information or other material that reveals much about the writer's thought content and facility with language. In contrast, if the text is copied, the content can be limited to neutral material that is the same for everyone. These differences in script content have been found to affect graphological interpretations.

Jansen (1973) found that psychologists who read only *typed* versions of spontaneous scripts were significantly better in predicting eighteen ratings than other judges (including experienced graphologists) who were given the actual writing, which included useful biographical information. This finding implies that the graphic features of the spontaneous samples actually reduced the accuracy of interpretation. Nevertheless, the accuracy of prediction was poor for all groups of judges. Keinan, Barak, and Ramati (1984) reported that psychologists who relied heavily on the autobiographical content of handwritten samples were as accurate in predicting officer training success as were graphologists who based their predictions on both the form and content of the spontaneous scripts. Again, neither group was able to predict success with significant accuracy. Ben-Shakhar et al. (1986) also studied the predictive value of autobiographical content by comparison with graphological analysis of script features. They too found that predictions based on content or on style were equally poor in predictive validity. They did identify several features of the writing samples that did improve prediction, but they were not formal script features. They were language usage qualities such as grammar, aesthetic use of language, and articulateness, all of which can be identified from typed script as easily as from handwritten samples. Rafaeli and Klimoski (1983) reported that autobiographical content did not increase predictive accuracy. In their study, handwriting analyses were equally poor in predicting sales productivity whether the scripts had neutral or autobiographical content and whether the judgments were made by experienced graphologists or by naive students.

Neter and Ben-Shakhar (1989) performed a meta-analysis of seventeen validity studies of handwriting analysis and concluded that graphologists performed at essentially random levels when using scripts with neutral content. Their judgments improved marginally when they used samples containing autobiographical content, but, even here, their predictions were not significantly different from those made by non-graphologists.

In summary, the preponderance of evidence indicates that more useful information is obtained from the autobiographical content and the language features displayed in handwriting samples than from formal script features. These non-graphic features can be determined equally well from typewritten or handwritten materials. Analysis of script features does not increase accuracy, and it may reduce the accuracy of judgments made on scripts that include biographical information.

Graphologists assert that validity studies of handwriting analysis should use well-trained, experienced graphologists. Some recommend that graduates of a particular training program such as Graphoanalysis be used in order to provide the most valid test of the interpretive system. This is a legitimate requirement if judgments are based on a variety of subtle features used in complex combinations that cannot easily be quantified for objective scoring and that, therefore, require both training and experience with the method of analysis. Similar recommendations have been made for validation studies of other projective techniques. If this claim is legitimate, then carefully designed validation studies should show that judgments made by well-trained, experienced judges are substantially more accurate than those made by naive, untrained judges.

Jansen (1973) reported that trained graphologists were no better than psychologists or laymen in predicting high- or low-energy levels from handwriting samples, and none of the groups showed significant accuracy. Vestewig, Santee, and Moss (1976) found that there were significant differences in the judgments made by six experienced graphologists on ten of fifteen criteria. The most experienced analyst failed to produce a single significant correlation out of fifteen, and no two analysts were in significant agreement on the same trait. Ben-Shakhar et al. (1986) used autobiographical writing samples and found no significant differences between the judgments made by personnel graphologists and a psychologist; both were equally poor. Keinan, Barak, and Ramati (1984) reported that experienced graphologists and psychologists made equally poor predictions from handwriting samples, although they used different features of the writing as the basis for their judgments. Both groups were somewhat better than lay judges who had no experience in assessing personality. Rafaeli and Klimoski (1983) found significant agreement (reliability) between naive students and experienced graphologists on three of ten possible judgments, but the judgments of both groups were equally faulty in predicting real estate work performance. The meta-analysis of seventeen studies by Neter and Ben-Shakhar (1989) showed that trained graphologists were no better than non-graphologists in making predictions from scripts with biographical content, and they were usually worse. Their predictions from scripts with neutral content were even more unsatisfactory.

In summary: there is no convincing evidence that lack of training in graphological analysis is responsible for failures to establish the validity of graphology as a technique for assessing personality and predicting behavior.

Some graphologists have argued that the personality concepts they are required to use in formal studies are often different from those they would normally use (e.g., Crumbaugh 1977a). This implies that graphologists are sometimes forced to make judgments in which they have little confidence and that the accuracy of their judgments should increase as their confidence increases. Vestewig, Santee, and Moss (1976) found, however, that although the six trained Graphoanalysts in their study expressed high confidence in their judgments, these judgments showed unacceptably low levels of predictive validity. Similarly, Eysenck and Gudjonsson (1986) found no correlation between the confidence ratings of a Graphoanalyst and the validity of her judgments. Thus, the evidence to date does not indicate that the validity of graphological judgments is related to the confidence with which they are made.

It is also of interest that, although naive judges can sort handwriting samples by gender with about 70 percent accuracy, handwriting analysts are reluctant to use gender as the basis for sorting script samples. For example, Crumbaugh (1977b) cites the following statement from *The Encyclopedic Dictionary for Graphoanalysts:* "And Graphoanalysis firmly teaches that it is absolutely impossible to determine reliably the sex of the writer by handwriting (1964, 192)." To which he adds: "Especially is this true today because of the blurring of sexual role differences in our current society." If graphologists who are trained in formal systems of handwriting analysis were unable to achieve the 70% accuracy rate of naive judges, serious doubt would be raised as to the validity of their systems of analysis.

Determining the validity of handwriting analysis and of other projective techniques is complicated by the fact that different systems of interpretation are used by different practitioners for inferring personality characteristics and predicting behavior. Therefore, the validity of each interpretive system must be tested independently. Klimoski and Rafaeli (1983) described three general approaches to the analysis of handwriting: (1) a trait or atomistic approach that ascribes specific personality attributes to specific graphic features; (2) a holistic approach that requires the analyst to generate an integrated, global view of the writing, from which the personality of the writer is inferred; and (3) the Graphoanalytic approach that combines both atomistic and holistic features.

The atomistic approach was used by Linton, Epstein, and Hartford (1962), who studied the personality correlates of two kinds of beginning strokes. They reported a significant correlation between the frequent use of a primary beginning stroke and psychological test indices of social conformity. Unfortunately, their study suffered from so many flaws in research design and data analysis that the significance of their findings is in doubt.

It may be the case that graphologists find some kinds of predictions easier to make than others. For example, it may be easier to sort handwriting samples into a few broad categories (e.g., psychotic, neurotic, normal) than to predict ratings of specific personality traits. However, if the sorting categories used represent an extreme contrast (e.g., between hospitalized psychotic patients and normal, healthy people), graphologists might be able to reach a high level of sorting accuracy simply by attending to gross signs of abnormality. The usefulness of an analytic system lies, however, not in its ability to distinguish extremes but in its ability to distinguish groups or individuals who are fairly similar to each other. Furthermore, sorting procedures can be carried out without specifying the bases on which the handwriting samples are placed in one or another category, so it may not be possible to determine whether sorting is based on clearly identifiable and reproducible criteria or on global, nonspecific intuitions.

Similar drawbacks are found in matching procedures, another relatively crude approach to validation. A judge, for example, might be given handwriting samples and work samples from each of four employees, his task being to match the handwriting sample to the work sample produced by the same employee. In addition to the problems inherent in sorting procedures, matching procedures are further limited, because the judgments made are not independent of one another. With each match that is made, the number of work samples left to be matched is reduced, thus, a correct match increases the probability of further correct matches, and an incorrect match reduces the probability of further correct matches.

Even when such crude validation methods are used, graphologists have failed to distinguish themselves. In Frederick's study (1965), writing samples were sorted into two extreme categories: hospitalized psychotic patients and normal controls. He found that the sorting accuracy of an experienced graphologist was no better than that of an untrained undergraduate, even when the graphologist made use of the content of the writing samples, whereas a clinical psychologist achieved a significant level of accuracy. The poor performance of the graphologist in this study echoes similar findings from a study by Pascal and Suttell (1947), in which the task was to discriminate psychotic from normal subjects.

More recently, Zdep and Weaver (1967) reported that the Graphoanalysts in their study were inaccurate in sorting the handwriting samples of successful and poor salesmen. Jansen (1973) also used a two-category sorting procedure in his studies, and he found that, with practice, graphologists, psychologists, and laymen alike could sort with an accuracy better than chance, but they were not accurate enough for the procedure to be used on an individual basis. This raises an important point: a method may show statistically significant results for *groups* of individuals, but the effects may be so small as to preclude its use in making predictions for a *particular* individual. In other words, an effect may be statistically significant but clinically insignificant, a common problem in personality assessment research. The literature dealing with the issue of effect size in graphology is reviewed by Dean in this volume (chap. 12).

Nevo (1989) used an improved matching procedure, in which close friends of ten writers were asked to match the handwriting samples of their friends to the interpretations derived from them, and then to rank the accuracy of their matches. Although Nevo reported positive findings, he warned that "Significant as the results of the matching were, it does not seem that the validity of the graphological analysis was very high. On the basis of these findings the practical application of graphology as a single psychodiagnostic tool cannot, in fact, be recommended: too many 'misses' are involved and the probability of getting a distorted personality description is too high" (1989, 1335). To date, sorting and matching approaches to handwriting validation have failed to show that sorting, even into extreme groups, can be made at an acceptable level of validity.

Predictions from handwriting samples to rating scores on specified dimensions of behavior are to be preferred to the use of matching or sorting techniques, because they allow for a more finely differentiated set of comparisons and for more sophisticated data analysis. Whereas sorting judgments are limited to inclusion or exclusion from several broad categories, ratings can cover a wider range of variation that reflects greater subtlety in human behavior. They are not without their disadvantages, however. The rating scales which are used to generate the criterion scores must be designed well enough to allow for high interjudge reliability before the scores derived from them can be used to test the validity of handwriting judgments. Thus, if supervisor ratings of job performance are used as the criterion for handwriting judgments, it must be established in advance that supervisors use their rating scales with high levels of intra- and interjudge reliability. If this is not done, it is not possible to determine whether the results of a study reflect the low reliability of the rating scale or the low validity of the handwriting analysis, or both. Most of the graphological studies that have used rating scales as criteria have not documented the rater reliability of the rating scales they have used. Nevertheless, these studies are worth considering.

Eysenck (1948) asked a graphologist to predict two measures of neuroticism from 176 handwriting samples obtained from army hospital patients: a neuroticism rating based on aggregated psychological test scores and neuroticism identified in psychiatric diagnoses. The graphologist was able to predict the aggregated test scores at a statistically significant level, but not the diagnosis of neuroticism. Zdep and Weaver (1967) used thirteen ratings in their attempt to validate the use of Graphoanalysis for identifying competent life insurance salesmen. As noted earlier, they found no evidence of validity in two of three studies, and the modest level of validity they reported for the third study was in error (their two Graphoanalysts failed to detect half the members of a criterion group for whom correct detection had a probability of 50 percent, thus failing to achieve even chance levels of correct judgment).

In an informal account, Sonneman and Kernan (1962) reported that the ratings made by a graphologist of the work performance of executives correlated significantly (.36–.48) with ratings made by their supervisors. Unfortunately, their study was flawed in a number of respects (e.g., writing samples were taken from personnel files that may have contained biographical information; ratings were made by only one graphologist), so their results should be viewed with caution. Drory (1986) reported significant correlations on ten of thirteen scales between supervisor ratings of work performance and judgments of sixty script samples that had been evaluated by a single, experienced graphologist. This study suffers from the same shortcoming as the Sonneman and Kernan study. When judgments are made by a single graphologist, one never knows whether it is the graphological method or the special talents and skills of the graphologist that have been validated.

In an attempt to validate handwriting predictions of the work performance of real estate salesmen, Rafaeli and Klimoski (1983) used twenty experienced graphologists to predict ratings on ten dimensions and four objective sales productivity measures. None of the forty relevant correlations reached significance. Keinan, Barak, and Ramati (1984) used graphologists' ratings to predict success in officer training in Israel and found that both graphologists and psychologists were equally inaccurate in predicting from handwriting samples.

Wellingham-Jones (1989) attempted to identify specific script features and clusters of features that would discriminate successful from unsuccessful women (subjectively defined). She reported thirty-seven correct predictions out of a possible sixty, but she failed to control statistically for the large number of comparisons she made. Furthermore, most of the differences found, even the statistically significant ones, were too small to be useful for discriminating among the individual women in her study. A revised version of this study appears as chapter 15 of the present volume. Neter and Ben-Shakhar (1989) found in their meta-analysis that graphologists and nongraphologists were equally poor in predicting such things as work performance and socio-psychological attributes from handwriting samples. The performance of the graphologists in their study was even worse when they had to base their judgments on scripts lacking autobiographical content.

Nor does the accuracy of prediction improve if graphologists are allowed to define the qualities they feel are most appropriate for the ratings. In the study by Zdep and Weaver (1967), graphoanalysts specified thirteen personality traits that they believed to be important for work in life insurance sales. When their ratings on these scales were compared with actual sales performance, no significant correlations were found. The graphoanalysts then studied the writing samples of the top three salesmen in order to identify important script features associated with the success. Using these features, they tried to select successful salesmen from the remaining pool of subjects, again without success. Finally, they identified script features associated with failure from the scripts of four failing salesmen and again searched the scripts of the remaining forty-six salesmen to identify successes and failures (i.e., those above and those below the cutoff point on the three traits associated with failure). Less than 50 percent of the actual failures were correctly identified, even though a hit rate of 50 percent would have been expected on the basis of chance. Thus, even when the graphologists were able to define their own criteria, the accuracy of their predictions did not reach acceptable levels.

A number of investigators have assessed the validity of handwriting analysis by examining the relationship between graphological judgments and scores obtained from psychological tests. One disadvantage that graphologists may report in using psychological test scores as validity criteria is that they require the use of psychological concepts or personality traits that are not commonly used by handwriting analysts, a problem previously noted when ratings are used as validity criteria. Graphologists may thus be forced to adapt their interpretations to categories that seem to be artificial or unnatural. Low levels of association between graphological analyses and psychological test scores may then be attributed to these conceptual problems rather than the inaccuracy of graphological analysis.

The extensive procedures previously described for validating psychological tests of personality have not been used in assessing the validity of handwriting analysis. Nor do graphological systems provide tables of normative scores with which the handwriting analyst can determine where in the range of observed handwriting features the handwriting features of each individual can be placed. There are, however, a number of studies that have attempted to relate the results of handwriting analyses to scores from well-established psychological tests.

A few studies have shown significant correlations between handwriting analyses and performance on standard personality tests. Linton, Epstein, and Hartford (1962) reported significant relationships between the use of a particular beginning stroke and a number of psychological test indices of social conformity. As noted earlier, however, their research was seriously flawed. In 1971, Lemke and Kirchner used fifty-nine specific script features to predict personality and mental ability measures from psychological tests. They reported "slightly significant" results for some measures and a significant correlation between vertical size of script and extroversion. Their results are problematic because they found only ten significant relationships from a total of 160 prediction formulas, a result no better than chance. Similarly, Williams, Berg-Cross, and Berg-Cross (1977) reported correlations between several graphic features and extroversion, introversion, and reflectivity, but they were unable to confirm other predicted relationships, and their study was compromised by the use of a sample that was too small for the analysis that was done.

In contrast to these (flawed) studies that report modest evidence for the concurrent validity of handwriting analyses with psychological tests, numerous other studies have been unable to document significant correlations between graphologists' conclusions and psychological test scores. Jansen (1973) found no significant correlations between graphological judgments and either a composite psychological test score or a personnel rating score. Vestewig, Santee, and Moss (1976) were unable to find significant correlations between the judgments of six graphoanalysts and fifteen variables on the Edwards Personal Preference Schedule. Similarly, Lester and McLaughlin (1976) and Lester, McLaughlin, and Nosal (1977) were unable to show significant correlations between graphological analyses and test scores of neuroticism and extroversion.

Extroversion became a popular trait for study by graphologists, following the early research by Cohen (1973), which suggested that it might be readily identified by handwriting analysis. Rosenthal and Lines (1978) were unable to find evidence of a connection between three script features and extroversion as measured by the Eysenck Personality Inventory. Furnham and Gunter (1987) studied three script features commonly identified in graphology texts as indicators of extroversion. They found a high level of interjudge reliability (.89) on the scoring of these features, but the predicted relationships to extroversion were not found, and in the matrix correlating thirteen theoretically important script features and four scores from the Eysenck Personality Questionnaire (EPQ), fewer correlations were significant than would be expected by chance.

Eysenck and Gudjonsson (1986) attempted to relate graphoanalystic predictions to scores on the EPQ, but they found a significant relationship for only one of four measures, Karnes and Leonard (chap. 16 in this volume) used an unusual validation procedure, in which they obtained judgments of colleagues from individuals who had known them for a long time and then had each person select the graphological reports that they believed were accurate descriptions of themselves and of their colleagues. They found that the frequency with which participants selected graphological reports as true was no greater than chance. In contrast, reports based on valid psychological tests are generally identified correctly at rates significantly better than chance.

In summary: the results of the many studies conducted to date provide little evidence for the validity of handwriting analysis as a means of assessing personality and predicting behavior. For the most part, these studies have shown little relationship between the results of graphological analyses and: (1) actual behavior, such as sales performance or success in training programs; (2) subjective ratings of work performance or psychological attributes; or (3) objective, reliable, and valid measures obtained from psychological tests. The few studies that do report significant relationships are, unfortunately, so flawed in research design that we can accept their findings only with serious reservations.

Despite the empirical evidence, reviewers who favor graphology often come to conclusions at variance with the very evidence they have reviewed. For example, Lockowandt (1976) examined a wealth of evidence concerning the reliability and validity of handwriting analysis and concluded that "The results of validity studies correlating individual characteristics with criteria are predominantly negative" (p. 28). Nevertheless, he ended his report on a hopeful note, suggesting that the particular graphologists used in validation studies may have been a major source of the difficulty in demonstrating validity, rather than the graphology method itself.

While differences among graphologists may indeed be part of the explanation, it is important to remember from the studies reviewed earlier that trained graphologists did not produce more accurate judgments or predictions than did untrained judges. Thus, lack of training in the techniques of graphology does not appear to be responsible for the failure to establish validity, although other significant differences among graphologists may be a contributing factor. Also, research that has investigated the possible role of other mitigating factors (such as type of validation procedure used, types of personality traits to be identified, or types of behavior to be predicted) have failed to identify a set of conditions under which graphological judgments have consistently proved valid.

Our reading of the empirical evidence, therefore, compels us to the conclusion that the ability of handwriting analysis to identify personality characteristics or to predict individual behavior has not been demonstrated.

REFERENCES

Allport, G. W., and P. E. Vernon. 1933. *Studies in Expressive Movement.* New York: Macmillan.

Bem, D. J., and A. Allen. 1974. "On Predicting Some of the People Some of the time: The Search for Cross-Situational Consistencies in Behavior." *Psychological Review* 81: pp. 506–520.

Ben-Shakhar, G., M. Bar-Hillel, Y. Bilu, E. Ben-Abba, and A. Flug. 1986. "Can Graphology Predict Occupational Success? Two Empirical Studies and Some Methodological Ruminations." *Journal of Applied Psychology* 71: pp. 645–653.

Block, J. 1971. *Lives through Time.* Berkeley, Calif.: Bancroft.

Blum, M. L., and B. Balinky. 1951. *Counselling and Psychology.* Englewood Cliffs, N.J.: Prentice Hall.

Boring, E. G., ed. 1950. *A History of Experimental Psychology.* New York: Appleton-Century-Crafts.

Campbell, D. P. 1971. *Handbook for the Strong Vocational Interest Blank.* Stanford, Calif.: Stanford University Press.

———. 1977. *Manual for the Strong-Campbell Interest Inventory.* Stanford, Calif.: Stanford University Press.

Campbell, D. T., and D. W. Fiske. 1959. "Convergent and Discriminant Validation by the Multitrait-Multimethod Matrix." *Psychological Bulletin* 56: pp. 81–105.

Cohen, R. 1973. *Patterns of Personality Judgment* trans. D. Schaeffer. New York: Academic Press.

Costa, P. T., and R. R. McRae. 1985. "Concurrent Validation After 20 Years: The Implications of Personality Stability for Its Assessment." In *Advances in Personality Assessment,* edited by J. Butler and C. D. Spielberger. Vol. 4. Hillside, N.J.: Lawrence Erlbaum Associates.

Crumbaugh, J. C. 1977a. "A reply to 'Validity and Student Acceptance of a Graphoanalytic Approach to Personality' by Vestewig, Santee, and Moss." *Journal of Personality Assessment* 41: pp. 351–352.

———. 1977b. "Comment on the Graphological Studies of Lester, McLaughlin and Nosal." *Perceptual and Motor Skills* 45: p. 494.

Dahlstrom, W. G., G. S. Welsh, and L. E. Dahlstrom. 1972. *An MMPI Handbook.* Vol. 1, revised. Minneapolis: University of Minnesota Press.

Drory, A. 1986. "Graphology and Job Performance: A Validation Study." In *Scientific Aspects of Graphology,* edited by B. Nevo, pp. 165–174. Springfield, Ill.: Charles C. Thomas.

Epstein, S. 1979. "The Stability of Behavior: I. On Predicting Most of the People Much of the Time." *Journal of Personality and Social Psychology* 37: pp. 1097–1126.

———. 1980. "The Stability of Behavior: II. Implications for Psychological Research." *American Psychologist* 35: pp. 790–806.

Exner, J. E. 1974. *The Rorschach: A Comprehensive System.* Vol. 1. New York: Wiley.

Eysenck, H. 1948. "Neuroticism and Handwriting." *Journal of Abnormal and Social Psychology* 43: pp. 94–96.

Eysenck, H. J., and G. Gudjonsson, 1986. "An Empirical Study of the Validity of Handwriting Analysis." *Personality and Individual Differences* 7: pp. 263–264.

Farberow, N. N. 1981. "Assessment of Suicide." In *Advances in Psychological Assessment.* Vol. 5, edited by P. P. McReynolds. San Francisco: Josey Bass.

Festinger, L. 1957. *A Theory of Cognitive Dissonance.* Evanston, Ill.: Row, Peterson.

Fluckiger, F., C. A. Tripp, and G. H. Weinberg. 1961. "A Review of Experimental Research in Graphology, 1933–1960." *Perceptual and Motor Skills* 12: pp. 67–90 (Monograph Supplement 1-V12).

Frederick, C. J. 1965. "Some Phenomena Affecting Handwriting Analysis." *Perceptual and Motor Skills* 20: pp. 211–218.

Furnham, A. 1986. "Response Bias, Social Desirability and Dissimulation." *Personality and Individual Differences* 7: pp. 385–400.

Furnham, A., and B. Gunter, 1987. "Graphology and Personality: Another Failure to Validate Graphological Analysis." *Personality and Individual Differences* 8: pp. 433–435.

Galbraith, D., and W. Wilson. 1964. "Reliability of the Graphoanalytical approach to Handwriting Analysis." *Perceptual and Motor Skills* 19: pp. 615–618.

Guilford, J. P. 1959. *Personality*. New York: McGraw.

Gough, H. G. 1957. *The California Psychological Inventory*. Palo Alto, Calif.: Consulting Psychologists Press.

Jansen, A. 1973. *Validation of Graphological Judgements: An Experimental Study*. Paris: Mouton.

Kangas, J., and K. Bradway. 1971. "Intelligence at Middle Age: A Thirty-eight Year Follow-up." *Developmental Psychology* 8: pp. 506–520.

Keinan, G., A. Barak, and T. Ramati. 1984. "Reliability and Validity of Graphological Assessment in the Selection Process of Military Officers." *Perceptual and Motor Skills* 58: pp. 811–821.

Kenrick, D. T., and D. C. Funder. 1988. "Profit from Controversy." *American Psychologist* 43: pp. 23–34.

Klimoski, R. J., and A. Rafaeli. 1983. "Inferring Personal Qualities through Handwriting Analysis." *Journal of Occupational Psychology* 56: pp. 191–202.

Klopfer, B., M. D. Ainsworth, W. G. Klopfer, and R. C. Holt. 1954. *Developments in the Rorschach Technique*. New York: Harcourt, Brace & World.

Knox, W. J., and R. Grippaldi. 1970. "High Levels of State or Trait Anxiety and Performance in Selected Verbal WAIS Subtests." *Psychological Reports* 27: pp. 375–379.

Lemke, E. A., and J. H. Kirchner. 1971. "A Multivariate Study of Handwriting, Intelligence and Personality Correlates." *Journal of Personality Assessment* 35: pp. 584–592.

Lester, D., and S. McLaughlin. 1976. "Sex-deviant Handwriting and Neuroticism." *Perceptual and Motor Skills* 43: p. 770.

Lester, D., S. McLaughlin, and G. Nosal, 1977. "Graphological Signs for Extroversion." *Perceptual and Motor Skills* 44: pp. 137–138.

Lezak, M. 1983. *Neuropsychological Assessment*. 2nd ed. New York: Oxford University Press.

Linton, H. B., L. Epstein, and H. Hartford. 1962. "Personality and Perceptual Correlates of Primary Beginning Strokes in Handwriting." *Perceptual and Motor Skills* 15: pp. 159–170.

Lockowandt, O. 1976. "Present Status of the Investigation of Handwriting Psychology as a Diagnostic Method." *J.S.A.S. Catalogue of Selected Documents in Psychology* 6(1): p. 4.

Lombroso, C. 1891. *The Man of Genius*. London: W. Scott; New York: Scribner.

Mischel, W. 1968. *Personality and Assessment*. New York: Wiley.

———. 1976. *Introduction to Personality*. 2nd ed. New York: Holt, Rinehart & Winston.

Mischel, W. 1984. "Convergences and Challenges in the Search for Consistency." *American Psychologist* 39: pp. 351–364.

Moore, M. 1985. "About the Sad State of Scientific Graphology." *Psychological Documents* 15(2): p. 2676.

Moss, H. A., and E. J. Susman. 1980. "Longitudinal Study of Personality Development." In *Constancy and Change in Human Development,* edited by O. G. Brim and J. Kagan, pp. 530–595. Cambridge, Mass.: Harvard University Press.

Mulvey, E. P., and C. W. Lidz. 1985. "A Critical Analysis of Dangerous Research in a New Legal Environment." *Law and Human Behavior* 9: pp. 209–219.

Murray, H. A. 1943. *Thematic Apperception Test Manual.* Cambridge, Mass.: Harvard University Press.

Neter. E., and G. Ben-Shakhar, 1989. "The Predictive Validity of Graphological Inferences: A Meta-Analytic Approach." *Personality and Individual Differences* 10: pp. 737–745.

Nevo, B. 1989. "Validation of Graphology through Use of a Matching Method Based on Ranking." *Perceptual and Motor Skills* 69: pp. 1331–1336.

Pascal, G. R., and B. Suttell. 1947. "Testing the Claims of a Graphologist." *Journal of Personality* 16: pp. 192–197.

Rafaeli, A., and A. Drory. 1988. "Graphological Assessments for Personnel Selection: Concerns and Suggestions for Research." *Perceptual and Motor Skills* 66: pp. 743–759.

Rafaeli, A., and R. J. Klimoski. 1983. "Predicting Sales Success through Handwriting Analysis: An Evaluation of the Effects of Training and Handwriting Sample Content." *Journal of Applied Psychology* 68: pp. 212–217.

Rorschach, H. 1942. *Psychodiagnostics,* translated by P. Lemkau and B. Kronenberg. New York: Grune & Stratton.

Rosenthal, D. A., and R. Lines. 1978. "Handwriting as a Correlate of Extroversion." *Journal of Personality Assessment* 42: pp. 45–48.

Saudek, R. 1929. *Experiments with Handwriting.* New York: William Morrow.

Sears, R. R. 1977. "Sources of Life Satisfaction of the Terman Gifted Men." *American Psychologist* 32: pp. 119–128.

Snyder, C. R. 1974. "Why Horoscopes Are True: The Effects of Specificity on Acceptance of Astrological Interpretations." *Journal of Clinical Psychology* 30: pp. 577–580.

Sonneman, U., and J. P. Kernan. 1962. "Handwriting Analysis—A Valid Selection Tool?" *Personnel* (Nov.–Dec.): pp. 8–14.

Sovik, N., O. Arntzen, and R. Thygesen. 1986. "Effects of Feedback." In *Graphonomics: Contemporary Research in Handwriting,* edited by H. S. R. Kao, G. P. Van Galen, and R. Hoosain. Amsterdam: North-Holland.

Tallent, N. 1958. "On Individualizing the Psychologist's Clinical Evaluation." *Journal of Clinical Psychology* 14: pp. 243–244.

Vestewig, R. E., A. H. Santee, and M. K. Moss. 1976. "Validity and Student Acceptance of a Graphoanalytic Approach to Personality." *Journal of Personality*

Assessment 40: pp. 592–597.

Wellingham-Jones, P. 1989. "Evaluation of the Handwriting of Successful Women through the Roman-Staempfli Psychogram." *Perceptual and Motor Skills* 69: pp. 999–1010.

Wiggins, J. S. 1973. *Personality and Prediction.* Reading, Mass.: Addison-Wesley.

Williams, M., G. Berg-Cross, and L. Berg-Cross. 1977. "Handwriting Characteristics and Their Relationship to Eysenck's Extroversion-Introversion and Kagan's Impulsivity-Reflectivity Dimensions." *Journal of Personality Assessment* 41: pp. 291–298.

Zdep, S. M., and H. B. Weaver. 1967. "The Graphoanalytic Approach to Selecting Life Insurance Salesmen." *Journal of Applied Psychology* 51: pp. 295–299.

11

Graphology and Personnel Selection

Richard J. Klimoski

Richard Klimoski begins this chapter by discussing what a consultant advising in the area of personnel selection must determine *before* testing of applicants can begin. Assembling a detailed *job description* is the consultant's first task, in order to identify the precise traits that are relevant to the job. After reading Klimoski's account of the complexity of this preliminary stage, the reader may wish to contrast this standard procedure among industrial psychologists with the *processual validation* approach suggested by Oskar Lockowandt in chapter 6. Nevertheless, the reader might ask whether the problems Dr. Lockowandt addresses in his chapter would arise in the first place if graphologists carefully and routinely followed the procedures described by Dr. Klimoski herein.

In the second part of his chapter, Klimoski reviews the accepted standards of industrial/organizational psychologists for determining the appropriateness of any personnel selection tool. The reader may wish to look also at Marilyn Bowman's treatment in chapter 10 of similar issues in the development of personality measures. Note that the standards Dr. Klimoski advocates in this chapter are the ones shared, in principle, by all the contributors to this volume—both graphologists and their critics. The dispute between the two groups really comes down to whether or not graphology meets these standards.

In his final section, Klimoski applies these standards to graphology. He cites a number of studies that test how well graphology meets these standards, including two studies conducted by himself and Anat Rafaeli, a practicing graphologist.

Note that scientific personnel selection employs multiple convergent measures and an ethical consultant would virtually never base a decision on a single indicator, graphology or any other.

INTRODUCTION

This chapter examines the application of graphology to personnel decisions in work organizations. Its focus is on the extent to which graphology is capable of assisting managers and personnel specialists in predicting and understanding performance on the job. In the context of personnel selection, this usually means trying to estimate the likely success of people who are applying for work. The overarching goal of the chapter is to prepare the reader to make more informed choices when offered graphological services in the personnel arena.

The main premise of the chapter is that, when offered for use in work organizations, graphological services should be viewed as any other potential device or program (e.g., selection testing or interviews) and subject to the same scrutiny. Thus, the first part of the chapter reviews the basic logic of personnel decision making. This will provide the context for comparing graphology. The second section will describe the standards that human resource specialists use to evaluate the appropriateness of any personnel selection device (including graphology). The third section reviews the evidence regarding the usefulness of graphology for personnel selection in light of these standards. A final section presents conclusions and offers recommendations for both proponents and opponents of graphological applications to personnel work.

THE NATURE OF PERSONNEL SELECTION

Scientifically based personnel selection principles have been available for over 70 years. By the second decade in this century in the United States, industrial/organizational psychologists such as Munsterberg (1913) and Scott (1911) were working with a variety of companies to improve the accuracy of personnel selection. Scott was later to use his expertise in advising the U.S. military during the First World War on the processing and screening of over 1,700,000 men. In the years since, a great deal of empirical research has been carried out on approaches to personnel selection. Moreover, a great deal of practical wisdom has also accumulated. Thus, by the 1980s, Schmidt, Hunter, and their colleagues (Schmidt and Hunter, 1981; Schmidt, Hunter, McKenzie, and Muldrow, 1979; Schmidt, Hunter, and Pearlman, 1982) were able to point out both the real (i.e., scientifically established) and financial benefits of systematic, professionally based personnel selection practices. For details, see Schmitt, Neal, and Klimoski (1991).

THE LOGIC OF PERSONNEL SELECTION

The logic of personnel selection is based on the very nature of modern complex organizations and on the notion of division of labor and job responsibilities (specialization) that has evolved over the years. It is also related to the practicalities and logistics of recruiting and hiring people.

Worker Requirements. Modern organizations, whether large or small, public sector or private enterprise, generally reflect the fact that products or services can best be produced or delivered if specific individuals are assigned to particular duties or tasks. Once assigned, various individuals' work activities or products are then integrated or coordinated by management policies or rules. The division of labor and the amount of specialization will vary, of course, and will depend upon such things as the particular goods or services involved, the tools or technology required, and, especially, management's beliefs about individual workers' capabilities and needs. As a result, in most organizations, different people do different things. To perform well at these various tasks, individuals must have appropriate capacities or capabilities. These factors are usually referred to as worker requirements.

Whether the job involved is that of a salesperson or a neurosurgeon, there will be a set of worker requirements. These include the knowledge, skills, abilities, needs, motives, and personality dispositions needed to perform. In other words, these are the important attributes of the people who are likely to be successful on the job.

There will be differences as to just which worker requirements are important from job to job. Some jobs place a heavy intellectual demand on incumbents. Others emphasize physical capacities or strong interpersonal skills. This means that, prior to recruiting or selecting individuals, personnel psychologists, or anyone else in the human resource area, must establish the particular set of requirements involved.

The preferred starting point for identifying worker requirements is to conduct a job analysis. There are a variety of ways to do this (Levine et al., 1983) but usually it involves a personnel specialist who will observe workers performing the job in question, examine the content of the job, conduct interviews with workers and their bosses, and occasionally make use of a specially constructed questionnaire to be completed by incumbents. A good job analysis is systematic, makes use of a variety of techniques, and is carried out by a qualified individual. The objective is to get as complete and valid a picture of a job as possible. Without this, efforts to recruit and select people will be seriously flawed.

The output of a job analysis is both a complete job description and a list of worker requirements. The former tells us what the person does on the job. The latter, as noted, are insights as to what it takes to do the job well.

Worker requirements can take various forms. They can involve particular types of knowledge, skills, or abilities, or they might reflect key aptitudes needed to attain or develop the former (through training or supervision).

In addition, requirements may include particular interests, values, needs, or motives. Thus, they describe the type of personality necessary to do the job on a day-to-day basis. An important point to remember is that worker requirements are determined by the type of work to be performed. They will exist and affect the likely success of individuals, whether we try to uncover them or not. The prudent organization usually makes an effort to get at them systematically.

Although a wide variety of worker requirements has been identified, for purposes of this chapter, it will be convenient to cluster them into two types. Personnel specialists often distinguish between what might be called "can do" requirements vs. "will do" requirements (Porter, Lawler, and Hackman, 1975). As you might surmise, the "can do" requirements are the knowledge, skills, and abilities which determine whether or not a person is likely to be ABLE to do the job, assuming that he or she puts out the necessary effort. This can be thought of as the capacity to perform. In fact, "can do" requirements limit the potential of an individual for effective job performance in important ways.

In contrast, other characteristics might be important for success because they determine how motivated a person is likely to be if placed on the job. Extensive research has established that interests, values, or needs must be fulfilled on the job for people to be motivated (Wanous, 1980). Thus, "will do" requirements describe the potential of the job to satisfy certain needs or, alternatively, the needs of certain types of individuals.

Any given job will typically have a mixture of "can do" and "will do" requirements. To be effective, a newly hired person will usually have to meet both criteria. In other words, if a person can't do the job (for lack of ability) it is unlikely that high levels of motivation alone will be sufficient. And, as you might expect, even if the individual does have the ability to do the job, he or she may not demonstrate the motivation or the inclination to do the job once placed there. There is ample evidence that fully capable individuals, hired into a job which fails to meet their needs, are very likely to quit in short order (Wanous, 1980).

MEASURING WORKER REQUIREMENTS

In staffing positions in work organizations, in general, we usually attempt first to establish the nature of worker requirements and then find ways of measuring both capacity and motivational requirements. Over the years, personnel specialists have developed different ways of measuring or estimating the extent to which applicants meet or exceed job requirements. Some of these approaches are more appropriate for assessing a candidate's capabilities, others his or her needs and values. Figure 1 lists some examples.

Type of Information Obtained	Type of Measure
Maximum Performance "Can Do"	Cognitive Tests Aptitude Tests Work Sample Tests Physical Ability Tests Assessment Centers
Both	Employment Interview Reference Checks
Typical Behavior "Will Do"	Biographical Data Personality Measures

Fig. 1. Measuring worker requirements.

A common approach to the "can do" assessments is to use what are called work samples and work sample tests. When staffing the position of a graphic artist or illustrator, we often ask to see the artist's previous work or portfolio. If most applicants are presumed to have relatively little actual job experience, the personnel specialist might design and develop a work sample test to get at key aptitudes (e.g., color perception) or skills (e.g., use of water colors) or both (Campion, 1972). Work samples and work sample tests are designed to index the candidates' capacity to perform important aspects of the job in question. Aptitude and ability tests are other common ways to measure capacity to perform.

The measurement of the candidate's suitability for a job in terms of needs and values has often involved the use of interest inventories and personality tests. In this regard, there are numerous standard measures that might be applied to the selection of personnel (e.g., the 16PF test). Occasionally, the job analysis might uncover special worker requirements for which there is no standard measure. Under these circumstances, professionals might be used to develop a new device. For example, Bernardin (1987) discovered that the job of telephone service representative required that the incumbent be able to tolerate a fair amount of pressure and hostility from irate customers (even verbal abuse). Because there was no standard measure for the personality that could deal with this kind of situation, he had to develop his own measure. This took the form of a self-report measure, part of which is reproduced in Figure 2.

Discomfort Sale

For each of the 20 sets of four situations listed, respondents were asked to circle the letters of the two situations—and only two—that would cause them the most aggravation or discomfort. Valid items are indicated with a (v).

1. a. You are shopping, can't find what you want and there isn't a salesperson in sight.
   b. You can't go out and party on weekends. (v)
   c. Having to listen to someone's point of view with which you disagree. (v)
   d. It rains the day you scheduled a picnic at the beach.
2. a. You must be indoors on a sunny day. (v)
   b. You are stood up for an appointment.
   c. You hear your neighbors argue. (v)
   d. You are the only employee to forget to get the boss a birthday card.
3. a. You are in an eight item express lane at the grocery and the person in front of you has 14 items.
   b. You have a long wait in a line before your number is called.
   c. Your boss yells at you about another person's mistake. (v)
   d. You have an 11:00 P.M. curfew on weekends. (v)
4. a. You are ill and have to miss work. You are docked for the time you missed. (v)
   b. A friend borrows something of yours and does not return it.
   c. You must get up at 6:00 A.M. and go to work. (v)
   d. The expressway is bumper to bumper and you are late for work.
5. a. You go to a theater and find the movie is sold out.
   b. You are required to work in a crowded, noisy room with no privacy. (v)
   c. Your work is closely monitored. (v)
   d. You are required to work in a room by yourself.
6. a. You are driving down the highway; someone cuts in front of you with only inches to spare.
   b. You work with someone who frequently uses obscenities. (v)
   c. Waiting at a railroad crossing for a long freight train.
   d. You have to repeat instructions several times. (v)
7. a. You have to be polite to a rude person. (v)
   b. Your charge account bill includes charges you did not make.
   c. Someone tries to tell you how to do something you know how to do very well.
   d. Circumstances require you to be indoors when you had scheduled a trip to the beach. (v)

Fig. 2.Assessing tolerance for stress in the job of a telephone customer service representative (from Bernardin, 1987).

Often, a given selection technique is used to get at a wide range of applicant qualifications. That is, it attempts to get at both the can do and will do aspects of the job. Thus, in most organizations, a selection interview is involved in the screening of candidates. In fact, in a carefully designed and conducted interview, a wide range of qualities may be assessed (Campion, Pursell, and Brown, 1988). An organization might use a test battery made up of different kinds of tests (ability and personality) to get at critical factors. Life history information (in the form of an application blank or a specially constructed questionnaire) and reference checks are also popular. When selecting from internal candidates, even co-worker descriptions have been found to be useful. All these approaches, when carefully developed and executed, have the potential to provide insights into both the capacity and the motivation of individuals.

One might consider graphology as a potential selection device, and apply the logic developed here. Based on the claims of proponents and current practices, it might best be classified as a way to assess personal dispositions and inclinations (i.e., the will do part of a person's qualifications). That is, graphology is frequently used as an attempt to get at a person's willingness to perform and the suitability of his or her temperament for the job. However, practitioners occasionally will use graphology in an attempt to index intellective qualities (e.g., critical thinking ability) as well. Other graphologists claim they can also predict absenteeism, pilfering, and drug use on the job.

ASSESSING THE SUITABILITY OF CANDIDATES

In practice, organizations stress key worker requirements in their advertisements for job openings and in their recruiting. By doing so, the goal is to generate sufficient interest among individuals who would potentially qualify as employees. The people who actually apply for the job are referred to as the applicant pool. If recruiting is successful, there will be many individuals in the applicant pool. A subset of these will indeed have the necessary qualifications. It is important that such a pool exists because the logic of personnel selection dictates that the organization must have the opportunity to pick and choose among individuals. They must have what is called a favorable selection ratio (number of job openings/number of applicants). To the extent that there are too few applicants, no selection device or program, no matter how good, will be of much use. The organization would have to take just about all of those available simply to have the jobs covered. Thus, in general, most companies will strive to enlarge the applicant pool as much as possible.

Assuming a favorable selection ratio, scientific selection procedures usually involve several phases. Each of these phases makes use of some assessment or screening mechanism; those candidates who compare favorably are then allowed to move up to the next phase. In this regard, the process is sequential and analogous to requiring a candidate to clear a number of hurdles before being given the status of a regular employee (see Fig. 3). To illustrate, one public utility company in the U.S. sends recruiters to college campuses to identify suitable candidates. In 1985 representatives of the company conducted 687 interviews (the first hurdle) at 14 schools. Out of this initial effort they found 220 acceptable. But for a variety of reasons (e.g., scheduling) only 50 were invited for a visit to the company's headquarters (a second hurdle). Fourteen individuals were offered a job. Once on the job, the new recruit would be reviewed and assessed each quarter (a third hurdle) and was only taken off probationary status (a fourth hurdle) after a period of 18–24 months.

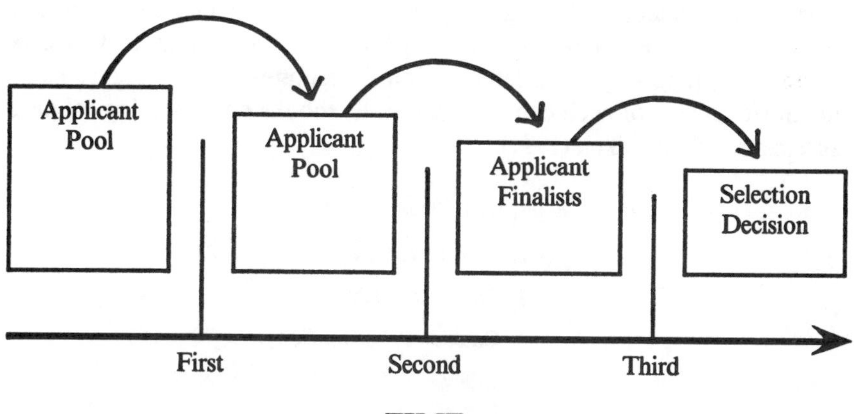

Fig. 3. Hurdles to overcome on the way to regular employee status.

Assessments at each point might involve any of a variety of tools or methods. In the example given, reference checks, resumes, tests, interviews, and ratings of on-the-job performance were all used at different stages in the process. To reiterate, the particular technique used at each hurdle was related to the worker requirements which had been previously identified as important to the job (in this case, being a manager). The stage in the sequence that a particular device was used was also determined (in part) by the belief that it was the best place to assess specific qualities with that technique. Thus, the organization in the example felt that certain skills (oral communications, decision making) and particular dispositions (being a self-starter, showing adaptability/flexibility) were basic to job performance in most jobs in the company. These were necessary (but not sufficient) qualities. Consequently, these were assessed early, at the time of the campus interview (and by relying on life history information, references, and insights gained in the interview itself). Only then did the company scrutinize the finalists for the characteristics important to specific jobs to be filled (usually during the visit to the job site).

ESTABLISHING THE USEFULNESS OF A SELECTION DEVICE

Prior to actually implementing a particular selection approach or adopting a specific device, it is important to establish that it will, in fact, be useful. This is the essence of personnel research in most organizations. Personnel specialists will do this by comparing what is known about the device to a set of standards. Several of these standards will be mentioned only briefly as they are detailed elsewhere in this book. Others will be given greater attention because they are somewhat peculiar to the personnel area. However, it is important to list them together as they will be applied to graphology in a later section. These are listed in Figure 4. Indepth treatments of each can be found in textbooks on psychological measurement such as Aiken (1991).

1. Reliability
2. Content Validity
3. Construct Validity
4. Criterion-Related Validity
5. Utility
6. Freedom from Bias
7. User Acceptance

Fig. 4. Establishing the usefulness of the selection device.

Reliability. The essence of reliability is consistency of measurement. More technically, reliability refers to the extent that data or information obtained with a particular measurement tool or selection device is free from errors (Schmitt, Neal, and Klimoski, 1991). There is a variety of ways to estimate reliability, several of which will be illustrated in a later section.

Content Validity. Whenever we want to be certain that a selection device is getting at all of the important worker requirements, we raise the issue of content validity. Technically, content validity refers to the degree to which the responses required by the test or measure are a representative sample of the whole domain of behaviors or knowledge of interest to us.

In the case of personnel selection, it means that we really are getting at the key traits or qualities needed for job performance.

Construct Validity. In many instances we assume that a selection device or measure is getting at some underlying theme, or, as professionals would call it, a "construct." Thus, an intelligence test is presumed to be measuring intelligence; an honesty test, honesty, and so on. Alternatively, an interview may or may not be used to assess the candidate's level or score on a construct. It would depend on what questions were asked and the kinds of inferences that are made. Establishing construct validity is somewhat of an inductive process whereby scores on a measure must be shown to relate in ways predicted by theory or logic to other scores or measures (Chronbach and Meehl, 1955). Equally important, a measure with good construct validity is expected to produce scores that are unrelated to other measures in a manner consistent with logic or theory. Thus, a valid measure of intelligence should produce scores that correlate with a standard or accepted measure of intelligence and, at the same time, be uncorrelated with measures of, say, physical strength.

Criterion-Related Validity. This refers to empirical evidence that the scores obtained with an assessment device are related to some important set of behaviors or some level of functioning. In personnel selection, persuasive evidence of criterion-related validity would be to show that scores on a selection device are, in fact, related to such things as job performance, regular work attendance, or longer job tenure.

Utility. Most selection devices are intended to be used for personnel decision making. The assumption is that by using the device, the organization is improving the likelihood that those people who are recommended for hire will be better than those who are rejected. But we expect even more. We assume that among those who are selected we will find a larger proportion of individuals who will be viewed as successful, once on the job, compared to what we are currently getting by using traditional methods. Utility refers to the extent that a measure does indeed fulfill this promise. We usually establish utility by demonstrating that we are making fewer selection errors by using the selection device than we would by not using it.

In personnel work there will always be some chance of making a decision error. No known system exists where this is not the case. In utility analysis, the particular kinds of errors made when using a selection device are examined.

There are two kinds of decision errors that may occur. One involves selecting someone for hire who, it is discovered later, is not a suitable employee. In fact, the individual may have to be fired. This kind of error is referred to as a "false positive" error. Alternatively, a manager or decision maker may, based on the evidence produced with a selection device, reject an individual who would have been a good employee. This is a "false negative" error.

An organization would have to determine which type of error is more important to avoid. This is, in part, a matter of business philosophy. But, it is also a matter of economics. That is to say, utility analysis will involve a computation of the expenses associated with recruiting, training, and terminating personnel relative to the benefits of average, below average, or superior performance from employees. It will also consider the "lost opportunity costs" of the excellent candidates who were turned away. Thus, a selection device with high utility is one that provides the appropriate balance between correct decisions with respect to these two types of errors (Schmitt, Neal, and Klimoski, 1991).

When selecting personnel, mistakes can indeed be costly. For example, a recent survey of U.S. personnel officers of large private companies revealed that, on average, it costs over $18,000 to dismiss an employee (Fowler, 1990). It is thus possible to estimate the money saved by using a particular device. However, a utility analysis would not only involve this figure (the benefits of avoiding mistakes) but also consideration of the actual expenses incurred in developing the measure and the recurring expenses associated with its use.

To be complete, estimating utility would also require us to consider the relative costs and benefits of alternatives. For instance, there might be some other, very inexpensive approach to selection that works almost as well.

Another aspect of cost/benefit analysis relates to just when in the selection process a given device might be used. That is to say, a more valid but expensive-to-administer device might be applied later in the recruiting/selection sequence where there are fewer candidates to consider (semi-finalists). A somewhat less valid, but very inexpensive measure might be administered at an earlier point as a screening device.

Freedom From Bias. In the United States today it is public policy to insure equal employment opportunities for all people, regardless of religion, gender, nationality, or ethnic background. It is also against the law to unfairly discriminate in employment practices. Thus, the impact of a selection device must be scrutinized to see if there are disproprtionate numbers of individuals in these protected classes who are adversely impacted (see chs. 17 and 18 for discussions of graphology in this context).

User Acceptance. Most of the standards listed, so far, have a strong technical component. In the case of user acceptance, we are simply stating that a selection device must be perceived as appropriate and fair to the people involved. This would include the larger pool of job applicants, those people ultimately hired, the current workers and managers of the organization, as well as the personnel specialists involved (recruiters, trainers). User acceptance is very often a function of the care taken in the development of the device. It is affected by the kind of evidence (quality and quantity) that exists for its validity. But, perceptions of fairness and appropriateness will also be related to how and by what means the selection tool was implemented or put into practice. Unilateral imposition of new hiring standards and/or the use of a particular screening program (e.g., drug testing via urine samples) is likely to reduce acceptance, irrespective of whatever validity or utility evidence exists.

The foregoing standards can be applied to any potential personnel-selection device or program. Usually, all would be relevant to some degree. An exception might be where we are not concerned with personnel constructs. Under these circumstances we would have less interest in construct validity. We might substitute instead evidence of content or criterion-related validity.

GRAPHOLOGY AND PERSONNEL SELECTION

After reviewing the claims of graphology with respect to personnel decisions and some of the assumptions made in its application to personnel work, its status will be assessed by applying the standards that have just been outlined. The emphasis will be on making use of research evidence published in refereed scientific journals (as opposed to personal testimonials, self-published promotional materials, or articles in journals in which authors can place anything by paying a fee).

CLAIMS OF THE PROPONENTS OF GRAPHOLOGY

Graphology has been proposed for or used in most areas of human endeavor. Klimoski and Rafaeli (1983) reviewed published research on the application of graphology to the areas of mental health, personality assessment, and intelligence measurement. Other chapters in this book attest to the variety of contexts in which it has been used. This section will focus on its use in personnel work and especially employee selection.

Applications to Personnel Work. As early as 1965, Thayer and Antoinetti reported that the insurance industry in the U.S. was experimenting with the use of handwriting analysis in personnel work. Jaekle (1974) lists several major U.S. firms (such as GE, Firestone, U.S. Steel, Southern Bell, and even the IRS) as involved with the practice. Somewhat later, Levy (1979) estimated that over 3,000 American firms had made use of graphology in personnel matters. He also wrote that 85 percent of all European companies routinely consider the recommendations of handwriting experts. Radar (1988) describes applications by a personnel search firm (Dunhill, in Boston) and a Houston-based firm (Greensheet, Inc.). Arnett (1989) reports on the use of handwriting analysis in the auto rental business (Thrifty Rent-a-Car). He also feels that there is increasing interest in handwriting analysis in personnel work as a result of the U.S. government's restrictions on the use of the polygraph in pre-employment screening.

It should be noted, however, that the claims regarding the extent and location of use of graphology are most often found in the popular press and such claims are often based only on opinions of those being interviewed. To put it another way, at this time there is very little in the way of systematic and documented evidence on prevalence of usage. It is fair to say, however, that the perception exists among many authors and managers that the application of handwriting analysis to personnel work is widespread.

The actual purpose for using handwriting analysis in personnel matters seems to be quite varied, at least if you take popular reports at face value. Shiela Kurtz, a graphologist practicing in New York City, is reported to offer services to screen job candidates, evaluate employees for promotion, determine an individual's compatibility for particular settings or assignments, and evaluate individuals as credit risks (Anonymous, 1979). Arnett (1989) sees applications of graphology to the assessment of job-relevant personality traits, the identification of a candidate's strengths and weaknesses, establishing the overall suitability of an individual for a job, and the estimating of risk or propensity to health disorders. Lynch (1985) concurs with the above lists of applications and includes most of them in his essay.

When it comes to charging for these services, the price appears to vary widely. Taylor and Sackheim (1988) report a cost of $30 to $300 per assessment. Gorman (1989) cites a range from $100-$500 per case. Arnett (1989) offers the largest variability of fees from $25-$1,000, depending on the amount of detail required.

It would seem reasonable that charges for graphological services to organizations could differ considerably. Personnel assessments using other, more traditional approaches (e.g., multi-aptitude test batteries) also vary in their costs to organizations. Charges usually depend on such factors as the quality or reputation of the firm supplying the assessments, the skill level of the individuals actually providing the analysis, the number of cases involved (there is usually a volume discount), the amount of detail requested by the company, the type of personnel (e.g., sales, management) to be assessed (and hence the risks associated with making a decision error), and the speed of reporting needed (there is usually a premium for rapid turn-around). Thus, costs for traditional assessments can range from $5 a case (for a self-administered, computer-scored, pre-qualifying quiz used in large numbers) to $2,000 (where a specially developed Assessment Center program is involved).

The wide variety of applications of graphology notwithstanding, the usual focus is the assessment of personality traits or dispositions. The review by Klimoski and Rafaeli (1983) uncovered an emphasis on the use of graphology to estimate such traits as determination, diplomacy, initiative, energy level, passivity, empathy, and sales drive. Braverman (1986) adds to this list such qualities as intuition, fluidity of expression, ambition, determination, susceptibility to influence, fear of failure, shallowness, and self-deception. Gorman (1989) stresses the use of handwriting analysis to assess honesty or dishonesty, although he refers to the possible detection of 20 different personal characteristics. Finally, Radar (1988) reports that there are potentially 300 traits that can be measured through handwriting.

In summary, graphology is used in support of a wide variety of personnel matters, but especially in screening applicants. Its costs vary considerably. But the focus is usually on the measurement of personal traits.

Working Assumptions. When graphology is used in personnel selection, there are a number of implicit or explicit assumptions that are made by proponents. At this point, it might be appropriate to review these briefly.

The most fundamental assumption is discussed throughout this book. That is, it is believed by proponents and disputed by skeptics that an individual's nature or personal qualities are reflected in handwriting. Proponents also believe that individuals trained in graphology can infer these traits from an analysis of handwriting. However, in applying graphology to the personnel area, additional things are assumed.

The first is that *job-relevant* traits or qualities are among those revealed in handwriting. Thus, the manager seeking advice from a graphologist usually wants insights with regard to a particular set of traits. These are what we have been calling worker requirements. A second assumption is that it is possible to estimate with some degree of accuracy a person's standing or "score" on each of these worker requirements. That is, it's not sufficient merely to determine that a person does or does not possess a particular quality, but it is necessary to know that he or she has more of certain qualities than others (or, at least, enough to do the job well). Proponents also believe that graphologists, as personnel consultants, have a good idea of how requirements combine to comprise the criterion behaviors of interest. To phrase it differently, they know what combination of qualities, and what particular levels of these qualities produce (for instance) good performance on the job. Finally, given that these key traits are estimated for a candidate, it is assumed that the graphologist can integrate the assessments in such a manner so as to accurately predict some criterion (job performance, absenteeism, theft, or likely job tenure).

When and Where Is Graphology Used? Personnel decision making has been characterized as a multistage or multiple-hurdle process. Candidates for jobs are usually evaluated at several points before they are given a job offer. A given selection device can be used at any stage of this process. Despite all that is written on handwriting analysis in the workplace, it is not clear just when and where in the sequence of things the graphologist gets involved. Yet, this would seem to be important not only to the graphologist but also to evaluating the impact of his or her service.

This point might be clarified by considering alternative scenarios. It is possible for the graphologist to be contracted to produce an initial screening of applicants. He or she would see script samples from all applicants for a job. The effective task here is, essentially, to eliminate those candidates who are not worthy of further consideration. All that's required is a fairly coarse estimate of the requisite traits or qualities. Alternatively, the graphologist might be asked to evaluate the finalists in the competition for a job. Here it is necessary to make fine-grained distinctions regarding the key traits. This is because the finalists are likely to be fairly similar in their qualifications.

These two situations also differ with regard to the amount of information available to the graphologist. While it is true that many graphologists claim to consider only the nature (not the content) of the candidate's handwriting sample, consultants to organizations usually have access to other records (Taylor and Sackhiem, 1988; Radar, 1988). In an extreme case, the graphologist, as personnel consultant, might not only have access to the candidate's application materials, but know something about the hiring manager's impressions, even his or her preferences among candidates. Thus, the assessments provided to the organization and the recommendations or predictions made regarding future job success could easily become affected by (or even based on) this extra-script information. When and how graphologists are used as consultants will affect the way we might want to evaluate the usefulness of graphology itself in the context of personnel work.

THE USEFULNESS OF GRAPHOLOGY IN PERSONNEL SELECTION

It is unfortunate that we have so little representative descriptive data on the actual practice of graphology in industry. Thus, the critique offered below will be based on research which has focused on looking at graphology in isolation, where inferences made from script samples alone have been studied. The evidence that is reported in scientific journals and reviewed here is, at most, relevant to establishing the potential value of graphology. It has less to say about the actual impact of graphological consulting, where other information may be available to the practitioner.

The evidence relative to the usefulness of graphology to personnel work will be organized around the standards described in an earlier section of this chapter. As will become clear, we really have very little good research on graphology in many key areas.

RESEARCH EVIDENCE ON RELIABILITY OF GRAPHOLOGICAL INFERENCES

Reliability is a necessary attribute for measurement in any area. In personnel research and practice, levels of reliability effectively set limits to the usefulness of a selection device. Operationally, lack of reliability makes a measure worthless. We would not be able to take scores or recommendations at face value. Such a deficiency also calls into question the very nature of the measurement area itself. That is to say, lacking evidence of reliability, the scores that we get on a measure must be thought of as arbitrary, in fact, without foundation.

Other chapters in this book have addressed the issue of reliability of graphological inferences in the general case. In this section, what is known about reliability from studies in the personnel area will be summarized.

Before this is attempted, however, it will be useful to distinguish among several types of reliability of importance to the application of graphology to personnel selection. While reliability can be defined as consistency of measurement, there are many ways that this can be operationalized. When discussing the reliability of graphological data in personnel work, we need to know what type is involved.

Intra-Judge Reliability. By intra-judge reliability we mean that the individual doing the analysis, the graphologist or graphoanalyst, is in fact, consistent in his or her assessments and predictions or decisions for the single case.

Figure 5 illustrates one approach to establishing reliability in the intra-judge sense. Script samples are first obtained from a group of individuals (e.g., applicants). The identity of the writers should not be known to the analyst. The researcher or manager would then obtain inferences or recommendations from the graphologist for this same group on two occasions. Note that the same script samples are used in this approach. To deal with the possibility of the influence of memory (which would serve to increase the similarity of inferences from the same scripts across the two occasions and hence increase apparent reliability) there would need to be a reasonable interval (e.g., one week) between the first and second attempt. Traditionally,

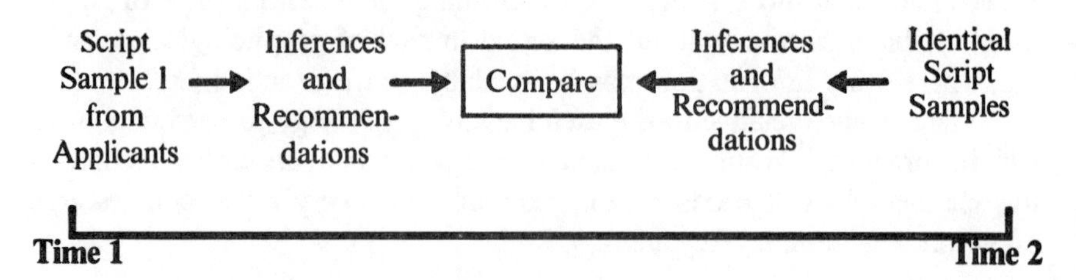

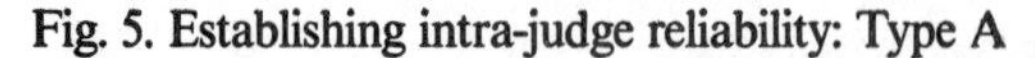

Fig. 5. Establishing intra-judge reliability: Type A

in this approach, the order of the presentation of the scripts is also varied between the two attempts. The investigator would then compare the assessment made by the graphologist of each writer, based on the same script sample. If the inferences are very similar, even exact, high intra-judge reliability could be claimed.

A second form of intra-judge reliability can be estimated. This is illustrated in Figure 6. In this case only one measurement period is involved. But two different samples of a script written by each applicant are used. In this method, the graphologist would be asked to assess both sets. This could be done simultaneously (i.e., the two sets are co-mingled) or sequentially (set one is done before set two but with little time between the work). Once again, the investigator would compare the inference from the first with those from the second set. A high correspondence would indicate high reliability.

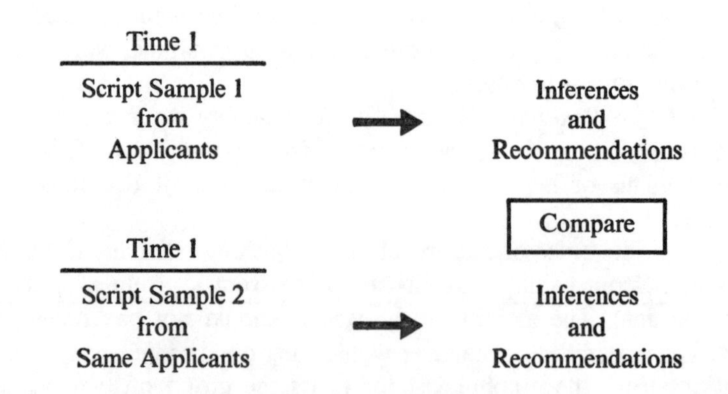

Fig. 6. Establishing intra-judge reliability: Type B.

One point that is implied by the above descriptions is that both approaches could be used to estimate the reliability of a particular graphologist. That is to say, graphologist "X" could be asked to provide evidence of both types. Alternatively, because many researchers are interested in the reliability of graphological inferences in general, a sample of graphologists would be asked to go through these exercises. In this case we would report (or ask to see) the average levels of inter-judge reliability.

There is very little empirical evidence with regard to the intra-judge reliability of graphological inferences in the personnel field. However, what little there is would seem to support the conclusions that such inferences are indeed reliable. For example, Neter and Ben-Shakhar (1989), in their review of the literature, summarize the work of Lockowandt and report intra-judge reliabilities ranging from .78–.88 (maximum r = 1.00).

It may be that the level of reliability would be affected by the nature of the inferences being made, however. For example, Nevo (1986) distinguishes script assessments that involve graphometric factors (e.g., letter size, letter shape, spacing); graphoimpressionistic characteristics (e.g., roundness, rhythm, pressure); and graphodiagnostic inferences (e.g., ego strength, honesty). It is quite likely that intra-judge reliabilities will be higher for the former type assessments than for the latter.

Still another factor to affect reliability would be the nature of the decision or recommendation being sought by the manager from the graphologist. If the latter is merely to recommend between two finalists, reliability is likely to be very high. But, if the manager is seeking elaborate diagnostic information (relative to a number of traits) for several candidates, we would expect poorer reliability.

Inter-Judge Reliability. Far more work has been done on examining the extent to which two graphologists, upon evaluating the same script sample(s), agree with one another. The paradigm for estimating inter-judge reliability is illustrated in Figure 7.

Overall, the evidence for the inter-judge reliability of graphological inferences in personnel research is supportive. Hofsommer, Holdsworth, and Seifert (cited in Neter and Ben-Shakhar 1989) found that inferences of "leadership ability" among 322 foremen estimated (on a 7-point scale) by three graphologists produced an average inter-judge agreement level of .74. Lockowandt, also cited in the same source, reported far lower agreements (average r = .39) among three graphologists estimating the likely success of technical school students. Galbraith and Wilson (1964) had three graphologists assess five attributes (e.g., persistence, dominance) from the script samples provided by 100 students. The median correlation was .78 (range from .61 for obstinacy to .87 for dominance). Rafaeli and Klimoski (1983)

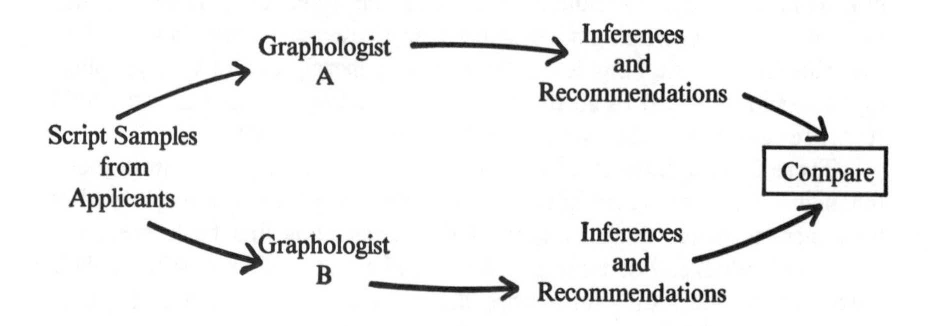

Fig. 7. Establishing inter-judge reliability.

in a study of real estate sales agents found a median correlation across 10 graphologists and 32 writers on ten factors of .45. An interesting aspect of this latter study is that, as a result of using so many graphologists (10), it was possible to contrast the levels of inter-judge agreement for analysts who used different analytic approaches. Somewhat surprisingly, it turned out that agreement levels among graphologists did not vary much as a function of the analytic paradigm involved.

Another aspect of the Rafaeli and Klimoski (1983) study that is worth mentioning is that they systematically examined the effects of script content. They questioned the assertion that graphologists only rely on script features and not script sample content. Thus, the real estate sales agents in this study were asked to provide two samples. One, of a traditional sort, was autobiographical in nature. The second was designed to be neutral with regard to the writer's background. Inter-judge agreement scores were then computed for the two types of scripts. Contrary to predictions, script content had only a modest effect on levels of agreement; even then, it was in the direction opposite to expectations. The median correlation for inferences from neutral scripts was .54; for the autobiographical scripts, .34. Finally, Nevo (1986) did find that inter-judge agreement levels were affected by the kind of assessment made. As discussed in the section on intra-judge reliability, the lowest ranges of reliabilities in his review were found for graphodiagnostic inferences (r= .30–.60). The highest for assessments of script features (r=.70–.90).

In summary, numerous studies have attempted to estimate the levels of inter-judge reliability that exists for graphologists working in the personnel area. The evidence implies that modest levels of this kind of reliability can be obtained. However, it also seems to be the case that the kind of assessment to be made by the graphologist will affect the results. Finally, at the present time there does not seem to be any research on the reliability of the actual employment recommendations made as a result of inference from handwriting.

EVIDENCE FOR CONTENT VALIDITY

Content validity issues have been largely ignored in research on applications of graphology to personnel work. In this context, content validity would be reflected in the degree of correspondence of the dimensions or factors assessed by the graphologist with those that are felt to be relevant to the job for which a candidate is being considered. In most of the available studies, the traits or factors to be assessed seem to have been chosen arbitrarily. They may have been selected based on tradition (e.g., past practice). Or the traits may reflect the preferences of the graphologists involved. Thus, the traits are ones that the graphologist feels that he or she can deal with. Recently, there appears to be an increasing amount of attention given by organizations to issues of honesty and integrity. As pointed out in an earlier section, handwriting analysts often are asked to focus on this area.

Theories of job effectiveness imply that the focus of graphological analysis for personnel selection should be on job-relevant traits. This can be accomplished by having the analyst use a set of traits that are somewhat universal to job success. For example, Drory (1984) obtained inferences on factors such as initiative, motivation, perseverance, etc., in an attempt to predict job performance for a sample of individuals working in a variety of jobs (machine operators, maintenance, clerical). While the traits were not specifically derived from an analysis of each of the jobs in question, they were job relevant, nonetheless. To put it another way, Drory's approach would seem to ensure some degree of content validity.

Far more appropriate, however, would be to have the graphologist work with only those traits that are indeed relevant to performance on a particular job. In the Raefeli and Klimoski (1983) study, this is exactly what was done. A single job, that of a residential real estate sales agent, was involved. A job analysis was performed and ten personal traits or characteristics were identified as important. These included such things as social confidence, sales (ego) drive, work management skills, vitality, and empathy. Each of these were defined and given to the graphologists as the focus of their work.

Notice that several of these factors are similar to those which have been traditionally assessed by graphologists (e.g., vitality). However, still others were peculiar to the job in question and consequently were new to the analysts involved.

There are clearly trade-offs involved in stressing content validity as a requirement for graphology as applied to personnel work. However, at the very least, graphologists should be asked to attend to those traits that they feel that they can assess and that are also job relevant. More will be said about this in the discussion of criterion related validity below.

EVIDENCE FOR CONSTRUCT VALIDITY

When a graphologist, relying on script samples, characterizes an individual in terms of traits, qualities, or dispositions, he or she is making use of constructs. A personnel manager does the same thing when discussing most job requirements or, for that matter, particular candidates for a job. Thus, it is important to know if, in fact, two such individuals are dealing with the same things. More fundamentally, we need to know if there is any evidence that particular constructs are involved in the assessment/selection process.

Establishing construct validity for a measure or for the output from a particular measurement device like graphology is not easy. Usually processes of induction are involved (Schmitt and Klimoski, 1991). Typically we look for patterns of evidence that ultimately convince us that the measure is really getting at the constructs (factors) of interest.

More operationally, the manager or investigator relates scores from a group of people obtained from a device (e.g., graphology) with information already known about this group. We would also look to see if such data are related to what we might obtain using well established and ostensibly valid instruments. Support for construct validity would exist when the information from the new measure (graphology) parallels what would be obtained from the traditional sources.

In such an analysis not only is it necessary that scores on the same traits or factors on the two sets of measures from the same group of people correspond to one another. Scores on factors believed to be different also should not relate to one another. Thus, we seek evidence of convergence (where appropriate) and divergence (discriminability). Clearly, to establish the construct validity of a measure or scores from a device requires that we have clear definitions of just what the constructs are and how various constructs should or should not inter-relate.

As noted in some of the other chapters in this book, there is a fair amount of research which has attempted to connect inferences or scores provided by graphologists to scores on standard tests or measures. For example, Lester, McLaughlin, and Nosal (1977) studied the relationship of 16 handwriting characteristics to the trait of extraversion as measured by a standard personality measure, the Edwards Personality Inventory. This approach was followed by Jansen (1973) and Rosenthal and Lines 1972). Alternatively, investigators might relate ratings or inferences made by graphologists to assessments made by other types of judges. Lomonaco, Harrison, and Klein (1973) used this strategy. They had graphologists examine script samples of individuals for whom they had personality descriptions. The latter had been derived by clinical psychologists using a standard projective test called the TAT.

The results of studies like this are summarized in other chapters in this book. Suffice it to say, there is only weak evidence (at best) for the construct validity of graphology. To put it another way, if a graphologist asserts that a person is high on a particular trait or quality, this may or may not be the case.

The research evidence available to evaluate the construct validity of trait inferences from handwriting applied to personnel work is very limited. What does exist is not very supportive. To illustrate, Rafaeli and Klimoski (1983) obtained from a group of 20 graphologists trait ratings based on script samples of nine factors relevant to the job of a residential real estate salesperson. They then related these ratings to a similar set made by the sales managers of the people who supplied the script samples. No significant correlations were found. In this same study, when graphologists' ratings were compared to self-assessments made by the writers of the script samples on the same trait dimensions, essentially, the same results were obtained. No correspondence could be established.

In a fairly elaborate and carefully controlled experiment, Ben-Shakhar, Bar-Hillel, Bilu, Ben-Abba, and Flug (1986) tried to assess the construct validity of script inferences in two ways. Similar to the Rafaeli and Klimoski study, these investigators examined the relationship of inferences regarding traits (job compliance and human relations) and of on-the-job performance that were made by three graphologists in their study to similar ratings made by managers of a sample of bank employees. They also got a set of evaluations from a psychologist as well. While the results are complex, they did find some pattern of correspondence for the graphologists' ratings with the standard they were using (supervisor assessments). However, this group did less well than the psychologist in the study. It is interesting to note that an employee selection test battery used by the bank at the time did the best job of predicting actual performance. Both the graphologists and the psychologist were less successful than this traditional method. As in the Rafaeli and Klimoski study, no data on discrimination validity was presented, however.

In the second part of the Ben-Shakhar et al. (1986) study, five graphologists received 40 scripts. They were asked to analyze them and to match each writer to one of eight professions. It was known to the investigators that each writer was actually very successful in one (and only one) of these. The matchings were statistically analyzed. It was found that the graphologists were not able to do any better at making correct matches than would be expected to be done by chance. As a side note, there was also low inter-rater agreement among the graphologists with regard to the matches. It too didn't differ from what would be expected by chance.

In conclusion, what little evidence exists with regard to the construct validity of graphology applied to personnel work does not support the claim for construct validity. But parametric studies of particular traits or of types of inferences have not been reported.

EVIDENCE FOR CRITERION-RELATED VALIDITY

This is a major factor in assessing the usefulness of a device in personnel work. In the context of personnel selection, we are usually interested in the criterion of job performance or effectiveness. Clearly, if graphology can be used to estimate future job performance, it would be valuable to managers of organizations.

As in the case of estimating reliability, there are a number of options for doing this for criterion-related validity. Three types will be characterized here: predictive, concurrent, and postdictive strategies. Generally, the differences in approach revolve around times at which predictor and criterion data are obtained. This distinction is highlighted in Figures 8, 9, and 10.

When it comes to personnel research, a predictive approach to establishing criterion-related validity would involve obtaining graphologists' script assessments at one point (time one), waiting for a period, and then collecting criterion (job performance) data. The two sets of data would then be related and checked for correspondence. The length of time required to wait will depend on the nature of the work and work performance. For instance, a manager might be able to tell just how effective a person is as a data entry clerk after only a few weeks. However it might take years to determine if a person will be a successful scientist.

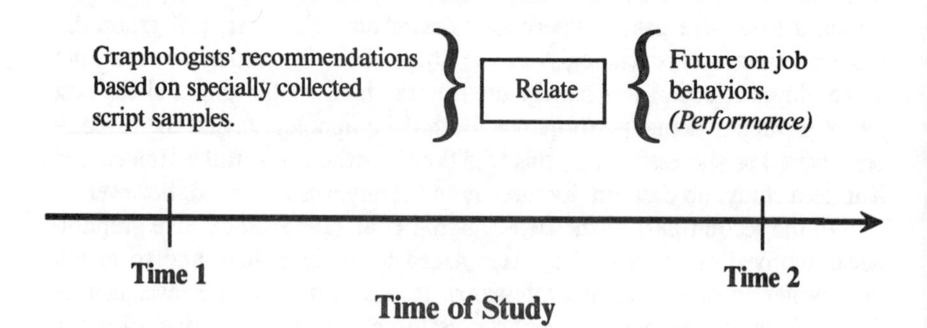

Fig. 8. Establishing predictive validity.

It is important to note that in a pure form of predictive strategy, all individuals in a validation study would be allowed to come onto the job. This would provide the maximum opportunity for an analysis to detect signs of validity. In most cases however, an organization cannot or will not permit this to happen. Instead, some screening will take place. Even in a validation study, individuals may be selected for employment based on traditional means (e.g., an interview). Those who do not do well in the interview will not be hired. As a result, the people who remain in the study (and for whom there would be job performance data) will only be a subset of the original group. More importantly, it is not a randomly established group but one that is likely to be better (on average) than the original. More technically speaking, this group will exhibit what is called a restriction of range in criterion scores. In effect, the poorest performers are, more likely than not, not represented, so the full range of possible performance is not manifest. The net result of all of this is that the potential for establishing criterion-related validity is reduced.

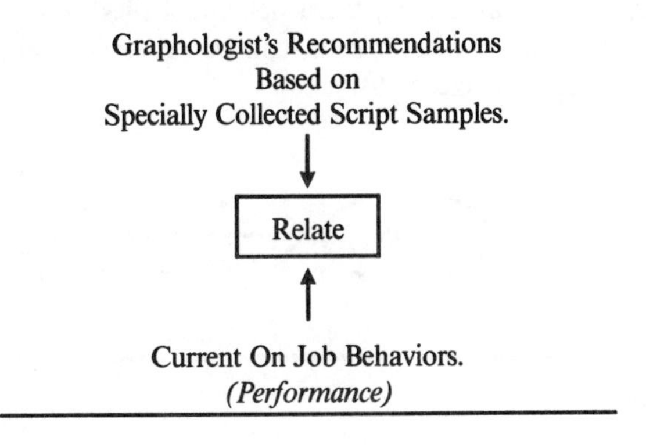

Fig. 9. Establishing concurrent validity.

There is a third circumstance where individuals in a validation study may be selected, not only using traditional means, but information from the test or device being evaluated may also be involved. Thus, in a validation study of graphology, some individuals might be rejected for employment based on the graphological inferences themselves. In this situation, the people allowed on the job and for whom there would be job performance data are not only a select group, they got their job, in part, because of their handwriting scores! This is a weak design for a validation study. An analysis of the data from such a group would tend to reveal higher than warranted correspondence between predictor (graphology) and criterion (job performance) measures. But this would be misleading. The results would be spurious and stem from what is essentially criterion contamination. (The same thing would occur if a supervisor knew of employees' graphology scores and allowed this knowledge to influence his or her ratings of job performance which are to serve as the criterion in the study.)

In a concurrent strategy, script samples would be taken from individuals currently on the job. Job performance information would be obtained at the same time. Inferences would then be analyzed and related to current performance (Figure 9). While criterion information would be known to investigators, it would not be known by the graphologist. If it were and such knowledge were allowed to influence the graphologist's assessments, we would have another form of criterion contamination.

A third form of a criterion-related validity study is possible. Because the bases of graphological inferences are script samples, it is feasible for the latter to be obtained for validation studies when, in fact, they were not intended for that purpose. Thus, in the postdictive strategy, handwriting samples from archives (e.g., from personnel files), ones that had been created at some point earlier in time, can be retrieved and related to current job performance. (Figure 10)

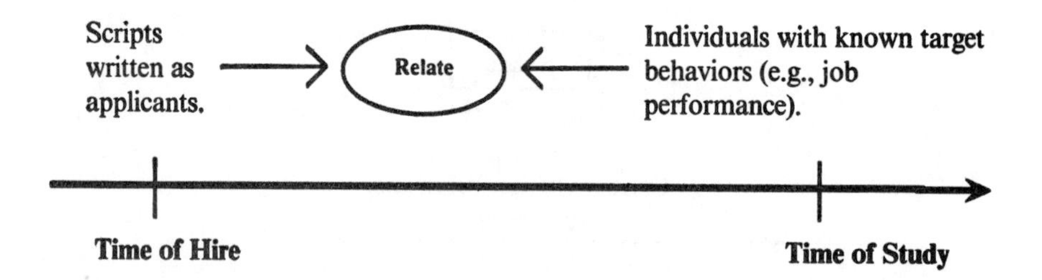

Fig. 10. Establishing postdictive validity.

All three validation approaches require some data regarding job effectiveness or job performance. This is an aspect of personnel research that has received a great deal of attention by industrial psychologists (Schmitt, Neal, and Klimoski, 1991). Thus, it is a topic of some complexity and cannot be fully developed here. What is important for the present discussion, however, is that in designing or implementing a validation study, or even in reviewing research evidence on criterion-related validity, the quality of the criterion measures themselves should not be taken for granted. Productivity data, supervisor ratings, peer ratings, customer reactions data are all options that can be used. Their appropriateness for a validation study and, once obtained, their quality should be scrutinized. Numerous techniques exist to do this (Schmitt, Neal, and Klimoski, 1991).

All three approaches to criterion-related validity also involve some mechanism for relating predictor and criterion scores. In some cases, this can take the form of a classification analysis. This would show to what extent a graphologist's assessments or recommendations correspond to discrete outcomes. If the assessment implies success, we would want to establish that the writer actually is (or will be) a success. If a failure is predicted, this also should indeed be the case. Thus, correspondence or validity can be represented in terms of "hits" or "misses." This type of analysis was performed by Ben-Shakhar et al. (1986), as described in the section on construct validity (see Figure 11).

Graphologist's assessments, prediction of performance, or recommendation.

	Actual Job Success: Yes	No
Hire	Hits	Misses
Reject	Misses	Hits

Fig. 11. Classification analysis.

More commonly, however, investigators use correlational analysis to establish the degree of correspondence involved. As a result, criterion-related validities are usually reported in terms of correlation coefficients.

The absolute size of correlation coefficients can range from .00 to 1.00, with the latter reflecting a perfect alignment of predictor scores (e.g., graphological recommendations for hire) and criterion scores (levels of job performance). In personnel selection research in general, it is unusual to obtain coefficients larger than .40 (Hunter and Hunter, 1984; Schmitt, Gooding, Noe, and Kirsch, 1984; Reilly and Chao, 1982). Note that uncovering a negative or a positive value of a given size would have equal practical utility (Figure 12).

Most rigorous research studies will not only report the size of a validity coefficient, but will also provide some indication that the obtained values are not likely to have occurred by chance. Usually this takes the form of conducting and reporting a test of statistical significance. The outcome of such tests are largely a function of the size of the sample of workers involved in the validation study. Thus, a coefficient of a given

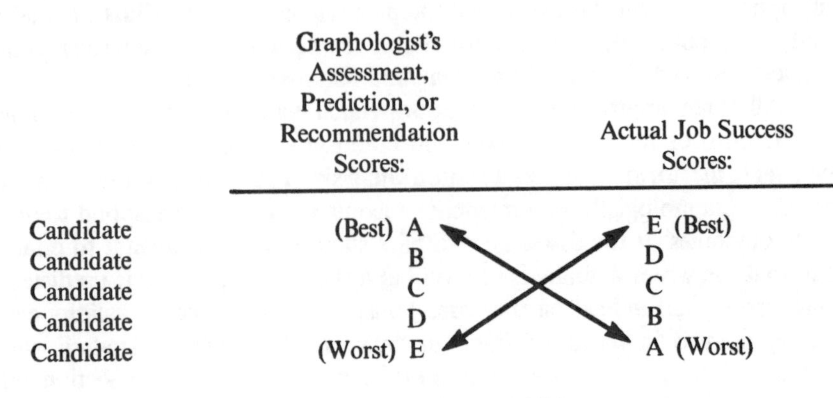

Fig. 12. Correlation analysis (r = +1.00 ⟷ 0 ⟷ -1.00)*

size (e.g., r = .35) for a small sample of cases (e.g., 25) is not given the same status as one for a larger sample as the values of a correlation coefficient are known to be unstable when the number of cases is small. Statistical tests involve an adjustment for sample size. (As an aside, most of the anecdotal arguments for and a great deal of the evidence in the popular press on the validity of graphology for personnel selection are based upon instances where small numbers of cases are involved. Thus the findings, positive or negative, are likely to be spurious.)

Most of the research on criterion-related validity has made use of the concurrent validation paradigm. This may reflect the fact that it is an easier and less time-consuming strategy to follow. Thus, Zdep and Weaver (1967), Rafaeli and Klimoski (1983), and Drory (1984) all collected script samples and criterion information at about the same time. To illustrate, Rafaeli and Klimoski (1983) visited real estate firms and arranged for sales agents to meet at a conference room where script samples were collected under controlled conditions (e.g., using pen on unlined paper in pad form). While this was being done, managers were rating each salesperson on a set of traits and on a scale of overall effectiveness. On the same visit, data on sales productivity for each agent (e.g., number of sales, dollar value of commissions earned, number of homes "listed") were recorded from company files.

The analysis of the relationship between graphological assessments and job effectiveness in the Rafaeli and Klimoski (1983) study revealed little support for claims of criterion-related validity. The trait inferences made by the 20 graphologists in the study were unrelated to the sales productivity

*As printed, the orders of predictions and clients' scores constitute a perfect negative correlation (r = -1.00). If the order of the righthand column were reversed, it would be a perfect positive correlation (+ 1.00).

and commissions data (median r = .06). Because the researchers were sensitive to the possibility that the traits to be rated might be unfamiliar to the graphologists (they had been derived from a job analysis), the latter were allowed to use what ever system they wished in order to directly estimate the effectiveness of each writer. They did not fare much better at this task either. Direct estimates of the effectiveness of the agents in the study made by the graphologists were also unrelated to actual productivity (median r =.04).

In their review of the more rigorously designed studies on the validity of graphology, Klimoski and Rafaeli (1983) reported at that time, ". . . given the evidence that we have, great reliance [for personnel work] on inferences based on script must be considered unwarranted" (p. 200). These authors could not find supportive scientific evidence for applying graphology to organizational problems. In a somewhat later effort, Nevo (1986) accumulated all the validity studies on graphology that he could locate that had been conducted in Israeli organizations. From the studies at his disposal, Nevo estimated the average validity coefficient (adjusting for differences in the sizes of the samples involved in each study) to be r =.14.

This is a more optimistic finding for proponents of graphology. If true, a value of this magnitude compares favorably to what has been uncovered for other, more traditional selection devices. Moreover, according to personnel selection theory, even a coefficient of this modest order of magnitude can have practical utility under certain circumstances (a favorable selection ratio—see Schmitt, Neal, and Klimoski, 1991). More recently however, Neter and Ben-Shakhar (1989) have convincingly reaffirmed the opposing position taken by Klimoski and Rafaeli (1983).

Neter and Ben-Shakhar conducted a statistical summary of all the studies that they could find that reported evidence of criterion-related validity in personnel work. All together, they uncovered 17 studies that met their standards for inclusion (e.g., they had to be empirical studies, report the results in the form of validity coefficients, clearly specify sample size and the type of criterion measures used). In this investigation, these authors used the technique called meta-analysis to control for such things as sample size and lack of reliability in order to reach conclusions regarding the best estimate of the validity of graphology as a predictor of job effectiveness (see also ch. 12, this volume). They examined the data for evidence of the validity of assessments made by others who were not graphologists (e.g., psychologists, lay people). They looked at differences in results associated with the type of job effectiveness criterion that investigators used. Finally, they contrasted studies conducted in a regular work versus a training setting.

In the 17 studies, a total of 63 graphologists and 51 non-graphologists were found to have evaluated 1223 scripts. Across all types of scripts and criteria, the predictive validities for graphologists were in the range of .14–.18. This is similar to Nevo's findings. However, if the type of script is considered, when graphologists were working with neutral (without biographical content) scripts, the predictive validity of their inferences was reduced to zero. Just as important, it was discovered that psychologists, with no knowledge of graphology ". . . outperformed the graphologists on all dimensions" (p. 737).

It was true that some graphologists were better at estimating performance than others. But this occurred in the case of non-graphologists as well. Neter and Ben-Shakhar (1989) argue that this has little to do with the validity of graphology. Finally, the type of setting also made a difference, but in complex ways. Essentially, the different groups of analysts (graphologists, psychologists, lay people) were differentially accurate in their predictions in the two settings.

In summary, there is little convincing evidence of the criterion-related validity of graphology when applied to personnel work.

EVIDENCE FOR UTILITY

To this writer's knowledge, there have been no studies which have attempted to demonstrate the utility of graphology, either in terms of reduced decision errors or of economic benefits. There are, however, a few studies comparing the performance of graphologists or graphology to alternative approaches to personnel decision making. Some of these have been alluded to already.

To illustrate, Rafaeli and Klimoski (1983) asked lay people (undergraduate students) to assess traits and estimate the effectiveness of the script writers in a manner that paralleled the task of the graphologists in their study. They found the interjudge agreement among students was less than among the graphologists. However, the data from both groups reflected the similar and low relationships with the various job performance criteria used in that study. Ben-Shakhar et al. (1986) contrasted the judgment of a clinical psychologist with those made by three graphologists. The clinician performed as well as the graphologists with regard to predicting supervisor ratings in specific areas. But she was somewhat better at estimating some of the global evaluations. These authors also contrasted the performance of all four human judges with predictions made based on the information that existed in organization's test files. It turned out that test data predicted performance as well as any of the judges.

In one final comparison, information extracted and coded from the scripts themselves (which were autobiographical in nature), when treated as a "test" of a person's background, outperformed all three graphologists in predicting a general evaluation and (in two of the three cases) in predicting the average of the ratings given each script writer by his or her supervisor. This "script content" index did about as well as the test battery information in predicting these criteria. Finally, the meta-analysis of Neter and Ben-Shakhar (1989), as pointed out above, found that graphologists possessed no special capability for predicting job performance and training criteria when compared to psychologists and lay-persons.

While these studies give us some insights regarding the comparative effectiveness of graphologists, it should be stressed that they do not really answer the essential questions about utility. We still don't know what kind of errors (if any) are reduced by using graphology to aid personnel decisions. This remains as a challenge for future work.

EVIDENCE OF FREEDOM FROM BIAS

To this writer's knowledge, there are no published studies of the differential impact of recommendations or decisions based on graphological inferences for different subgroups of people (e.g., males/females, native born/foreign born). For example, Reilly and Chao (1982) had nothing to say about graphology in their review of the fairness of various selection devices. While most graphologists wish to know the gender and the native language of the script writer (Klimoski and Rafaeli, 1983), there seems to be little evidence one way or another that this knowledge affects their trait ratings or their recommendations.

EVIDENCE REGARDING USER ACCEPTANCE

If one takes at face value the reports in the popular press, it would appear that the use of graphology by organizations in Europe and Israel is widespread and that its application to personnel work by U.S. companies is on the increase. On this basis, it would be tempting to assert that the acceptance of graphology for personnel decisions is great. However, to do so would be a mistake.

It has already been cautioned that reliable survey data on the use of graphology in industry does not exist. Moreover, just because so many managers may make use of a device or program does not mean that all the parties involved in the hiring process are amenable to it. The fact is, we don't know. There don't seem to be any studies on this issue.

There may be strong cultural differences which moderate the acceptance of a technique or service like graphology. In the United States, at least, there is an increased concern for the rights of potential and actual employees. This includes the rights to privacy (Stone and Stone, 1990). The surreptitious use of script samples would seem to violate most Americans' sense of propriety and fair play. And, even if an organization does make public its reliance on graphology, it is possible that individuals in the U.S. will challenge its relevance to personnel decisions, particularly if they felt disadvantaged in the process (see also chs. 17 and 18, this volume). Courts in the U.S. are currently willing to hear such challenges (Arvey, 1979). Thus, it would seem that an organization should have some persuasive reasons to use any non-traditional (for the U.S.) approach as a basis for selection. And, if it does make use of one, it will need to have the data to back up any claims of "business necessity."

The last point may be a key to user acceptance. Personal preferences or national values notwithstanding, it is likely that acceptance of graphology as part of a personnel selection program, like in any other case (e.g., honesty testing, drug testing), will be strongly influenced by evidence that it is needed (there are not more conventional alternatives), and that it is effective (there is convincing evidence that decisions based on graphology are related to job behaviors or performance). Based on the published literature reviewed above, such a case cannot be made.*

OVERALL CONCLUSIONS

There are several points that have been made throughout this review. In this section, the more important ones will be recapitulated in order to make clear the status of graphology as a method for aiding personnel decisions.

1. Proponents of graphology are strong advocates for its application to organizations, particularly in the realm of personnel decision making.
2. There is the perception, in the popular press at least, that an increasing number of companies are using graphology and the services of graphologists as consultants.
3. There is a well-developed theory and a technology available for making and assessing the quality of personnel decisions. This in-

*The editors of this volume have seen several cases where the professional reputations and career advancement of personnel managers have been harmed by the public outcry that arose when it was revealed that they were employing "unscientific" graphological services that have not passed the validation tests described in this chapter.

cludes a set of standards that can and should be applied to the analysis of claims made for any tool, device, or program to be used for personnel work.

4. As a rule, proponents of graphology do not offer credible empirical evidence to support claims of the usefulness of graphology for personnel work. When data or analysis are forthcoming, they are usually of insufficient completeness or scope to assess graphology relative to these standards.
5. When the credible empirical evidence is reviewed, summarized, and analyzed relative to these standards (as was done in this chapter), most claims for graphology as applied to personnel decisions are not supported.

A skeptic reading this chapter could reasonably conclude that there is little value to graphology for personnel work. Given the available evidence, he or she would be correct. For example, there is very little support for the construct, content, and criterion-related validity of graphological inferences. More importantly, there is no research on the utility of graphology relative to other approaches to personnel decision making. Thus, a "business case" for graphology cannot be made.

On the other hand, a proponent of graphology might find some solace in some of the findings that have been summarized. For example, modest levels of inter-judge agreement among graphologists have been documented. If they concur, however, in making invalid inferences from people's script, this agreement is hardly of much value. More importantly, it appears that some graphologists are able to estimate some organizationally relevant criteria (such as job performance and success in training) and do it about as well as others who would claim professional status (e.g., psychologists). The evidence that it is use of graphology per se that permits *some* graphologists to exceed chance in their estimates is insufficient at this time.

All things considered, at this period in time, a manager receiving solicitations for graphological services or seeking assistance in personnel decision making would be wise to heed the American credo "Caveat Emptor" —let the buyer beware. The prudent manager would examine claims closely and require documentation regarding these claims. Toward this end, the standards described and used in this chapter, and the data summarized relative to these standards, will provide a useful point of reference. To put it bluntly, careful empirical analysis, not personal beliefs or positive personal experiences, should guide the decision to adopt graphology as a solution to personnel problems.

PROBLEMATIC ISSUES

There are several questions that have been raised throughout this chapter that need to be resolved before the advocate of graphological services can hope to be credible in the eyes of the prudent manager:

A. What is graphology (as applied to personnel work)?

B. Who is qualified to offer services to industry?

C. What is the role of script sample features?

D. What is the nature of involvement of graphologists in personnel decisions?

E. Are graphologists willing to use better research designs to try to document the validity of graphology?

Fundamentally, just what is graphology? As outlined in other chapters, there are a variety of philosophical orientations, epistemologies, and techniques that are covered under the rubric. Just how this question gets answered has numerous implications for both research and practice. For example, Rafaeli and Klimoski (1983) had at least three approaches reflected in the work of the 20 graphologists in their study. However, most investigators use only one or two graphologists. And, rarely is the notion of professional orientation to graphological analysis (i.e., the particular school of handwriting analysis being employed) stressed in the published research.

In a related vein, another issue is to resolve just who is qualified to offer such services. As highlighted elsewhere in this book, there are very few barriers to entry into the field of graphology. Any number of individuals may claim to have expertise in this area. More specifically, it would seem that, as is the case in most fields, competency in one domain will not ensure the same in another one. That is to say, graphologists with no experience or expertise in personnel matters may nonetheless offer services of this type. While a number of certification programs for graphologists exist, there is no evidence that these do in fact insure competence in consulting for organizations.

With regard to the technology of graphological analysis, the issue of script sample features deserves special attention. As a rule, many graphological texts are quite specific regarding the conditions that should exist in order to obtain high-quality samples for analysis. For instance, script samples should be spontaneous (not represent copied work), they should be of sufficient length, the work should be done in pen on unlined paper from a pad or tablet, etc. However, it's not clear that this is what happens in practice. The conditions of script sample derivation are rarely described in testimonials. They are often poorly described in research. The point is that if graphological analysis is to be fairly characterized and to be offered on a regular basis as a service to organizations, some element of standardization must exist.

A particular concern with regard to script samples has to do with the nature of their content. Rafaeli and Klimoski (1983) make a strong a priori case that the content of scripts, usually of a biographical nature, could be contributing to whatever validities might be obtained in studies of graphology. Their study did reveal some impact of script content on the assessments made by the students in their research but not for the graphologists. But, it might be recalled that both groups showed little capacity to predict the actual job performance of script writers. In contrast, in their extensive review Neter and Ben-Shakhar (1989) make a convincing case that script content does make a difference, and in the direction theorized by Rafaeli and Klimoski (autobiographical content facilitates prediction). Clearly, the content issue needs to be resolved.

The nature and point of involvement of the graphologists who are offering services to organizations has already been characterized in this chapter as problematic. As consultants to organizations, graphologists can assist managers in personnel decision making in any number of ways. But, therein lies a dilemma. When assessing the usefulness of graphology for personnel work, it is difficult to separate the technique and what it can offer from the effectiveness of the consulting habits and skills of the practitioner. In particular, graphologists, as consultants, often have access to a great deal more information regarding candidates than what can be inferred from script samples. They may review an application form. They may meet the candidate. They may know the impressions and opinions held by the hiring manager of the candidate. It is quite reasonable to assume that their recommendations are affected by this non-script intelligence. The prudent manager needs to evaluate the claims of the graphologist in light of his or her "modus operandi." And the manager must scrutinize the evidence offered to see if it comes from studies of graphological analysis per se, or from studies where graphology just happened to have been used.

In this regard, it may be that the best design for research on the effectiveness of graphology as applied to personnel matters might not be the relational study, but the field experiment (Schmitt, Neal, and Klimoski, 1991). Thus, data on the correlations between graphological inferences and job performance (the type of data reviewed in this chapter), even if it were to be reassuring to proponents, would not be accepted as definitive. Instead, what would be more appropriate is a rigorously designed and executed demonstration that graphological services, when delivered in a standardized way, really do improve the quality of personnel decisions, relative to alternatives in use. Given that the work lives and careers of individuals are at stake, demonstrated effectiveness of this sort is what the prudent manager should require before adopting graphology as a solution to staffing problems. At this time such demonstrations have not yet been reported.

REFERENCES

Aiken, L. R. 1991. *Psychological Testing and Assessment.* 7th ed. Boston: Allyn and Bacon.

Anonymous. 1979. "Reading between the Lines—What Your Handwriting Reveals." *Credit and Financial Management* 81(1): pp. 14–15.

Arnett, E. 1989. "For More Employers, the Scrawl Is All." *Washington Post,* July 14.

Arvey, R. D. 1979. *Fairness in Selecting Employees.* Reading, Mass.: Addison Wesley.

Bar-Hillel, M., and G. Ben-Shakhar. 1986. "The A Priori Case against Graphology." In *Scientific Aspects of Graphology,* edited by B. Nevo. Springfield, Ill.: Charles Thomas.

Ben-Shakhar, G., M. Bar-Hillel, Y. Bilu, E. Ben-Abba, and A. Flug. 1986. "Can Graphology Predict Occupational Success? Two Empirical Studies and Some Methodological Ruminations." *Journal of Applied Psychology* 71(4): pp. 645–653.

Bernardin, H. J. 1987. "Development and Validation of a Forced Choice Scale to Measure Job Related Discomfort among Customer Service Representatives." *Academy of Management Journal* 30(4): pp. 162–173.

Braverman, Louis L. 1986. "Graphonanalysis—Let It Help You More." *Life Association News* 81(6): pp. 131–132.

Campion, J. R. 1972. "Work Sampling for Personnel Selection." *Journal of Applied Psychology* 56(1): pp. 40–44.

Campion, M., E. Pursell, and B. K. Brown. 1988. "Structured Interviewing: Raising the Psychometric Properties of the Employment Interview." *Personnel Psychology* 41(1): pp. 25–42.

Cronbach, L. J., and P. E. Meehl. 1955. "Construct Validity in Psychological Tests." *Psychological Bulletin* 52: pp. 281–302.

Drory, Amos. 1984. "Validity of Handwriting Analysis in Predicting Job Performance." Unpublished manuscript.

Fowler, E. M. 1990. "Careers: Personnel Executives on the Rise." *New York Times,* May 9.

Galbraith, D., and W. Wilson. 1964. "Reliability of the Graphoanalytic Approach to Handwriting Analysis." *Perceptual and Motor Skills* 19(2): pp. 615–618.

Gorman, C. 1989. "Honestly, Can We Trust You?" *Time,* January 23: p. 44.

Hunter, J. E., and R. F. Hunter. 1984. "Validity and Utility of Alternative Predictions of Job Performance." *Psychological Bulletin* 96: pp. 72–98.

Jaekle, L. 1974. "The Write Approach." *Pacific Business* 64(1): pp. 36–38.

Jansen, A. 1973. *Validation of Graphological Judgments: An Experimental Study.* Paris: Mouton.

Kalogerakis, G. 1984. "Enthusiasm Is Sweeping the T-Bars." *Commutator's Journal* 2: pp. 2–34.

Klimoski, R. J., and A. Rafaeli. 1983. "Inferring Personal Qualities through Handwriting Analysis." *Journal of Occupational Psychology* 56: pp. 191–202.

Lester, D., S. McLaughlin, and G. Nosal. 1977. "Graphological Signs for Extroversion." *Perceptual and Motor Skills* (44(1): pp. 137–138.

Levine, E. L., R. Ash, H. Hall, and S. Sistrunk. 1983. "Evaluation of Job Analysis Methods by Experienced Job Analysts." *Academy of Management Journal* 26(2): pp. 339–347.

Levy, L. 1979. "Handwriting and Hiring." *Dun's Review:* pp. 72–79.

Lomonaco, T., R. Harrison, and F. Klein. 1973. "Accuracy of Matching TAT and Graphological Profiles." *Perceptual and Motor Skills* 36: pp. 703–706.

Lynch, B. 1985. "Graphology—Towards a Hand-picked Workforce." *Personnel Management* 17(3): pp. 14–18.

Munsterberg, H. 1913. *Psychology and Industrial Efficiency.* Boston: Houghton-Mifflin.

Neter. E., and G. Ben-Shakhar. 1989. "The Predictive Validity of Graphological Influences: A Meta-Analytic Approach." *Personality and Individual Differences* 10(7): pp. 737–745.

Nevo, B., ed. 1986. *Scientific Aspects of Graphology.* Springfield, Ill.: Charles Thomas.

Porter, L., E. Lawler, and J. Hackman. 1975. *Behavior in Organizations.* New York: McGraw-Hill.

Radar, E. 1988. "Hire-oglyphics." *U.S. Air Magazine* (January): pp. 12–15.

Rafaeli, A., and R. J. Klimoski. 1983. "Predicting Sales Success through Handwriting Analysis: An Evaluation of the Effects of Training and Handwriting Sample Content." *Journal of Applied Psychology* 68(2): 213–217.

Reilly, R. R., and G. T. Chao. 1982. "Validity and Fairness of Some Alternative Employee Selection Procedures." *Personnel Psychology* 35: pp. 1–62.

Rosenthal, D. A., and R. Lines. 1978. "Handwriting As a Correlate of Extroversion." *Journal of Personality Assessment* 42: pp. 45–48.

Schmidt, F., and J. Hunter. 1981. "Employment Testing: Old Theories and New Research Findings." *American Psychologist* 36(10): pp. 1128–1137.

Schmidt, F., J. Hunter, and K. Pearlman. 1982. "Progress in Validity Generalization: Comments on Callender and Osburn and Further Developments. *Journal of Applied Psychology* 67(6): pp. 835–845.

Schmidt, F., J. Hunter, R. McKenzie, and T. Muldrow. 1979. "Impact of Valid Selection Procedures on Workforce Productivity." *Journal of Applied Psychology* 64(6): pp. 609–626.

Schmitt, N., R. F. Gooding, R. A. Noe, and P. M. Kirsch. 1984. "Meta-Analyses of Validity Studies Published between 1964 and 1982 and the Investigation of Study Character Clusters." *Personnel Psychology* 37: pp. 407–422.

Schmitt, N., J. Neal, and R. J. Klimoski. 1991. *Research Methods in Human Resources Management.* Cincinnati: South-Western Publ.

Scott, W. D. 1911. *Increasing Human Efficiency in Business.* New York: Macmillan.

Stone, E. F., and D. L. Stone. 1990. "Privacy in Organizations: Theoretical Issues, Research Findings and Protection Strategies." In *Research in Personnel/Human Resources Management,* vol. 8, edited by G. Ferris and K. Rowland.

Taylor, M. S., and K. L. Sackheim. 1988. "Graphology." *Personnel Administrator* 33(5): pp. 71–76.

Thayer, P. N., and J. A. Antoinetti. 1965. "Graphology." *The Industrial Psychologist* 2: pp. 33–34.

Wanous, J. P. 1980. *Organizational Entry: Recruitment, Selection, and Socialization of Newcomers.* Reading, Mass.: Addison-Wesley.

Zdep, S., and H. Weaver. 1967. "The Graphoanalytic Approach to Selecting Life Insurance Salesmen." *Journal of Applied Psychology* 51(3): pp. 295f.

12

The Bottom Line: Effect Size

Geoffrey A. Dean

In this chapter, Dean explains what evidence is required to reasonably conclude that graphology "works." He begins by pointing out that our real question is *how well* graphology works, since when we decide to use graphology, we always have alternatives—if nothing else, we have our common-sense methods of assessing personality. So, what we want to know is whether graphology works better than the competitors. He explains, without excessive use of technical statistical terms, the notion of *effect size,* which gives us a way of measuring the effectiveness of one method of generating predictions against another. We often lose sight of the fact that a statistically significant result merely tells us that the effect was unlikely to be due to chance. It does not tell us what the non-chance factor is, nor does it tell us whether the effect is large enough to be useful in any practical sense. Thus Dean warns us not only to beware of falsely claimed effects, but also of "true-but-trivial" effects.

The reader may wish to examine also Dale Beyerstein's discussion of the rationale behind the scientific method in chapter 8, as well as Dean, Kelly, Saklofske, and Furnham in chapter 13 for a discussion of the biases which lead our common sense astray when we attempt to examine the efficacy of a method of personality assessment such as graphology. The evidence presented in the latter chapter makes a case for the need for the more sophisticated measures of efficacy discussed here by Dean.

Dean applies these standards to a discussion of a broad spectrum of studies of graphology. The results are summarized in Appendix B. He also comments on other surveys of graphological studies *(meta-analyses).* The reader can compare Dean's observations and conclusions with those of Lockowandt in chapter 5.

INTRODUCTION: LIFE ON THE BOTTOM LINE

> Scientists have known for centuries that a single study will not resolve a major issue. Indeed, a small sample study will not even resolve a minor issue. Thus, the foundation of science is the cumulation of knowledge from the results of many studies.
>
> —Hunter, Schmidt, and Jackson

This chapter goes straight to the bottom line. To what extent does graphology work? It looks at the technicalities of testing graphology, surveys over 200 experimental studies, and compares the results with those of other approaches such as personality tests, peer ratings, and astrology. The conclusions are summarized in the last section. For technical readers the more important technical details are covered by notes.[1] First a look at what the books have said over the years.

VIEWS OF GRAPHOLOGISTS

Graphology books leave you in no doubt that graphology works:

> There can be no doubt that . . . certain peculiarities of handwriting run so unfailingly and so unexceptionally parallel to certain traits of character that from them we may by analogy assume the corresponding traits of character.[2] (Saudek 1925:42)

> An accurate picture of the *real* you. . . . You will be surprised how successful you will be [at graphology] after even a small amount of practice. (Holder 1958:3,13)

> A sure-fire way of getting the real low-down . . . will give you true pictures of what they [people] really are. . . . an aid in vocational guidance . . . personnel selection . . . marriage [guidance]. (Olyanova 1960:9,15)

> Long ago reputable scientists admitted the unmistakable relationship between one's handwriting and one's character. (Jeanne Dixon in Kurdsen 1971:5)

> Discover traits . . . find immediate clues to the personality . . . Even a strange signature at the bottom of an official letter can tell you whether the writer is kind, timid, aggressive or sexy. Graphology is a recognized aid to psychology in many countries. (Lowengard 1975:3,8)

> A wonderful potential for help and personal exploration . . . an objective evaluation of personality strengths and weaknesses . . . covers aspects of personality not covered in other tests. (Paterson 1976:20,87–88)

The range of potential interpretative capacities is already much larger through graphology than through other psychological methods. (Schwieghofer 1979:10)

[Graphology] brings into focus the secrets of your basic character, emotional makeup, intellectual gifts, creative abilities, social adjustment, material values, neurotic conflicts, parental hang-ups, sensuality, sexuality, and much, much more. (Surovell 1987:11)

Your handwriting is all-revealing. To the trained eye it lays open your secret mind. Every whirl or line you pen exposes your true character and personality to the graphologist. . . . Handwriting analysis can help you in your search for whatever it is you want out of life. (Marne 1988:7)

In short, graphology is objective, accurate, true, internationally recognized, quick, easy, helpful, all-revealing, wider-ranging than other tests, confirmed by reputable scientists, and much, much more. Or so the books lead us to believe. Now for a word from reputable scientists.

VIEWS OF SCIENTISTS

Scientists have been investigating graphology since the 1900s:

The claims of the graphologists are frequently very extravagant. . . . The more pretentious works are predominantly *a priori* deductions from very general principles. (Hull and Montgomery 1919:63–64)[3]

The average graphological analysis is especially difficult to validate . . . Verbal self-contradictions appear frequently . . . and the terms employed often seem to obscure rather than reveal the personality. (Allport and Vernon 1933:210–211)

Every text on graphology examined by the author presents the analysis of handwriting as a test of personality; yet not one of them offers norms, not one of them presents figures showing the reliability and validity of their test, not one of them bothers to define their personality variables. (Pascal 1943:124)

The boundlessness of the graphologist's faith, the enormity of his claims, must make the cautious scientist hesitate . . . much of the evidence . . . cannot be regarded as more than suggestive. Too frequently the controls have been insufficiently stringent, the number of handwritings used too small to give results free from serious sampling errors, and the criteria for validation themselves too much lacking in both reliability and validity to make comparisons fruitful. (Eysenck 1945:70,72)

> Research in the area of handwriting and personality has lingered long and prospered rarely. Scattered studies have continued to appear through the years, yet somehow we have not progressed very far towards reaching decisions concerning the nature of relationships between the two. (McNeil and Blum 1952:476)

> [Graphologists] claim that the usefulness of graphology is proved if the writers themselves, or their acquaintances, accept their personality sketches as accurate. This is quite unconvincing to the psychologist. (Vernon 1953:58)

> A vast number of articles have been written on handwriting in many languages, but few rigorous experimental studies have been done. . . . it is difficult to draw many conclusions since the methods used and the criterion variables investigated have been highly diversified. (Fluckiger et al. 1961:67)

> With few exceptions, the quality of research in the area is not high. . . . when researchers are more rigorous . . . the results have not been supportive of the usefulness of inferences based on script. (Klimoski and Rafaeli 1983:200)

> There is a growing body of empirical research literature on graphology. It is almost uniformly negative as regards graphologists' claims. (Hines 1988:294)

It seems there are two sides to every story. But why should the two sides be so conflicting?

RESOLVING THE CONFLICT

How can graphologists be so sure that graphology works if the empirical research literature is "almost uniformly negative"? Two reasons are given in the next chapter:

1. Human cognitive skills are not equal to the task graphologists have set themselves. Human judgmental biases have created false beliefs. (Here bias means *systematic error* not *prejudice.*)
2. There are many non-graphological reasons why graphology seems to work, none of which requires that graphology be true.

Another reason is that, as any graphology book will show, graphologists seem generally unaware of the empirical research, whereas their critics are not. So what *is* the empirical research? Is it really "almost uniformly negative"? To answer these questions we start by looking at how the research was done in the first place, that is, at how graphology is tested. This occupies the next two sections.

MEASURING EFFECT SIZE: THE TECHNICALITIES OF TESTING GRAPHOLOGY

APPROACHES TO TESTING GRAPHOLOGY

Handwriting is said to indicate ability and behavior. In other words to see the script is to know the person. To determine more precisely what graphology claims to do, Jansen (1973) read graphology books (in English, Dutch, and German); talked to graphologists; and examined 62 graphological analyses selected at random. He concluded that:

> the claims of graphology extend to practically all character aspects and cover at least all major personality areas. (Jansen 1973:13)

To test such claims there are two basic approaches to assessing scripts and people, namely subjective (guessing) and objective (measuring):

1. Subjective. Uses *impressions* of things such as rhythm and energy. Why measure when you can guess?
2. Objective. Uses *measurements* of things such as slant and E (extroversion). Why guess when you can measure?

Figure 1. *Four Ways of Testing Graphology*

Two approaches (subjective and objective) to two target areas (scripts and human behavior) give four ways of testing graphology. Each combination except top right has been widely used, the most popular by a small margin being bottom left.

On the left generally is holistic graphology, based on the whole script, approached by tests that include matching handwriting interpretations to their owners. On the right generally is analytic graphology, based on individual signs, approached by tests that include testing the sign interpretations listed in graphology books.

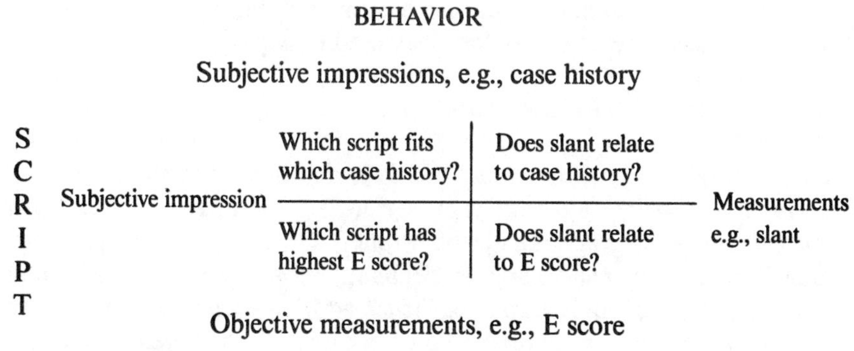

BEHAVIOR

Subjective impressions, e.g., case history

SCRIPT	Subjective impression	Measurements e.g., slant
Subjective impressions, e.g., case history	Which script fits which case history?	Does slant relate to case history?
Objective measurements, e.g., E score	Which script has highest E score?	Does slant relate to E score?

Objective measurements, e.g., E score

The two approaches combine to give four ways of testing graphology, as shown in Figure 1, of which all but one have been widely used. The choice of approach has traditionally been embroiled in an analytic-holistic controversy over the best way to assess scripts, with pros and cons briefly as follows:

Analytic approach (tests isolated script features)

Pro: Test is readily defined and standardized. All researchers can do it the same way, so we know what is happening.
Most graphology books list isolated features.
Modern multivariate techniques allow for interaction.
Accuracy is readily determined.
Con: Isolated features play no part in modern graphology.

Holistic approach (tests the whole script)

Pro: This is the way modern graphologists work.
Con: Test is impossible to define or standardize. No two graphologists work the same way, so what is happening?
Not more than five scripts can be compared at one time.[4]
Success is influenced by external cues, atypical differences, stereotypes that happen to fit, and small samples.
Success could mean subjective impressions are 10 percent accurate or 100 percent accurate, but there is no way of telling which.

In their everyday work most graphologists favor the holistic approach to assessing scripts and abhor the analytic approach. Fair enough. But for *testing* graphology the above cons against the holistic approach are so severe that Brengelmann (1960) could conclude "the holistic-analytic controversy is a pseudo-problem." That was thirty years ago, yet today the controversy still continues. For the present purpose we will accept that both approaches are necessary for a balanced testing of graphology.

ASKING THE RIGHT QUESTIONS

To test graphology we must ask the right questions. We should not ask *is graphology true?* (Answer: what is truth?) Or *does it work?* (Answer: can thousands of graphologists be wrong?) Or *is it real?* (Answer: you sound like a blind man feeling an elephant.) Instead we should ask about *extent*. To what extent is graphology true? To what extent do graphological judgments agree with each other? To what extent do they predict behavior?

To what extent does graphology do better than other tests? In short, we should ask about *effect size.*

An effect size is a number that, unsurprisingly, tells us how big the effect is. A big effect, like a bucket of water on a cigarette butt, is useful. A small effect, like the same bucket in a city blaze, may be of no use at all. Unfortunately effect sizes are conspicuously missing from graphology books, whose authors generally behave like used-car salesmen—yes, lady, this beauty is for you, gleaming chrome, dazzling paint job, never mind the engine.[5] In this chapter we are taking a long hard look under the hood.

MEASURING EFFECT SIZE

An effect size indicates the extent to which one thing is associated with another. It is commonly expressed as a *correlation,* a number between +1 and -1, defined as follows:

+1 perfect correlation
0 no correlation
-1 perfect inverse correlation

All correlations have the advantage of being independent of the original units of measurement. So they can be directly compared with other correlations.[6] Box 1 shows how it works.

To obtain an effect size, someone has to test graphological indications against reality, using procedures as described in any book on experimental design, e.g., Miller (1984). This is hard and demanding work, which is one reason why busy graphologists have better things to do. Depending on the test, the outcome will be either an effect size or something that can be converted to an effect size. Whether it means anything depends on your controls and sample size, coming up next.

CONTROLS TELL THE STORY

Controls are what stop you generating nonsense. They are called *controls* because they control the possibility of mistaking spurious effects for the real thing. Predicting sunshine with an amazing 90 percent accuracy means nothing if you live in the desert. Neither does matching pairs of writers with 100 percent accuracy if one is sober and the other is blind drunk. So tests of graphologists and their readings need controls which repeat everything using nongraphologists and bogus readings. Otherwise you cannot tell whether the results are due to graphology or to something else.

Box 1. *Examples of Effect Sizes*

r	Example	Source
1.00	Feet vs. meters or 100% hits	
.95	Arm length right vs. left	1
.70	Adult height vs. weight	1
.60	Educational attainment } husbands	2
.50	Physical attractiveness } vs. wives	2
.40	City size vs. incidence of jaywalking	3
.30	Height of husbands vs. wives	1
.20	IQ vs. appreciation of music	4
.10	IQ vs. head size	5
.00	Coin tossing or 50% hits	

Sources: 1. Jensen (1984); 2. Feingold (1988); 3. Mullen et al. (1990); 4. Williams et al. (1938); 5. Van Valen (1974); Passingham (1979).

At top, an effect size of 1.00 means the correlation is perfect, as between feet and meters. You always get 100 percent hits. At bottom, an effect size of .00 means there is no correlation at all, as between the tosses of two coins. You average 50 percent hits or exactly chance. So an effect size of .00 is rock-bottom useless.

In between are the effect sizes observed in human affairs, rounded to simplify comparison. At .95 is the near-perfect correlation between right and left arm lengths, which supports our everyday observation that any difference is small. At .70 is the less-perfect correlation between height and weight—heavyweights tend to be tall and lightweights tend to be short, but there are individual exceptions. And so on, down to the almost negligible correlations for IQ vs. music appreciation and head size, where one variable is not a useful guide to the other. A negative effect size means that more of one gives less of the other, such as -.20 for job satisfaction vs. absenteeism (Hackett 1989), and -1.00 for daylength vs. nightlength.

In technical terms effect size r has a simple interpretation. If x and y are measured in standard deviations, then r is the slope of the line relating y to x, namely $y = rx$. In practical terms this means that an effect size of .40 is 40 percent as useful as an effect size of 1.00, or perfect prediction (Hunter and Schmidt 1990:200–201). The symbol r was first used over a century ago when it stood for regression.

If you find effect sizes inscrutable, try this easy conversion to hit rates. Rosenthal and Rubin (1982) show that, for tossing a coin, the hit rate corresponding to correlation r is (50 + 50r) percent, which gives the conversions used above:

Effect size	-.60	-.40	-.20	.00	.20	.40	.60
Hit rate (50% expected)	20%	30%	40%	50%	60%	70%	80%

Thus an effect size of .40 is like averaging (50 + 50 × .40) = 70 percent heads all the time. An effect size of .00 is like averaging (50 + 50 × .00) = 50 percent heads all the time, or exactly chance.

For example, a study may show that authentic readings are seen as accurate, but so what? So are bogus readings. For sobering examples see Crowley (1991), McKelvie (1990), Vestewig et al. (1976), and the second experiment by Karnes and Leonard in chapter 16, where authentic graphoanalytic readings were found to be even more Barnum than Barnum. Box 2 will give you a feel for this sort of thing.

Box 2. *Pick the Genuine Graphoanalysis*

One statement in each pair is from a handwriting analysis by a master graphoanalyst which the subject rated as "quite startling in its accuracy" (Warner and Swallow 1989). The other is from the classic set of Barnum statements, i.e., statements of universal validity, assembled by Forer (1949) largely from a newstand astrology book. Forer's aim was "to demonstrate the ease with which clients may be misled by a general personality description into unwarranted approval of a diagnostic tool." Can you tell which statements are from the genuine graphoanalysis?

Kind and considerate with an apparent optimistic outlook, you nevertheless keep yourself and your emotions under control.	At times you are extroverted, affable and sociable, while at other times you are introverted, wary, and reserved.
While you have some personality weaknesses, you are generally able to compensate for them.	You feel deeply, but you prefer to hide your feelings and find it difficult to express them.
You seek to maintain dignity and poise in situations where you feel inferior. This can lead to tension.	Disciplined and self-controlled outside, you tend to be worrisome and insecure inside.
At times you have serious doubts as to whether you have made the right decision or done the right thing.	Some incidents affect you deeply while others of a similar nature hardly do so at all.
You tend to be reticent, but you do need people, and want to lead a life of some significance.	You have a great need for people to like and admire you. Security is one of your major goals.

You probably found it impossible to choose with any confidence, which illustrates the need for controls when assessing the accuracy of graphological interpretations. For the answers look under Warner and Swallow (1989) in the list of references. Chance score is 2.5 hits. One reader in 32 should get 0 or 5 hits by chance alone.

SAMPLE SIZE IS CRUCIAL

A sample that is too small can ruin everything before you even start. Try this simple exercise:

1. Imagine that half the population writes large, and half writes small, regardless of sex.
2. Imagine collecting a sample of 20 handwritings.

Owing to chance variations your sample will not contain *exactly* the same proportions (50 percent male and 50 percent large) as the population, any more than 20 coin tosses always gives 10 heads. If it happens to contain an excess of males and large writings, you would wrongly conclude that males tend to have large writing. Furthermore your chance of being wrong increases as the sample size N decreases. For example, to get a proportion in the range 45–55 percent for both sex and size, your chance is a reassuring 92 percent at N = 200 but only 25 percent at N = 20. The last means that on average 75 percent of such samples would give wrong answers.

In other words sampling variations are like magic—out of nothing they can produce results that are interesting, exciting, full of promise, and totally spurious. The sample size needed to avoid spurious results depends on the effect size and can be calculated.[7] For graphology the answer is typically over 200, which almost no studies manage to achieve. As we shall see later, this has predictable consequences. Next we come to a tiresome but necessary distinction between reliability and validity.

RELIABILITY VS. VALIDITY

Reliability and validity have special meanings in experimental work:

Reliability= *consistency,* the agreement between repeated measurements.
Validity = *accuracy,* the agreement between measurement and reality.

If we cannot agree on how slanted a handwriting is, then looking at slant is a waste of time, like planning a holiday but disagreeing on where to go. If we agree on slant but not on the interpretation, we are no better off. Disagreement means the measure is *unreliable*—we never get the same answer twice. By contrast a *reliable* measure gives us the same answer nearly every time. Obviously when testing graphology we want as much reliability as possible.

But reliability is not everything. The number of coins in your pocket can be measured very reliably (you get the same answer every time) but is useless for predicting the weather. So high reliability does not necessarily mean high validity. On the other hand low reliability *always* means low validity, because an unreliable test gives us different answers every time, so we cannot be sure they mean anything. Thus graphologists who disagree on what slant means are useless for interpreting slant, just as tipsters who disagree on their tips are useless for winning bets.

Now comes the clever part. If we measure both reliability and validity as a correlation, the maximum possible validity is the square root of the reliability. If the reliability of tipsters is .25, the maximum possible validity in using their tips is $\sqrt{(.25)}$ or .50—a useful finding because it sidesteps the problems of validation (agreement is easy to measure, but truth is something else).[8] On the other hand, the validity so calculated is only an upper bound (the tipsters may agree but still be wrong), so it tends to greatly overestimate the validity actually observed.[9]

In general, validity means the same as effect size. A tipster with a validity of .50 has an effect size of .50, meaning his tips correlate .50 with the winners. The terms are interchangeable, but effect size is easier to understand.[10]

RELIABILITY: HOW RELIABLE IS RELIABLE?

To be acceptable, how reliable must a test be? In general no psychological test becomes widely accepted unless its reliability exceeds .80. But it depends on the situation. Meehl (1972:159) points out that doctors still measure blood pressure despite a poor test-retest reliability caused by instrumental defects, differences in resting state, and individual differences in technique. It is simply more useful to know blood pressure with a reliability of say .65 than it is to know wrist width with a reliability of say .98. On the other hand doctors must offset the unreliability by taking many measurements, say three times a day for a week, before believing what they see. Also .65 would be unacceptable if .80 were available elsewhere. So it depends on the situation.

Nevertheless for the psychological testing of *individuals* (are you prone to anxiety?) .80 is a good starting point. For making decisions about *groups* (are old people generally more anxious than young people?), reliabilities down to .50 may be acceptable. Anything below .40 is generally regarded as useless, because the error rate is then too high for the results to mean anything.[11] As shown next, the key word is *individuals*.

EFFECT SIZE: HOW USEFUL IS USEFUL?

To be useful, how large must an effect size be? Again, it depends on the situation. If you are laying carpet, a correlation of .90 between your tape measure and reality would give dimensions accurate to only ±20 percent. So .90 would be far too low. But if you are betting at roulette, an effect size of .20 in your favor would on average take all of one hour to convert twenty dollars into a million. So .20 could be needlessly high.

Furthermore, it depends on whether the situation involves individuals or groups. For *individuals,* if you are testing personality or ability, the minimum effect size generally regarded as being useful is around .40. Also .40 is the minimum correlation that the average person can detect between columns of figures or shapes, which needs .85 before nearly everyone can detect it, see next chapter. So as a guide we can reasonably adopt .40 as the minimum useful effect size for any technique applied to individuals.

For *groups* the thinking is different. Here applying an effect size is like detecting it in reverse. Just as a small effect needs a large sample to reliably *detect* it, so it needs a large sample to reliably *apply* it. If we have a single situation such as buying a car, we need a large effect size (i.e., between our information and reality) to maximize the chance of getting a hit (i.e., not buying a lemon). But if we have many situations such as planting seeds, we can accept a smaller effect size because the large sample evens out the impact of individual misses. To put it another way, it is safer to play Russian roulette once with two chambers loaded than many times with one chamber loaded.

So what is the minimum useful effect size for groups? If the group is big enough the answer is *anything larger than zero.* Thus tests which have effect sizes too small for individual use can still be usefuly applied to groups. For a company that hires many people each year, hiring on the basis of such tests (as opposed to hiring at random) has substantial dollar value.[12]

So far so good. Now comes the frustrating part, where among other things we catch up with the predictable consequences of using small samples.

THE FINE PRINT: OR THE HIDDEN DELIGHTS OF SURVEYING EXPERIMENTAL STUDIES

YES, GRAPHOLOGY IS PLAUSIBLE, BUT SO WHAT?

In principle graphology is eminently plausible. Unlike astrology and palmistry, it relies on an actual sample of behavior. And if the differences are large enough, it would be unreasonable *not* to see them reflected in handwriting. Take the two biggest single determinants of human behavior and destiny, namely, sex and intelligence. Many studies have shown that non-graphologist judges can pick sex from handwriting with 60 to 70 percent accuracy (effect size .20 to .40), or even more when only their most confident judgments are counted, as in the following examples:

Author	Sample	No. of judges	Mean % correct	Ditto, confident judgments only
Downey 1910	200 envelopes	13	67.4%	75.1%
Young 1931*	50 brief lists	50	61.0%	
Goodenough 1945	115 same paragraph	20	69.6%	81.0%

*Cues: Careless untidy angular = male. Careful tidy rounded = female.

Similarly many studies have shown that lay and graphologist judges can judge intelligence from handwriting with comparable accuracy, the effect size averaging around .30 (Michel 1969). As expected, it gets easier as the IQ differences increase, leading to an increase in the effect size:

Author	Judges	Subjects	IQ	r
Michel 1969:44	7 rankers	7	91–128	.27
Castelnuovo-Tedesco 1948	6 raters	100	68–132	.59

Studies of sex and IQ are summarized in Appendix D.

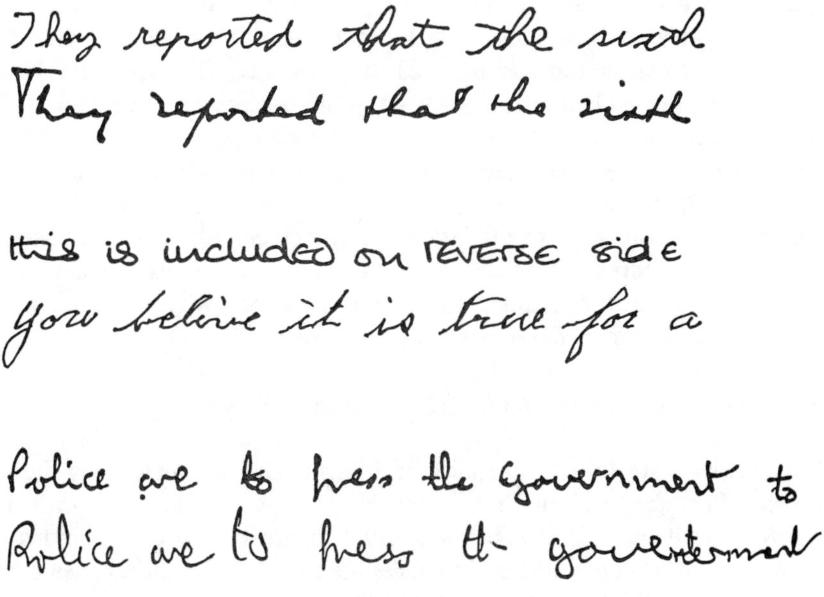

They reported that the sixth
They reported that the sixth

this is included on REVERSE side
you believe it is true for a

Police are to press the government to
Police we to press the governtement

Figure 2.

Big differences are just as detectable in other areas. Thus it is unsurprising that people prematurely aged by concentration camps should have a disturbed handwriting, typically oversized or complicated, with breaks and tremors (Paul-Mengelberg 1956, Ratzon 1986). Figure 2 shows how easy it is to distinguish between extreme IQs, between the artistry of the artist and the tremor of the alcoholic, and between being sober and blind drunk. (Here I will ignore the problem that it is even easier face to face, in which case it is pointless to look at handwriting.) Furthermore, from the bottom example in Figure 2, it is easy to understand why poor handwriting gets you lower marks. It is also easy to understand this interesting 1930 court case from Germany:

> A farmer was living on bad terms with his neighbour. To offend him he deliberately sowed seeds on his neighbour's field in the form of libellous words. The seeds grew to plants which were in the exact pattern of the offender's handwriting. The court accepted this as evidence and legal proof of the offender's identity, and he was convicted. (Singer 1974:27)

If graphologists had no greater claims than these, then nobody could complain. But there is a huge leap of faith between a teacher's failing of a pupil whose handwriting she cannot decipher, and a graphologist's conclusions about your honesty, leadership, musical ability, performance in marriage, and so on, if only because there is no reason to believe such qualities find expression in handwriting. Even neat appearance and neat writing, both clear products of motor movement, seem poorly related—the observed correlation was only .23 for 30 females (Brown 1921), Neat-in-Dress scores and predictions by six graphologists correlated only .32 for 13 males and, disconcertingly, -.28 for 35 females (Vestewig et al. 1976), while 200 doctors in their neat surgeries had significantly *less* legible writing than 500 nondoctors, the corresponding correlation being -.20 (Goldsmith 1976).[13] So there seems little hope for claims like Albert Einstein's "prodigious memory is revealed in the careful dotting of his i's" (Olyanova 1960:193). But in this chapter ours is not to reason why, only to survey the evidence. Which is not as easy as it may seem.

SURVEYING EXPERIMENTAL STUDIES BY META-ANALYSIS

Suppose we have found 50 studies of a particular effect. Typically the reported effect sizes will all be different. How do we decide which ones are correct? Until the mid-1970s it was usual to attribute such variations to differences in *situation,* like testing males here but females there. Then came a revolution in thinking. It was realized that much of the variation between studies was due to differences in *statistical variables* such as sample size and measurement reliability. As a result a special method of analysis, called meta-analysis (rhymes with better), was invented to tackle this problem. Meta-analysis quickly became the preferred method for surveying research results, and by 1984 about 300 meta-analyses had been conducted in diverse areas from medical research to finance (Hunter and Schmidt 1990:41). Entering the keyword *meta-analysis* into the PsycLIT computerized database would have returned 0 titles in 1976, 50 in 1983, and 900 in 1991—and that is just for psychology. Meta-analysis is used later to survey graphology research.

Meta-analysis takes a set of effect sizes and removes the statistical variability. It then tests any remaining variability to see if it is genuine. If it is, further tests can be made to identify the underlying causes, and thus track down the variables which matter. The whole point of meta-analysis is that it reaches better conclusions than those reached in individual studies. Which is why it is used here. The first step is to retrieve all relevant research studies, which is easy to say but not easy to do.

RETRIEVING GRAPHOLOGY RESEARCH STUDIES

To retrieve research studies the usual approach (followed here) is a computerized search of literature databases, a methodical gleaning of references from the works thus uncovered, and so on down the line until nothing further appears, plus writing to people. Then it is off to the university library to photocopy the cited studies from the original journals, and (at least in theory) you are up and running. For popular orthodox subjects like personnel testing this can produce hundreds of studies based on a total of many thousands of subjects, sometimes even hundreds of thousands (Schmidt et al. 1981). Such data bases are so large that the indications become extremely trustworthy. But in graphology it is not so easy:

1. Computerized data bases rarely extend much before 1970 and therefore do not cover the important early work in graphology. Nor do they cover studies reported in graphology journals, which are excluded for the same reason that astrology journals are excluded, namely, the general absence of even minimum standards of scientific reporting.

2. Studies of graphology are so highly scattered across journals and countries that retrieval is difficult. Not even national libraries can subscribe to every scientific journal (all 100,000 of them, somewhat more than in 1700 when the total was 8). So knowing a study exists is no guarantee you can retrieve it. For example, in their reviews of reliability Lester (1981)

cites 12 studies and Nevo (1986a) cites 25 studies. Both authors tried to be comprehensive, but only 3 studies are common to both. In principle any study can be retrieved given enough resources like money and someone to do all the work, but we may then discover it suffers from the next three problems.

3. Many studies are not relevant. For example, Eysenck (1945) cites 30 studies that are "the most important 10%" to have appeared since 1933, but only 10 report effect sizes. You cannot tell from the title. Similarly, Miller's (1982) bibliography of 2321 graphology items (roughly 40 percent English, 30 percent German, and the rest mostly French), including books and journals, is of no use because he does not identify research studies reporting effect sizes.

4. Many studies are impossible to assess. For example they omit important details, or omit controls, or, as Klimoski and Rafaeli (1983) put it, they suffer from "significant methodological negligence." Examples are given in note 14.

5. Journals may tend to reject studies with negative findings. Or they may favor the better-designed studies. Either way, the retrieved studies may be a biased sample of the studies actually carried out, in the same way that shiny maggot-free apples in the supermarket are a biased sample of those on the trees. This is called the *file-drawer problem* (Rosenthal 1979), after the file drawers supposedly crammed with negative studies rejected by cruel editors.[15]

Despite these problems I managed to retrieve over 60 reliabilities and nearly 140 effect sizes, usually directly from published studies but occasionally secondhand from reviews. To give you a feel for what lies behind the dry-as-dust figures ahead, next are a few selected details from these published studies, most of them reflecting the delights of small sample sizes.

NOW YOU SEE IT, NOW YOU DON'T

Small sample sizes ($N<100$) are common in graphology studies because they are quick and easy. They also give erratic and unreliable results, which means that for every study with a particular result there is usually another which contradicts it. For example:

Does heavy writing pressure indicate an aggressive nature? The answer is *no* according to Hull and Montgomery (1919) but *yes* according to Downey (1919), a difference which is easily explained by small sample sizes:

Hull and Montgomery 1919	Light = aggressive	r = .17	p = .53	N = 17
Downey 1919	Heavy = aggressive	r = .23	p = .25	N = 28

What size of handwriting indicates emotionality? The answer is *small* according to Taft (1967) but *large* according to Furnham and Gunter (1987):

Taft 1967	Small = emotional	r = .2	p = .07	N = 86
Furnham and Gunter 1987	Large = emotional	r = .19	p = .13	N = 64

Here the sample sizes are larger than in the previous case, but not enough to give reliable results. For even larger samples the effect size approaches zero (Crowley 1991, Stabholz 1981), which supports the view that the disagreement is mostly due to sampling variations:

Crowley 1991	Small = emotional	r = .03	p = .78	N = 93
Stabholz 1981	Large = emotional	r = .01	p = .86	N = 316

Do artistic people have artistic writing? The answer is *yes* according to Meloun (1935), who gives only sketchy evidence, but *no* according to Lester (1981:75), who gives no evidence at all despite having complained about Meloun's sketchy evidence.

Can nongraphologists judge emotionality? Middleton (1941) found they tended to get the *right* answers, but Vine (1974) found they tended to get the *wrong* answers, both at an impressive level of significance:

Middleton 1941	5 levels of emotionality.	r = .31	p = .006	N = 78
Vine 1974	6 levels of emotionality.	r = -.4	p = .001	N = 63

Do confident writers omit i-dots? Lemke and Kirchener (1971) found *yes* for 103 students, r = .20, one of the better results in a study that generated 160 effect sizes, only a handful of which are reported. But two years later Kirchener and Lemke (1973) found *no* for 72 alcoholics and schizophrenics, conveniently referring the reader to their Figure 1 for details—except there is no Figure 1.

Take twenty close friends and have a graphologist interpret five of their handwritings. Can the others tell which interpretation is which? The answer is *yes* according to Bobertag (1929) but *no* according to De Groot (1947), a difference which is entirely explained by the tiny sample size:[16]

Bobertag 1929	15 others averaged 81% hits	hits expected by chance = 20%
De Groot 1947	13 others averaged 23% hits	

Does confidence increase the accuracy of graphological judgment? Eysenck (1945) found *yes* for his graphologist filling out a personality test for 50 handwritings, whereas Eysenck and Gudjonnson (1986) found *no* for another graphologist doing the same for 99 handwritings. However others tend to find *yes,* e.g., Jansen (1973) and Vestewig et al. (1976), which is as it should be if there is something in it, even though the correlation between confidence and hit rate averaged only about .30.

When is an expert not an expert? Rafaeli and Klimoski (1983) tested 20 graphologists, of whom "Twelve had previous experience in personnel selection . . . All were considered experts in the field." But Rafaeli and Drory (1988), referring to the same study, say most of them "had little if any experience with graphology as a selection tool." So now you see it, now you don't. Perhaps the answer lies in the popular definition of expert, where x is the unknown and spurt is a drip under pressure.

Can poor results be made to look good? Of course they can. As already noted in note 14, there are numerous strategies, for example, you can toss out your controls or, in an emergency, your entire results. More subtly, you can focus on significance and ignore effect size. Less subtly, you can make unsupported assertions, as do LoMonaco et al. (1973) when they rate the empirical literature on graphology (whose bad press was aired earlier) as "predominantly favorable."

The good news is that the above problems are what meta-analysis is designed to cope with. Meta-analysis cuts through the confusion and gets straight to the bottom line. In what follows we look at the results, reliability first. For technical readers the technicalities of meta-analysis are described in note 17, the correction for artifacts in notes 18–21, and the interpretation of meta-analytic results in note 22.

THE BOTTOM LINE: THE RESULTS OF EXPERIMENTAL STUDIES OF EFFECT SIZE

RELIABILITY OF GRAPHOLOGY

Reliability is the agreement between repeated tests. By searching the literature I managed to locate 23 articles that reported reliabilities, plus a further 18 articles and dissertations whose results were obtained secondhand, mostly from the reviews by Lester (1981) and Nevo (1986a). These yielded a total of 66 reliabilities; see Appendix A. The mean reliabilities (weighted by sample size) obtained by meta-analysis are shown below. Details of how each study was processed are given in note 23.

Feature tested	Mean reliability, same scripts			No. of scripts	
	Test-retest same judges	Agreement diff judges	All	Mean	Total
Objective e.g. slant*	.87 (5)**	.85 (12)	.86 (17)	58	989
Subjective e.g. rhythm	.69 (3)	.60 (3)	.64 (6)	94	566
Interp e.g. extrovert	.59 (4)	.42 (15)	.44 (19)	40	756
Interp, lay judges	.66 (4)	.30 (16)	.36 (20)	46	923

*Based on the mean of typically ten or more instances of each feature.
**Mean is .74 (4) if retested using *fresh* scripts within two months.

( ) = number of studies

The above results show that when two or more people measure *objective* features such as slant or slope in a sample of handwriting, the correlation between their results is quite high. So such measurements tend to be reliable. As expected, the correlation drops somewhat for *subjective* features such as rhythm and connectedness, and drops still further for *interpreted* features such as extroversion. So while judges may agree closely on the degree of slant or slope, they agree less closely on what it means, which of course is what matters. As expected, the agreement between different judges is consistently worse than between repeats by the same judge.[24] Similarly, compared with lay judges, graphologist judges show better agreement on interpretation, but not much better (.42 vs. .30).

For a graphological consultation the relevant reliability in the above table is .42, or close to useless (see "Reliability: How Reliable Is Reliable?" above). It is based on 15 studies, so it cannot be easily dismissed as unrepresentative. In which case, unless graphologists improve their reliability, graphology will remain unacceptable for use with individuals.

EFFECT SIZE OF GRAPHOLOGY IN PERSONNEL SELECTION

A meta-analysis of graphology in personnel selection has been performed by Neter and Ben-Shakhar (1989). By searching the literature, and by contacting active researchers, they managed to locate 13 articles and dissertations that investigated effect size at an acceptable standard. To be acceptable the work had to:

1. Compare graphological predictions of work performance with an independent criterion such as supervisor ratings or training success.
2. Report correlations or enough data for their calculation.

3. Report sample size.
4. Report the content of the handwriting sample.

In most cases the script used for the handwriting analysis was part of a job application, whose content may have influenced the graphological judgment. So Neter and Ben-Shakhar were careful to analyze separately all studies using neutral scripts. By further searching I managed to locate another 3 articles to make a total of 16, which yielded a total of 35 effect sizes; see Appendix B. Meta-analysis gave the following mean effect sizes, the categories being those of Neter and Ben-Shakhar:[25]

		Handwriting judged by				No. of scripts	
Test	Neutral scripts?	Graph	Psych	Lay	All	Mean	Total
Whole script vs work perf	No	.158 (17)	.178 (5)	.173 (4)	.165 (26)	68	1758
	Yes	.086 (6)	.11 (1)	.022 (2)	.073 (9)	102	920
( ) = number of studies		Weighted mean			.134 (35)	77	2678

Each effect size is the mean correlation (weighted by number of scripts) between work performance as predicted from the handwriting (by graphologists, psychologists, or laypersons), and reality as determined by supervisor ratings or success during job training. Not surprisingly they are very similar to those found by Neter and Ben-Shakhar (1989).[26] The above results show that:

1. Effect sizes are too low to be useful.
2. Nongraphologists are generally as good as graphologists.
3. Effect size is much reduced by using neutral scripts.

The last suggests that much of any validity is due to information in the scripts and not to graphology. In other words, contrary to what graphologists say, content *does* influence judgment.[27]

EFFECT SIZE OF GRAPHOLOGY IN PREDICTING PERSONALITY

To date no meta-analysis of graphology in predicting personality has been reported. Therefore I repeated the previous meta-analysis, this time on studies that compared graphological predictions of personality with an independent criterion such as self-ratings, peer-ratings, or personality test scores. Studies of sex and IQ were excluded (these yielded 10 and 14 effect sizes respectively; see Appendix D).

By searching the literature I managed to locate 47 articles and dissertations that investigated effect size at the same acceptable standard as before, plus 6 more from secondhand sources, total 53, of which 4 are shared with the previous section. These yielded a total of 72 effect sizes; see Appendix C. To be more than fair to graphology, studies were included even when methodological shortcomings could reasonably be suspected of inflating the success rate, e.g., Eysenck (1945), Crumbaugh and Stockholm (1977), and Wellingham-Jones (1989).[28] About ten works cited in reviews could not be obtained and therefore could not be included. Half were dissertations not accessible through Dissertation Abstracts International and the rest were pre-1930 German articles. However, according to the reviews they were as frequently negative as positive, so their omission should be of little consequence. Meta-analysis gave the following mean effect sizes for the same categories as before:[29]

Test		Neutral scripts?	Handwriting judged by Graph	Psych	Lay	All	No. of scripts Mean	Total
Signs vs. predicted trait				.082 (11)		.082 (11)	76	835
Whole script vs. personality		No	.139 (14)	.269 (4)	.064 (5)	.135 (23)	60	1386
		Yes	.066 (10)	–.05 (1)	.106 (7)	.068 (18)	47	854
Match to personality	Script	Yes	.205 (2)	.076 (2)	.044 (3)	.076 (7)	15	107
	Interp	Yes			.146 (13)	.146 (13)	19	244
( ) = number of studies					Weighted mean	.104 (72)	48	3426

Each effect size is the mean correlation (weighted by number of scripts) between personality as predicted from the handwriting (by graphologists, psychologists, or laypersons), and the actual personality as determined by self-ratings, peer-ratings, or personality tests. The above results show that:

1. Effect sizes are too low to be useful.
2. Nongraphologists are generally as good as graphologists.
3. Effect size is reduced by using neutral scripts.
4. Signs (individual features) are no worse than neutral scripts.
5. Sample sizes for matching tests are dismally low.

Included in Appendix C, but not shown above, are 7 omnibus studies of signs where large numbers of signs were correlated with large numbers of traits in the hope of finding something. A total of 1519 correlations were observed but the number reaching significance at the $p \leq .05$ level is slightly less than chance (74 vs. 76).[30] This suggests that, if effective signs exist, there are not many of them.

The results of this and the previous section show consistently that nongraphologists are generally as good as graphologists. Isn't this the worst possible news for graphology? Answer: not if the traditionally impoverished researcher could afford to test only inexperienced amateur graphologists of dubious repute. For how can you test graphology properly if you don't use *real* graphologists? A good point. Now read on.

ARE PROFESSIONALS BETTER THAN AMATEURS?

As it happens, most studies did *not* use inexperienced amateurs. Instead they used only experienced professional graphologists, typical descriptions being "well-known" (Bobertag 1929, Eysenck 1948); "experienced" (Cox and Tapsell 1991); "years of experience" (Drory 1986); "better qualified than most" (Eysenck 1945); "ample experience of personnel selection and [according to their peers] all able" (Jansen 1973); "highly experienced certified graphologists" (Kimmel and Wertheimer 1966); and "professional" (LoMonaco et al. 1973, a modest description for the then president of the American Association of Handwriting Analysts).

Furthermore, the graphologists often helped in designing the experiment to make it as realistic as possible. For example, Kimmel and Wertheimer (1966) held a joint conference among the graphologists, raters, and experimenters "to decide *which* particular personality characteristics would be rated, and precisely *how* they were to be defined and rated." For his four lengthy experiments (they took seven years), Jansen (1973) had a panel of four graphologists and four psychologists establish the initial approach, criticize each experiment when it was finished, and suggest improvements for the next (for the record the results were consistently dismal). To select a mutually acceptable task, Goldberg (1986) and his graphologist "spent a day together examining each of the tests, inventories, and questionnaires that were available."

In other words, researchers generally *have* been careful to test real graphologists under realistic conditions, so their poor results cannot be explained by lack of expertise. Similarly we cannot conclude that professionals are generally better than amateurs. Here is an example:

In one of the few studies that used amateurs, Nevo (1989) had judges match 10 persons to interpretations by student graphologists, and obtained an encouraging mean effect size of .34. But when Nevo and Benitta (1991) repeated the experiment with 12 persons and 3 professional graphologists, the mean effect size dropped to only .01. As usual the sample sizes are too small for comfort, but the results illustrate the point.

This poor performance by professionals is consistent with the findings of Garb (1989), who reviewed 55 studies of validity vs. experience in the clinical assessment of personality. In general, experienced clinicians were no more accurate than students across a wide variety of judgments including interviews, therapy sessions, biographies, and personality test results. Which sets the tone for what comes next.

IS GRAPHOANALYSIS BETTER?

Graphoanalysis is the trademarked name of a particular U.S. school of graphology founded in 1929. It is a strongly holistic method in which the graphologist converts a multitude of cues into a global whole. According to Crumbaugh and Stockholm (1977) it "has been more systematically developed, presented in greater detail, more effectively taught, and better researched, than any other method of handwriting analysis." Peeples (1991) found that 13 Graphoanalysts were slightly less in agreement with each other (mean r=.29) than were 13 psychogrammists (r=.36) and 11 gestaltists (r=.46), but since this was based on a single script no general conclusion is possible.

Of the 35 personnel selection studies and 61 non-sign personality studies surveyed here, 9 involve Graphoanalysts. Matching these studies in design are 21 involving other kinds of graphologists. Meta-analysis of these 9 Graphoanalytic studies (7 with neutral scripts) and the 21 equivalent non-Graphoanalytic studies (18 with neutral scripts) gave the following mean effect sizes and standard deviations:

9 Graphoanalytic studies	.071 sd.049 (387 scripts)	by t-test
21 non-Grapholanalytic studies	.101 sd.121 (853 scripts)	t=.71, p=.48

The difference is nonsignificant and in the wrong direction to suggest that Graphoanalysis has advantages over other kinds of graphology.

ARE EXTERNAL CRITERIA BETTER THAN INTERNAL CRITERIA?

In chapter 6 Lockowandt concludes that:

1. *Internal* criteria (e.g., personality and IQ tests) are of questionable validity. Therefore,
2. Only *external* criteria (e.g., peer and supervisor ratings) should be used to validate graphology.

When you see the validity comparison in my Tables 2 and 3 you may be inclined to disagree with Lockowandt's first point. And if you noted Lockowandt's own dismissal of ratings in chapter 5 to explain the disappointing results of Birge (1954), you may be inclined to disagree with his second point also. No matter. If internal criteria really are useless, then the effect sizes for studies using personality tests (*internal* criteria) should be consistently worse than those for studies using peer and supervisor ratings (*external* criteria). Since the studies surveyed here contain plenty of both, Lockowandt's claim can be put to the test.

Accordingly, I extracted every study where judgments by graphologists were compared against an independent criterion. Studies involving individual signs or nongraphologists were of course excluded. I then segregated the extracted studies into those using personality tests vs. those using peer and supervisor ratings. Excluded were matching tests, and tests where the criterion was not clearly one or the other, e.g., psychiatric diagnoses, examination grades, and success in training. The result was 15 studies using tests (6 with neutral scripts) and 16 studies using ratings (3 with neutral scripts). Meta-analysis gave the following mean effect sizes and standard deviations:

15 studies with internal criteria	.115 sd.093 (806 scripts)	by t-test
16 studies with external criteria	.102 sd.137 (794 scripts)	t=.31, p=.76

The difference is nonsignificant and in the wrong direction to support Lockowandt's claim.

OVERALL MEAN EFFECT SIZE

The results so far have shown no significant difference in effect size between predicting work performance and predicting personality, or between graphologists and nongraphologists, whereas there is a significant difference between neutral and non-neutral scripts.[31] Therefore for convenience they can be combined as follows:

Test	Neutral scripts?	Effect size		sd	No. of scripts Mean	Total
Signs vs. predicted trait		.082	(11)	.075	76	835
Whole script vs. work performance or personality	No	.152	(49)	.111	64	3144
	Yes	.080	(47)	.114	45	2125
( ) = number of studies	Weighted mean	.117	(107)	.114	57	6104

The above results are based on 107 studies (from 65 published and unpublished articles over the period 1905–1991), over 6100 scripts, nearly 200 graphologists, and nearly 600 psychologists and laypersons. At the going rate for everyone's time this represents over a million dollars just for looking at scripts. The above results are displayed visually in Figure 3 using the plots suggested by Light and Pillemer (1984).

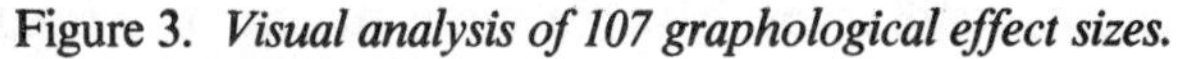

Figure 3. *Visual analysis of 107 graphological effect sizes.*

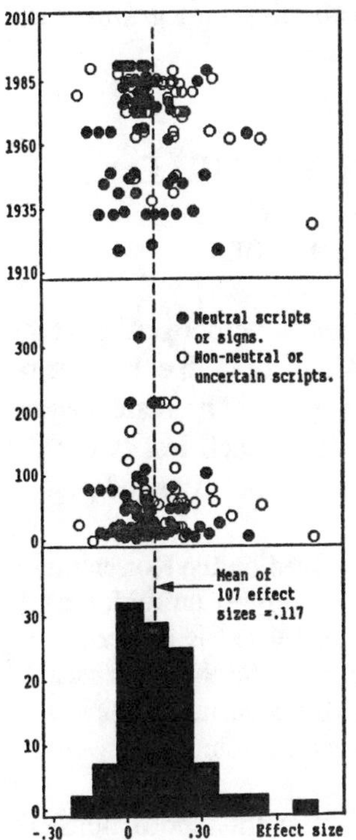

Effect size vs. year of study. As methods improve over time, so the results should converge on the truth with a corresponding decrease in scatter. But no such convergence or decrease is evident, suggesting that future studies will be equally dismal.

Effect size vs. number of scripts. As sample size increases, sampling errors decrease, so the plot should resemble an inverted funnel. And it does. There are fewer extreme results on the left than on the right, suggesting that some publication bias exists.

Distribution of effect sizes. The distribution is orderly, suggesting that most of the variability is due to sampling error, which of course agrees with the meta-analytic results. The bar width is too coarse to resolve the neutral/non-neutral difference (discernible in the other plots), so there is a single peak only.

The above results suggest that the best representative effect size for graphology using neutral scripts, and corrected for a criterion reliability of .60, is $.080/\sqrt{(.60)} = .10$, or say .12 to allow for range restriction and other attenuating artifacts. This (at last) is the bottom line. Of course many studies used test criteria more reliable than .60, and had no range restriction (or were already corrected for it where it was extreme). Furthermore, no allowance has been made for publication bias.[15] So this estimate may be optimistic.

So what does a corrected effect size of .12 tell us? It tells us that, in general, when used for predicting personality and work performance, graphology delivers $50 + 50 \times .12 = 56$ percent hits vs. 50 percent expected by chance—hardly a dazzling performance. Any null studies stashed away in file drawers will make the results even worse. Unretrieved studies may or may not improve things, but to save the day many dozens would be needed, all with effect sizes approaching 1.00—hardly something that over the years would have escaped notice by reviewers. So on balance it seems that an effect size around .12 is here to stay.

However, in fairness we must ask whether other techniques do any better. If selection interviewers, clinicians, IQ testers, inkblot readers, astrologers, palmists, and so on have no more success at this sort of thing than graphologists do, then we can hardly point the finger at graphology. So let us find out.

GRAPHOLOGY VS. THE REST OF THE WORLD

RELIABILITY: GRAPHOLOGY VS. OTHER TECHNIQUES

Table 1 shows how graphology compares in reliability with 14 other techniques. For use with individuals, tests in the top half of Table 1 are generally acceptable while those in the bottom half are not. The results show that graphology is roughly comparable with the Rorschach test (what do you see in this inkblot?), of which Jensen (1964:75) concluded as follows:

> . . . the 40 years of massive effort which has been lavished on the Rorschach technique [over 3,000 published studies by 1964] has proven unfruitful, at least so far as the development of a useful psychological test is concerned. [Therefore] . . . it seems not unreasonable to recommend that the Rorschach be altogether abandoned in clinical practice, and that students of clinical psychology not be required to waste their time learning the technique.

The same would now seem to apply to graphology. For the record, Jensen's 1964 comments about the Rorschach test had no effect, at least not in North America, where if anything the Rorschach's popularity in graduate clinical psychology courses rose between 1974 and 1984; see Ritzler and Alter (1986).[32] For recent comments about the future of the Rorschach test, and why it is unlikely to be abandoned, see Howes (1981) and Hertz (1986).

PREDICTING WORK PERFORMANCE: GRAPHOLOGY VS. OTHER TECHNIQUES

Table 2 shows how graphology compares in effect size with 15 other techniques for predicting work performance, such as cognitive tests, assessment centers, peer ratings, and interviews. The values for graphology are

Table 1. *Reliability. Graphology vs. Other Techniques.*

Technique	Mean agreement between judges		Source
Rating sex with 1% error	.98		
Achievement batteries	.92 (32)	Test-retest agreement on same subjects	1
Cognitive ability (IQ) tests	.90 (63)		1
Self-ratings of ability	.90 (24)		2
Aptitude batteries	.88 (22)		1
Personality inventories	.85 (43)		3
Structured interviews	.82 (25)		4
Rankings of ability	.80 approx.[33]		5
Unstructured interviews	.61 (9)		4
Ratings of ability	.48 (23)[34]		2
Mean agreement on:	*Interpretation*	*Features*	
Graphology	.42 (15)	.85 (12)	
Rorschach (inkblots)	.36 (7)	.84 (24)	6
TAT (ambiguous pictures)	–	.70 (45)	7
Palmistry	.11 (1)	.89 (4)	8
Astrology	.11 (27)	–	9

( ) = number of studies.

Sources: 1. Helmstadter (1966); 2. Harris and Schaubroeck (1988), Rothstein (1990); 3. Eysenck and Eysenck (1964), Helmstadter (1966); 4. Wiesner and Cronshaw (1988); 5. Kane and Lawler (1978), Nathan and Alexander (1988); 6. Jensen (1959, 1964), Reznikoff et al. (1982), Parker et al. (1988); 7. Murstein (1963); 8. Dean (1985), Symaniz (1980); 9. Dean (1986), Kelly et al. (1990).

taken from the preceding section "Effect Size of Graphology in Personnel Selection." The results show that graphology is outperformed by almost everything. Only predictions based on age are worse.

PREDICTING PERSONALITY AND IQ: GRAPHOLOGY VS. OTHER TECHNIQUES

Table 3 shows how graphology compares in effect size with 10 other techniques for predicting personality and IQ, such as the Eysenck Personality Inventory, IQ tests, Rorschach inkblots, and astrology. The values for graphology are taken from the preceding section "Effect Size of Graphology in Predicting Personality." Also included in the lower half are some related effect sizes for general interest. The results show that, compared to graphology, some techniques (astrology, phrenology) do worse, while others

Table 2. *Predicting Work Performance: Graphology vs. Other Techniques*

Effect size	N	Technique	Source	Sample
.43 (.70)	61	Cognitive test vs. success in training[35]	1	31535
(.53)	425	Cognitive test plus psychomotor test	2	32124
.35 (.45)	27	Assessment center	3,4	c.1700
.35 (.63)	32	Structured individual interview	5	7873
.32	48	Work sample or biography or peer rating	4	5771
.24 (.50)	144	Cognitive test	1	10564
.23 (.35)	47	Self-ratings	6	4941
.21	32	Personality test[36]	4	4065
.18 (.26)	8	References from previous employers	2,7	5389
.18	5	Projective technique vs. various criteria	7	335
.17	26	Graphology using non-neutral scripts		1758
.11 (.20)	19	Unstructured individual interview	5	2303
.10	3	SVIB vocational interest inventory	2	1789
.07	9	Graphology using neutral scripts		920
-.01	425	Age (adults only)	2	32124

N = number of studies. Effect size is the mean correlation between prediction and actual work performance, the latter being measured by supervisor ratings unless otherwise indicated. ( ) = effect size corrected for attenuation by the original authors.[37] Cognitive tests (same as IQ tests) measure mental ability. Psychomotor tests measure mostly dexterity and coordination. Structured interviews use preset questions and associated rating scales. Work sample tests measure performance on a sample of work, e.g., typing a letter. The listed effect sizes usually hide individual variations. Thus biographies (akin to CVs) are better at predicting wages, and worse at predicting tenure, than the .32 above. For the present purpose these variations do not affect the broad indications.

Sources: 1. Schmidt et al. (1981); 2. Hunter and Hunter (1984); 3. Cohen et al. (1974) via 2; 4. Schmitt et al. (1984); 5. Wiesner and Cronshaw (1988); 6. Harris and Schaubroeck (1988); 7. Reilly and Chao (1982).

(all recognized tests) do better, usually much better.[38] For predicting personality, even physiognomy has a higher effect size than graphology, suggesting that a single glance at the face is generally more useful than several hours spent analyzing the handwriting.

The comparison in Table 3 confirms our earlier suspicion, namely, that the effect size of graphology is too small to be useful. Interestingly, contrary to the unanimous claims of graphologists,[39] graphology's best performance is in predicting sex, no doubt helped by good criterion reliabil-

Table 3. *Predicting Personality and IQ: Graphology vs. Other Techniques*

Effect size	N	Technique	Source
.65	5	Wechsler IQ test vs. high school grades	1
.56	13	Eysenck Personality Inventory vs. self/peer ratings	2
.52	8	Wechsler IQ test vs. college grades	1
.46	30	MMPI vs. clinical ratings	3
.34	726	Law School Ability Test vs. 1st year law grade	4
.34	13	Rorschach vs. IQ, personality test, clinical ratings	3,5
.29	14	Graphology vs. IQ test	6
.15	17	Physiognomy vs. IQ, personality test, peer ratings	7
.14	23	Non-neutral scripts } Graphology vs. personality test, ratings, matchings	
.09	38	Neutral scripts } Graphology vs. personality test, ratings, matchings	
≤.05	79	Astrology vs. IQ, personality test, case histories	8
.00	1	Phrenology measures vs. peer ratings	9
-.05	9	Palmistry vs. personality test, self-ratings	10
		Some related effect sizes:	
.90	10	Social desirability of trait vs. perceived accuracy	11
.75	19	Readability score vs. grade required for comprehension	12
.72	119	IQ scores between identical twins	13
.51	116	IQ scores between nonidentical twins	13
.50	122	Personality scores between identical twins	13
.48	134	Behavioral therapy vs. outcome	14
.32	10	Graphology vs. sex (lay predictions from handwriting)	6
.30	23	Improving teamwork vs. job satisfaction (corrected r=.58)	15
.22	119	Personality scores between nonidentical twins	13
.19	16	Humanistic therapy vs. outcome	14
.10	21	Sun sign effect (role playing) vs. EPI extroversion	2
.0003	597	ESP vs. random number generators	16

N = number of studies. Effect size is the mean observed correlation between prediction and the indicated criterion. MMPI = Minnesota Multiphasic Personality Inventory. Rorschach = inkblot test. Physiognomy = judging from appearance, not body build, for which the effect size is slightly higher.[40] Astrology = individual features (signs, houses, aspects) and the birth chart as a whole, not Gauquelin planetary effects, for which the effect size is typically .05 (Kelly et al. 1990). Phrenology = judging from head shape. Humanistic therapy includes psychodynamic, client-centered, encounter, and gestalt therapies. When corrected for attenuation the effect sizes in the upper part of this table are about 10 to 30 percent larger. The listed effect sizes often hide considerable individual variations but for the present purpose this does not affect the broad indications.

Sources: 1. Frank (1983); 2. Summarized in Dean (1986); 3. Parker et al. (1988); 4. Linn et al. (1981); 5. Jensen (1964); 6. See Appendix D; 7. Dzida and Kiener (1978), Estes (1938), Hull (1928), Landis and Phelps (1928), Mason (1957), Michel (1969), Pinter (1918), Ray (1958), Vernon (1953); 8. Dean (1986), Kelly et al. (1990); 9. Cleeton and Knight (1924); 10. Dean (1985), Misiak and Franghiadi (1953), Seifer (1977), Symaniz (1980), Wilson (1983), Wolff (1941); 11. Edwards (1967); 12. Klare (1974); 13. McCartney et al. (1990); 14. Shapiro and Shapiro (1982); 15. Neuman et al. (1989); 26.

Box 3. *Not All Effect Sizes Are What They Seem*

The *criterion* is the yardstick used to measure the effect size. Because all criteria are imperfect, the observed effect size will be less than its true value, in the same way that wearing boxing gloves worsens dexterity with chopsticks. So an observed effect size will be misleading unless its associated imperfections are kept in mind. In other words, not all effect sizes are what they seem. The main imperfections to be considered are as follows:

Criterion reliability, or the agreement between repeated test scores, or ratings, or whatever. Examples are given in Table 1. This imperfection typically reduces the observed effect size to between 75 and 95 percent of what it would otherwise be.[16]

Range restriction. Samples in real life are often restricted in range, e.g., to the top 20 percent of job applicants. This reduces the overall signal without necessarily reducing the noise, which reduces the observed effect size. Range restriction is visible in Table 3, where IQ vs. high school grades has a higher effect size than IQ vs. college grades, due to selection of college students. Conversely in the laboratory the middle 30 to 90 percent of samples may sometimes be chopped out. This enhances the variation between ends, which increases the observed effect size. Range restriction can be more important than criterion reliability.[17]

Mismatch. If the criteria cover many traits or many aspects of work performance, but the test measures only some of these, then the test cannot possibly correlate highly with the criteria. Mismatch is visible in Table 2, where age cannot possibly correlate with *everything* (or even most things) relevant to work performance.

Owing to the above imperfections, observed effect sizes may be only 50–70 percent of the true effect size. For example in Table 3, efforts to improve teamwork vs. resulting job satisfaction (r=.30) seems to have a slightly smaller effect size than graphology vs. sex (r=.32). But because the criteria involved are subject to all of the above, whereas sex is not, the true effect size is much superior (r=.58). To facilitate comparison, any important obstacles like this one have been noted in the tables.

ity; see Box 3. But as Loewenthal (1982:85) notes, "it is hard to think of situations where this would be really useful."

ARGUMENTS OF THE GRAPHOLOGISTS

The preceding results are undeniably dismal. When faced with such results, supporters of graphology have traditionally never lacked arguments to explain them away. Their main arguments, with counterarguments in parentheses, are as follows:

- Methodology may be suspect (only sometimes true).
- Experimenters may be hostile. (Some were graphologists.)

- Graphologists may be inexperienced. (Some were world famous.)
- Traits are not enough—the whole picture must be looked at. (Many studies have done exactly that.)
- Criteria are a problem. (But not enough to hinder discovery of graphology in the first place.)
- Criteria may not be valid. (Does not worry other techniques.)
- We need *better* criteria. (Like what?)
- Graphology reaches areas inaccessible by other methods. (Nonfalsifiable.)
- Client does not understand the graphologist. (Find another graphologist.)
- Situation was unrealistic. (Now you tell us.)
- More experiments are needed. (Only if results are inconsistent, but they are not.)
- Only graphologists can judge graphology. (So who judges murder?)

However, in this case it is hardly plausible to suppose that, across 107 effect sizes, such factors could consistently attenuate a *useful* effect to the extent implied. If graphology was as good as graphologists claim, it should shine through regardless. But it does not.

COMPARISON WITH OTHER REVIEWS

How do the present results compare with those of other critical reviews? Over the years the following English-language books (denoted by *) and articles have critically reviewed the status of graphology in detail:

Allport and Vernon (1933)	59	references
Bell (1948)	137	references
Wolfson (1951)	55	references
Fluckinger et al. (1965)	105	references
Lockowandt (1976)	123	references
Lester (1981)*	240	references
Klimoski and Rafaeli (1983)	45	references
Nevo et al. (1986)*	310	references

Three of the above review articles were quoted in the Introduction, where they showed increasing negativity over the years as the number of experimental studies increased. This trend is in agreement with the present results. However, in striking disagreement is the review by Lockowandt (1976), reprinted with minor editing in chapter 5, who concludes: "With strict methodology, however, handwriting has shown itself to be highly valid in many different respects." Ironically this optimism is immediately dispelled in chapter 6, where Lockowandt notes that "While going through individual cases in our research seminar, we keep coming across judgments of fully trained graphologists which prove to be completely incorrect." Nevertheless there is disagreement. To resolve it, consider the following:

To assess a particular study the minimum information needed is sample size, observed correlation, number of judges, and type of script (neutral or non-neutral). Lockowandt cites over 20 reliability studies but gives sample size and correlation for only 6 vs. my 66. For a similar number of validity studies including sex and IQ he gives sample size and correlation for only 3 vs. my 138. For around 30 other studies such as twin studies he gives none at all. On such crucial points as sampling error, type of script, cross-validation in factor analytic studies, and range restriction in extreme groups, there is a deafening silence. These points are crucial because each can artificially inflate the observed correlation. Furthermore, other than one of his own works, there is no reference more recent than 1972, so in effect the last 20 years of research (in graphology, in psychology, in everything) are ignored. Also ignored is the general superiority of other techniques, as documented earlier. In other words Lockowandt is highly selective, and *this* is why our conclusions differ. If the result is favorable he spells out the detail. Otherwise the result is merely "greater than chance performance" or "positive" or "informative" or hidden by galloping prolixity. Your choice of conclusion about validity will depend on whether you prefer 2 percent of the evidence (chapter 5) or as near 100 percent of the evidence as possible (this chapter).[41]

Now for the books. After surveying some 200 studies, Lester (1981:122) concludes: "At the present time, it does not appear that handwriting will be a useful tool in diagnosis." However, *if* it were proven valid, it would have "a potentially great future in psychological and psychiatric assessment." It is hard to disagree. But so would reading tea leaves.

After editing his 19-author anthology, Nevo (1986:241) is equally ambivalent: "After nearly one hundred years of investigating the psychodiagnostic value of handwriting behavior, and after almost two hundred years of the practical application of graphology, it is still unclear whether these methods are, or could be, valid." But in a review of Nevo's book, Hirsch (1987:842) was not convinced: ". . . any job-related information that a graphological analysis could extract can probably be obtained more directly by other measures, which also provide additional job-related information not contained in the handwriting sample."

Similarly, to an informed and impartial observer, the research results summarized in this chapter will seem consistent and not at all unclear. The conclusion they point to will seem glaringly obvious and very simple, as indicated next.

CONCLUSION: SPELLING OUT THE BOTTOM LINE

The results of this meta-analysis of over 200 graphology studies can be summarized as follows:

Yes, graphology *is* valid . . .	(there *is* an effect, but at least some of it is due to content not graphology)
. . . but not valid enough . . .	(the representative effect size of .12 for neutral scripts is not nearly big enough)
. . . or reliable enough . . .	(the mean agreement on interpretation of .42 is not nearly good enough)
. . . to be useful.	(other methods are better)

This does not of course deny the possibility that some as yet untested graphological technique may work, or that certain graphologists may achieve success in tests where others have failed. In which case the onus is on graphologists to demonstrate it. Nor does it deny the therapeutic utility of graphological beliefs—if invalid beliefs worked for something as invasive as bloodletting, they will certainly work for graphology. What *is* denied is the practical utility of graphology as practiced by most graphologists. In terms of adequate effect sizes, the claims made in graphology books are mostly false. In other words it seems that graphology has much in common with the Emperor's New Clothes.

Should graphologists wish to challenge the above conclusion, all they need do is present a meta-analysis of properly controlled tests that demonstrates an adequate effect size. Nothing else will do.

Before leaving this chapter you may like to re-read the views of graphologists and scientists quoted in the Introduction, and draw your own conclusions.

NOTES

1. About these notes. These notes provide technical details for technical readers, and useful information for anyone wishing to test graphology, especially those without access to a university library. However they do not provide basic information such as how to calculate a correlation coefficient, which can be found in any introductory book on statistics. In addition, some references are annotated where this would be helpful. There are another 40 notes, so a bookmark will help you whizz to and fro.

2. Unfailing parallels. As an example, Saudek notes how pasty writing (thick and blurred due to holding pen far from nib) *always* indicates sensuality. "For the last seventy years graphologists of all countries have recognized this sign as unfailing, and . . . [it] has certainly been verified in hundreds of thousands of cases without exception" (Saudek 1925:42).

3. A pioneering study. The study by Hull and Montgomery (1919) was among the first to test individual features and raised a storm of protest. It had "only remote relation to most of the claims of graphologists and practically none at all to their methods of work" (Allport and Vernon 1933:186). It had "the obvious intent of debunking graphology" (Castelnuovo-Tedesco 1948:171). So it was "unscientific from the viewpoints of graphological and experimental theory alike" (Sonnemann 1950:11), being merely "not-to-be-taken-seriously handwriting games" (Lockowandt 1976 and in summary to chapter 5 of this book).

But inspection of the actual study tells a different story. Hull and Montgomery begin with a survey of existing studies, and conclude that "we may not . . . safely ignore the claims of graphologists" because there is "at least a weak relation between handwriting and certain traits of character." They noted that previous studies had tested the skill of graphologists, so by contrast they set out to test "the truth of certain graphological theories, i.e., certain correlations alleged to exist between specific traits of handwriting and traits of the writer's character." Their test involved 17 male university students, all members of the same medical fraternity, who copied the same 108-word paragraph and ranked each other on six traits (ambitious, proud, bashful, forceful, persevering, reserved). The mean rankings for each trait were then correlated with the relevant ranked measure such as slope and the thickness and width of t-bars. In hindsight the sample size is too small, otherwise the test is as carefully done as any recent test.

According to the above critics, the theories tested were merely straw men. In fact they were chosen because they involved traits "susceptible of objective measurement and being among the less improbable of the relations alleged," and each is supported by typically 2–5 references to reputable works (with page numbers) where the theory is advanced. The three most widely held of the theories tested are still widely held, but the observed correlations were neither significant nor even in the right direction, namely, –.20 for upward sloping lines = ambitious, –.06 for heavy t-bars = forceful, and –.02 for closed a's and o's = reserved. The authors end cautiously by noting that tests of theories are not the same as tests of graphologists, so their results are not necessarily in conflict with the positive results cited in their introduction. Despite which they were accused of rampant debunking.

4. Ways of matching. As N the number of cases increases, the number of possible matches increases as N^2, rapidly increasing the processing load and rapidly decreasing the average difference between each match. For this reason judges find it difficult to match more than 5 cases at a time, whether as 5 descriptions to be matched to another 5 descriptions (Crumbaugh and Stockholm 1977:404) or as 5 descriptions to be matched to people you know (LoMonaco 1973:705). So the total sample is best divided into sets of no more than 5 cases each.

However this reasonable conclusion is not supported by Allport and Vernon (1933:229), who used scripts from 23 college freshmen selected for diversity of background. They matched the 23 script interpretations with information from peer-ratings, test scores, and interviews, and then rematched them after dividing the 23 interpretations at random into three roughly equal subsets. The hit rate (as effect size kappa, see below) of 1st, 2nd, and 3rd choices showed no clear improvement over using the undivided set:

Choices	1st	1st+2nd	1st+2nd+3rd	Mean
Undivided set	.05	.13	.08	.09
Three subsets	.11	.09	.00	.07

Weinberg et al. (1962) suggest a new matching technique in which the judge selects not one but several matches for each case, the number being chosen by the judge and then kept the same for each case. Used matches are not eliminated and may be re-used without limit. When finished, the judge selects the best single match for each case, but this time without re-use. The difference between the two results allows cues to be identified much more easily than with the standard matching method. However, their actual results for 15 scripts showed no improvement over matching one sketch to each script:

	Judge A		Judge B	
Sketches matched to each script	1	3	1	4
Effect size as kappa	.21	.21	.14	.13

Usually the results of a matching test are given as observed vs. expected hits, in which case they can be converted to an effect size known as *kappa* (Cohen 1960), given by kappa = (O-E)/(N-E), where O = observed hits, E = expected hits, and N = number of matches. Thus if 5 interpretations matched against 5 subjects gives 2 hits, and expected hits = 1, then kappa = (2–1)/(5–1) = .25. Actually kappa is a measure of *agreement* rather than *association,* but for hits and misses they are identical. If near misses can be defined (which is seldom the case), they can be allowed for by a related measure known as *weighted kappa* (Cohen 1968), whose calculation is too complex to be summarized here. Ordinary kappa ignores near misses, so when near misses can be counted it gives a somewhat smaller effect size than weighted kappa.

A method due to Halevi (1965) automatically generates near misses and takes them into account. For each target the interpretations are ranked in order of fit, where best fit = rank 1, second best = rank 2, and so on. The effect size g is given by $g = 1 - 2 \times (\text{sum of } (k-1) / N(N-1))$ where k = rank of the correct match for each target, and N = number of targets. Like a correlation, g can take any value between +1 and −1. However, like biserial r and tetrachoric r, its associated variance differs from that for Pearson r, which means that too many of them (not a problem here) will bias an analysis of variance as used in meta-analysis (Hunter and Schmidt 1990:206). According to my computer simulations, this defect does not apply to kappa.

Recently Cox and Tapsell (1991) have proposed an ingenious alternative that avoids all the above problems. The scripts are paired with their matching sketches, then half of them are re-paired by sex and age but otherwise at random. Each judge rates the similarity of each pair on a 7-point scale, where 1 = certainly two different people, and 7 = certainly the same person. This allows large samples to be used without exhausting the judges. The judges' ratings are then compared with reality using point biserial r. Cox and Tapsell tested this approach on 50 scripts using 3 nongraphologist judges, and obtained mean point biserial r = .09. For a useful survey of matching methods see Swentzell and Roberts (1964).

5. Blind eyes. Nobody should be surprised to learn that the hardest things to find in graphology books are facts, although to be fair some psychology books are just as bad. Even scientific graphologists keep quiet about effect sizes. Thus Fluckiger et al. (1961) survey over 100 studies, while Bradley (1988, 1989) presents a one-page summary of each of 199 studies, both without citing a single effect size even though plenty were available. Crumbaugh (1986:56), reprinted in chapter 7, refers to the "substantial validation evidence" offered by several studies but stops short of quoting an actual effect size. This seeming inability to be specific exists even at the top. Thus Moore (1985) wrote to seven international graphology organizations asking for details of controlled studies which validated the use of graphology in personnel selection. Only four replied, namely Handwriting Analysts International [USA], the American Association of Handwriting Analysts, Societa Internazionale di Psicologia della Scrittura, and the Israeli Graphological Institute. Not one provided the requested details.

6. Types of correlation. There are various measures of correlation depending on the type of data. For example *Spearman rho* for ranked data, *kappa* (see note 4) for hits and misses, *Pearson r* (product moment) for two continuous variables, *point biserial r* if one is dichotomized, and *phi* if both are dichotomized. Their calculation is explained in any statistics textbook. Rosenthal (1984:24–26) gives methods of estimating Pearson r from reported data when no correlation is given.

7. Calculation of sample size. The calculation is complicated if exact results are required; see Schmidt et al. (1976) for Pearson r and Donner (1984:201) for phi. But as an approximation the minimum sample size N required to detect effect size E is given by $N = K/E^2$ where E is the effect size you hope to observe, not the one obtained after correcting for attenuation, and N is variously the number of pairs (Pearson r), a+b+c+d (phi), or number of observations (kappa with an

expectancy of .5, otherwise $N=K/E^2 \times P/(1-P)$ where P=expectancy).

The value of K depends on how certain you want to be of detecting E. To detect E in 4 out of 5 tests at a two-sided significance level of .05, which is the normal criterion, put K=9. To detect E in 19 out of 20 tests at a two-sided significance level of .01, put K=18. For example to detect phi=.20 using the normal criterion, minimum N is about $9/.20^2$ or 225, the exact value being 214. In technical terms K is roughly 15 percent more than $(z_\alpha+z_\beta)^2$, where z_α and z_β are the corresponding standard scores, e.g., $z_\alpha=1.96$ and $z_\beta=.84$ for the above normal criterion.

Later we will find that graphological sample sizes are typically N=60 or less, which is too small for comfort. But small sample sizes are not unique to graphology and may be the most common failing in validation research generally. For example, the median of N=68 found for 427 published studies of employment tests is barely adequate to detect the typical effect size of around .30 (Lent et al. 1971).

8. Sidestepping the problems of validation. Here is an example. In note 2, graphologists were agreed that thick, pasty writing *always* indicates sensuality, which suggests excellent validity. However, pasty writing is variously characterized by *heavy* pen pressure (Sonnemann 1952:48, Olyanova 1969:123) or *light* pen pressure (Roman 1952:265, Paterson 1976:49), so judges guided by pen pressure could not possibly agree. In other words the guideline could not be more unreliable, so it cannot be valid. I could find no study of thickness vs. sensuality, but Hull and Montgomery (1919) found that thickness correlated .45 with shyness for 17 male university students. If sensual university students tend not to be shy, then this result is in the wrong direction.

9. Deriving an upper bound to validity. The true validity of a test, as measured perfectly by a perfect criterion, is given by $v/(\sqrt{(r)} \times k)$, where v = observed validity, r = test reliability, and k = attenuation as explained in notes 18–21. Simple arithmetic shows that only if true validity = 1 and k = 1 will the observed validity approach $\sqrt{(r)}$, which is therefore an upper bound. In practice both true validity and k are typically 1, and the criterion is never perfect nor perfectly measured. So the upper bound tends to be more like $\sqrt{(r)}/2$.

10. Misrepresenting effect size. With crooked thinking it is easy to make the use of effect sizes look ridiculous. Thus Yeaton and Sechrest (1981) note that the observed effect size of .13 between job punctuality and Type A people (who tend to be late) is quite tiny. But for a company employing 1000 people at $10 per hour, this supposedly tiny lateness translates into lost time worth about $140,000 a year. Which they suggest is not tiny at all. Therefore effect size is not a practical measure because it "fails to convey any sense of practical worth." However, they fail to mention that the total wages bill is $90 million a year, of which $140,000 represents 0.15 percent, a genuinely tiny figure compared to say annual inflation.

11. Interpreting reliability. Reliability affects the confidence we can have in a test score. Suppose there is a difference of D between the scores of two individuals on the same test. Let r be the test reliability and sd be the test standard deviation, i.e., the standard deviation of the test scores for a large sample of people. The standard deviation of D is given by $\sqrt{(2 \times (1-r))} \times sd$, provided sd does not vary with test score. From this we can calculate the standard score z = D/(standard

deviation of D) and hence the probability that D is real. Some example probabilities in percent are shown below:

Reliability	.20	.40	.60	.80	.90	.95
D/sd = 0.5	31	35	42	57	74	89
D/sd = 1.0	57	64	74	89	97	>99
D/sd = 2.0	89	93	97	>99	>99	>99

Suppose a personality test has a standard deviation of 5 points. If two individuals have scores 5 points apart, then D/sd = 5/5 or 1.0. If the test reliability is .80, then from the above table it is 89 percent probable that the difference is real.

12. Dollar value of an effect size. In personnel selection a number of methods have been devised to relate dollar value to effect size. From Hunter and Hunter (1984), the annual saving in dollars due to hiring people on the basis of tests, as opposed to hiring at random, is given by annual saving in dollars = Ntrsz where N=number of persons hired each year, t=average tenure in years, r=true effect size (i.e., corrected for attenuation), s=standard deviation of job performance in dollars (typically 40 to 70 percent of annual wage), and z=average standard score for the proportion of applicants who are hired. Thus if 10 percent are hired, z will be the average standard score beyond p=.10 one-sided, given by (ordinate of the normal curve at p)/p, here .176/.10 = 1.76. If 100, 50, 20, 5 percent are hired the value of z is 0, .80, 1.40, 2.08. For the U.S. federal government in 1980, N=460,000 persons, t=6.52 years, and s=.40 × $13,598. Roughly the top 10 percent of applicants are hired, so z=1.76. Entering these values into the equation shows that the saving in 1980 due to hiring via tests with an effect size r, as opposed to hiring at random, was about $28 billion. The mean effect size of U.S. government ability tests is .55, so the saving was about $15 billion, or 4 percent of the total federal budget. Cascio and Ramos (1986) present a simple method of estimating s, the most difficult component to estimate. Other approaches allow for overheads, taxes, the cost of assessment, and so on; for example, see Cronshaw and Alexander (1985) and Burke and Frederick (1986).

A related concern is productivity. Hunter et al. (1990) found that in low complexity jobs like package wrapping the top 10 percent of workers are twice as productive as the bottom 10 percent. As job complexity increases so does the difference in productivity. Thus in medium complexity jobs like claims evaluation the ratio is four times, and in high complexity jobs like law the ratio is ten times or more, always assuming that the bottom 10 percent can learn the job in the first place. Large differences will of course increase the benefits of valid selection tests.

13. Handwriting legibility. Fifty years earlier Kirk (1926) had 20 judges rate 1000 Philadelphia handwritings against standard legibility examples from the Ayres Measuring Scale for Handwriting, scaled 10 (perfectly illegible) to 90 (perfectly legible) in steps of 10. The distribution of the resulting 100 legibilities was bell-shaped and symmetrical, mean 47.1 sd 12.9. The worst writers were 20 clergymen

(mean 35.1) and 42 doctors (35.9). The best writers were 7 housekeepers (51.4) and 202 teachers (51.1). Overall 606 females (49.7) were neater than 394 males (43.0), thus supporting the sex differences noted by others. Only 186 of the 1000 (and only 3 of the 42 doctors) met the minimum standard of 60 judged acceptable for social correspondence.

14. Examples of studies impossible to assess. Lester et al. (1977) claim their results are nonsignificant but give no actual results. In their matching test Cantril and Rand (1934) use only scripts that matched in the first place. Good agreement is reported between handwriting indications and teacher ratings (Von Kügelgen 1928), therapist descriptions (Wells 1946), and personality scores (Pang and Lepponen 1968), but in each case there are no controls to establish chance agreement. Williams et al. (1977) factor-analyzed a sample of 46 scripts, which is far too small for such analysis (Comrey 1988). They also omit essential information like observed correlations and which method they used. In Wellingham-Jones (1989), reprinted in chapter 15, the graphologist knew some of the subjects, the subjects were selected by graphologists (in fact 23 percent *were* graphologists), the script content was not controlled, and scoring was not done blind. Peeples (1990) uses a sample size of 1. Oosthuizen (1991) uses 10 graphological signs of *noncognitive* personality to predict *cognitive* exam results by multiple regression, but overcomes this fatal handicap by not testing his results on a fresh sample. Such studies (many more could be cited) are impossible to assess. One wonders why anyone bothered.

15. File-drawer problem. The number of missing studies (new, unreported, or unretrieved) with null results needed to bring the retrieved studies to overall nonsignificance ($p.>05$) is shown by Rosenthal (1979) to be roughly 19 × number of significant studies $p \leq .05$ – number of nonsignificant studies $p > .05$, Rosenthal suggests that bias is unlikely if the answer exceeds (10 + 5 × number of retrieved studies). This makes the plausible assumption that file drawers throughout the world are unlikely to have more than five times as many studies as the reviewer. For example if we retrieved 100 studies, all of them significant at $p \leq .05$, we would need 19×50=950 null studies stashed in file drawers to reduce them to nonsignificance, or rather more than the plausible limit of 10+5×100=550. However, Hunter and Schmidt (1990:512) note that this approach looks at *significance* whereas the real issue is *effect size.* Therefore it is more useful to know how many missing null studies are needed to reduce the mean effect size to inutility. If we have retrieved k studies whose mean effect size is r, the number n of null studies needed to reduce r to some critical level c is given by $n = k\ (r/c - 1)$. For example, if our 100 studies have mean r=.40, and we adopt c=.20 as indicating inutility, then $n = 100(.40/.20-1) = 100$ null studies are needed to reach it, a much smaller number than the 950 based on significance.

But is the file-drawer problem a *real* problem? Hunter and Schmidt (1990:507) examined many hundreds of effect sizes in personnel selection, and found no difference between unpublished reports and articles published in journals. Rosenthal (1984:41–45) found much the same for many hundreds of effect sizes in 12 areas of education and psychology, although dissertations and theses (which are usually classified as unpublished) averaged 40 percent lower. Glass (1980) surveyed nine meta-analyses involving over 2000 effect sizes in education and psychology, and in every case theses were lower than journal articles, averaging 25 percent lower. For academic achievement research, theses averaged 15 percent lower (White 1982). Greenwald (1975) took the direct approach and surveyed 36 authors and 39 referees of articles submitted to the *Journal of Personality and Social Psychology* during three months in 1973. He found that, compared to researchers with negative results, those with positive results were *four times* as likely to simply give up, and were *eight times* as likely not to submit them for publication. So the better the results the more likely they are to be published. As an extreme case he cites parapsychology, which is so plagued by publication bias that "no reasonable person can regard himself as having an adequate basis for a true-false conclusion."

So, depending on the area, the file-drawer problem can indeed be a real problem. For graphology and personnel selection, the data of Neter and Ben-Shakhar (1989) show a mean effect size of .24 for 10 published studies (most with non-neutral scripts, mean N=61), significantly larger than the mean of .07 for 7 unpublished studies (all with non-neutral scripts, mean N=77). The samples are too small to be sure but they suggest that, for graphology at least, published studies do tend to have better results. This is compatible with the findings given later in Figure 3. On this basis the mean effect sizes reported later are likely to be optimistic.

16. More on Bobertag. Actually Bobertag (1929) gave the five scripts to six graphologists, and each of the 15 others matched the resulting 30 sketches to the subjects. Of the 450 matchings, 80.7 percent were correct. When the five writers had to pick their own sketch, three got everything right. At first sight this is a remarkable result. However, although the sketches from each graphologist were randomized, no graphologist was mixed with another. So the matchings were not independent. Furthermore the results are inflated by having *many* graphologists, *many* raters, and *few* scripts, when what is required is *many* scripts. In reality there are only 5 matchings, not 450, of which about 4 are correct—a result easily caused by atypical cues. Unfortunately Bobertag gives no details of how the subjects were selected, or how the matchings were done, so it is impossible to judge what might be happening.

17. How meta-analysis works. Meta-analysis can take several different forms, some of which do not consider sampling error. My procedure was the bare-bones procedure of Hunter and Schmidt (1990:107–112), which includes small improvements on Hunter et al. (1982:41–47). It begins by establishing an effect size r and sample size N for each study. It then calculates the following:

Weighted mean r	= sum of (N × r for that N) / total N
T Total variance	= sum of (N × (r − mean r)^2) / total N
S Sampling error variance	= (1 − (mean r)^2)^2 / (mean N − 1)
Vr percent variance remaining after removing sampling error	= 100 × (T−S)/T.

Ideally the effect size we want from each study is the correlation between predictor and reality, not reality as measured by imperfect criteria. But imperfect criteria (test scores, ratings, whatever) are all we have. In principle we can correct for these imperfections, in which case the subsequent calculations differ from those above, but in practice the necessary data are usually unavailable. To show how it works, corrections are described in the next four notes. Corrected effect sizes are usually described as "corrected for artifacts" or "corrected for attenuation." Many other imperfections exist such as typographical and computational errors, but they are generally (not always) minor; see Hunter and Schmidt (1990:43ff).

18. Correction for criterion reliability. The *criterion* (test scores, ratings, whatever) is the yardstick used to measure the effect size. Suppose a test correlates .50 with a criterion that happens to be measured with reliability .60. Then instead of observing r=.50 we will observe $r=.50 \times \sqrt{(.60)}$, or .39. Reversing the arithmetic converts observed r=.39 into corrected $r=.39/\sqrt{(.60)}=.50$. Examples of criterion reliabilities are given later in Table 1.

19. Correction for range restriction. Suppose an *unrestricted* sample shows effect size r. Restrict the sample by chopping subjects from one end of the range or from the middle. The observed effect size for the *restricted* sample will then be rk, where k is roughly as follows (calculated from Schmidt et al. 1976):

k for % of range lost	=10%	30%	50%	70%	90%	True r
Lost from one end	0.85	0.75	0.65	0.55	0.45	.1 to .6
Lost from middle	1.05	1.20	1.35	1.55	1.95	.1 to .3
Lost from middle	1.05	1.15	1.25	1.35	1.55	.4 to .6

Valid only if the variable is normally distributed.

Chopping from one end *reduces* r. Chopping from the middle *increases* r. For example, in the general population the effect size for predicting IQ from handwriting vs. actual IQ is around .30. Suppose we chop over 50 percent from the low end, as we do when using university students as subjects. The expected effect size is now reduced to $.30 \times .65 = .20$, where .65 is the value of k for a loss of 50 percent from one end. Reverse the arithmetic to obtain true r = observed r/k.

20. Correction for criterion coarse grouping. A reduction in r akin to range restriction also occurs if a *continuous* criterion is chopped into a discrete N-point scale, but not if the criterion is naturally discrete, eg left-right or male-female. Here true r = observed r/g, where g is as follows (Guilford 1965:353):

N	2	3	4	5	7	11
g	.816	.859	.916	.943	.970	.988

Valid only if the variable is normally distributed.

Thus if the continuous criterion is measured on a 3-point scale, true r = observed r/.859. If in addition the criterion reliability is .60, and half the range has been chopped from one end (so k=.65), overall true r = observed $r/(.859 \times \sqrt{(.60)} \times$

.65) = 2.3 × observed r, a substantial difference. For practical purposes it is of course meaningless to apply further corrections for *predictor* reliability and coarse grouping, since no such predictor could actually exist.

21. Effect of extreme base rates. If one or both of our measures (of behavior, of handwriting) are dichotomized, then extreme base rates (e.g., the incidence of using green ink) can cause the calculated effect size to be too low, leading us to wrongly conclude that nothing important is happening (MacLennan 1988). Fortunately this is not a consideration in the studies surveyed here, but it could have been. In general if both variables are dichotomized into a 2×2 table, i.e., where phi is the measure of effect size, then if any cell = 0, or if the ratio largest/smallest >5, the underestimation by phi may be severe. No formal corrections have been proposed, but the possibility of underestimation in a particular case can be checked by determining the maximum possible phi. If phi is positive and abcd are the cell frequencies:

1. Calculate $x = \sqrt{((c+d)/(a+b))}$ and $y = \sqrt{((b+d)/(a+c))}$.
2. If $b \geq c$, maximum possible phi is x/y.
3. If $b < c$, maximum possible phi is y/x.

If phi is negative, swap a with c, and b with d. Then proceed as above and make the answer negative. The more the answer differs from 1 the greater the underestimation. If there is underestimation then we can replace phi by a more robust measure such as Yule's colligation, given by $(k-1)/(k+1)$ where $k=\sqrt{(ab/bc)}$, see Alexander et al. (1985). Ideally we should have avoided extreme base rates by designing the experiment properly in the first place.

22. Interpretation of meta-analysis results. To help track down the variables which matter, Hunter and Schmidt (1990:68) provide this useful rule-of-thumb approach. Look at your results (calculated as in note 17) and ask: Is the sampling error variance more than 75 percent of the total variance? (Put another way, after removing the sampling error variance, is the remaining variance less than 25 percent of the total variance?) If *yes,* the variation among r's is due to sampling fluctuations (i.e., chance) and other artifacts, not to differences between studies. If *no,* there is a genuine difference between studies, in which case we can divide the studies into two groups to maximize a particular difference. If this eliminates the within-group variation (i.e., the variance of the individual groups is now less than the variance of the combined groups), then that particular difference is the culprit. However, as noted by Hunter and Schmidt (1990:449), this approach is not very sensitive, so it is better to divide the data on rational grounds in advance to see if the outcomes differ. This is the approach used here.

For a detailed and very readable discussion of meta-analysis, see Schmidt et al. (1985a), with further points in Hunter and Schmidt (1990). Another readable discussion appears in Green and Hall (1984), and in Light and Pillemer (1984), who also cover other methods of reviewing research including visual displays. For an intriguing test of meta-analysis see Schmidt et al. (1985b), who divided a large database of N=1455 into individual "studies" of N=30 and N=68. The overall r for N=1455 was .22, yet the individual rs for N=30 varied all the way from –.16 to .61, showing the enormous variation caused by small sample sizes. Meta-analysis correctly estimated the original effect size and sampling errors whereas traditional techniques failed.

23. How each study was processed. Ideally we want to know how reliability and effect size varies with:

1. Type of judge. Are graphologists better than psychologists?
2. Type of judgment. Is the whole script better than signs?
3. Type of script. Are content scripts better than neutral scripts?
4. Type of source material. Are originals better than photocopies?

And so on. But authors vary enormously. Some give breakdowns, some give means, others give medians. Some measure slant in degrees, others as present or absent. Some measure personality by ratings, others by tests. In general this makes it impossible to combine studies other than broadly by type of judge, type of judgment, and type of script, thus ignoring type of source material, and even then each category averages only half a dozen studies. The procedure I followed for each study was as follows:

1. Identify the particular combination of judge, judgment, and script types. Many authors look at more than one combination.
2. Take the given mean or median (reliability or effect size as the case may be), or compute a mean if several results are given.

Thus each study is represented for each combination by one reliability or one effect size, and the term *number of studies* means the number of handwriting samples, not the number of published articles. If results for three separate samples are given in the same article, they count as three studies, not one. If the same sample is judged by graphologists and again by laypersons, it counts as one study under *graphologists* and one study under *laypersons.*

No correction was made for *criterion reliability* because the required data was mostly unavailable. Occasionally there was extreme *range restriction,* usually by chopping out the middle to improve sensitivity, in which case it was corrected; see note 19. Otherwise no correction was made. In principle making a correction changes the calculation of sampling error variance as given in note 17, but the number of corrected cases were too few to make much difference.

Choice of data: Some authors report only a single effect size, so no choice is possible. Others may report effect sizes for several scales and for a single global judgment, in which case is the latter taken or the mean of the former? Generally I took the global one provided it was representative. It is here that subjective judgment becomes necessary in what should ideally be a nonsubjective procedure. Since graphologists will suspect negative bias, while debunkers will suspect positive bias, all effect sizes used in the meta-analyses are listed in the Appendices to allow independent scrutiny.

24. Reliabilities and sampling error. My meta-analysis of these reliabilities found significant differences between studies in about half of the categories. That is, of the reliabilities listed in Appendix A, half have Vr values exceeding 25 percent (Vr = percent variance remaining after removing sampling error), suggesting that genuine differences exist between studies; see note 22. But rating slant and slope is more precise than rating arcades and garlands, and 7-point scales are more precise than present-absent scales. So when such diverse techniques are lumped together, as here, it is hardly surprising that meta-analysis detects the difference.

25. Origin of categories. Neter and Ben-Shakhar (1989), in advance of meta-analysis, divided their studies into the categories shown. That is, the categories were set by them, not by their meta-analysis. To allow comparison I used the same categories. Would meta-analysis of the 35 personnel studies lumped together have produced the same categories? No, because it detected no true difference between studies, the Vr value being zero, showing that all the variance was accounted for by sampling error. This would normally suggest caution when interpreting the difference between neutral and non-neutral scripts. However, as detailed in note 31, a t-test shows that the difference is significant (p=.03). Apart from confirming the greater sensitivity of dividing studies in advance, see note 22, this means we can have some confidence that the difference is real.

Many other categories are possible. For example Rafaeli and Drory (1988) suggest looking at types of: graphologists, writers (sex, age, race, handedness, personality), jobs, context (culture, situation), and criteria. It sounds wonderful, but there are problems. (1) Testing all possible combinations would require a sample exceeding the total world population. (2) Even if graphology was thus shown to be optimum for young non-smoking gentlemen graphoanalysts, elderly left-handed neurotic Israeli ladies, middle management jobs in equal-opportunity engineering companies, and numerical scores on the Myers-Briggs Type Indicator, on past performance it is unlikely that working graphologists would take the slightest notice. (3) Such fine tuning is justified only if graphology seems likely to compare favorably with other techniques. But it does not; see Tables 1-3. (4) Nevertheless, Neter and Ben-Shakhar (1989) did meta-analyze across individual judges to see if breakdown by setting (work vs. training) and by graphologist (Israeli vs. other) had any effect. The last is of interest because the Israeli graphologists worked with scripts in Hebrew, written from right to left, whereas the other graphologists worked with scripts in English, Dutch, or German. However, the results were too ambiguous to allow a conclusion. The only breakdown with clear results was neutral vs. non-neutral scripts.

Which is not to say that looking at particular other categories may not be productive, and in later sections this is put to the test. Recently, Crowley (1991) looked at 91 female writers divided into high and low social desirability, and found that those wishing to be seen favorably by others had markedly flamboyant handwriting, i.e., large and regular like the script often used in ads to promote a prestigious product. This suggests that they had adjusted their style to project the desired image, a skill also noted by Lowenthal (1975). The correlations between handwriting and various personal qualities (personality, verbal reasoning, occu-

occupational interests, work values) were significantly different between the two groups, suggesting that those wishing to be seen favorably used flamboyance to project a good image, especially if they were also extroverted, non-anxious, and low on verbal reasoning, whereas those who were indifferent used flamboyance to signal their independence, love of freedom, and rejection of work-related values. These results suggest that image-projection may be a major source of contamination in graphology studies. If so, then graphologists can hardly use it in reverse, because the personality thus revealed by the handwriting is actually fabricated, not authentic, and therefore is precisely what graphology claims *not* to indicate. Unfortunately no other study divided writers on social desirability, so this promising lead could not be examined further.

26. Comparison with Neter and Ben-Shakhar (1989). Both our meta-analyses followed the bare bones procedure of Hunter et al. (1982), but we differed in two respects: (1) They used the median effect size from each study, whereas I used the mean effect size. (2) They did not correct for extreme range restriction. However, their results (shown below for the general evaluation dimension from their Table 3) are very close to mine (if anything my effect sizes tend to be larger), showing that the differences are of little consequence:

	Neutral scripts?	Graph	Psych	Lay
Whole script vs. work prof	No	.153 (16)	.180 (5)	.136 (5)*
	Yes	.033 (2)		
Difference, mine – theirs	No	.005	–.002	.037
	Yes	.053		

*Sic. But only 4 studies are listed in their Table 1.

Neter and Ben-Shakhar also meta-analyzed the effect size for each individual judge instead of averaging them as here. The mean effect sizes were slightly higher by an average of .02, and their comparison made graphology look even worse, otherwise the outcome was unchanged.

27. More on content. One detail from Experiment 4 by Jansen (1973:173–174) is of interest here. Six psychologists matched *typewritten transcripts* of nine scripts with supervisor ratings on 18 personality variables. Their mean effect size was .21, whereas another six psychologists who matched the *original scripts* averaged only .06, little different from six graphologists who averaged .09. In this case it seems that handwriting hindered more than it helped. The subjects were adults who had been selected for extreme ratings from a large parent group.

28. Examples of inflated results. Eysenck (1945) had a graphologist fill out a personality test from the handwriting of each of 50 neurotics. The result was 62 percent hits vs. 50 percent expected by chance, effect size as kappa = .23. However, Wolfson (1951:423–424) notes that the test contained many items related to neuroticism (e.g., Easily startled? Easily rattled? Mood ups and downs?), and that

these scored the most hits. This suggests that success was inflated by knowing the subjects were neurotic, especially as a repeat experiment using non-neurotics, i.e., where such cues could not apply, gave chance results (Eysenck and Gudjonsson 1986). Crumbaugh and Stockholm (1977) had an independent graphologist select most of their subjects and obtain the scripts, which immediately introduces the opportunity for selection bias (would *you* knowingly select cases that disproved *your* pet beliefs?). For Wellingham-Jones (1989) see note 14. Further sobering examples of inflation due to faulty procedures are given by Secord (1949) and Nevo (1986:203–215).

29. Effect sizes and sampling errors. Meta-analysis of the 72 studies lumped together showed that the Vr value was zero, showing that all the variance was accounted for by sampling error. As detailed in note 31, a t-test between neutral and non-neutral scripts was only marginally significant (p=.09), whereas it was significant (p=.03) for the personnel results. This reduced sensitivity is explained by the smaller sample sizes, which averaged N=48 vs. N=77 for personnel tests. In other words they were almost too small to detect any difference.

30. Significance of one result among many. Perform 1000 tests on random data and count the number of results that are significant at the .05 level. Even though the data are random, we can expect on average to obtain .05 × 1000 = 50 such results purely by chance. Only if we get significantly more than 50 such results can we claim that something special is happening. As a guide, if you make N tests then your best result will not be genuinely significant unless it is significant at the p=.05/N level. See Wilkinson (1951). In recent years this approach (and variations thereof) has become known as the Bonferroni method.

31. Differences between effect sizes. By t-test the two-sided significance of the differences between the means are as follows. For this test we use the observed standard deviations (sd), i.e., uncorrected for sampling error:

Personnel vs. personality: no significant difference.

Neutral scripts?	No .165 sd.119 (26) vs. .135 sd.098 (23)	t=0.96	p=.34
	Yes .073 sd.046 (9) vs. .068 sd.149 (18)	t=0.10	p=.92

Neutral vs. non-neutral scripts: significant difference.

Personnel	.073 sd.046 (9) vs. .165 sd.119 (26)	t=2.24	p=.03
Psychology	.068 sd.149 (18) vs. .135 sd.098 (23)	t=1.73	p=.09

Signs vs. matching tests: no significant difference.

	.082 sd.075 (11) vs. .146 sd.141 (13)	t=1.35	p=.19

32. Rorschach reliability. But all may not be lost. Weiner (1991), editor of the *Journal of Personality Assessment* (originally the *Rorschach Research Exchange and the Journal of Projective Techniques*), noted that clear criteria can produce reasonable agreement on Rorschach scores. Therefore "Reports of Rorschach research that . . . indicate less than 80% agreement . . . will be returned for further

work before being accepted for publication." The corresponding correlation is .60–.80, depending on the agreement expected by chance, somewhat less than the .84 reported in Table 1.

33. Reliability of rankings. Kane and Lawler (1978) reviewed the literature on peer evaluation and found only two studies that examined the reliability of rankings by the same judge (mean .92), and none for the reliability between judges. Nathan and Alexander (1988) surveyed the validity of ratings, rankings, and other criteria from hundreds of studies of clerical occupations. They give no reliabilities, but their results indicate that the mean reliability of rankings is nearly twice the mean reliability of ratings (.48 in Table 1), i.e., about .80 to .90.

34. Inter-rater reliability. Ratings of personality are about the same. Many things affect inter-rater reliability, for example halo effects (bias due to liking or attractiveness), how visible the characteristic is, how well each rating point is described, and especially length of acquaintance. Rothstein (1990) analyzed performance ratings for 9975 supervisors and found that reliability rose rapidly during the first six months of acquaintance. It was effectively constant after one year, although small increases occurred even after five years, the asymptotic limit being .60. The mean for all ratings was .52, in good agreement with the Table 1 figure of .48. After surveying many hundreds of occupational studies, Ghiselli (1966) suggested that reliabilities were typically .70 to .80, which a few years later he amended to .60 to .80 (Ghiselli 1973). Currently .60 is commonly used when actual reliabilities are unavailable (Schmidt et al. 1985a).

The reliability of ratings can be increased by having teams of raters. If r is the reliability between individual raters, the reliability between teams of n raters is $nr/(1+(n-1)r)$, which is known as the Spearman-Brown formula. Thus an r of .45 increases to .62 for n=2 and to .80 for n=5. Useful practical hints about the use of ratings are given by Cronbach (1970:571ff).

35. Prediction of success in a training course. The effect size for cognitive tests vs. success in training (.70 corrected for attenuation) is larger than vs. work performance (.50 corrected). This is because training puts more emphasis on cognitive skills such as learning and remembering, which are of course directly tapped by the cognitive test. Indeed, when Ree and Earles (1991) looked at the training success of 78,041 U.S. Air Force enlistees in 82 jobs, they found that nine specific ability tests such as arithmetic reasoning and mechanical comprehension added little to the prediction affored by cognitive ability alone. Such findings further weaken the case for graphology.

36. Work performance and personality tests. Personality tests are generally poor predictors of work performance, see Guion and Gottier (1965). But they can be good predictors of other work-related qualities. For example McHenry et al. (1990) found that cognitive ability tests were best at predicting general work performance for 4039 enlisted soldiers (r=.47 vs. .15 for personality tests, or .65 vs. .25 corrected for attenuation), while personality tests were best at predicting responsibility, perseverance, and capacity for hard work (r=.31 vs. .11 for cognitive ability tests, or .32 vs. .16 corrected). Similarly, Barrick and Mount (1991) found that conscientiousness is a consistently valid predictor regardless of occupation.

37. Correction of effect sizes in Table 2. Typically only 10 percent of studies report criterion reliability and range restriction. So meta-analysts correct for these artifacts by assuming the delinquent 90 percent are no different, which may or may not be the case. This means that the corrected effect sizes in Table 2 are somewhat uncertain, especially when N (number of studies) is small.

38. Other methods are better. Whether predicting aptitude or personality, the best pencil-and-paper tests are invariably more accurate, quicker and cheaper than graphology, which in the U.S.A. costs $35–$300 per assessment (cost is from Taylor and Sackheim 1988:74), or in the U.K. around £200 for a Graphoanalysis covering personality, thinking patterns, imagination, goals, fears, defenses, integrity, social traits, and aptitudes (Warner 1991). For example, in his review of several dozen graphological studies of IQ, Michel (1969:52) notes that IQ "is traced more economically and with higher validity by other techniques, since evaluation of intelligence on the basis of graphology hardly seems to be of any usefulness." And Eysenck (1948) notes that the emotionality judgments for 176 subjects by Mrs. F, a famous long-established European graphologist, bore no relation to psychiatric diagnoses (r=.02), whereas individual objective tests showed good agreement up to .57, and a battery of 17 tests showed .73. These objective tests are now largely obsolete, but they included things like measuring dark vision, persistence (write S's and reversed S's as fast as you can for two minutes), and body sway when blindfolded, all of which correlate with emotionality. He comments "When it is further remembered that these objective tests are of short duration (2 to 5 minutes each), and that they can be combined and multiplied at will [to improve accuracy], while the graphological analysis is extremely time-consuming, the relative superiority of the tests as opposed to the analysis will perhaps become apparent." And that was in 1948, when such tests were inferior to the pencil-and-paper tests available today.

Recent developments in testing methods promise to widen the gap still further. For a readable review see Murphy (1988). For example, computerized tests can measure abilities difficult to measure by pencil-and-paper tests, such as basic information processing and spatial visualization. Other computerized tests can generate narrative reports (Butcher et al. 1985), although unsurprisingly they are not universally popular among clinicians (Matarazzo 1986). Computers can also generate psychodiagnoses from interview questions administered by laypersons without any clinical experience, thus greatly reducing costs (Robins et al. 1981). Finally the computerized development known as Item Response Theory is having a major impact in the laboratory if not yet in the workplace. Classical test theory is based on test scores, that is, on the overall response to a number of individual items. From the scores comes the model of personality. By contrast IRT is based on *providing* responses to individual test items, and takes into account random disturbances. From the model of personality comes the individual item responses. In effect IRT allows tests to be separated from people, thus delivering personality freed from the quirks of a particular test (Hambleton and van der Linden 1982).

39. No, we cannot predict sex. For example, Olyanova (1960:15) says "The *sex*—whether male or female—is not revealed in handwriting. Neither is the *age* of the writer." Paterson (1976:90) says "'No graphologist or handwriting expert

can tell the age or sex of a writer." Roman (1952:5) says "Neither the chronological age nor the sex of a writer can be ascertained from his [sic] script." Bar-Hillel and Ben-Shakhar (1986:274) make the pointed comment that, because even lay persons can diagnose a writer's sex with some accuracy, "It would therefore seem reasonable to expect graphologists to be willing—and able—to predict a writer's sex from handwriting. That they refuse to do so reflects, under a charitable interpretation, their preference for predicting deep-lying unobservables to their observable correlates and perhaps even a disavowal of the relevance of behavioral criteria to the evaluation of their assessments."

40. Physiognomy in Table 3. Body build correlates around .10 with IQ (Rees 1960:375–376) and .20 to .30 with extroversion and emotionality (Eysenck 1970:346), so that unstable introverts tend slightly to be tall and narrow while stable extroverts tend slightly to be short and wide. Correction for attenuation increases the latter effect size to around .30 to .50, or large enough to be visible, which may explain the old English saying "Fat and merry, lean and sad." But then so does starvation. Conversely, the correlation of .10 between body build and IQ is not large enough to be visible, so it is unremarkable that the old Italian proverb "Fat heads, lean brains" is in the wrong direction. Secord et al. (1954) found that, as expected, people showed good agreement when judging purely physical features such as *light-dark complexion* or *height of eyebrows.* Interestingly, they showed equally good agreement when judging inferred traits (i.e., stereotypes) such as *honest face* or *intelligent look.* As a result the correlation between physical appearance and the inferred traits reached a dramatic .60 or more, thus confirming the power of stereotypes. But as shown by the physiognomy effect size of .15 in Table 3, these powerful stereotypes are powerfully inaccurate. For a review of the prominent role of appearance in forming stereotypes, and of recent trends toward an ecological theory of physiognomy (childlike faces are perceived to have childlike qualities such as warmth, honesty and submissiveness), see Berry and McArthur (1986).

41. Help wanted. If you know of any study that has been missed, please send details to the editors, if possible enclosing a photocopy of the original study, for which postage and photocopying expenses will be reimbursed. If the study is a lengthy one, just the title page and results pages will do, in which case make sure they include the details indicated by the headings in the relevant Appendix. The study will then be included in an updated meta-analysis in the second edition of this book, and your help will be acknowledged. Write to: Dr. Barry L. Beyerstein, Department of Psychology, Simon Fraser University, Burnaby BC, Canada V5A 1S6. Fax 604-291-3427.

REFERENCES

Alexander, R. A., G. M. Alliger, K. P. Carson, and G. V., Barrett. 1985. "The Empirical Performance of Measures of Association in the 2×2 Table." *Educational and Psychological Measurement* 45: pp. 79–87.

Allport, G. W., and P. E. Vernon. 1933. *Studies in Expressive Movement.* New York: Macmillan. Graphology is reviewed on pages 185–211, with 59 references, plus another 142 unrelated to graphology.

Anderson, L. D. 1921. "Estimating Intelligence by Means of Printed Photographs." *Journal of Applied Psychology* 5: pp. 152–155.

Bar-El, N. 1984. "Interrelations among Graphological Judgments, Psychological Assessments and Self-Ratings of Personality." MA thesis, Tel Aviv University. Cited by Nevo (1986a).

Barnes, G. E. 1984. "A Brief Note on Two Often Ignored Principles That Tend to Attenuate the Magnitude of Correlations." *Personality and Individual Differences* 5: pp. 361–363.

Barrick, M. R., and M. K. Mount. 1991. "The Big Five Personality Dimensions and Job Performance: A Meta-Analysis." *Personnel Psychology* 44: pp. 1–26.

Bayne, R., and F., O'Neill. 1988. "Handwriting and Personality: A Test of Some Expert Graphologists' Judgements." *Guidance and Assessment Review* 4(4): pp. 1–3. Additional data kindly supplied by Dr. Rowan Bayne.

Bell, J. E. 1948. "The Analysis of Handwriting." Chapter 14 in *Projective Techniques: A Dynamic Approach to the Study of the Personality.* New York: Longmans, Green, pp. 291–327. 137 references.

Ben-Shakhar, G., M. Bar-Hillel, Y. Bilu, E. Ben-Abba, and A. Flug. 1986. "Can Graphology Predict Occupational Success? Two Empirical Studies and Some Methodological Ruminations." *Journal of Applied Psychology* 71: pp. 645–653. The same study but with additional reliability coefficients appears in G. Ben-Shakhar, M. Bar-Hillel, and A. Flug. "A Validation Study of Graphological Evaluation in Personnel Selection." In Nevo (1986: pp. 175–191).

Berry, D. S., and L. Z. McArthur. 1986. "Perceiving Character in Faces: The Impact of Age-related Craniofacial Changes on Social Perception." *Psychological Bulletin* 100: pp. 3–18.

Binet, A. 1906. *Les révélations de l'écriture d'après un contrôle scientifique.* Paris: Alcan. Cited by Downey (1910).

Birge, W. R. 1954. "An Experimental Inquiry into the Measurable Handwriting Correlates of Five Personality Traits." *Journal of Personality* 23: pp. 215–223.

Bobertag, O. 1929. *Ist die Graphologie zuverlässig?* Heidelberg: Kampmann. Cited by Allport and Vernon (1933:201).

Borenstein, Y. 1985. "The Utility of Graphological Assessment As a Selection Tool in the Israeli Defence Forces." MA thesis, University of Haifa. Cited by Keinan (1986) and by Neter and Ben-Shakhar (1989).

Bradley, N. 1988. "99 Studies in Handwriting and Related Topics." Published by the author, 91 Hawksley Avenue, Chesterfield, Derbyshire S40 4TJ, England.

———. 1989. "100 Studies in Handwriting and Related Topics." Published by the author, see above. In preparation is a further volume "101 Studies in Handwriting and Related Topics."

Brandstatter, H. 1969. "On Diagnosing Integration of Personality from Handwriting." *Psychologische Rundschau* 21: pp. 159–172. Cited by Nevo (1986:257).

Brengelmann, J. C. 1960. "Expressive Movements and Abnormal Behavior." In *Handbook of Abnormal Psychology,* edited by H. J. Eysenck. London: Pitman, pp. 62–107. Graphology is reviewed on pages 82–85.

Briggs, D. 1970. "The Influence of Handwriting on Assessment." *Educational Research* 13: pp. 50–55.

Broom, M. E., B. Thompson, and M. T. Bouton. 1929. "Sex Differences in Handwriting." *Journal of Applied Psychology* 13: pp. 159–166.

Brown, L. E. 1921. "An Experimental Investigation of the Alleged Relations between Certain Character Traits and Handwriting." AB thesis, University of Wisconsin. Cited by Hull (1928: pp.. 149–151).

Burke, M. J., and J. T. Frederick. 1986. "A Comparison of Economic Utility Estimates for Alternative SD Estimation Procedures." *Journal of Applied Psychology* 71: pp. 334–339.

Burnup, R. H. 1974. "Handwriting Characteristics as Predictors of Personality Patterns." Thesis, University of Missouri, Kansas City. Cited by Stabholz (1981: p. 59).

Butcher, J. N., L. S. Keller, and S. F. Bacon. 1985. "Current Development and Future Directions in Computerized Personality Assessment." *Journal of Consulting and Clinical Psychology* 53: pp. 803–815.

Cantril, H., H. A. Rand, and G. W. Allport. 1933. "The Determination of Personal Interests by Psychological and Graphological Methods." *Character and Personality* 2: pp. 134–143.

Cantril, H., and H. A. Rand. 1934. "An Additional Study of the Determination of Personal Interests by Psychological and Graphological Methods." *Character and Personality* 3: pp. 72–78.

Cascio, W. F., and R. A. Ramos. 1986. "Development and Application of a New Method for Assessing Job Peformance in Behavioural/Economic Terms." *Journal of Applied Psychology* 71: pp. 20–28.

Castelnuovo-Tedesco, P. 1948. "A Study of the Relationship Between Handwriting and Personality Variables." *Genetic Psychology Monographs* 37: pp. 167–220.

Cleeton, G. U., and F. B. Knight. 1924. "Validity of Character Judgments Based on External Criteria." *Journal of Applied Psychology* 8: pp. 215–231.

Cohen, J. 1960. "A Coefficient of Agreement for Nominal Scales."*Educational and Psychological Measurement* 20: pp. 37–46.

———. 1968. "Weighted kappa: Nominal Scale Agreement with Provision for Scaled Disagreement or Partial Credit." *Psychological Bulletin* 70: pp. 213–220.

Comrey, A. L. 1988. "Methodological Contributions to Clinical Research." *Journal of Consulting and Clinical Psychology* 56: pp. 754–761.

Cox, J., and J. Tapsell. 1991. "Graphology and Its Validity in Personnel Assessment." Paper presented at the BPS Occupational Psychology Conference, Cardiff, January 1991.

Crider, B. 1941. "The Reliability and Validity of Two Graphologists." *Journal of Applied Psychology* 25: pp. 323–325.

Cronbach, L. 1970. *Essentials of Psychological Testing,* 3rd ed. New York: Harper and Row.

Cronshaw, S. F., and R. A. Alexander. 1985. "One Answer to the Demand for Accountability: Selection Utility as an Investment Decision." *Organizational Behaviour and Human Decision Processes* 35: pp. 102–118.

Crowley, T. 1991. "The Influence of Social Desirability on the Relationships Between Handwriting and Personal Qualities." *Personality and Individual Differences* 12: pp. 881–885.

Crumbaugh, J. C. 1986. "Graphoanalytic Cues." In Nevo (1986: pp. 47–58).

Crumbaugh, J. C., and E. Stockholm. 1977. "Validation of Graphoanalysis by Global or Holistic Method." *Perceptual and Motor Skills* 44: pp. 403–410.

Dean, G. 1985. "Can Astrology Predict E and N? 2. The Whole Chart." *Correlation* 5(2): pp. 2–24. Palmistry test is on page 20. A total of 14 palmists made 1–2 yes/no judgments of personality on each of 13 color slides showing the hands of extreme personalities.

———. 1986. "Can Astrology Predict E and N? 3. Discussion and Further Research." *Correlation* 6(2): pp. 7–52. A detailed survey of the evidence, including a comparison with palmistry, graphology and orthodox methods. 110 references, most of them annotated.

De Groot, A. D. 1947. "Een experimenteel-statistische toetsing van karakterologische (grafologische) rapporten." *Nederlands Tijdschrift van Psychologie* 2: pp. 380–473. Cited by Jansen (1973:3).

Donner, A. 1984. "Approaches to Sample Size Estimation in the Design of Clinical Trials—A Review." *Statistics in Medicine* 3: pp. 199–214.

Downey, J. E. 1910. "Judgments on the Sex of Handwriting." *Psychological Reviews* 17: pp. 205–216.

———. 1919. "Character and Handwriting." *Psychological Bulletin* 16: pp. 28–31.

Drory, A. 1986. "Graphology and Job Performance: A Validation Study." In Nevo (1986: pp. 165–173).

Dzida, W., and F. Kiener. 1978. "Strategien der Verwertung nonverbaler Informationen zur Persönlichkeitsbeurteilung." *Zeitschrift für experimentelle und angewandte Psychologie* 25: pp. 552–563.

Edgell, S. E., and S. M. Noon. 1984. "Effect of Violation of Normality on the *t* Test of the Correlation Coefficient." *Psychological Bulletin* 95: pp. 576–583.

Edwards, A. L. 1967. "The Social Desirability Variable: A Review of the Evidence." In *Response Set in Personality Assessment*, edited by I. A. Berg. Chicago: Aldine, pp. 48–70.

Eisenberg, P. 1938. "Judging Expressive Movement: I. Judgments of Sex and Dominance-Feeling from Handwriting Samples of Dominant and Non-dominant Men and Women." *Journal of Applied Psychology* 22: pp. 480–486.

Esroni, G., A. Rolnik, and E. Livnat. 1985. "Studies Evaluating the Validity of Graphology in a Voluntary Military Unit." A paper presented at the 20th Israeli Psychological Association Conference. Cited by Neter and Ben-Shakhar (1989).

Estes, S. G. 1938. "Judging Personality from Expressive Behavior." *Journal of Abnormal and Social Psychology* 33: pp. 217–236.

Eysenck, H. J. 1945. "Graphological Analysis and Psychiatry: An Experimental Study." *British Journal of Psychiatry* 35: pp. 70–81.
———. 1948. "Neuroticism and Handwriting." *Journal of Abnormal and Social Psychology* 43: pp. 94–96.
———. 1960. *Handbook of Abnormal Psychology: An Experimental Approach.* London: Pitman.
———. 1970. *The Structure of Human Personality.* 3rd edition. London: Methuen.
Eysenck, H. J., and S. B. G. Eysenck. 1964. *Manual of the Eysenck Personality Inventory.* London: University of London Press.
Eysenck, H.J., and G. Gudjonsson. 1986. "An Empirical Study of the Validity of Handwriting Analysis." *Personality and Individual Differences* 7: pp. 263–264.
Feingold, A. 1988. "Matching for Attractivness in Romantic Partners and Same-Sex Friends: A Meta-Analysis and Theoretical Critique." *Psychological Bulletin* 104: pp. 226–235.
Feldt, L. 1962. "The Reliability of Measures of Handwriting Quality." *Journal of Educational Psychology* 53: pp. 288–292. Concerned with, e.g., clarity of form and size in the handwriting of elementary school children. Of little relevance to graphology.
Fischer, G. 1962. "Die faktorielle Struktur der Handschrift." Doctoral dissertation, Vienna University. Cited by Nevo (1986:255).
———. 1964. "Zur faktorielle Struktur der Handschrift. *Zeitschrift für experimentelle und angewandte Psychologie* 11: pp. 254–280. Cited by Nevo (1986:255).
Fluckiger, F. A., C. A. Tripp, and G. H. Weinberg. 1961. "A Review of Experimental Research in Graphology 1933–1960." *Perceptual and Motor Skills* 12: pp. 67–90, 105 references.
Flug, A. 1981. "Reliability and Validity of Graphology in Personnel Selection." MA thesis, Hebrew University of Jerusalem. Cited by Nevo (1986:258).
Forer, B. R. 1949. "The Fallacy of Personal Validation: A Classroom Demonstration of Gullibility." *Journal of Abnormal and Social Psychology* 44: pp. 118–123. The Barnum statements used in Box 2 are those numbered 11, 4, 6, 7, and 1+13.
Frank, G. 1983. *The Wechsler Enterprise: An Assessment of the Development, Structure, and Use of the Wechsler Tests of Intelligence.* Oxford: Pergamon.
Frederick, C. J. 1965. "Some Phenomena Affecting Handwriting Analysis." *Perceptual and Motor Skills* 20: pp. 211–218.
Furnham, A., and B. Gunter. 1987. "Graphology and Personality: Another Failure to Validate Graphological Analysis." *Personality and Individual Differences* 8: 433–435. Additional details including resolution of conflict between table and text were kindly supplied by Dr. Adrian Furnham.
Galbraith, D., and D. Wilson. 1964. "Reliability of the Graphoanalytic Approach to Handwriting Analysis." *Perceptual and Motor Skills* 19: pp. 615–618.
Garb, H. N. 1989. "Clinical Judgment, Clinical Training, and Professional Experience." *Psychological Bulletin* 105: pp. 387–396.
Gesell, A. L. 1906. "Accuracy in Handwriting, as Related to School Intelligence

and Sex." *American Journal of Psychology* 17: pp. 394–405.
Ghiselli, E. E. 1966. *The Validity of Occupational Aptitude Test.* New York: Wiley. Important comments on this and the next reference appear in Pearlman et al. (1980).
———, 1973. "The Validity of Aptitude Tests in Personnel Selection." *Personnel Psychology* 26: pp. 461–477.
Goldberg, L. R. 1986. "Some Informal Explorations and Ruminations About Graphology." In Nevo (1986: pp. 281–293).
Goldsmith, H. 1976. "The Facts on the Legibility of Doctors' Handwriting." *Medical Journal of Australia* [no vol. nos.], part 2: pp. 462–463.
Goodenough, F. L. 1945. "Sex Differences in Judging the Sex of Handwriting." *Journal of Social Psychology* 22: pp. 61–68.
Green, P. E., V. R. Rao, and D. E. Armani. 1971. "Graphology and Marketing Research: A Pilot Experiment in Validity and Inter-judge Reliability." *Journal of Marketing* 35: pp. 58–62.
Greene, B. F., and J. A. Hall. 1984. "Quantitative Methods for Literature Reviews." *Annual Review of Psychology* 35: pp. 37–53.
Greene, J., and D. Lewis. 1980. *The Hidden Language of Your Handwriting.* London: Souvenir Press, p. 252.
Greenwald, A. G. 1975. "Consequences of Prejudice against the Null Hypothesis." *Psychological Bulletin* 82: pp. 1–20.
Guilford, J. P. 1965. *Fundamental Statistics in Psychology and Education,* 4th ed. New York: McGraw-Hill.
Guion, R. M., and R. F. Gottier. 1965. "Validity of Personality Measures in Personnel Selection." *Personnel Psychology* 18: pp. 135–164.
Hackett, R. D. 1989. "Work Attitudes and Employee Absenteeism: A Synthesis of the Literature." *Journal of Occupational Psychology* 62: pp. 235–248.
Halevi, H. 1964. "Studying Graphology via Matching Technique." MA thesis, Hebrew University of Jerusalem. Summarized in Nevo (1986: p. 244).
Helevi, H. 1965. "An Alternative Approach to the Method of Correct Matching." *Psychometrika* 30: pp. 67–90.
Hambleton, R. K., and Q. J. van der Linden. 1982. "Advances in Item Response Theory and Applications: An Introduction." *Applied Psychological Measurement* 6: pp. 373–378.
Harris, M. M., and J. Schaubroeck. 1988. "A Meta-Aanalysis of Self-Supervisor, Self-Peer, and Peer-Supervisor Ratings." *Personnel Psychology* 41: pp. 43–62.
Harvey, O. L. 1933. "The Measurement of Handwriting Considered as a Form of Expressive Movement." *Character and Personality* 2: pp. 310–321.
Helmstadter, G. C. 1966. *Principles of Psychological Measurement.* London: Methuen, p. 85. The values cited are those obtained by Helmstadter in the early 1960s "by simply recording reported reliabilities for well known tests in each of several areas."
Hertz, M. R. 1986. "Rorschachbound: A 50-Year Memoir." *Journal of Personality Assessment* 50: pp. 396–416.

Hines, T. 1988. "Pseudoscience and the Paranormal: A Critical Examination of the Evidence." Buffalo, N.Y.: Prometheus Books.

Hirsch, R. H. 1987. "Review of Nevo (1986)." *Personnel Psychology*, 40: pp. 838–842.

Hoepfner, R. 1962. "An Empirical Study of the Contents of Handwriting." Thesis, University of Southern California. Cited by Stabholz (1981: p. 53).

Hofsommer, W., R. Holdsworth, and T. Seifert. 1962. "Zur Bewahrungskontrolle Graphologischer Diagnosen." *Psychologische Beitrage* 7: pp. 397–401. Cited by Neter and Ben-Shakhar (1989).

Hofsommer, W., and R. Holdsworth, 1963. "Die Validität der Handschriftenanalyse bei der Auswahl von Piloten." *Psychologie und Praxis* 7: pp. 175–178. Cited by Neter and Ben-Shakhar (1989).

Holder, R. 1976. *You Can Analyze Handwriting*. North Hollywood: Wilshire.

Hönel, H. 1977. "Grundrhythmus und Kriminelle disposition in der Handschrift." *Zeitschrift für Menschenkunde* 41: pp. 1–55. Re-analyzed by Nevo (1986: pp. 203–215).

Howes, R. J. 1981. "The Rorschach: Does It Have a Future?" *Journal of Personality Assessment* 45: pp. 339–351. The answer was yes.

Hull, C. L. 1928. *Aptitude Testing*. London: Harrap.

Hull, C. L., and R. B. Montgomery. 1919. "An Experimental Investigation of Certain Alleged Relations between Character and Handwriting." *Psychological Reviews* 26: pp. 63–74.

Hunter, J. E., and R. F. Hunter. 1984. "Validity and Utility of Alternative Predictors of Job Performance." *Psychological Bulletin* 96: pp. 72–98.

Hunter, J. F., and F. L. Schmidt. 1990. *Methods of Meta-Analysis: Correcting Error and Bias in Research Findings*. Newbury Park, Calif.: Sage. An updated and enlarged version of next reference.

Hunter, J. E., F. L. Schmidt, and G. B. Jackson. 1982. *Meta-Analysis: Cumulating Research Findings Across Studies*. Beverly Hills, Calif.: Sage.

Hunter, J. E., F. L. Schmidt, and M. K. Judiesch. 1990. "Individual Differences in Output Variability as a Function of Job Complexity." *Journal of Applied Psychology* 75: pp. 28–42.

Jansen, A. 1973. *Validation of Graphological Judgments: An Experimental Study*. Paris and The Hague: Mouton.

Jensen, A. R. 1959. "The Reliability of Projective Techniques: Review of the Literature." *Acta Psychologica* 16: pp. 108–136.

———. 1964. "The Rorschach Technique: A Re-evaluation." *Acta Psychologica* 22: pp. 60–77. Repeats much of the data in the previous reference but includes validity and an update.

———. 1981. *Straight Talk about Mental Tests*. London: Methuen, pp. 19–34.

Kane, J. S., and E. E. Lawler. 1978. "Methods of Peer Assessment." *Psychological Bulletin* 85: pp. 555–586.

Karnes, E. W., and S. D. Leonard. 1991. "Graphoanalytic and Psychometric Personality Profiles: Validity and Barnum Effects." Chapter 16 in this book.

Keinan, G., A. Barak, and T. Ramati. 1984. "Reliability and Validity of Graphological

Assessment in the Selection Process of Military Officers." *Perceptual and Motor Skills* 58: pp. 811–821.,
Keinan, G. 1986. "Graphoanalysis for Military Personnel Selection." In Nevo (1986: pp. 193–201).
Kelly, I. W., G. A. Dean, and D. H. Saklofske. 1990. "Astrology: A Critical Review." In *Philosophy of Science and the Occult,* edited by P. Grim. 2nd ed. Albany, N.Y.: State University of New York, pp. 51–81. 80 references. Page 55 updates the survey by Dean (1986).
Kimball, T. D. 1973. "The Systematic Isolation and Validation of Personality Determiners in the Handwriting of School Children." Thesis, University of Southern California. Cited by Stabholz (1981: pp. 58–59). Summarized in *Dissertation Abstracts International* 34: pp. 6450–6451.
Kimmel, D., and M. Wertheimer. 1966. "Personality Ratings Based on Handwriting Analysis and Clinical Judgment: A Correlational Study." *Journal of Projective Techniques* 30: pp. 177–178.
Kinder, J. S. 1926. "A New Investigation of Judgments on the Sex of Handwriting." *Journal of Educational Psychology* 17: pp. 341–344.
Kirchner, J. H., and E. A. Lemke. 1973. "I-dots in the Handwriting of a Clinical Sample." *Perceptual and Motor Skills* 36: pp. 548–550.
Kirk, J. G. 1926. "Handwriting Survey to Determine Grade Standards." *Journal of Educational Research* 13: pp. 181–188 and 259–272.
Klare, G. R. 1974. "Assessing Readability." *Reading Research Quarterly* 10: pp. 62–102.
Klimoski, R. J., and A. Rafaeli. 1983. "Inferring Personal Qualities through Handwriting Analysis." *Journal of Occupational Psychology* 56: pp. 191–202. 45 references.
Kurdsen, S. 1971. *Graphology The New Science.* New York: Galahad.
Landis, C., and L. W. Phelps. 1928. "The Prediction from Photographs of Success and of Vocational Aptitude." *Journal of Experimental Psychology* 11: pp. 313–324.
Lemke, E. A., and J. H. Kirchner. 1971. "A Multivariate Study of Handwriting, Intelligence, and Personality Correlates." *Journal of Personality Assessment* 35: pp. 584–592.
Lent, R. H., H. A. Aurbach, and L. S. Levin. 1971. "Predictors, Criteria, and Significant Results." *Personnel Psychology* 24: pp. 519–533.
Lester, D., S. McLaughlin, and G. Nosal. 1977. "Graphological Signs for Extraversion." *Perceptual and Motor Skills* 44: pp. 137–138.
Lester, D. 1981. *The Psychological Basis of Handwriting Analysis: The Relationship of Handwriting to Personality and Psychopathology.* Chicago: Nelson-Hall. 240 references of which 40 are nongraphological. Very readable but summaries of published articles often lack detail and are sometimes inaccurate.
Light, R. J., and D. B. Pillemer. 1984. *Summing Up: The Science of Reviewing Research.* Cambridge, Mass.: Harvard University Press.
Linn, R. L., D. L. Harnisch, and S. B. Dunbar. 1981. "Validity Generalization and Situational Specificity: An Analysis of the Prediction of First-Year Grades

in Law School." *Applied Psychological Measurement* 5: pp. 281–289.
LoMonaco, T., and R. Harrison. 1973. "Accuracy of Matching TAT and Graphological Personality Profiles." *Perceptual and Motor Skills* 36: pp. 703–706.
Lockowandt, O. 1976. "Present Status of the Investigation of Handwriting Psychology as a Diagnostic Method." *JSAS Catalog of Selected Documents in Psychology* 6(1): p. 4. Reprinted with minor editing in chapter 5 of this book.
Lowenthal, K. 1975. "Handwriting and Self-presentation." *Journal of Social Psychology* 96: pp. 267–270.
——. 1982. "Handwriting as a Guide to Character." In *Judging People: A Guide to Orthodox and Unorthodox Methods of Assessment,* edited by D. M. Davey and M. Harris. London: McGraw-Hill, pp. 83–96.
Lorr, M., L. T. Lepine, and J. V. Golder. 1953. "A Factor Analysis of Some Handwriting Characteristics." *Journal of Personality* 22: pp. 348–353.
Lowengard, M. 1975. *How to Analyze Your Handwriting.* London: Marshall Cavendish.
Mabe, P. A., and S. G. West. 1982. "Validity of Self-Evaluation of Ability: A Review and Meta-Analysis." *Journal of Applied Psychology* 67: pp. 280–296.
MacLennan, R. N., 1988. "Correlation, Base-Rates, and the Predictability of Behavior." *Personality and Individual Differences* 9: pp. 675–684.
Mann, W. 1961. "A Continuation of the Search for Objective Graphological Hypotheses." Thesis, University of Ottawa. Cited by Stabholz (1981: p. 53).
Marne, P. 1988. *The Concise Graphology Notebook.* Slough: Foulsham.
Mason, D. J. 1957. "Judgments of Leadership Based upon Physiognomic Cues." *Journal of Abnormal and Social Psychology* 54: pp. 273–274.
Matarazzo, J. D. 1986. "Computerized Clinical Psychological Test Interpretations: Unvalidated Plus All Mean and No Sigma." *American Psychologist* 41: p. 96. With subsequent debate in 42: pp. 192–193.
McCartney, K. M., M. J. Harris, and Bernieri. 1990. "Growing Up and Growing Apart: A Developmental Meta-Analysis of Twin Studies." *Psychological Bulletin* 107: pp. 226–237.
McHenry, J. J., L. M. Hough, J. L. Toquam, M. A. Hanson, and S. Ashworth. 1990. "Project A Validity Results: The Relationship Between Predictor and Criterion Domains." *Personnel Psychology* 43: pp. 335–354.
McKelvie, S. J. 1990. "Student Acceptance of a Generalized Personality Description: Forer's Graphologist Revisited." *Journal of Social Behavior and Personality* 5: pp. 91–95.
McNeil, E. B., and G. S. Blum. 1952. "Handwriting and Psychosexual Dimensions of Personality." *Journal of Projective Techniques* 16: pp. 476–484.
Meehl, P. E. 1972. "Reactions, Reflections, Projections." In *Objective Personality Assessment: Changing Perspectives,* edited by J. N. Butcher. New York: Academic Press, pp. 131–189. For the technical problems of blood pressure measurement see O'Brien and O'Malley (1979).
Meloun, J. 1935. "Does Drawing Skill Show in Handwriting?" *Character and Personality* 33: pp. 194–213.
Michel, L. 1969. "Empirische Untersuchungen zur Frage der Übereinstimmung und

Gültigkeit von Beurteilungen des intellektuellen Niveaus aus der Handschrift." *Archiv für die gesamte Psychologie* 121: pp. 31–54. For a shorter updated version in English, but without physiognomy results, see L. Michel, "Intellectual Abilities and Handwriting," in Nevo (1986: pp. 217–229).

Middleton, W. C. 1941a. "The Ability of Untrained Subjects to Judge Neuroticism, Self-Confidence, and Sociability from Handwriting Samples." *Character and Personality* 9: pp. 227–234.

———. 1941b. "The Ability of Untrained Subjects to Judge Intelligence and Age from Handwriting Samples." *Journal of Applied Psychology* 25: pp. 331–340.

Miller, J. H. 1982. *Bibliography of Handwriting Analysis: A Graphological Index.* Troy, N.Y.: Whitson, 432 pages. An annotated list of 2,321 references, not 100 percent comprehensive.

Miller, S. 1984. *Experimental Design and Statistics,* 2nd ed. London: Methuen. Readable and inexpensive.

Misiak, H., and G. J. Franghiadi. 1953. "The Thumb and Personality." *Journal of General Psychology* 48: pp. 241–244.

Moore, M. 1985. "About the Sad State of Scientific Graphology." *Psychological Documents* 15 (2), MS No. 2676.

Mullen, B., C. Copper, and J. E. Driskell. 1990. "Jaywalking as a Function of Model Behavior." *Personality and Social Psychology Bulletin* 16: pp. 320–330.

Murphy, K. R. 1988. "Psychological Measurement: Abilities and Skills." In *International Review of Industrial and Organizational Psychology 1988,* edited by C. L. Cooper and I. T. Robertson, pp. 213–243. New York: Wiley.

Murstein, B. I. 1963. *Theory and Research in Projective Techniques (emphasizing the TAT),* pp. 139–148. New York: Wiley.

Nathan, B. R., and R. A. Alexander. 1988. "A Comparison of Criteria for Test Validation: A Meta-Analytic Investigation." *Personnel Psychology* 41: pp. 517–535.

Neter, E., and G. Ben-Shakhar. 1989. "The Predictive Validity of Graphological Inferences: A Meta-Analytic Approach." *Personality and Individual Differences* 10: pp. 737–745. See note 26.

Neuman, G. A., J. E. Edwards, and N. S. Raju. 1989. "Organizational Development Interventions: A Meta-Analysis of Their Effects on Satisfaction and Other Attitudes." *Personnel Psychology* 42: pp. 461–489.

Nevo, B. 1986. *Scientific Aspects of Graphology: A Handbook.* Springfield, Ill.: Thomas. An anthology of 19 authors including Nevo. About 310 references not counting those duplicated between chapters, of which about 190 are on validity and methodology.

———. 1986a. "Reliability of Graphology: A Survey of the Literature." In Nevo (1986: pp. 253–261).

———. 1986b. "Graphology Validation Studies in Israel: Summary of 15 Years of Activity." Paper presented at the 21st International Congress of Applied Psychology, Jerusalem.

———. 1988. "Yes, Graphology Can Predict Occupational Success: Rejoinder to Ben-Shakhar et al." *Perceptual and Motor Skills* 66: pp. 92–94.

———. 1989. "Validation of Graphology through Use of a Matching Method Based on Ranking." *Perceptual and Motor Skills* 69: pp. 1331–1336. Same study as reported briefly in B. Nevo and H. Halevi (1986). "Validation of Graphology through the Use of Matching Method Based on Ranking." In Nevo (1986: pp. 241–246).

Nevo, B., and R. Benitta. 1991. "Rank-Ordered Matching in Validity Studies of Personnel Selection Devices: A Proposed Model and Some Empirical Results." Pre-publication draft kindly supplied by Professor Baruch Nevo.

Newhall, S. M. 1926. "Sex Differences in Handwriting." *Journal of Applied Psychology* 10: pp. 151–161.

O'Brien, E. T., and K. O'Malley. 1979. "ABC of Blood Pressure Measurement." *British Medical Journal* 1979 (2): pp. 851–853.

Olyanova, N. 1960. *The Psychology of Handwriting*. New York: Sterling.

———. 1969. *Handwriting Tells*. London: Peter Owen.

Oosthuizen, S. 1990. "Graphology as Predictor of Academic Achievement." *Perceptual and Motor Skills* 71: pp. 715–721.

Pang, H., and L. Lepponen. 1968. "Personality Traits and Handwriting Characteristics." *Perceptual and Motor Skills* 26: p. 1082.

Parker, K. C. H., R. K. Hanson, and J. Hunsley. 1988. "MMPI, Rorschach, and WAIS: A Meta-Analytic Comparison of Reliability, Stability, and Validity." *Psychological Bulletin* 103: pp. 367–373. Their five Rorschach studies came from the *Journal of Personality Assessment* 1970–1981. I added three more studies by extending the survey to 1990. There is no overlap with Reznikoff et al. (1982).

Pascal, G. R. 1943. "The Analysis of Handwriting: A Test of Significance." *Character and Personality* 12: pp. 123–144.

Pascal, G. R., and B. Suttell. 1947. "Testing the Claims of a Graphologist." *Journal of Personality* 16: pp. 192–197.

Passingham, R. E. 1979. "Brain Size and Intelligence in Man." *Brain, Behavior and Evolution* 16: pp. 253–270.

Paterson, J. 1976. *Interpreting Handwriting*. London: Macmillan.

Paul-Mengelberg, M. 1965. "Die Symptome der Veralterung in der Handschrift." *Zeitschrift für Menschenkunde* 29: pp. 3–27. Summarized by Lockowandt in chapter 5 of this book.

———. 1986. Personal communication to Nevo (1986: p. 257).

Pearlman, K., F. L. Schmidt, and J. E. Hunter. 1980. "Validity Generalization Results for Tests Used to Predict Job Proficiency and Training Success in Clerical Occupations." *Journal of Applied Psychology* 65: pp. 373–406.

Peeples, E. E. 1990. "Training, Certification, and Experience of Handwriting Analysts." *Perceptual and Motor Skills* 70: pp. 1219–1226.

Perron, R., and H. De Gobineau. 1957. "Study on Identification and Diagnosis of Epilepsy by Means of Handwriting Analysis." *Travail Humain* 29: pp. 323–338. Cited by Nevo (1986: p. 256).

Pinter, R. 1918. "Intelligence as Estimated from Photographs." *Psychological Review* 25: pp. 286–296.

Powers, E. 1933. "Matching Sketches of Personality with Script." Chapter 10 in Allport and Vernon (1983: pp. 212–223).

Prystav, G. 1969. "Beitrag zur faktoren analytischen Validierung der Handschrift." Doctoral dissertation, University of Freiburg. Cited by Nevo (1986: 256).

Rabin, A., and H. Blair. 1953. "The Effects of Alcohol on Handwriting." *Journal of Clinical Psychology* 9: pp. 284–287. Scripts were obtained from 28 adult males before and after drinking to a blood alcohol level of .05–.17 percent, and each pair was judged by 8 nongraphologists. The mean number judged correctly was 26.9 or 96 percent, range 26–28.

Radin, D. I., and R. D. Nelson. 1989. "Evidence for Consciousness-Related Anomalies in Random Physical Systems." *Foundations of Physics* 19: pp. 1499–1513. A meta-analysis of random number generator studies.

Rafaeli, A., and A. Drory. 1988. "Graphological Assessments for Personnel Selection: Concerns and Suggestions for Research." *Perceptual and Motor Skills* 66: pp. 743–759.

Rafaeli, A., and R. J. Klimoski. 1983. "Predicting Sales Success through Handwriting Analysis: An Evaluation of the Effects of Training and Handwriting Sample Content." *Journal of Applied Psychology* 68: pp. 212–217. Additional data kindly supplied by Professor Richard Klimoski.

Ratzon, H. 1986. "Handwriting Analysis of Holocaust Survivors." In Nevo (1986: pp. 127–139).

Ray, W. S. 1958. "Judgments of Intelligence Based on Brief Observations of Physiognomy." *Psychological Reports* 4: p. 478.

Ree, M. J., and J. A. Earles. 1991. "Predicting Training Success: Not Much More than g." *Personnel Psychology* 44: pp. 321–332.

Rees, L., 1960. "Constitutional Factors and Abnormal Behavior." In Eysenck (1960: pp. 344–392).

Reilly, R. R., and G. T. Chao. 1982. "Validity and Fairness of Some Alternative Employee Selection Procedures." *Personnel Psychology* 35: pp. 1–62.

Reznikoff, M., E. Aronow, and A. Rauchway. 1982. "The Reliability of Inkblot Content Scales." In *Advances in Personality Assessment,* Vol. 1, edited by C. D. Spielberger and J. N. Butcher. Hillsdale, N.J.: Erlbaum. There is only a small overlap with Jensen (1959, 1964).

Ritzler, B., and B. Alter. 1986. "Rorschach Teaching in APA-approved Clinical Graduate Programs: Ten Years Later." *Journal of Personality Assessment* 50: pp. 44–49.

Robins, L. N., J. E. Helzer, J. Croughan, and K. S. Ratcliff. 1981. "National Institute of Mental Health Diagnostic Interview Schedule." *Archives of General Psychiatry* 38: pp. 381–389.

Roman, K. G. 1952. *Handwriting: A Key to Personality.* New York: Pantheon.

Rosenthal, D. A., and R. Lines. "Handwriting as a Correlate of Extraversion." *Journal of Personality Assessment* 42: pp. 45–48.

Rosenthal, R. 1979. "The 'File Drawer' Problem and Tolerance for Null Results." *Psychological Bulletin* 86: pp. 638–641.

———. 1984. *Meta-Analytic Procedures for Social Research.* Beverly Hills, Calif.: Sage.

Rosenthal, R., and D. B. Rubin. 1982. "A Simple, General Purpose Display of

Magnitude of Experimental Effect." *Journal of Educational Psychology* 74: pp. 708–712.

Rothstein, H. R. 1990. "Interrater Reliability of Job Performance Ratings: Growth to Asymptote Level with Increasing Opportunity to Observe." *Journal of Applied Psychology* 75: pp. 322–327.

Saudek, R. 1925. *The Psychology of Handwriting*. London: Allen and Unwin.

Schmidt, F. L., J. E. Hunter, and V. W. Urry. 1976. "Statistical Power in Criterion-related Validation Studies." *Journal of Applied Psychology* 61: pp. 473–485.

Schmidt, F. L., J. E. Hunter, and K. Pearlman. 1981. "Task Differences as Moderators of Aptitude Test Validity in Selection: A Red Herring." *Journal of Applied Psychology* 66: pp. 166–185.

Schmidt, F. L., J. E. Hunter, K. Pearlman, and H. R. Hirsch. 1985a. "Forty Questions about Validity Generalization and Meta-Analysis." *Personnel Psychology* 38: pp. 697–798. Includes comments from others and authors' replies.

Schmidt, F. L., B. P. Ocasio, J. M. Hillery, and J. E. Hunter. 1985b. "Further Within-Setting Empirical Tests of the Situational Specificity Hypothesis in Personnel Selection." *Personnel Psychology* 38: pp. 509–524.

Schmitt, N., R. Z. Gooding, R. A. Noe, and M. Kirsch. 1984. "Metaanalyses of Validity Studies Published Between 1964 and 1982 and the Investigation of Study Characteristics." *Personnel Psychology* 37: pp. 407–422.

Schweighofer, F. 1979. *Graphology and Psychoanalysis: The Handwriting of Sigmund Freud and His Circle.* New York: Springer. Comments on the handwriting of Freud and about 40 others.

Secord, P. F. 1949. "Studies of the Relationship of Handwriting to Personality." *Journal of Personality* 17: pp. 430–448.

Secord, P. F., W. F. Dukes, and W. Bevan. 1954. "Personalities in Faces: 1. An Experiment in Social Perceiving." *Genetic Psychology Monographs* 49: pp. 231–279.

Seifer, M. 1977. "Dominant Personality Characteristics and Their Relationship to Thumb Size." *Journal of Occult Studies* (later *Metascience Quarterly,* now defunct) 1: pp. 242–256. Summarized in Dean (1986).

Shapiro, D. A., and D. Shapiro (1982). "Meta-Analysis of Comparative Therapy Outcome Studies: A Replication and Refinement." *Psychological Bulletin* 92: pp. 581–604. Therapy outcome is a hotly debated issue, so see also the debate in *Psychological Bulletin* 1990, 107: pp. 106–113.

Shilo, S. 1979. "Prediction of Success on a Moshav According to Graphological Scores as Compared to Prediction of the Same Criterion by Psychological Scores." Internal Research Report, Hadassa Institute for Career Guidance Counselling, Jerusalem, Israel. Cited by Nevo (1986b).

Singer, E. 1969. *A Manual of Graphology.* London: Duckworth.

Smith, M .L. 1980. "Publication Bias and Meta-Analysis." *Evaluation in Education* 4: pp. 22–24.

Sonnemann, U. 1950. *Handwriting Analysis as a Psychodiagnostic Tool.* London: Allen and Unwin.

Sonnemann, U., and J. P. Kerman. 1962. "Handwriting Analysis—A Valid Selection Tool?" *Personnel* 39: pp. 8–14.

Stabholz, M. S. 1981. "Individual Differences in the Handwriting of Monozygotic and Dizygotic Twins in Relation to Personality and Genetic Factors." MPhil Thesis, Institute of Psychiatry, University of London.

Strolovitch, I. 1980. "Impact of Personal Variables and Job Variables on the Predictive Validity of Some Personnel Selection Practices for Scientific-Technical Positions." MA thesis, the Technion, Israel. Cited by Neter and Ben-Shakhar (1989).

Super, D. E. 1941. "A Comparison of the Diagnoses of a Graphologist with the Results of Psychological Tests." *Journal of Consulting Psychology* 5: pp. 127–133.

Surovell, H. 1987. *Lovestrokes. Handwriting for Love, Sex, and Compatibility.* New York: Harper & Row.

Sussams, P. 1985. "Graphology and Psychological Tests: Part 2—The Correlation Experiment." *The Graphologist* [UK] (1)3: pp. 10–12.

Swentzell, R., and A. H. Roberts. 1964. "On the Interaction of the Subject and the Experiment in the Matching Model." *Psychometrika* 29: pp. 87–101.

Symaniz, A.J. 1980. "A Study Concerned with Investigating the Potential Diagnostic Value of Palmar-analysis." Honors psychology thesis, University of Adelaide, South Australia. Summarized in Dean (1986).

Taft, R. 1967. "Extraversion, Neuroticism, and Expressive Behavior: An Application of Wallach's Moderator Effect to Handwriting Analysis." *Journal of Personality* 35: pp. 570–584.

Taylor, M. S., and K. K. Sackheim. 1988. "Graphology." *Personnel Administrator* (5)33: pp. 71–76 (May 1988). [Each month starts from page 1].

Van Valen, L. 1974. "Brain Size and Intelligence in Man." *American Journal of Physical Anthropology* 40: pp. 417–424. The correlation with *brain* size is larger than that with *head* size.

Vernon, P. E. 1953. *Personality Tests and Assessments.* London: Methuen.

Vestewig, R. E., A. H. Santee, and M. K. Moss. 1976. "Validity and Student Acceptance of a Graphoanalytic Approach to Personality." *Journal of Personality Assessment* 40: pp. 592–598.

Vine, I. 1974. "Stereotypes in the Judgement of Personality from Handwriting." *British Journal of Social and Clinical Psychology* 13: pp. 61–64.

Von Kügelgen, G. 1928. "Graphologie und Berufseignung." *Industrielle Psychotechnik* 5: p. 311.

Wallner, T. 1961. "Reliabilitätsuntersuchungen an metrisch nicht messbaren Handschriftvariablen." *Zeitschrift für Menschenkunde* 25: pp. 1–14 and 49–78. Cited by Nevo (1986: 257).

———. 1962. "Neue Ergebnisse experimenteller Untersuchungen über die Reliabilität von Handschriftvariablen." *Zeitschrift für Menschenkunde* 26: pp. 257–269. Cited by Nevo (1986: p. 257).

———. 1963. "Über die Validität Graphologischer Aussagen." *Diagnostica* 9: pp. 26–35. Cited by Neter and Ben-Shakhar (1989).

Warner, L. 1991. Information kindly supplied by Lawrence Warner, President of the International Graphoanalysis Society in the UK.

Warner, L., and J. Swallow. 1989. "Graphoanalysis: Can It Save You Money and Help to Increase Effectiveness?" *Sundridge Park Management Review* [UK], Summer 1989: pp. 11–18. From the top, the graphoanalysis statements are LRLRL. The statements received minor editing, e.g., to substitute "you are" for "the writer is"; otherwise their original sense and order is unchanged. Although the excerpt presented by Warner and Swallow is only two paragraphs from a 3-page interpretation, it is clearly intended to show what graphoanalysis can do, so some generalization is warranted. Both authors are qualified graphoanalysts.

Weinberg, G. H., F. A. Fluckiger, and C. A. Tripp. 1962. "The Application of a New Matching Technique." *Journal of Projective Techniques* 26: pp. 221–224.

Wellingham-Jones, P. 1989. "Evaluation of the Handwriting of Successful Women through the Roman-Staempfli Psychogram." *Perceptual and Motor Skills* 69: pp. 999–1010. Reprinted in chapter 15 of this book.

Wells, F. L. 1946. "Personal History, Handwriting and Specific Behavior." *Character and Personality* 14: pp. 295–314.

White, K. R. 1982. "The Relation between Socioeconomic Status and Academic Achievement." *Psychological Bulletin* 91: pp. 461–481.

Wiesner, W. H., and S. F. Cronshaw. 1988. "A Meta-Analytic Investigation of the Impact of Interview Format and Degree of Structure on the Validity of the Employment Interview." *Journal of Occupational Psychology* 61: pp. 275–290. The reliability and validity of *unstructured* (i.e., traditional) interviews is much lower at .61 (9 studies) and .11 (19 studies), respectively.

Wilkinson, B. 1951. "A Statistical Consideration in Psychological Research." *Psychological Bulletin* 48: pp. 156–158.

Williams, E. D., L. Winter, and J. M. Woods. 1938. "Tests and Literary Appreciation." *British Journal of Educational Psychology* 8: pp. 265–284. See page 282. Sample was 256 schoolgirls aged 11–17.

Williams, M., G. Berg-Cross, and L. Berg-Cross. 1977. "Handwriting Characteristics and Their Relationship to Eysenck's Extraversion-Introversion and Kagan's Impulsivity-Reflectivity Dimensions." *Journal of Personality Assessment* 41: pp. 291–298.

Wilson, G. D. 1983. "Finger-Length as an Index of Assertiveness in Women." *Personality and Individual Differences* 4: pp. 111–112.

Wolff, C. 1941. "Character and Mentality as Related to Hand-Markings." *British Journal of Medical Psychology* 18: pp. 364–382.

Wolfson, R. 1951. "Graphology." In *An Introduction to Projective Techniques, and Other Devices for Understanding the Dynamics of Human Behavior,* edited by H. H. Anderson and G. L. Anderson. New York: Prentice-Hall, pp. 416–456. 55 references of which only about a dozen are on validity.

Yeaton, W. H., and L. Sechrest. 1981. "Meaningful Measure of Effect." *Journal of Consulting and Clinical Psychology* 49: pp. 766–767.

Young, P. T. 1931. "Sex Differences in Handwriting." *Journal of Applied Psychology* 15: pp. 486–498.

Zdep, S. M., and H. B. Weaver. 1967. "The Graphoanalytic Approach to Selecting Life Insurance Salesmen." *Journal of Applied Psychology* 51: pp. 295–299.

APPENDIX A

RELIABILITY OF GRAPHOLOGY

All the studies meta-analyzed in the text are summarized below. Reliability is expressed as a correlation, decimal point omitted.

Blank	=	source gives no details.
Judges	=	graphologists unless otherwise indicated.
Signs	=	individual handwriting features tested, e.g., slant.
Traits	=	traits established by ratings or personality tests.
Wtd mean	=	mean weighted by number of scripts.

a	Assumed equal to the mean to avoid wasting a useful result.
e	Estimated from range or other source details.
sd	Standard deviation of mean before removing sampling error.
Vr	Variance remaining after removing sampling error; see note 17.
*	Data obtained from secondary sources; see annotated reference.

Reliability of Objective Features (e.g., slant)

		—— Number of——			Reliability		
	Source	Scripts	Signs	Judges	Range	Mean	Interval
Test-retest agreement for same judges	DIFFERENT SAMPLES, DIFFERENT TIMES						
	Fisher 1964*	25a			80 93	84	1 week
	Harvey 1933	20	15	1	47 85	73	2 months
	McNeil & Blum 1952	40	9	2	26 80	64	1 month
	Nevo 1986 vs. global	15		15		89	1 week
	4 studies mean N=25	100 total		18	Wtd mean	75 sd 10	Vr 17%
	SAME SAMPLE						
	Fischer 1962*						
	Timm 1967*	74a				90	split half
	Prystav 1969*						
	Mann 1961*	30	4	1		89	test-retest
	Hoepfner 1962*	100	1	1		80	test-retest
	Rosenthal & Lines 1978	58	3	1	82 92	90	split half
	Wallner 1975*&	107	11	1		90	test-retest
	5 studies mean N=74	369 total		4	Wtd mean	87 sd 04	Vr 59%
Agreement between different judges	Birge 1954	50	5	2	94 99	97	
	Furnham & Gunter 1987	64	13	2		89	
	Galbraith & Wilson 1964	100	5	3	46 91	78	
	Hoepfner 1962*	100	1	2		87	2 weeks
	Kimball 1974*	32	61	2		73	
	McNeil & Blum 1952	20	7	2	40 99	85	
	Nevo 1986:256	15	11	2	85 99	95	
	Oosthuizen 1991	69	10	2		89	
	Perron & de Gobineau 1957*	2	12	6		90	
	Rosenthal & Lines 1978	58	3	2	91	93e	
	Williams et al. 1977	47	11	2	92	95	
	Zdep & Weaver 1967	63	13	2	50 85	64	
	12 studies mean N=52	620 total		29	Wtd mean	85 sd 10	Vr 84%

Reliability of Objective Features (e.g., rhythm)

	Source	—— Number of —— Scripts	Ftres	Judges	Reliability Range	Mean	Interval
Test-retest agreement for same judges	Honel 1977*	111	2	1	81 82	81	10 months
	Prystav 1969*	56	3	1	15 86	39e	
	Timm 1967*	83a				73	
	3 studies mean N=83	250 total		2	Wtd mean	69 sd 16	Vr 88%
Agreement between different judges	Honel 1977*	111	2	5	25 63	44	
	Paul-Mengelberg 1986*	105a	3		70 85	78e	
	Wallner 1961, 1962*	100	1	5		59	
	3 studies mean N=105	316 total		10	Wtd mean	60 sd 14	Vr 80%

Reliability of Interpretation (e.g. extroversion)—For IQ see Appendix D

	Source	—— Number of —— Scripts	Traits	Judges	Reliability Range	Mean	Interval
Test-retest agreement for same judges	GRAPHOLOGIST JUDGES						
	Crider 1941	12	16	1	64 94	82	1 month
	Goldberg 1986	21	32	1		17	1 month
	Jansen 1973:58 Expt 1+2	5	1	6		54	1 year
	Sonnemann & Kerman 1962	37	5	1	64 85	77	15 years
	4 studies mean N=19	75 total		9	Wtd mean	59 sd 27	Ve 68%
	LAY JUDGES						
	Dzida & Kiener 1978	45	1	22		56	4 weeks
	Goldberg 1986	21	32	2	18 29	24	1 month
	Jansen 1973:58 Expt 1+2	5	1	10		41	1 year
	Reichold 1969*	90	5	1	78 88	83e	3 months
	4 studies mean N=40	161 total		35	Wtd mean	66 sd 21	Vr 82%
Agreement between different judges	GRAPHOLOGIST JUDGES						
	Bar-El 1984*	10	14	8	33 64	51	
	Ben-Shakhar et al. 1986	80	4	3		40	
	Borenstein 1985*	214	1	3	33 58	46e	
	Brandstatter 1969*	84	24	2		71	
	Crider 1941	9	16	2		18	
	Flug 1981*	58	1	3		30	
	Green et al.1971	7	20	7	–24 51	21	
	Hofsommer et al.1965*	57	1	3		39	
	Jansen 1973:34 Expt 1	15	1	10		21	
	Jansen 1973:57 Expt 2	20	1	10		14	
	Jansen 1973:90 Expt 3	20	1	10		32	
	Jansen 1973:173–4 Expt 4	9	18	6		45	
	Keinan et al.1984	65	13	6	21 37	29	
	Peeples 1990	1	16	37	07 63	37	
	Rafaeli & Klimoski 1983	32	11	2	23 51	42	
	15 judges mean N=45	681 total		112	Wtd mean	42 sd 14	Vr 19%

LAY JUDGES					
Bar-El 1984*	10	14	8		18
Borenstein 1985*	214	1	3	16 28	22e
Dzida & Kiener1978	45	1	22		31
Jansen 1973:57 Expt 2	20	1	10		17
Jansen 1973:90 Expt 3	20	1	10		19
Jansen 1973:173–4 Expt 4	9	18	6		14
Kienan et al.1984	65	13	6	09 20	14
Middleton 1941a	10	3	72	27 63	44
Middleton 1941b	20	1	98		36
Vine 1974	6	2	63	31 60	46
10 studies mean N=42	419 total 298			Wtd mean 23 sd 07	Vr Nil
PSYCHOLOGIST JUDGES					
Borenstein 1985*	214	1	3	46 48	46e
Jansen 1973:34 Expt 1	15	1	10		29
Jansen 1973:57 Expt 2	20	1	20		24
Jansen 1973:90 Expt 3	20	1	10		28
Jansen 1973:173–4 Expt 4	9	18	6		30
Keinan et al.1984	65	13	6	17 36	25
6 studies mean N=57	343 total 55			Wtd mean 39 sd 10	Vr Nil

APPENDIX B

EFFECT SIZE OF GRAPHOLOGY IN PERSONNEL SELECTION

All the studies meta-analyzed in the text are summarized below. Effect size is expressed as follows, decimal points omitted:

cc	contingency coefficient	ph	phi coefficient
g	Halevi's g	r	Pearson r
ir	intraclass correlation	rp	point biserial r
k	Cohen's kappa	rs	Spearman rho for ranks
kw	Weighted kappa	rt	r by $r=\sqrt{(t^2/t^2+df)}$

- c Corrected for range expansion.
- e Estimated from significance level.
- sd Standard deviation of mean before removing sampling error.
- u Uncorrected value (if available).
- Vr Variance remaining after removing sampling error, see note 17.
- x Scripts not identical but content cues deleted.
- ? Source gives no details.
- * Data obtained from secondary sources, see annotated reference.
- † Graphologists were graphoanalysts.

Under criterion, tr = trainees, ratings = supervisor ratings.

	—Number of—			—Effect size—			Neutral	
Source	Scripts	Judges	Sample and criterion	Type	Range	Mean	scripts?	Method
GRAPHOLOGIST JUDGES								
Ben-Shakhar et al. 1981	58	3	Bank-global ratings	r		21	n	
Borenstein 1985*	214	3	Military tr-grades	r		14	n	
Drory 1986	60	1	Drinks plant-ratings	r	13 55	36	n	
Esroni et al. 1985*	23	1	Military-success	ph		19	n	
Esroni et al. 1985*	125	1	Military-ratings	ph		01	n	
Esroni et al. 1985*	49	1	Military-rtgs & success	r		03	n	
Esroni et al. 1985*	45	1	Military-ratings	r		06	n	
Hofsommer et al.1962*	54	?	Forester tr-grades	rs		55	n	
Hofsommer&Holdsworth 1963*	141	1	Pilot tr-success	rp		20	n	
Jansen 1973:91 Expt 3	20	10	Commercial-ratings	ph		23c	n	
Jansen 1973:173-4 Expt 4	9	6	Administration-ratings	rs		09	n	
Keinan et al.1984	65	6	Military tr-success	r	06 36	23	n	
Rafaeli & Klimoski 1983	55	20	Real estate-sales	r	-15 25	03	n	
Shilo 1979*	15	?	Moshav-success	?		18	n	
Sonnemann & Kerman 1962	37	1	Executives-ratings	r	35 48	43	n	
Strolovitch 1980*	25	2	Technical-ratings	r		-19	n	
Wallner 1963*	89	2	Executive tr-ratings	r		05	n	
17 studies mean N=64	1084	61+			Wtd mean 158 sd 147			Vr 30%
Ben-Shakhar et al. 1981	36	5	Successful professionals	k	01 18	08	y	Pick profession
Borenstein 1985*	214	3	Military tr-grades	r		12	y	
Cox & Tapsell 1991	50	2	Exec-9 assessment rtgs	r	-20 22	00	y	
Rafaeli & Klimoski 1983	55	20	Real estate-sales	r	-09 26	09	y	
Super 1941	24	1	Students-SVIB	ph		-02	x	Pick vocation
Zdep & Weaver 1967†	63	2	Insurance-sales	r	01 12	08	y	6 success traits
6 studies mean N=74	442	33			Wtd mean 086 sd 045			Vr Nil
PSYCHOLOGIST JUDGES								
Ben-Shakhar et al.1981	58	1	Bank-global ratings	r		24	n	
Borenstein 1985*	214	3	Military tr-grades	r		16	n	
Jansen 1973:91 Expt 3	20	10	Commercial-ratings	ph		21c	n	
Jansen 1973:173-4 Expt 4	9	6	Administration-ratings	rs		06	n	
Keinan et al. 1984	65	6	Military tr-success	r	11 26	19	n	

5 studies mean N=73	366	26				Wtd mean 178 sd 035		Vr Nil
Borenstein 1985*	214	3	Military tr–grades	r		11	y	
1 study means N=214	214	3				Wtd mean 11 sd 000		
LAY JUDGES								
Borenstein 1985*	214	3	Military tr–grades	r		20	n	
Jansen 1973:91 Expt 3	20	10	Commercial–ratings	ph		23c	n	
Jansen 1973:173–4 Expt 4	9	6	Administration–ratings	rs		07	n	
Keinan et al. 1984	65	6	Military tr–success	r	–12 17	08	n	
4 studies mean N=77	308	25				Wtd mean 173 sd 053		Vr Nil
Borenstein 1985*	214	3	Miitary tr–grades	r		02	y	
Cox & Tapsell 1991	50	3	Exec–9 assessment rtgs	r	-18 39	03	y	
2 studies mean N=132	264	6				Wtd mean 022 sd 004		Vr Nil

APPENDIX C

EFFECT SIZE OF GRAPHOLOGY IN PREDICTING PERSONALITY

All studies meta-analyzed in the text are summarized below. Symbols are the same as in Appendix B.

Key to Method

Rate script	= rate script vs personality ratings or test scores.
Decide A or B	= subject is A or B, judge must decide which.
Fill out test	= graphologist uses script to fill out personality test.

Key to Personality Tests:

ACL	Adjective Check List
AS	Allport's Ascendance-Submission
CPI	California Psychological Inventory
EdPI	Edwards Personality Inventory
EPI	Eysenck Personality Inventory
EPQ	Eysenck Personality Questionnaire
MBTI	Myers-Briggs Type Inventory
SV	Study of Values
SVIB	Strong Vocational Interest Blank
TAT	Thematic Apperception Test

Test Objective Signs (e.g. slant)

	–Number of–			–Effect size–			Number of results		
Source	Script	Signs	Tested vs these traits	Type	Range	Mean	Total	Sig*	Exp
TEST MANY SIGNS, NO PREDICTED DIRECTION, MEAN IS ABSOLUTE MEAN									
Birge 1954	56	22	6 peer-related extremes	rt	19c		132	10	6.6
Furnham & Gunter 1987	64	13	E,N,P,L, by EPQ	r	-19 24	09	52	1	2.6
Harvey 1933	20	15	E by AS test	r	-24 19	11	15	0	0.8
Lemke & Kirchener 1971	103	16	10 by unspecified test	r			160	9	8.0
Lester et al. 1977	111	16	E,N by EPI	rp			16	0	0.8
McNeil & Blum 1952	119	17	11 by projective test	ph	24e		352	17	17.6
Pascal 1943	22	22	36 by clinical ratings	r	-56 60		792	37	39.6
7 studies mean N=71	495	121	Mean number of signs=17		Absolute mean 095		1519	74	76.0
TEST SPECIFIC SIGNS, A POSITIVE EFFECT IS IN PREDICTED DIRECTION									
Brown 1921*	30	5	5 by peer ranking	rs	-05 23	11			
Burnup 1974*	83	1	MZ size vs E by EPI	r		19			
Crowley 1991	93	4	E by EPQ	r		07			
Downey 1919	28	9	5 by peer ranking	rs	23 61	38			
Furnham & Gunter 1987	64	4	E by EPQ	r	03 15	09			
Lester et al. 1977	111	1	Slant vs E by EPI	r		08			
Harvey 1933	20	4	E by AS test	r	-17 08	-04			
Hull & Montgomery 1919	17	6	6 by peer ranking	rs	-45 38	-02			
Rosenthal & Lines 1978	58	3	E by EPI	r	-13 11	01			
Secord 1949	15	11	11 by peer rating	r	-39 30	-05			
Stabholz 1981:105	316	6	Size vs E by EPQ	r	-05 19	06			
11 studies mean N=76	835	54			Wtd mean 082 sd 075			Vr Nil	

*Sig = Number of significant results with 2-sided p $\leq$ .05, Exp = expected number.

Judge Whole Script for Particular Traits

Under criterion, t = traits or scales. For judgment of sex and IQ see Appendix D.

Source	—Number of— Scripts	Judges	Criterion	——Effect size—— Type	Range	Mean	Neutral scripts?	Method
GRAPHOLOGIST JUDGES								
Bar-El 1984*	28	?	Personality tests	?		16	n	
Ben-Shakhar et al. 1981	58	3	Supervisor ratings 24t	r	06 42	21	n	
Crider 1941	18	2	Test scores 16t	rs	15 27	20	n	
Goldberg 1986	170	1	ACL,CPI,SVIB results 54t	r		02	n	
Green et al.1971	7	7	Self-ranked traits 20t	rs	-21 51	24	n	Rate script
Keinan 1986†	56	3	State anxiety score	r		13	n	
Peeples 1990	1	37	16PF scores 16t	r		-13	n	
Rafaeli & Klimoski 1983	70	20	Supervisor ratings 10t	r	-16 20	08	n	
Wellingham-Jones 1989	112	1	Recognized success	rt	-16 64	20	n	
Bayne & O'Neill 1988	16	6	6 clear MBTI-peer types	k	-40 14	-02	n	
Eysenck 1948	176	1	Neurotic or normal?	r		21	n	
Frederick 1965	80	1	Psychiatric case or not?	k		20	n	Decide A or B
Jansen 1973:36 Expt 1	15	10	Energetic-lethargic	ph		01c	n	
Jensen 1973:59 Expt 2	20	10	extremes by test	ph		10c	n	
14 studies mean N=59	827	102				Wtd mean 139 sd 081		Vr Nil
Cantril et al. 1933	50	1	SV test scores 5t	r	-06 40	21	y	
Kimmel & Wertheimer 1966†	22	1	Peer ratings 5t	r	-27 53	06	y	Rate
Rafaeli & Klimoski 1983	70	20	Supervisor ratings 10t	r	-10 10	00	y	script
Vestwig et al. 1976†	48	6	EdPI scores 15t	r	-23 21	00	y	
Frederick 1965	80	1	Psychiatric case or not?	k		-10	y	
Lester et al. 1977†	39	1	EPI E extremes = 1t	k	(08u)	05c	y	Decide A or B
Pascal & Suttell 1947	20	1	Psychotic or normal?	k		20	y	
Eysenck 1945 Method 1	50	1	N by personality test	k		24	y	
Eysenck & Gudjonsson 1986†	99	1	E,N,P,L by EPQ = 4t	r	-06 22	05	y	Fill out test
Sussams 1985	20	4	E,N by EPI = 2t	r	23 38	30	y	
10 studies mean N=50	498	37				Wtd mean 066 sd 117		Vr Nil
PSYCHOLOGIST JUDGES								
Ben-Shakhar et al.1981	58	1	Supervisor ratings 24t	r	-08 42	28	n	Rate script
Frederick 1965	80	1	Psychiatric case or not?	k		35	n	
Jansen 1973:36 Expt 1	15	10	Energetic-lethargic	ph		06c	n	Decide A or B
Jansen 1973:59 Expt 2	20	20	extremes by test = 1t	ph		07c	n	
4 studies mean N=43	173	32				Wtd mean 269 sd 107		Vr Nil
Frederick 1965	80	1	Psychiatric case or not?	k		-05	y	Decide A or B
1 study means N=80	80	1				Wtd mean -050 sd 000		
LAY JUDGES								
Goldberg 1986	170	2	ACL,CPI,SVIB results 54t	r		02	n	Rate
Keinan 1986	56	6	State anxiety score	r		13	n	script
Eisenberg 1938	60	10	Dominant/nondominant?	k	(15u)	11c	n	
Frederick 1965	80	1	Psychiatric case or not?	k		08	n	Decide A or B
Jansen 1973:59 Expt 2	20	10	Energetic or lazy?	ph		05c	n	
5 studies mean N=77	386	29				Wtd mean 106 sd 197		Vr Nil
Castelnuovo-Tedesco 1948	104	6	Rorschach scores 3t	cc	29 37	33	y	
Dzida & Kiener 1978	45	22	Aggression test scores	r		10	y	
Lowenthal 1975	11	5	Self-rated traits 5t	rs		13	y	Rate script
Middleton 1941	20	72	Extreme test scores 3t	r	-15 31	05c	y	(08u)
Vine 1974	6	63	E&N extreme scores = 2t	rs	-40 30	04c	y	(05u)
Frederick 1965	80	1	Psychiatric case or not?	k		-15	y	Decide
Pascal & Suttell 1947	20	25	Psychotic or normal?	k	-60 60	02	y	A or B
7 studies mean N=39	276	194				Wtd mean 106 sd 197		Vr 34%

Match Script or Interpretation to Person or Sketch

Under method, int = graphological interpretation, scr = script, sketch = personality description by close acquaintance, sometimes supported by tests or interviews, gr = graphologists.

	—Number of—			——Effect size——			Neutral	Items per
Source	Scripts	Judges	Method	Type	Range	Mean	scripts?	matching
GRAPHOLOGIST JUDGES MATCH SCRIPTS								
Cantril & Rand 1934	6	26	Match scr to extreme type	k		28c	y (56u)	6
Powers 1933	10	17	Match script to sketch	k	-11 44	16	y	10
2 studies mean N=8	16	43			Wtd mean	205 sd 058	Vr Nil	
PSYCHOLOGIST JUDGES MATCH SCRIPTS								
Eysenck 1945 Method 5	10	10	Match script to sketch	k		-08	y	5
Weinberg et al. 1962	15	2	Match script to sketch	k	14 21	18	y	15
2 studies mean N=13	25	12			Wtd mean	076 sd 127	Vr Nil	
LAY JUDGES MATCH SCRIPTS								
Cantril & Rand 1934	6	26	Match scr to extreme type	k		00c	y (01u)	6
Powers 1933	10	168	Match script to sketch	k	-11 56	09	y	10
Secord 1949	50	5	Match script to TAT	k		04	y	5
3 studies mean N=22	69	199			Wtd mean	044 sd 023	Vr Nil	
LAY JUDGES MATCH INTERPRETATIONS								
Bobertag 1929*	5	15	Match int by 6gr to person	k		76	?	30
Cox & Tapsell 1991	50	3	Pick matches in 100 pairs	rp	-05 23	09	y	2
Crumbaugh & Stockholm 1977†	30	3	Match int to person	k	-17 58	18	y	5
De Groot 1974*	5	13	Match int to person	k		04	?	5
Eysenck 1945 Method 4	50	8	Match int to person	k		18c	y (11u)	4-6
Halevi 1964*	7	7	Rank 7 int to fit person	k		50	x	7
Karnes & Leonard 1991†	9	9	Pick own int from 9	k		-02	n	9
LoMonaco & Harrison 1973	10	85	Match int to TAT	k		25	y	5
Nevo 1989	10	10	Rank 10 int to fit person	g		34	y	10
Nevo & Benitta 1991	12	24	Rank 6 int by 3gr to fit p	g		01	n	6
Allport & Vernon 1933:228	23	1	Match int to sketch	k		12	x	23
Allport & Vernon 1933:231	12	8	Pick own int from 12	k		-10	x	12
Vestewig et al.1976†	21	21	Rate two int (one yours)	rt	-11 35	09	y	2
13 studies mean N=19	244	207		Wtd mean		146 sd 141	Vr Nil	

APPENDIX D

EFFECT SIZE OF GRAPHOLOGY IN JUDGING SEX AND IQ

The studies of sex and IQ meta-analyzed in Table 3 are summarized below. Effect size is expressed as kappa with decimal point omitted. Symbols are the same as in Appendix B. Unlike in Appendices A–C, no attempt has been made to be exhaustive.

Judgment of Sex from Handwriting

Source	Handwriting sample	No. of judges	Mean % correct	Effect size
Binet 1966	180 envelopes	10	69.8	40
Broom et al.1929	40 same sentence	24	69.9	40
Castelnuovo-Tedesco 1948	100 same two paras	6	68.1	36
Downey 1910	200 envelopes	13	67.4	35
Eisenberg 1938	60 same passage	10	71.7	43
Gesell 1906	50 high school	16	62.6	25
Goodenough 1945	115 same paragraph	20	69.6	39
Kinder 1926	100 same sentence	20	68.4	37
Newhall 1926	200 addresses	92	57.0	14
Young 1931	50 brief lists	50	61.0	22
10 studies mean N = 110	1095 total, Vr=23%	261	Wtd mean	323

Judgment of IQ from Handwriting (all studies are from Michel 1969)

Source	Handwriting sample	No. of judges	Neutral scripts?	Effect size
RELIABILITY, GRAPHOLOGIST JUDGES				
Mields 1964	24 women	18	n	60
Schneevoight 1968	18 men	12	?	75
RELIABILITY, PSYCHOLOGIST OR LAY JUDGES				
Michel 1969	20 adults	7	n	57
Schneevoight 1968	18 men	12	?	52
INDIVIDUAL SIGNS				
Lockowandt 1966	100 children vs IQ tests		?	20–35
Oinonen 1961	122 children extreme IQs (38u)		?	29c
Timm 1967	80 adults vs IQ tests		?	24–37
GRAPHOLOGIST JUDGES				
Michel 1969	20 adults vs. WAIS/ratings		n	16
Mields 1962, 1964	24 adults vs. WAIS		n	33
Rasch 1957	114 adults vs. ratings		?	29
Schonfeld & Simon 1935	100 children vs. IQ tests		n	34
Schneevoight 1968	18 men vs. IQ tests		?	36
Von Foerster 1927	70 children vs. IQ tests		?	29
Wallner 1965 Expt 1	118 adults vs. IQ tests		?	20
Wallner 1965 Expt 2	88 adults vs. IQ tests		n	20
Wallner 1965 Expt 3	91 adults vs. IQ tests		n	23

PSYCHOLOGIST OR LAY JUDGES				
Castelnuovo-Tedesco 1958	100 adults IQ 68–132 (59u)		y	43c
Schneevoight 1968	18 men vs. IQ tests		?	40
14 studies mean N=76	1063 total, Vr=Nil	Wtd	mean	286

13

Graphology and Human Judgment

G. A. Dean, I. W. Kelly,
D. H. Saklofske, and A. Furnham

In this paper the authors are concerned with the kinds of biases in perception and judgment that can make us think that we know something when we do not. Many of these biases are responsible for false beliefs in ordinary life. However, the most interesting problems with our reasoning identified here are the ones that lead us to posit correlations between two things—such as backward-slanting handwriting and a certain personality trait—whether or not these correlations actually exist. Many points made here that apply to graphology can be generalized to both pseudosciences and bad science. Almost all scientific claims involve correlations.

The authors argue that most of the correlations regularly claimed by graphologists *could not* be discerned by graphologists. First of all, some of the correlations reported in the scientific literature as vindications of graphological claims are so small that they simply would not have been noticed prior to controlled statistical studies on quite large populations. (Further evidence for this claim is to be found in Dean's chapter on effect sizes that precedes this one.) So how did graphologists come to make these claims for years, prior to these tests being done? The present authors, as well as Barry Beyerstein in chapter 9, provide an answer to this.

Dean et al.'s second reason why graphologists were not in a position to notice these correlations depends upon the fact that graphologists usually examine at least 15, and sometimes as many as 55, features of handwriting in order to make a judgment about the writer; and they maintain that these features mean different things when they are found along with other features on their list. (This is the presupposition of "holism" discussed in chapter 8.) Thus they do not examine features one by one, they must juggle all the features on their list at the same time. But the simple fact is that research has shown that people are not capable of keeping a list of all these features in their heads as they examine features of handwriting, let alone keeping straight all the combinations and permutations of them that would seem to be necessary if graphology were really correct. Graphologists, despite their often-made claims to the contrary, must be selecting from the data they examine, and they do not usually report using an algorithm to weigh these factors in their judgments. They instead talk of "intuition" and the "clinical judgment" used by the skilled clinical diagnostician. The authors of chapter 13 make their most disturbing point here: they make use of the results of over 100 studies which show that experts in a wide range of fields do not use the procedures they *think* they are using to select and weigh the conflicting criteria involved in their judgments; and that they are often outperformed in making these judgments by simple algorithms of the sort a computer can use. So, graphologists, as well as many other practitioners whose reputations depend on these supposed abilities involved in "clinical judgment," have food for thought.

INTRODUCTION: VIEWS OF JUDGMENT AND HOW GRAPHOLOGISTS DO IT

> Given the extraordinary ability of the human mind to make sense out of things, it is natural occasionally to make sense out of things that have no sense at all.
>
> —Richard Furnald Smith

This chapter is about how graphologists and their clients make judgments. Not *what* they do, but the judgment processes *underlying* what they do. We look at three crucial areas, namely, (1) detecting correlations (which is how graphology arose); (2) combining correlations into predictions (which is how graphology is applied); and (3) human biases (which graphologists don't tell you about) in assessing the predictions. The results throw new light on systems like graphology and astrology that claim to indicate your character without necessarily making your acquaintance. On the way we discover how easy it is to be fooled, so we end with hints on protecting yourself from the known ways of fooling yourself. But first a quick peek at human judgment then and now.

HUMAN JUDGMENT THEN AND NOW

Around 1600 William Shakespeare gave this rousing view of human judgment (taken from Slovic 1972):

> What a piece of work is man! How noble in reason! How infinite in faculties! In form and moving, how express and admirable! In action, how like an angel! In apprehension, how like a god! The beauty of the world! The paragon of animals! (*Hamlet,* Act 2, Scene 2)

Three centuries later the 1978 Nobel prizewinner in economics, Herbert Simon (1957), gave this somewhat different view:

> The capacity of the human mind for formulating and solving complex problems is very small compared with the size of problems whose solution is required for objectively rational behaviour in the real world—or even for a reasonable approximation to such objective rationality.

On these two views Armstrong (1978:74) comments:

> On almost any basis one would choose Shakespeare! He is more poetic than Simon; he is more widely read; and his position is more popular. The only thing that Simon has going for him is that he is right.

Unfortunately we act as if Simon were wrong. We act as if human judgment was always accurate. But the primary aim of human judgment is not accuracy but the avoidance of paralyzing uncertainty (hence the popularity of religion). We hate uncertainty so much that our judgment processes are geared to speed and confidence—but at a price. They work well in simple situations like deciding who won the ball game or what hat to buy. But they fail in complex situations like deciding the chance of a recession or the validity of a graphology reading. To see why, we look first at how graphologists make their judgments.

HOW GRAPHOLOGISTS MAKE THEIR JUDGMENTS

A serious handwriting analysis may take several hours. Typically the aim is to describe either the client's entire personality or the part relevant to a given area such as employment. There is no single method or approach, but having considered pen, paper, age, sex, handedness, nationality, and aim of the analysis, the graphologist typically proceeds in three broad steps as follows:

1. Gain an initial overall impression.[1]
2. Examine each of typically 20 features such as size and slant.
3. Combine the indications into a global assessment.

The most important step is the last. A golden rule in graphology is that no one graphological feature means anything by itself. In fact Singer (1969:39) says "It should be printed three times at the beginning and end of each chapter in every book on graphology." Thus whatever is suggested by feature A may be modified by features B and C. So each feature must be carefully juggled against everything else before judgment is made. The final judgment is thus a synthesis of isolated features or discrete signs into a meaningful whole or gestalt.

But even that may be simplistic. Some graphologists hold that each feature has a double meaning (basically good vs. bad, such as generous vs. extravagant) depending on the standard of writing. An original and harmonious hand is good. A trite and discordant hand is bad. Other graphologists hold that each feature has many meanings depending on the area involved, such as physical, intellectual, social, or spiritual—in which case the juggling process must be repeated for each area (Singer 1969:81–84).

Never mind. What matters is that graphologists say that handwriting features *interact*. So the whole is more than the sum of its parts, which means it is futile to study isolated features.[2] McNeil and Blum (1952) give a selection of quotes to illustrate such views, and make the following pithy comment:

> While we are quite willing to grant that the whole may represent more than the sum of its parts, it is difficult to see how discrete signs, valueless in themselves, can suddenly be transformed by artful intuition into a highly functional, significant gestalt.

That was in 1952. Since then research into human judgment (which is what this chapter is all about) has thrown much light on what may be happening. We look first at detecting correlations, that is, at how graphologists derived their discrete signs in the first place.

DETECTING CORRELATIONS: OR HOW DO YOU KNOW FORWARD SLANT MEANS EXTROVERTED?

IS YOUR CORRELATION REALLY NECESSARY?

If systems like graphology, astrology, and palmistry are used as entertainment or as an excuse for unburdening your soul, it hardly matters whether extroversion is *really* indicated by forward-slanted writing or Sagittarius rising or short fingers. But if they are presented as being not merely helpful but also true (which is usually the case) then the system *requires* a correlation between each feature and the person; Otherwise the system is pointless, for without such a correlation no feature could mean anything.

In graphology the correlation between each feature and the person is said to be based on observation, despite occasions when this process "was surrendered to metaphysics and armchair speculation" (Roman 1952:9), to say nothing of the huge difficulty, generally unrecognized by graphologists, of assessing the person; see chapter 10 in this book. For our purpose it does not matter whether the feature is a discrete sign or a motor pattern or an overall gestalt or whatever. What matters is that everything begins by detecting a correlation. So how good are we at detecting correlation? And exactly what do we detect? We start with the simplest case, namely detecting correlation in yes/no data using slant as an example.

DETECTING CORRELATION IN YES/NO DATA

When reduced to yes/no data, forward-slanted writing and extroversion can combine in four possible ways as follows:

Forward slant	Extrovert		Example	
	Yes	No	Yes	No
Yes	a	b	35	20
No	c	d	10	10

Correlation phi = (ad-bc) / $\sqrt{((a+b)(c+d)(a+c)(b+d))}$

On the left, abcd are the observed totals for each of the four combinations. As shown by the equation, the correlation between slant and extroversion cannot be determined unless *all* of the four cells are considered. And all four cells are equally important. But most people consider only cell a, while a few consider cell a and one other. Hardly anyone considers all four *even when all four are provided* (Smedslund 1963, Ward and Jenkins 1965, Arkes and Harkness 1983). Look at the (fictitious) example on the right. Does extroversion go with forward slant? The high total of 35 in cell a gives the impression that the correlation is high and useful. But the other cells indicate otherwise—while nearly 80 percent of extroverts have forward slant, so do nearly 70 percent of introverts. In fact the correlation is only .12, which for practical purposes is quite useless.

In other words, without formal training we are hopeless at detecting correlations in yes/no data. If asked whether redheads are hot tempered, or prayers are answered, hardly anyone considers even-tempered brunettes or non-prayed-for answers. Yet no special correlation can exist unless redheads differ from brunettes in the incidence of temper, and praying from not praying in the incidence of answers.[3]

Faust and Nurcombe (1989) point out that the utility of any sign (in this case the graphological indication) depends on two things, namely, (1) the correlation, and (2) the base rate, the rate of occurrence in the base population. Thus for 2000 members of the British Mensa the base rates are 2 percent for colored ink (red, green, or purple), 8 percent for left-handedness, 14 percent for left-slanted writing, and 52 percent for right-slanted writing (Paterson 1976). For areas of graphological interest like managerial ability, the base rate in the general population is typically 10 percent or less. For such low base rates a sign may increase accuracy only if the correlation between sign and managerial ability exceeds about .4 or .5. If it does not, as is invariably the case (see preceding chapter), then *using graphology may make the prediction worse.* This is such an unexpected but crucial point that we explain it at length in note 4.

Detecting Correlation in Paired Data

When the data are *not* neatly summarized in a table, our ability to detect correlation is even worse. Does giving Tom an apple make him happy? We can detect correlation between these two events only if they occur less than a few seconds apart, they are quantifiable, and the correlation is high enough (Holyoak and Nisbett 1988:61–62). Figure 1 suggests that correlations in paired data are not reliably detected until they exceed about .4, which is rather higher than the correlations of .3 typically observed between trait and behavior in comparable data, i.e., for a group of people in a single situation.[5] Even correlations around .7, which are considered strong by psychologists, are missed by one person in four. Only when the correlations reach .85 and above are they detected by almost everyone.

At this point a problem arises. As shown in the preceding chapter, the observed correlations between personality and graphological features (whether discrete or global) are typically around .2 or less, far too small to be reliably detected. So how did graphologists discover them in the first place? How can countless graphology books imply that the correlations are strong when they are not? The answer is next.

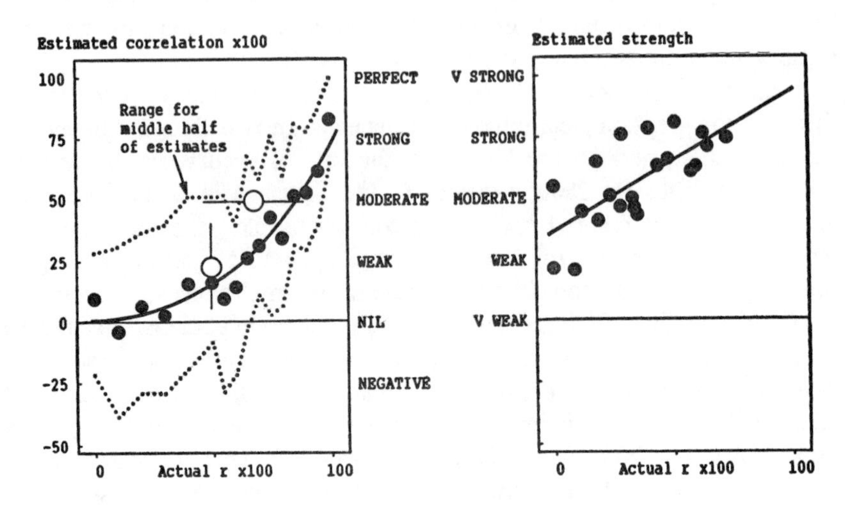

Figure 1. How Good Are We At Detecting Correlation?

Left: Detecting correlation in numbers, drawings, and timing. Jennings et al. (1982) asked 64 undergraduates to look at 16 sets of paired data whose correlation varied from 0 to 1. Each set contained 10 items, either pairs of simple numbers, or drawings of men holding walking sticks. In each case the subjects could study the data for as long as they liked. There was also a spoken letter followed by a tone. The subjects had to estimate on a scale of 0-100 the correlation between the numbers, between the figure height and stick length, and between the alphabet position and tone duration. The results showed no consistent differences so they are plotted together. For each of the 16 actual Pearson r correlations (horizontal axis) there is a black dot showing the mean correlation estimated by the 64 subjects (vertical axis).

The two open circles show the results of a similar study by Oakes (1982). *Lower circle:* 30 psychologists guessed the correlation between two sets of numbers 1-12, whose correlation was .50. *Upper circle:* Another 30 psychologists arranged two sets of numbers 1-12 to give a guessed correlation of .50. The bars indicate the standard deviation.

The main features are as follows: (1) The two studies are in reasonable agreement. (2) The range of individual estimates is very large, showing that judgment was difficult and uncertain. (3) Correlations are consistently *under*estimated, i.e., poorly detected. The relationship seems to be non-linear, albeit less so in the Oakes study, so that weak correlations are proportionately much harder to detect than strong ones. Thus the correlations typically observed in graphology (.0 to .2) are generally beyond unaided detection.

Right: Detecting correlation in behavior. Epstein and Teraspulsky (1986) asked 88 undergraduates to estimate the correlation between various behaviors on a scale of 1 = very weak to 5 = very strong. The correlations had been previously determined for a separate sample of 63 students or 51 problem boys, and ranged from .00 to

.73, e.g., general high activity vs. fights readily (.18), neat desk vs. neat notes (.44), number talked to at lunch vs. number talked to at dinner (.63). For each of the 21 observed Pearson r correlations (horizontal axis) there is a black dot showing the mean strength as estimated by the 88 subjects (vertical axis).

The main features are as follows: (1) Zero correlations are rated weak to moderate, which is probably due to illusory correlation; i.e., the subjects believed the behaviors were correlated when in fact they were not. This is confirmed by the lefthand graph, where the data sets are not subject to illusory correlation, and the curve shows no inflation at zero correlation. (2) The dots are scattered due to the small sample sizes for criteria and estimates, but there is no obvious curvature as in the lefthand graph, probably because the vertical scale is not tied to actual numbers. (3) Nevertheless the vertical scales of both graphs are broadly similar, as are their mean slopes. So the two graphs are broadly consistent. Overall their message is clear, namely, *we are generally poor at detecting correlation.*

Box 1. *Test your skill*

Below are six sets of 10 number pairs similar to those used by Jennings et al. (1982 in Figure 1). Look first at the 10 vertical pairs in the AA row and estimate the correlation between them. That is, how well does one A row keep in tune with the other A row? Then do the same for the BB and other rows. Which row has the highest correlation, AA or BB, CC or DD, EE or FF? All correlations are positive and between 0 and .7, so in each case your answer should be between 0 and .7.

```
A 5 5 1 8 2 2 5 7 2 4       C 5 6 5 5 5 6 3 4 9 4        E 5 1 5 2 1 8 2 6 9 3
A 4 4 8 5 1 4 2 6 4 6 B     C 2 9 4 6 9 9 8 4 5 1 D      E 2 8 3 3 3 8 1 4 4 4 F
  1 7 8 6 1 5 1 6 9 4 B       6 1 9 1 7 4 9 4 3 3 D        2 9 5 9 1 7 5 9 7 7 F
```

For the record, the Pearson r correlation for paired data is given by $r = (a-bc/n)\ \sqrt{(d-b^2/n)}\ \sqrt{(e-c^2/n)}$, where abcde = sum of xy, x, y, x^2, y^2 respectively, x and y = values of each pair, and n = number of pairs. Because we cannot juggle so many variables, it will not escape your notice that knowing this equation is no help at all.

Now test your skill at picking randomness with this example from Wagenaar (1988:92). A coin is tossed 50 times. Which of the following five sequences is the most likely? Answers to both tests are given in note 6.

1. hxhxhxxhxhxhxxhxhxhxxhhxhxhxhhxhxxhhxxhxhxhxhxxx
2. hxhhxhhxxhhhxxxhxxxhxxhxxhxhxhhxhhhxhhhxxhxxhxhxhx
3. hxhxhhxhhhhhxxxhhxhxhxxhxhhxxxxhxhxxxhhhxxhxxxhxxh
4. xhhhxxhxhxxhxhxhhhxhhxxxhxhhhhxhhhhhhxhhxxhxxxxxxh
5. xxhhhhhxhxxxhhhhxxhhhxxhxxxxxxxhhhhhxxxxxxhhhxxhhh

DETECTING CORRELATIONS WHERE NONE EXISTS

We make up for our poor ability to detect a real correlation by a spectacular ability to see correlation where none exists. The only requirement is that we know (or think we know) the answer in advance regardless of whether true or not. It also helps if our data is ambiguous and vague, as it will be if nothing is *measured.* For example, if we believe that redheads are hot tempered, then ambiguous behavior can be seen as hot tempered, and vaguely red hair can be seen as red—or the opposite, depending on what we want to see. Confirmation of our belief then follows automatically, especially as we are not disposed to consider even-tempered brunettes.

Consider the Draw-a-Person technique (Machover 1951). You draw a person on a sheet of blank paper, and its size, detail, clothing, etc. supposedly reveal your inner conflicts. Thus close-set eyes mean you have a suspicious nature, big eyes indicate paranoia, and a big head means you worry about intelligence. However, dozens of studies have found these to be stereotypes which are in fact false—*people with such features do not draw such pictures* (Chapman and Chapman 1971, Aiken 1989). The point is that such stereotypes are pervasive and almost impossible to eradicate.[7] In other words if we think we know the answer then accurate judgment is impossible. That is why scientific blind trials (i.e., where experimenters are deliberately not told what is being tested) are necessary when the outcome is crucial, as in testing new drugs.

The phenomenon of believing-is-seeing is called *illusory correlation.*[8] Less illusory are the problems it can cause (see Figure 2). The belief or stereotype can come from anywhere—myths, superstition, rumors, something we read, even experience (see below). . If we believe that forward slant or Sagittarius rising or short fingers indicates an extrovert, then our observations will confirm it even if our belief is false.[9,10] So no matter what others may say, our belief is here to stay, as for this clinical psychologist quoted by Chapman and Chapman (1971):

> I know that paranoids don't draw big eyes in the research labs, but they sure do in my office.

We say more about stereotypes later. In the meantime, if it still seems preposterous that your judgment could be biased by knowing the answer in advance, try the simple test given in note 11.

But what if no stereotypes exist? Does this free us from the tyranny of illusory correlation? Unfortunately not, for this is where *experience* can generate illusory correlations due to a learning process that works like this. Suppose we try our hand at graphology, and our first reading is successful. Since the outcome is good, we try more readings. Even if we tend to be unsuccessful, the occasional success is enough to keep us trying. This process is called *operant conditioning,* where a behavior (graphology)

Figure 2. How Illusory Correlation Can Be Bad for You

The eminent graphologist Nadya Olyanova was consultant to many American psychiatrists and businesses. Two former pupils describe her as having

> a highly developed ability to sift the wealth of data, and to coordinate and summarize it. In finding common denominators and arranging them by order of importance, she demonstrates the remarkable capacity of the human mind at the height of alertness. (Olyanova 1969:x)

> Perhaps the most important characteristic of Miss Olyanova's techniques in general is that they are so largely a product of her long experience analyzing not hundreds, but thousands of handwritings. (Olyanova 1960: 220)

Her pupils imply that an alert mind and huge experience are sufficient to guarantee accuracy. So what about her neglect (common to nearly all graphologists) of the scientific approach?[12] Olyanova gives this diagram showing the relation of slant to extroversion:

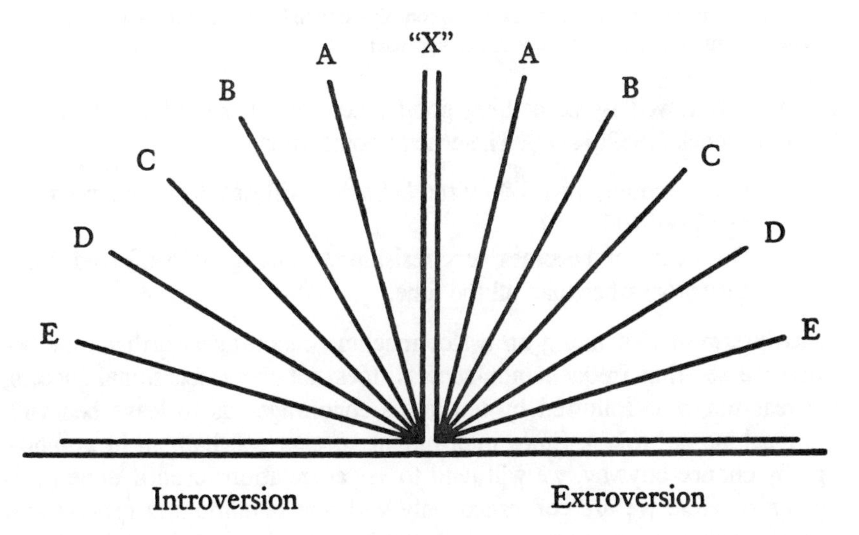

Extroverts are "social, gregarious, impulsive, and demonstrative." Introverts are "undemonstrative, reticent, and withdrawn. . . . they . . . usually reflect before taking action." These descriptions are a close match to the extroversion measured by personality tests such as the Eysenck Personality Inventory, so we confidently expect a sizable correlation between slant and test scores. But what we actually get is very close to chance:

Source	Subjects	Mean age	Correlation	p
Harvey (1933)	20 students	21 years	.02 vs. AAS	.93
Lester et al. (1977)	111 students	22 years	.08 vs. EPI	.41
Rosenthal and Lines (1978)	58 students	19 years	-.13 vs. EPI	.33
Furnham and Gunter (1987)	64 adults	early 30s	.10 vs. EPQ	.44

These results indicate that if you judge extroversion by slant, your accuracy is no better than that of tossing a coin. But it gets worse. Olyanova asserts that two people are compatible only if their slants are alike:

There can seldom be compatibility when one person writes leftward and the other rightward. . . . they would have too little in common emotionally, temperamentally, and in interests to ensure a lasting relationship in marriage. . . . Attractions between extroverts and introverts rarely jell. (Olyanova 1969:92)

No hedging here with the futility of looking at isolated features! But compatibility is unrelated to extroversion. For married couples the correlation is around .5 for intelligence and .3 for height, but only .1 at most for extroversion (Eysenck and Wakefield 1981). So even if slant did indicate extroversion, it would be irrelevant to compatibility. In other words the above assertions, delivered with all the authority of an alert mind and huge experience, are wrong twice over. The point is, Olyanova had thousands of clients. How many relationships suffered needlessly from her illusory correlations and neglect of the scientific approach?

is closely followed by something good (success), thus reinforcing the behavior (Alcock (1982:94–97). The crucial points are:

1. The outcome must follow the behavior without delay but need not be related to it.
2. The behavior becomes very resistant to change if reinforced *intermittently* rather than all the time.

Thus intermittent winning on a slot machine encourages further play because we see that frequent non-success does not deny occasional success, whereas ten wins followed by ten losses encourages us to leave believing the machine is broken. Since intermittent success will happen in graphology by chance anyway, we will tend to see correlations even if none actually exist. Here we are concerned only with the conditioning *process* and not with the many ways (of which illusory correlation is only one) of being persuaded that graphology works, for which see later.

Operant conditioning is a powerful process. No reasoning ability is required (even the lowest animals learn in this way), which can cause problems. For when the time interval between two events is short, *learning* occurs automatically, so if no actual relation exists we have to make a conscious effort to overcome such learning. Alcock (1982:16-20) suggests that operant conditioning plays a major role in the development of magical beliefs and superstition generally.

Having observed our correlations, real or illusory, we are now ready for the next step, namely combining them into a prediction.

COMBINING CORRELATIONS INTO PREDICTIONS

HOW MANY CORRELATIONS ARE WE LOOKING AT?

To obtain a judgment, graphologists have to juggle many features at once. So do astrologers, palmists, and orthodox clinicians. According to the books the number of features to be juggled is considerable, as shown below:

Graphology	15–55, typically 20	Number of features to be juggled before proper judgment can be made.
Astrology	20–120, typically 40	
Palmistry	27–70, typically 40	
Phrenology	27–92, typically 39	
Rorschach	5×10, i.e., from 10 blots	
Personality tests	1–20, typically 5–10	

However, our short-term memory cannot juggle more than about 7±2 features at a time, as is apparent whenever we try dialing an unfamiliar 10-digit telephone number.[13] If the features have little in common, we have trouble in juggling even *two* of them. For example, when people are asked to compare circles of various sizes containing spokes at various angles, they tend to look at size *or* angle but not both (Shepard 1964). As a result the information content of the above techniques (except personality tests with few scales) *always* exceeds our capacity to handle it.

This means that practitioners cannot possibly do what they say they do, namely, juggle all relevant features. Even with a memory aid such as pencil and paper, which would always be used in serious work, their task is not much easier. Instead they are forced to do what their golden rule expressly forbids, namely, be selective.[14] For the moment we will ignore this problem and look at the ways in which we transform parts into wholes, starting with intuition.[15]

INTUITION: APPREHENSION BY MEANS UNKNOWN

Common to the first five systems listed above is the supposed faculty of intuition, also called insight or hunch or gut feeling, which is frequently assumed by experts and generously attributed to the entire female sex. Its key features are (1) everything happens in your head, and (2) answers pop up out of nowhere.

However, since the 1930s there has been evidence that intuition comes not from nowhere but from previous experience.[16,17] The relevant experience may not be quickly remembered or its existence even recognized, in which case the incubation process so helpful in problem solving may merely reflect the time needed for (unconscious) retrieval. Similarly the supposed effortless, unanalyzable, and instant nature of intuition means nothing; driving a car requires endless decisions of exactly this nature, but from our first fumbling steps at learning to drive they clearly owe nothing to intuition as traditionally conceived.

For these reasons most cognitive psychologists discount intuition. For example Dawes (1988:204), a leading expert in judgment psychology, comments that unless the person relying on intuition has good evidence for its validity, meaning sound experimental data rather than plausible arguments, then the use of intuition "is in my view arbitrary, stupid, and unethical."

A useful clarification is provided by Cook (1982), who points out that the confusion surrounding intuition would disappear if it was redefined as "a skill so thoroughly learned that one is not conscious of its operation." The alternative to intuition is inference.

INFERENCE: APPREHENSION BY THINKING

Human inference is made on the basis of (1) what we see, and (2) what we know. We see that Mary Lou wears glasses. We know that people who wear glasses are brainy. Therefore Mary Lou is brainy.

However there are problems. What we see may be wrong (the glasses are only safety spectacles) or what we know may be wrong (not everyone who wears glasses is brainy). Actually nearsightedness *is* associated with high IQ but the correlation is only around .2 (Jahoda 1962, Karlsson 1978), which emphasizes our next point.[18] Co-occurrences in real life are far from perfect, so we should always think in tendencies and in shades of gray. But there is abundant evidence that we cannot do this (Kahneman and Tversky 1973). Instead we use black and white, and persist in using our favorite information long after we have evidence of its inutility. For example, we tend to see smoking vs. lung cancer not as a gray tendency but as either black (cancer cures smoking) or white (grandma smoked 50 a day and lived to be 95).

Our attempts to combine information can lead to peculiar judgments, especially when its relevance is uncertain. Is a man likely to assault his friends if he is aggressive when drunk? Probably. If he is aggressive but a good darts player? Probably not! (from Bromley 1986:247).

Our problems do not end there. People are good at picking predictors but bad at combining them. As explained next.

COMBINING PREDICTORS: PEOPLE VS. EQUATIONS

A predictor is something we use to predict something else. Thus wrinkles, false teeth, and gray hair are predictors of old age. When we have many predictors we combine them in clever ways. For example, we ignore wrinkles if caused by sunbathing, ignore false teeth if due to an accident, suspect hair dye if an old person's hair is not gray, and so on. This cleverness sets us apart from machines, or so we like to believe.

But we are wrong. In reality people are so bad at *combining* predictors that their results are consistently worse than simply *adding* predictors.[19,20] This remarkable finding has been tested in over 100 studies involving all kinds of judgment from people to economic trends, and in all but 6 cases (mostly medical) the finding has been confirmed (Dawes et al. 1989). When equation is pitted against expert using the same codable predictors,[21] the equation is always as good and usually better. Table 1 gives examples. In fact, the findings are so controversial yet so consistent that a former president of the American Psychological Association could comment:

> There is no controversy in social science that shows such a large body of qualitatively diverse studies coming out so uniformly in the same direction as this one. When you are pushing 90 investigations, predicting everything from the outcome of football games to the diagnosis of liver disease, and when you can hardly come up with half a dozen studies showing even a weak tendency in favor of the clinician, it is time to draw a practical conclusion, whatever theoretical differences may still be disputed. (Meehl 1986)

Naturally the findings are an affront to vested interests. Who would dare imagine that an equation could outperform the experience, sensitivity, and intuitive skills of the human expert? Certainly not the expert.[22] Related findings (Dawes et al. 1989) add to the affront. Minimally-trained people do as well as experts (see also Faust and Ziskin 1988, and Garb 1989, for reviews relevant to personality assessment). Accuracy is unrelated to confidence. When equation judgments are partialled out of expert judgments, the result is usually close to zero, indicating that experts have noth-

Table 1. Examples of expert judgments vs. equations.

Area	N	Judgment	No. of experts	Correlation with Experts	Correlation with Equation
Academic	90	Student performance.	80	.35.	60
Astrology	120	Extroversion and emotionality.	45	.01	.14*
Economics	60	Which firm will go bankrupt?	43	.50	.64
Graphology	52	Job performance.	3	.19	.30**
Medical	193	How soon will patient die?	3	.00	.42
MMPI	861	Neurotic or psychotic?	29	.28	.34
Shapes	180	Ellipse size and color.	6	.84	.97

*Vs. age **Vs. 9 variables such as army rank and neatness of writing.

The above table shows the correlation between actual outcome and the outcome predicted by (1) experts and (2) an equation using the same data. No matter what area is involved, the equation outperforms the experts in each case. MMPI = Minnesota Multiphasic Personality Inventory, a widely-used test of disturbed personality.

From top, sources are Wiggins and Kohen (1971), Dean (1985), Libby (1976) and Goldberg (1976), Ben-Shakhar et al. (1986), Einhorn (1972), Goldberg (1965), Yntema and Torgerson (1961).

ing useful to add. Indeed, letting experts revise the equation judgment usually makes it worse. This does not make experts redundant—they are still needed to select the predictors. Armstrong (1978:85) suggests that the place of experts "is in saying how things are (estimating current status), rather than in predicting how things will be (forecasting change)."

But what if no equation is available? Can anything be done to improve the experts? Shanteau (1988) studied experts recognized by their peers as being the best (in auditing, business management, livestock judging, nursing, personnel selection, or soil judging) and found several characteristics that set them apart from lesser experts. For example, they could home in on the relevant information, were always right up to date with the latest developments, and knew which problems to tackle and which to avoid. *They also used strategies designed to overcome cognitive limitations.* For example, they sought feedback from associates, learned from past successes and failures, used aids such as written records to aid judgment biases, focused on avoiding really bad mistakes rather than on being exactly right, and solved large problems by dividing into parts and then reassembling the partial solutions. Shanteau suggests that novices will become genuine experts only if their natural thinking patterns match the above. Some of these patterns may be teachable, others such as those requiring creativity may not. Nevertheless, the general failure of experts when pitted against equations suggests that, for most of us, equations are the best option. For a review of how to choose between using experts and equations or both, with many examples and helpful suggestions, see Kleinmuntz (1990).

Even the crudest of equations can be surprisingly effective. Thus Dawes (1979) could predict marital happiness by lovemakings/week minus arguments/week, whereas neither predictor was effective alone. The trick is to pick the right predictors and know how to add. But why should equations perform better than people?

WHY SHOULD EQUATIONS PERFORM BETTER THAN PEOPLE?

Let us be clear what these studies are telling us. They tell us that two basic patterns underlie apparently complex human judgments:

1. Judges do not use the process they think they use.
2. Simply adding the predictors usually outperforms the judges.

Judges think they use more than simple weighting and adding. For example, if A then X=Y, but if B then X=Z. But tests reveal a different story. For example, analysis of the way physicians diagnose ulcers from X-ray photos (Hoffman et al. 1968), or decide to release patients (Rorer et al. 1967), showed that most of the time they just added up their favorite cues, despite their claims to the contrary. The problem of course is that judges seldom agree on the relevant cues and on their weighting.[14]

We can now see why equations perform better than people. They simulate what we actually do, i.e., add up our favorite cues. But they do it more consistently. When people make complex judgments as in graphology, the proliferation of cues overwhelms their capacity to be consistent. Give us more than one or two interrelated cues to juggle and we are lost. Indeed it is difficult not to get lost even when the cues are *not* interrelated (Slovic 1974). By contrast an equation never gets lost. It is always consistent. It can handle any degree of complexity, never gets tired, and is never distracted by irrelevant cues. So it is not surprising that equations outperform experts using the same cues.

Having combined our correlations into a prediction, we are now ready for the final step, namely assessing the results. At this point we take on board a staggering number of biases, discussed next. We start with a look at some testimonials on graphological judgments.

BIASES IN HUMAN JUDGMENT: OR HOW TO BE WRONG WITHOUT EVEN TRYING

TESTIMONIALS: CAN COUNTLESS CLIENTS BE WRONG?

Graphologists believe in graphology because it seems to work. Their belief is not based on scientific evidence, for if it were, there would be little or no belief. Instead their belief rests on face validity, where graphology *looks* like it should work, and on the satisfaction of clients, a process called *personal validation* (Bar-Hillel and Ben-Shakhar 1986, Ben-Shakhar et al. 1986). Not surprisingly, opinions on the result are divided. On the one hand there are opinions like this one from John Mansfield, a British producer of TV documentaries on personality assessment:

> . . . graphologists are still their own worst enemy as far as gaining recognition goes. Much of their published work is based on little, if any, experimentally proven evidence; remarkably few scientifically controlled studies have been undertaken; and many books and articles purporting to be written by qualified, responsible graphologists are so crammed with wild generalizations that, however titillating they may be, they deter serious study. . . . Tragically for the prestige of graphology, it is precisely because everyone has a sneaking belief that it makes sense that charlatans have found it an easy way to make a living, particularly when they present their findings in the ambiguous terms of a newspaper horoscope wherein every reader can see some element of truth. (Mansfield 1975:73)

On the other hand there are testimonials from satisfied clients:

> "[The graphologist] told me some things that were of such a personal nature I was surprised he would know. . . .He said 'Here are some things you might be afraid of. . . . here are some situations you're going to run into.' " (Purvis 1987)
>
> The president of a savings and credit union says, "We find [the graphologist] very, very accurate, uncannily so." (Purvis 1987)
>
> The personnel director of another credit union says, "At first I thought it was black magic . . . but after seeing it work, it's obviously not." (Griffin 1988)
>
> A seventeen-year-old youth on the brink of suicide says, "I thought no one cared; I knew no one would believe me. Couldn't talk about it to anybody. Then somebody looked at my handwriting and told me what was going on in my head." (Hollander and Parker 1989)

> The managing director of a British employment agency which uses graphology says the analysis of his own handwriting "was remarkably accurate. It also added to self-knowledge and has since contributed to greater effectiveness in doing my job." (Reid 1983)[23]

Furthermore there are testimonials from eminent men such as these taken from Severn (1913:6) and Hungerford (1930):

> Thomas Edison: "I never knew I had an inventive talent until graphology told me. I was a stranger to myself until then."
>
> Andrew Carnegie: "Not to know yourself graphologically is sure to keep you standing on the Bridge of Sighs all your life."
>
> Alfred Russel Wallace: "The graphologist has shown that he is able to read character like an open book . . . with an accuracy that the most intimate friends cannot approach."
>
> Edgar Allen Poe: "Graphology is no longer to be laughed at. . . . it has assumed the majesty of a science and as a science ranks among the most important."

Impressive stuff. After all, these people have been there. *They know.* Despite what Mansfield says, are you not convinced that graphology works? Before you answer, be aware that we have doctored the eminent quotes—every reference to *graphology* is actually to *phrenology,* a system of reading character from brain development as shown by head size and shape. The point is, the claims of phrenology are now known to be wrong.[24] So a bulge here or a depression there cannot mean what it is supposed to mean. If eminent men of the highest standing can testify to nonexistent effects, then what price testimonials?

More to the point, how can an invalid system like phrenology *seem* valid? The answer is simple—*personal validation is hopelessly unreliable.* The validity we perceive can be due to many factors, none of them related to the factor supposedly responsible (Hyman 1977, Marks and Kammann 1980). As a result the system can be totally invalid yet totally accepted.[25] The factors actually responsible are generated by our judgment biases, discussed next. Some apply to judgment in general. Others apply to the judgment of personality descriptions. We look at these in turn.

BIASES IN GENERAL JUDGMENT

We cannot attend to everything, so our judgment must be selective to avoid overload. Otherwise we would drift forever in a sea of possibilities so vast that the idea *fire causes burns* would be no more likely than the idea *ice causes baldness.* What happens is that we attend to a manageable subset selected by our ideas (which may be wrong), by our problem (which makes us look here rather than there), and by our cognitive ability (which may be inadequate), all of which generate bias.[26] Here bias means *systematic error* not *prejudice.*

People are quite good at things that require only counting. As marbles are drawn at random from a bag, we can estimate their average size or the proportion of red quite well. But once we start using *data drawn from memory* we become subject to the following biases:

1. *Vividness.* We attend more to things that are noticeable or vivid. You decide to buy car X because 1000 readers of *Consumer Reports* liked it. By chance you meet someone who hates their X. It leaks, rattles, belches smoke, guzzles gas, and is always breaking down. Suddenly you decide against buying X, even though your database of 1000 has been incremented by only one. Tornadoes make the headlines whereas asthma does not, so you guess that tornado deaths are more common than asthma deaths. You are wrong (Fischoff 1988:177). Vivid images always have more impact, and we remember them for reasons other than their actual frequency (which is what matters). This is known as the availability heuristic (*heuristic* comes from the Greek and means an *aid to discovery*).

It has an interesting corollary. To us our situation is more vivid than our personality, whereas the personality of others is more vivid than their situation. So we attribute *our* behavior to situation but *their* behavior to personality (Jones 1976). This is called the fundamental attribution error. Among other things it is a further complication for those claiming to see personality in handwriting.

2. *Representativeness.* We go by looks and ignore base rate, the rate of occurrence in the base population. At the Massachusetts Institute of Technology you meet Tom, who looks like a poet. Is he a poet or a physicist? To answer poet is to ignore base rate—physicists are much more common at MIT than poets. Are you amazed by psychic predictions? To answer yes is to ignore base rate—the incidence of fraud among psychics is high (Brandon 1983). You toss four coins and get HTTH. Is this more likely than HHHH? It looks more likely but in fact both are equally likely. The apparent representativeness blinds us to the actual frequency (which is what matters). This is known as the representativeness heuristic.

3. *Stereotypes.* Once we perceive a person as old or Irish or having neat writing, or a car as expensive or a good runner or a lemon, then a great number of attributes follow *automatically,* some right, some wrong. Such preconceptions of what to expect are called stereotypes, useful short-cuts that we use to avoid our pet hates of uncertainty and having to think. Thus there are stereotypes for almost everything from laundry detergents to restaurants. And they work. Coke and Pepsi stereotypes prevail over taste differences (Woolfolk et al. 1983). Ada and Mason are seen as better therapists than Gladys and Fritz (Gladding and Farrar 1982). Lisa and David get 5 percent better marks than Bertha and Hubert for the same essays (Harari and McDavid 1973). Neat writing gets 15 percent better marks than untidy writing for the same essays (Briggs 1970). Mouth curvature is seen as kind, friendly and easygoing, and thin lips as conscientious (r= .7 for both, Secord et al. 1954). A dramatic example of visual stereotypes was discussed earlier in note 7.

The important features of stereotypes are as follows: (1) They are part of the human way of judgment. (2) They do not arise from our observations, because our ability to detect correlation is too poor. Instead they arise from what some person (or book, newspaper, TV program, song, or joke) told us. (3) Even if the stereotype is totally false, we always meet confirming cases in cell a by chance alone, so the stereotype is almost impossible to eradicate. Especially as confirmation of any *part* of it will be seen as evidence for *all* of it—one red hot momma in a sea of tight-lipped matrons is all we need. (4) Explanations (male chauvinists are pigs because . . .) serve to maintain the stereotype. (5) Like other beliefs, stereotypes are acted on (see above examples). For all these reasons, stereotypes are pervasive and a potent source of bias. All too easily are we like the psychoanalyst who accused clients who came late of hostility, those who came early of defensiveness, and those who came on time of compulsiveness (from Nisbett & Ross 1980:242).

4. *Sample size.* We recognize that people are more variable than peas, and that to make a reliable judgment we need more people than peas (Nisbett et al. 1983). But once past the first few, we think that a small sample of 10 is as good as a larger one of 100 (it is not), and that the difference between a random sample and one selected to prove a point is unimportant (it is hugely important). This failing is sarcastically called the law of small numbers (Tversky and Kahneman 1971), in distinction to the statistical law of large numbers which says the bigger the sample the better it represents the population it came from.

5. *Inflation of coincidence.* In a Paris hotel we are amazed to meet a long-forgotten school friend. The co-occurrence of *this* city, *this* place, and *this* friend seems wildly improbable. But in reality the co-occurrence of *a* city, *a* place, and *a* friend is not so unlikely (Marks and Kamman 1980:165, Falk 1981). A woman won the New Jersey lottery twice in four months, for which *her* chance was an amazing 1 in 17 million million. But many millions of people buy U.S. lottery tickets, and the chance that *some* person will win twice in their lifetime is better than 50:50 over a 7-year period (quoted by Diaconis and Mosteller 1989).[27] There is also a strong egocentric influence—we find our coincidences more amazing than your coincidences, and our coincidences amaze us more than they amaze others, even when they are between random numbers and are therefore truly meaningless (Falk 1989).

6. *Order.* We try to create order even when it does not exist. If we take a fair coin and toss 5 heads in a row, we feel the next toss is bound to redress the balance. But we are wrong. This is called the gambler's fallacy, because the probability of heads is a constant .5 regardless of what went before (Yackulic and Kelly 1984).

7. *Overconfidence.* We tend to be overconfident in our judgments. Thus we can be 100 percent confident in our reply to general-knowledge questions even though our accuracy averages only 80 percent (Fischoff et al. 1977). This overconfidence applies even in physics, where current values for several constants such as the speed of light lie well beyond one standard deviation of many earlier values (Fischoff 1988:173–175). For a long time the British national electricity supply suffered from its engineer's overconfidence in predicting the time taken to overhaul electric generators, even though the predictions were made long after each overhaul had started. It now multiplies their predictions by two (Kidd 1970).

Box 2. *De-biasing your data analysis*

If you snoop around in data looking for something interesting then your biases are bad news. Diaconis (1988) suggests you try the following remedies:

- Graph the results so you can *see* what is happening.
- If you tried N tests, multiply your individual p values by N.
- Test the findings from one half of the sample on the other half.
- Compare your results with those of similar or nearly similar studies.
- Replicate on fresh data, or if unavailable, on random data.

BIASES IN JUDGING DESCRIPTIONS OF PEOPLE

Whatever the system, be it graphology, astrology, palmistry, or a personality test, the end result is a prediction of what we are like. If it seems accurate, then we are persuaded that the system works. What could be simpler? How could we possibly be wrong? As we shall see, the answer is *very easily*. Such judgments are subject to so many biases that a detailed description of just some of them has occupied entire books, for example (in order of decreasing readability) Armstrong 1978, Dawes 1988, Hogarth 1987, Sternberg and Smith 1988, Kahneman et al. 1982, Nisbett and Ross 1980. So what follows is a brief survey only. An overview with some additional biases appears in Table 2.

Before we start, two points need to be made. First, the biases apply to person descriptions from any source, not just graphology. Second, each bias varies in effectiveness depending on the situation and the people involved. So in a particular case some may be trivial and others may be irrelevant. However, they *all* operate in the direction of reinforcing belief, with *no* opposing biases other than the informed critical mind, which of course is not a bias in the sense used here. For convenience we list them in alphabetical order.

1. *Asking the wrong questions*. Or how we accentuate the positive. If graphology says a person is extroverted, we tend to test it with extroverted questions (do you go to parties?), rather than introverted questions (do you read books?). Since introverts occasionally do extroverted things, the answer (yes I go to parties) will necessarily confirm graphology. In other words we tend to test graphology with strategies that are bound to *confirm* it (Glick and Snyder 1986), whereas it would be more efficient to use strategies that would *disconfirm* it.[28] This is the same as "not considering all four cells" discussed earlier in "Detecting Correlation in Yes/No Data."

2. *Aunt Fanny effect*. Or bigger is better. Superfluous statements that say nothing (you have trouble performing optimally under stress; you have unconscious hostile urges) should prompt the alert reader to think "So has my Aunt Fanny!" (Tallent 1958). This is similar to the Barnum effect (see next) except the intent is not to satisfy the reader but to pad out the reading. If size impresses, then we will be impressed.

Table 2. Twenty-six ways to convince clients that graphology works.

Principle	Factor	How it works
Cues	Cold reading	Let body language be your guide.
	Hot reading	Let the content give the game away.
Disregard for reality	Illusory validity	Sound argument yes, sound data no.
	Procrustean effect	Force your client to fit his writing.
	Regression effect	Winter doesn't last forever.
	Selective memory	Remember only the hits.
Faith	Placebo effect	It does us good if we think it does.
	Predisposition	Preach to the converted.
Generality	Barnum effect	Statement has something for everybody.
	Variability	Everybody has something for statement.
Gratification	Client misfortune*	The power of positive thinking.
	Rapport*	Closeness is its own reward.
Invention	Illusory correlation	Know the answer in advance.
	Non-falsifiability	Safety in numbers.
Packaging	Aunt Fanny effect	Bigger is better.
	Dr. Fox effect	Blind them with science and humor.
	Face validity	It works if it looks like it should.
	Halo effect	The importance of first impressions.
	Social desirability	I'm firm, you're obstinate, he's !!!
Self-fulfilling prophecies	Hindsight bias	Once seen, the fit seems inevitable.
	Projection effect	Find meaning where none exists.
	Self-attribution	Role play your handwriting.
Self-justification	Charging a fee*	The best things in life are not free.
	Cognitive dissonance	Reduce conflict—see what you believe.
Testing	Missing out cells	Ask only confirming questions.
	Ignorance	Yes we have no way of checking validity.

*Not discussed in text but mechanism will be self-evident.

The above table shows there are many non-graphological reasons why clients should be satisfied by a graphology reading, none of which require that graphology be true. But if clients are going to be satisfied, then graphologists can hardly fail to believe in graphology. In this way a vicious circle of reinforcement is established whereby graphologists and their clients become more and more persuaded that graphology works. A graphologist typically spends years learning to read handwriting and thus has ample chance to respond to such reinforcement. (Adapted and enlarged from Dean 1987).

3. *Barnum effect.* Or how we accept vague statements as being specific for us when in fact they apply to everybody. Named after P. T. Barnum's circuses which had a little something for everybody. A typical Barnum statement is "You tend to be critical of yourself." Sundberg (1955) identified the most readily accepted types of statement as follows:

Favorable:	You are forceful and well-liked by others.
Vague:	You enjoy a certain amount of change and variety.
Double-headed:	You are generally cheerful and optimistic but get depressed at times.
Typical:*	You find that study is not always easy.

The Barnum effect is pervasive and has attracted over 60 studies; for reviews see Dickson and Kelly (1985) and Furnham and Schofield (1986). Not unexpectedly, the result of accepting Barnum statements is an increase in belief. For example, McKelvie (1990) gave the same set of Barnum statements to 108 students as a supposed interpretation of their handwriting. As a result their belief in graphology rose from 3.6 to 4.7 (mean standard deviation 1.5) on a 7-point scale of 1 (not at all) to 7 (completely).

In general the acceptance of Barnum statements is strongly increased if: (1). the *reading* is general, favorable, and short, and is said to apply specifically to the client. (2) The *favorability* suits the client's personality. Beware unfavorable items (you are not an independent thinker) unless the client is introverted, emotional, or fatalistic (Furnham 1989). However, the occasional unfavorable item adds plausibility provided it is also very general (Hyman 1977:31). (3) The *client* is naive and insecure. (4) The *situation* is intimidating, as for students in class or when the reading is expensive.

Acceptance is weakly increased if: (1) The *reader* is confident and of high status. This works only if the statements are favorable. (2) The *method* is mysterious. Thus a projective test (what do you see in this inkblot?) is more mysterious than an interview. (3) The *data required* are as exact as possible. Thus statements supposedly based on month of birth are accepted less readily than those supposedly based on year, month, day, and minute of birth (Snyder 1974). (4) The reading contains *qualifiers* such as "but", "nevertheless", and "in spite of" (Rim 1981).

Acceptance is little affected by the sex of the participants, and by whether the reading is oral or written or computerized.

Many of the above features fit graphology exactly. But why are Barnum statements so readily accepted? The answer is not because we are gullible but because the statements fit—and if they fit they will be accepted.

*In this case of students.

Here it is vital to distinguish between *accurate* statements and *trivial* statements.[29] Barnum statements are accurate but trivial; i.e., they say nothing really important or specific. They do not tell us how we differ from others, which is what matters. If we judge only on accuracy, then Barnum statements tend to win when pitted against interviews (Gage 1952) and personality tests (Sundberg 1955). But if we also judge on triviality, they lose (Furnham and Schofield 1986:175). So we are not completely gullible. That is the good news. The bad news is that we tend *not* to judge on triviality unless prompted.

In graphology, individual-feature interpretations may appear specific, such as *cautious* or *wasteful* or *shy* or *vain,* but in combination they tend to become Barnum statements. Note also that we have all been each of these things at some time or another. However, the problem is not unique to graphology. Due to the universality of human traits it is difficult to avoid at least some Barnum statements in any personality description. The trick is to focus on traits that make a person different (Tallent 1958) and to distinguish between accuracy and triviality.

4. *Client predisposition.* Or preaching to the converted. A predisposition to believe in graphology must already exist among clients or they would not have contacted a graphologist in the first place. Furthermore, it is a common experience among graphologists that their clients tend to be uncritical. Hence there will be little to stop the predisposition becoming a reality.

5. *Cognitive dissonance.* Or the need to justify our decisions. If we believe in graphology, then it is painful to find discrepancies between our belief and reality, especially when graphology readings cost us money. So we search (unconsciously or otherwise) for personal attributes to match the graphology. Given the variability of human nature, the search can hardly fail. Cognitive dissonance is among the most potent of the effects listed here (Dean 1987:259–260).

6. *Cold reading.* Or how body language tells the story. Here the graphologist uses cues (e.g., pupil dilation and hand movements) leaked by the client to home in on the truth (Hyman 1977, Dutton 1988). Such cues may be used quite unwittingly. Thus Neher (1980) concluded from observations of astrology/palmistry/Tarot/etc. readers that they were often "astute, sensitive individuals who pick up subtle clues leaked by the client. Usually neither the reader nor the client is consciously aware of this communication process, which therefore can result in a reading that seems mysteriously perceptive." The point is that a skilled cold reader can produce

a totally convincing reading very similar to a graphology reading (and probably more accurate) but without using graphology (Nelson 1971).[30] In which case it cannot be claimed that graphology plays an essential part in the reading process. This would not of course apply to readings written down before the client arrives, or to readings by mail order, especially if addressed to specific abilities.

7. *Dr. Fox effect.* Or how style can be more important than content. Dr. Fox was an actor who was coached to give a meaningless one-hour talk on games theory to 55 psychiatrists and social workers (Naftulin et al. 1973). He looked distinguished, sounded authoritative, and lectured charismatically with much jargon, enthusiasm, jokes, and references to unrelated topics. His talk was highly entertaining but deliberately meaningless. Yet the audience found it to be clear and stimulating, and nobody realized it was nonsense. In other words an expressive presentation can persuade us to see meaning where none exists. The Dr. Fox effect explains why Evans (1973) could remark of L. Ron Hubbard (whose style was exactly that of Dr. Fox) that "one gets the feeling that were Hubbard to stand on the platform and recite the telephone directory backwards he would still receive a standing ovation." To the extent that a graphologist is authoritative, witty, and entertaining, clients will be seduced into believing what they hear. The Dr. Fox effect also extends to writing, where perceived prestige increases with increasing unintelligibility (Armstrong 1979).

8. *Face validity.* Or if it looks right, then it is right. Thus a new radio looks functional even if its batteries are dead. Graphology certainly has face validity, with features that look like they *should* work, a lengthy history, impressive jargon, national organizations, national and international conferences, and a huge literature.[31] To the unwary the effect is dazzling.

9. *Halo effect.* Or how one favorable trait causes us to infer the presence of others. Numerous studies have shown that we are more likely to believe a person if they are warm rather than cold, if they are authoritative rather than indecisive, if they are well-dressed rather than dowdy, and if they are encountered in prestigious surroundings rather than non-prestigious ones. In other words packaging can work wonders for graphologists, their claims, and their products (Cooper 1981, Kelly and Renihan 1984).

10. *Hindsight bias.* Or the I-knew-it-all-along effect. Once we know the answer we find plenty of evidence to support our judgment, so we feel we knew it all along when in fact we did not (Fischoff 1982). Once a match has been found between handwriting and person, it will be hard

to see how it could be any other way. In which case the graphologist gains a strong impression that the match was inevitable, and thus gains unwarranted confidence in graphology. Once a match has been found, the rest of the sequence from bias to conviction follows automatically. Hindsight bias is important because we are unaware of it, it affects everybody, it limits our ability to learn from experience, and it is not affected by strategies designed to reduce it, such as providing prizes or advance warnings. The last means that any graphologists who read this are unlikely to be influenced by it.

Of course for hindsight bias to operate a match must exist between handwriting and person. But given the large number of features that can be seen in handwriting, and the variability of personality (most of us have been everything at one time or another), some match is inevitable. No matter whether our slant indicates we like or dislike people around us, we can always find instances where it is true.

11. *Hot reading.* Or with all this input who needs graphology? Graphologists need to know in advance the client's age, sex, handedness, and nationality. Some may also require brief medical, educational, and social details as well. Such data alone can lead to predictions of modest validity, especially if the writing sample contains personal data, as is usually the case if it forms an application for employment. Thus a survey of 17 studies of personnel selection showed that graphologists were generally outperformed by psychologists using the same writing, even though both did poorly, suggesting that any validity was due to content alone (Neter and Ben-Shakhar 1989). This point is examined further in the preceding chapter.

12. *Ignorance is bliss.* Or believing what you cannot prove. Large-scale clients of graphologists, such as companies and organizations, are seldom able to check each reading against the truth (Bar-Hillel and Ben-Shakhar 1986). Criteria for predictions such as honesty may be unavailable, there may be no time for checks, the candidate may be rejected out of hand, and so on. In which case the reading cannot fail to be accepted provided it sounds good and matches our ideas of what people are like.

13. *Illusory correlation.* Or seeing only what we want to see because we know the answer in advance. This most potent effect was discussed earlier in "Detecting Correlation Where None Exists."

14. *Illusory validity.* Or making ostensibly sound judgments from unsound data. If a graphologist is judging whether a person should be a librarian, his confidence is determined by how well the handwriting fea-

tures happen to match his librarian stereotype, even though the features and stereotype may lack validity. A good fit will thus produce an illusion of validity (Tversky and Kahneman 1974). The important point is that the illusion persists even when we should know better. Thus a psychologist can feel confident about projective tests or unstructured interviews even though a vast literature shows both to be highly fallible. Similarly, after reading a graphological description of personality, we feel we know the person and can predict his behavior, even though graphology is unproven and personality is generally a poor predictor of behavior in a specific situation.

But if the validity is an illusion, why don't we notice it? One good reason is illusory correlation (see previous item). Another is that even though a stereotype may be unsound it can boost accuracy as well as confidence. Asked to say what Tom will do, we invoke the stereotype and say what people in general will do—meaning we play with Barnum statements. As noted under *Barnum effect,* the result is usually more accurate than a specific prediction (Gage 1952). So the illusion will persist. Conversely, if we are prevented from using stereotypes, our accuracy is drastically reduced. The effect of stereotypes can be minimized by rating all subjects on one trait at a time, so later ratings will be less influenced by earlier ones.

15. *Nonfalsifiability.* Or why graphology cannot possibly be wrong. Should the graphologist make a wrong statement he has an endless supply of plausible explanations as follows:

Client does not know himself. Graphologist is not infallible.	This shifts the blame from graphology to the participants.
Another feature is responsible. Manifestation is nontypical.	This puts the blame on the ambiguity of the indication.

In an emergency he can always turn to his bookshelf. For example, depending on whether you believe Lowengard (1975) or Greene and Lewis (1980), red ink indicates *vitality and affection* or a *disturbed personality,* and green ink indicates *harmonious and adaptable* or *different and nonconforming.* Such strategies make the whole process nonfalsifiable. Once the reading has begun, the end result can hardly fail to support graphology. No matter what the client now believes, the graphologist's belief in graphology remains unassailed.

16. *Placebo effect.* Or how anything will do us good if we think it will. From the Latin *I will please.* Thus a gelatine capsule filled with table

salt, and given with the assurance that it will bring sleep, will actually do so for about 1 person in 3 (Melzack and Wall 1983). Here it is the faith itself, not the doctrine, which is the effective agent (Prioleau et al. 1983). Placebos are effective even when people know they are receiving them (Levine and Gordon 1984). In fact, the effect is so potent (whether in medicine or psychotherapy or graphology) that entire books have been written about it and the special experimental strategies needed to cope with it (e.g., Spiro 1986). If people have a strong need to believe in graphology, then that alone will be enough to convince them of its validity.

17. *Procrustean effect.* Or forcing the client to fit his handwriting. After the mythical Procrustes who stretched his guests' limbs or lopped them off to fit his bed. Much easier than you might think.[10] It can also work over time. Knowing that a person should be X (when in reality they are not), we behave in a way that elicits X, thus producing a self-fulfilling prophecy. For example, a waiter who suspects you are a poor tipper may give poor service, thus helping his suspicion come true.

18. *Projection effect.* Or finding meaning where none exists. Hyman (1977) points out that in order to comprehend anything we have to make sense out of what is normally a disorderly array of inputs. Because the inputs are so numerous, to survive we have to be selective. The problem with this necessary process occurs when no actual message is being conveyed, because we then manage to find meaning where none exists, as when we see images in clouds or in vague interpretations. Ironically, the vulnerability to being led astray may increase with the ability to comprehend and hence with intelligence. But the problems do not end there. As Hyman (1981) and Connor (1984) point out, words and sentences do not exist like chunks of rock but have to be interpreted before they mean anything. Thus the message we receive is determined by our previous programming, that is, by the experiences and expectations we draw on to give it meaning. Thus normally trivial statements (you have problems with money) may seem deeply meaningful.

19. *Regression towards the mean.* Or the natural alternation of ups and downs. If today is very windy, it will most likely be less windy tomorrow. So the natural tendency is for extreme situations to become less extreme, i.e., to regress towards the mean (Tversky and Kahneman 1974). Thus football players who do poorly in one game will tend to do better in the next (so our criticism will seem to work), whereas those who did brilliantly will tend to do worse (so our praise will seem premature). Similarly, if clients consult a graphologist when their fortunes are low, they

are likely to improve anyway. Because regression is generally unrecognized, clients will tend to attribute their improvement to graphology.

20. *Role playing effects.* A variant of the self-fulfilling prophecy. If we write with a forward slant, and we know this supposedly indicates extroversion, we tend to see ourselves as more extroverted than would otherwise be the case (see Jones 1986). The effect probably varies greatly from one person to the next, but overall it is important because it can affect independent measures such as personality tests (Delaney and Woodyard 1974, Layne and Ally 1980). Thus the effect is sufficient to explain the apparent correlation of about .1 between test scores and astrological signs (Eysenck and Nias 1982). The effect is also known as self-attribution.

21. *Selective memory.* Or remembering the hits and not the misses. Here our memory is selective not because of inherent bias (although this can occur; see previous section and note 26) but because we think that striking coincidences cannot occur by chance (Marks and Kamman 1980:165; Falk 1981). In a graphology reading the number of things that can exist in both handwriting and person are so large that some kind of striking hit is more than likely. This will not be recognized as a statistical artifact and so will be remembered as evidence for graphology. The misses will of course be forgotten or explained away. Assisting our selective memory is the operant conditioning process discussed earlier, where behavior becomes resistant to change if reinforced intermittently rather than all the time. Since intermittent success will happen in graphology by chance anyway, our chances of becoming hooked are excellent, leaving selective memory to finish the job.

22. *Social desirability effects.* Or the nicer the statement the greater its acceptance. People agree very closely on what they see as desirable or undesirable, and this agreement is maintained across age groups, class, and culture (Edwards 1967: 48–70). On average, social desirability is roughly equal in effect to the statement itself, and the correlation between desirability and acceptance is around .9, which is extremely high. Thus to make people believe what you say, tell them they are *cautious, self-controlled, and thrifty* rather than *timid, inhibited, and stingy.* In other words be positive rather than negative. Since a golden rule in graphological counseling is *be positive*, this can be an unexpectedly potent influence. For example Green et al. (1971) got 7 graphologists and 7 adult subjects to rank themselves on 20 traits such as cautious, conceited, dependable, and stubborn (note the differences in social desirability). The graphologists then ranked each subject on the same traits using graphology. The results showed that

the graphologists' self-ranking matched the subjects' self-rankings better than the rankings based on graphology (the mean correlations were .49 and .24). Green et al. conclude that an approach based on social desirability "appears to do better than the one based on training and experience in graphology."

23. *Variability effects.* Or how we can usually find something to match any statement. All people have a rich repertoire of behavior, and how they behave at any given time depends on experience, situation, and personality. Everyone is shy in one situation and bold in another, and so on. Thus we can usually find aspects of ourselves that will match almost any statement within a broadly qualified range, thus reducing the chance of it being wrong (Marks and Kammann 1980:189). The effect is aided by the imprecision of language. Are we shy because we dislike crowds or shy because we are scared?

* * *

We end this survey with two points. First, the word *gullibility* does not appear above because it implies an element of wanton frailty, whereas most of the biases reflect fundamental human qualities. Second, our survey has revealed many reasons why people should see graphological readings as valid, none of which require that there be any truth in graphology as such. Of course these reasons do not mean that graphology is invalid. They mean only that a large number of variables have to be controlled before conclusions are possible. In other words, graphologists have to show that their results have an adequate effect size, and that they cannot be accounted for by non-graphological factors.[32]

At this point there will be an obvious question in readers' minds. If we are so hopelessly biased, how do we ever get to Friday, let alone walk on the moon? A good point. However, as noted by Hogarth (1987), our judgment skills are perfectly adequate for cooking meals ro playing chess, but not for the information explosion.[33] Once the information becomes complex as in graphology, or the outcome becomes *really* important as in to bomb or not to bomb, then we need help. Which brings us to our final section.

HOW TO PROTECT YOURSELF FROM THE KNOWN WAYS OF FOOLING YOURSELF

ASSESSING WHAT YOU SEE

Short of running your own controlled experiment, try this:

1. Be aware of your biases. Do not believe what you see.
2. Consider your emotional involvement. Hell hath no fury like a cherished belief under attack.
3. Ask where the sample came from. If small or non-random, forget it, i.e., suspend judgment.
4. Ask what all four cells look like. If not available forget it. If available, look at effect size. See preceding chapter.
5. Consider base rates, then use control groups to provide an objective basis for comparison. If not possible, forget it.

For example, apply the above to the previous testimonials, and their bias will be apparent. As another example, consider the following claims:

> Extroverts are right slanted.
> Graphology readings describe the person.
> Clients are satisfied.

Here we need to know the sample source and size, how the variables were measured, and the following:

Whether introverts are also right slanted
(so there is nothing special about extroverts).
Whether wrong graphology readings also describe the person
(so there is nothing special about authentic readings).
Whether clients can be dissatisfied.
Whether there are non-graphological explanations for client satisfaction
(so there is nothing special about graphology).

Until such questions are answered, no conclusions are possible.

HOW TO BE CRITICAL

Marks and Kamman (1980:223–226) suggest that you ask the person advocating an idea the following questions:

1. Why do you believe in it? This puts the burden of proof on the claimant.
2. What evidence would you accept as proving your idea wrong?
3. Are there other explanations that could produce the same result?
4. Where did your idea come from? Is the source credible?

Such questions should be asked at all graphology lectures. Bear in mind that the aim is not to win but to learn.

Hyman (1987) makes the following suggestions:

1. Do your homework. Know what you are talking about.
2. Examine your aims. Is it the truth or your ego at stake?
3. Be fair and honest. Attack the claim, not the claimant.
4. Avoid emotion. Let the facts speak for themselves.
5. Above all, be constructive. Specify improvements.

Truzzi (1987) makes the following comments:

1. In science the burden of proof lies with the claimant.
2. The more extraordinary the claim, the stronger the evidence required.
3. If your verdict is *not proved,* meaning that the claimant's evidence is insufficient, you make no claim and have no burden to prove anything. But if your verdict is *disproved,* you make a claim and must bear the burden of proof.
4. Be as critical of the ordinary as of the extraordinary. For example, consider not only graphology but also personality tests, and make a truly scientific comparison.

CONCLUSION: THIS CHAPTER IN A NUTSHELL

For graphology as traditionally practiced, we conclude that:

1. Graphological effects are too small to have been reliably observed.
2. Graphological features are too numerous to be reliably combined.
3. Assessment of the match between graphology and the person suffers from too many biases to allow valid conclusions.

In other words, from start to finish the system is beyond unaided human judgment. Human cognitive skills are simply not equal to the task graphologists have set themselves and routinely claim to have accomplished. So what we read in graphology books deserves disbelief. The remedy is clear —graphologists need appropriate strategies such as the scientific approach to control judgment errors. But from what we have said about human biases, we predict that graphologists will be unconvinced.[34,35] Paraphrasing Dean and Mather (1985), we can say:

> Graphologists are like phrenologists. Their systems cover the same ground, they apply them to the same kinds of people, they turn the same blind eye to the same lack of experimental evidence, and they are convinced for precisely the same reasons that everything works. But despite glowing testimonials from eminent people the phrenologists were wrong. So why shouldn't critics conclude for precisely the same reasons that graphologists are wrong? This is an honest question that graphologists have yet to answer.

Perhaps the issue facing graphology is not whether graphological beliefs are true, but whether the beliefs *need* to be true. If they do not need to be true, as is suggested by present evidence, then graphology will be left without a leg to stand on.

NOTES

1. For example, strong or weak, harmonious or unbalanced. However, having specified this first step, even to the extent of holding the script upside down to avoid bias by its contents, the graphologist Klara Roman (1952:119–124) notes that such initial judgments "prove to be the main sources of error in graphological analysis." So the value of this first step is unclear.

2. If it is futile to study isolated features, it is not clear how their meanings (which fill the pages of graphology books) could have been derived in the first place. According to Olyanova (1960:13): ". . . over a period of many hundreds of years, men and women of intellect and intuition used handwriting as a means of judging character. From their intuitive findings a set of rules developed and it is by these that the student of graphology is guided today." However, to claim individual knowledge of so many *interacting* variables is like claiming to know the effect of each of 20 chemical elements on every feature of every plant in your garden regardless of climate. The task is clearly beyond unaided human ability. The good news is that interaction can be tested directly using ANOVA techniques (short for analysis of variance), which reduce the variation in a set of data to components whose relative importance we wish to assess. The bad news is that such tests provide no evidence for interaction. Thus for 13 features such as size and slant in the handwriting of 64 adults vs. personality test scores for extroversion and emotionality, there was no evidence that interaction improved the fit (Furnham and Gunter 1987). Furthermore, different features that supposedly indicate the same

thing should tend to cluster, i.e., correlate with each other. Letter size (area) and width are physically related, so it is hardly surprising they correlate about .60 (Taft 1967). But the correlations between three physically unrelated features (letter width, letter slant, line slope), all supposedly indicative of extroversion, are all close to zero and thus show no evidence of clustering:

	Width vs. slant	Width vs. slope	Slant vs. slope	
Lorr et al. 1953	.06	–.03	–.03	N=200
Rosenthal and Lines 1978	.16	.07	–.08	N=58

So these features *cannot* be indicating the same thing, be it extroversion or anything else, which suggests that the general interaction of handwriting features may be a myth. However, for the present purpose this is of no conseuqence.

3. A good example of error due to missing out cells is biorhythms, the idea that people are subject to cycles of 23, 28, and 33 days starting from birth. Despite the impressive counts in cell a promoted by proponents, a review of 13 studies involving a massive 25,000 events and all four cells showed no hint of a biorhythm effect (Hines 1979).

4. In the absence of signs the best predictor is the base rate itself, given by (a+c)/n, where n=a+b+c+d. If the base rate exceeds 50 percent, the best prediction is *yes;* otherwise the best prediction is *no.* The base rate for literacy exceeds 50 percent, so in the absence of signs our best prediction is *yes this person can read.* The base rate for murder is much less than 50 percent, so our best prediction is *no this person is not a murderer.*

Enter signs. Surprisingly, the best predictor may still be the base rate, and using graphology may only make our prediction worse. To see why, suppose we are using graphology to distinguish between 90 innocent people and 10 murderers. In terms of cells abcd their handwriting will either set them free or send them to jail as follows:

		Murderer	Innocent
Graphological indication	Murderer = Jail	a	b
	Innocent = Free	c	d

correlation between graphology and murder
$$= (ad-bc)/\sqrt{((a+b)(c+d)(a+c)(b+d))}$$

Method. We can play the base rate for murderers, which in our sample is 10 murderers per 100 people, so a+c=10. Or we can use graphology, for which we will pretend there are correlations of .00 to 1.00 between handwriting features and murder. Now when we use graphology, we must send 10 people to jail, so a+b=10. Since a+b+c+d=100, we can calculate the remaining unknowns a and d by working backwards from our pretend correlations, which gives the following results:

Method		Hits		Misses		
		Murderers in jail a	Innocents set free d	Murderers set free c	Innocents in jail b	Total errors c+b
Base rate		0	90	10	0	10
Graphology where correlation between writing and murder is perfect result	.00	1	81	9	9	18
	.11	2	82	8	8	16
	.44	5	85	5	5	10
	1.00	10	90	0	0	0

In the first line we play the base rate. Since the base rate is 10 percent, and 10 percent is less than 50 percent, our best prediction is *this person is not a murderer.* We jail no innocent people, but we jail no murderers either. Overall we make 10 errors, all of them unjailed murderers.

In the remaining lines we use graphology. Here we can make two kinds of errors, namely a *wrong no* (setting murderers free) and a *wrong yes* (jailing innocent people). If we care only about jailing murderers (too bad if we jail innocent people as well), then column a shows that any increase in correlation increases the number of mailed murderers, so even a tiny correlation can help.

But if we also care about not jailing innocent people, tiny correlations do not help at all, for using graphology will increase accuracy only if the error rate (c+b)/n is less than the base rate (a+c)/n, that is, *only if b*< a. As shown in column c+b, this occurs only when the correlation between handwriting and murder exceeds about .44; otherwise we make more errors than by playing the base rate. Similarly if the base rate is 1 percent or less, we need correlations exceeding about .50; otherwise using graphology will make our predictions worse. These findings apply equally to astrology, palmistry, and any other technique that uses signs.

In this sample the incidence of handwriting features indicating murder has to be 10 percent because graphology has to jail 10 people in our sample of 100. If the incidence happened to be less than 10 percent, then graphology would of course jail fewer murderers and fewer innocents, and the opposite if it was more than 10 percent.

5. Two points are important here. First, if we are sneaky about sampling then we can get any correlation we like. For example, a graphology test for the position of psychology professor would presumably report higher correlations if the applicants were a professor, a schoolboy, and a dog than if they were three professors. So the correlations cited here assume an unbiased sample. Second, the typical correlation of .3 between trait and behavior in a single situation is low because behavior nearly always depends on more than one trait. Our going to a particular party depends not only on our fondness for parties but also on the kind of party, our availability, our good nature (which is why we were invited), our inter-

est in a concurrent movie, and so on. It is a property of correlation that, as the number of things which determine our behavior increases, the correlation with any one of them must decrease to leave room for the others. Thus if there are 3 or 4 independent determinants, then the maximum possible correlation with any one of them is generally around .5 or .45 respectively (Ahadi and Diener 1989).

6. Answers to *Test Your Skill.* The highest correlation in each pair is BB, CC, FF. The difficulty increases from left to right, and you probably noticed how juggling even ten pairs of numbers is an impossible task. Alternatively you may have stored mental pictures of each set divided into pairs and trios, which makes juggling easier. All correlations are in the nil-to-weak range of Figure 1, but in each case the highest correlation is much higher than those typically observed between personality and graphological features. The actual Pearson r correlations are AA.04 BB.63, CC.29 DD.00, EE.20 FF.51. Only BB is statistically significant with p=.05 exactly, df=8.

In the coin-tossing test, the correct answer is sequence 4. Sequences 1–3 have too many short runs. Sequence 5 has too many long runs. When Wagenaar (1988:92–93) gave an extended version of this test to 203 subjects, the preference for sequences 1,2,3,4,5 was 4,29,37,27,3 percent respectively. When the responses were divided into above or below the correct answer, a large majority of 86 percent preferred too many short runs. This suggests that we tend to see long runs as non-random (and therefore due to some outside factor) when in fact they are genuinely random, thus generating erroneous beliefs.

7. In one famous study (Chapman and Chapman 1967) groups of 56 college students were given 45 Draw-a-Person drawings each with six personality statements. The students had to work out the meaning of features such as head size. But unknown to them the statements involved stereotypes that were deliberately unrelated to the drawings. For example, the statement "worried about intelligence" appeared just as often for small heads as for big heads. However, nearly every student saw the stereotype relationships even though they did not exist, and continued to see them despite anti-stereotype strategies such as repeating the exercise, sorting the drawings into piles for closer study, and being offered money for accuracy. Even when the statements totally opposed the stereotype, so that "worried about intelligence" appeared *only* for small heads, the students still saw the stereotype relationship, albeit to a somewhat lesser extent. In other words, they saw only what they expected to see. The same result was observed for ink blots and in verbal studies. The important point is that these experiments made it easy to avoid stereotypes. But the students failed miserably, so there is no reason to suppose we do any better in daily life.

8. Being fooled by illusory correlation is a fundamental human quality that has perpetrated all kinds of false beliefs such as N–rays and polywater (Kohn 1986). N–rays were a new type of radiation supposedly emitted by a very hot platinum wire enclosed in an iron tube. Polywater was a supposedly new form of water produced by condensing ordinary water in quartz capillaries. Initially both received support from dozens of independent studies. Interest ran high until further studies showed they did not exist, whereupon they were abandoned. Despite

these crushing findings, the discoverer of N-rays kept going for 25 years until his death (Hines 1988). Such is the power of illusory correlation. Anastasi (1988) comments, "Illusory correlation is a special example of the mechanism that underlies the survival of superstition . . . This mechanism may actually interfere with the discovery and use of valid diagnostic signs in the course of clinical observation by clinicians who are strongly identified with a particular diagnostic system."

9. This would not apply if the correlation was enormously high, like .9 between not-slanted and not-extroverted, because our belief would then be too frequently and too obviously wrong. Thus nobody believes that weight is unrelated to height, for which the correlation is about .7. But such an argument does not apply here, because the whole point of illusory correlation is that the true correlation is near zero.

10. Relevant here is our ability to link any trait to any behavior. Gergen et al. (1986) asked university students how a given trait could explain a given attitude or behavior, both of which (unknown to the students) had been picked at random. The results showed that any trait could plausibly explain any attitude and any behavior including opposite behaviors. For example, the *hostile* person *avoids social groups* because he hates people, and *seeks social groups* because he needs people to attack. There were typically 3–6 plausible explanations for a given link. For example, the *lonely* person agrees that *luck determines who is boss* because he is covering up (why admit to social inadequacy?), logical (luck is the easy way), or incapacitated (not familiar with social processes).

11. This test is from Marks and Kamman (1980:178) and shows how a single casual cue can organize an entire performance. The following poem is from Dooling and Lachman (1971). Read it carefully and try to make sense of it:

> With hocked gems financing him
> Our hero bravely defied all scornful laughter
> That tried to prevent his scheme
> Your eyes deceive he said
> An egg not a table correctly typifies
> This unexplored domain.
> Now three sturdy sisters sought proof
> Forging along sometimes through calm vastness
> Yet more often over turbulent peaks and valleys
> Days became weeks
> As many doubters spread fearful rumors
> About the edge
> At last from nowhere winged creatures appeared
> Signifying momentous success.

If you found no satisfactory meaning, go to note 36. But beware—after note 36 this poem will never be the same again.

12. The *non*scientific approach is the way graphologists have always done it, namely: (1) Examine handwritings. (2) Find interesting features like slant. (3)

Conclude it means something, like extroversion. By contrast the scientific approach is much more systematic and rigorous. It also recognizes and controls our biases. The steps are: (1) Define problem. Is slant related to extroversion? (2) State hypothesis. Forward slant = extroverted. (3) Collect data, e.g., 200 handwritings and personality test scores. (4) Analyze results statistically. To what extent is the hypothesis supported? Scientific and nonscientific approaches differ not in their ideas but in the methods used to test them.

13. Our short-term memory can hold only about 7±2 items at a time, whether numbers, letters, or words (Miller 1956). Some people manage only 4–5 while others manage 10 or more. Alternatively, we tend to manage only as much as we can say in 1.5 seconds (Baddeley 1982). Unless continuously rehearsed, half the items are gone after about 7 seconds, and all are gone after about 20 seconds (Peterson and Peterson 1959, Murdock 1961). Adding new items displaces existing ones. So give us more than about 7 items to juggle and we are lost. For example, with your eyes shut to stop inadvertent cheating, try multiplying 52×9 in your head. This involves storing 7 digits (namely 52,9 and the two intermediate products 18,45), which is just within the 7-item limit. So most people can do it. Now try 52×49. This involves storing about twice as many digits, or well beyond the 7-item limit. So most people fail. Stage mentalists succeed by using special techniques, for example 52×49 is seen as 52×7×7 or as (52×50)–52.

14. Graphologists stress the interaction between cues and the need for combining individual cues. So do astrologers and palmists. But when Dean (1985:19) submitted birth charts or hand prints to live panels of astrologers (total N=39) or palmists (total N=14), together with questions like *extrovert or introvert?* it was clear that they were swayed by the presence or absence of relatively few cues. And because they used different cues, disagreement was the rule. Thus it was not uncommon for alternate panel members to vote alternate ways, or for half the audience to vote one way and the other half to vote the other way, which incidentally had no evident effect on their faith in their craft. For the record, their overall accuracy was no better than chance.

15. Here we use intuition in the popular sense of a quasi-psychic process. This differs from psychology, where *intuitive* means *done in your head.*

16. Birch (1945) describes an interesting test of insight. Six laboratory-raised chimpanzees are put one at a time into a cage containing a stick. Outside beyond reach there is food. Will they use the stick to get it? Each animal is given half an hour. The first four have no history of stick-using, and in each case the answer is no. The fifth has used sticks before and gets the food within 12 seconds. The sixth has no history of stick-using and reaches for the food without success. After four minutes his thrashing arm brushes the stick and moves the food slightly. He stops, pushes the stick against the food, and sees it move. A few more trials and the food is his. The four unsuccessful animals are then given sticks to play with for the first time in their lives. After three days the use of sticks is old hat. The food test is then repeated, and all get the food within seconds. Conclusion: there is no insight that does not go back to actual experience. As you might imagine, the bigger the similarity between problem and experience the better the in-

sight (Holyoak and Koh 1987). And the insight that brings a truly creative achievement may come only after months or years of uneventful labor and general floundering. Thus Newton did not suddenly happen on the law of gravitation in his mother's orchard. Instead it came "by thinking on it continually." See Ochse (1990:252–256).

17. But what about leaps of imagination, like predicting life on other planets? Surely they transcend the need for prior experience? Yes indeed. Since the time of the visionary scientist Emanuel Swedenborg (1688–1772), many hundreds of intuitives have documented such leaps in hundreds of books. The results are generally glowing descriptions of exotic landscapes, undiscovered moons, and abundant life (usually humanoid), most of them conflicting and all of them wrong (see Gardner 1988). Such is the penalty for transcending experience. Furthermore, if we really could leap there would be no casinos, because our leaping would put them out of business. We know this because the mathematics professor E. O. Thorp (1966) noticed that the odds on blackjack made no allowance for the decrease in the card deck as the game progressed. By keeping a tally of the cards played he was able to win consistently, just as if he could leap on demand. This led to a crisis among casinos, and ultimately he was banned from playing. Casinos were forced to change the game (e.g., by using multiple decks and more frequent shuffling) to foil those who used his methods. Interestingly, despite these changes, there remains a widely-publicized optimal strategy that should allow players to win in the long run. But due to their judgment biases (which favor other strategies), players refuse to believe the optimal strategy will work (Wagenaar 1988:15). So in casinos at least, chance is alive and well, and leaping is conspicuous by its absence.

18. Furthermore, farsightedness is associated with lower IQ and is roughly twice as prevalent as nearsightedness at age 16. In general only nearsighted people need glasses in the street, and only farsighted people need glasses in the library. So the relationship glasses = brains should apply in the street but not in the library—except that libraries tend to attract high verbal IQs, thus confounding the issue. Interestingly, people wearing glasses are perceived *initially* as being more intelligent (Thornton 1944), but the effect of glasses wears off as we collect a larger sample of behavior (Argyle and McHenry 1971).

19. Adding predictors will not work unless (1) the predictors are roughly proportional to the quality predicted, which is nearly always the case (if not, e.g., due to skew, they can be transformed to suit); (2) they are scaled in the same direction; and (3) they are converted to standard scores to eliminate differences in scaling. The standard score of a predictor is (actual value – mean value)/standard deviation. The accuracy is remarkably insensitive to weighting, so it is usual to give each predictor equal weight to avoid bias from measurement error. If there are N predictors, then (sum of the N standard scores)/N = standard score of the quality predicted. Optimal weights can be derived by regression analysis but will generally not improve accuracy unless (number of cases/number of predictors) exceeds 20. See Dawes (1979).

Alternatively the predictors can be adjusted to avoid the use of standard scores. If each predictor is given equal weight, then predicted rating = k + sd of ratings

$\times (a_1/s_1 + a_2/s_2 + \ldots)/N$ where k = mean rating − sd of ratings $\times (m_1/s_1 + m_2/s_2 + \ldots)/N$, s = sd of predictor, m = mean value of predictor, a = actual value of predictor, and N = number of predictors

For example, Dawes (1971) looked at the evaluation of 384 applications for entry to graduate courses in the University of Oregon. Although the Admissions Committee considered many variables including letters of recommendation, their admission rating was well predicted by

admission rating = .0032 graduate exam score + 1.02 mean grade +
.0791 crude index of undergraduate institution.

Other coefficients (of .0006, .76 and .2518 respectively) produced even better predictions of subsequent graduate performance than the Committee ratings. Dawes suggested that, if this represented a policy which the Committee endorsed, then much effort would be saved by publicizing the equation and discouraging people with low scores from applying.

20. If we have lots of predictors to choose from, how many should we use? The usual approach is to assemble as many predictors as possible, and then identify the best combination by multiple regression analysis. It sounds easy but there is a tricky problem—due to measurement errors and sampling fluctuations, the sample *always* contains false correlations that can grossly bias the overall result. False correlations exist even when the sample consists of random numbers, i.e., pure noise. For example, Freedman (1983) analyzed ten sets of random data, each having 50 predictors and a sample size of 100. The mean overall correlation between criterion and combined predictors (i.e., between noise and noise) should have been zero, but thanks to false correlations it was a staggering .69. This agrees with the expected value of .70 given by $\sqrt{((k-1)/(N-1))}$, where k = number of predictors and N = sample size (Kachigan 1986:230). Similarly, an overall correlation of .60 with graphology would normally delight any graphologist, but it would mean nothing if obtained using 20 handwriting features and 50 subjects, because on average we would expect $\sqrt{(19/49)} = .62$ by chance alone. If we have tested k predictors and pick the best n, the correlation expectd by chance is not much less than if we use all k, being very roughly $\sqrt{(a/(N-1))}$, where $a=(k+n)/2$.

Because a sample always contains false correlations, the top predictors found by our analysis may be in error. So they must always be checked against a fresh sample. Furthermore, predictors are useful only if they add something new. Suppose we predict the area of playing fields by measuring their length with a steel tape. Obviously we do not include length estimated by eye, because it adds nothing new and would reduce accuracy. By contrast, we might include *width* estimated by eye, because it adds something new and could increase accuracy. However, predictors tend to correlate with each other. Playing fields tend to be of standard shape, so length tends to be strongly correlated with width. So as we add more and more predictors, starting with the strongest, we usually get more and more error but less and less new information, with the whole picture being continuously biased by false correlations due to measurement errors and sampling fluctuations. Consequently we can never be sure that the weaker predictors are not adding more error than they are worth. For this reason it is usually not practical to use more than 4 or 5 predictors, especially when predictors cost time and effort to obtain (Baggaley 1964:54).

The above considerations are bad news for those who defend graphology by saying they use it only with other evidence. When we add graphology to other predictors such as personality tests that have a higher validity, we *lower* rather than *raise* the overall accuracy, in the same way that eyeball estimates lower the accuracy of our steel rule. So unless graphology is known to be more valid than our other predictors, or is known to cover a new area, its use can only reduce the overall accuracy of our predictions.

21. If expert judgments occasionally appear superior to an equation, this is because the experts use more predictors than the equation. So the qualifier *using the same codable predictors* is important.

22. If equations are better than experts, why are they not more used? Meehl (1986) suggests seven reasons—sheer ignorance, threat of unemployment, threat to dignity, we don't do it that way, it is inhuman, my way feels better, and I hate computers. Kleinmuntz (1990) adds a further reason—in many cases no equation is available.

23. Reid (1983) also presents selected anecdotes from his employment agency files after 15 years of using graphology. For example, a manager saved by graphology after a bad interview was a great success in his new job, an executive whose malpractice was indicated by graphology was removed in the nick of time, an older candidate had his references and medical condition confirmed by graphology, and graphology pointed to deceit by a consultant that was subsequently confirmed.

24. In the brain there are modules that do highly specific things like recognize speech or recognize faces (Fodor 1983), but they are quite different from the faculties such as acquisitiveness, vanity, and veneration modularized by phrenology. The faculties do not correspond to the way the brain works, nor does personality break down in the way required by phrenological theory. So the whole thesis of phrenology is illusory. For example, a fundamental claim of phrenology is that size is a measure of power. Leading textbooks such as Fowler (1895) and Sizer and Drayton (1893), both of which sold over 100,000 copies, vigorously assert that, other things being equal, brain size indicates mental power. Severn (1913:20), who in over 25 years as a practicing phrenologist examined over 100,000 heads, says "Persons of commanding mentality invariably have heads above the average size." Who would dare question such intimidating sources? Yet scientific studies of IQ vs. brain size, estimated from *head* size just as a phrenologist would, have consistently found the correlation to be around .1, or effectively zero, although the true correlation between *brain* size and IQ, i.e., after correction for the unreliability of the measures, may be higher (Van Valen 1974, Passingham 1979). So the claimed association between size and power could not possibly have been observed by phrenologists. Indeed, their observations should have denied it. That it persisted was another triumph for illusory correlation.

Nevertheless, in the 1830s phrenology was far more popular in the U.S.A. and Britain than graphology is today. Like graphology, it attracted people of intelligence and a vast literature wherein every criticism was furiously attacked. Flugel (1965) comments, "The failure of phrenology, with the implied immense amount of misdirected effort and ill-informed enthusiasm, was the price that had to be paid for this neglect of scientific caution." Unfortunately, this neglect of scientific caution is raging out of control among graphologists and their teaching institutions. For example, fifty years ago Jacoby (1939) could say, "There are graphologists who allow of no objection whatsoever to graphology, discard all criticism, and will never admit that there are limitations to the work of a graphologist. They are inclined to treat anybody doubting the one or the other point in graphology as their personal enemy." More recently, in an address to the British Institute of Graphologists, the psychologist Pamela Sussams (1984) could say, "you have decided to be a scientific body, yet some of you, sometimes, have appeared to me to speak and behave as if it is a religious one . . . [which says] we have the way, the truth and the light, only believe and all will be revealed to you."

25. Personal validation is validation by subjective experience, not by scientific tests. We see that the reading fits and conclude that graphology works. What could be simpler and more convincing? But as shown in this chapter, it is not nearly that simple, and our convincing conclusion can be dead wrong. Graphology (and astrology, palmistry, phrenology, the Tarot, and so on) rest entirely on personal validation, never on scientific tests, whereas for properly devised personality tests the opposite applies. Beware the difference.

26. These findings arose from the cognitive revolution of the 1950s and the birth of artificial intelligence. Before then the talk was on stimulus and response. Now it is on things like the selective filtering of experience, and strategies for handling information. Perception is seen as a set of ideas and models on which we act until they are proved wrong, in which case we change them. That is, we do not merely receive experience, we use it selectively to test models. These models are basically labor-saving devices that collapse the information into manageable chunks. They determine to some extent what we see and how much. For example, in a given landscape the geologist will see rocks, the developer will see building sites, and the artist will see meaning. So what is more important in determining perception, the model or the information input? The answer is the model. For example, suppose we see a slippery wet road ahead. Because the image on our retina is neither slippery nor three-dimensional, the perception must be generated by selecting the model that best fits the cues. So perception is not simply seeing. Instead it is a matter of guessing followed by adjustments if we find the wrong model was chosen, as for example when the shadowy figure in our bedroom turns out to be a coat hanging behind the door. This explains hindsight bias—once the choice of models has been biased by the experience, it reintroduces itself into the original perception. The problem is that guessing from inadequate data can go off the rails, as when it generates fiction, because the fiction is not easily dispelled by knowing the truth. Although we may know when our perception is wrong, this does not correct the perception. In other words, intellect and perception are almost separate processes. No wonder we need the scientific approach to keep us on the rails. (Miller 1983)

27. Suppose two people meet and compare notes. Coincidences could involve countless topics such as same birthday, same job, same car, and so on. If a topic has N categories, e.g., for birthdays N = 365, there is a 50 percent chance of at least one coincidence if the sum of 1/N for each topic exceeds 0.35, and a 95 percent chance if it exceeds 1.5 (Diaconis and Mosteller 1989). If all N's are the same, e.g., 10 makes of car and 10 brands of toothpaste, only 0.35N topics are needed for a 50 percent chance of at least one coincidence, and 1.5N topics for a 95 percent chance. Because possible topics can be multiplied almost indefinitely (same color dress, same make, same style, same size, same number of buttons, and so on), this makes coincidences of one kind or another almost inevitable. For a lengthy discussion of coincidences with many examples and much useful data, see Watson (1981).

28. The surprises do not end there. Studies have shown that if we are basically skeptics, our belief will be modified by subsequent evidence. But if we are believers, our belief will persist because positive evidence will be remembered, whereas negative evidence (like much of this book) will be ignored (Russell and Jones 1980, Glick et al. 1989). On this basis, regardless of the evidence, graphology is not going to go away. On the other hand, we should not underestimate the power of really vivid facts. As Bertrand Russell (1952) cogently observed, "We were told that faith could remove mountains, but no one believed it; we are now told that the atomic bomb can remove mountains, and everyone believes it." Nor should we underestimate the cunning of psychologists. Suppose we believe that men make better bosses than women. If our belief is entrenched, contrary questions (why do women make better bosses than men?) will have no effect. So Swann et al. (1988) use questions that are simply more extreme (why do men *always* make better bosses than women?). Because we resist change, we think up reasons against this extreme view—and unwittingly change our beliefs in the opposite direction. Interestingly, the authors show that the change is a true shift in position, not just a recognition that more extreme views exist. So the next time you meet an entrenched graphologist, ask questions like: Why are isolated features always so accurate? Why do small differences in pen and paper have such enormous effects? Why is it possible to make judgments from a photocopy? Why do different approaches always give the same result? Why is it impossible to judge sex? Why does graphology deny free will?

29. Accuracy and triviality can combine in four ways as shown below:

	Trivial and general	*Important and specific*
Accurate:	You have two legs.	Your verbal IQ is way above average.
Inaccurate:	You hate chocolate.	Yesterday you committed suicide.

The effect of triviality and generality is well illustrated by an experiment conducted in 1928 by Meili, supervisor of the Rousseau Institute in France, long before the Barnum effect was named. Meili set out 68 very diverse items such as will, fear of storms, aptitude for maths, sense of color, response to weather, aptitude for teaching, and respect for the opinion of others. He wrote the 68 items on 50 sheets of paper, giving each item a score (1–5) picked at random, but taking care that the middle scores occurred more frequently than the extremes. Without looking at the results, he wrote on the back of each sheet the name of a psychology student at the Institute. He then gave the sheets to the students as a test of graphology: "A sample of your handwriting was sent to a graphologist. Here are the results. Please give your opinion, and your own rating for each of the items."

The results showed that over half the students found most of the items to be perfectly accurate. Of the 2516 random items, 53 percent agreed perfectly with the self-ratings, while a further 25 percent were only 1 point apart, the mean difference being 0.73 points. Only 6 percent were 3 or more points apart. Meili concludes pithily, "Fictitious diagnoses, determined by chance, will satisfy subjects to a large extent if one follows the following rules: Give the interpretation in the vaguest possible terms; always prefer poorly-defined and difficult-to-check qualities; choose the most uniform qualities possible, i.e., where individual differences are the least marked. . . . One will thus find a certain number of qualities which would be of no risk in an interpretation." (Quoted by Ferrière 1946:66–67.) In other words, in modern terms, they would be ideal Barnum statements.

30. Steiner (1989), a magician and expert cold reader, gave fake Tarot card readings at a party. Someone who was impressed asked if he could also read palms. His answer, although crude, makes the point. "I have studied the craft of cold reading and am skilled in the art. With equal grace and confidence, I can read buffalo shit."

31. For example, Miller (1982) gives a 430-page annotated list of 2321 references to books and journals in over 6 languages, and Gille-Maisani (1989) gives a 60-page bibliography covering books and journals from eight countries. The latter does not include the several hundred articles that have appeared in scientific journals.

32. This need not be difficult. For example, if wrong profiles (whose nature is of course concealed) are accepted as readily as correct profiles, it cannot be claimed that graphology plays much part in the process. Kelly and Saklofske (1989) gave three graphological profiles to each of 10 female subjects aged 21 to 42. One was theirs, the other two were matched on age and chosen at random. The graphologist claimed that his profiles were always accurate. But only three subjects picked the correct profile, which is no better than guessing. By contrast, people do tend to pick the correct profile when based on a valid personality test; see Furnham and Schofield (1986:175).

33. Funder (1987) gives this useful visual analogy. The two horizontal segments are the same length. On paper the lower segment *appears* shorter, but on a real railroad track it *is* shorter. Without this bias we would misjudge real size and distance, so we would crash airplanes and cars and trip over railroad tracks. Similarly, without our judgment biases we would be overloaded by the need for (usually unavailable) data, so everyday life would grind to a halt. In general our biases lead us seriously astray only when we enter non-everyday areas like rail-

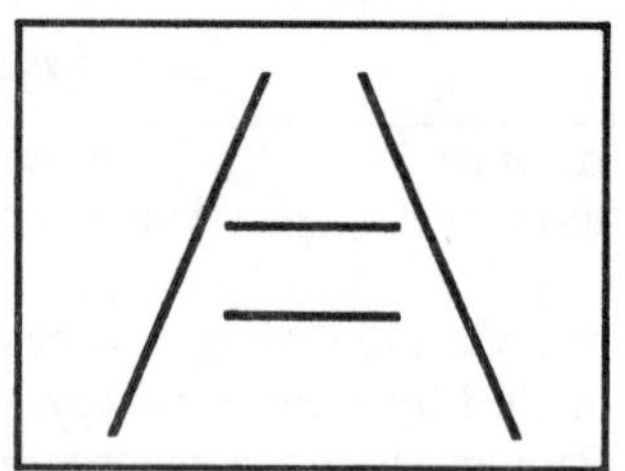

road tracks on paper or evaluating graphology.

34. Just as Rorschach (inkblot) testers remain unconvinced despite published studies showing the test to be unreliable and invalid—the correlation with independent measures is typically .3 at best (Jensen 1964). Furthermore, such tests can reveal more about the judge than about the subject (Hamilton and Robertson 1966). Nevertheless, in the USA about six milllion Rorschach tests were given in 1964. Dawes (1988:234), a former user, comments that "the use of Rorschach interpretations in establishing an individual's legal status and child custody is the single most unethical practice of my colleagues. It is done, widely. . . . it violates what I believe to be a basic ethical principle in this society—that most people are judged on the basis of what they do, not on the basis of what they feel, think, or might have a propensity to do. And being judged on an *invalid* assessment of such thoughts, feelings, and propensities amounts to losing one's civil rights on an essentially random basis." Graphologists please note.

35. Dawes (1988:243–253) suggests that the Rorschach test persists because plausibility is more powerful than disconfirming evidence. For example, a clinical psychologist quoted by Chapman and Chapman (1971) said, "I'll trust my own senses before I trust some journal article." This is especially true when vested interests are involved (note 22). So Dawes suggests that the best way to attack a belief based on plausibility is not to provide disconfirming evidence but to provide a *new* plausible hypothesis. Thus the Draw-a-Person test has been largely abandoned because the hypothesis *unusual person = inner conflicts* was displaced by the more plausible (and better supported) *unusual person = lack of artistic ability.* Dawes (1988:240–243) notes that graphology too is based on plausibility. However, the hypothesis *handwriting = personality* has no accepted rival such as *handwriting = hand shape,* which tends to be implausible because foot or mouth writing show features similar to hand writing—the correlations are around .6 or .2 respectively (Lyons 1964). But without a rival hypothesis we tend to brush aside any evidence against our cherished beliefs. So what can we do? Dawes suggests the trick is to estimate two probabilities, namely pT, the probability of getting the existing evidence if *handwriting = personality* were *true,* and pF, the corresponding probability if it were *false.*

Here pT and pF will be between 0 and 1, and the evidence should be *reliable* evidence, meaning scientific tests and not personal validation. If $pT>pF$, then we think the hypothesis is more likely to be true than false, and vice versa if $pT<pF$. For example, if the hypothesis were true to the extent claimed by graphologists, we might estimate the probability of getting the existing dismal evidence as fairly low, say $pT=.2$. If the hypothesis were false, or at least not true to the extent claimed by graphologists, we might estimate the same probability as fairly high, say $pF=.8$. Since $pT>pF$, we think the hypothesis is more likely to be false than true.

36. Read the poem in note 11 again but this time ignore the fact that it is about Christopher Columbus. You will find that you cannot, neither now nor in a year's time. Your judgment is totally affected by knowing the answer in advance. Also, it now seems impossible that anyone could not identify Christopher

Columbus from the poem. No wonder graphologists find that handwriting perfectly reflects the person.

REFERENCES

Ahadi, S., and E. Diener. 1989. "Multiple Determinants and Effect Size." *Journal of Personality and Social Psychology* 56: pp. 398–406.

Aiken, L. R. 1989. *Assessment of Personality*. Toronto: Allyn & Bacon.

Alcock, J. E. 1981. *Parapsychology: Science or Magic?* Oxford: Permagon. A readable account of the fallibility of human judgment is on pp. 90–104.

Anastasi, A. 1988. *Psychological Testing*. 6th ed, p. 260. New York: Macmillan.

Argyle, M., and R. McHenry. 1971. "Do Spectacles Really Affect Our Judgements of Intelligence?" *British Journal of Social and Clinical Psychology* 10: pp. 27–29.

Arkes, H. R., and A. R. Harkness. 1983. "Estimates of Contingency between Two Dichotomous Variables." *Journal of Experimental Psychology: General* 112: pp. 117–135.

Armstrong, J. S. 1978. *Long-range Forecasting: From Crystal Ball to Computer*. Wiley: New York. Extremely readable, nearly 800 rated and annotated references, essential reading for anyone interested in human judgment.

———. 1979. "Unintelligible Research and Academic Prestige: Further Adventures of Dr. Fox." Paper presented to the 1979 TIMS/ORSA conference in New Orleans.

Baddeley, A. 1982. *Your Memory: A User's Guide*, p. 175. London: Sidgwick & Jackson.

Baggaley, A. R. 1964. *Intermediate Correlational Methods*. New York: Wiley.

Bar-Hillel, M., and G. Ben-Shakhar. 1986. "The *A Priori* Case against Graphology: Methodological and Conceptual Issues." In *Scientific Aspects of Graphology*, edited by B. Nevo, pp. 263–279. Springfield, Ill.: Thomas.

Ben-Shakhar, G., M. Bar-Hillel, Y. Bilu, E. Ben-Abba, and A. Flug. 1986. "Can Graphology Predict Occupational Success? Two Empirical Studies and Some Methodological Ruminations." *Journal of Applied Psychology* 71: pp. 645–653.

Birch, H. G. 1945. "The Relation of Previous Experience to Insightful Problem-Solving." *Journal of Comparative Psychology* 38: pp. 367–383.

Brandon, R. 1983. *The Spiritualists: The Passion for the Occult in the 19th and 20th Centuries*. Buffalo, N.Y.: Prometheus Books.

Briggs, D. 1970. "The Influence of Handwriting on Assessment." *Educational Research* 13: pp.50–55.

Bromley, D. B. 1986. *The Case-Study Method in Psychology and Related Disciplines*. New York: Wiley.

Chapman, L. J., and J. P. Chapman. 1967. "Genesis of Popular but Erroneous Psychodiagnostic Observations." *Journal of Abnormal Psychology* 72: pp. 193–204.

Chapman, L. J., and J. Chapman. 1971. "Test Results Are What You Think They Are." *Psychology Today* (November 1971): pp. 18–22, 106–110. Reprinted in Kahneman et al. 1982, pp. pp. 230–248.

Connor, J. W. 1984. "Misperception, Folk Belief, and the Occult: A Cognitive Guide to Understanding." *Skeptical Inquirer* 8 (Summer): pp. 344–354.

Cook, M. 1982. "Perceiving Others: The Psychology of Interpersonal Perception." In *Judging People: A Guide to Orthodox and Unorthodox Methods of Assessment,* edited by D. M. Davey and M. Harris, pp. 67–82. Maidenhead Berks, UK: McGraw-Hill. See p. 77.

Cooper, W. H. 1981. "Ubiquitous Halo." *Psychological Bulletin* 90: pp. 218–244.

Dawes, R. M. 1971. "A Case Study of Graduate Admissions: Applications of Three Principles of Human Decision Making." *American Psychologist* 60: pp. 180–188.

———. 1979. "The Robust Beauty of Improper Linear Models in Decision Making." *American Psychologist* 34: pp. 571–582.

———. 1988. *Rational Choice in an Uncertain World.* New York: Harcourt Brace Jovanovich.

Dawes, R. M., D. Faust, and P. E. Meehl. "Clinical versus Actuarial Judgment." *Science* 243: pp. 1668–1674.

Dean, G. 1985. "Can Astrology Predict E and N? The Whole Chart." *Correlation* 5 (2) (1985): pp. 2–24.

———. 1987. "Does Astrology Need to Be True? Part 2: The Answer Is No." *Skeptical Inquirer* 11: pp. 257–273. See p. 263.

Dean, G., and A. Mather. 1985. "Superprize Winners Part I: And a New Prize to Challenge the Critics." *Astrological Journal* 28(1): pp. 23–30.

Delaney, J. G., and H. D. Woodyard. 1974. "Effects of Reading an Astrological Description on Responding to a Personality Inventory." *Psychological Reports* 24: pp. 1214.

Diaconis, P. 1988. "Theories of Data Analysis: From Magical Thinking through Classical Statistics," pp. 1–36. Suggested remedies are from pp. 12–22.

Diaconis, P., and F. Mosteller. 1989. "Methods for Studying Coincidences." *Journal of the American Statistical Association* 84: pp. 853–861.

Dickson, D. H., and I. W. Kelly. 1985. "The 'Barnum Effect' in Personality Assessment; A Review of the Literature." *Psychological Reports* 57: pp. 367–382.

Dooling, J. D., and R. Lachman. 1971. "Effects of Comprehension on Retention of Prose." *Journal of Experimental Psychology* 88: pp. 216–222.

Dutton, D. L. 1988. "The Cold Reading Technique." *Experientia* 44: pp. 326–331.

Edwards, A. L. 1967. "The Social Desirability Variable—A Review of the Evidence." *Response Set in Personality Assessment,* edited by I. A. Berg. Chicago: Aldine.

Einhorn, H. J. 1972. "Expert Measurement and Mechanical Combination." *Organizational Behavior and Human Performance* 7: pp. 86–106.

Epstein, S., and L. Teraspulsky. 1986. "Perception of Cross-Situational Consistency." *Journal of Personality and Social Psychology* 50: pp. 1152–1160.

Evans, C. 1973. *Cults of Unreason,* p. 70. New York: Farrar Straus and Giroux.

Eysenck, H. J., and D. K. B. Nias. 1982. *Astrology: Science or Superstition?* pp.

50–60. New York: St. Martin's Press.

Eysenck, H. J., and J. A. Wakefield. 1981. "Psychological Factors as Predictors of Marital Satisfaction." *Advances in Behavior Research and Therapy* 3: pp. 151–192 (a study of 566 couples).

Falk, R. 1981."On Coincidences." *Skeptical Inquirer* 6(2): pp. 18–31.

———. 1989. "Judgment of Coincidence: Mine versus Yours." *American Journal of Psychology* 102: pp. 477–495.

Faust, D., and B. Nurcombe. 1989. "Improving the Accuracy of Clinical Judgment." *Psychiatry* 52: pp. 197–208.

Faust, D., and J. Ziskin. 1988. "The Expert Witness in Psychology and Psychiatry." *Science* 241: pp. 31–35.

Ferrière, A. 1946. *L'Influence des Astres.* Tome 1 de Typocosmie. Nice: Editions des Cahiers Astrologiques.

Fischoff, B. 1982. "Debiasing." In Kahneman et al. 1982.

———. 1988. "Judgment and Decision Making." In Sternberg and Smith 1988, pp. 153–187.

Fischoff, B., P. Slovic, and S. Lichtenstein. 1977. "Knowing with Certainty: The Appropriateness of Extreme Confidence." *Journal of Experimental Psychology: Human Perception and Performance* 20: pp. 159–183.

Flugel, J. C. 1964. *A Hundred Years of Psychology,* 3rd ed., p. 37. London: Duckworth.

Fodor, J. A. 1983. *The Modularity of Mind.* Cambridge: Cambridge University Press.

Fowler, L. N. 1895. *Fowler's New Illustrated Self-Instructor in Phrenology and Physiology,* p. 39. London: Fowler.

Freedman, D. A. 1983. "A Note on Screening Regression Equations." *American Statistician* 37: pp. 152–155.

Funder, D. 1987. "Errors and Mistakes: Evaluating the Accuracy of Social Judgment." *Psychological Bulletin* 101 pp. 75–90.

Furnham, A. 1989. "Personality and the Acceptance of Diagnostic Feedback." *Personality and Individual Differences* 10: pp. 1121–1133.

Furnham, A., and B. Gunter. 1987. "Graphology and Personality: Another Failure to Validate Graphological Analysis." *Personality and Individual Differences* 8: pp. 433–435.

Furnham, A., and S. Schofield. 1986. "Accepting Personality Test Feedback: A Review of the Barnum Effect." *Current Psychological Review of Research* 7: pp. 162–178.

Gage, N. L. 1952. "Judging Interests from Expressive Behavior." *Psychological Monographs* 66(18): whole no. 602.

Gage, H. N. 1989. "Clinical Judgment, Clinical Training, and Professional Experience." *Psychological Bulletin* 105: pp. 387–396.

Gardner, M. 1988. *The New Age: Notes of a Fringe Watcher,* pp. 252–263 on "Psychic Astronomy." Buffalo, N.Y.: Prometheus Books.

Gergen, K. J., A. Hepburn, and D. C. Fisher. 1986. "Hermeneutics of Personality Description." *Journal of Personality and Social Psychology* 50: pp. 1261–1270.

Gille-Maisani, J-C. 1989. *Psychologie de l'Ecriture.* Paris: Payot. 347 pp.

Gladding, S. T., and M. K. Farrar. 1982. "Perceptions of Common and Unusual First Names of Therapists." *Psychological Reports* 50: pp. 595–601.

Glick, P., and M. Snyder. 1986. "Self-Fulfilling Prophecy: The Psychology of Belief in Astrology." *Humanist* (May/June): pp. 20–25, 50.

Glick, P., D. Gottesman, and J. Jolton. 1989. "The Fault Is Not in the Stars: Susceptibility of Skeptics and Believers in Astrology to the Barnum Effect." *Personality and Social Psychology Bulletin* 15: pp. 572–583.

Green, P. E., V. R. Rao, and D. E. Armani. 1971. "Graphology and Marketing Research: A Pilot Experiment in Validity and Inter-Judge Reliability." *Journal of Marketing* 35: pp. 58–62.

Greene, J., and D. Lewis. 1980. *The Hidden Language of Your Handwriting,* p. 252. London: Souvenir Press.

Goldberg, L. R. 1965. "Diagnosticians vs. Diagnostic Signs: The Diagnosis of Psychosis vs. Neurosis from MMPI." *Psychological Monographs* 79. 28 pp.

———. 1976. "Man versus Model of Man: Just How Conflicting Is That Evidence?" *Organizational Behavior and Human Performance* 16: pp. 13–22. A re-analysis of Libby (1976).

Griffin, K. 1988. "What They See Is What You Write." *Enterprise* (November 1988): pp. 22–25. See p. 23.

Hamilton, R. G., and M. H. Robertson. 1966. "Examiner Influence on the Holtzman Inkblot Technique." *Journal of Projective Techniques and Personality Assessment* 30: pp. 553–558.

Harari, H., and J. W. McDavid. 1973. "Name Stereotypes and Teachers' Expectations." *Journal of Educational Psychology* 65: pp. 222–225.

Harvey, D. L. 1933. "The Measurement of Handwriting Considered as a Form of Expressive Movement." *Character and Personality* 2: pp. 310–321.

Hill, B. 1981. *Graphology.* London: Hale, p. 56.

Hines, T. 1979. "Biorhythm Theory: A Critical Review." *Skeptical Inquirer* 3(4): pp. 26–36.

———. 1988. *Pseudoscience and the Paranormal: A Critical Examination of the Evidence,* p. 11. Buffalo, N.Y.: Prometheus Books.

Hoffman, P. J., P. Slovic, and L. G. Rorer. 1968. "An Analysis of Variance Model for the Assessment of Configural Cue Utilization in Clinical Judgment." *Psychological Bulletin* 69: pp. 338–349.

Hogarth, R. M. 1987. *Judgement and Choice: The Psychology of Decision.* 2nd ed, pp. 1–3. New York: Wiley.

Hollander, P. S., and R. Parker. 1989. "Handwriting: Fingerprints of Character." *The World and I* (June 1989): pp. 244–251.

Holyoak, K. J., and K. Koh. 1987. "Surface and Structural Similarity in Analogical Transfer." *Memory & Cognition* 15: pp. 332–340.

Hungerford, E. 1930. "Poe and Phrenology." *American Literature* 2: pp. 209–231.

Hyman, R. 1977. "Cold Reading: How to Convince Strangers That You Know All About Them." *The Zetetic* (now *The Skeptical Inquirer*) 1(2): pp. 18–37.

Hyman, R. 1981. "The Psychic Reading." In *The Clever Hans Phenomenon: Communication with Horses, Whales, Apes, and People,* edited by T. A. Sebeok and R. Rosenthal, pp. 169–181. New York: New York Academy of Sciences.

———. 1987. "Proper Criticism." *Skeptical Briefs* 3: pp. 4–5. Reprinted in Hyman, R. *The Elusive Quarry: A Scientific Appraisal of Psychical Research,* pp. 437–441. Buffalo, N.Y.: Prometheus Books 1989.

Jacoby, H. J. 1939. *Analysis of Handwriting: An Introduction into Scientific Graphology,* p. 44. London: Allen and Unwin.

Jahoda, G. 1962. "Refractive Errors, Intelligence and Social Mobility." *British Journal of Social and Clinical Psychology* 1: pp. 96–106.

Jennings, D. L., T. M. Amabile, and L. Ross. 1982. "Informal Covariation Assessment: Data-Based versus Theory-Based Judgments." In Kahneman et al. 1982, pp. 211–238.

Jensen, A. R. 1964. "The Rorschach Technique: A Re-evaluation." *Acta Psychologica* 22: pp. 60–77.

Jones, E. E. 1976. "How Do People Perceive the Causes of Behavior?" *American Scientist* 64: pp. 300–305.

———. 1986. "Interpreting Interpersonal Behavior: The Effects of Expectancies." *Science* 234: pp. 41–46.

Kachigan, S. K. 1986. *Statistical Analysis.* New York: Radius Press.

Kahneman, D., and A. Tversky. 1973. "On the Psychology of Prediction." *Psychology Review* 80: pp. 237–251.

Kahneman, D., P. Slovic, and A. Tversky. 1982. *Judgment under Uncertainty: Heuristics and Biases.* New York: Cambridge University Press.

Karlsson, J. L. 1978. *Inheritance of Creative Intelligence.* Chicago: Nelson-Hall.

Kelly, I. W., and P. Renihan. 1984. "Elementary Credibility for Executives and Upward Mobiles." *The Canadian School Executive* 3(10): pp. 16–18.

Kelly, I. W., and D. H. Saklofske. 1989. "Small Scale Study of a Graphologist Using Wrong Profiles." Unpublished study, Dept. of Educational Psychology, University of Saskatchewan, Saskatoon, Canada S7N 0W0.

Kidd, J. B. 1970. "The Utilization of Subjective Probabilities in Production Planning." *Acta Psychologica* 34: pp. 338–347.

Kleinmuntz, B. 1990. "Why We Still Use Our Heads Instead of Formulas: Toward an Integrative Approach." *Psychological Bulletin* 107: pp. 296–310. A comprehensive review with 231 references.

Kohn, A. 1986. *False Prophets: Fraud and Error in Science and Medicine,* pp. 18–20 and 26–30. Oxford: Basil Blackwell.

Layne, C., and G. Ally. 1980. "How and Why People Accept Personality Feedback." *Journal of Personality Assessment* 44: pp. 541–546.

Lester, D., S. McLaughlin, and G. Nosal. 1977. "Graphological Signs for Extroversion." *Perceptual and Motor Skills* 44: pp. 137–138.

Levine, J., and N. Gordon. 1984. "Influence of the Method of Drug Administration on Analgesis Response." *Nature* 312: pp. 755–756.

Libby, R. 1976. "Man versus Model of Man: Some Conflicting Evidence." *Organizational Behavior and Human Performance* 16: pp. 1–12 and 23–26.

Lorr, M., L. T. Lepine, and J. V. Golder. 1953. "A Factor Analysis of Some Handwriting Characteristics." *Journal of Personality* 22: pp. 348–353.
Lowengard, M. 1975. *How to Analyze Your Handwriting,* p. 26. London: Marshall Cavendish.
Lyons, J. 1964. "Recognition of Expressive Patterns as a Function of Their Mode of Expression." *Journal of Consulting Psychology* 28: pp. 85–86.
Machover, K. 1951. "Drawing of the Human Figure: A Method of Personality Investigation." In *An Introduction to Projective Techniques,* edited by H. Anderson and G. Anderson. New York: Prentice-Hall.
Mansfield, J. 1975. *Selfscape,* p. 73. London: Weidenfeld and Nicolson.
Marks, D., and R. Kammann. 1980. *The Psychology of the Psychic.* Buffalo, N.Y.: Prometheus Books.
McKelvie, S. J. 1990. "Student Acceptance of a Generalized Personality Description: Forer's Graphologist Revisited." *Journal of Social Behaviour and Personality* 5: pp. 91–95.
McNeil, E. B., and G. S. Blum. 1952. "Handwriting and Psychosexual Dimensions of Personality." *Journal of Projective Techniques* 16: pp. 476–484.
Meehl, P. E. 1986. "Causes and Effects of My Disturbing Little Book." *Journal of Personality Assessment* 50: pp. 370–375.
Melzack, R., and P. Wall. 1983. *The Challenge of Pain.* New York: Basic Books.
Miller, G. A. 1956. "The Magical Number Seven, Plus or Minus Two: Some Limits on Our Capacity for Processing Information." *Psychological Reviews* 63: pp. 81–97.
Miller, J. 1983. *States of Mind: Conversations with Psychological Investigators.* London: British Broadcasting Corporation.
Miller, J. H. 1982. *Bibliography of Handwriting Analysis: A Graphological Index.* Troy, N.Y.: Whitston.
Murdock, B. B. 1961. "The Retention of Individual Items." *Journal of Experimental Psychology* 62: pp. 618–625.
Naftulin, D. H., J. E. Ware, and F. A. Donnelly. 1973. "The Doctor Fox Lecture: A Paradigm of Educational Seduction." *Journal of Medical Education* 48: pp. 630–635.
Neher, A. 1980. *The Psychology of Transcendence,* p. 230. Englewood Cliffs, N.J.: Prentice-Hall.
Nelson, R. A. 1971. *The Art of Cold Reading, and A Sequel to the Art of Cold Reading.* Calgary: Hades.
Neter, E., and G. Ben-Shakhar. 1989. "The Predictive Validity of Graphological Inferences: A Meta-Analytic Approach." *Personality and Individual Differences* 10: pp. 737–745.
Nisbett, R. E., and L. Ross. 1980. *Human Inference: Strategies and Shortcomings of Social Judgment.* Englewood Cliffs, N.J.: Prentice-Hall.
Nisbett, R. E., D. H. Krantz, D. Jepson, and Z. Kunda. 1983. "The Use of Statistical Heuristics in Everyday Inductive Reasoning." *Psychological Review* 90: pp. 339–363.
Oakes, M. 1982. "Intuiting Strength of Association from a Correlation Coefficient."

British Journal of Psychology 73: pp. 51–56.

Ochse, R. 1990. *Before the Gates of Excellence: The Determinants of Creative Genius.* Cambridge: Cambridge University Press.

Olyanova, N. 1960. *The Psychology of Handwriting,* p. 220. New York: Sterling Publishing.

———. 1969. *Handwriting Tells.* London: Peter Owen.

Passingham, R. E. 1979. "Brain Size and Intelligence in Man." *Brain Behavior and Evolution* 16: pp. 253–270.

Paterson, J. 1976. *Interpreting Handwriting,* pp. 61, 78, 79, 81. London: Macmillan.

Peterson, L. R., and M. J. Peterson. 1959. "Short-Term Retention of Individual Verbal Items." *Journal of Experimental Psychology* 58: pp. 193–198.

Prioleau, L., M. Murdock, and N. Brody. 1983. "An Analysis of Psychotherapy versus Placebo Studies." *Behavioral and Brain Sciences* 6: pp. 275–310.

Purvis, A. 1987. "Right Writing the Key to Right Choice." *Vancouver Sun* (6 October): p. D1.

Reid, J. 1983. "Use of Graphology." *Personnel Management* (October 1983): p. 71.

Rim, Y. 1981. "Who Believes in Graphology?" *Personality and Individual Differences* 2: pp. 85–87.

Roman, K. G. 1952. *Handwriting: A Key to Personality.* New York: Pantheon.

Rorer, L. G., P. J. Hoffman, H. R. Dickman, and P. Slovic. 1967. "Configural Judgments Revealed." *Proceedings of the Annual Convention of the American Psychological Association.* Washington, D.C.: APA.

Rosenthal, D. A., and R. Lines. 1978. "Handwriting as a Correlate of Extraversion." *Journal of Personality Assessment* 42: pp. 45–48.

Russell, Bertrand. 1952. *The Impact of Science on Society,* p. 25. London: Allen andUnwin.

Russell, D., and W. H. Jones. 1980. "When Superstition Fails: Reactions to Disconfirmation of Paranormal Beliefs." *Personality and Social Psychology Bulletin* 6: pp. 83–88.

Saudek, R. 1925. *The Psychology of Handwriting,* pp. 1–4. London: Allen and Unwin.

Secord, P. F., W. F. Dukes, and W. Bevan. 1954. "Personalities in Faces: I. An Experiment in Social Perceiving." *Genetic Psychology Monographs* 49: pp. 231–279.

Severn, J. M. 1913. *Popular Phrenology,* p. 6. London: Rider.

Shanteau, J. 1988. "Psychological Characteristics and Strategies of Expert Decision Makers." *Acta Psychologica* 68: pp. 203–215.

Shepard, R. D. 1964. "On Subjectively Optimum Selections among Multivariate Alternatives." In *Human Judgments and Optimality,* edited by M. W. Shelly and G. L. Bryan, pp. 257–281. New York: Wiley.

Simon, H. A. 1957. *Models of Man: Social and Rational,* p. 198. New York: Wiley.

Singer, E. 1969. *A Manual of Graphology.* London: Duckworth.

Sizer, N., and H. S. Drayton. 1893. *Heads and Faces, and How to Study Them.*

A Manual of Phrenology and Physiognomy for the People, p. 7. New York: Fowler & Wells.

Slovic, P. 1972. "From Shakespeare to Simon: Speculations—and Some Evidence—about Man's Ability to Process Information." Revised version of a paper presented at the Ninth Meeting of the Institute of Management Sciences, Houston, Tex., April 1972. Copies available from Oregon Research Institute, P.O. Box 3196, Eugene, OR 97403.

———. 1974. "Hypothesis Testing in the Learning of Positive and Negative Linear Functions." *Organizational Behavior and Human Performance* 11: pp. 368–376.

Smedslund, J. 1963. "The Concept of Correlation in Adults." *Scandinavian Journal of Psychology* 4: pp. 165–173.

Smith, R. F. 1975. *Prelude to Science: An Exploration of Magic and Divination,* p. 24. New York: Scribner.

Snyder, C. R. 1974. "Why Horoscopes Are True: The Effects of Specificity on Acceptance of Astrological Interpretations." *Journal of Clinical Psychology* 38: pp. 577–580.

Spiro, H. 1986. *Doctors, Patients and Placebos.* New Haven: Yale University Press.

Steiner, R. A. 1989. *Don't Get Taken! Bunco and Bunkum Exposed: How to Protect Yourself,* p. 57. El Cerrito, Calif.: Wide-Awake Books.

Sternberg, R. J., and E. E. Smith, eds. 1988. *The Psychology of Human Thought.* Cambridge: Cambridge University Press.

Sundberg, N. D. 1955. "The Acceptance of 'Fake' versus 'Bona Fide' Personality Test Interpretations." *Journal of Abnormal and Social Psychology* 50: pp. 145–147.

Sussams, P. 1984. "Graphology and Psychological Tests: Part 1—Some Pitfalls in Personality Assessment." *The Graphologist* 2(4): pp. 3–5.

Swann, W. B., B. W. Pelham, and T. R. Chidester. 1988. "Change through Paradox: Using Self-Verification to Alter Beliefs." *Journal of Personality and Social Psychology* 54: pp. 268–273.

Taft, R. 1967. "Extraversion, Neuroticism, and Expressive Behaviour: An Application of Wallach's Moderator Effect to Handwriting Analysis." *Journal of Personality* 35: pp. 570–5874.

Tallent, N. 1958. "On Individualizing the Psychologist's Clinical Evaluation." *Journal of Clinical Psychology* 14: pp. 243–244.

Thornton, G. R. 1944. "The Effect of Wearing Glasses upon Judgments of Personality Traits of Persons Seen Briefly." *Journal of Applied Psychology* 28: pp. 203–207.

Thorp, E. O. 1966. *Beat the Dealer.* New York: Vintage Press.

Truzzi, M. 1987. "Zetetic Ruminations on Skepticism and Anomalies in Science." *Zetetic Scholar* 12/13: pp. 7–20. Comments are from pages 16–19.

Tversky, A., and D. Kahneman. 1971. "Belief in the Law of Small Numbers." *Psychological Bulletin* 76: pp. 105–110.

———. 1974. "Judgment under Uncertainty: Heuristics and Biases." *Science* 185: pp. 1124–1131.

Van Valen, L. 1974. "Brain Size and Intelligence in Man." *American Journal of Anthropology* 40: pp. 417–424.

Wagenaar, W. A. 1988. *Paradoxes of Gambling Behaviour.* Hillsdale: Lawrence Erlbaum. Contains many examples of judgment biases among casino and other gamblers, with a useful review on pp. 107–114.

Ward, W. C., and H. M. Jenkins. 1965. "The Display of Information and the Judgment of Contingency." *Canadian Journal of Psychology* 19: pp. 231–241.

Watson, P. 1981. *Twins: An Investigation into the Strange Coincidences in the Lives of Separated Twins.* London: Hutchinson, pp. 101–190. Very readable but no index.

Wiggins, N., and E. Kohen. 1971. "Man vs. Model of Man Revisited: The Forecasting of Graduate School Success." *Journal of Personality and Social Psychology* 19: pp. 100–106.

Woolfolk, M. E., W. Castellan, and C. I. Brooks. 1983. "Pepsi versus Coke: Labels, Not Tastes, Prevail." *Psychological Reports* 52: pp. 185–186.

Yackulic, A., and I. W. Kelly. 1984. "The Psychology of the 'Gambler's Fallacy' in Probablistic Reasoning." *Psychology* 21: pp. 55–58.

Yntema, D. B., and W. S. Torgerson. 1961. "Man-Computer Cooperation in Decisions Requiring Common Sense." *IRE Transactions of the Professional Group on Human Factors in Electronics* HFE-2(1): pp. 20–26.

14

Handwriting Is Brainwriting. So What?

Barry L. Beyerstein

In debates between skeptics and proponents of handwriting analysis, one of the most frequent defenses offered by graphologists is that "handwriting is brainwriting." In this chapter Barry Beyerstein provides a critique of that argument from the perspective of a physiological psychologist. Physiological psychology is the interdisciplinary field that seeks to elucidate the brain mechanisms involved in psychological phenomena such as cognition, perception, memory, emotions, personality, motor movements, arousal, etc. This chapter provides a review of research in the neurosciences and psychology that shows why the "brainwriting" argument not only fails as a plausible rationale for handwriting analysis, but in fact weakens the graphologists' case because its central assumptions are questioned by modern research into the neural substrates of personality and writing.

INTRODUCTION

Graphologists often defend their craft with the assertion that "handwriting is brainwriting" (e.g., Lockowandt, this volume, chap. 5; Matousek 1987, 1). If by advancing this truism they were claiming nothing more than the undeniable fact that handwriting is controlled by the brain, I would have no objection. But by use of this rhetorical device, graphologists obviously wish to imply much more, namely, the non sequitur that because the brain is responsible for our psychological makeup as well as our writing, script formation necessarily reveals deep secrets about our personal habits, talents, and predilections.

Despite its surface plausibility, closer inspection reveals that this gambit merely asserts that which is yet to be proved. The burden of proof for the claim that minute details of writing correlate with psychological, social, or medical phenomena remains firmly with those who promote graphology as an evaluative or predictive tool, and on this point skeptics find the evidence insufficient.[1] The introduction by graphologists of the true but misleading assertion that "handwriting is brainwriting" diverts attention from the real issue: the paucity of methodologically adequate research supporting their techniques. The mere proclamation that writing is controlled by the brain provides no reason to believe that particular signs on a page are related to unique neurophysiological entities and, therefore, to highly specific personal qualities (especially when different schools of graphology disagree as to what the same signs mean).

"THOSE WHO IGNORE HISTORY ARE CONDEMNED TO RELIVE IT"

The attempt by the graphological community to cloak itself in neurological garb is reminiscent of a long line of questionable diagnostic and self-improvement schemes whose authors have tried to enhance their credibility by claiming unearned affiliation with brain research (Beyerstein 1990). Naive "neurologizing" is so prevalent among "pop-psychologists' seeking a patina of authority for unproven speculations that Miller (1986) coined the term "neurobabble" for those attempts to usurp the prestige of neuroscience without understanding its principles. In placing themselves in such unenviable company, graphologists do little to advance their claim to scientific respectability.

In this chapter, I contrast the tacit assumptions underlying the "handwriting is brainwriting" justification with current neurological perspectives on personality and writing. In so doing, I question whether neuroscience does indeed offer an acceptable rationale for graphology. It is ironic that by appealing to neuroscience, graphologists actually weaken their case, for in order for handwriting analysis to draw support from brain research, the cerebral mechanisms responsible for writing, cognition, and personality would need to be organized in ways that clash with well-established principles of neurophysiology and neuroanatomy.

A THEORETICAL BASIS FOR GRAPHOLOGY?

Among the reasons critics cite for doubting the validity of graphology are the failure of its proponents to produce an acceptable theory to account for why it appears to work, and the fact that graphology neither draws upon nor contributes to progress in related fields such as psychology, neurophysiology, biomechanics, biocybernetics, and graphonomics.[2] One of the hallmarks of a legitimate science is that its data and theory mutually support (rather than contradict) those of related disciplines (Bunge 1984).

If graphologists wish to be taken seriously by the scientific community, they will first have to:

(a) present replicable, methodologically sound research to document the links they postulate between writing and psychological variables;
(b) account satisfactorily for the large number of careful studies that have failed to find such relationships (cf. Karnes and Leonard, this volume, ch. 16; Neter and Ben-Shakhar 1989; Furnham 1988);
(c) adequately rule out alternative explanations[3] for graphology's apparent successes in everyday settings; and then, *and only then,*
(d) provide a plausible and falsifiable theory to explain their findings.

Only if robust correlations between written signs and psychological attributes could be empirically established would it be worth attempting a theoretical explanation by reference to brain mechanisms. But even then, such attempts are likely to founder because the kind of personality constructs used by graphologists are not only questionable in themselves (see Bowman, this volume, ch. 10), but are of a sort that is difficult, if not impossible, to relate to mechanisms at the neural level.

In fields such as graphology, where supporting data are equivocal at best, plausibility of the underlying theory and compatibility with established research become the paramount arbiters of scientific status. Though graphologists have not, to my knowledge, tried to develop (or test) the implications of their "handwriting is brainwriting" argument, it and the related "expressive movement" rationale (discussed below) come as close to theoretical statements as I have found in this essentially ad hoc field. Thus it is worth unpacking and examining these assertions to see if they could constitute an acceptable theoretical rationale for graphology.

WHAT DOES THE BRAINWRITING ASSERTION IMPLY?

It should be emphasized that although the brainwriting argument is true as far as it goes, it cannot, by itself, sustain the explanatory burden graphologists place upon it. The fact that handwriting is controlled by the central nervous system is necessary, but not sufficient, for their purpose, as can be seen from the following.

No educated person seriously doubts that handwriting is controlled by the brain, but so are coughing, yawning, spitting, and vomiting. Why, then, should writing deserve special status as a putative window on character and talent? The reason many have accorded it this distinction in advance of the usual verification is, I submit, that writing seems as though it *ought* to correlate with personality, whereas so many other behaviors controlled by the brain do not.[4] Writing is multifaceted, as is personality; it exhibits the kind of variation across and consistency within individuals that makes it an intuitively attractive candidate for character reading. Moreover, handwriting offers a wealth of detail for metaphorical generalization to behavior, the "pop-psychologist's" stock in trade (see B. Beyerstein, ch. 9, this volume). Moreover, it does not seem unreasonable that sloppy, artistic, or even bold people might reveal some of these qualities in their handwriting. As a source of testable hypotheses these inferences may not be inherently absurd, but their truth or falsity is an empirical question to be established by research, not proclaimed by fiat. And, to date, the evidence is questionable. Furthermore, what quirks of penmanship could distinguish the deceitful from the honest, the cold from the compassionate, or the promiscuous from the faithful? And why?

The brainwriting argument allays the unease many laypersons might feel when such questions arise because it appears to carry the imprimatur of legitimate research. It impresses the neurologically untutored because it is easy to imagine that writing movements and personality could somehow be linked (because of their common reliance on the brain), whereas it is more difficult to conceive of plausible mechanisms to link character with lines on the palm or the position of the stars. Nonetheless, for those of us directly involved with the neurosciences, the brain-writing–personality nexus is extremely dubious, a priori, for reasons discussed below. Before pursuing those objections, brief mention should be made of a related graphological claim to legitimacy, the "expressive movement" argument.

EXPRESSIVE MOVEMENTS AND GRAPHOLOGY

Graphologists also seek credibility by analogizing their practices to orthodox research that suggests that some gestures are related to broad aspects of comportment. Though the strength of the relationship remains controversial, a few very general correspondences between mannerisms and other social tendencies have been noted (Kirkcaldi 1985). While these studies are valid within their own domain, the support they lend to graphology is tenuous. The weak and rather indefinite relationships reported in the expressive-movement literature cannot be stretched to justify the fine-grained character depictions produced by graphologists.

In his review of the expressive-movement research, Brebner (1985) noted modest correlations between certain gestures and very general inclinations such as extroversion and introversion.[5] However, he found that even these frail relationships could be overridden by transient emotional states and situational factors. Such clues to personality as could be inferred from movements were far too inexact to justify the willingness of graphologists to label people potential thieves, child molesters, or drug abusers. In fact, it is extremely unlikely that such complex behavioral patterns have a particular neuroanatomical locus that could reliably evoke specific gestures, or, for that matter, specific writing features.

In the only study reviewed by Brebner that involved graphic behavior, it was found that outgoing, sociable people tended to fill more of a page with their "doodlings." However, there was no suggestion in his extensive review that more subtle attributes like honesty, loyalty, or benevolence express themselves gesturally.[6] Brebner also noted that untrained people can glean all there is to infer from expressive movements simply by observing them for a few minutes. Thus there is no need to hire graphologists to uncover such readily obtainable information, and its precision is hardly sufficient to justify the involvement of graphologists in marital, employment, or parole decisions.

Even if the correlations between personality and expressive movements were stronger and more specific, the onus would still be on graphologists to show how minute facets of handwriting relate to these global gestures, let alone to highly specific personality traits. This they have notably failed to do. It goes without saying that the willingness to pronounce someone sexually deviant, violence prone, or a security risk based on such flimsy extrapolations from gestures to writing behavior is unconscionable and is not condoned by the expressive-movement researchers.

Graphologists might be tempted to claim as support for their endeavors the research on facial expressions that has demonstrated relatively precise ties between muscle configurations and psychological qualities. But here too they would encounter serious obstacles. Distinctive facial expressions are produced by activity in brain systems that mediate anger, disgust, happiness, etc. (Ekman 1980). The basic facial code is innate and similar across many diverse cultures. Presumably, it was favored by natural selection because this way of broadcasting inner feelings promoted survival by enhancing social cooperation (Buck 1985). But, as with the gestural behaviors discussed earlier, no professional training is needed to read facial signals. Furthermore, they evolved to indicate moment-to-moment emotional changes, not the enduring personality styles that graphologists wish to infer. Support from other superficial similarities between handwriting and facial expressions crumbles with the realization that the usefulness of facial expressions depends upon the invariance of the inborn facial code across individuals, whereas it is minute idiosyncrasies in the acquired skill of writing that graphologists insist are revealing.

Similar arguments arise with regard to brain mechanisms that imbue speech with its recognizable emotional timbre. Inasmuch as this must involve connections between emotional mechanisms of the brain and the musculature of speech, could this finally be the elusive prototype for graphology? To see why not, we must look more closely at how this brain system works.

Loss of right temporal lobe function can strip a person's speech of its emotional tonality while leaving its meaningfulness intact (Dimond 1979; Sacks 1985, 83).[7] Lesions of the left temporal lobe spare the ability to recognize the emotional qualities in the speech of others but devastate the ability to understand its content. The fact that no training is required for normal production and recognition of these speech qualities and that identifiable areas of the brain are devoted to them are obvious differences vis-a-vis graphology. Discerning graphological signs requires formal training, and I know of no reports of specific brain lesions that obliterate the ability to make graphological judgments and nothing else. A final reason for doubting facile analogies between graphology and this aspect of oral communication arises from the fact that the brain's emotional apparatus blends the same affective flavoring unformly across any given utterance, rather than differentially modulating one morpheme for aggressiveness and another for kindliness, and so on. The latter would need to be the case for graphologists to derive any comfort from this research.

Before leaving this section, we should be reminded how convincingly skilled actors and manipulative sociopaths can learn to mimic body language, facial expressions, and tone of voice so as to create false personas. This should give pause to graphologists who invoke the expressive-movement rationale to support the claim that they can "see through" a writer's attempts to disguise his or her script in order to mask unsavory tendencies (assuming that writing could expose them in the first place.)[8] That said, let us return to the central assumptions of the "handwriting is brainwriting" argument.

THE BRAIN AND PSYCHOLOGICAL PROCESSES

Graphologists and their critics can agree that individual differences in personality, abilities, and dispositions derive from structural and functional relationships in the brain.[9] Some of these are innate, others are learned and stored as permanent modifications in brain circuitry. The field of physiological psychology provides ample evidence that the attributes of concern to graphologists are—like all thoughts, feelings, motives, skills, memories, perceptions, and movements—products of brain states (Carlson 1986; Oakley 1985). Even though the central programming of writing and the psychological traits that graphologists claim to discern are both due to brain states, the question remains as to whether specific writing movements are matched in a one-to-one fashion with any other personal attributes.

For the statement "handwriting is brainwriting" to offer any meaningful support for graphology, several preconditions would need to be satisfied. First, every psychological dimension upon which graphologists pass judgment (e.g., optimism, conservatism, piety) would need to be associated with a unique entity in the brain.[10] This was once a popular view in neurology but has long since been abandoned (as will be discussed shortly). Each of these anatomical representations of a trait, unlikely as they are, would in turn need to be hard-wired to a neural program that executes a particular set of writing movements. Granting for the moment this improbable scenario, it would still be necessary, in order for graphology to be a useful diagnostic tool, that these connections be invariant across all people in a given culture. Otherwise, there would be no reason to expect the same pen strokes from everyone who shares the psychological trait in question.[11] As we shall see, the sort of brain organization necessary to satisfy these conditions is hard to reconcile with current data on how psychological functions are mapped out in the brain. In fact, as Ben-Shakhar et al. (1986) remind us, if reliable relationships were found between handwriting and personality traits, they would pose a major theoretical challenge for modern psychology and neurology to accommodate them.

Though proponents of the brainwriting argument seem unaware of it, their thesis presupposes a particular position with respect to the age-old debate about localization of functions in the brain (Krech 1962; Rosner 1974). As it shares this tenet—and its attendant problems—with a once popular, but now discredited, school of trait assessment, a brief historical digression seems in order.

LOCALIZATION OF FUNCTION—A FALSE START

In the last century, a widely acclaimed character-reading system emerged from the discovery that different mental operations are handled by separate parts of the brain. Phrenology, the most egregious overextension of this legitimate notion of functional specialization, was the handiwork of Franz Joseph Gall (1758–1828). Gall was a leading neurophysiologist of his day whose many worthwhile discoveries have, unfortunately, been overshadowed by his phrenological follies.[12] He tried to explain personality by postulating circumscribed "organs" in the brain, each devoted to a "faculty" such as "secretiveness," "reverence," "self-esteem," or "benevolence" (Leahey and Leahey 1983, ch. 4). It is my contention that, in order for writing to correlate with psychological dispositions, a similarly dubious allocation of traits to isolated brain sites would be required.[13]

Gall proceeded logically from flawed premises: viz., that "faculties" were innate, possessed in varying degrees by everyone, and that each was segregated in a unique brain region. One's outstanding endowments were thought to stem from enlargement of the responsible "organs" which, in turn, should be marked by protuberances of the overlying skull. Thus, anyone's intimate makeup could be established by "reading" the shape of his or her cranium.

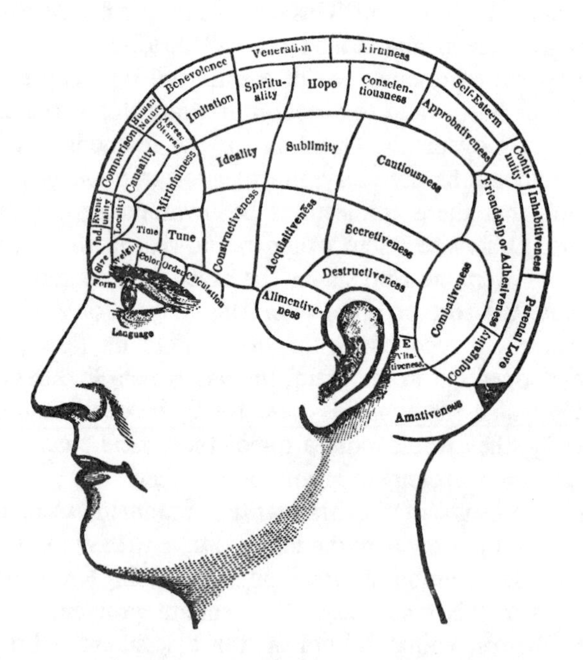

Figure 1. Thirty-seven faculties: the phrenological "organs"

Gall's initial assumptions were not unreasonable for his time, but he (and especially his overzealous followers) carried them to absurd lengths. Their unshakable faith in the theory led them to see confirmation where there was none and to discount the negative evidence provided by others.[14] In addition to their failure to subject their ideas to rigorous testing, the phrenologists were doomed by several other misapprehensions. One was the assumption that common-sense, essentially literary, depictions of human peculiarities could adequately describe and explain the complexities of human personality. Another was their belief that such depictions would be sufficiently stable across social situations to permit reliable predictions of behavior. Similar assumptions have not fared well at the hands of modern researchers (see Bowman, this volume, ch. 10), but they remain central to most graphological notions of personality. Even if the phrenologists had not erred in their conceptualization of traits and in their assumption that they live in little islands of enlarged cortex, their head-reading system would have been rendered useless by the fact that the outer shape of the cranium does not follow exactly the contour of the underlying brain.

Doubtful as the phrenologists' program was, it still left them better off than the graphologists in one respect—an enlarged phrenological organ simply had to produce an excess of its associated feelings. These urges could then be expressed in a variety of voluntary or involuntary ways. Thus, the phrenologists were spared the difficulty of suggesting a plausible mechanism whereby each "organ/faculty" could be invariably fixed to an output as specific as a unique writing movement.

Graphologists who rely on testimonials from famous supporters could do well to ponder the impressive list of those who staunchly defended phrenology in its heyday (cf. Edwardes 1977, pp. 131–138; Leahey and Leahey 1983, chs. 3 and 4; and Dean et al., this volume, ch. 13). The fact that intelligent people can be easily misled when they stray beyond their fields of expertise makes this sort of endorsement much less impressive than it might otherwise seem.

Despite its abandonment by mainstream physiological psychology, phrenology continues to enjoy devoted adherents, largely because its all-encompassing simplicity appeals to the impatient and its anti-establishment flavor attracts the envious and uncredentialed. Anyone offering the average citizen an allegedly powerful tool for manipulating others by exposing "what they are really like" invariably attracts an eager clientele (Beyerstein 1990). If vendors offer benefits shunned by scientific experts and even promise to evaluate people without their knowledge, so much the better for sales.

LOCALIZATION OF FUNCTION—THE CONTEMPORARY VIEW

Cerebral localization of function is a well-documented fact, but the brain's functional units in no way correspond to the "faculties" proposed by the phrenologists and implicitly assumed by graphologists (Krech 1962; Posner et al. 1988; Gazzaniga 1989). Studies of brain damage and experiments using electrophysiological, imaging, and cerebral bloodflow measures of brain structure and activity indicate that the functions localized in the brain are narrow subcomponents of psychological processes rather than the global attributes and dispositions dear to prescientific character readers. Graphologists could sidestep this difficulty if it did not immensely complicate any brain theory that could account for their alleged trait-writing correspondences.

Modern brain research shows that the elementary operations underlying complex mental functions are strictly localized and that these dispersed subroutines are assembled into different temporary networks as their contributions are required. The brain can be thought of as a collection of modules, each performing a fragment of tasks such as facial recognition or linguistic analysis (Gazzaniga 1989; Posner et al. 1988). In other words, broad abilities and dispositions do not reside in any single area of the brain, but their constituent operations do. Evidence for this kind of dynamic organization poses grave difficulties for the simplistic assumption of graphologists that minute features of writing could denote complex abilities, because there is no single, enduring center devoted exclusively to each of these abilities or traits. In other words, there is nothing that could easily be hard-wired to writing movements. This is essentially the same problem that thwarted neurosurgeons who naively thought violent behavior could be eliminated by surgically removing an allegedly overactive "aggression center" in the brain; no such convenient target exists (Valenstein 1973). We turn next to a consideration of the implications for graphology of this modular organization of the brain.

BIOLOGICAL THEORIES OF PERSONALITY

There is much reason to doubt the outmoded notion that people possessed of, say, a compassionate nature are so inclined because of a hyperactive "compassion center" in their brains. If, as I believe, personality differences do ultimately reflect brain differences, they must be much more subtle than the one center–one trait model proposed by the phrenologists and implied by graphologists of the brainwriting persuasion.

These days, students of the biological bases of personality think the plethora of overt character types reflects various blends of activity from a more modest number of temperamental systems in the brain (see, e.g., Mangan 1982; Derryberry and Rothbart 1988). Just as all colors of the spectrum can be produced by appropriate mixtures of a few primary hues, dissimilar personalities can result from varying strengths of a few neural systems, in a manner akin to the cognitive networks described in the preceding section. These temperament modules evolved to regulate physiological states and to motivate appropriate survival behaviors. Though their aggregate effect is the biological substrate of personality, the actual function each module performs bears little resemblance to any recognizable personality style. The sum of genetically determined "set points" in the different systems produces characteristic emotional responses to novelty, threat, deprivation, reward, and other biologically significant stimuli. These interact with learned attitudes to produce the behavioral consistencies we call personality.

Given their more primitive arousal, motivational, and emotional responsibilities, these temperament networks are found mainly in subcortical limbic areas (i.e., the evolutionarily older core of the brain that is most similar in human and infrahuman species). The cognitive modules are mostly cortical and serve perceptual awareness and the planning and execution of voluntary actions that satisfy limbic urgings.

Although theorists differ on specifics, they broadly agree about how idiosyncratic mixtures of these temperament systems could affect personality. Jeffrey Gray (1982), for instance, shows how individual differences in a "behavioral inhibition" system found in limbic areas can interact with arousal and motivational mechanisms in ways that could explain the personality dimensions proposed by Hans Eysenck (see Brody 1988, ch. 5). These interactions affect general orientation to the environment and increase the probability of certain kinds of responses to threat, novelty, punishment, and reward. They also set general excitability levels and affect readiness to learn about particular stimuli. Externally, they appear as inclinations to be impulsive, anxiety prone, or introverted as opposed to extroverted.

Tucker and Williamson (1984) have related neurochemical aspects of these subcortical activation and arousal systems to individual differences in specialization of the right and left cerebral hemispheres. They show how personal styles could be affected by interactions among subsystems governing response to novelty and reward, rate of habituation, filtering extraneous stimuli, maintaining vigilance, and the like. These subsystem interactions bias the relative importance of internal versus external controls on behavior, with obvious consequences for personality.

Extrapolating from studies of drug effects, brain damage, genetic selection, and other manipulations in animals, Cloninger (1986) argues that various human typologies can be derived from responsiveness in three separate but interacting subcortical systems. The novelty-seeking system, mediated by the neurotransmitter dopamine, regulates exploratory drives and the level of arousal generated by new stimuli. Those high in activity of this system are strongly motivated to avoid monotony. The second system, controlled by the neurotransmitter serotonin, mediates self-protectiveness. People with a robust harm-avoidance system generally choose their options with an overriding concern for averting punishment and unpredictable situations. The "harm-avoider" thus learns to inhibit behavior that might lead to punishment, excessive novelty, or loss of reward. Reward dependency, characterized by low activity in the norepinephrine tracts of the brain, is associated with a strong need to please others and a low tolerance for delay of gratification. Among other things, a reward-dependent person finds it difficult to abandon previously rewarded behaviors.

Cloninger has speculated about the types of personality that might result from various "set points" in his three systems. For instance, a person dominated by need for novelty but less driven by a need for constant reward might appear opportunistic and unconventional, whereas someone high in both needs might be an impassioned, self-indulgent attention seeker. Similarly, one low in need for both novelty and frequent reward would tend to be modest, unimaginative, and reclusive.

Kagan and colleagues (1988) extended a similar biological perspective to explain shyness, a human trait that remains quite stable throughout life. Faced with unfamiliar events or persons, some people typically become timid and withdrawn, whereas others are gregarious and affectively spontaneous. Kagan et al. drew upon research showing that animals who become cautious and socially avoidant when they encounter unexpected changes have hypothalamic-limbic mechanisms that are innately easy to arouse. They predicted that socially inhibited children might have similar hair triggers for certain sympathetic nervous system reactions, muscle tensions, and neuro-hormone secretions involved in the fight-or-flight response. The expected patterns, consistent with inherited differences in limbic arousability, were found to distinguish shy from outgoing children, further supporting a biological basis for the widely studied traits of extroversion and introversion.

It is clear that the biological component of personality is derived from *quantitative* interactions among several diverse brain systems possessed by everyone, not from *qualitatively* different trait controllers that some possess and others do not (and which could more easily command their own unique writing programs). Even if a temperament module could become linked with a writing trait, the link would be very difficult for a graphologist to discern because what any given module is actually doing for the individual bears little resemblance to the various overt behaviors it affects. Two people equally high in activity in one module could have quite different personalities because they differed in the quantitative inputs from a second or third. These two individuals would display the same written sign, but appear quite unalike nonetheless. The quantitative nature of these multiple contributors to a trait also makes it difficult to see how they could determine something as qualitative as an embellishment of a letter.

Of course, people's idiosyncratic experiences contribute importantly to their adult personality as well, creating a further problem for graphological theorists to explain: how can life's vicissitudes lead to modifications in writing in the first place, let alone produce the same modifications in everyone with a shared background?

In this section we have seen that the kinds of character traits portrayed by graphologists are not controlled by unitary centers that could easily be attached to specific writing movements. Having writing traits determined by quantitative interactions among the dispersed motivational and emotional mechanisms that actually underlie personality would represent a neural control problem of horrendous magnitude and no conceivable evolutionary value. For the brainwriting justification to make sense, graphologists would have to point to neural pathways that could lock these farflung temperament systems onto equally dispersed control systems for handwriting. It is to the latter that we now turn.

BRAIN MECHANISMS AND WRITING

Writing is a secondary, graphic representation of language, or, a re-encoding of another more basic code.

> As a code, language symbolizes experiences. This code can then be represented through a system of sounds combined to form words and sentences. However, these sounds (which are themselves a code) can be rerepresented as visual, rather than auditory, symbols. That is, reading and writing are codes for hearing and speaking, which themselves are codes for the actual experience or ideas (the referents). (Reed 1986, 17)

Reed (1986) classifies linguistic communication according to the receptive and expressive modalities employed. The auditory-oral system, comprised of hearing and speech, is the most common way of using language. It supplies the foundation for the visual-graphic system, the derivative ability to read and write.

Evolutionarily and developmentally, speech predates writing. Constructing visual signs to stand for auditory symbols emerged from primitive picture writing as recently as three to five thousand years ago (Ellis 1985). Long before that, the neural substrates of the auditory-oral system evolved as genetically organized features of the brain's cognitive apparatus—as evidenced by the fact that normal children require only minimal exposure to the arbitrary codes of a particular linguistic community to become proficient in their native tongue. By contrast, writing and reading must be laboriously taught and practiced, long after the auditory-oral system has attained a high level of sophistication. Even today, the power of manipulating written symbols remains a minority accomplishment (Critchley 1970, 1263).

Like all complex motor skills, writing demands painstaking attention to individual movements as it is being learned. With practice, writing comes to require little conscious monitoring and as this automatization progresses, letter formations become personalized. This process raises another problem for any theory of graphology because it must explain why a student's personality mechanisms supposedly force him or her, unconsciously, to deviate from the teacher's standard strokes in exactly the same way as all psychologically similar persons. Non-graphologists offer a much more convincing and parsimonious explanation for why individual differences in script formation emerge as we learn to write. For example, in their mathematical model of writing, Edelman and Flash (1987) show how slight biases in biocybernetic brain/muscle programs could interact with biomechanical factors to individualize writing strokes in ways that graphologists would insist are personality driven. The biocyberneticists require none of the convoluted inputs from motivational systems that the graphologists do in order to account for individual differences in writing. Furthermore, biocyberneticists show how the same control modules could contribute to different writing strokes that would need to be controlled separately if—as graphologists believe—they derive from quite different trait mechanisms.

If writing is a learned extension of the brain's cognitive apparatus, one would expect that its neural control systems would receive their input from perceptual, linguistic, and memory areas rather than the motivational/personality ones suggested by graphology. This is supported by the fact that writing disorders (other than those resulting from damage to systems controlling the hand and arm) are most likely to accompany disruption of linguistic areas. These can include the mechanisms that imbue the strokes with meaning or the translational functions that encode acoustic, visual, or semantic information into motor commands (cf. Luria 1970, 328). The resulting syndromes are known as "agraphias" or "dysgraphias," depending on the type and severity of the deficit (Critchley 1970, ch. 22). The fact that dysgraphia is usually, though not inevitably, associated with receptive or expressive speech disorders shows that they share some, but not all, neural substrates.

If writing were linked to peculiarities of personality as graphologists maintain, brain damage that alters personality should have predictable consequences for writing, and vice versa. My search of published clinical case reports revealed no support for this notion. On the contrary, brain damage that profoundly alters personality can leave a patient's writing unchanged and gross disruptions of writing can occur in the absence of personality changes. In cases where both personality and writing are affected, there is no systematic relationship between losses of one kind and the other. Damage to the frontal lobes or their limbic connections is most likely to alter global personality (Damasio and Van Hoesen 1983), whereas it is injury to motor or language systems or to the parietal regions toward the rear of the cortex that disrupts writing.

Ogle (1867, in Roeltgen and Heilman 1985) was a pioneer in classifying writing disorders produced by injury to higher brain centers. By relating specific deficits to sites of damage, he derived the first comprehensive neurological model of writing. Recent technological advances have improved the precision of his picture of the distributed brain networks that serve writing.

The writing system, like the other brain networks discussed earlier, is dispersed and modularized (see Luria 1970; Ellis 1982; Roeltgen and Heilman 1985; Paradis 1987). Since there are visual, auditory, cognitive, linguistic, and motor subcomponents to the act of writing, it is not surprising that there can be a variety of partial deficits, depending upon which modules or interconnecting pathways are damaged. For instance, it is not unusual for a brain-injured patient to be able to spell a word orally but not in writing, even if he or she retains the ability to form individual letters. Other patients can write letters and words dictated to them but are unable to copy them from visual examples.

Some brain lesions affect the translation of acoustically stored information into the basic graphemic units[15] used by motor programs for writing. These patients are unable to write pronounceable nonwords (e.g., "blarg") but can still write irregular words such as "knife" that cannot be spelled by converting their auditorily stored form to its graphemic equivalent. Other patients, whose injuries disconnect hand/arm control from the memory banks that contain these atypical spellings (but spare access to phonetic systems), might hear and understand the word "laugh" but only be able to write it as "laf" (Ellis 1982). Roeltgen and Heilman (1985) have developed a comprehensive model of writing control in the brain by correlating dysfunctions such as these with specific anatomical sites of damage.

Since graphologists claim to look only at script formation and distribution, we can concentrate on modules that control these features. Dysfunctions of the pyramidal motor system (cortical muscle control areas and their efferent pathways) and extrapyramidal motor systems (basal ganglia, cerebellum) can cause writing to become undeciperable, even if the perceptual/cognitive input is normal (Roeltgen and Heilman 1985). In these cases, performance on other tasks requiring manual dexterity will be similarly degraded.

When perceptual input to the motor systems for writing is interrupted by localized damage to the brain, different problems arise. Disruption of brain mechanisms that process spatial relationships drastically affects writing (Ellis 1982; Luria 1970, ch. 8; Roeltgen and Heilman 1985). Parietal lobe damage on the nonlinguistic side of the brain affects orientation of letters and lines on the page, including various combinations of irregular slants and baselines, duplication of strokes (particularly the vertical strokes of the letters *m*, *n*, and *u*), sequestering of script to one side of the page, inappropriate insertions of spaces in words, abnormally small or large script, pressure variations, and difficulty in combining correctly formed strokes into proper letters. Effects such as these are of particular interest because they show that the sorts of features upon which graphologists base their judgments are sensitive to alterations in spatial perception systems, not systems related to personality.

Injury to the parietal area on the linguistic side of the brain produces quite different dysgraphias, characterized by difficulty in producing graphemes, the basic units of writing. Letters are adequately formed, but their sequence, and hence the meaning they convey, is jumbled.

Graphologists I have debated are impressed by the fact that a person's writing on a page and on a blackboard are recognizably similar (as, allegedly, are the same person's writing done with either hand or even, some say, by hand and foot!). This, they assert, indicates that there are idiosyncratic central programs for writing, as indeed there are. However, what this individuality of script most likely indicates is that the complex programming of biomechanical relationships, speeds of movement trajectories, etc. (Edelman and Flash 1987) is performed at a relatively high level, before the command sequence is fed into one of several possible motor output systems. Once again, graphologists point to an interesting phenomenon that prejudges nothing one way or the other about their hypothetical personality-writing correspondences.

GRAPHOLOGY AND OTHER AREAS OF SCIENCE

In this chapter I have argued that concern for consistency with relevant scientific research has been sadly lacking in graphological thought. Graphologists' unfamiliarity with reliable, easily obtainable information on the psychophysiology of personality and writing has led them to base their major theoretical justification upon outmoded concepts. This sort of insularity must cast serious doubt upon the scientific pretensions of the field. If this criticism seems unduly harsh, I could point to further evidence: e.g., the failure of graphologists to anticipate evolutionary arguments against their implicit brain theory.

Given that the structure of the human brain is the culmination of a long series of selective pressures (cf. Oakley and Plotkin 1979), we must ask what survival advantage would have been conferred by specifying an elaborate system of interconnections between control routines for minute aspects of writing and the motivational/emotional networks that underlie personality. The amount of genetic information, structural material, and metabolic resources required to develop and maintain the required "labeled lines" in the brain would be enormous. As nature has been notoriously loathe to squander investments of that magnitude for minimal evolutionary payoffs, it is incumbent upon graphologists to suggest how such a costly and cumbersome arrangement would have enhanced fitness. Theorists who propose intricate connections between the facial musculature and limbic mechanisms, or similar connections that infuse speech with its emotional timbre, were able to point to just such a payoff—improved social communication. How would natural selection have worked to fashion neural substrates for writing-personality correspondences so subtle that they only became apparent to specially trained observers in the last few hundred years? For what purpose was this alleged arrangement in place before our ancestors first devised the art of writing and before there were graphologists to supply the needed exegesis?

And, finally, because writing is a learned, arbitrary rerepresentation of a similarly arbitrary auditory code, it is twice removed from any genetically determined cognitive function—hardly an ideal arena for natural selection to work. Is it not more reasonable to think of writing as one of many possible uses to which this general purpose, user-programmable part of the brain can be put?

The kind of lockstep control by ancient parts of the brain over more recent additions implied by graphology's trait-writing correspondences also flies in the face of another well-established evolutionary trend. As vertebrate species developed increasingly elaborate brains, they began to rely correspondingly less on automatic, stereotyped behaviors to satisfy motivational states. Using trial and error to select the most efficient approaches proved to be a more effective survival strategy for higher mammals than the kind of hard-wired links between motives and micromovements suggested by graphology. Phylogenetically recent cortical additions that allow us to generate a mental representation of the environment greatly broadened the range of strategies for achieving goals. The result, as someone once put it, is that "our ideas can die in our stead." The cerebral cortex with its symbolic representational systems, of which writing is a learned expression, is the culmination of a trend that has loosened the bonds between motivational/emotional/personality mechanisms and any particular behavior fragments that could express them. Tying our most recently evolved and uniquely human capacities to older brain systems in the unyielding way graphology demands would mitigate the flexibility brain evolution has made possible. Inasmuch as writing is a quite recent acquisition—and a learned, conventional one at that—it seems odd that the human brain, the only one to have evolved the necessary substrate, would have saddled it with exquisitely deterministic links of such dubious value.

Now, it might be countered that writing itself exhibits just this sort of rigidity within individuals, which of course is true. But that rigidity is typical only within functional modules, and we have seen that in this instance it results from automatization of carefully practiced routines. What these stereotyped behavioral routines become temporarily attached to is anything but rigid in our highly plastic species.

Of course, if people with certain personalities chose voluntarily to express their predominant characteristics by means of certain writing conventions, the foregoing would be less problematic, but this would not sit well with the expressed belief of most graphologists that writing movements are unconscious and automatic.[16] Furthermore, this view hardly jibes with our subjective experience that few of us actively chose to write the way we do. And, finally, if the putative personality-script correspondences are not innate and unconscious, it strains credulity even further to accept the notion that everyone with a given trait would learn to express it via the same arbitrary writing convention.

CONCLUSION

In deciding among conflicting claims, it is often worth asking what must be abandoned as well as what will be accepted if we embrace one alternative over another. Other chapters in this collection have presented data in favor of and against the practical utility of graphology. Here, I have argued that in order to accept graphology as a valid method of discerning human strengths and weaknesses, one would have to consign a century of well-documented data in psychology and the neurosciences to the rubbish heap. The fact that so much of what we have learned about the neurological underpinnings of personality must be wrong if graphology is right does not automatically rule out graphology's claims. But, surely, it makes the gravity of accepting them such that a prudent observer would demand a specially high standard of proof before concluding that graphology is valid and that the whole edifice of psychobiological research, which serves us so well in so many areas, is in need of drastic revision. In my opinion, that standard has not been met.

It is ironic that so many graphologists should think the "handwriting is brainwriting" argument is one of their best lines of defense when it represents some of the most tempting chinks in their armor.

NOTES

1. See, e.g., chapters by Bowman, Dean, Dean et al., Klimoski, and Karnes and Leonard in this volume.

2. "Graphonomics" is the name chosen by the recently founded association of psychologists, physiologists, bioengineers, educators, and computer scientists devoted to research on handwriting. It is significant that this interdisciplinary taskforce invited no graphologists to join, cited no work by graphologists in its conference proceedings (Kao et al., 1986), and, despite demonstrations by members of the group that certain errors in children's writing predict later academic problems, did not even mention the possibility that handwriting might correlate with personality. Perusing graphologists' works, I have been unable to locate any who seem conversant with the published research of this highly relevant scientific organization.

3. One important alternative is "the Barnum Effect"—see Dean et al., and Karnes and Leonard, this volume.

4. See chapters by D. Beyerstein, Bowman, Dean et al., and Klimoski in this volume for discussions of the dangers of relying on this kind of "face validity" to justify psychological testing methods.

5.. Furnham and Gunter (1987) tested the ability of graphology to discern extroversion and introversion. They found that the results did not exceed chance expectancy. For a review of many other graphological failures to detect these most robust of all personality dimensions, see Furnham (1988).

6. In a related vein, it is a prevalent misconception that sexual orientation is discernible from body language (e.g., the stereotypes of the "swish" gay male or "butch" lesbian), but research shows that attributions based on this kind of folk-psychology are inaccurate most of the time (Krajeski 1981).

7. With respect to graphological claims, it is worth noting that therapists who work with these patients typically find no alterations in their handwriting

despite profound changes in personality. This underscores the fact, discussed above, that writing is a learned re-representation of speech. As such, its neural mechanisms are not innately intertwined with the emotional/motivational systems in the brain that affect personality and the emotional qualities of speech.

8. And would not this alteration of writing eliminate the undesirable behavior anyway? According to many highly touted "graphotherapists" (e.g., de Sainte Colombe 1972, pg. v): "You can correct your worst faults and strengthen your character by changing your handwriting."

9. By this, I do not mean to deny that many consistencies in behavior that might be called personality traits are, in fact, under control of regularities in the environment. But even these reactions are mediated by perceptual, motivational, memory, and motor systems of the brain.

10. Even if, say, "perseverance" could be said to have a unique brain locus, why would the property of "being a security risk" be any more likely than "vegetarianism" to have a brain area devoted to it and thus to command writing features all its own?

11. This sort of invariance is unlikely enough, but there is a further problem. How would this dubious "trait mechanism" in the brain "know" that it should become wired to neural programs for forming a particular letter, line arrangement, etc. in every writer of the Roman alphabet and attached to quite different features in programs for pictographic writing (which, as Paradis [1987] shows, are located in different brain sites) in those who happened to be born in another culture? Even within writers of Roman script, there are characteristic writing conventions in different countries and historical periods (Goldberg 1986). Obviously, these differences must be learned—otherwise, why would immigrants display the characteristics of their homelands and their children write with the national markings of their adopted lands? How could a group of hypothetical "personality neurons" unerringly sort out this myriad of demands, and why would they bother?

12. Though his own construal of the relationship between brain structure and mental endowment was fatally flawed, Gall deserves credit for promoting popular acceptance of the notion that individual differences are rooted in specializations of the brain. For equating mental states with brain states, Gall endured many attacks from religious leaders who assumed mind was a property of the immaterial soul.

13. I grant that one could conceive of a way in which numerous sites contributing to nonlocalized personality traits could be rigidly linked to equally dispersed writing mechanisms (if graphologists' accuracy were good enough to demand an explanation at the neural level). But such an arrangement would be far-fetched indeed. There is no independent evidence for it, and the required number and specificity of nerve tracts would be staggering. And we would still have to ask what purpose such a profligate use of genetic information and brain tissue would serve. Before graphologists invoke the brainwriting argument, they should at least show how such a cumbersome substrate could be laid down during brain development, long in advance of acquiring one of many possible learned programs for writing. If these dubious but necessary interconnections are not specified by

genetic instructions during early development, why would the brain bother to enshrine them later?

14. Once again, this demonstrates the necessity of "blind" measurements in situations where judgments of this sort are being made (see Dale Beyerstein's discussion in ch. 8).

15. Graphemes are the written equivalents of phonemes in spoken language.

16. To abandon the claim that writing unconsciously conforms to inner aspects of character would undermine the graphologists' contention that they can see through attempts to disguise writing because we inadvertently reveal these attributes in our script.

REFERENCES

Ben-Shakhar, G., M. Bar-Hillel, Y. Bilu, E. Ben-Abba, and A. Flug. 1986. "Can Graphology Predict Occupational Success? Two Empirical Studies and Some Methodological Ruminations." *J. of Applied Psychology* 714(4): pp. 645–653.

Beyerstein, B. L. 1990. "Brainscams: Neuromythologies of the New Age." *Intl. J. of Mental Health.* 19(3): pp. 27–36.

Brebner, J. 1985. "Personality Theory and Movement." In *Individual Differences in Movement,* edited by B. D. Kirkcaldy. Lancaster, U.K.: MTP Press.

Brody, N. 1988. *Personality: In Search of Individuality.* San Diego: Academic Press.

Buck, R. 1985. "Prime Theory: An Integrated View of Motivation and Emotion." *Psychological Review* 92(3): pp. 389–413.

Bunge, M. 1984. "What Is Pseudoscience?" *The Skeptical Inquirer* 9(1): pp. 36–46.

Carlson, N. R. 1986. *Physiology of Behavior.* 3rd ed. Boston: Allyn & Bacon.

Cloninger, R. 1987. "A Systematic Method for Clinical Description and Classification of Personality Variants." *Archives of General Psychiatry* 44: pp. 573–588.

Critchley, M. 1970. *Aphasiology and Other Aspects of Language.* London: Edward Arnold.

Damasio, A. R., and G. W. Van Hoesen. 1983. "Emotional Disturbances Associated with Focal Lesions of the Limbic Frontal Lobe." In *Neuropsychology of Human Emotions,* edited by K. Heilman and P. Satz. New York: Guilford Press.

Derryberry, D., and M. Rothbart. 1988. "Arousal, Affect, and Attention as Components of Temperament." *Journal of Personality and Social Psychology* 6: pp. 958–966.

de Sainte Colombe, P. 1972. *Grapho-therapeutics: The Pen and Pencil Therapy.* New York: Popular Library.

Dimond, S. 1979. "Symmetry and Asymmetry in the Vertebrate Brain." In *Brain, Behaviour and Evolution,* edited by D. Oakley and H. Plotkin, pp. 189–218.

Edelman, S., and T. Flash. 1987. "A Model of Handwriting." *Biological Cybernetics* 57: pp. 25–36.

Edwardes, M. 1977. *The Dark Side of History: Magic in the Making of Man.* New York: Stein and Day.

Ekman, P. 1980. *The Face of Man: Expressions of Universal Emotions in a New Guinea Village.* New York: Garland STPM Press.

Ellis, A. W. 1982. "Spelling and Writing (and Reading and Speaking)." In *Normality and Pathology in Cognitive Functions,* edited by A. W. Ellis. New York: Academic Press, pp. 113–146.

Furnham, A. 1988. "Write and Wrong: The Validity of Graphological Analysis." *The Skeptical Inquirer* 13: pp. 64–69.

Furnham, A., and B. Gunter. 1987. "Graphology and Personality: Another Failure to Validate Graphological Analyses." *Personality and Individual Differences* 8: pp. 433–435.

Gazzaniga, M. S. 1989. "Organization of the Human Brain." *Science* 245: pp. 947–952.

Goldberg, L. 1986. "Some Informal Explorations and Ruminations about Graphology." In *Scientific Aspects of Graphology,* edited by B. Nevo, pp. 281–293. Springfield, Ill.: Charles Thomas.

Gray, J. A. 1982. *The Neuropsychology of Anxiety: An Inquiry into the Functions of the Septo-hippocampal System.* Oxford: Clarendon.

Kagan, J., R. Reznick, and N. Sidman. 1988. "Biological Bases of Childhood Shyness." *Science* 240: pp. 167–171.

Kao, H. S. R., G. P. van Galen, and R. Hoosain. 1986. *Graphonomics: Contemporary Research in Handwriting.* North Holland: Elsevier.

Kirkcaldi, B. D., ed. 1985. *Individual Differences in Movement.* Lancaster, U.K.: MTP Press.

Krajeski, J. 1981. "Identifying Homosexuals by Mannerisms." *Medical Aspects of Human Sexuality* 7: p. 52.

Krech, D. 1962. "Cortical Localization of Function." In *Psychology in the Making; Histories of Selected Research Problems,* edited by L. Postman, pp. 31–72. New York: Knopf.

Leahey, T. H., and G. E. Leahey. 1983. *Psychology's Occult Doubles: Psychology and the Problem of Pseudoscience.* Chicago: Nelson-Hall.

Luria, A. 1970. *Traumatic Aphasia: Its Syndromes, Psychology, and Treatment.* The Hague: Mouton.

Mangan, G. L. 1982. *The Biology of Human Conduct: East-West Models of Temperament.* Oxford: Pergammon Press.

Matousek, R. 1987. *Graphology and the Phenomenon of Writing.* Self-published. 820 W. Maple St., Hinsdale, Ill. 60521.

Miller, L. 1983. "Neurobabble." *Psychology Today* (April): pp. 70–72.

Neter, E., and G. Ben-Shakhar. 1989. "The Predictive Validity of Graphological Inferences: A Meta-Analytic Approach." *Personality & Individual Differences* 10(7): pp. 737–745.

Oakley, K., ed. 1985. *Brain and Mind.* London: Methuen.

Oakley, K., and H. Plotkin, eds. 1979. *Brain, Behaviour and Evolution.* London: Methuen.

Paradis, M. 1987. "The Neurofunctional Modularity of Cognitive Skills: Evidence from Japanese Alexia and Polyglot Aphasia." In *Motor and Sensory Processes of Language,* edited by E. Keller and M. Gopnik. Hillsdale, N.J.: Lawrence Erlbaum, pp. 277–289.

Posner, M. I., S. E. Peterson, P. T. Fox, and M. E. Raichle. 1988. "Localization of Cognitive Operations in the Human Brain." *Science* 244: pp. 1627–1631.

Reed, V. A. 1986. *An Introduction to Children with Language Disorders.* New York: Macmillan.

Roeltgen, D. P., and K. M. Heilman. 1985. "Review of Agraphia and a Proposal for an Anatomically-Based Neuropsychological Model of Writing." *Applied Psycholinguistics* 6: pp. 205–230.

Rosner, B. 1974. "Recovery of Function and Localization of Function in Historical Perspective." In *Plasticity and Recovery of Function in the Central Nervous System,* edited by D. Stein, J. Rosen, and N. Butters. New York: Academic Press.

Sacks, O. 1985. *The Man Who Mistook His Wife for a Hat and Other Clinical Tales.* New York: Harper and Row.

Tucker, D., and P. Williamson. 1984. "Asymmetric Neural Control Systems in Human Self-Regulation." *Psychological Review* 91(2): pp. 185–215.

Valenstein, E. S. 1973. *Brain Control.* New York: Wiley.

Section Five

Representative Research by Graphologists and Critics

15

Evaluation of the Handwriting of Successful Women Through the Roman-Staempfli Psychogram

Patricia Wellingham-Jones

This study is included as an example of a recent attempt to validate the methods of a particular graphological school, as published in a refereed psychology journal. This chapter is a modified version of Dr. Wellingham-Jones's paper published originally in *Perceptual and Motor Skills* 69 (1989):999–1010.

As with the experiment published in chapter 16, the reader should carefully scrutinize the methodology. The hypothesis tested in this experiment is that successful women write differently from not-so-successful women. Thus, the prediction to be tested is: "[S]ignificant differences between the two groups would be found for six syndromes. . . ." (p. 425) Of course, if graphology is worth anything as a predictor of personality traits, we would expect that graphology by itself could predict these traits in advance of the graphologist knowing them. But this claim is not tested in the experiment reported here: "Several of the participants were known to the investigator, but not closely acquainted." (p. 427). Note that nothing is said in the paper about the graphologist reviewing the handwriting samples *blind*—that is, without knowing the identities of the writers. And we should never simply assume that this is the case, just because a properly controlled experiment would be done this way. Also, this study provides no evidence for the central claim of graphology that it is the features of the *handwriting* itself that provide the graphologist with the information used to construct the personality profile. Note on p. 425 that the subjects wrote about success or on random topics, but composed the passages themselves: "It was stressed that voluntary (noncopied or dictated [sic],[1] informal) writing was needed." Thus there was a wealth of cues—spelling, grammar, style—in the content of the writing, which could be used to determine the personal attributes quite irrespective of what the graphological theory in question has to say about the actual features of the handwriting. Those readers who are not trained in any version of graphology may wish to try an informal "experiment" to demonstrate how information supposedly irrelevant to graphology can provide information for guesses about a writer's personality: Read the two handwriting samples in Figure 2A and 2B on p. 428, without reading the captions below the samples. Guess which is the example of the successful, and which is the unsuccessful person's handwriting. Also, make a list of traits you associate with each writer. Now, read the captions below the samples. Look at the samples again, and try not to see the traits mentioned in these captions! (For another example of this *illusory correlation,* see note 9 of chapter 13 by Dean, Kelly, Saklofske, and Furnham).

Previous studies have shown that such personal qualities as adaptability, asseriveness, common sense, creativity, independence, intelligence, resourcefulness, leadership drive, and risk-taking are more highly developed in people who achieve their goals in life than in those who do not (see References for a selection of relevant articles, and Wellingham-Jones, 1989, for a complete bibliography). The present study was designed: (1) to discover what, if any differences exist between women who are considered successful and women from the population at large; and (2) to determine whether qualities that are important for achieving success are relevant to self-judgments of success. Personality characteristics of the participants in the study were determined by handwriting analysis, using the Roman-Staempfli Psychogram.

THE ROMAN-STAEMPFLI PSYCHOGRAM

The Roman-Staempfli Psychogram was developed in the 1950s by the European graphologist and psychologist Klara G. Roman and her associate, George Staempfli. The Psychogram was designed to show the functional interrelatedness of graphic characteristics, which may be interpreted as a profile of personality (Roman 1968: 516–524). The Psychogram provides a scoring system and a "map" of the personality. It allows the graphologist to make objective ratings and to integrate material in a meaningful way. The charting system assembles individual components of the handwriting sample into groups or syndromes of functionally related graphic indicators. Although significant in its own right, each syndrome is actually inseparable from every other syndrome, and each is subordinate to the overall pattern of the Psychogram. Roman referred to this pictorial rendering of a writer's personality as the "Profile-in-the-Circle."

The circular Psychogram is divided into segments which reflect the visual pattern of writing. They correspond to the symbolic use of space, and they are placed so as to be symbolically meaningful. Mental characteristics and the corresponding graphic indicators are in the upper half of the circle. Biologically rooted characteristics appear in the lower half of the circle. Introversion, the self, mother, past, and tension are represented in the left half of the circle. Extroversion, the world, father, future, and release appear in the right half of the circle. See Figure 1 on the next page.

Some indicators can be measured to a fairly refined degree by instruments such as the graphodyne, a device developed by Roman to measure pressure; some can only be matched to standard forms. Some indicators have accepted standards of judgment, such as 3 mm for the height of middle-zone letters in a writing sample. Indicators are rated on a scale of 1 to 5, from zero expression to average performance at 2.5, to over-expression at 5 (Roman 1956, 1961). These raw scores are doubled to obtain a total score.

The result is a synthesis of graphic indicators and their corresponding personality traits which yields a personality profile. The Psychogram depicts the personality of the writer as a dynamic whole. The qualities of achievement and success reported in the literature are also measured in the Psychogram both directly and indirectly.

HYPOTHESIS

It was hypothesized that the Psychogram scores of successful women would be significantly different from those of less successful women along some dimensions, but not all. In addition, it was predicted that significant differences between the two groups would be found for six syndromes: Intellect, Ego, Emotional Release, Inhibitions/Overcontrol, Repression, and Control, but not for two others: World Directedness and Libido-Vitality-Drives.

METHOD

There were two criteria for participation in this study. To be included in the successful group, a woman had to see herself as successful or she had to be considered successful by others. The expression "high achiever" was deliberately avoided, because a secondary object of the study was to learn what women themselves consider success to be. Dictionary definitions of personal success focus on outcomes such as the attainment of wealth, fame, or position. In this study, friends or family members nominated women

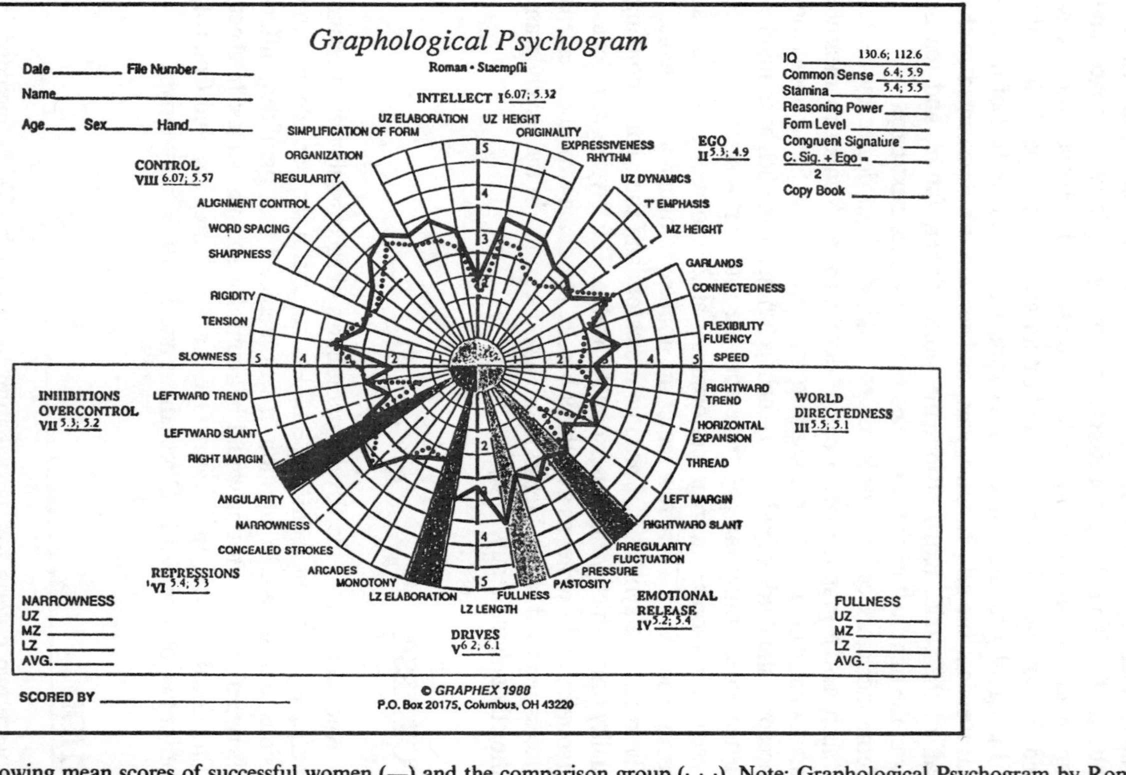

Fig. 1. Psychogram showing mean scores of successful women (—) and the comparison group (· · ·). Note: Graphological Psychogram by Roman-Staempfli. © 1988 by Graphex. Permission to reprint by Ellen Bowers, Ed.D. and Graphex. Where no dots appear, the mean scores of the two groups were the same.

for the successful group, because they had achieved recognition, competence, or power in their work or personal lives; because they were considered to function better than average; or because they seemed to handle their lives competently. When questioned, the women themselves agreed with these observations but said they felt that success was an inner glow of satisfaction with their lives rather than external evidence of achievement. Success meant different things to different women. For some, success meant raising healthy children, for others it was linked directly to job satisfaction, and for still others inner tranquility was the criterion. Only two women in the group volunteered for the project.

The women in the comparison group were chosen either because they did not see themselves as markedly successful, or because they were considered by others to lead lives of only average or less than average success. Some of the women in the comparison group were identified by acquaintances; others were the authors of handwriting samples in the author's collection or in the collections of other psychologists.

Handwriting samples were either volunteered by the participants or were collected from their acquaintances in response to requests at graphological meetings, in graphological journals, and in correspondence. The samples came from women located across North America and from all walks of life. The content of the samples varied; some women wrote about success, others on a variety of topics. It was stressed that informal, spontaneous (noncopied or dictated) writing was needed. Examples are shown in Figure 2A and 2B. Several of the participants were known to the investigator, but not closely acquainted. The investigator had not previously analyzed any of the writings.

Table 1 shows the demographic characteristics of the 70 successful and 42 comparison women. All were Caucasian, and ages for both groups ranged from 19 to 80 yrs. The women were married, divorced, or single. Economic status ranged from welfare recipient through moderate wealth. Some were employed; some were not. Some had children; some did not. Many in the successful group were well known and respected in their fields; others were not known outside their immediate area.

One graphologist (the author) analyzed the handwriting samples of all participants in the study using the Roman-Staempfli Psychogram and nine additional graphological indicators:

Personal pronoun I	t-bar	t-stem
Baseline garlands	ovals	e
Buckles (k,s,p)	j and LZ loops	f

The measurement criteria of the Roman-Staempfli Psychogram indicators are generally well known to graphologists. Other qualities, such as IQ, common sense, and stamina, are calculated by combining and averaging scores from

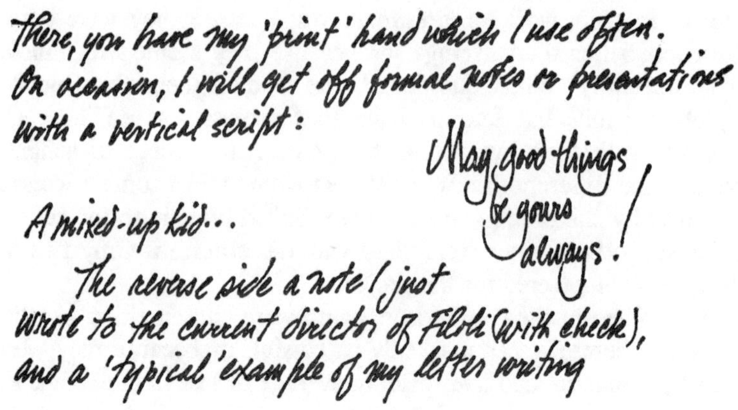

There, you have my 'print' hand which I use often.
On occasion, I will get off formal notes or presentations
with a vertical script:

May good things
be yours
always!

A mixed-up kid...

The reverse side a note I just
wrote to the current director of Filoli (with check),
and a 'typical' example of my letter writing

Fig. 2A. The handwriting of a 74-yr.-old woman reflects her artistic temperament (she is an active landscape designer, artist, and author) in its high form level, individuality, and aesthetic placement on the page. The rhythmic writing swings with health, vigor, and enthusiasm, hallmarks of the successful woman.

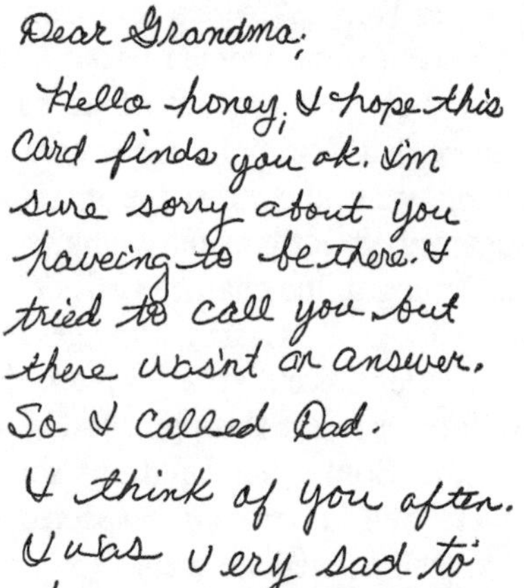

Dear Grandma,
Hello honey; I hope this
Card finds you ok. I'm
sure sorry about you
haveing to be there. I
tried to call you but
there wasn't an answer.
So I called Dad.
I think of you often.
I was very sad to
hear you were there.
I'll write you Very
often. and try to Visit

Fig. 2B. The writing of an unhappy and insecure 30-yr.-old woman accurately depicts her inner fears and tension in angular forms, leftward tendencies, jerky rhythm, and variable spacing. Her strong dependency needs are seen in right slant, excessively full and looped ovals, exaggerated but weak personal pronoun I, and the clinging to the left margin with some long initial strokes. She has a history of failed relationships and alcohol.

TABLE 1

DEMOGRAPHIC CHARACTERISTICS OF 70 WOMEN IN SUCCESS GROUP AND 42 IN COMPARISON GROUP

Characteristic		Success	Comparison
Age, yr.	18—19	1	0
	20—29	1	6
	30—39	19	9
	40—49	13	11
	50—59	15	7
	60—69	15	4
	70—79	3	4
	80 and over	2	0
	Unknown	0	1
Marital Status	Married	46	20
	Single	12	13
	Divorced	7	4
	Unknown	5	5
Children	Have children	42	26
	Do not have children	16	9
	Unknown	12	7
Handedness	Right	61	30
	Left	4	2
	Unknown	5	10:
Occupation	Artist	5	0
	Banker	1	2
	Editor	2	0
	Educator	6	1
	Executive	3	0
	Graphologist	16	1
	Health	2	2
	Homemaker	7	9
	Horticulturist	2	2
	Librarian	0	2
	Manager	4	0
	Own Business	11	0
	Retired	0	1
	Student	1	0
	TV personality	2	0

TABLE 1 (CONTINUED)

DEMOGRAPHIC CHARACTERISTICS OF 70 WOMEN IN SUCCESS GROUP AND 42 IN COMPARISON GROUP

	Characteristic	Success	Comparison
Occupation	Welfare recipient	0	4
	Worker	3	12
	Writer	5	0
	Unknown	0	6

the Psychogram. The nine additional indicators were adapted from the graphometric system of graphology and were graded for width, height, and exaggeration of form on a 5-point scale. Data were analyzed statistically using the one-way analysis of variance program in the Statistical Package for the Social Sciences.[2]

RESULTS

The data presented in Tables 2 and 3 indicate that of the 38 graphological indicators on which successful and less successful women were expected to differ, significant differences were found for 24 indicators. More predictions were confirmed for those indicators on which successful women were expected to score *higher* than the comparison group (22 of 27, or 81.5%) than for those indicators on which they were expected to score *lower* (2 of 11, or 18.2%). Of the 14 indicators for which no significant differences were expected, the hypothesis was confirmed in 10 cases (71.4%; see Table 4). In the remaining four cases, successful women scored higher than the less successful women.

Of the six syndromes (clusters of graphological indicators) on which the two groups of women were expected to be significantly different, only three predictions were confirmed: Intellect, Ego, and Control. On all three of these syndromes, successful women scored higher than the women in the comparison group (see Table 5). For the other three syndromes (Emotional Release, Inhibitions, and Repressions), there were no differences between the groups. Of the two syndromes on which successful and less successful women were expected not to differ, one (Libido-Vitality-Drive) was confirmed; the other (World-Directedness) was not. In the latter case, successful women again scored higher than the less successful women.

TABLE 2

SCORES PREDICTED TO BE SIGNIFICANTLY HIGHER FOR THE SUCCESSFUL GROUP THAN FOR THE COMPARISON GROUP

Graphological Indicator	Success		Comparison		F
	M	SD	M	SD	
Organization	6.5	.94	6.0	1.15	6.98†
Simplification	6.6	.97	5.9	1.09	13.98†
Originality	6.7	.87	5.9	.73	26.67†
Expressiveness	6.7	.93	5.8	1.11	18.81†
Rhythm	6.1	1.01	4.6	1.06	57.56†
Upper Zone Dynamics	5.6	.79	4.6	.76	39.81†
"I" Emphasis	5.4	.72	4.9	.76	10.49†
Flexibility/Fluency	6.1	1.29	4.8	1.21	27.57†
Right Trend	5.6	1.12	5.1	1.22	4.61*
Speed	5.3	.83	4.7	1.00	10.49†
Pressure	5.4	.77	5.6	.69	2.81
Fullness	7.1	1.10	7.1	1.16	.01
Angularity	6.2	1.08	5.6	1.10	8.23†
Sharpness	5.3	.59	5.0	.81	5.39*‡
Word Spacing	5.5	.72	5.1	.97	6.55†
Alignment Control	6.5	.90	5.8	1.13	13.28†
Regularity	7.0	1.14	6.4	1.61	5.14*‡
IQ	130.6	11.31	112.6	8.82	77.83†
Common Sense	6.4	.61	5.8	.72	17.54†
Stamina	5.4	.76	5.5	.96	.03
PPI	5.6	1.18	5.1	1.12	5.83*
t-bar	6.2	1.27	5.4	1.58	8.98†
t-stem	6.2	.88	5.6	.94	10.93†
f	6.4	1.09	5.8	1.26	6.88†
j	6.9	1.74	6.6	1.96	.62
e	5.3	.97	4.7	1.04	8.77†
Ovals	5.5	1.09	5.6	1.15	.14

*$p < .05$.
†$p \leq .01$.
‡Violated homogeneity of variance assumption although considered reportable.

TABLE 3

SCORES PREDICTED TO BE SIGNIFICANTLY LOWER FOR THE SUCCESSFUL GROUP THAN FOR THE COMPARISON GROUP

Graphological Indicator	Success		Comparison		F
	M	SD	M	SD	
Irregularity, Fluctuation	5.0	1.13	5.3	1.44	1.60
Narrowness	6.4	1.21	6.4	1.30	.03
Monotony	4.6	.83	5.0	1.29	3.64
Right Margin	5.3	1.53	5.3	2.05	.01
Left Slant	4.0	2.62	2.8	2.95	4.95*
Slowness	4.8	.83	5.3	1.05	8.13†
Tension	6.3	.88	6.4	.79	.27
Rigidity	5.3	.75	5.5	.92	2.31
Left Trend	5.9	1.19	5.8	1.34	.56
Buckles	5.4	1.09	5.0	1.45	2.37
Baseline	5.2	.97	5.1	.97	.33

$^*p < .05$ $^\dagger p < .01$.

TABLE 4

SCORES PREDICTED TO SHOW NO SIGNIFICANT DIFFERENCES BETWEEN THE SUCCESSFUL GROUP AND THE COMPARISON GROUP

Graphological Indicator	Success		Comparison		F
	M	SD	M	SD	
Upper Zone Elaboration	5.9	.64	5.4	.77	13.51†
Upper Zone Height	3.9	1.21	3.6	1.53	1.08
Middle Zone Height	5.0	1.40	5.2	1.66	.31
Garlands	6.7	.88	6.9	1.16	1.76
Connectedness	5.1	1.58	5.2	1.79	.01
Horizontal Expansion	5.2	1.17	5.1	1.54	.00
Thread	6.0	1.13	5.3	1.35	7.96†
Left Margin	4.5	1.98	3.7	1.61	4.49*
Right Slant	5.2	2.27	5.4	2.66	.23
Pastosity	5.1	.62	5.1	.84	.00
Lower Zone Length	5.4	1.40	5.3	1.93	.21
Lower Zone Elaboration	6.0	.88	5.9	1.14	.33

TABLE 4 (CONTINUED)

SCORES PREDICTED TO SHOW NO SIGNIFICANT DIFFERENCES BETWEEN THE SUCCESSFUL GROUP AND THE COMPARISON GROUP

Graphological Indicator	Success		Comparison		F
	M	SD	M	SD	
Arcades	4.7	.75	4.5	.77	3.82*
Concealed	5.0	.58	5.2	.55	1.78

$^{*}p < .05$.
$^{\dagger}p \leq .01$.

TABLE 5

MEAN SCORES OF GROUPS BY SYNDROME

Syndrome	Success		Comparison		F
	M	SD	M	SD	
Control	6.1	.62	5.6	.87	12.74†
Ego	5.3	.65	4.9	.53	14.42†
Emotional Release	5.2	.60	5.4	.62	2.15
Inhibitions	5.3	.70	5.2	.90	.41
Intellect	6.1	.46	5.3	.40	75.53†
Repressions	5.4	.37	5.3	.41	1.20
Libido-Vitality-Drive	6.2	.85	6.1	1.17	.22
World-directedness	5.5	.71	5.1	.78	6.43†

$^{*}p < .05$.
$^{\dagger}p \leq .01$.

The Roman-Staempfli Psychogram shown in Figure 1 presents the mean scores of both groups of women.

DISCUSSION

The results of this study suggest that the qualities found by other investigators to be important in the perceived achievement of success are indeed expressed in the writing samples of highly achieving women and that they can be measured by the Psychogram plus other graphological indicators. Scores for such qualities as originality, expressiveness, rhythm, flexibility, organization, and simplification of form were significantly higher in the writings of the successful than of the less-successful women. Successful women also showed less rigidity and slowness. Other characteristics such as pastosity, fullness, lower zone length, and narrowness were shared by both groups (see Figure 1).

The four graphological indicators which were expected to be similar for the two groups but which were actually different were: (a) The successful group used far more personal flourishes and dynamics (upper zone elaboration). (b) Signs of diplomacy and ability to handle awkward situations (thread) were more evident for the successful group. (c) Although both groups scored lower than average on arcades (a dignified and self-protective connecting stroke), the comparison group used this form less often than the successful group. (d) Both groups scored lower than average on width of left margin, indicating a certain need for security or caution before starting a project, but hesitancy to proceed was somewhat greater in the comparison group than in the successful group.

There were 14 indicators for which the predicted differences between the groups were not confirmed. These findings indicate that personality or behavioral qualities such as energy and stamina (pressure and lower zone length), and tension and self-protectiveness (narrowness, tension, left trend) are observed in equal degree in both groups. However the reasons for these similarities may be quite different for the two groups of women (e.g., socioeconomic pressures, self-esteem needs, achievement motivation).

In addition, the data identify areas of personality functioning that do not seem to be associated with perceived success or failure; at least, not as indicated by these women. Personality characteristics which both groups shared include physical and psychic energy, tension, rigidity, defenses against fears, traditional female amiability and receptiveness, need for feedback, curiosity, and emotional release.

The results of this study suggest that achievement or success can be inferred fairly easily from measures used in graphological analysis. Specific behavioral traits, such as assertiveness, decisiveness, and risk-taking, are associated with perceived success, and they are readily apparent in handwriting samples. The actual feelings of success, however, are more subtle, and they are not necessarily accompanied by those outward signs which others consider as indicative of achievement. Further, these perceptions of success and well-being are not independent of life's fears and problems. For successful women, these fears and problems may be overridden by the drive to push ahead, whereas low-achieving women (who nonetheless may view themselves as relatively successful) may find life's challenges more problematic.

This study was subject to several limitations that follow-up studies should seek to avoid. First, many of the handwriting samples included signatures. Although signatures are important for complete analyses, they may introduce bias into analyses conducted for research purposes, and they should be omitted or hidden until the analyses have been completed. Second, in order to collect a sufficiently large number of handwriting samples, it was necessary to admit to the study women who were known to the graphologist. The graphologist also knew whether the samples came from women in the successful or the comparison group. Future studies should use blind scoring of handwriting samples; that is, scoring without knowledge of the group membership of the writer. And, finally, the writing samples were scored by only one graphologist, because there are few research-trained graphologists in the United States who can spend the many hours required for scoring.

This study suggests intriguing possibilities. It indicates that personality and behavioral characterisitics associated with achievement and success can be identified by properly trained graphologists and that other aspects of personality functioning can be similarly detected. Such information could be used in psychological counseling, personnel profiles, vocational counseling, assessment, monitoring of behavior, and in other areas where knowledge of perceived success would be useful.

NOTES

1. Meaning "not copied and not dictated."—Eds.

2. Fisher's exact method was used to address whether agreement with the predictions was as a result of chance or not. Because the test is specifically designed for a small number of comparisons and this study involved many, the results were inconclusive. Jeanette Alosi's help in the statistical analysis is gratefully acknowledged.

16

Graphoanalytic and Psychometric Personality Profiles: Validity and Barnum Effects

Edward W. Karnes and S. David Leonard

Chapter 16 presents two experiments prompted by the senior author's curiosity about a news report concerning several prominent local citizens who expressed great satisfaction with a graphoanalyst's personality reading based on their handwriting. Knowing that the so-called "Barnum Effect" can produce a strong but illusory sense of accuracy in such readings (see also Bowman, chapter 10, and Dean et al., chapter 13) he suspected that this might have been responsible for the graphoanalyst's rave reviews. From this conjecture came several predictions discussed in this chapter. First, if graphologists can depict personality accurately as they claim, clients should be able to exceed chance in correctly selecting their own character sketch from an anonymous batch of such analyses. Second, people who know these clients well should also be able to identify their friends' profiles in a similar "blind" test. Third, it is reasonable to assume that if graphologists' descriptions are in fact specific to the individuals for whom they were done, they should be less acceptable as personality portrayals if given to randomly selected individuals than intentionally vague, global sketches that are known to be acceptable to virtually everyone.

In Experiment One, Karnes and Leonard compare their subjects' success rates in identifying their own graphological profiles with those when they tried to identify their own profiles derived from two standard psychological tests. The authors also compare subjects' confidence in the accuracy of their identifications when they make correct as opposed to incorrect identifications.

In Experiment Two, the authors ask whether graphological profiles contain enough unique information about the client that they would not serve as equally good descriptors for anyone else. They compare subjects' ratings of applicability to themselves when they receive a randomly selected personality sketch from one of four different sources. One group received standard psychometric profiles that had been prepared for someone else, other groups received graphoanalytic profiles that were done for people in Experiment One or for the people in the Denver newspaper "test," and the remainder received vague "Barnum-type" personality descriptions. The group given the profiles derived from valid psychological tests rated them the poorest match with themselves (because they contained specific descriptions that apply to another individual), whereas those who received the graphoanalytic and Barnum-type profiles rated them much more accurate descriptions of their own personality (because of their widely applicable generality). In fact, the graphoanalytic profiles proved just as universally acceptable as the Barnum sketches. This was true whether or not the subjects thought the sketch they had just read was their own or that it had been intended for someone else. Interpretations of these findings are presented along with a discussion of their implications for use of graphology as a diagnostic or job placement tool. (cf. Klimoski, chapter 11).

As with Wellingham-Jones' study in chapter 15, the reader is encouraged not only to examine the authors' conclusions, but also to pay close attention to the methodological details of the experiments (see Dale Beyerstein's evaluative criteria in chapter 8 and Geoffrey Dean's in chapter 12). A single study practically never settles a scientific controversy and since the two studies in Section Five of this book come to different conclusions about the value of graphology, the reader will have to decide which carries the greater weight. Note that Wellingham-Jones was testing the hypothesis that graphologists can discern personality traits from script, whereas Karnes and Leonard were testing the aforementioned hypotheses which could account for customer satisfaction with graphology even though it cannot pass properly controlled tests. Because support for Karnes and Leonard's hypotheses would cast doubt on Wellingham-Jones' conclusions, the reader must examine each chapter on its own merits and in light of how it is supported or contradicted by research reviewed elsewhere in this book. One's provisional decision, pending further research, should be based on a number of methodological considerations.

First, do the statistical procedures meet the criteria listed by Geoffrey Dean in chapter 12? Karnes and Leonard used a relatively small sample size of nine subjects in their first experiment and found that people could not exceed chance in identifying their own or their acquaintances' graphological profiles. Subjects did better in identifying their own psychometric profiles, but this difference did not quite reach statistical significance. While the direction of this result is consistent with many similar studies that did reach statistical significance, the experiment should be replicated with a larger group of subjects before definitive conclusions can be drawn. However, testing with a large group of subjects whether or not close colleagues can recognize each other's profiles would present another problem. On the one hand, in order to find subjects who satisfy the "familiarity" criteria for inclusion in the test, the sample size cannot be very large (how many people do you know that intimately?) But, on the other hand, statisticians would prefer the sample size to be much larger. Karnes and Leonard discuss ways around this problem for future research. Their second experiment has the sort of sample size recommended by Dean in chapter 12 and provides much more telling evidence against graphology.

Other elements to compare (where applicable) in weighing the conclusions of chapter 16 against those of chapter 15 are the following. How were the key variables in the experiment chosen and operationalized? How were the subjects, the graphologists, the psychometric measures, and the handwriting samples selected? What steps were taken to prevent "leaking" to the graphologist relevant information other than what might be contained in the scripts themselves? (E.g., were the ratings done "blind" and was the evaluated material stripped of all useful biographical cues?) How was the criterion of accuracy determined for the different procedures being evaluated? What controls were in place to minimize the effects of unintentional bias on the part of the experimenter and/or subjects?

In choosing sides in the graphology debate, it is insufficient merely to tally up the "box score" of papers reporting positive versus negative results. As Dean (chapter 12) emphasizes, the methodological soundness of each study must be evaluated first to see if it can count as evidence at all.

INTRODUCTION

Handwriting analysis is once again the subject of public controversy because an increasing number of businesses have begun to consult graphologists in personnel matters. This use of graphology has been particularly offensive to civil libertarians who see it as an evasion of laws that have restricted the use of invalid tests in the workplace. After successfully opposing the use of polygraphs on the grounds of unreliability, opponents see "lie detectors" being replaced by an assessment technique with even less scientific credibility, graphology.

As the critics in this volume show, the overwhelming majority of scientific experts consider graphology unproven; e.g., few reputable texts in the field of psychological measurement even mention graphology, let alone accept it as a valid science. Nonetheless, many non-scientists working in personnel selection feel that graphology has demonstrated its worth in everyday settings. Frequently, this conviction is based on a graphological sketch of the personnel manager that seemed "amazingly accurate." Sometimes it also stems from satisfaction with employees hired on the recommendation of a graphologist. Althoughs anecdotes of this sort may be true as far as they go, they do not constitute scientifically acceptable evidence for the validity of graphology. To see why they cannot count, we must consider how the rules for obtaining and evaluating data in scientific disciplines differ from those of everyday decision making.

The scientific method evolved to help discern real from apparent relationships in the world. It accomplishes this by ensuring that samples to be studied are representative, observations are systematic, and possible alternative causes for the phenomena under study are eliminated. It demands that putative effects be repeatable under controlled conditions. These rules are necessary in order to counter our strong tendency to perceive illusory relationships in complex situations, simply because we wish or expect them to be there. The scientific method also allows us to distinguish causality from mere coincidence. While it cannot claim infallibility, it is certainly the most reliable way of gaining knowledge we have, and it has the additional advantage of being self-correcting over time. The reader may wish to pursue these issues further by consulting Dale Beyerstein's discussion in chapter 8.

Proponents of graphology (see Section Two, this volume) assert that their methods are sufficiently like those of psychology, particularly in the area of projective testing, that graphology deserves to be considered a branch of psychology. The critics counter that while the two disciplines bear certain superficial similarities, graphology is essentially a pseudoscience. They base this on the magical underpinnings of handwriting analysis (see chapters 2, 3, and 9), the failure to produce a plausible theory of graphology (see chapters 8, 9, and 14), and, above all, the shortage of methodologically sound evidence for its validity (see Section Four of this volume).

A PRIORI DOUBTFULNESS OF GRAPHOLOGY

There are many aspects of graphology that strike critics as implausible from the outset. These doubts have supplied the impetus to seek alternate explanations for graphologists' apparent successes (e.g., the Barnum Effect discussed below). One of these sore points is the lack of a credible theory to account for the posited correspondences between writing and personality. Evaluating graphological claims is made difficult by this lack of a unified theoretical position and by the frequent factional disputes over meanings of various signs and the relative merits of interpreting individual components of letters to specific traits versus relying on the graphologist's "holistic" impressions. Thus a study demonstrating the inadequacy of one type of graphology is often endorsed by rival schools who still claim that their own brand of analysis would have passed.

The "Brainwriting" Rationale. The graphologists' main attempt at theorizing has been the so-called "brainwriting hypothesis." This is the assumption that because personality and writing are both controlled by the brain, writing necessarily reveals character. As Barry Beyerstein points out in chapter 14, no competent neurophysiologist would deny that both writing and personality depend on brain functions. But this is no different from any other human activities. If we carry the "brainwriting" argument to its logical conclusion, we might just as reasonably claim to read details of someone's character from the way he or she walks down the street. Certainly, different people have recognizable ways of walking (see next paragraph). Should we therefore refer to walking as "brainstepping"? The mere fact that the brain controls writing movements offers no guarantee that writing is a valid indicator of personality. The burden of proof that it is rests with the graphologists, whose evidence to date has been quite unconvincing.

The "Uniqueness" Argument. Graphologists also trade on the undeniable individuality of a person's script by assuming that the uniqueness of both writing and personality implies some sort of correspondence between the two (see Nickell, chapter 4). Appealing though this leap of faith may be, readers with a historical bent will recall the failures of several other systems that attempted to read character from equally unique attributes; e.g., Caesar Lombroso (1831–1901) thought he could recognize criminal tendencies from distinctive facial features. Modern criminologists and psychologists have completely abandoned Lombroso's theories because research found that facial features, despite their uniqueness, are useless as predictors of character. Extending our earlier walking analogy to the graphologists' "uniqueness" argument, consider the following. In his graduate student days, one of the authors used to surprise fellow students by addressing them by name before they entered his field of view. He was able to recognize them from the distinctive sounds of their gait as they traversed the hallway leading to his office. This obviously unique behavior provided no basis for inferring the walker's honesty, piety, or conscientiousness, however.

"You're as bad as we are." Another ploy used by graphologists to deflect attacks is to concede that their procedures lack empirical support but to argue that they are no worse than those of orthodox psychologists and psychiatrists. This is misleading because there are degrees of wrongness. To admit that the diagnostic methods of psychology and psychiatry are not perfect provides no support for graphology, which must stand or fall on its own merits.[1] The claims of psychologists and psychiatrists to discern traits and syndromes should be, and are, rigorously tested (see chapters 10, 11, and 12). Their professional journals are replete with experiments

providing evidence for and against various theories and practices. As a result, many once-popular tests in psychology and psychiatry have been abandoned and others continue to undergo extensive modification. Despite the fact that some questionable methods have not yet been abandoned by all mainstream practitioners, this does not abrogate the requirement for psychological techniques to prove their effectiveness empirically. As pointed out in chapter 9, it is the fact that graphologists have virtually never abandoned any of their oldest precepts that makes the field most suspect. Sciences progress, pseudosciences remain stagnant.

"We play by different rules." When all else fails, graphologists often fall back on the argument that empirical verification is unnecessary because graphology is an art rather than a science. If graphology were only a parlor game like a ouija board, or a harmless foible like belief in the Easter Bunny, this argument could be tolerated, but it is unacceptable for several reasons. First, whether it be art or science, graphology makes claims about relationships in the world and is therefore required to back them up with evidence. Second, graphologists sell their services to the public for purposes that seriously affect people's happiness and welfare. Citizens whose livelihoods or reputations are at stake have a right to demand proof of competence from any professional who can stigmatize them in this way. And finally, those who pay for graphologists' services have the right to know that they are not being victimized by flim-flam artists or by sincere but deluded pseudoscientists. What standards could reasonably decide these issues, other than those of empirical validation?

Graphologists also alienate the scientific community with their ad hominem responses to criticism, such as branding critics as narrow minded or claiming that detractors are simply protecting their own turf. In chapter 8, Dale Beyerstein deals with such failures to answer the substance of principled criticisms. The scientists' rejoinder is that until graphologists meet conventional standards of proof, they have no right to demand acceptance by the scientific community—the burden of proof is always with the claimant.

"Caveat emptor." It is odd that people who have grown wary of financial institutions that promise unbelievable returns often fail to extend this skepticism to the sphere of psychological and medical services. Here, as elsewhere, the maxim of the consumer advocate David Horowitz applies: "If it sounds too good to be true, it probably is." The more a technique promises, the closer it should be scrutinzed, and the extravagance of graphologists' claims puts them squarely in this category. E.g., their ads proclaim, "It opens up the entire personality like an X-ray photograph," and "It is a technique to scrutinize the unconscious." Such claims are vague but seem to promise a great deal. Other statements such as the one that eight to ten lines of writing can reveal someone's mental abilities, business

aptitude, personal fears and foibles, moral shortcomings, and how well he or she will interact with the boss are more precise but are presented without even the standard of proof one would normally demand of a used car salesman. Such grandiose claims immediately arouse suspicion in those who have seen similarly overblown assertions fail consistently in the past.

CONCERNS FROM SCIENTIFIC TEST DEVELOPERS

Chapters 10, 11, and 12 of this volume specify the requirements for a scientifically valid psychological test, so our treatment here can be brief. When the distribution of scores on a test that claims to predict how well people will perform on some task (called "the criterion") turns out to correlate well with their eventual performance on that task, we say the test has demonstrated validity. It can thenceforth be used in good conscience, where applicable, to help decide among competing job candidates, provide marital advice, make parole decisions, etc. But assessing the validity of a test is much more complicated than it may seem at first glance.

Let us assume, for instance, that we are to hire six persons from a pool of twenty-four applicants. Suppose that we hire the six highest scorers on Test *Z* and find that they perform well on the job. Does this prove that Test *Z* is a good selection device (i.e., is a valid predictor of criterion performance)? To see why the foregoing scenario provides necessary but not sufficient grounds for approving the test, we must also consider the possibilities of "the road not taken." In other words, how would the rejected applicants have performed, had they been given the opportunity? Cost considerations usually preclude such a test in the corporate world, but in the development stage that should precede any application of a test in the real world, this kind of evaluation is absolutely necessary. Without such evidence, simple satisfaction with a test on the part of a personnel manager is no proof of its validity. The following example shows why.

The matrices of Table 1 provide a range of possible results for all 24 applicants had they been hired for a trial period. Note that the outcomes depicted in matrices *a*, *b*, *c*, and *d* would provide the same evidence if only the six high-scoring individuals were hired. Clearly, the usefulness of Test *Z* also depends on how the low scorers perform, not just on how well the high scorers do. Yet, if only the latter are hired, as is typically the case when companies consult graphologists, we will never know if the test tells us anything about the adequacy of the applicants for the job. As Dean et al. emphasize in chapter 13, it is essential in determining the presence or the absence of a relationship that we note the cases of non-occurrence as well as cases of occurrence. It is at this stage of basic research, prior to any application, where graphologists have failed to prove their worth.

Table 1

Possible Matrices of Number of Successful Cases When Hiring Individuals Scoring High and Low on "Test Z"

	Job Performance							
	Scenario a.		Scenario b.		Scenario c.		Scenario d.	
Test Scores	Good	Poor	Good	Poor	Good	Poor	Good	Poor
High	6	0	6	0	6	0	6	0
Low	18	0	15	3	9	9	0	18

Note that for the cases in matrix *b* of Table 1, a very minor change in the performance of the high scorers would make the probability of success the same for high and low scorers. That is, if one of the high scorers performed less well on the job, the ratios of good to poor among both high and low scorers would be identical. Thus there would be serious doubts about the relationship of scores on Test *Z* to performance on the job. Even in set *c*, a numerically small change in performance would result in questions about the validity of the test. This raises the question of how it is possible to determine whether or not the results of an experiment truly represent the state of the world.

Hypothesis Testing. In most cases where one is conducting a formal test to decide whether a relationship exists or not, one begins with two opposing hypotheses. One is that the relationship exists (i.e., some non-random factor is operating to produce the observed results); the alternative, or "null hypothesis," is that it does not exist (i.e., the observed distribution of scores is most likely due to random variation). When the data have been collected, a statistic is calculated that will tell the researcher the probability that the observed result would have occurred if nothing but chance were operating. For instance, suppose a graphologist selects two groups of people, one of which she claims are good leaders and the other poor leaders. If we are evaluating the claim that the graphologist can make such distinctions, we would state the alternative hypotheses as follows: "The differences between these groups on the criterion (an accepted indicator of leadership) are large enough to be unlikely to be due to chance," versus the null hypothesis that "the observed differences are due to nothing more than chance variations." If we fail to reject the null hypothesis, we are, in effect, saying that the observed differences are sufficiently likely to have occurred by chance that it is reasonable to conclude that the graphologist has failed to substantiate her claim. By convention, scientists reject the null hypothesis if the statistical test determines that the observed differences between groups would occur by chance alone only five times out of a hundred. Details of the technique and rationale for this procedure are available in any statistics text (e.g., Keppel 1991).

The Need for Control Groups. Even if a statistical test provided satisfactory evidence that the graphologist had exceeded chance in detecting some trait, that by itself would not prove that his success was due to his graphological judgment rather than some other way of gaining information about the subjects. E.g., were there useful clues in the contents of the handwriting samples or in the background data supplied? This underscores the need for something else that distinguishes a formal test from anecdotal observations—the principle of scientific control. If we wish to conclude that variable *X* is the cause of effect *Y*, we must rule out (or "control for," as a scientist would say) other possible variables that could have produced it. In the case of graphology, we would also need to demonstrate that subjects' acceptance of graphological readings is due to their accuracy and precision rather than to something else, such as the Barnum Effect, discussed below. It was this lack of such controls in a local newspaper's informal test of a graphologist that prompted us to undertake the experiments presented later in this chapter.

Procedures like the foregoing are essential before conceding the validity of any psychological measurement technique and that is why every job candidate should demand that any selection test he or she is subjected to can pass these criteria. As Geoffrey Dean's review in chapter 12 clearly shows, this is something graphology cannot do.

THE BARNUM EFFECT

When personnel managers are informed of graphology's numerous failures on well-controlled validity tests, they frequently discount such criticisms because the graphologist's character sketch seemed "amazingly correct and precise." These executives might be less impressed with this seeming accuracy if they were aware that a group of randomly selected people, given the same description, would find it equally applicable to themselves. Indeed, this has been demonstrated repeatedly with groups ranging from college students (Forer 1949) to personnel managers (Stagner 1955). The subtle psychological processes that underlie this so-called "Barnum Effect" are discussed by Dean and his co-authors in chapter 13. It is also known in the psychological literature as the "subjective validation effect" or the "personal validation effect."

The term "Barnum Effect" was popularized by Paul Meehl (1950) who reminded fellow psychologists that conventional personality measures also benefit from these spurious impressions of validity and ought not to be accepted unless they can pass tests that control for subjective validation. Meehl warned against tests that seem accurate merely because their assertions are vague enough (despite their seemingly precise language) that they invite the client to unconsciously "fill in the gaps." This is easy for them to do because such assertions are true, in some form, of most people in the population. This is the same phenomenon that contributes illusory accuracy to pronouncements of fortune tellers, astrologers, and mediums and forms the basis of a very effective form of stage magic called "Cold Reading" (Hyman 1977).[2]

One of the first demonstrations of the compelling nature of subjective validation was provided by Forer (1949) who told student volunteers that the personality description they received had been derived from a graphological analysis of a sample of their writing. Though they all received the same intentionally vague, internally contradictory sketch, there was overwhelming agreement that it was remarkably accurate. Forer cautioned that:

> The positive results obtained from personal validation can easily lull a test analyst or a therapist into a false sense of security which bolsters his conviction in the essential rightness of his philosophy or his diagnostic prowess. . . . A great danger arises when the confirmation of a prediction is extended uncritically to the instrument or conceptual system or person making the prediction. Such uncritical extension occurs too frequently in the clinical field. (p. 118)

Since Forer demonstrated the power of subjective validation, many studies have examined the factors that contribute to this willingness to accept general statements as though they were specific, revealing depictions of ourselves (see reviews by Snyder et al. 1977, Dickson and Kelly 1985; and by Dean et al., chapter 13, this volume). The effect is so robust that subjects will even concede the accuracy of a putative test whose items have no obvious connection to personality. E.g., Delprato's (1975) subjects were merely required to circle certain digits in a long list. They were then given a general character description, allegedly derived from their performance, and asked to rate the whole procedure as a means of testing personality. Sixty percent of the subjects rated it as good or excellent. This result is so easy to obtain that one of the present authors often uses this procedure as a class demonstration of the subjective validation effect.

Investigators such as Greene (1977) have noted that the uniformly high accuracy ratings in demonstrations like the foregoing could be because the statements may indeed be correct for the individuals concerned. But even if its descriptions do fit a person quite well, this does not necessarily indicate that graphology (or any other insufficiently validated technique) is an acceptable way to measure personality, select people for specific jobs, or recommend them as mates. The reason is that such tests cannot *differentiate* among individuals. As Forer (1949) reminds us, ". . . a universally valid statement is a description of a cultural group rather than a personal psychological datum."

Many studies (e.g., O'Dell 1972) have found that people consider Barnum-type generalities to be better descriptions of themselves than more realistic profiles derived from well-validated scales that *do* measure specific traits. Merrens and Richards (1970) suggested that this is so because subjects may see discrepancies between specific statements about their traits and their self-perceptions, whereas the global statements arouse no such dissonance.

The ease with which intelligent, educated people can be misled by the Barnum Effect makes it clear why personal testimonials, such as those relied upon extensively by graphologists, are worthless as scientific evidence. Along with the increasing media interest in graphology, there has been, for the most part, a deplorable lack of critical analysis of its claims. In the city of Denver alone, articles and programs have uncritically published the following claims by advocates of the school of handwriting analysis known as Graphoanalysis:[3]

- Personnel officers in major companies use graphology in hiring and promotion decisions. According to the *Wall Street Journal,* the following companies have used handwriting analysis: New England Mutual Life Insurance Co., the New York Branch of the Equitable Life Assurance Co., Sears Roebuck and Co., U.S. Steel, and the Bendix Corporation.

- The police use graphology in criminal investigations (but see Nickel's comments on this in chapter 4).

- Graphology is also used extensively elsewhere in the legal system (see chapters 4, 9, and 17, this volume). E.g., judges use it in sentencing decisions and in regard to educational and vocational matters for juvenile offenders. Lawyers use it to help select jurors and evaluate the criminal mind. Graphologists have also been consulted in parole decisions.

- The U.S. Government hired a Denver graphoanalyst to provide personality profiles in regard to the Watergate scandal.

- Graphotherapy (changing one's handwriting style) effectively corrects learning disabilities and personality disorders. One Denver judge was so impressed that he often made graphotherapy a condition of parole.

- Graphoanalysis can determine marital compatibility.

- Handwriting exercises can alleviate pain, improve marital difficulties, and treat declining sexual performance.

- Graphoanalysis is 97 percent accurate: "One page of handwriting unerringly reveals more than all the psychological tests combined."

Many of these claims that important people use graphology are undoubtedly true, but this supplies no compelling evidence for its validity. After all, President Reagan used an astrologer too! Many of the foregoing claims are so fanciful as to call the entire enterprise of handwriting analysis into question, but they serve to belie the common misconception that the dispute over graphology is only of academic interest. Obviously, it has serious consequences for those who may be unfairly denied positions or falsely accused (see also chapter 1).

TESTING GRAPHOLOGY

The authors have been intrigued by the broad public acceptance of graphology despite its poor track record in properly controlled tests. Given the research reviewed in Section Four of this book that seriously questions the validity of graphology, one must ask why the public reception has been so favorable. We think this is because graphology can be quite impressive in casual demonstrations that do not control for subjective validation effects or "leakage" of clues from sources other than the script itself. Thus we decided to explore some of the ways in which graphology could gain a spurious aura of validity.

We chose to test a graphologist who is a follower of the Graphoanalytic method. That was because this school has been responsible for some of the most immoderate assertions in the media and because it is most vocal in asserting its scientific status.[4] In addition, it was a Graphoanalyst who had received such enthusiastic endorsements in the informal tests done by the Denver newspaper. Realizing that the high praise in this uncontrolled demonstration could have been due to the Barnum Effect,[5] we decided to pursue this possibility.

We set out in Experiment One to improve on the methods used in our local newspaper's test of graphology. Therein, six prominent citizens submitted samples of their writing for blind rating by a Graphoanalyst. They then commented on the accuracy of their own personality profiles. All the comments were laudatory; e.g., "That's great," "Isn't that deep?—I think it's very accurate." Although this demonstration served to enhance public belief in graphology, it is woefully inadequate as a scientific test. It included no control for the Barnum Effect—simply asking each person to pick out his or her own profile after reading all six would have made the test more credible. So we instituted this blind selection procedure among our other controls.

Given the ease with which people are led to feel that almost any personality profile describes them accurately, the possibility arises that this is because most of us are not sufficiently aware of our own personality makeup. Thus, in addition to having each individual try to select his or her own profile out of an anonymous stack, we also tested the ability of a group of well-acquainted individuals to identify each others' profiles. This procedure was followed with profiles produced by a Graphoanalyst and by two well-validated personality tests.

In Experiment Two, we tested the hypothesis that randomly selected recipients will find a graphologist's profiles just as general, and hence as applicable to themselves, as intentionally vague Barnum-type profiles. We also predicted that profiles derived from valid psychological tests would (because they do contain more specific information) be less acceptable to randomly chosen recipients than the graphologist's descriptions if given to randomly chosen recipients. And finally, we tested a proposition, derived from the literature on the Barnum Effect, that acceptability of global personality sketches is affected by one's belief that the profile was produced specifically for them.

EXPERIMENT ONE

METHOD

Experiment One had several purposes. First, it provided needed materials for the larger-scale study, Experiment Two. Second, it also provided an opportunity to check the reliability of the Graphoanalyst's readings; i.e., to see if similarly trained graphologists would arrive at the same conclusions from the writing samples. Finally, it provided the opportunity for a small-scale pilot study, replicating earlier studies of the Barnum Effect but with two additional conditions that could be worth incorporating into future research. One of these was to have individuals very familiar with the participants try to match the descriptions to their owners as well as the more usual procedure where people try to identify their own profiles. The other was to compare participants' success in identifying their own and others' graphological profiles relative to their success with psychometrically derived profiles. We also asked participants to express their degree of confidence in their ascriptions, for later comparison with their accuracy scores. Because the sample sizes in Experiment One were small, the results were not expected to be definitive and are presented here as a recommended paradigm to pursue in future research with larger sample sizes.

Subjects. Participants in the experiment were nine college administrators who had worked closely with one another in the same unit for about ten years. Five were male and four were female. All submitted handwriting samples for Graphoanalysis and also took two standard psychometric tests of personality: the California Psychological Inventory (CPI) and the Myers-Briggs Type Indicator (MBTI).

Handwriting Samples and Analysis. The handwriting samples were one-page, two-paragraph essays containing each person's attitudes concerning legal prohibition of smoking in public.[6] The samples were evaluated blind (i.e., without names) by a prominent handwriting analyst from Denver, Colorado, who is certified by the International Graphoanalysis Society. The graphologist knew the purpose of the experiment and was paid the normal fee for preparing the personality profiles.

Reliability Checks for Handwriting Analyses. The requirement of test reliability is dealt with extensively in chapters 10 and 11 of this volume. The reliability of the Graphoanalyst's technique used in this study was evaluated in two ways. A second Graphoanalyst, who did not know the identity of the preparer, compared the handwriting samples with the personality descriptions and evaluated the overall accuracy and suitability for purposes of the experiment. The first Graphoanalyst's work was rated as excellent and no suggestions for improvement were offered. A third certified graphologist was then given the script samples and graphological profiles in unmatched sets and asked to match each sample of writing to its corresponding personality synopsis. This graphologist correctly matched seven of the nine pairs, a success rate that is highly improbable by chance alone.[7] Thus we accept that this Graphoanalytic technique demonstrates what is called inter-rater reliability. Note that this says nothing about the correctness of the ascriptions (i.e., the method's "validity" as discussed in chapters 10, 11, and 12), only that practitioners trained in the same method are consistent in their assignment of the same traits to features of handwriting.

Scoring of Psychometric Tests. The MBTI was scored by the Center for Applications of Psychological Type. A computerized narrative personality report was prepared by the Center for each participant. Before participants judged them, these narratives were retyped on standard bond paper with the usual four-letter type designation omitted from the telescript.

The CPI was scored by Behaviordyne of Palo Alto, California, and a computer generated psychodiagnostic report was prepared for each participant. Because these psychodiagnostic reports were designed for use by correctional counselors, all references of a forensic nature were omitted when the reports were retyped on standard bond paper. The retyped personality profiles from the CPI and the MBTI were stapled together and names were replaced by an identification code affixed to each one.

Evaluation Procedure. The participants evaluated the Graphoanalytic profiles first. Each participant was given all nine profiles and a scoring sheet that contained sections for the self-selection and co-worker selection tasks. In the self-selection task, the participants were allowed to choose one or more profiles as possibly their own and were asked to rate each profile chosen, according to their degree of confidence that it was theirs. The co-worker selection process involved matching the code letters for the profiles to the names of the members of the group. Participants were given one week to complete these tasks and were asked not to discuss their choices among themselves.

The psychometric profiles were evaluated by the same procedure used with the Graphoanalytic profiles. Sadly, one of the participants died prior to evaluating the psychometric personality profiles, so the self-selection and co-worker matching was completed by only eight individuals. They were given one week to complete the task. After its completion, the participants were debriefed and the correct profiles for each person were revealed.

RESULTS OF EXPERIMENT ONE

Graphoanalytic Profiles. In the self-selection process, the average number of profiles each participant selected as possibly being his or her own was 3.67. Three persons included their own profiles among those they considered to be possibly their own. Assuming that, on average, one could select one's own profile (i.e., a hit) by chance one in nine tries, the probability that three or more individuals would do so by chance alone is 0.623. In other words, if these individuals were to pull three profiles out of a hat 1,000 times in a row, this many or more hits would be expected on 623 of those attempts. Obviously, this does not suggest that the participants were able to recognize the profile the Graphoanalyst had done for them with any certitude.

Even though the ability to recognize one's own Graphoanalytic profile did not exceed chance expectancy, it could still be asked whether the confidence one has in a correctly selected profile might not be superior to that expressed when the selected profile was somebody else's. This does not seem to be the case. We compared the subjects' mean confidence ratings for their hits with those for incorrect selections (false alarms). The mean confidence rating for hits was 2.67, which is slightly below the midpoint of the range, and the mean rating for false alarms was 3.35, which indicated somewhat more than average certainty. Thus it appears that under conditions designed to reduce the Barnum Effect, people are less willing than they are under everyday conditions to accept, unequivocally, the profiles derived for them by a Graphoanalyst.

Matching Graphoanalytic profiles to co-workers was also quite difficult. Of the 72 assignments of profiles to co-workers, only five were correctly matched, a hit rate of 0.07.

Psychometric Profiles. An interesting comparison with the selection of profiles derived from Graphoanalysis is provided by those obtained from the psychometric tests. An average of only 1.75 profiles were selected by the eight persons participating in this phase of the study. This suggests that the psychometric profiles were less general than the Graphoanalytic ones. Their greater specificity gave the subjects a better chance of identifying their own profiles. Four of the eight participants correctly identified their own profile. Assuming each person selected, on average, 1.75 profiles as possibly their own, the probability of selecting his or her own by chance alone would be 0.22. Therefore the probability that four or more would be correctly identified is 0.075. This is slightly greater than the 1 in 20 probability scientists conventionally set as the borderline for considering an outcome too unlikely to have been due to chance. However, because the sample size in this pilot study was small, it would be wise to reserve judgment about the adequacy of psychometric techniques for describing personality in self-selection paradigms. Our preliminary results cast no doubts on the validity of the CPI or MBTI as personality tests because both have already passed the rigorous tests of reliability and validity that legitimate psychometricians demand before marketing a test.

Matching of psychometric profiles to other participants was also somewhat easier than matching Graphoanalytic profiles. Of the 56 possible matches that could be made, 13 were correct. The hit rate in the peer selection phase was 0.23 for the psychometric profiles as opposed to 0.07 with the Graphoanalytic profiles. Although the small sample size in this pilot study does not allow a definitive decision of the relative merits of the two approaches, there is certainly no indication of the superiority of the Graphoanalytic technique as claimed by its advertising. The trends established in this small scale study suggest that if it were replicated with an adequate sample size, the participants' superior performance with the psychometrically derived report would prove statistically significant. This would be consistent with the results of the meta-analysis of graphological versus psychometric effect sizes reported by Dean in chapter 12.

EXPERIMENT TWO

In tests of the Barnum Effect, subjects are typically asked to provide some sort of personal information and later to rate the accuracy of global personality descriptions purportedly derived from it. In most studies (see the review by Dean et al., chapter 12), everyone received the same generalized sketch, and almost everyone rated it a very good portrayal of themselves.

Experiment Two followed this time-honored procedure, but included additional groups of subjects who were given different personality descriptions of varying degrees of specificity. The Barnum Effect has been shown to depend on a number of factors. The feedback should be applicable to the general population but phrased in ways that seem more specific, and the recipient should believe that the statements were derived individually for them. Because most members of the general public are not familiar with the difficulties in establishing test validity exemplified in Table 1, the majority will not test the possibility that their descriptions would be as applicable to their friends and neighbors as to themselves. Thus they will consider the presenter (whether graphologist, palmist, astrologer, or psychologist) to be a discriminating judge of character.

As some have suggested (e.g., Forer 1949; Meehl 1956), the global personality descriptions are essentially statements about commonalities in a given culture. If so, such generalizations ought to be acceptable to most members of the culture, whereas a truly specific description would be accepted only by that subset who shared the unique cluster of attributes and experiences described. Thus it is reasonable to assume that profiles derived for particular individuals by a valid technique would be less acceptable than global descriptions when both are presented to randomly selected individuals (cf. O'Dell 1972).

METHOD

Subjects in Experiment Two were recruited from the students in lower-division psychology courses at Metropolitan State College in Denver, Colorado. A total of 276 volunteers participated in the experimental condition and 235 in the control condition.

In the experimental group, subjects submitted a short sample of their handwriting and were told that a certified graphologist would derive a personality description for them. They were told that because these would be blind evaluations the graphologist would be unaware of their gender, so all profiles would be written in the masculine gender. One week later each student received a personality description with his or her name typed at the top. The students were asked to read the profile carefully and to rate its overall accuracy on a seven-point scale, with one being the lowest and seven the highest accuracy. In fact, the descriptions they received were not based on their writing samples, but were selected randomly from one of the following four categories of profiles.

1. *Barnum Profiles (BP).* An ambiguous, general personality sketch consisting of thirteen statements that had been used in previous studies of the Barnum Effect.

2. *Graphoanalytic Profiles Done for Prominent Local People (GPP).* These were six descriptions prepared by a Denver graphologist and featured in a local newspaper article describing this informal test of graphology.

3. *Graphoanalytic Profiles of College Administrators (GCA).* The nine profiles produced by a certified Graphoanalyst for the participants in Experiment One.

4. *Psychometric Profiles (PP).* Sixteen personality profiles produced from the California Personality Inventory (CPI) and Myers-Briggs Type Indicator (MBTI) tests taken by the participants in Experiment One.

Students in the experimental condition were randomly assigned to groups that received one of the profile types described above. Those in the control condition (referred to as the "self-relevance condition" in Table 2) were also randomly assigned a profile from one of the foregoing groups. The name had been removed and the subjects were told that the profile was that of another person. Nonetheless, they were asked to rate how well they felt it described their own personalities. Both groups used a seven-point rating scale, with higher numbers representing greater accuracy.

RESULTS OF EXPERIMENT TWO

The results of Experiment Two were analyzed using the statistical technique known as Analysis of Variance (ANOVA) (Keppel 1991). This procedure compares the differences between groups receiving different treatments to the internal variability of scores among subjects within the different treatment conditions. A statistical measure of differences among cases is the variance. It is derived by squaring the differences between each pair of values in the data set and taking the mean of those squared values. It is assumed that the greater the difference among pairs of cases within groups treated alike, the higher the probability that any mean differences between the groups who received different treatments would also be due to random variation. In other words, in order to conclude that any differences among conditions are not merely due to happenstance, the variance between groups must be large relative to that within groups.

As shown in Table 2, there were a total of eight conditions in Experiment Two: four types of personality profiles and two different "relevance" conditions (Self: "this profile was done for you" vs. Other: "this profile was done for someone else").

Table 2

Mean Acceptability Ratings for Personality Profiles

	Believed Relevance of Profile to Self or Other	
Profile Type	Relevant to Self Mean	Relevant to Other Mean
Barnum (Global)—**BP**	6.17	4.88
Graphoanalytic (College Administrators)—**GCA**	5.80	5.47
Graphoanalytic (Prominent People)—**GPP**	5.94	5.25
Psycometric Profiles—**PP**	5.11	3.40

The ANOVA technique allows us to compute four subcomponents of the overall variance: (1) a component related to the individual differences in ratings among all subjects; (2) a component based on whether perceived accuracy was affected by the belief that the profile was done for themselves or someone else (its "relevance" to self); (3) a component based on which of the four profile types a subject evaluated; and (4) a component based on whether or not the perceived accuracy of the various profile types was affected differently if participants believed that the profile they were reading was their own or someone else's.

Component (4) is referred to as the "interaction" of profile type with its relevance. The statistical significance of the interaction, or lack thereof, determines whether the overall effect of one variable in an experiment can be considered in isolation or must be interpreted in light of the different values of another experimental variable. In the present instance, absence of a significant interaction would permit us to consider the different effects of the various profile types without concern for the effect of subjects' belief that the statement were relevant to themselves or someone else. Presence of an interaction would require us to examine the comparison among different profile types separately for subjects in the experimental and control conditions.

In an ANOVA, the *F* statistic is computed in order to determine the probability that the observed results would have occurred if only random fluctuations were affecting subjects' ratings. The average value for *F* if the experimental manipulations have no discernible effect (i.e., only random variation is present) is 1.0. As mean differences among groups in the various experimental conditions become large (in any direction), the value of *F* increases. The probability of obtaining large *F*s is small,[8] so when a large *F* is obtained, we can be confident that the observed differences among groups in the experiment were unlikely to have been chance occurrences. Therefore we say these differences are "statistically significant" and conclude that the different experimental treatments had reliably different effects. In Experiment Two, the obtained *F* value (using an unweighted means ANOVA) for the interaction of relevance and profile type was less than 1.0, and therefore not statistically significant. So we proceeded to test the effects of the other variables without differentially considering them in light of the relevance factor.

The relevance factor produced an *F* value of 64.61. With 503 degrees of freedom,[9] for the denominator term of the *F* ratio, such a value is extremely improbable (< 1 in 10,000) if the difference between these two groups were accidental. Accordingly, we can conclude, as expected, that the assumption that a profile is relevant to one's self as opposed to someone else affects the degree to which it is perceived as accurately describing one's self.

The "Profile Type" factor (BP, GPP, GCA, or PP) also produced a statistically significant difference, with an F value of 28.38 (again with 503 degrees of freedom for the denominator of the F ratio). Because random variation should produce such a result only once in 10,000 times, we can reasonably conclude that the contents of the profile affected the subjects' willingness to accept it as an accurate reflection of their personalities. Thus assured that there are statistically significant differences among groups that received the different profile types, we performed additional tests to reveal exactly where those differences lay. These supplementary tests provided no reason to believe that the subjects who received the Graphoanalytic profiles (GPP or GCA) rated them any differently than did the subjects who received the Barnum profiles (BP). In all specific comparison tests, the F values were less than 1.0. This is compatible with the assumption that any differences among them were due to random fluctuations. The similarities in mean acceptability ratings for the Barnum and Graphoanalytic profiles are apparent in Table 2.

The differences in mean accuracy ratings between the group that received the psychometric profiles (PP) and each of the other groups (BP, GPP, and GCA) were statistically significant (all Fs>15). The probability of this being due to chance is less than 0.001. The logical inference from these results is that when people received a randomly selected psychometric profile, they reliably rated it as a less accurate description of themselves than Barnum-type generalities or someone else's Graphoanalytic profile. In other words, psychometric data are particular to the person who took the test; with graphological profiles and Barnum sketches, "one size fits all."

DISCUSSION

No single experiment, or even a modest series of experiments, provides a definitive answer to a broad question such as whether or not handwriting analysis is a valid technique for evaluating personality. This underscores the need for large-scale meta-analyses of published results such as that conducted by Dean in chapter 12, and for studies to be replicated with ever improved methodologies. The experiments reported in the present chapter demonstrate the sorts of factors that must be controlled before it can be concluded that handwriting analysis (or any other character-reading technique) provides any unique information about people's personalities.

The present experiments indicate that when people are told that a randomly selected personality profile is their own, they will tend to see elements in the description that match their personalities. The higher mean ratings given by all groups that were led to believe the sketches were relevant to themselves (see table 2) support this conclusion. Furthermore, descriptions that contain global generalities that are common to almost everyone in our culture will be considered more accurate than those which provide more specific, concrete information. Intentionally vague Barnum-type statements and the pronouncements of a certified Graphoanalyst were equally acceptable to randomly selected recipients, but profiles derived from well-validated psychometric instruments were significantly less likely to be embraced under the same conditions.

Of particular interest with respect to the newspaper's informal "test" of graphology with the Denver celebrities was the fact that our subjects showed no significant difference in applicability to themselves between the Barnum profile and the Graphoanalyst's descriptions done for this demonstration. This suggests that, despite claims of astounding specificity, the GPP profiles were as global and non-specific as the intentionally vague Barnum statements. Furthermore, the Graphoanalytic profiles produced for the college administrators in Experiment One were rated essentially the same in applicability to self as the Barnum and GPP descriptions. This suggests that although there are enough differences among profiles produced by Graphoanalysts that fellow practitioners can determine which scripts they were derived from, there is not much in them that differentiates members of the same culture from one another. A common failing, even among those who should know better, is the tendency to mistake the occurrence of a consistent result with respect to a single variable as indicating that a relationship exists between that variable and another one we desire to predict. Unless it can be demonstrated that manipulation of one variable produces lawful differences in the other variable, we have not shown the validity of the relationship, no matter how consistent our measurement of the predictor variable.

The overall results of Experiment Two are precisely what one would expect from the assumption that the more non-specific the contents of the profile, and the more one is led to believe that it is relevant to one's self, the greater the tendency to embrace it as an accurate depiction of one's personality. Although it could be argued that the Graphoanalytic profiles for the prominent Denver citizens were not definitely shown to be that global in nature, the results of Experiment One strongly suggest that the profiles derived by the same technique for the college administrators were more universally applicable than those based on the psychometric tests. In addition, if one presumes that the more specific the profile, the less acceptable it would be to any randomly selected individual, and if the Graphoanalytic profiles were indeed uniquely descriptive of the writer, then they should have been rated as less accurate than the Barnum profile, which they were not.

We cannot rule out the possibility that here, as in any experiment that exceeds the 5 percent confidence interval conventionally required for statistical significance, the lack of a difference between the Barnum and Graphoanalytic profiles was simply an aberration due to sampling error (known to statisticians as a "Type 2 error"). However, there are several reasons to doubt this possibility. First, there is the fact that our results are consistent with those of many other published tests of graphology reviewed by the authors in Section Four of this volume. Moreover, as sample sizes become quite large, as they were in Experiment Two, sample means tend to be closer and closer approximations to the true means of the populations from which they were drawn. And finally, there were 14 Graphoanalytic profiles used in this experiment. While one or two of them might be similar to the Barnum profile, if graphologists produce highly specific descriptions there should be a sufficient number that were in fact unique to produce a statistical difference vis-a-vis the Barnum profile.

Of course, if the graphological community finds our conclusions unpalatable, the same option is open to them as to any investigator who feels the results of a study are methodologically flawed or may be due to a Type 2 statistical error: replicate the study, improving the methodology. In Experiment One, for instance, a larger sample size should be used, though this is much easier said than done. It would create practical difficulties in obtaining a sufficiently large group, all of whom knew each other intimately enough to judge the accuracy of the graphological profiles. This might necessitate, instead, getting a separate group of close acquaintances for each person the graphologists describe and have this group choose their friends' profile from an array of others. Though this could make the experiment quite unwieldy, it would partially get around another possible problem with the procedure used in Experiment One. That is a problem of "restricted range." It is conceivable that people who work together are more alike in various ways than members of a group randomly selected off the street. This would make even valid depictions of them more similar than usual, and thus more difficult to discriminate correctly. This problem, of course, applies equally to the Graphoanalytic and the psychometric profiles. The subjects in Experiment One did considerably better with the latter than the former, although the difference only approached rather than reached statistical significance. We predict that with a larger sample size, discrimination using the psychometric data would be statistically significant but the graphological results would remain statistically non-significant.

In deciding contentious issues in science, the a priori probabilities of the alternatives are also relevant. It is generally agreed that extraordinary claims demand extraordinary proof. The aforementioned objections to graphology on theoretical grounds are sufficiently daunting to demand far more than anecdotal evidence. Another reason for demanding a very high standard of proof from graphologists is that their pronouncements can have significant consequences for people's reputations, professional advancement, and general well-being. Vigorously advertising, as they do, a product that makes claims of breadth and accuracy that no reputable psychologist would make panders to a vast audience desperate for quick fixes to the hardships and uncertainties of life. People who would not think of buying a toaster without consulting *Consumer Reports* are curiously willing to put much more serious matters in the hands of advisors who cannot pass the simplest empirical tests (such as blind evaluations that control for placebo and Barnum effects). In this chapter we have shown some reasons why graphology in everyday settings, and even in poorly controlled experiments, can seem deceptively accurate. Unless a service, in conventional psychology or its numerous fringe imitators, can document its claims under conditions that prevent such spurious appearances of accuracy, it has no ethical right to sell its wares to the public. We contend that graphologists have not lived up to the required standard of proof.

NOTES

1. Another difference—emphasized by Klimoski (this volume)—is that a competent psychologist would rarely, if ever, rely on a single technique, even to measure a single attribute of a client, whereas graphologists claim they can depend entirely on one method, handwriting analysis, as a measure of everything. E.g., psychologists use different tests to assess different attributes of a client (such as intelligence, aptitudes, personality, psychopathology, etc.). Graphologists' assertions that handwriting analysis works in all of these disparate domains lowers their credibility even further.

2. Actual examples of the subjective validation effect are contained in chapter 13.

3. "Graphoanalysis" is capitalized because it is a registered trademark of the International Graphoanalysis Society (IGAS) of Chicago. IGAS advocates a global or "holistic" approach to discern traits from writing (see Crumbaugh, chapter 7). Practitioners become certified by the IGAS by completing a home study course. The basic course requires approximately 1,000 hours of study, and an additional 1,000 hours is required for the optional master's course.

4. As shown by quotations in chapter 9, officials of the International Graphoanalytic Society (IGAS) condescendingly dismiss competing graphological systems as unscientific parlor games.

5. Knowing that all participants were prominent public personalities would also supply useful clues for conscious or unconscious inferences, even if the analyst

was not aware of their names. E.g., none of these people was likely to be a shrinking wallflower.

6. Note that this procedure allows some advantages to the graphologist from the outset, because what subjects express on this controversial issue, and how they express it, could provide some clues to personality quite independently of what may or may not be revealed by their script alone. Also, if the writer admitted that he or she was a smoker, this could supply additional useful information because it is known that smokers and non-smokers tend to differ on certain personality variables (e.g., smokers, as a group, tend to be more extroverted). As an alternative, subjects could be asked to copy a set piece instead, but graphologists complain that this distorts variables of interest to them. It would be quite revealing to see if graphologists could distinguish, under blind and controlled conditions, copy from spontaneously written pieces. If the graphologists had demonstrated any appreciable success in the present study, it would have required another control experiment to rule out the possibility that their success had stemmed from inferences derived from the content, rather than from the bare features of the writing itself.

7. There are 9! (9 factorial) or 362,880 possible matches that could have been made, but only 36 ways in which seven correct matches could be made. Thus the probability that these graphologists could have achieved the observed hit rate by random matching is approximately one in 10,000.

8. What statisticians consider to be a large F value becomes smaller as the number of cases studied in the experiment increases. This is reflected in a term called "degrees of freedom" that enters into the mathematical formulas in the ANOVA (Keppel 1991).

9. This value is determined by the number of subjects and conditions in the experiment (see Keppel 1991).

REFERENCES

Delprato, D. J. 1975. "Face Validity of Test and Acceptance of Generalized Personality Interpretations." *Journal of Personality Assessment* 39 (4): pp. 345–348.

Dickson, D. H., and I. W. Kelly. 1985. "The 'Barnum Effect' in Personality Assessment: A Review of the Literature." *Psychological Reports* 57: pp. 367–382.

Forer, B. 1949. "The Fallacy of Personal Validation: A Classroom Demonstration of Gullibility." *Journal of Abnormal and Social Psychology* 44: pp. 118–123.

Greene, R. L. 1977. "Student Acceptance of Generalized Personality Interpretations." *Journal of Consulting and Clinical Psychology* 45: pp. 965–966.

Hyman, R. 1977. " 'Cold Reading': How to Convince Strangers You Know All about Them." *The Zetetic* (Spring/Summer): pp. 18–37.

Keppel, G. 1991. *Design and Analysis: A Researcher's Handbook*. 3rd ed. Englewood Cliffs, N.J.: Prentice-Hall.

Meehl, P. E. 1956. "Wanted: A Good Cookbook." *American Psychologist* 11: pp. 262–272.

Merrens, M. R., and W. S. Richards. 1970. "Acceptance of Generalized versus 'Bona Fide' Personality Interpretations." *Psychological Report* 27: pp. 691–694.

O'Dell, J. W. 1972. "P. T. Barnum Explores the Computer." *Journal of Consulting and Clinical Psychology* 38: pp. 270–273.

Richards, W. S., and M. R. Merrens. 1971. "Student Evaluation of Generalized Personality Interpretations as a Function of Method of Assessment." *Journal of Clinical Psychology* 27: pp. 457–459.

Snyder, C. R., R. J. Shenkel, and C. R. Lowery. 1977. "Acceptance of Personality Interpetations: The 'Barnum Effect' and Beyond." *Journal of Consulting and Clinical Psychology* 45: pp. 104–114.

Stagner, R. 1955. "The Gullibility of Personnel Managers." *Personnel Psychology* 11: pp. 347–352.

Section Six

Graphology and the Law

17

Legal Implications of Graphology in the United States

John D. Reagh

In this chapter, John D. Reagh reviews the most significant U.S. federal and state law, as well as the common law, for its implications for the practice of graphology. Reagh emphasizes that many of his conclusions are speculative, since there is not a large body of precedent to use to predict the courts' rulings. The relevant Canadian law is reviewed by Robert Carswell in chapter 18. In the present chapter, graphology as used in hiring is considered: the recourses open to a job applicant who alleges defamation, discrimination, or invasion of privacy, and those open to an employer who considers that he or she has been saddled with an unsuitable employee because of the recommendation of a graphologist. The same considerations apply when graphology is used to judge loan applications or suitability of a renter of an apartment. Reagh considers the trend in the courts to employ graphologists as questioned document examiners—a confusion deplored by Nickell in chapter 4—and as expert witnesses to testify to the psychological states of witnesses, and for advice on jury selection. Reagh points out that the use of graphology in the courts is by no means endorsed by the majority of the legal profession; and its justification requires a demonstration of its scientific validity. However, the jury is still out on this question.

INTRODUCTION

The expert analysis of handwriting has long played a role in the law. The interpretation and authentication of handwritten documents and the detection of alterations and forgeries are common ingredients of lawsuits, and much has been written about such applications of handwriting analysis. The law has dealt less often with the practice of analyzing handwriting to determine the mental and physical characteristics of the writer. Whether or not such analysis is accurate, the fact that graphology is sometimes relied upon in matters which profoundly affect people's lives is enough to justify legal scrutiny.

This book demonstrates that graphology is the subject of learned disagreement, and in our society most controversial practices will soon find themselves the subject of litigation. Because the use of graphology in our economic life is relatively new, there is little legal precedent. Also, each state has its own courts, statutes, and common law; so important details will vary from state to state. Therefore, this chapter will not be a comprehensive survey of the law but, rather, an attempt to predict some of the directions we might expect the law to take. I hope that it will provoke thought both by those who practice graphology and by those who may become the subject of graphological analysis, so that they will be sensitive to their legal rights and responsibilities.

I will discuss graphology as it is used (1) in the evaluation of employees for jobs, credit, or rental housing; and (2) in the courtroom, either to analyze jurors and witnesses or to serve as expert testimony. These uses of graphology will have serious implications for whether or not graphology "works."

THE USE OF GRAPHOLOGY IN EMPLOYMENT, CREDIT, AND RENTAL HOUSING

Let us start with a hypothetical example from the field of employment, but keep in mind that the legal considerations raised by our example and by the law cited are basically the same for those applying for credit or rental housing.

Hiram Fast, the personnel manager of Widgets, Inc., has seen an advertisement for Write Stuff Inc., which claims that its graphologists can determine job applicants' aptitudes, personality traits, and suitability for particular jobs merely by examining their handwriting. Mr. Fast is impressed by these claims and sends handwriting samples of several job applicants to Write Stuff for analysis.

Ms. Candi Date applies to Widgets, Inc. for a job as a bookkeeper and provides a half-page handwritten essay as part of her application. After analyzing Ms. Date's writing, Write Stuff reports that Ms. Date is unsuited for the bookkeeping job. According to Write Stuff, Ms. Date makes friends easily and is extroverted, but she is not a detail person and is bad with figures. Furthermore, she is likely to steal from her employer, and she shows a tendency toward sexual deviancy. After reading the Write Stuff report about Ms. Date, Mr. Fast hires Mr. Art Cursive, whom Write Stuff reported to be introverted, loyal, diligent, reliable, and honest. Six months later, Mr. Cursive disappears with the company payroll. Our scenario might lead to several interesting lawsuits.

CANDI DATE VS. WRITE STUFF, INC.: DEFAMATION

The disappointed job applicant might sue Write Stuff, Inc. and the individual graphologist for defamation. Defamation is any false statement, written (libel) or spoken (slander), that is made to a third person and that tends to expose a person to public hatred, contempt, or ridicule, or causes that person to be shunned or avoided, or to be injured in his or her business or occupation.

Write Stuff, Inc. and the individual graphologist who wrote Ms. Date's analysis made a written statement and communicated that statement to Mr. Fast, a third party. In our example, the report resulted in Ms. Date's failure to get the job with Widget, Inc., thereby injuring Ms. Date in her occupation. In addition, Write Stuff's statement that Ms. Date has a tendency to sexual deviancy could also be libelous because it potentially exposes her to public hatred, contempt, or ridicule.

It is important to keep in mind that, despite Ms. Date's injury, Write Stuff's report was not defamatory *unless it was false.* Write Stuff's ultimate defense would be to prove the truth of its statements. Before the court gets to the question of truth, however, it must consider whether Write Stuff was protected by a legal privilege when it reported to Widget about Ms. Date.

There are certain situations in which, as a matter of public policy, the law gives extra protection to free expression. For example, participants in judicial proceedings, in legislative proceedings, or in the conduct of their duties as executive officers of government are given absolute privileges to speak out in the conduct of their official duties, without fear of defamation suits. Such a privilege is *absolute* in the sense that it has no exceptions or loopholes.

The law also provides a variety of *qualified* or *conditional* privileges. A qualified privilege protects a statement made in good faith when it is on a subject in which the speaker or writer has an interest or a duty, if the statement is made to a person with a corresponding interest or duty. In addition, the statement must be limited in scope to the protected purpose and communicated only to the proper parties.

It is frequently held that a communication which defames the character of an employee or a job applicant may be protected by a qualified privilege. To qualify for the privilege, the person making the statement must have either a pecuniary interest or a duty to speak to the employer. The statement will be privileged even though it is false, unless the defendant acted with knowledge of its falsity or with reckless disregard of whether it is false. For example, a qualified privilege will cover a supervisor's report about the conduct or performance of a subordinate. Also, judicial precedent recognizes that outside consultants such as Write Stuff and the individual graphologist are covered by a qualified privilege to report the findings they were hired to make.

In *Thibodeaux v. S.W. Louisiana Hospital Assn.*, 488 So. 2d 743 (La. App. 3 Cir. 1986), the defendant hospital, located in Louisiana, hired Newman & Associates (a firm licensed to conduct lie detector tests in Texas) to test employees. Newman tested numerous hospital employees and reported that four were not completely truthful in their answers. The hospital fired the four employees, who then sued Newman, the hospital, and others. The plaintiffs claimed that Newman had defamed them, but the court found that Newman was protected by a qualified privilege. The court explained at page 748:

> [Newman] enjoyed a position of privilege in that regard and may not be held liable for the disclosure. There is a clear unrebutted showing that Newman did not make a defamatory statement concerning the plaintiff. Even were the opposite the case, it was made in good faith, to one having a corresponding interest, by one having a duty in that regard, and defendant would not be liable therefore even if the information should later turn out to be incorrect.

A qualified privilege may be lost if the speaker did not believe his statement, if he did not have a reasonable reason to believe in the truth of the statement, if the statement was not relevant to or went beyond the scope of the situation, or if it was excessively publicized. There may be some question about whether Ms. Date's alleged sexual deviancy was relevant to her fitness as a bookkeeper. Certainly, the graphologist must take care to limit his report to matters which are relevant to the inquiry at hand. Publication of irrelevant but damaging information might not be protected by the privilege. Even relevant statements might lose their privilege, if the publisher acted recklessly or dishonestly.

The test for overcoming a qualified privilege was explained more fully in *McDermott v. Hugly,* 561 A.2d 1038 (Md. 1989), U.S. cert. den. 1989. In this case, a candidate for a job as a mounted policeman was examined by a psychologist who had been hired as a consultant by the police department. The psychologist reported that the candidate had a fear of horses. After the candidate failed to get the job, he sued the psychologist for defamation. The court noted that communications arising out of the employer-employee relationship are protected by a qualified privilege:

> A person may lose that qualified privilege, however, if the plaintiff can demonstrate that the publication is made for a purpose other than to further the social interest entitled to protection or can prove malice on the part of the publisher. Regarding the scope of "malice", "Knowledge of falsity or reckless disregard of truth is the standard by which the malice required to defeat the conditional privilege defense is to be measured in cases of private defamation."[1]

In order to win her case, Ms. Date would have to prove that the graphologists either knew that their report was false—an unlikely event—or that they had a reckless disregard for the truth of their report. Either of these issues could place the practice of graphology on trial.

The court might then consider the scientific evidence regarding the usefulness and accuracy of graphology, the extent of training or experience of the graphologist, the graphologist's "track record," and other evidence of success or failure. Ms. Date might prevail if she could prove by a preponderance of the evidence that the graphologist could not reasonably have believed he could accurately determine Ms. Date's qualities merely by examining a sample of her handwriting. Even if Ms. Date succeeded in defeating the qualified privilege, the graphologists would still have a chance to prove the truth of their report which is, after all, the ultimate defense to a claim of defamation.

CANDI DATE VS. WIDGETS, INC.: DISCRIMINATION

Title VII of the Civil Rights Act of 1964 prohibits discrimination in employment and public accommodation based on race, color, religion, sex, or national origin. Although state and municipal statutes sometimes expand on these categories, Title VII remains the basic anti-discrimination law of the land.

> It shall be an unlawful employment practice for an employer—(1) to fail or refuse to hire or to discharge any individual, or otherwise to discriminate against any individual with respect to his compensation, terms, conditions, or privileges of employment because of such individual's race, color, religion, sex, or national origin; or (2) to limit, segregate, or classify his employees or applicants for employment in any way which would deprive or tend to deprive any individual of employment opportunities or otherwise adversely affect his status as an employee, because of such individual's race, color, religion, sex, or national origin. (Sec.42 U.S.C. Sec. 2000e-2(a))

Other statutes prevent unwarranted discrimination against the handicapped.

Graphology could run afoul of these laws in a variety of ways. Most fundamentally, the use of graphology could either intentionally or innocently introduce discrimination into an employer's employment practices. Intentional discrimination is, of course, illegal but, most often, hard to prove. The Supreme Court has decided, however, that intent is not required. In *Griggs v. Duke Power Co.,* 402 U.S. 424 (1971), the employer based job assignment decisions on professionally developed general intelligence and mechanical comprehension tests. The result was that blacks were assigned predominantly to the lower paying jobs.

The U.S. Supreme Court decided that the purpose of Title VII was to eliminate the consequence of discrimination, not simply the motive. The Court held at page 432 that "good intent or the absence of discriminatory intent does not redeem employment procedures . . . that operate as 'built-in head winds' for minority groups and are unrelated to measuring job capability." The Court went on to conclude that once the adverse or discriminatory effect had been established, the employer had the burden to prove "that any given requirement [has] a manifest relationship to the employment in question." Duke Power failed to carry its burden and was found liable for the "disparate impact" its employment tests had on minority groups.

In *Albermarle Paper Co. v. Moody,* 422 U.S. 405 (1975), the Court considered what an employer must show to establish that pre-employment tests which are discriminatory in effect, but not in intent, are sufficiently job-related to survive a challenge under Title VII. To demonstrate that a test is "job-related" the employer must show "by professionally acceptable methods [that the test results are] predictive of or significantly correlated with important elements of work behavior which comprise or are relevant to the job or jobs for which candidates are being evaluated" (supra. at page 431). This standard raised the issue of professional validation of employment tests, a subject of substantial difficulty.[2]

If the use of graphology results in a statistically significant tendency to disfavor any protected minority, the employer could be required to prove the validity of the test. Indeed, the employer would be liable for any discrimination that resulted, even though an outside agent performed the tests.

The Equal Employment Opportunity Commission Office of Personnel Management, and the Departments of Justice and the Treasury have adopted "Testing Guidelines" by which personnel tests are evaluated. Generally, the Guidelines favor professionally developed ability tests which can be shown to be job-related. Courts and enforcing agencies will also favor a test which is supported by a professional job analysis. Under the Guidelines, a test will not be validated by the tester's promotional literature, frequency of the test's use, testimonials, credentials of the testers, or anecdotal accounts of successful results.

As a practical matter, when employers hire graphologists, the employers should require graphologists to provide the data which would validate the test should it ever be challenged. The graphologist should also demonstrate the ability to defend the test in court, if necessary. In particular, there should be data that show that the test measures what it claims to measure and that what it measures is in fact related to job performance.

There is reason to fear that, by its nature, graphology can inadvertently cause discrimination based on race, national origin, age, or physical handicap. All these personal attributes can directly or indirectly affect handwriting and thereby influence the results of handwriting analysis.

For example, handwriting is taught differently in different parts of the United States and throughout the world. Therefore, handwriting is to some extent a reflection of the race and national origin of the writer.

> The general character of handwriting is influenced by the system of writing studied during an individual's formative period of life, the amount and quality of family tutelage, and how handwriting is used by a person during his or her everyday endeavors. (Muehlberger 1989)

> Style characteristics may be used to determine the nationality of the writer or, more correctly, the country where he was taught to write. (Harrison 1958, 289)

It follows that to analyze a job applicant's handwriting accurately, you must know about his national origin, schooling, and family background. Questions into such areas would be offensive to many people, would appear discriminatory on their face, and would invite litigation. The alternative is to make assumptions about the cultural factors which influenced the formation of the applicant's handwriting and risk the inaccuracy which could result from mistaken assumptions.

INVASION OF PRIVACY

Even if the handwriting analysis is perfectly correct and, therefore, not defamatory, and if it has no improper discriminatory effect, an employee or candidate could still have a legal complaint that his or her privacy had been invaded.

> One who intentionally intrudes, physically or otherwise, upon the solitude or seclusion of another or his private affairs or concerns, is subject to liability to the other for invasion of his privacy, if the intrusion would be highly offensive to a reasonable man. (*Phillips v. Smalley Maintenance Serv. Inc.*, 711 F. 2d 1524 [11th Cir. 1983])

Of course, a person's handwriting is usually not considered private. After all, it is intended in most cases to be shown to others. On the other hand, graphology purports to extract from handwriting information which is not apparent to most readers, including information which most people would consider private in the extreme.

The greatest risk occurs if there is disclosure of such private information. The right of privacy protects persons from the public disclosure of private facts even if the disclosure is true. Thus, invasion of privacy could be claimed if the graphological report were widely distributed to the general public or to a narrower group of the employee's work associates, friends, and acquaintances. Generally, evaluations of employees or applicants are not distributed widely enough to raise such a privacy issue. It is also possible that the mere inquiry into areas of personal privacy would be actionable, if the inquiry is not limited to areas which are clearly related to work performance.

Finally, it could be argued that an applicant has the right to know the manner of examination to which he or she will be subjected. This putative right is not always satisfied by companies making use of graphology for personnel selection. Sometimes companies will ask in their advertisement for a handwritten cover letter without telling the job applicant what the letter is for—in fact, this request is often a signal that the letter will be sent to a graphologist. A court might well be disturbed by the surreptitious analysis of a job applicant's handwriting. Such secret analysis would either reveal details of the applicant's life, attitudes, or personality in greater depth than the applicant might expect or, at least, cause the prospective employer to form opinions of the applicant's characteristics, which may or may not be founded. Simple fairness dictates that a job applicant be told how much of his privacy he must surrender to apply for a job, so that he has a chance to choose between privacy and employment. An employer should warn the applicant if a handwriting sample will be analyzed and should inform him of the kinds of information that will be sought from the sample.

There are numerous statutes in the United States which regulate or prohibit the administration of honesty tests as conditions of employment. These statutes vary considerably, and employers and graphologists should take care to examine the local law to avoid violations.

In *State by Spannaus v. Century Camera,* 309 NW 2d 735 (Minn 1981), the state of Minnesota sued an employer and its consultant for conducting polygraph examinations of employees. Minnesota statute prohibited employers from requiring employees to take "polygraph, voice stress analysis, or any test purporting to test honesty." The employer argued that this statute denied the company its constitutional rights and that the language of the statute was too vague.

The court upheld the statute, in general, holding that the state had a substantial public interest in encouraging the maintenance of a harmonious labor climate, protecting employees' expectations of privacy, and discouraging practices that demean the dignity of employees. On the other hand, the court held that the term "any test purporting to test honesty" was overly broad and undefined, and it limited the effect of the statute to tests and procedures which purported to assess honesty by measuring physiological changes in the subject tested. This decision left open the possibility that a more clearly worded statute could prohibit graphological testing of employees or candidates.

WIDGETS, INC. VS. WRITE STUFF, INC.: MALPRACTICE

In our example, Write Stuff advertised that handwriting analysis could determine, with a high degree of reliability, job applicants' intellectual capacity, honesty, reliability, motivation, and even physical and mental health. Unfortunately, Write Stuff reported that Art Cursive, the successful applicant, was reliable and honest. Mr. Cursive got the bookkeeping job and stole the payroll. If Write Stuff promised foolproof results, they could be liable for breach of that warranty.

Even if Write Stuff were more careful with its promises, they might still be liable for the damage caused by Mr. Cursive. If the handwriting analyst promises to generate a psychological profile of the job applicant from the applicant's handwriting, then, arguably, the analyst could be expected to live up to the same standards of professional skill as would be expected of a psychologist or psychiatrist. In effect, the handwriting analyst is claiming to function as a psychologist, though by alternate means. He may well find himself judged by those standards and compelled in court to defend the scientific validity of his methods in comparison to the traditional methods of psychological analysis.

GRAPHOLOGY IN THE COURTROOM

GRAPHOLOGY AS A TOOL FOR LAWYERS

Lawyers are always eager to find tools which will give them added insight into the veracity and motivations of witnesses, the attitudes or prejudices of jurors, and the secrets an opposing party wants to conceal. Graphology claims to be able to grant all of these wishes, and lawyers have been repeatedly urged to sample its benefits.

> Graphologists are most familiar in the courtroom as questioned document examiners. They are also sometimes used to help select juries. Increasingly, they are hired as expert witnesses to testify about personality characteristics. (Moore 1988)

Ms. Moore has written several other articles in *Case & Comment* extolling the virtues of graphology for the legal profession, and similar articles appear from time to time in the legal press (see, for example, Forte 1989, 10). Even in the legal profession, however, graphology is not universally accepted.

> Barristers and solicitors, as well as other professionals, are precluded by ethics from utilizing graphology as a component of a selection or testing procedure due to its lack of validity. (Quesnel and Lawrence 1990, 248)

GRAPHOLOGISTS AS EXPERT WITNESSES

The rules of evidence permit experts to testify about their findings. Rule 702 of the *Federal Rules of Evidence* provides:

> If scientific, technical, or other specialized knowledge will assist the trier of fact to understand the evidence or to determine a fact in issue, a witness qualified as an expert by knowledge, skill, experience, training, or education, may testify thereto in the form of an opinion or otherwise.

In a proper case psychologists have testified about the mental capacities of a subject. Polygraph (lie detector) and voice stress analysis test results have also been admitted into evidence, although such evidence is very controversial. The reliability of these tests is often called into question, as would certainly be true for graphology.

Warren v. Hartnett, 561 SW 2d 860 (TX Civ App 1977, reh den 1978), was a will contest over a holographic (handwritten) will. A handwriting expert was called upon to testify that, based upon the handwriting in the will, the decedent was an alcoholic and that her alcoholism had reduced her mental capacity so that she was unable to understand her business. The court held that the expert's opinion was without probative value because the expert had never met the decedent. The court was not impressed by the expert's experience in working with alcoholics, and it held at page 863:

> We cannot give this testimony any probative effect. The evaluation of abnormal mental conditions is peculiarly within the field of *medical* science, particularly psychology, and also, perhaps, abnormal psychology, but we are aware of no recognized field of scientific inquiry which permits divination of mental capacity by persons whose expertise is limited to handwriting analysis. [Emphasis in the original]

Before graphology is widely accepted as a proper basis for expert testimony, the scientific community will have to reach a consensus that graphology is capable of making reliable findings.

CONCLUSION

Graphology is claimed to be a powerful tool for the analysis of aptitudes, attitudes, and personality. Such power or even the claim of such power carries a heavy burden of responsibility. To the extent that the results of handwriting analysis are accurate or at least believed to be accurate, they will have a potent effect on people's lives. Practitioners of graphology should understand that the legal system will hold them responsible for the consequences of their analyses and conclusions. They should take care to establish the accuracy of their methods and to apply those methods in a responsible manner.

NOTES

1. This formulation of the rule follows the *Restatement (Second) Torts* (1977), an influential treatise covering tort law.

2. See "Courts, Psychologists, and the EEOC's Uniform Guidelines: An Analysis of Recent Trends Affecting Testing as a Means of Employee Selection," *Emory Law Journal* 203 (1987): p. 36.

REFERENCES

Forte, Lowell. 1989. "Lawyers Turn to Graphologist for Expertise." *California Law Business* (Monday, November 13, 1989).

Harrison, W. R. 1958. *Suspect Documents: Their Scientific Examination.* London, U.K.: Sweet & Maxwell, Ltd.

Meuhlberger, Robert J. 1989. "Class Characteristics of Hispanic Writing in the Southeastern United States." *Journal of Forensic Sciences* 34 (March): pp. 371–376.

Moore, Maurine. 1988. "Your Witness, Counselor." *Case & Comment* (January-February).

Quesnel, Lionel J., and Wade C. Lawrence. 1990. "Graphology, Personnel Selection and Litigation." *Solicitor's Journal* 134 (March 2): p. 248.

18

Graphology: Canadian Legal Implications

Robert S. Carswell

Robert S. Carswell explores the Canadian Criminal Code and other federal and provincial statutes and legislation relevant to graphology. Since the vast majority of graphologists sincerely believe in what they are doing, even if what they believe is false, they would not be considered to be engaging in fraud under the Canadian Criminal Code. However, there may be civil proceedings that could be brought against graphologists. For example, the graphologist may be liable for damages if a graphologist recommends someone for employment who turns out to be much less competent or honest than the evaluation indicated, and the company suffers as a result. Carswell explores what would have to be proved if such a suit were to be successful.

It is possible that some graphologists could run afoul of provisions of provincial consumer protection laws. As well, graphologists who diagnose medical or psychiatric conditions from handwriting may be prosecuted under provincial statutes governing the medical profession. Employers using graphology in personnel decisions may violate discrimination provisions in the human rights codes of some provinces. Carswell explores these possibilities.

Readers may wish to compare the Canadian legal implications for the use of graphology with those in the United States, discussed by John Reagh in chapter 17.

INTRODUCTION

If, as some of the contributors to this book assert, graphology lacks scientific validity, then its practitioners may run the risk of civil liability to those who suffer damages as a result of its use. They may even find themselves in contravention of legislation intended to protect consumers or, in extreme cases, they may be charged with a criminal offense. In this chapter, I will describe in very general terms some of the Canadian laws on this subject.

CIVIL LIABILITY OF GRAPHOLOGISTS

It is easy to imagine a company losing money as the result of hiring the wrong person on the basis of his handwriting. Say, for example, an accomplished thief is hired for a sensitive executive position involving the handling of significant amounts of money, on the advice of an independent graphologist who reported that the handwriting had all the requisite indications of honesty and competence. If it happens that the executive in question bilks the company of some thousands of dollars, does the company have a good civil case to recover that money from the graphologist? Or, if the executive was bonded, will the bonding company, after payment to the employer, have that recourse? To take a less obvious example, suppose that a company, again relying on the advice of a graphologist, hires a new vice-president in charge of sales. Although his *t*'s may be perfectly crossed and his words perfectly slanted and broken, the sales of the company may suffer if he is incompetent. Will the company have a case to recover from the graphologist its losses or the decline in its revenues?

In both the common law and civil law systems in Canada, the company will be obliged to prove three principal elements: first, that the graphologist was negligent or intentionally at fault; second, that the company suffered damages; and third, that these damages were caused by that negligence or fault.

Proving damages may be easy if the employee has simply gone to Brazil with the company's funds. It will be considerably more difficult if the employee has been merely incompetent, but this is a familiar challenge for the legal and accounting professions.

To prove fault or negligence on the part of the graphologist, the company would have to show that the graphologist was not able, as he claimed, to identify or measure the intelligence, qualifications, or competence of a prospective employee, and that in fact he did not do so. Establishing the fact that the graphologist did not do what he claimed to do would, I suppose, be relatively easy, at least in the case of fraud. Merely showing that the employee defrauded the company or was incompetent may bring with it a presumption that the graphologist's advice was wrong. Normally, a consultant's fault consists in his lack of expertise or in his negligence in applying the principles of his field of expertise to the particular case. Indeed, if the graphologist has analyzed the handwriting poorly, this argument could be used. More interesting, however, would be the assertion that graphology is not a science, that it cannot substantiate its claims. In this event, the plaintiff's claim would be that the graphologist was negligent or disingenuous in thinking that graphology could produce valid information.

Against these arguments, the graphologist will raise many of his own. Most important, he will argue that he was only an advisor, that the hiring of the executive was strictly the company's doing; that if there were previous instances of fraud and defalcation or indications of incompetence, the company should have noted them and acted accordingly (even though this argument would implicitly admit the uselessness of the handwriting analysis). Just as the law does not require a psychologist or a lawyer to guarantee the results of his interventions, so too the accuracy of a graphologist's advice is not guaranteed. He will also assert that he himself has all the necessary training and knowledge (having passed all the required correspondence courses of a bona fide graphological society) to act as a qualified graphologist, and that he applied all the skills of his profession to the particular case. He may add that the employee must have undergone a change in character after his handwriting analysis, because at the time of the test his character was obviously unblemished.

In addition, the graphologist may argue that the company was itself at fault, that there was at least contributory negligence on its part. For example, he may say that the company should have noticed the employee's fraudulent or incompetent tendencies soon after his hiring, notwithstanding the graphologist's glowing report. Again, he may claim that the company created opportunities for theft and fraud by not having in place a system for determining or detecting such actions. The company will have to be prepared to counter these allegations.

Finally, the company will have to show a link between the graphologist's fault and the damages the company has suffered. Again, this will be relatively straightforward where the employee has absconded with its funds, but very much more difficult where general incompetence has given rise to a diminution of revenues. In the case of the vice-president in charge of sales, for example, the graphologist will be tempted to argue that the company's losses were due to unfair competition, or poor products, or a general economic decline, or someone else's incompetence.

In all of this, the burden of proof will, generally speaking, lie on the company. It will not be up to the graphologist to show that he gave sound advice and that the company did not suffer because of it, but rather the company will have to prove, on the balance of probabilities, that the graphologist was at fault and that the company suffered damages as a result of that fault.

Discharging this burden will be particularly difficult where the company wishes to call into question the very legitimacy of the graphologist's field of expertise. This will mean calling witnesses who are themselves sufficiently expert that they can credibly refute the principles of graphology. How does the company choose such an expert witness? Normally, an expert from the same field would be used to discredit the testimony of the defendant, but this option is not available when the profession itself is being attacked. Some philosophers, and in particular, philosophers of science, may be eminently qualified to give expert evidence on the topic, but their own expertise may not be scientific. I suspect that the Courts would rather hear from established scientists, even in unrelated fields such as physics, who are sufficiently prestigious that their judgment would be regarded as impeccable. Better, perhaps, to have the Dean of the Faculty of Science testify, or the Chairman of the Department of Psychology, than a less eminent academician.

The graphologist, for his part, will also call upon experts, doubtlessly other graphologists and—if he can find one or two to testify on his side—scientists or other academicians, to prove the legitimacy of his expertise. He will also be tempted to produce satisfied customers, but the Courts should be persuaded to disregard anecdotal evidence of this sort. Indeed, the company should object to any such testimony as inadmissible because it is neither expert nor pertinent to the particular litigation.

As everyone knows, the costs of civil litigation are high. If the company wins, it would normally be able to recover some of those costs (not all of them) from the graphologist. By the same token, if it loses, it would be obliged to pay costs to the winning side. The prospect of high costs and the uncertainty inherent in litigation undoubtedly act as strong disincentives to an employer who might otherwise wish to sue a graphologist. There is also the possibility that even if a judgment is obtained, the graphologist may not have the money to satisfy it.

Whether for these reasons, or because few companies have used the services of graphologists (notwithstanding frequent claims to the contrary), or (conceivably) because companies are satisfied with the advice they get, I am not aware of any civil litigation in Canada involving graphologists.

EMPLOYER'S LIABILITY FOR DISCRIMINATION

In Canada, as elsewhere, employers must be careful not to discriminate illegally in their hiring practices. For example, Section 15 of the *Canadian Charter of Rights* provides as follows:

> Every individual is equal before and under the law and has the right to the equal protection and equal benefit of the law, without discrimination and in particular, without discrimination based on race, national or ethnic origin, colour, religion, sex, age or mental or physical disability.

Where an employer uses a graphologist's report to choose between two prospective employees who are otherwise similarly qualified, then if it can be shown that graphology is not a legitimate science, a case can be made that the unsuccessful employee was the victim of discrimination. The other employee was, in effect, chosen over him for no reason at all.

In 1982, the Supreme Court of Canada was called upon to determine whether certain occupational qualifications or requirements were discriminatory under *The Ontario Human Rights Code* (*The Ontario Human Rights Commission v. Etobicoke* [1982] 1 S.C.R. 202.). The Court discussed criteria for determining non-discriminatory qualifications (in the context of age discrimination) in the following terms:

> A bona fide occupational qualification must be imposed honestly, in good faith, and in the sincerely held belief that it is imposed in the interests of adequate performance of the work involved with reasonable dispatch, safety and economy and not for ulterior or extraneous reasons that could defeat the Code's purpose. The qualification must be objectively related to the employment concerned, ensuring the efficient and economical performance without endangering the employee or others. Evidence as to the duties to be performed and the relationship between the aging process and the safe, efficient performance of those duties is imperative, with statistical . . . evidence being of more weight than the impressions of persons experienced in the field.

If graphology is unscientific, the imposition of a handwriting test can hardly be said to "be objectively related to the employment concerned."

CRIMINAL LIABILITY

Whereas the majority of graphologists are sincere believers in the value of graphology, there may be some who engage in fraud. Section 380.(1)

of the *Criminal Code* of Canada provides that anyone guilty of criminal fraud is guilty of an indictable offense and liable to imprisonment for up to fourteen years, where the amount in question exceeds $1,000. (The penalties are less severe if the amount is less than $1,000). Fraud, in turn, is defined in the Code in the following terms:

> **380.**(1) Every one who, by deceit, falsehood or other fraudulent means, whether or not it is a false pretence within the meaning of this Act, defrauds the public or any person . . . of any property, money or valuable security.

The key words are "deceit, falsehood or other fraudulent means." They are, of course, open to multiple interpretations, and it will be up to judges and juries to decide whether they will fit the particular case if charges are laid against a graphologist. Over the years, however, the decisions of the Canadian courts have provided some guidance.

We know, for example, that one of the essential elements of the infraction is that the victim must have been deprived of property or money. The fact that the victim is only temporarily dispossessed (because, for example, the accused pays back the amount of his fees) will not be a defense. Equally, the fact that the victim was negligent and could have prevented the fraud by being more vigilant is not a defense (and not one likely to be raised by a graphologist in any event).

In the case of a fraudulent graphologist, the deprivation of money would appear relatively easy to prove. The fraudulent advice was given and paid for. The victim is the client, and the money of which he was defrauded is the graphologist's fee for services. It could be argued too that the graphologist defrauded the *public*. Knowingly making false claims that graphology will assist employers in hiring and firing may result in losses, and the courts have held that it is not necessary to show that the accused personally profited or benefited from the fraud. It is not even required to show a loss; a *risk* of loss is sufficient.

It is not enough, of course, to prove that a graphologist has caused a loss or a risk of loss through his actions; it must also be proven that he was dishonest, that he employed "deceit, falsehood or other fraudulent means." The classic definition or description of the offense is given in *Re London & Globe Finance Corp.* [1903] 1 Ch. 728:

> To deceive is, I apprehend, to induce a man to believe that a thing is true which is false, and which the person practising the deceit knows or believes to be false. To defraud is to deprive by deceit: it is by deceit to induce a man to act to his injury.

Accordingly, the Crown would have to prove that the graphologist's claim to be able to determine a person's qualities by his handwriting is false. It is not the particular advice that constitutes the fraud, but rather the pretext that the theory on which the advice is based is of value. The fraud, in other words, would lie in the knowing use of a theory which is false.

Proving criminal intent (*mens rea*) is an essential part of most criminal offenses. The irony is, of course, that far from knowing that the tenets of graphology are false, many graphologists believe them to be true. The Crown is in the curious position of having to prove (beyond a reasonable belief, as we will see) that the accused really does *not* believe in what he preaches. It will not be enough to show that graphology cannot live up to its claims; neither will it be enough to show that the particular graphologist's claims are preposterous; rather, it will be necessary to show that the graphologist is not sincere. The ignorant believer in graphology will avoid conviction because of his ignorance; the clever non-believer will avoid conviction because it will be very difficult to prove his lack of sincerity.

A closely related issue came before the Canadian Courts in the fortunetelling case of *Labrosse* v. *The Queen*.[1] This case involved the Criminal Code provision which makes an offense of fortunetelling *when it is fraudulent*. What happened was that an investigator from the Montreal police force visited the apartment of a clairvoyant named Lucette Labrosse. After ascertaining his astrological sign and having him cut a deck of cards several times, she made some precise predictions: that he would get married and have two children, that at the age of about 50 he would have kidney problems, and that one of his work companions would have an accident. She also advised him not to accept a job offer he had received, but rather to keep his present job at the James Bay hydroelectric project. For all of this information, the policeman was charged $15.00.

At her trial before the Montreal Municipal Court, Labrosse admitted that she had foretold the future, for payment, but denied that she had done so fraudulently. Three of her satisfied clients, a journalist, a cook, and an unemployed nurse, told the Court that she had accurately predicted future events on the basis of card-reading and palmistry. Thus the defense maintained that not only did she truly believe she had powers of prediction, but also that she truly had those powers.

The chief judge of the Municipal Court, Mr. Justice Tourangeau, found her guilty from the bench and fined her $100. In an oral judgment, he said that "the accused knows full well that she has no basis for her claim to be able to predict what will happen in people's futures," and "the fact of claiming to find in cards or in the lines of a hand the unforeseen occurrence of events of which a person has no knowledge whatsoever, is absolutely without scientific foundation."[2]

Labrosse instructed her lawyer to appeal this decision. As permitted by the Criminal Code, there was a new trial before a higher Court, the Quebec Superior Court. Again, Labrosse admitted she had foretold the policeman's fortune and had charged him for it, but denied having acted fraudulently. In a very brief judgment,[3] the Superior Court judge agreed with her that no proof had been made of any fraudulent utterances. Accordingly, he reversed the verdict of the Municipal Court and acquitted her.

The prosecution then appealed this judgment to the Court of Appeal of Quebec. In a split decision the Court of Appeal reversed the decision of the Superior Court and restored the conviction imposed by the Municipal Court. Both majority judges asserted that in fortunetelling, the fraud is in the pretext, not in the prediction. As Mr. Justice Bernier put it, "fraud does not lie in the falsity of the utterances in predictions but in the acts and things done and remarks made to make one believe in the power to know and predict the future." What was necessary for a conviction, according to the other majority judge, Mr. Justice Mayrand, was proof that the accused "acted in a fashion to make others believe that she possessed the power or gift" of divination. Of this proof, there was an abundance.

Labrosse then appealed the judgment to the Supreme Court of Canada. Unfortunately for those of us in the legal profession who would have preferred a definitive statement of the law, the Supreme Court could scarcely have been more laconic: "given the finding of fact by the trial judge that (translation) 'the accused knows full well that she has no basis for her claim to be able to predict what will happen in peoples' futures,' we are agreed that the defense of honest belief is not open on the facts of this case." The door, therefore, is open to such a defense in the future, not just in fraudulent fortune-telling prosecutions, but also in those involving fraudulent graphology.

One procedural point should be made here. Under Canadian criminal law, anybody may file a criminal complaint, so long as he has reasonable and probable grounds for believing that a criminal offense has been committed, but this does not guarantee that a summons or warrant will be issued. The authority of a Justice of the Peace is required for that purpose. If the Justice considers that no case has been made out, the case will simply not proceed.

LIABILITY UNDER CONSUMER PROTECTION LAWS

If a graphologist advertises his skills, claiming that handwriting analysis reveals qualities of a person's character and that businesses worldwide rely on graphology for hiring, and if these claims are false, then members of the public may be able to take advantage of consumer protection laws which prohibit false advertising.

In Canada, there is both federal and provincial legislation on this subject. In Quebec, for example, the *Consumer Protection Act* contains the following interesting provisions:

> **219.** No . . . advertiser may, by any means whatever, make false or misleading representations to a consumer.
>
> **220.** No . . . advertiser may, falsely, by any means whatever,
>
> (a) ascribe certain special advantages to . . . services;
>
> (b) hold out that the . . . use of . . . services will result in pecuniary benefit . . .
>
> **222.** No . . . advertiser may, falsely, by any means whatever, . . .
>
> (c) hold out that . . . services have been furnished
>
> **239.** No . . . advertiser may, by any means whatever, . . .
>
> (d) rely upon data or analysis falsely presented as scientific.

The key words here, of course, are "false" and "falsely." As is proper, the burden is once again on the prosecutor to prove that the advertisements in question are based on falsehood. Although the facts need not be proven beyond a reasonable doubt, it will still be difficult, as noted above, to prove to the satisfaction of the Court that graphology is unscientific.

I mention this Quebec statute because I am aware of a prosecution under it based on pseudoscientific claims, *Procureur Général* v. *Centre d'Enquêtes Internationales de Parapsychologie (C.D.I.P.) Ltée.* In this case, the defendants had published newspaper advertisements claiming the power to predict the winning numbers in lotteries. They were found guilty of false advertising under Section 219 and, accordingly, were ordered to publish a notice stating that the defendant was not able to predict the winning numbers.

As in the case of criminal proceedings, prosecutions under consumer protection legislation may have to be undertaken by government authorities, so the first step will be to convince these authorities that the advertising in question is false. In particular, note Section 239 of the Quebec statute, or its equivalent in other provincial legislation, which explicitly refers to pseudoscientific analysis.

The applicable federal legislation in Canada is the *Competition Act*, Section 36 of which prohibits any "representation to the public that is false or misleading in a material respect." This is a criminal offense, requiring proof of the facts beyond a reasonable doubt, but the offense is one of strict liability, not requiring proof of intent to deceive or mislead the public.

MEDICAL DIAGNOSES

If graphologists go so far as to diagnose physical or mental disorders, they may also find themselves in violation of statutes governing the medical profession. Every province has laws prohibiting the illegal practice of medicine, and there are many reported cases involving pseudoscientific medical theories, from pyramid power to diagnosis by channeling. Even if graphology is not a pseudoscience, its practitioners should not be diagnosing cases of schizophrenia or epilepsy if they wish to avoid prosecution under these laws, unless of course they are also qualified medical doctors.

CONCLUSION

If a person is seeking a remedy for damages from those who use graphology in ways that are harmful, Canadian law provides several possible routes that might be pursued. I emphasize "possible" here because I have uncovered nothing that specifically mentions graphology in the relevant case law cited above. Since the workplace is so important and affects so much of our interests, it is the source of much civil litigation and criminal prosecution. The fact that graphology has not entered the courts yet may be a sign either that proponents of graphology are overestimating its use in Canada as a tool in personnel matters, or that its use is too recent to have come to the attention of the courts. However, if graphology moves from the parlor, where it served as an innocent amusement, into the workplace where significant interests are at stake, we can expect litigation in Canadian courts along the lines of those described in this chapter.

NOTES

1. File no. 18–902 of the Montreal Municipal Court. The judgment is unreported. The transcription of the oral judgment can be found in an annex to the joint record in the Court of Appeal.
2. The quoted sentences (with the exception of the last one in this section) are unofficial translations from the French.
3. File no. 36–016–80.
4. File no. 500–10–000082–816.

5. Reported at [1987] 1, S.C.R. 310.
6. Court of Sessions of the Peace, Montreal, file no. 500–27–017076–896.

Contributors

BARRY L. BEYERSTEIN received his Ph.D. in experimental and biological psychology from the University of California at Berkeley. He teaches in the Psychology Department at Simon Fraser University in Burnaby, British Columbia, and does research in the Brain Behavior Laboratory and Drug Studies Laboratory at S.F.U. His research interests include the brain mechanisms of consciousness and the psychobiology of addiction. Dr. Beyerstein serves as a scientific consultant to the Committee for the Scientific Investigation of Claims of the Paranormal (CSICOP) and is a member of the CSICOP Executive Council. He is also chair of the Society of British Columbia Skeptics. Dr. Beyerstein has held several fellowships and has been awarded the gold medal of the British Columbia Psychological Association and the Donald K. Sampson Memorial Award of the British Columbia College of Psychologists. At present, he sits on a committee of the latter organization that will recommend guidelines for protecting the public from abuses of psychological testing, including that of being subjected to scientifically unsound tests.

DALE F. BEYERSTEIN teaches philosophy at Vancouver Community College, Langara Campus, in Vancouver, B.C., Canada. He did his M.A. at the University of Toronto. His main interests are in medical ethics and critical thinking. He is on the Boards of the Society of British Columbia Skeptics, an organization that provides scientific responses to occult and pseudoscientific claims, and the British Columbia Civil Liberties Association, which he served for several years as Chairman of the Access to Information and Privacy subcommittee.

MARILYN L. BOWMAN received her Ph.D. from McGill University. She teaches and does research at Simon Fraser University in Burnaby, British Columbia. She specializes in the areas of personality theory, psychological measurement, and clinical psychology. Dr. Bowman has served as Chair of the Psychology Department at S.F.U., Director of the Clinical Psychology Program, Associate Dean of Graduate Studies, Acting Vice-President, and as a member of the university's Board of

Governors. Dr. Bowman has also served on the Board of Directors of the Canadian Psychological Association and was elected a fellow of that association.

ROBERT S. CARSWELL is a partner in the Montreal law firm of Beyers Casgrain. He specializes in commercial law. He is a founding member of the Quebec Skeptics and has contributed to *The Skeptical Inquirer* on the legal status of fortunetelling.

JAMES C. CRUMBAUGH is a Certified Graphoanalyst and a clinical psychologist at the Veterans Administration Medical Center in Gulfport, Mississippi. He has authored many general works on Graphoanalysis and has done several research projects on Graphoanalysis. Dr. Crumbaugh practices Graphoanalysis, a school of graphology distinct from that practiced by Wellingham-Jones (chapter 15) and Lockowandt (chapters 5 and 6).

GEOFFREY A. DEAN received his Ph.D. in analytical chemistry from the University of London. After ten years as a research scientist in various countries around the world, he started another career in technical writing and editing, which he describes as "making complex things simple, not simplistic." His classic two-part examination of astrology, originally published in *The Skeptical Inquirer* and widely regarded as the best ever done, has been reprinted in *The Hundredth Monkey* anthology published by Prometheus Books.

ADRIAN FURNHAM received his D.Phil. from Oxford University and taught at Oxford until he assumed his present position as Reader in Psychology at University College, London. He has held a wide range of visiting professorships and is on the editorial board of several international journals. A fellow of the British Psychological Society and a director of the International Society for the Study of Individual Differences, he ranks among the most frequently cited psychologists in the U.K. for his over 200 articles and ten books. Among these are reports of several tests of handwriting analysis that found it inadequate as a means of measuring personality traits.

EDWARD W. KARNES received his Ph.D. in experimental psychology from Temple University. He is a professor and former Chair of the Department of Psychology at Metropolitan State College in Denver, Colorado. In addition to his teaching and research duties, Professor Karnes is a frequent consultant to industry and the courts in various areas of applied psychology.

IVAN KELLY, whose Ph.D. is from the University of Calgary, is Professor of Educational Psychology at the University of Saskatchewan, Saskatoon, Canada. Kelly specializes in statistics and research design, and is the Chairman of the Astrology Subcommittee of the Committee for the Scientific Investigation of Claims of the Paranormal (CSICOP) and has authored many critical works on astrology, alleged lunar effects on behavior, and the "Barnum Effect."

RICHARD KLIMOSKI received his Ph.D. in industrial and organizational psychology from Purdue University and is currently Professor and Vice-Chairman of the Psychology Department at the Ohio State University in Columbus, Ohio. He is the author of numerous articles and co-author, with J. Schmitt and J. Neal, of the 1991 textbook, *Research Methods in Human Resources Management* (Cincinnati: South-West Publishers). Dr. Klimoski is active in many professional societies and has served on the executive committee of the Personnel and Human Resources Division of the National Academy of Management.

S. DAVID LEONARD received his Ph.D. from the University of Iowa. He is on the faculty of the Department of Psychology of the University of Georgia in Athens, Georgia. His primary interests are in experimental psychology, particularly the area of learning.

OSKAR LOCKOWANDT is a Professor of Psychology in the Faculty of Psychology and Sports Science at the University of Bielefeld in Germany. He received his Ph.D. in psychology in 1966 from the University of Freiburg. His supervisor was Dr. Robert Heiss. In addition to his work on graphology, Dr. Lockowandt's academic research centers around the humanistic psychology of Abraham Maslow. Dr. Lockowandt has published two books, both in German and not (yet) translated into English. One book is on happiness, and the second is a personal reflection on self-actualization, which grew out of a year-long series of daily readings of Maslow's descriptions of self-actualized people and meditations on these readings.

JOE NICKELL teaches business and technical writing at the University of Kentucky. His doctoral dissertation, at that institution, focused on aspects of "literary investigation," including dating and authenticating written texts. These academic pursuits grew out of his earlier career as an investigator for a world-famous detective agency. He is a registered Questioned Document Examiner, which explains his interest in chapter 4 in distinguishing between questioned examination and graphology. Dr. Nickell employs his investigative skills on a wide range of paranormal claims, and is the author of *Inquest on the Shroud of Turin* (1987), and (with John F. Fischer) *Secrets of the Supernatural* (1988). He has also published articles in *The Skeptical Inquirer, Journal of Police Science and Administration, Identification News, Pen World*, and other periodicals. He is also a calligrapher, with an extensive collection of historical documents, books on penmanship, and antique writing materials. These interests motivated his latest book, *Pen, Ink and Evidence* (Lexington: The University Press of Kentucky, 1990).

ZHANG JING PING is a senior student in the English program of the Department of Foreign Languages and Literatures, Jilin University, Changchun, People's Republic of China.

JOHN D. REAGH has a physics degree from Stanford University and a law degree from the University of Chicago. He has practiced commercial law in Seattle, Washington, for 15 years and worked as an investment banker and as counsel for a contact lens manufacturer where he also wrote computer software for the optical design and manufacture of contact lenses. His law practice has emphasized contracts, bankruptcy, and intellectual property.

DONALD H. SAKLOFSKE received a Ph.D. from the University of Calgary and is a professor of Educational Psychology at the University of Saskatchewan in Saskatoon, Saskatchewan. He also holds associate memberships in the Psychology Department and the Department of Education of Exceptional Children at the University of Saskatchewan, and lists among his research interests the measurement of individual differences in personality, intelligence, and cognitive processes.

PATRICIA WELLINGHAM-JONES is a graphologist living in Tehema, California. She is a former psychiatric nurse and received her Ph.D. from Columbia Pacific University, where she is presently a faculty mentor. Dr. Wellingham-Jones is a practitioner of the Roman-Staempfli school of graphology.

Subject Index

Name Index